the ONION®

AD NAUSEAM

COMPLETE NEWS ARCHIVES • VOLUME 14

the ONION®
AD NAUSEAM

COMPLETE NEWS ARCHIVES • VOLUME 14

EDITED BY
Robert Siegel

WRITTEN BY
Robert Siegel, Carol Kolb, Todd Hanson, John Krewson,
Maria Schneider, Tim Harrod, Mike Loew, Joe Garden,
Chris Karwowski, Rich Dahm, Chad Nackers

GRAPHICS BY
Mike Loew, Chad Nackers

DESIGNED BY
Andrew Welyczko

ADDITIONAL MATERIAL BY
Josh Greenman, Dan Guterman, Barry Julien,
Peter Koechley, Sean Quirk, Dave Sherman, Ben Wikler

COPY EDITOR
Stephen Thompson

MADE POSSIBLE BY
Peter Haise

SPECIAL THANKS
Ken Artis, Juli Aulik, Brian Belfiglio, Tyondai Braxton, Christine Carlson, Jen Cohn,
Chris Cranmer, Ian Dallas, Scott Dikkers, Dan Friel, Daniel Greenberg, Tim Hughes, Allison Klaas,
Annik LaFarge, Kurt Luchs, Lindsay Mergens, Sean Mills, David Miner, Michael O'Brien, Philip Patrick,
Keith Phipps, Adam Powell, Nathan Rabin, Tasha Robinson, Steve Ross, David Schafer,
Tom Scharpling, Camille Smith, Dorianne Steele, Scott Templeton

BOXTREE

This book uses invented names in all stories, except notable public figures who are the subjects of satire. Any other use of real names is accidental and coincidental.

First published 2003 by Three Rivers Press, New York, New York. Member of the Crown Publishing Group, a Division of Random House, Inc.

First published in Great Britain 2003 by Boxtree
an imprint of Pan Macmillan Ltd
Pan Macmillan, 20 New Wharf Road, London N1 9RR
Basingstoke and Oxford
Associated companies throughout the world
www.panmacmillan.com

ISBN 0 7522 1587 6

9 8 7 6 5 4 3

A CIP catalogue record for this book is available from the British Library.

Designed by The Onion
Printed and bound in Great Britain by the Bath Press, Bath

House Haunted By Elks Club Members

see LOCAL page 10B

Hank Williams Jr. Honored By Institute For Football Preparedness

see SPORTS page 3C

Monster Truck Chased Down By Torch-Wielding Regular Trucks

see LOCAL page 2B

STATshot

A look at the numbers that shape your world.

Top Halloween Costumes, Women 18-34

1. Sexy French maid
2. Sexy cat
3. Sexy witch
4. Sexy hobo
5. Sexy ketchup bottle
6. Sexy prostitute
7. Sexy Mother Teresa
8. Sexy bus driver
9. Sexy Teenage Mutant Ninja Turtle

the ONION®

VOLUME 37 ISSUE 39   AMERICA'S FINEST NEWS SOURCE™   1–7 NOVEMBER 2001

Teen Who Just Discovered Led Zeppelin Starting To Piss Off Friends

Left: The Zeppelin-loving Campa.

GURNEE, IL—Mark Campa, 16, who has listened to and talked about Led Zeppelin almost exclusively since discovering the '70s rock group over the summer, is "really starting to piss off" his friends, sources reported Monday.

"I've got nothing against Zep—they're awesome," said James Savich, 16, a longtime friend of Campa's. "But Mark acts like he's the first person ever to really get into them when

he's, like, the 59 billionth."

Campa was first exposed to the band in June when older brother Bryan returned from college and started playing *Led Zeppelin II* while lifting weights in the garage. After one listen, Campa was reportedly hooked, buying his own copy and playing it incessantly for weeks.

Campa's Led Zeppelin fixation soon manifested itself in myriad ways, with the teen playing only Led Zeppelin in his car, drawing the *Led*

see TEEN page 5

Gore Delivers Emergency Presidential Address Into Bathroom Mirror

Above: Gore delivers his make-believe address to the American people.

CARTHAGE, TN—Urging the American people to have "courage, faith, and resolve in this time of trial," Al Gore delivered an emergency presidential address into his bathroom mirror Tuesday.

"My fellow Americans, our enemies have struck at the heart of our great democracy," Gore solemnly intoned into his electric razor during the not nationally televised address. "They have attacked our citizens, our cities, and the most prominent symbols of our pride and prosperity. In so

doing, they sought to tear us apart. But they have done just the opposite."

Punctuating his opening statements with a dramatic pause intended to bolster the resolve of a wounded nation, Gore applied shaving cream to the beard he had grown during his time out of the spotlight.

"We have, in recent days, seen tragedy and infamy on a scale equal to any in American history," said a proud, defiant Gore as he shaved. "Yet we have also seen heroism and selfless-

see GORE page 6

Restaurant Turns Out To Be Spanish, Not Mexican

Above: The Spanish restaurant accidentally patronized by the taco-loving Mangurten (inset) and his wife.

SCRANTON, PA—Bob and Debra Mangurten expressed confusion and frustration Monday, when the restaurant Don Quixote turned out to be Spanish, not Mexican.

"Where are the tacos?" Bob, a 33-year-old Scranton telephone repairman, asked waiter Pedro Cruz while scanning the menu. "What kind of Mexican place doesn't have tacos?" Cruz politely explained to him that tacos were not on the menu because tacos are not indigenous to Spanish cuisine.

"Turns out, the place was Spanish, which, apparently, is different," Debra later recalled. "How the heck were we supposed to know that?"

After ordering two Mountain Dews and requesting more time to look over

see RESTAURANT page 3

1

Fear Of Mail

The U.S. Postal Service has emerged as the primary means of spreading anthrax, sparking fear among mail carriers and millions of Americans. What do *you* think?

Rich Pfloeg
Carpenter

"I've been terrified to open my mail lately. Especially the stuff from Verizon."

Frank Dawson
Business Owner

"As owner of America's third-largest mail-order baking-soda distributorship, I am deeply concerned."

Keith Howe
Cashier

"To think that just a short time ago, the biggest worry in opening your mail was that a package might contain a spring-propelled boxing glove that knocked you unconscious."

Dana Dunst
Systems Analyst

"I was wondering why some moonsuit-wearin' motherfucker handed me a Lenscrafters flyer this morning."

Andrea Vincent
Podiatrist

"We should write 'Return To Sender' on any anthrax-laced letters. That'd show 'em."

Thomas McEntyre
Publisher

"As a major New York media power player, I'd better see an envelope full of anthrax on my desk by noon tomorrow, or I'm gonna be seriously pissed."

Increasing NYC Tourism

New York has suffered a sharp decline in tourism since Sept. 11. What is the city doing to attract visitors?

- Assuring would-be visitors that Broadway is quickly going bankrupt and will soon be gone
- Sending "shame on you" letter to all Americans who visited Grand Canyon in past month
- Launching new hard-sell "U ♥ NY" campaign
- Applying soothing lanolin to rough areas in the South Bronx
- Omitting phrase "jam-packed, urine-reeking subway platforms" from tourism ads
- Courting Midwesterners with slogan "New York: The Milwaukee Of The East Coast"
- Playing up world-class restaurants and museums, downplaying threat of mass bioterrorism apocalypse
- Guaranteeing visitors at least one B-level-celebrity sighting during visit
- Unveiling new TV ad boasting, "I'll gladly risk death to visit the New York Transit Museum!"
- Making it clear just how real the danger is that New York may no longer be number one

---

⌀ the ONION®
America's Finest News Source.™

Herman Ulysses Zweibel
Founder

T. Herman Zweibel
Publisher Emeritus
J. Phineas Zweibel
Publisher
Maxwell Prescott Zweibel
Editor-In-Chief

Hang In There! You Live In The Richest Nation In The World!

By Darcy Wyatt

Ever have "one of those days"? You know the kind: The boss is screaming, "I want it yesterday!," the kids have the flu, and your hair is sticking up on end like Don King's. Well, on those days, it's important to keep things in perspective. After all, you live in the richest, most powerful nation in the whole gosh-darn world!

You may have a run in your pantyhose, and the floor of your car may be covered with a week's worth of Styrofoam coffee cups, but you shouldn't be a frowny Frank. Keep that chin up, and remember that our country has more than 1.3 million military personnel on active duty and the most advanced weapons systems on Earth. That should turn anyone's frown upside-down.

Even on a Monday—heck, even on a *rainy* Monday—our nation has nearly three times the purchasing power of Japan, which has the world's second largest economy. That's gotta make you smile. So hang in there!

Speaking of "Hang In There!," have you ever seen the poster with the picture of the kitten hanging from the branch? I have it on the wall of my cubicle at the insurance agency. It re-

> **Now, I'm not saying I never complain. There are lots of things that make me mad.**

minds me to keep reaching for the stars, even when I feel discouraged. Sure, life's an uphill battle. Sometimes, you want to throw your hands up and say, "I give up!" But at those moments, you owe it to yourself to give it another try.

Psst... I've got a secret remedy for a case of the blues. First, buy yourself a treat. Ice cream, flowers, a foot-massage kit—it doesn't matter what, so long as it's something you love. Then, take a look at the latest statistics from the World Health Organization. At least in your country, you don't have a one-in-three chance of being HIV-positive, like the people in some places! Did you know that AIDS will account for 44.7 percent of adult deaths in South Africa this year and is projected to account for 78.6 percent by 2010? Not in America, though! That's why, around these parts, every day is a rainbow day!

Sometimes, it feels like I can't do anything right. This morning, for example, I dropped my toast on the floor. (Guess which side it landed on.) Then, when I got to work, I realized I'd forgotten my desk keys—again! I was this close to getting seriously down on myself when I remembered something I definitely *have* done right in my life: I was born in the U.S.A.! Just think where I could've been born: North Korea, Estonia, Cambodia, Burkina Faso. I could be dead by now, killed by starvation, malaria, tidal wave, rebel insurgents, drought, civil war, well poisoning, a land mine... I

> **Keep that chin up, and remember that our country has the most advanced weapons systems on Earth.**

won't bore you, but the list goes on and on!

You know that old saying, "Life begins at 40"? Well, not in Sierra Leone! The life expectancy there is 38! I don't think we're in Kansas anymore, Toto!

Did you know that the U.S. makes up only 4 percent of the world's population, yet we have one third of its automobiles and consume one-quarter of its energy supply? Keep that in mind the next time you get passed over for that big promotion at work!

Now, I'm not saying I never complain. There are lots of things that make me mad. Like waiting in line. It drives me absolutely batty! Doesn't it seem like every time you get in line at the post office, the line you pick winds up moving half as fast as the one next to it? But if you switch to the other line, the one you'd been in suddenly starts moving! At times like that, I just close my eyes and think about our country's 3.9 million miles of paved roads, enough to circle the Earth at the equator 157 times.

Yes, whenever I need a super-duper pick-me-up, I just think about my elite status as an American citizen. That never fails to put the feather back in my cap. Sure, there's a war going on and lots of other problems, but let's keep in mind that over the past 20 years, our economy has grown at a faster rate than at any other time in our history. That means when Friday comes, it's time to celebrate with a happy-hour raspberry margarita at Applebee's! Why not? I'm from America, the wealthiest country in the entire world! ⌀

Awkward Farewells Exchanged On Disliked Coworker's Last Day

Above: The departing Mooney (center) is surrounded by indifferent coworkers.

NEW BRITAIN, CT—Paula Mooney, 29, a not particularly popular Sentinel Savings & Loan mortgage underwriter, was the recipient of awkward goodbyes from coworkers Monday, her last day with the company.

Mooney, who in two and a half years with Sentinel "never quite hit it off with the gang," was given a polite but emotionless going-away party near her workspace. Featuring an Entenmann's chocolate cake, Hi-C fruit punch, and a good-luck card signed by whomever happened to be at their desks when it was passed around, the 15-minute gathering met the minimum standards for a farewell fete.

"I never had any deep, personal grudge against Paula," said Barb Rid-

> "There was just something about her that rubbed me the wrong way. I don't know, there was a certain coldness about her."

nak, 48, one of the nine Sentinel employees who chipped in to buy Mooney a $13 picture frame as a going-away gift. "But there was just something about her that rubbed me the wrong way. I don't know, there

see COWORKER page 4

RESTAURANT from page 1

the menu, the couple debated whether to stay or just pay for the drinks and find a Mexican restaurant.

"I had my heart set on tacos," Bob said. "But we were too hungry to get back in the car and drive all the way across town to Chi-Chi's, so we decided to stay put and make the best of things. Besides, Deb and I had agreed to try new things together, so I guess that counts."

Upon returning with the Mangurtens' soft drinks, Cruz suggested that they start off with some *tapas*, which he described to the bewildered pair as "Spanish-style appetizers."

"Why don't they just have chips and salsa for the appetizer?" Bob asked. "Instead, they have stuff like prosciutto and melon, and steamed mussels. That sounds like something you wouldn't eat on a dare."

"I'm scared I'm going to order the wrong thing, and these prices don't exactly encourage experimentation," Debra said. "The way the restaurant looks on the outside, you'd never know it was the kind of place where

> Though the words "authentic Spanish cuisine" are printed on Don Quixote's door, Bob said the restaurant should make more of an effort to make its identity clear to patrons.

you'd feel nervous ordering."

After studying the menu for nearly 25 minutes, Bob ordered sea bass and Debra ordered Paella Valenciana, chosen because she recalled hearing the

> "Why don't they just have chips and salsa for the appetizer?" Bob asked. "Instead, they have stuff like prosciutto and melon, and steamed mussels. That sounds like something you wouldn't eat on a dare."

term *paella* on an episode of *Seinfeld*. Fifteen minutes later, her entree, a mixture of seafood, chicken, sausage, rice, saffron, and assorted vegetables and spices, was brought out and served tableside directly from a sizzling pan.

Reaction was lukewarm.

"It was fine, I suppose," Debra said. "It didn't hit the spot like some quesadillas would have, but we could have done worse."

"I guess it doesn't matter at this point," Debra continued. "They got our money either way."

Though the words "authentic Spanish cuisine" are printed on Don Quixote's door, Bob said the restaurant should make more of an effort to make its identity clear to patrons.

"When you walk into a place called Don Quixote and see all the crazy, colorful stuff on the wall, you figure it's a place to get normal Mexican food," he said. "Then, you open up the menu and you're like, what's with all this seafood? They should call it 'Don Quixote's Not-Mexican Restaurant,' so people will know exactly what they're getting. Or not getting."

Debra, who said she had been in the

Above: Mangurten, who "really wanted some tacos," eats herb-crusted sea bass with mashed yams.

mood for a beef enchilada with molé sauce, agreed.

"I think it's just plain sneaky giving the place a Mexican name and making it look like a Mexican place. The least they could do is have a few things like chimichangas and burritos on the menu, for all the people who walk in here by accident. You shouldn't have to fool people to get them to eat at your restaurant. That's just bad business."

Ed Brulley, a longtime friend of the Mangurtens, said this is not the first time the pair has been duped by a restaurant.

"I took them to a great Szechuan place, and they were upset about it not having sweet-and-sour chicken or chow mein," Brulley said. "I told them that's Cantonese style, and that this was authentic Szechuan. They looked at me like *I* was from China. I don't think they realize different parts of a country have different styles of dishes. They certainly don't realize that countries that speak the same language don't always have the same food."

Added Brulley: "God help them if they ever accidentally stumble into a Cuban joint."

3

was a certain coldness about her. And a phoniness. When you talked to her, she always came off kind of, well, surface-y."

After avoiding eye contact with Mooney for the entire party, Ridnak encountered her in the women's rest room shortly before quitting time. In spite of her distaste for the departing Mooney, Ridnak forced a grin and gave her an awkward goodbye.

"I said something like, 'It's going to be different not having you around.' Which I guess, technically, is true," Ridnak said. "Then, she gave a little nervous laugh and shrugged slightly. She didn't really say much, Miss Personality that she is. I guess she felt just as uncomfortable as I did."

Added Ridnak: "I'm not even exactly sure why she's leaving here. I think somebody said she's moving to Texas to be with her boyfriend, but I'm not positive."

Another employee who exchanged banal pleasantries with Mooney was receptionist Alana Hodge, 22. According to Hodge, Mooney was "her usual strange self."

"She asked me if her old phone extension was going to be retired,"

> "I said something like, 'It's going to be different not having you around.' Which I guess, technically, is true," Ridnak said. "Then, she gave a little nervous laugh and shrugged slightly. She didn't really say much, Miss Personality that she is."

Hodge said. "I said we'd probably just give it to whoever takes her place. Then I asked her why she was asking. After this awkward silence, she explained that she was joking, saying that she was such a legend, her extension would be retired. I was like, 'Oh.'"

In addition to criticizing Mooney's personality, coworkers used her departure as an opportunity to surreptitiously snipe about her work habits.

"At least we won't have anyone at Sentinel who thinks lunch hour is 70 minutes long," said personal-lending representative Eric Martel, 36. "I loved how she was always the last person back from lunch but the first person out the door at quitting time."

Mary Hoeving, 41, another personal-lending representative, said that when she saw Mooney's cleaned-out workspace, it was the first time she'd seen it clean since her March 1999 hiring.

"She was so disorganized," Hoeving

> "She seemed okay enough to me," coworker Steve Melville said. "Then again, we worked in different parts of the office, so I didn't see her all that often."

Above: The hastily decorated Entenmann's cake that was served at Monday's going-away party.

said. "I think she kept her desk messy to look like she was working hard, but most people around here knew otherwise."

While a majority of employees were glad to see Mooney go, some were merely indifferent.

"She seemed okay enough to me," said Steve Melville, 40, a computer-network consultant. "Then again, we worked in different parts of the office, so I didn't see her all that often."

The most dreaded portion of the day was quitting time, when the staff was forced to say its final goodbyes. Afraid that she would have to hug

Mooney on her way out of the office, Hodge took an elaborate, circuitous route to avoid passing Mooney's desk, slipping away undetected. Others shared her fear but nevertheless mustered limp waves and wan smiles. Ridnak urged Mooney not to be a stranger, telling her that if she ever "happen[s] to be in the neighborhood, [she] should swing by the office."

"I really don't know why I said that," Ridnak said. "After all, if she ever dropped by, I'd make myself plenty scarce. Not that she'd ever drop by, but still." ∅

NEWS IN BRIEF

Terrorism Storylines Being Added To TV Shows As Quickly As They Were Dropped

LOS ANGELES—Less than two months after frantically excising any allusions to terrorism, network executives are scrambling to add terror-related storylines to TV shows, sources reported Monday. "We're working around the clock to squeeze in a special episode where a Libyan with ties to Al Qaeda threatens to blow up the D.A.'s office," said *Law & Order* producer Dick Wolf, who on Sept. 15 scrapped an episode of the NBC drama in which a character utters the word "bomb." "We've got to stay on top of this thing." Next week, *Spin City*, which last month pulled an episode featuring a shot of the World Trade Center, will air a "very special" one-hour episode in which Mayor Winston is infected with anthrax.

School Principal Pauses For Applause That Never Comes

WILLIAMSPORT, PA—During a speech before Medford Middle School students Tuesday, principal Arthur Morehouse paused for applause that never came. "So let's all join together and show the kind of spirit that made Medford the most academically improved middle school in the entire Williamsport area!" said Morehouse, raising his hands. After three seconds of silence, Morehouse added, "Well, moving on," and proceeded to speak for 20 minutes on the importance of keeping the lunchroom clean.

Parents Regret Letting Child Name Dog

MANKATO, MN—Bruce and Gail Kreuter expressed regret Monday over their decision to let their 8-year-

old son Brian choose the name of the family's new cocker spaniel, Hitmontop. "He named the damn thing after his favorite Pokémon," Bruce said. "What's more, apparently, Hitmontop isn't even a *dog* Pokémon: It's some cartoon guy who kicks people." Gail said she should have seen this coming when Brian named his goldfish Garlic Junior.

CIA Admits It's Good At Overthrowing Stuff, Not So Much The Intelligence

LANGLEY, VA—Central Intelligence Agency director George Tenet conceded Monday that the organization excels at overthrowing foreign governments but isn't so hot at the actual intelligence gathering. "Iran, Zaire, Guatemala, Chile, Indonesia, Greece, Panama, Australia, Haiti... we're real good at toppling regimes," Tenet said.

"But just collecting your basic data about who's up to what in the U.S. and whatnot, that's not our strong suit." Tenet added that if the U.S. needed to "swoop in and take out Colombia's current government, man, we could have that done by the weekend."

Family Now Openly Wondering When Grandma Will Die

ATHENS, GA—After years of silent speculation, Trotter family members openly wondered Monday when ailing family matriarch Helen Trotter would die. "I'd say sometime in the next six months," Trotta's granddaughter Emily told her brother Zach after a visit to Valley View Nursing Home. "No way she'll hang on more than a year." Reports indicate that the Trotters hope the 88-year-old stays alive at least until after Christmas so it doesn't force a change of travel plans. ∅

This Marriage-Counseling Scam Is A Real Moneymaker

By L. Phillip Udall

There's a sucker born every minute, and as a National Board For Certified Counselors-licensed marriage counselor, I know that better than anyone. For 22 years, I've bilked troubled couples out of their hard-earned cash by actually convincing them that their marital problems have a solution and that I can give it to them. Yep, this marriage-counseling scam is a real money-maker!

I hate to give away my secrets, but I'll let you in on the basics, just so you can see what an amazing racket I have going. It's so simple, anyone can pull it off.

First, you've got to find a school that offers a master's degree in counseling. They have them all over the country, and most of them will accept just about anybody. For just a little bit of money up front—believe me, you'll recoup your investment hundreds of times over—they'll let you in on all the secrets of the big marriage-counseling swindle. They'll tell you what to say, show you what books to have lining your office shelves, and teach you time-tested techniques from all the old pros and big rollers in the biz.

After you get your degree, the next step is to take the National Counselor Examination for Licensure and Certification. Once that's done, it's time to start making the green! Get yourself some puppets and big foam bats and shit like that. (I'm not going to tell you where I got mine, because I have my own special type of rag doll I like to use, and I don't want anybody moving in on my hustle.) Set yourself up in a nice little office with some couches and lacquered diplomas and a receptionist up front just to make everything look legit. Then sit back and watch the cash roll in.

I have no idea why this works, but it does. Basically, all you do is sit there and listen. I'm serious! A good 75 percent of my "job" is listening as some miserable husband-and-wife team drones on about their problems. Every once in a while, you say something like, "Well, what are some things Don could do to make you feel like he appreciates you?" Or, "Don, did you even know Wendy felt this way?" The rest of the time, it's just keep the eyes open, nod, and cash the checks.

Last week alone, my haul was a cool $4,500, and I made it just sitting on my ass. Check this out: These couples pay me $200 an hour, and I get paid whether I solve their problems or not. If they leave crying their eyes

out, I get paid. If they end up getting divorced... *paid!*

Wait, it gets even better. Rather than scam a bunch of couples for

> **For 22 years, I've bilked troubled couples out of their hard-earned cash by actually convincing them that their marital problems have a solution.**

$200 and then flee, setting up my "office" on some other corner, I actually stay in one place and make repeat customers out of them! Some of them, I've had coming in on a weekly basis for years! This month alone, it's $200, $200, $200, $200... thank you, Mr. and Mrs. Abramson, and don't let the glass door with my name tastefully stenciled on it hit you on the ass on the way out.

I know what some of you are thinking. How can you prey on these innocent people? Hey, I didn't ask them to be born so stupid! That's their own damn fault! Or, as I find out with a lot of them, it's their parents' fault. (When in doubt, trace it back to the

parents.) It's like they're begging to be ripped off.

Take this one gullible couple I had in here today. The Ortons. The husband says he feels "smothered." The wife, meanwhile, says she's "not self-actualized" in the marriage, whatever the hell that means. So I let them jabber on for a good 20 minutes while I think about the hot speedboat I'm planning to buy. Finally, I ask, "Well, how much time do you spend together?" Turns out, they both work out of their home, and not only do they have no mental or physical boundaries to separate work time and social time, but they also have almost no autonomous recreational interests.

So what do I do? You're gonna love this. I tell them to take out a piece of paper and draw up a schedule that includes "Together Time" and "Independence Time." Do you know how much thought I put into that genius advice? Zero. Zip. Nothing. For that, I got 200 smackeroos! The best part is, as they were leaving, I said, "Come back next week, and we'll see how that schedule is working." Ha, ha! They actually thanked me as they walked out!

As a break from counting my money, I've been working on a book called *Family Foundations: Building The Base That Will Sustain Your Marriage For A Lifetime.* When it hits bookstores, I'll be pulling in the

chump change all across the country. The publisher will do my work and just send me the check. Ka-ching!

Yeah, I've got a pretty sweet thing

> **I know what some of you are thinking. How can you prey on these innocent people? Hey, I didn't ask them to be born so stupid! That's their own damn fault! Or, as I find out with a lot of them, it's their parents' fault.**

going here. Of course, any time you're running a scam on someone, you've got to keep in mind that it won't last forever. No matter how good it is, eventually, somebody's gonna sniff you out. That's why I've been socking away a little of the dough every month, just in case someone catches on to me. If that day ever comes, you can find me in Key West, a bottle of suntan lotion in one hand and a drink in the other.

See ya, suckers! ∅

TEEN from page 1

Zeppelin IV runes on his arm, and spending $73 at the Kane County Fair ring toss in an effort to win a *Swan Song* mirror.

According to friends, Campa's newfound love of the band has caused him to behave in a "dicklick" fashion.

"Last Saturday night, a bunch of us were driving around cranking the new Slipknot when Mark popped the

> **Campa was first exposed to the band in June when older brother Bryan returned from college and started playing *Led Zeppelin II* while lifting weights in the garage. After one listen, Campa was reportedly hooked.**

tape out and started messing with the radio," said Rick Eglund, 17. "I was like, 'Dude, what's your problem?' He said it was time for WLUP's 'Get The Led Out,' and that he never

missed it. I told him he was gonna miss it that night. Then, he tried to stop me from putting the tape back into *my own stereo.* I had to pull over and force him to switch seats with Dan [Alberman]."

"The stupid thing is, at the time, we were driving Mark home," Eglund continued. "He has all their CDs, so he could've listened to Zep all night if he'd just waited five minutes. I guess he had to prove what a big fan he is."

In addition to naming his '91 Prelude the "Honda Of The Holy" and renaming his cat of four years "Bonzo" as an homage to late Led Zeppelin drummer John "Bonzo" Bonham, Campa has irritated friends with his constant barrage of Led Zeppelin trivia.

"In the past week alone, I've learned that Keith Moon came up with the band's name, Jimmy Page is in the movie *Blowup,* and 'All Of My Love' is about Robert Plant's son Karac, who died from a viral infection," Savich said. "And if I hear Mark tell us about the 'mudshark incident' one more time, I'm gonna kill him. Everybody knows *Hammer Of The Gods* is bullshit, anyway."

Campa has also developed a habit of pointing out Led Zeppelin connections to seemingly non-Zeppelin-re-

> **"It could be worse, I guess. He could've gotten into the Grateful Dead. Or Floyd. Just imagine if he walked around all day quoting *Dark Side Of The Moon.* Christ."**

lated items.

"I downloaded the *Lord Of The Rings* trailer and, next thing you know, Mark goes into this whole thing about how 'The Battle Of Evermore' references the book *Lord Of The Rings,*" Alberman said. "I had to re-start the trailer after he was done because no one got to see it. It's getting to the point where you're almost afraid to go to a movie with Mark because John Paul Jones' second cousin might be an extra in it."

Added Eglund: "It could be worse, I guess. He could've gotten into the Grateful Dead. Or Floyd. Just imagine if he walked around all day quoting *Dark Side Of The Moon.* Christ." ∅

GORE from page 1

Above: Gore confers with top advisors Simba and Stripe.

ness on a scale equal to any in human history."

Gore, who last week pretended to pledge an additional $1.5 billion in federal aid to New York City, then switched off his razor and pulled out his toothbrush.

"We must honor our fallen heroes by devoting ourselves fully to the causes of liberty and freedom," said Gore, brushing his teeth with small circular motions. "And we must resolve to ensure, as Lincoln said, that government of the people, by the people, and for the people shall not perish from the Earth."

After a long silence, Gore said, "God bless America," and spat.

Gore, who narrowly lost the controversial 2000 presidential election to George W. Bush, then adjourned to the dining room, where he held a closed-door meeting with his top advisors, Simba and Stripe.

Since not taking office in January, Gore's accomplishments on both the domestic and foreign fronts have earned him high praise among fellow family members. His State Of The Union address of June 19 was hailed by wife Tipper as "very nice," despite it having been delivered in his sleep. His late-August tax-reform proposal was generally well received by daughter Kristin, who came across it on the back of a pizza-delivery menu. And his handling of the Sept. 11 tragedy and its aftermath has earned him a 100 percent approval rating within the Gore household.

"He's really risen to the occasion, that's for sure," said Gore housekeeper Virginia Evans, who spent nearly half an hour listening to Gore's anti-terrorism plan after being named his "Secretary Of State" last Thursday. "'President Gore' has taken some

bold, decisive steps to help the American people in this time of crisis."

"All you have to do is see the man rake leaves into piles representing the various members of the international coalition, and you suddenly feel the nation is in good hands," said Gore son-in-law Andrew Schiff. "Or, you

Since not taking office in January, Gore's accomplishments on both the domestic and foreign fronts have earned him high praise among fellow family members.

know, would be, if things had gone differently in Florida and with the Supreme Court and all."

Schiff also lauded the emergency federal-law-enforcement table of organization Gore drew in his mashed potatoes during a recent family dinner as "a masterpiece of delegation and efficiency."

"He's unbelievable, the way he's taken charge," Schiff said. "It's truly amazing how much good he's imagined doing for this country."

Gore's bathroom-mirror speech, his 16th such address since Sept. 11, is widely considered to be the almost-president's most emotional and stirring yet.

"I thought it was very moving," Tipper said. "It was exactly what the nation would have needed to hear in the wake of this horrible tragedy, I suppose." ∅

INGOT from page 2

amounts of blood. Passersby were amazed by the unusually large amounts of blood. Passersby were amazed by the unusually large amounts of blood. Passersby were amazed by the unusually large amounts of blood. Passersby were amazed by the unusually large amounts of blood. Passersby were amazed by the unusually large amounts of blood. Passersby were amazed by the unusually large amounts of blood. Passersby were amazed by the unusually large amounts of blood. Passersby were amazed by the unusually large amounts of blood. Passersby were amazed by the unusually large amounts of blood. Passersby were amazed by the unusually large amounts of blood. Passersby were amazed by the unusually large amounts of blood. Passersby were amazed by the unusually large amounts of blood. Passersby were amazed by the unusually large amounts of blood. Passersby were amazed by the unusually large amounts of blood. Passersby were amazed by the unusually large amounts of blood. Passersby were amazed by the unusually large amounts of blood. Passersby were amazed by the unusually large amounts of blood. Passersby were amazed by the unusually large

amounts of blood. Passersby were amazed by the unusually large amounts of blood. Passersby were amazed by the unusually large amounts of blood. Passersby were amazed by the unusually large amounts of blood. Passersby were amazed by the unusually large amounts of blood. Passersby were amazed by the unusually large amounts of blood. Passersby were amazed by the unusually large

Correction:
Alleged cannibal.

amounts of blood. Passersby were amazed by the unusually large amounts of blood. Passersby were amazed by the unusually large amounts of blood. Passersby were amazed by the unusually large amounts of blood. Passersby were amazed by the unusually large amounts of blood. Passersby were amazed by the unusually large amounts of blood. Passersby were amazed by the unusually large amounts of blood. Passersby were

see INGOT page 9

Lara Flynn Boyle's Publicist Warns Interviewer Upfront

see PEOPLE page 9D

KFC Responds To Stockpiling Trend With 576-Piece Bucket

see PRODUCTWATCH page 11C

Neutered Cat Instinctively Protects Empty Scrotum

see LOCAL page 3E

Googly Moogly: Great?

see LOCAL page 4C

STATshot

A look at the numbers that shape your world.

Worst Excuses For Needing Hug

1. Got incorrect change back
2. Favorite porn actress retired
3. Just vomited down front of favorite shirt
4. Moving into higher tax bracket
5. Still upset about 1946 death of writer Damon Runyon
6. On trial for sexual assault again
7. Forgot your name

the ONION ®

VOLUME 37 ISSUE 40   AMERICA'S FINEST NEWS SOURCE™   8–14 NOVEMBER 2001

U.N. Report:
70 Percent Of World's Population Could Use All-Star Benefit Concert

GENEVA, SWITZERLAND—According to a study released Monday by the U.N. Economic and Social Council, 4.2 billion people—a full 70 percent of the planet's inhabitants—could use an all-star benefit concert.

"Whether ravaged by war, disease,
see BENEFIT page 11

Above: Michael Jackson during the finale of last month's "United We Stand" benefit concert. Right: A group of benefit-concert-needing Bosnian refugees.

Above: Self-proclaimed Afghanistan expert Michael Schloegel.

Area Man Acts Like He's Been Interested In Afghanistan All Along

LEXINGTON, KY—According to friends and colleagues, for nearly two months now, Michael Schloegel has been acting like he was interested in Afghanistan long before Sept. 11.

"Ever since the attacks, he's been making like he's been a Central Asia expert for years," said Lisa Reames, a longtime friend of the 30-year-old University of Kentucky graduate student. "Like, the other day, he was saying how after the Soviets left Afghanistan, an alliance of *mujahideen* set up a new government. Then, he said he remembers when the Soviet-backed government replaced President Barbrak Karmal with Muhammad Najibullah in '86. Yeah,
see AFGHANISTAN page 10

Woman Has Perfect Clip Art For Party Invitation

Above: Riverside Property Management's Irene Smalls.

CHILLICOTHE, MO—Irene Smalls, 45, an office manager at Riverside Property Management, announced Monday that she has found the "perfect clip art" for the invitation to an upcoming office Thanksgiving party.

Slated for officewide distribution this Friday, the invitation to the Nov. 21 celebration features clip-art images of a turkey, a pile of leaves and a rake, a "horn of plenty," and light-hearted cartoons of boy and girl pilgrims.

"I honestly think this is the best invitation I've ever done," Smalls said. "Everything's there: pilgrims, Thanksgiving food, autumn stuff. It's a perfect balance."

Riverside Property Management's unofficial party organizer, Smalls

spent nearly two days deciding which copyright-free illustrations to choose from the company's collection of clip-art booklets and Office Depot-purchased CD-ROMs.

"Choosing art for an invitation is trickier than you'd think," Smalls said. "It should be tasteful but not stuffy, fun but not juvenile."

Offering insight into her artistic process, Smalls revealed that she nixed an image of a Norman Rockwell-like family seated at a dinner table for thematic reasons.

"The dinner scene was nice, but since this party will be a casual office gathering with punch and cupcakes, I didn't think it quite fit," Smalls said. "Then again, I guess you could argue
see CLIP ART page 11

7

Ashcroft's Vague Warnings

U.S. Attorney General John Ashcroft has issued several vague warnings of "credible threats" of terrorism, urging Americans to stay on alert. What do *you* think?

Virginia Innes
Teacher

"I applaud Ashcroft for his warnings. How else would I know when to be on alert for terrorist activity? Look—look how on-alert I am right now."

Brent Cleveland
Doctor

"I thought Ashcroft's most recent warning of possible terrorist attacks was calm and controlled enough, if you ignored the dark, spreading stain on the front of his trousers."

Todd Booth
Roofer

"So Ashcroft didn't specifically mention anything about the Golden Gate Bridge, five pounds of weapons-grade plutonium, or next Thursday afternoon? Cool."

Iris MacNaughton
Graphic Designer

"Does Ashcroft know something we don't? What is it? Never mind, I don't want to know. Wait, yes, I do—tell me! Tell me now! No, don't! No! Mary had a little lamb, little lamb, little lamb..."

Henry Davidson
Cashier

"Gee, the things Ashcroft says seem reasonable enough when they scroll across the bottom of the screen during *Friends*."

Christopher Adams
Systems Analyst

"The whole damn country's been paranoid about terrorism ever since the whole damn country was devastated by terrorism."

Oprah Makes A Correction

Oprah Winfrey recently withdrew her selection of Jonathan Franzen's *The Corrections* for her book club. What did Franzen do to get dropped?

▶ Kept calling it "Oprah's Book Cult"

▶ In NPR interview, described Winfrey as resembling a "chocolate-covered bulldozer"

▶ Let slip that he was a straight, white male who had never been sexually abused

▶ Expressed eagerness to appear on *The Oprah Winfrey Show* "the minute it stops sucking"

▶ Kept stopping by Barnes & Noble and ripping the Oprah's Book Club seals off copies of the book

▶ Refused to cry during appearance on show

▶ Wasn't sure if depressed, alienated housewives would understand novel about depressed, alienated people

▶ *New Yorker* editor David Remnick warned Franzen that if he went on *Oprah*, he couldn't be in the Big Brainy Writers' Club anymore

▶ Kept making the sort of non-groveling remarks to which Winfrey is unaccustomed

Ⓐ the ONION®
America's Finest News Source.™

Herman Ulysses Zweibel
Founder

T. Herman Zweibel
Publisher Emeritus
J. Phineas Zweibel
Publisher
Maxwell Prescott Zweibel
Editor-In-Chief

If I Don't Get My Medium-Rare Shell Steak With Roasted Vegetables In The Next 10 Minutes, The Terrorists Have Already Won

Waitress, I realize you're very busy and no doubt have a lot on your mind. God knows, everyone does these days. But what this country needs

By Bernard Kloss

right now is a return to normalcy. We need to work, laugh, and eat the way we did before Sept. 11. That's why it's absolutely vital that I get my medium-rare shell steak with roasted vegetables in the next 10 minutes. Because if I don't, well, then the terrorists have already won.

These are hard times for all of us. Some days, I can barely bring myself to send back my tuna sandwich for having too much mayo or too little tarragon. Yet to hang my head in defeat and eat a sandwich that fails to meet my personal specifications is exactly what they want us to do. They want us to give up and admit defeat. I don't know how you were raised, but when life deals me a blow, I pick myself up, dust myself off, and demand that the kitchen reheat my lobster bisque. That's the way I am, and I'm not going to let some fundamentalist wacko halfway around the world change that.

> You have to understand that keeping Americans from getting a finely marbled cut of tenderloin, de-boned and seared to perfection, in a timely manner is phase three of the terrorists' plan.

You have to understand that keeping Americans from getting a finely marbled cut of tenderloin, de-boned and seared to perfection, in a timely manner is phase three of the terrorists' plan. The first was the destruction of our most powerful political and financial symbols. The second was to shake our confidence in our government's ability to protect us. The third is to prevent us from enjoying the high standards of service that customers here at Joe's Steak Pit have come to expect.

Don't you realize that by giving me poor service, you're giving poor service to America itself? Until you can learn to get me a decently chilled Pinot Grigio, maybe you should take that American-flag pin off your apron. Your entire kitchen staff is making a mockery of everything

> Do you want the blood of our forefathers to have been spilled for nothing? Well, if you can't bring us the entrees we need to rebuild our strength as a nation in the next five minutes, you might as well move to Afghanistan.

those stars and stripes stand for. You should feel ashamed wearing such a pin. You should also comp us free desserts to make up for the long wait.

At this crucial juncture in our nation's history, we have to come together as one. Only then do we stand a chance of getting through this. Also, we need a busboy over here ASAP to refill our water. If not, the fine line between quality service and chaos will not only be crossed, but stomped on. Without constant beverage refills, we might as well tear up the constitution and declare this great land of ours a theocratic dictatorship. Surely, the busboy understands the connection between prompt water refills and liberty, doesn't he? Perhaps you can remind him.

Do you want the blood of our forefathers to have been spilled for nothing? Well, if you can't bring us the entrees we need to rebuild our strength as a nation in the next five minutes, you might as well move to Afghanistan and join in one of their American-flag-burning rallies. Because that's what you're really doing.

I understand you got our appetizers to us relatively quickly, but that's only half the battle. Right now, you need to go to the waitress station and ask yourself some difficult questions. Namely, are you part of the problem or part of the solution?

Also, we need some fresh rolls when you get a chance. ∅

Model-Train Hobby Becomes Model-Train Habit

When Leon Gehr began dabbling in model trains, his family wasn't terribly concerned, confident he could handle it.

BILLINGS, MT—Though he insists he can handle it, Leon Gehr's model-train pastime has crossed the line from hobby to habit, Gehr family sources reported Monday.

"Leon just isn't the same person anymore," said Penny Gehr, 48, Leon's wife of 21 years. "All he ever thinks about is where he's going to get his next few feet of nickel silver snap-together track. It's all-consuming. I want my husband back."

"I'd been dabbling in die-cast metal cars for years, and then one day, about three years ago, I thought to myself, 'Boy, it sure would be fun if these cars could run,'" said a glassy-eyed Gehr, his arms covered with railroad-track marks. "The fella at the hobby store said to me, 'What you want is a model railroad.' From that day forward, I was hooked. Now, I'm a big railhead."

When Gehr began dabbling in model trains, his family wasn't terribly concerned, confident he could handle it.

"Dad experimented for years with cars and even model airplanes, so I didn't think a whole lot of it," said Cory, his 19-year-old son. "It was always a weekend thing, something

Last winter, Gehr converted his family's basement rec room into a maze of twisting tracks and miniature houses. He began to stay up until all hours of the night gluing branches onto miniature trees.

he did for kicks. If I'd only known what the model trains would do to him, how addictive they are, I would have organized an intervention long ago."

For the first two and a half years, Gehr's model-railroad use appeared to be under control. Eventually, however, the trains began to take over.

Above: Model-train addict Leon Gehr poses with his stash.

"At first, Leon would buy just a flatbed here or a tanker there. Then, it started to pick up," Penny said. "Before long, he was doubling the number of cars he was bringing home, then tripling. Without us knowing it, he'd crossed the Rock Island line."

"Leon and I used to grab a beer or watch a ballgame together," friend Jason Gammon said. "At some point, he gave all that up and just withdrew into his own world—one on a 1:48 scale."

Last winter, Gehr converted his family's basement rec room into a maze of twisting tracks and miniature houses. He began to stay up until all hours of the night gluing branches onto miniature trees. On more than one occasion, he was late to work because of his habit, sleeping through his ringing alarm clock after staying up until 2 a.m. on a bridge-painting binge.

The breaking point came two weekends ago, when Gehr drove six hours to the Montana Model Railroad Association convention in Missoula.

"I begged him not to go, but he wouldn't listen," Penny said. "He said he had to find a Lionel Pennsylvania Flyer Train Set Model 6-3191 and that he'd do anything for it. He slipped out when I was still asleep and left a note saying he wanted to 'get an early start.'"

The back of the note, however, painted an even more disturbing picture. In the frenzied scrawl of a man possessed were written the words, "Precision can motor / Transformer controlled forward / Neutral and reverse / Operating headlight and puffing smoke unit / Detailed molded tender body with stamped metal frame and operating air whistle. Must get 40-WATT TRANSFORMER!!!"

The night after he left, Penny received a call from her husband, who said he'd decided to stay the night in Missoula. When he finally got home 36 hours later, his eyes were bloodshot and he'd blown more than $600 on Bachmann O-scale Cityscenes building kits.

"I finally gave him an ultimatum," Penny said. "I said, 'Either the model trains go or I go.'"

Even when threatened with losing his wife, Leon continued to deny he has a problem.

"Penny likes to give me the business about how much money I spend on these trains, but what she doesn't realize is that they're an investment," Gehr said. "I could make some real money someday if I ever decided to turn around and start selling."

"I just know he's going to do something stupid and get in way over his head. He's going to throw away everything he's worked so hard for," Penny said. "That Sam Gilchrist is the one I blame for this."

Gilchrist, who works at the East Towne Mall's Hobby Haven, intro-duced Gehr to model railroading.

"Sam and the others who hang out at the hobby shop all day have dragged Leon down into the dirt with

> **"Leon and I used to grab a beer or watch a ballgame together," friend Jason Gammon said. "At some point, he gave all that up and just withdrew into his own world—one on a 1:48 scale."**

them," Penny said. "Now, my husband is a train careening out of control."

Unbeknownst to Penny, Gilchrist recently informed Gehr that he has a job waiting for him at Hobby Haven if he ever wants it.

"If I worked at the Hobby Haven, I could just hang out and talk to people about trains all day," Gehr said. "I know it sounds crazy, but I could make a lot of money working on commission. Plus, I'd get the employee discount. And if I ever did get tired of it, I know I could quit at any time." ∅

fucking right. I'm sure he was aware of that when he was 15."

Friends concede that the intelligent and well-read Schloegel may well have known something about Afghanistan prior to the crisis, but they say he is exaggerating the depth of this knowledge.

"I'm sure Mike knew more about [Afghanistan] than I do," roommate Ben Ware said. "He probably knew what the capital was and maybe some real basic stuff about the Taliban. But I lived with him over the summer, and I don't recall him ever going off about the history of the Northern Alliance like he does these days."

Ware said Schloegel is often seen carrying books related to the crisis, including such current bestsellers as Karen Armstrong's *Islam: A Short History* and Ahmed Rashid's *Taliban*. Ware said he is "99.9 percent sure" that Schloegel purchased the books in recent weeks.

"Yesterday, he was saying something about Al Qaeda, and then he says, 'There's some very interesting stuff about them in Cooley's *Unholy Wars: Afghanistan, America And International Terrorism*, which I read last year,'" Ware said. "It was so obvious he was going out of his way to mention when he read it. And what's with the last-name-only reference to the author? Like I'm supposed to know who 'Cooley' is? Like I'm actually supposed to believe that Mike knows who Cooley is? Please."

According to Reames, within days of the Sept. 11 attacks, Schloegel began to speak frequently of the history of the Afghan people. She said he implored people to not hate Arabs, urging them to "try to understand the historical conditions that led to this unfortunate situation."

"Mike said to me, 'The land has been filled with turmoil for thousands of years, since Darius I and Alexander The Great first used Afghanistan as the gateway to India,'" Reames recalled. "'Islamic conquerors arrived in the 7th century, and Genghis Khan and Tamerlane followed in the 13th and 14th. Then, we all know what happened in the 19th century: the three Anglo-Afghan Wars—let's see, 1839-42, 1878-80, and 1919—which just made everything worse.'"

While Reames called Schloegel's desire to understand world politics commendable, she said "lately it's been too much."

"Afghan history seems very interesting, and I'm glad he's into it," Reames said. "But he doesn't have to lord it over everybody, prefacing everything with, 'As I'm sure you already know…' He should just say, 'As I now know because I just read it on cnn.com about five minutes ago…' Sheesh."

Another blatantly contrived moment came Monday, when Schloegel told friends he has always wanted to visit Afghanistan but "probably won't be able to go any time soon."

"It's really too bad that Afghanistan is plunged in strife and turmoil,"

> Schloegel is often seen carrying books related to the crisis, including such current bestsellers as Karen Armstrong's *Islam: A Short History* and Ahmed Rashid's *Taliban*. Ware said he is "99.9 percent sure" that Schloegel purchased the books in recent weeks.

Schloegel said. "It's actually an amazingly beautiful place. The country is split east to west by the beautiful snowcaps of the Hindu Kush mountain range, rising in the east to heights of 24,000 feet."

In spite of evidence that his expertise is only recently gained, Schloegel continues to rail against the ignorance of others.

"It's really sad how little people know about the world around them," Schloegel said. "Take the recent anthrax attacks, which I saw coming from a mile away. It's all laid out in

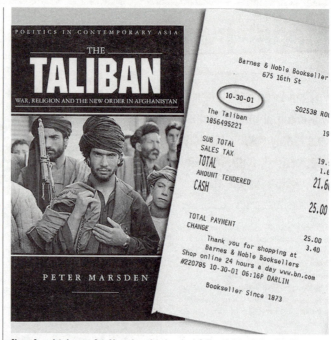

Above: A receipt shows an Oct. 30 purchase date for a book Schloegel claims to have bought three years ago.

Miller, Engelberg, and Broad's *Germs: Biological Weapons And America's Secret War*. In it, the authors make it plain that our government knew about the threat of just such an attack as early as 1991. But did anybody listen, much less do anything? Sadly, no."

This is not the first time Schloegel has suspiciously claimed current-events expertise. Last November, he spontaneously became an expert in ballot-counting procedure and election law, and earlier this year, he "wouldn't shut up" about global warming and the history of the Kyoto Protocol. ∅

NEWS IN BRIEF

Flood Of Cheap Afghan Heroin To Arrive Just In Time For Recession

NEW YORK—The nation's smack addicts received welcome news Monday, when *The Wall Street Journal* reported that the war in Afghanistan has opened the floodgates for cheap Afghan heroin, just in time for the coming recession. "Even if their stock portfolios are dwindling, America's junkies can take heart in the fact that the Taliban is embarking on a massive heroin sell-off, slashing prices dramatically," *Wall Street Journal* reporter Tom Petzinger said. "So even if GE drops to $20 a share, keep in mind that heroin has dropped to $50 a gram." Ed Evans, a recently laid-off Detroit auto worker and longtime heroin addict, called the report "real great, uh, that's unnnnhhf…"

Olive Garden Voted Best Italian Restaurant In Annual *Milwaukee Magazine* Awards

MILWAUKEE, WI—For the second straight year, Olive Garden took top honors in the "Best Italian Restaurant" category in *Milwaukee Maga-*zine's annual "Best Of Milwaukee" poll. "For authentic Italian cuisine and friendly service (they call it Hospitaliano), the Blue Mound Road Olive Garden is the one to beat," wrote the magazine, whose readers voted for the chain restaurant over such local stalwarts as Mimma's Cafe and Balistreri's. "Once again, Olive Garden is Milwaukee's finest." High marks were also given to the Mayfair Mall Chi-Chi's, voted "Best Date Spot" for the third year running.

Weird Coworker Apparently Likes Walking Two Miles To Work Every Day

SACRAMENTO, CA—Despite owning a car and receiving frequent offers of rides from coworkers, State Farm Insurance claims adjuster Jonathan Kiel inexplicably prefers to make the daily two-mile trek to work on foot. "I know he's got a car, and he certainly earns enough for a monthly bus pass," coworker Colin Damrush said, "but for some freaky, mind-boggling reason, he insists on walking a distance of almost two miles every day—to *and* from work." Damrush said he and others in the office suspect Kiel is part of "some weird Luddite cult."

JCPenney Abandons 45-Second Sale

PLANO, TX—JCPenney announced Monday that it is discontinuing its "45-Second Sale," in which all store items are 60 percent off from 1:00:00 p.m. to 1:00:45 p.m. "The 45-second sale drew very strong customer response," JCPenney CEO Allen Questrom said Monday. "Regrettably, only a handful of shoppers actually got to capitalize on our fantastic bargains due to the horrific injuries they sustained during the cashier stampede. In the future, Questrom said, JCPenney sales would be two minutes long at an absolute minimum.

Actor's Parents Proud He's Playing A Doctor

SOUTHFIELD, MI—Gail and Milt Greenblatt, parents of soap-opera star Brett Green, are beaming with pride that their son is a doctor on ABC's *All My Children*. "Dr. Cord Montgomery graduated from Harvard Medical School at the top of his class," Gail told a neighbor Monday. "What's more, he's the youngest surgeon at Pine Valley's top hospital." Milt expressed relief that his son has left behind the "rough crowd" he ran with last fall as a bully on *Gilmore Girls*. ∅

BENEFIT from page 7

natural disaster, or just plain grinding poverty, there are a whole heck of a lot of people out there in desperate need of a star-studded fundraiser at Madison Square Garden," ECOSOC president Martin Belinga-Eboutou said. "Or, if not that, a Quincy Jones-produced remake of 'What's Going On' featuring everyone from P. Diddy to 'N Sync to U2's Bono."

Belinga-Eboutou pointed to the recent success of Concert For New York City, a five-and-a-half-hour extravaganza featuring such superstars as Elton John, Mick Jagger, Backstreet Boys, Paul McCartney, and Destiny's Child, among others. Earnings from the benefit, which aired on VH1 and will soon be released as a double-disc CD, are expected to surpass the $150 million raised in last month's all-star *America: A Tribute To Heroes* telethon.

"If we could get something like that going in the 315,583 places on the globe the U.N. has identified as 'in crisis,' we'd really have something," Belinga-Eboutou said.

Belinga-Eboutou cited Gujarat, the Indian state where a January earthquake killed an estimated 100,000 people and left nearly one million homeless, as an example of a region that could use a night of star-studded "compassiontainment."

"If Jerry Seinfeld could see it in his heart to toss off a few of his trademark observational one-liners for the needy people of Gujarat, it would greatly alleviate the suffering they

have endured," Belinga-Eboutou said. "And the rock stylings of a reunited Who would be much appreciated, as well."

Last week, the U.N. established an exploratory committee to begin the arduous task of assigning stars to the world's trouble spots. However, with the ratio of needy locales to bankable stars standing at 4,390 to 1, an estimated 800 two-hour concerts per celebrity would be required over the next year to set things right in the world. These figures are also contingent upon no further natural or man-made catastrophes occurring during that time period.

Though only in its initial stages, the deployment of stars has already begun. Last week, R&B sensation Pink was dispatched to Indonesia to raise money for the families of the 350 asylum-seeking refugees who drowned in an overcrowded boat last month, while Arista recording artist Dido is slated to perform Nov. 27 in war-torn Macedonia. In addition, the '80s new-wave band Soft Cell has agreed to reunite for three December shows in AIDS-ravaged South Africa.

New York concert promoter Ron Delsener, who is in talks to organize more than 22,000 relief concerts on behalf of the U.N., said the logistical problems such a humanitarian effort would present are considerable.

"There just aren't any adequate venues for, say, an Ozzy Osbourne show in Sierra Leone," Delsener said. "No stadiums, no arenas, not even a

large auditorium. And have you ever tried tracking down a pyrotechnics expert with a union card in sub-Saharan Africa? It's practically impossible."

Delsener also noted that the cost of providing adequate security at such a

> "If we could get something like that going in the 315,583 places on the globe the U.N. has identified as 'in crisis,' we'd really have something," Belinga-Eboutou said.

concert would be greater than the gross national product of the nation in need.

In spite of such challenges, Third World leaders are urging musicians to do whatever they can.

"It is up to each and every star to pitch in," said Nicaraguan president José Arnoldo Alemán Lacayo, whose drought-ravaged country will soon receive help in the form of Eagle-Eye Cherry. "From heavy hitters such as Billy Joel and Bruce Springsteen to young upstarts like Macy Gray, the world needs all the singers it can get."

The world's impoverished received more good news Monday, when George Harrison, whose 1971 Concert For Bangladesh was the first all-star fundraiser, said plans are underway for a follow-up show.

"I've already talked to Ringo [Starr] and Eric Clapton, and Tom Petty appears to be interested, too," Harrison said. "The Concert For Bangladesh was such a big success, there's no reason to think that this upcoming Concert For Albania, Algeria, Angola, Armenia, Azerbaijan, Belarus, Belize, Benin, Bolivia, Bosnia and Herzegovina, Botswana, Bulgaria, Burkina Faso, Burundi, Cambodia, Cameroon, Central African Republic, Chad, Colombia, Congo, Costa Rica, Côte d'Ivoire, Croatia, Cuba, Djibouti, Egypt, El Salvador, Eritrea, Ethiopia, Gabon, Gambia, Georgia, Ghana, Guatemala, Haiti, Honduras, India, Indonesia, Iran, Iraq, Jamaica, Kazakhstan, Kenya, Kyrgyzstan, Laos, Latvia, Lesotho, Liberia, Libya, Lithuania, Macedonia, Malawi, Mali, Mexico, Mongolia, Morocco, Mozambique, Myanmar, Namibia, Nepal, Nicaragua, Niger, Nigeria, North Korea, Pakistan, Panama, Paraguay, The Philippines, Romania, Russia, Rwanda, Senegal, Serbia and Montenegro, Sierra Leone, Slovakia, Slovenia, Somalia, Sri Lanka, Sudan, Tajikistan, Tanzania, Thailand, Tunisia, Turkey, Turkmenistan, Uganda, Ukraine, Uzbekistan, Vietnam, Yugoslavia, Zaire, Zambia, and Zimbabwe won't be just as great." *∅*

CLIP ART from page 7

that our office is like one big family, so it's appropriate. In the end, though, I decided that if I used it, the reason probably wouldn't come across. So you see, it just depends how you look at it. There are lots of shades of gray when you're talking about clip art."

Smalls also left out an image of a Native American man carrying ears of corn.

"I didn't want to make [leasing agent] Joseph [White], who's one-

Below: The invitation.

quarter Indian, feel uncomfortable," Smalls said. "I think a lot of that 'Heap Big Injun' stuff reminds him of the sad things that happened to his people."

Smalls said her formidable clip-art-selection skills are the result of years of trial and error. In 1987, she learned a valuable lesson when choosing images for a church pancake-breakfast flyer.

"I wanted it to be eye-catching, so I went to Bartz Party Supply and

picked out some classy pictures from their clip-art book, including a couple ballroom-dancing, two hands clinking champagne glasses, and a top hat with white gloves and a cane," Smalls said. "Now, that would've worked just dandy for a wedding or New Year's Eve invitation, but, as I found out the hard way, not for a pancake breakfast. Only eight people showed up, and some parishioners complained that they

thought the breakfast was going to be a ritzy affair. They were too intimidated to attend."

Rather than give up, Smalls resolved to "stick it out and get better at clip art." She now boasts of being able to find the ideal clip art for any occasion.

"I love to rise to any clip-art challenge," Smalls said. "Birthdays, weddings, anniversaries, July 4... you name it, I've got the perfect clip art for it. I even have a Star Of David for our Jewish friends."

Smalls' appreciation of clip art is heartening to Mitch Sklar, a Buffalo, NY, freelance artist who creates illustrations for the clip-art market.

"We clip artists work in near-total anonymity: No one knows who we are, and we barely ever know who's out there enjoying our clip artistry," said Sklar, who designed the leaves and rake Smalls used for her invitation. "So when I hear that someone appreciated my work enough to use it in their PTA newsletter or blood-donation sign-up sheet, I feel really proud."

Smalls takes equal pride in her creations.

"Making invitations and flyers is the most rewarding thing about my job, I think," Smalls said. "Even though I can barely draw a stick figure, doing this stuff makes me feel like a real creative artist." *∅*

Thanksgiving Party!

WHEN: Wednesday, November 21, 5:30 pm
WHERE: Break Room

See You there!

I'm No Tali-fan!

The Outside Scoop
By Jackie Harvey

Item! Terrorism has hit these shores, and I for one am ready to put my foot down and say enough! I don't care if I become a target for terror as a result of my stance. I think this is the time for action, not silence. So I've put an **American flag** on my car, one on my mailbox, and one on my dog. Take that, **Osama Ben Laden!**

Does Osama have any idea just how many millions of Americans strongly support America? If he ever came here and saw all the flags on every street, he'd quickly find out. Then he'd go running back to wherever it is he came from! And, hey, just how is that name spelled, anyway? I've seen Osama and Ossama and Usama. Here's a suggestion for the media: Spell it **J-E-R-K**.

I don't know about you, but I must have eaten my weight in **peanut-butter sandwiches** over the past month or so.

All this terrorism and war has really put a damper on the **Emmy Awards**. They were scheduled twice and cancelled twice. But in true American fashion, the Emmy people have decided that the show must go on! And so it will, sometime in late November, I think. In case you want one person's opinion on what to expect, assuming they happen (or haven't already happened), take out your scorecards and get ready for **Jackie Harvey's 2001 Emmy Prediction Picks!**

Best Drama Series? Let's look at the nominees. They are **ER**, **Law And Order**, **Tony Soprano**, **Practice Makes Perfect**, and **West Wings**. Well, before Sept. 11, I would've said *ER*, if only for their bold choice of going widescreen. However, I think nowadays the nation needs the healing, calming influence of our other president, **Josiah Bartlett**. I predict the academy will keep this in mind and give Commander-In-Chief Bartlett the big gold one. *Tony Soprano* is okay, but it has a bit too much harsh language for me to endorse it.

For **Best Actress In A Movie Or Miniseries**, look no further than Sir Judi Dench. I'm pretty sure she's been nominated.

And for **Best Actress In A Drama Series**? Please! It could only be **Eileen Brenneman** from **Chasing Amy**. I picked her because a girl in my high school had the same name, and she was pretty nice. Well, that wasn't the only reason, but it was a pretty big factor.

And if this isn't **Becker's** year for **Best Comedy Show**, I may stop watching the Emmys altogether. (Aw, who am I kidding? Emmy, I'd never turn you away!)

That's all the advice I feel comfortable giving you, because for all I know, you might be in an **Emmy Pool** against me!

Have you heard about this **"Terror Sex"**? I understand it was a big thing for a while after the tragedy. Otherwise, why would **Salon** have run an article about it? I guess it makes sense that people would do that. After all, in the words of **Stephen Crosby-Stills**, if you can't be with the one you love in times of international terrorism, love the one you're with.

> ### Does Osama have any idea just how many millions of Americans strongly support America? If he ever came here and saw all the flags on every street, he'd quickly find out.

Item! I'm just wild about Harry! **Harry Potter**, that is! Okay, so I've never read any of the books, and I haven't seen the movie. But there's so much hullabaloo surrounding it all, I'm quite certain that if I had read the books or seen the movie, I'd be wild enough about Harry for that clever play on words to be true.

It looks like those **reality-TV shows** are really taking a whomping from those old-fashioned **regular-TV shows**. After **Rudy** and the **Wisconsin truck-driving woman with the huge husband** squared off on **Survivor I** and racy bartendress Kimmi was booted off **Survivor II**, I lost all interest. Who's going to win **Temptation Island 2**? I am... because I'm not watching!

Item! **Britney Spears'** new album is due out soon, and rumor has it we can look forward to a **sexy image makeover** from the young singing sensation! I don't know about you, but I can't wait to see what she's got in store for us!

You know how the **New York Police Department** is abbreviated **NYPD**? Well, I was surprised to find out that the fire department is the **FDNY**, not the NYFD. Funny how that works.

Item! **Kevin Spacey** has a new movie out. It's called **K-PAX**, and the verdict is... it's K-OK! I saw it over the weekend, and Spacey really delivers, looking up at the stars in wide-eyed wonderment. He also smiles a lot, in this really wise way that tells you that he understands the human spirit. It's great to see somebody doing that sort

Your Horoscope

By Lloyd Schumner Sr.
Retired Machinist and
A.A.P.B.-Certified Astrologer

Aries: (March 21–April 19)
Life is just a big joke to you, which wouldn't be so bad if it wasn't the one about the chicken crossing the road.

Taurus: (April 20–May 20)
You will spend virtually all of your money, time, and effort before learning that fashion is not very important.

Gemini: (May 21–June 21)
The famous saying actually says that golf is "a good walk spoiled," not "a waste of time and an annoyance to the pig." Let the poor pig out of your golf bag.

Cancer: (June 22–July 22)
It's not easy being a loving, giving, trusting person in this world. On the other hand, it's no picnic working in advertising, either.

Leo: (July 23–Aug. 22)
Don't worry too much about what tomorrow may bring, as nobody can tell the future. Except the stars, of course, and they aren't telling.

Virgo: (Aug. 23–Sept. 22)
People who say you drive like your car is an extension of your penis have never seen your brain-surgery work.

Libra: (Sept. 23–Oct. 23)
The ancient Greeks tell us that there were two basic forms of human love, *eros* and *agape*. But, apparently, they told you something different.

Scorpio: (Oct. 24–Nov. 21)
You will score a major victory at work when you're able to produce documentation proving that the appropriate person has died and made you God.

Sagittarius: (Nov. 22–Dec. 21)
Try to listen more carefully and openly to what other people think, even if they're completely wrong.

Capricorn: (Dec. 22–Jan. 19)
You experience a truly Chekhovian moment when you witness a devout couple praying over the grave of their atheist son. It won't affect you much, though.

Aquarius: (Jan. 20–Feb. 18)
There are many people who claim they'd rather be fishing, but you seem to actually mean it.

Pisces: (Feb. 19–March 20)
You will experience inner turmoil after reading way too much into a statement filled with vague, undefined terms.

of thing now that **Robin Williams** has disappeared off the face of the Earth.

Anyway, I usually use my last paragraph, or **"graph"** as we call it in the biz, to give you a teaser for my next column. Instead, I'm using it to make an urgent plea to check out a show on **Broadway**. They could really use your support. Hey, for $115 plus service charge, where else can you see stars like **Reba McEntire** and **Tom Wopat** whoop it up in **Annie Get Your Gun**? Or **Bernadette Peters** in **whatever she's starring in these days**? Nowhere except New York City! So if you're in the area, go see a show. It's the most patriotic thing you can do short of enlisting in the armed services.

And the **Red Cross** could still use your blood! Please donate now if you haven't already. I'd do it myself, but I faint at the sight of a needle.

Well, that's it for now. So keep 'em waving, **men** and **women**, **boys** and **girls**. And remember: America is still number one for ringing freedom and waving wheat fields and fruited plains and pie. Not just apple, but every kind of pie! See you next time... on the outside! *✎*

HAMMOCK from page 10
of blood. Passersby were amazed by the unusually large amounts of blood. Passersby were amazed by the unusually large amounts of blood. Passersby were amazed by the unusually large amounts of blood. Passersby were amazed by the unusually large amounts of blood. Passersby were amazed by the unusually large amounts of blood. Passersby were

---

Are socks in fashion this season?

---

amazed by the unusually large amounts of blood. Passersby were amazed by the unusually large amounts of blood. Passersby were amazed by the unusually large amounts of blood. Passersby were amazed by the unusually large amounts of blood. Passersby were amazed by the unusually large amounts of blood. Passersby were amazed by the unusually large amounts of blood. Passersby were

see HAMMOCK page 15

Congress To Meet At Feingold's House Today

see NATION page 6A

Hot-Dog Craving Ends After First Bite

see EATS page 10E

Wedding Ring Mistakenly Left Inside Prostitute

see LOCAL page 4D

Man Waxes Patriotic, Truck

see LOCAL page 5D

STATshot

A look at the numbers that shape your world.

What Are We Feeling That Would Be Better Expressed In German?

1. Dread of something inevitable yet benign
   Fuerchtenünabwendbarfreundlich
2. The wish to see all suffer for the crimes of one
   Schadenallemeinverbrechen
3. Laughter at something one knows in one's soul is not funny
   Lachenaüfkomischsnichtspaßheit
4. Shame over eating last piece of Black Forest cherry cake
   Schwarzschamekirschkuchenessen

THE ONION • $2.00 US • $3.00 CAN

0 74470 94595 6

---

the ONION®

VOLUME 37 ISSUE 41   AMERICA'S FINEST NEWS SOURCE™   15–21 NOVEMBER 2001

6,000 Runners Fail To Discover Cure For Breast Cancer

ATLANTA—In spite of their diligent, dedicated running, the 6,000-plus participants in Sunday's 5K Race For The Cure did not find a cure for breast cancer.

Hopes were high, given the excellent weather and record turnout for the 11th annual event, but no viable cure for the disease was discovered along the 3.1-mile course.

"We were particularly hopeful of locating the cure somewhere around the two-and-a-half-mile mark," race organizer Jill Broadbent said. "At that point, the route goes right past Northside Hospital and within a block of several Emory University oncology facilities. That seemed the most promising place to perhaps spot a breast-cancer cure. Regrettably, the runners were unable to do more than momentarily glimpse in researchers' windows as they passed by."

At 10 a.m., participants gathered outside the Georgia Dome and proceeded to search through much of downtown Atlanta, including a one-mile stretch

see CANCER page 16

Above: Race For The Cure runners take off in search of a breast-cancer cure.

Spaghetti-Os Discontinued As Franco-American Relations Break Down

PARIS—With talks collapsing at the 11th hour, Franco-American relations hit an all-time low Monday, casting the future of Spaghetti-Os-brand canned pasta in serious doubt.

"Thus far, three months of negotiations have yielded bitter fruit," French minister of foods Guy Charpentier said. "Despite concessionary offers from both sides, no acceptable compromise has been reached on a number of key issues, including sauce tanginess,

sodium levels, and pasta-ring size. As a result, the sort of friendly Franco-American partnership necessary to produce the neat, round spaghetti one can eat with a spoon may no longer be possible."

U.S. Canned Goods Secretary James Miller echoed

Charpentier's sentiments with a terse, "Uh-oh... Spaghetti-Os are in grave jeopardy."

see SPAGHETTI-OS page 16

Above: French prime minister Lionel Jospin and U.S. Canned Goods Secretary James Miller at last month's Franco-American conference. Left: Spaghetti-Os.

Luann Creator Wrestling With How To Address Terrorist Crisis

SAN MARCOS, CA—Greg Evans, creator of the popular *Luann* comic strip, continues to struggle to find the right way to address the events of Sept. 11 and their aftermath, the cartoonist reported from his home Monday.

"I definitely feel an obligation to address this tragedy—through Luann's eyes," said Evans, referring to Luann DeGroot, the inquisitive and outspoken teen whose adventures appear daily in more than 300 newspapers nationwide. "It's a real high-wire act: entertaining, informing, and providing emotional support to my readers all at the same time. But it's a chal-

lenge I have no choice but to rise to."

"I'm so lucky to have this public forum," Evans continued. "With it, however, comes responsibility. I must not let my readers down."

Though he has been wrestling with it for weeks, Evans has yet to integrate the current crisis into either the plotline about Luann's crush on Aaron Hill or the subplot about Bernice's budding romance with Zane.

"Zane is the strip's first character in a wheelchair, so I think it would send a terrible message to suddenly drop his storyline," Evans said. "I definitely have to find a way to work this in, though. Like the rest of the country, the gang at Pitts High School would

see LUANN page 17

Left: The creator of *Luann* in his studio.

13

Could Osama Get The Bomb?

Last week, President Bush disclosed that Osama bin Laden has been trying to acquire nuclear weapons. What do *you* think of the possibility?

"Come on, how's a multi-millionaire with close ties to the world's most ruthless, amoral arms dealers gonna get his hands on a nuclear device?"

Larry Messick
Systems Analyst

"If so, he missed his chance: The Emmys were a few weeks ago."

Barry Frees
Plumber

"Let me guess what's next: bin Laden has an asteroid the size of the moon, and he's aiming it straight at the Earth."

Kim Welker
Speech Therapist

"Shit, we should be trying to find this guy."

Dan Butler
Landscaper

"As a lifelong New Yorker, I must admit that central Kansas is not without a certain rustic, remote charm."

Ronald Foray
Advertising Executive

"What's this? I'm sorry, I stopped paying attention to the news about three weeks ago out of sheer psychological self-preservation."

Lois Vanderpyl
Architect

The Post-Office Cash Crunch

Reeling from a post-Sept. 11 drop in mail volume, the U.S. Postal Service faces a $3 billion deficit. What is the USPS doing to improve its bottom line?

- Following Suriname's lead and issuing limited-edition Dave Matthews stamp
- Cutting that lazy-ass, do-nothing Mr. Zip from the payroll
- Staying open past 5 goddamn o'clock so people can stop by on their way home from work, for Christ's sake
- Introducing lickable $20 stamp with "special majik adhesive" on back (first one free)
- Launching new ad slogan: "You Could Just E-mail, But Then You'd Be Contributing To The Ongoing Fragmentation Of American Society Through Mechanization"
- Finally releasing controversial "Shut Up, Bitch" stamp
- Hiring employees who don't obviously hate people

⌀ the ONION®
America's Finest News Source.™

Herman Ulysses Zweibel
Founder

T. Herman Zweibel
Publisher Emeritus
J. Phineas Zweibel
Publisher
Maxwell Prescott Zweibel
Editor-In-Chief

14

I Do So Adore The Adult Theatre

Ah, the adult theatre! As a discriminating patron of the adult arts, nothing compares to a night out enjoying the lights, glamour, and pelvic

By Denny Wexler

gyrations of the adult theatre. Each performance is a glorious release, filling me with the joy and elation that only high smut can deliver.

Let me describe my perfect Saturday evening to you. It starts off with an early dinner, followed by a Bud tall boy or three. Then, it's off to the adult theatre to delight in some hot, throbbing facial action. Nothing could be more satisfying! If done properly, the adult theatre lifts the soul, frees the spirit, and engorges the genitals. Yes, only the adult theatre can transform the dull routine of the Everyman into something truly magical through staged acts of moaning, heaving, and fucking and sucking.

By any chance, did you happen to catch the Chrysti & Sindi Sextravaganza at Club Platinum last Thursday? Spectacular! Truly a night to remember. The musical numbers were exquisitely choreographed, as if angels themselves had descended from above to guide the action. Ever graceful, Chrysti glided gracefully up and down the brass pole to the strains of Mystikal's "Shake Ya Ass."

And Sindi? Oh, she was magnificent! From the moment she took the stage, a vision in rhinestone pasties, she held everyone transfixed. I don't exaggerate when I say that she brought the house down with her show-stopping lollipop number. But the third act was the true *coup de grace*: Their bodies intertwined in sapphic splendor, Chrysti and Sindi wowed the crowd with their human-totem-pole trick. It was almost more than I could bear... a feast for all the senses!

Those who think adult theatre is only for those upper-crust types who attend live dramatic performances are quite mistaken. The adult theatre is for everyone, and it thrives in any number of formats. Much like an official cast recording can bring home all the magic of a Broadway musical, the adult theatre can be enjoyed at home with videotapes. In fact, many of the best adult dramatic productions are exclusive to home viewing.

Take, for example, *Motel Sex*, starring adult-theatre legend Asia Carrera. You could never find a production like that mounted onstage. The reason is simple: In order to capture the essence of a motel, it is necessary to use a real motel, and no stage set can achieve the level of verisimilitude demanded by adult-theatre connoisseurs. Oh, there are those purists who say you cannot duplicate the adult-

theatrical experience within an electronic medium, but I say home viewing, when done properly, is every bit as good as a live show.

There are those who charge that the adult theatre is superficial. They claim it's all artifice, nothing but a lot of *sturm und tang* with no real substance undergirding it all. These so-called "critics" are sorely misinformed. If only they would let go of their conventional, preconceived notions of what "good theatre" is, they would see the beauty and timelessness of such tales as *Cum-Crazed Slurp Sluts Vol. 14*.

Still skeptical? As Exhibit A, I pre-

> There are those who charge that the adult theatre is superficial. They claim it's all artifice, nothing but a lot of *sturm und tang* with no real substance undergirding it all.

sent to you the straight-to-video feature *Farrah's Anal Adventure*. I don't exaggerate when I say it made me dizzy with paroxysms of ass-eating joy! I also recently caught a big-screen showing of the classic *Behind The Green Door*, starring the Grand Dame of adult theatre herself, the lovely Marilyn Chambers. While I have seen the film at least 15 times, it never fails to raise my spirits and lower my pants.

I would be remiss if you, gentle reader, were to walk away from this column with the impression that every work of adult theatre is a fully realized piece of art worthy of plaudits. Sadly, this is not so. Take, for example, *Blow By Blow*, a regrettable 1997 Vivid Video misfire set in the world of boxing. The film's actors spend far too much time using their mouths for wooden dialogue and not nearly enough for hot oral action. Fortunately, I wasn't stuck watching *Blow By Blow*, as, along with it, I rented three superior titles: *Night Creams*, *Fresh And Tasty #31*, and *Knee-Pad Nymphos*. Let's just say I'm still cleaning the walls of my room.

Still not convinced? Still cling to the belief that adult theatre is not for you? So be it! Clearly, some people were meant for Salisbury steak while others were meant for filet mignon. Well, you can keep your Salisbury steak, because the adult theatre is the life for me! ⌀

Man Pretends To Hit On Woman He'd Like To Hit On For Real

BATON ROUGE, LA—Employing a silly voice and jocular manner to suggest a lack of serious intentions, Dennis Vukelich, 29, pretended to hit on a woman he'd like to hit on for real Monday.

> "Aimee is a really great girl," Vukelich told coworker Bill Pearce during a recent after-work get-together at Bennigans. "She'll be a wonderful mother to our 10 children."

"Ah, at last we're alone," Vukelich, a due-diligence manager at C&H Accounting, jokingly told coworker Aimee Broussard in the office copier room. "I've waited for this moment all my life."

"Let's make beautiful music together," continued Vukelich, holding a stapler like a microphone and launching into a rendition of Barry White's "Can't Get Enough Of Your Love Babe" while Broussard laughed.

"Dennis is so funny," said Broussard, who met Vukelich in February when she joined C&H Accounting as an administrative assistant. "He cracks me up so much."

Several weeks after meeting Brous-

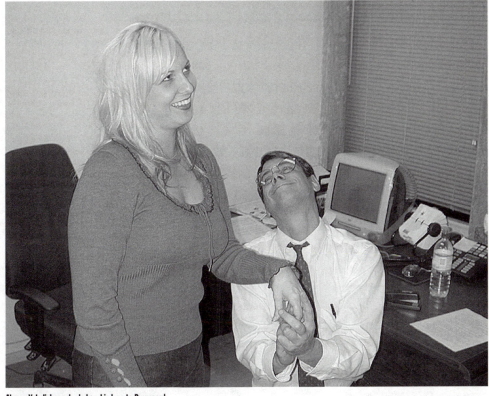

Above: Vukelich mock-pledges his love to Broussard.

sard, Vukelich began pretending to pursue the 26-year-old blonde.

"Aimee is a really great girl," Vukelich told coworker Bill Pearce during a recent after-work get-together at Bennigans. "She'll be a wonderful mother to our 10 children."

Broussard, who was sitting within earshot at the time, playfully slapped at Vukelich, prompting him to pretend to pour his half-empty Corona over her head.

Like Vukelich, Broussard is single, having recently ended a two-year relationship with her former live-in boyfriend. But despite Broussard's

eligibility, and Vukelich's frequent complaints about his lack of a girlfriend, Vukelich said he has no intentions of pursuing her.

"Aimee and I are just good friends," Vukelich said. "Besides, she gets asked out by tons of really good-
see MAN page 16

U.S. To Arab World: 'Stop Hating Us Or Suffer The Consequences'

WASHINGTON, DC—In a strongly worded ultimatum Tuesday, President Bush warned the Arab world to "stop hating the United States or suffer the consequences." "You have exactly 10 days to put aside your deep-rooted resentment and rage toward America and learn to like us," said Bush in a message broadcast live to 17 Arab nations via Al-Jazeera. "If you fail to comply, prepare to have the full might of the U.S. military brought down upon you." Bush also threatened to carpet-bomb any Arab region whose populace continues to be angry about America's longtime bombing campaign against Iraq and the decade-long U.S. sanctions that have led to the malnutrition deaths of tens of thousands of Iraqi children.

Ugly Man With Huge Penis Unsure How To Get The Word Out

AUBURN, ME—Overweight and balding Ira Groff, 37, is unsure how to get the word out about his 11-inch penis. "In theory, I could fumble around in my wallet for something and then—whoops!—an extra-large condom falls out," the acne-scarred Groff said Monday. "But that would come off as staged." Groff has also pondered wearing tighter pants, leaving penile-reduction-surgery brochures around his workspace, or sporting a button that reads, "Ask Me About My Huge Cock."

Plan To Make Snacks Last Through Opening Credits Fails

EDEN PRAIRIE, MN—In spite of his best intentions, moviegoer Brad

Schuyler failed to make his snack supply last beyond the opening credits of *Monsters, Inc.* Monday. "The *Harry Potter* trailer came on, and I guess I just got excited," said Schuyler, 26, who took his last bite as the words "Written By Dan Gerson" appeared on the screen. "Maybe I should have bought more than a box of Sno-Caps and a 32-ounce Coke, but the stuff costs so much." Next time he sees a film, Schuyler said he will not start eating until the studio logo appears.

Argument About Capital Of Australia Occurs 10 Feet From Encyclopedia

ORD, NE—Brothers Jeff and Adam Clink spent 20 minutes fiercely debating the capital of Australia while standing 10 feet from the family's World Book encyclopedia Monday. "You're high," Jeff, 18, told Adam. "It's

Sydney." Adam, who said he is "99.99 percent sure" that Melbourne is the capital, conceded that one city might be the capital of the Australian continent and the other the capital of the nation.

Steve Vai Impresses The Hell Out Of Neighborhood Kids

GLENDALE, CA—Rock guitarist Steve Vai wowed a group of neighborhood children with his spectacular guitar pyrotechnics Monday. "His behind-the-head guitar solo was so wicked," said Jimmy Hetzel, 11, one of six children blown away by Vai's fretboard wizardry. "He also did this thing where he held the guitar between his legs and played it with a bow." The impromptu performance is believed to be the most impressive display of its kind since September 2000, when Joe Satriani "showed off a few licks" at a Southfield, MI, bar mitzvah. ∅

CANCER from page 13

of Peachtree Road, before finishing cureless at the Capitol building.

Among those disappointed by Sunday's failed attempt was Gene Worth, a Germantown, TN, real-estate agent who drove 450 miles to participate in his seventh Race For The Cure.

"I worked out for three months, focusing my full energies on preparing for this race," Worth said. "I switched to a vegan macrobiotic diet just to be in top shape. Three kilometers in, I felt great, like this was going to be the year we cured it. I did break my personal 5K record, but even that wasn't enough. Then, after I crossed the finish line, I watched other racers finish, but they came in empty-handed, as well."

Broadbent was quick to dispute characterizations of the run as a failure.

"As we like to say, today brought us one 5K run closer to the cure," Broadbent said. "We may not have cured it yet, but one of these times, we will. When faced with a setback like this, we need to pick ourselves up, dust

> **Among those disappointed by Sunday's failed attempt was Gene Worth, a Germantown, TN, real-estate agent who drove 450 miles to participate in his seventh Race For The Cure.**

ourselves off, and run another five kilometers."

Added Broadbent: "If even one patient went into remission as a result of thousands of people running around Atlanta, then it's all worth it."

The race was the latest disappointment in a dismal two-week stretch for athletic-based medical research. On Nov. 1 in Dallas, an estimated 3,000 cyclists were unable to isolate the portion of the human genome responsible for Alzheimer's disease. Three days later in Boston, some 200 rowers from 27 different colleges gathered on the Charles River in an unsuccessful attempt to eliminate AIDS. And a pair of Nov. 9 regattas in San Diego and Miami failed to cure cystic fibrosis and heart disease, respectively.

Runs against cancer and other diseases have been popular since 1976, when Olympic runner Bill Rodgers discovered the formula for Interferon Beta—effective in the treatment of multiple sclerosis—at the base of Nobska Point Lighthouse while running the Falmouth (MA) Road Race. Rodgers went on to win the Nobel Prize For Medicine for his discovery, despite losing the race itself to Alberto Salazar. ⌀

SPAGHETTI-OS from page 13

An ambitious Franco-American joint venture, Spaghetti-Os have been a source of tension between France and the U.S. since August, when the 10-year accord governing its production expired. U.S. delegates have re-

> **From 1965 to 1968, a panel of top U.S. food engineers painstakingly developed the four sizes of Os while France's most esteemed chefs developed the distinctive tomato-and-cheese sauce.**

fused to renew the pact unless numerous revisions are made, including a 60-40 split of profits.

"We contribute a majority of the ingredients, including all of the thiamine mononitrate, ferrous sulfate, and enzyme-modified butter—not to mention all the paper for the labels—so we should get a majority of the proceeds," Miller said.

At 11 a.m. Monday, operations at L'Usine Des Os, the world's largest Spaghetti-Os manufacturing plant, ground to a halt, leaving the world with as little as a week's supply of Spaghetti-Os in reserve. Meanwhile,

French efforts to replace the O-shaped pasta with plain, easier-to-produce long spaghetti have proven fruitless, with the U.S. threatening to withhold Ravioli-Os from French supermarkets if there is an "embarg-O."

The international dispute casts a pall over the proud and storied history of Spaghetti-Os. A symbol of trans-Atlantic friendship dating back to 1965, the canned lunchtime staple began as a cooperative effort between U.S. president Lyndon Johnson and French president Charles de Gaulle, who shared the conviction that the convenient pasta meal was a delicious and nutritious way to maintain good Franco-American relations.

From 1965 to 1968, a panel of top U.S. food engineers painstakingly developed the four sizes of Os while France's most esteemed chefs developed the distinctive tomato-and-cheese sauce. When finally unveiled at a White House dinner, Johnson hailed Spaghetti-Os as "the zesty, flavorful glue that holds our two nations together in peace." Subsequent development of meatball and sliced-frank varieties of the product only added to its enduring mythos.

After years of mutual amity, however, the Age Of Spaghetti-Os may have finally come to an end. More fuel was added to the fire earlier this month, when U.N. Secretary Of Quick-Heating Prepared Foods Stefan Fredriksen openly questioned the Franco-American venture in the November issue of *Bon Appetit.*

"In an age when Kellogg's Pop Tarts™ are being dropped on the impoverished people of Afghanistan, the notion that the U.S. and France would devote so much of their resources to the production of circular spaghetti is ludicrous," Fredriksen said.

In a stopgap attempt to alleviate the crisis, Italian minister of cuisine Hector Boyardee offered the Franco-American alliance an emergency airlift of "ABCs & 123s"-brand precooked pasta. French officials declined the offer, however, due to their American counterparts' insistence on

> **When finally unveiled at a White House dinner, Johnson hailed Spaghetti-Os as "the zesty, flavorful glue that holds our two nations together in peace."**

pronouncing "123s" "one, two, threes" rather than "un, deux, troises." In a recent speech to European convenience-food authorities, French President Jacques Chirac also preemptively rejected any Italian offer of pasta shaped like Spider-Man™. ⌀

MAN from page 15

looking guys. She probably wouldn't be the least bit interested in me. Then again, we do have pretty undeniable chemistry."

In addition to his blossoming friendship with Broussard, Vukelich has been cultivating his friendships with other coworkers of late. Though he had never before thrown a party at his apartment, Vukelich has hosted three coworker gatherings since Broussard joined the C&H Accounting team in February. This summer, he

> **Though he had never before thrown a party at his apartment, Vukelich has hosted three coworker gatherings since Broussard joined the C&H Accounting team in February.**

was also instrumental in organizing three weekend outings, one of which was cancelled when Broussard was unable to attend.

"Aimee has really been a great addition to our gang at work," Vukelich

said. "It's good to have someone new around to motivate us to do things."

Carl Gaston, a due-diligence senior at C&H, encouraged Vukelich to open himself up to the possibility of a relationship with Broussard.

"Dennis should just ask Aimee out already," coworker Carl Gaston said. "He's always joking about it, but he should just do it."

Vukelich rebuffed Gaston's suggestion.

"Oh, come on!" Vukelich said. "Maybe in the future something might develop. But for now, it's not even a possibility. Unless she hit on me first so I knew she was interested."

Attempting to explain why he and Broussard get along so well, Vukelich cited their common interests.

"Aimee comes from a small town, and so do I, so we can really relate on that level," Vukelich said. "There's other stuff, too, like TV shows we both watch, and restaurants and music we both like."

Vukelich said he possesses other qualities that make him attractive to Broussard as a friend.

"I may not be the best-looking guy in the world, but in friendships—and many relationships, too, actually—that doesn't matter so much," Vukelich said. "Women look for other things in a man, like sense of humor and a kind, generous nature. And Aimee definitely knows I have those things."

Now entering its 10th month, the friendship continues to grow. Last Friday, Vukelich invited Broussard to attend a Paul Simon concert with him—the first time he has asked her to do something outside of work as a pair.

> **"Oh, come on!" Vukelich said. "Maybe in the future something might develop. But for now, it's not even a possibility. Unless she hit on me first so I knew she was interested."**

"I had an extra ticket, so I figured, 'What the heck,'" Vukelich said. "No reason to waste it, right?"

Unfortunately, Broussard had "other plans" the night of the event.

"Dennis was sweet to offer, but I lied and said my mom was in town," Broussard said. "I just don't think I could handle him for a whole night alone. At work, with lots of other people around, he's great. But for us to go to a concert or something, just the two of us, that'd be kind of weird." ⌀

16

LUANN from page 13

certainly be forever changed by what's happened."

"So many possibilities are running through my mind," Evans continued. "Should I have Luann talk to Bernice and Delta about this? Or should I provide guidance for the teens in the form of Miss Phelps or Mr. Fogarty? Should Luann be tough, or should she show vulnerability? These are the sorts of questions that, as an artist, I

> "So many possibilities are running through my mind," Evans continued. "Should I have Luann talk to Bernice and Delta about this? Or should I provide guidance for the teens in the form of Miss Phelps or Mr. Fogarty?

grapple with every day."

Evans has also considered using Luann's parents as a means of broaching the subject.

"I was thinking Luann's dad could call one of his dreaded family meetings," Evans said. "Then, instead of lecturing the kids about dragging mud through the house, he could hold a little 'rap session,' where he and Mrs. DeGroot encouraged the kids to talk about their feelings toward what America is going through. Still, my instincts tell me that's not the way to go. When I hit on the right take, I'll know it in my gut."

One of the most widely respected names in the comic-strip community, Evans has earned a reputation for his refusal to back down from relevant social issues. According to United Feature Syndicate's promotional packet, Evans "has been praised for his amusing, insightful portrayals of the issues that teens face—everything from reaching puberty to dealing with peer pressure, drugs, and alcohol."

"Fortunately, the folks over at United Feature Syndicate trust me and give me a tremendous amount of creative latitude," Evans said. "I'm very lucky to be working with supportive people who respect and understand my vision, and who let me say whatever it is that's on my mind."

In spite of the supportive atmosphere, Evans has yet to make his 'statement,' unable to decide which aspect of the nation's ongoing turmoil to address.

"Not only are there the deaths of thousands, but there's also the war and fears of more attacks," Evans said. "Perhaps I'm better off dealing with such a momentous topic in a book, where I'd have unlimited space. But that would mean the work wouldn't reach my readers now, when they need it most."

Above: A page from Evans' sketchbook.

To avoid alienating his more sensitive readers, Evans said he would avoid specifics, just as he avoided using the words "menstruation" and "period" in his memorable series of strips, "Luann Gets Her First."

> One of the most widely respected names in the comic-strip community, Evans has earned a reputation for his refusal to back down from relevant social issues.

"Instead of a scary word like 'anthrax,' I'd say 'affliction' or 'illness,'" Evans said. "People would know what I meant."

For all his determination to address the current crisis, Evans admitted that a small part of him is tempted to not mention it at all.

"Maybe an alternate universe where

this never happened is exactly what the American people need," Evans said. "In Luann, I could give them that escape, that safe haven from all the horror. But in my heart of hearts, I feel like that would be taking the easy way out."

Evans said he takes comfort in the fact that he is not alone in his struggle.

"This is something that all of us in the comics community are dealing with right now," Evans said. "I've talked about it with a number of my

colleagues, including [Funky Winkerbean creator] Tom Batiuk and [Arlo & Janis creator] Jimmy Johnson. Jimmy asked me how I planned to make sense of this all, and I told him, 'I don't know, Jimmy. I just don't know.' He replied, 'Greg, none of us do.'"

Added Evans: "I feel like the eyes of the whole country are on me. And I don't want to do the wrong thing. When I was just a high-school art teacher, I never dreamed I'd have so much power and responsibility." ∅

CAT MEMOIR from page 15

of blood. Passersby were amazed by the unusually large amounts of blood. Passersby were amazed by the unusually large amounts of blood. Passersby were amazed by the unusually large amounts of blood. Passersby were amazed by the unusually large amounts of blood. Passersby were amazed by the unusually large amounts of blood. Passersby were amazed by the unusually large amounts of blood. Passersby were amazed by the unusually large amounts of blood. Passersby were amazed by the unusually large amounts of blood. Passersby were amazed by the unusually large amounts of blood. Passersby were amazed by the unusually large amounts of blood. Passersby were amazed by the unusually large amounts of blood. Passersby were amazed by the unusually large

amounts of blood. Passersby were amazed by the unusually large amounts of blood. Passersby were

This cake wasn't originally meant to be erotic.

amazed by the unusually large amounts of blood. Passersby were amazed by the unusually large

see CAT MEMOIR page 19

Ask A High-School Student Who Didn't Do The Required Reading

By Randy Friel

Dear High-School Student Who Didn't Do The Required Reading,

I recently discovered that two of my coworkers are carrying on an office affair. Now, normally, this sort of thing would be none of my beeswax, but I have reason to suspect that they're actually doing some of their "carrying on" on other employees' desks! I often show up in the morning to find papers disheveled, and one time, I found part of what I'll tactfully call a "suspicious-looking wrapper" on my mousepad. What should I do?

Upset In Upper Darby

Dear Upset,

What is *Tom Sawyer* about, you ask? Well, basically, the book *Tom Sawyer* is about the olden days, back in the days of Huckleberry Finn. Back then,

> All in all, George Orwell did a great job, and *Animal Farm* is a Signet Classic in every sense of the word, and well worth the $5.99 purchase price. It's so good, in fact, that if I was in Canada, I would be happy to pay the higher price of $7.99.

many people were so poor, they had no shoes and often wore only overalls with no shirt. The main character, whose name is Tom Sawyer, was so poor, he had to paint something to earn money. Which is tough work, as I know, because I once had to paint a garage, and it took a long time. It's too bad times were so tough when the Sawyers were around, but it's important to keep in mind that this was the olden days. I would say things have certainly changed since the book took place, what with TV and movies and all. Things were simpler back then, for sure, but people like the ones in the book *Tom Sawyer* were pretty happy living the way they did. What's that? How would I respond to charges that *Tom Sawyer* is racist? Well, in the book *Tom Sawyer*, there is some of that, but we need to keep in mind as readers of today that that kind of thing is unacceptable. At the same time, though, that's how things were back then, so the book is also like a

history book, if you think about it that way.

Dear High-School Student Who Didn't Do The Required Reading,

My son was recently diagnosed with Faloni's Syndrome. Our family knew nothing about this disease when he contracted it, and only now are we learning how easy prevention is. Would you please let your readers know that a simple blood test can determine the presence of FS in a person's blood, and that anyone with a family history of Faloni's should get checked?

Concerned In Canoga Park

Dear Concerned,

Animal Farm, by George Orwell, is a Signet Classic in which animals take over the farm. In the book, animals are used to represent communists and people represent Democrats. I would say that using animals to represent communists was a pretty good idea, because, historically, communists tried to do a lot of animalistic things, like aim nuclear bombs at America, and that is like something an animal on a farm might do. Portraying communists as animals who try to run things instead of humans is a good way to make a point. The best scene in the book was probably when some of the various animals on the farm set out to create a paradise of progress, ideals, and equality. Anyone who knows history knows how that really turned out. Not only George Orwell, the author, deserves credit, but Russell Baker for his excellent introduction. Edmund Wilson from *The New Yorker* sure knew what he was talking about when he said the book was "Absolutely first-rate... on par with Voltaire and Swift." All in all, George Orwell did a great job, and *Animal Farm* is a Signet Classic in every sense of the word, and well worth the $5.99 purchase price. It's so good, in fact, that if I was in Canada, I would be happy to pay the higher price of $7.99. If you liked "Voltaire and Swift," then you will love *Animal Farm*.

Dear High-School Student Who Didn't Do The Required Reading,

My aging mother has grown somewhat eccentric since Dad died three years ago. Among her more extreme habits: She's begun crocheting obsessively, up to 10 hours a day. She's also stopped speaking to several of her oldest, dearest friends, calling them "silly." I know she's dealing with a devastating loss, but I just don't like to see her turn inward like this. What can I do?

Heartsick In Hampton

Your Horoscope

By Lloyd Schumner Sr.
Retired Machinist and
A.A.P.B.-Certified Astrologer

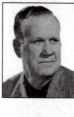

Aries: (March 21–April 19)
Your so-called "perfect crime" will be utterly transparent to anyone who's read pages 823-828 of *O'Hara's Fundamentals Of Criminal Investigation.*

Taurus: (April 20–May 20)
Plato claimed that our ideas are borne of our souls and not derived from our experience, but you get most of yours from the TV.

Gemini: (May 21–June 21)
Eventually, it will occur to you that every interesting thing that's happened in your life actually happened to someone around you, and you just watched.

Cancer: (June 22–July 22)
The point isn't that the emperor is unclothed, nor is it that no one dares acknowledge this. The point is that people think a naked emperor is sexier.

Leo: (July 23–Aug. 22)
You will be kept in the supermarket after it closes and forced to retake all the taste tests until you pass.

Virgo: (Aug. 23–Sept. 22)
You will experience great prosperity after realizing that people's best impulses can be used against them.

Libra: (Sept. 23–Oct. 23)
The letter code CAG is used to signify the amino acid glutamine. This will be extremely important next Thursday.

Scorpio: (Oct. 24–Nov. 21)
It turns out, you don't die if you hit the ground while falling in a dream. You merely lie in a pool of blood and bone shards until you wake up hours later.

Sagittarius: (Nov. 22–Dec. 21)
You will take refuge from a storm at a lonely roadside tavern, where strangers will regale you with some of the most boring stories you've ever heard.

Capricorn: (Dec. 22–Jan. 19)
Next Friday in the Kmart employee breakroom, you will be moved by a thought so achingly beautiful that you dare not share it with anyone, ever.

Aquarius: (Jan. 20–Feb. 18)
Sooner or later, you're going to have to 'fess up to those who blame Yoko Ono for breaking up The Beatles and tell them the terrible things you and Pete Best did.

Pisces: (Feb. 19–March 20)
The stars indicate, as tactfully as possible, that you may not have much of a future as a lyric poet.

Dear Heartsick,

Dune, by David Lynch, is the book I've chosen to read for my book assignment. *Dune*, which contains many hundreds of pages, is a really freaky book about the future. This one particular guy had to put his hand in a box, and he trips like it's burning up. Then, he had to learn fighting from a guy who reminded me quite a bit of Captain Picard. This fat guy with insane acne is trying to take everything over, somewhat like Darth Vader. But unlike Darth Vader, he got kind of gay on this other guy in a chapter of the book that was not my particular favorite. There's also a talking slug in a tank that you have to see to believe. The spaceships had cool design and the girl was pretty cute. You should read *Dune* or, even better, *Starship Troopers.*

Randy Friel is a high-school student whose syndicated advice column, Ask A High-School Student Who Didn't Do The Required Reading, appears in more than 250 newspapers nationwide. ∅

PLUNKED from page 15

of blood. Passersby were amazed by the unusually large amounts of blood. Passersby were amazed by the unusually large amounts of blood. Passersby were amazed by the unusually large amounts of blood. Passersby were amazed by the unusually large amounts of blood. Passersby were amazed by the unusually large amounts of blood. Passersby were

> I'd give your life to save this country.

amazed by the unusually large amounts of blood. Passersby were amazed by the unusually large amounts of blood. Passersby were amazed by the unusually large amounts of blood. Passersby were amazed by the unusually large amounts of blood. Passersby were amazed by the unusually large amounts of blood. Passersby were amazed by the unusually large amounts of blood. Passersby were

see PLUNKED page 24

18

90 Percent Of Americans Now Wearing Laminated ID Badges

see NATION page 6A

Lesbian Hen Enjoying Hen House

see LOCAL page 4C

Bruce Banner Reacts Predictably To Unrequested Perfume Sample

see PEOPLE page 8D

STATshot

A look at the numbers that shape your world.

Top Rumors About Tom Cruise

1. Sees the letter "R" backwards
2. Had self cloned so he could fellate self
3. Is carved from soapstone
4. Isn't terribly bright and gets talked into crazy, scam-artist pseudo-religions fairly easily
5. Is heterosexual

the ONION®

VOLUME 37 ISSUE 43 — AMERICA'S FINEST NEWS SOURCE™ — 29 NOV.–05 DEC. 2001

Report: Economically Disadvantaged Men More Skilled At Communicating Attraction To Women

BOSTON—According to a Boston University study released Monday, men from lower-income backgrounds are significantly more skilled at communicating their attraction to women than their middle- and upper-class counterparts.

"Many people would assume that the relative dearth of educational opportunities available to men in lower economic strata would result in inferior communication skills," said Boston University social anthropologist Dr. Mary Schoen, co-author of the study. "To the con-

Gender Watch

trary, our research finds that they are up to four times more adept at conveying their interest in women than men with higher incomes."

Lower-income men, Schoen said, have a variety of phrases at their disposal to clearly and concisely communicate their attraction to members of the opposite sex. Among them are, "Slow down so I can get a look at you," "Mmmm, you are lookin' fiiiine today," and "I wouldn't mind a piece-a dat."

"Cultures in which the written word

is not stressed generally tend to develop a greater oral tradition," Schoen said. "Never before, however, has the propensity been placed in a socioeconomic context, specifically with regard to how certain demographic subsets are better able to articulate their desire to get with that hot little mama over there in the red dress."

The study found that 95 percent of men who earn less than $18,000 a year were able to loudly and publicly voice their approval of specific body parts on women. By contrast, a paltry 3 percent of men who earn more than

see STUDY page 22

Third-Grade Scientists Successfully Vaporize Water

GRESHAM, OR—In a breakthrough that has electrified the world's 10-and-under scientific community, Mrs. Wagner's third-grade class successfully vaporized water under controlled classroom conditions Monday.

"Um, the coolest thing was when we got to light the fire that made the water disappear," said Jake Squirek, 9, a member of the Gresham Elementary School experimental-research team. "Then it boiled, then it turned into steam, which is the gas form of water."

"Clouds are like steam, only not hot," said fellow scientist Pam McKee, 8. "Water is called H2O in sci-

ence."

The experiment began with researcher Brittany Chase, 8, transferring approximately 50cL of water from the hallway drinking fountain into an Erlenmeyer flask. The water was then poured into a test tube placed on a stand over a Bunsen burner.

Despite offers from numerous members of the third-grade team, the burner was lit by Mrs. Wagner. Within two minutes, the contents of the flask began to boil, and shortly thereafter, the water vaporized and turned to steam.

According to Mrs. Wagner, the experiment was designed to illustrate the prin-

see SCIENTISTS page 24

Above: Scientists Jake Squirek (left) and Tommy Mautz announce their findings at a schoolwide assembly in the gym.

Above: The latest anthrax scare, in Connecticut. Right: Rosling and Ward.

Breakup Put Off Until Bioterrorism Scare Is Over

NEW CASTLE, PA— Shaken and needing companionship in this time of national crisis, Jordan

Rosling, 26, announced Monday that he has decided to postpone breaking up with longtime girlfriend Allison Ward until the current bioterrorism scare is over.

"I've been thinking of calling it off with Allison for a while, but the time just never seemed right," Rosling said. "Now that we might experience another Black

see BREAKUP page 22

Sept. 11 Charities Under Fire

The Red Cross and other aid groups are under fire for giving only a portion of the billions that have poured in since Sept. 11 to the attacks' victims. What do *you* think?

"Hey, I felt great when I gave that money. Isn't that all that matters?"

Leslie Gottfried
Sales Associate

"See? That's why giving actual money to a charity is a bad idea. I donated 10 tennis lessons instead."

Andrew Dillon
Tennis Pro

"I recently donated to a Sept. 11 online charity and was afraid that the money wouldn't all go to the victims. But the folks at savinpeopleandshit .com assured me it would."

Don Matthius
Office Manager

"All I can say is, if the money I gave goes to some Indian kid orphaned by a monsoon instead of a Sept. 11 victim, I'm gonna be fuckin' pissed."

Barb Rocket
Painter

"This is why I don't trust the Red Cross. From now on, anyone who needs blood can come straight to me."

Richard Risley
Lawyer

"Well, these vague accusations and rumors seal it: I'm never donating to a charity again."

Marcus Murphy
Systems Analyst

Reality TV On The Decline

After nearly two years of ratings success, reality TV programs are losing out to traditional sitcoms and dramas. Why?

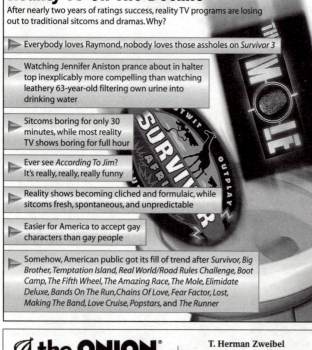

▶ Everybody loves Raymond, nobody loves those assholes on *Survivor 3*

▶ Watching Jennifer Aniston prance about in halter top inexplicably more compelling than watching leathery 63-year-old filtering own urine into drinking water

▶ Sitcoms boring for only 30 minutes, while most reality TV shows boring for full hour

▶ Ever see *According To Jim*? It's really, really, really funny

▶ Reality shows becoming cliched and formulaic, while sitcoms fresh, spontaneous, and unpredictable

▶ Easier for America to accept gay characters than gay people

▶ Somehow, American public got its fill of trend after *Survivor, Big Brother, Temptation Island, Real World/Road Rules Challenge, Boot Camp, The Fifth Wheel, The Amazing Race, The Mole, Elimidate Deluxe, Bands On The Run, Chains Of Love, Fear Factor, Lost, Making The Band, Love Cruise, Popstars,* and *The Runner*

 **the ONION**®

America's Finest News Source.™

Herman Ulysses Zweibel
Founder

T. Herman Zweibel
Publisher Emeritus
J. Phineas Zweibel
Publisher
Maxwell Prescott Zweibel
Editor-In-Chief

Ah, The Beauty Of The Fall TV Season

Is there anything that compares to the majesty of the fall TV season?

In late October, when the last of the repeats fade into darkness, it's time to

By Bridget Cascoli

pour a cup of hot tea, pull a favorite blanket up over your knees, and sit back and watch the network programming change. What a welcome relief it is after all those oppressively hot months of sizzling summer blockbusters!

Sure, the summer movie season, with its exciting trips to the multiplex and dramatic box-office showdowns, has its charms. But by the time the fall season rolls around, I'm good and ready for a break from all that. Fall is when the colors of my Sony 36-inch TV really come alive.

There's so much beauty to behold during the fall TV season: the deep brown of Jessica Alba's hair, the vibrant red and amber hues of Kelsey Grammer's sweater vests, the rustling of Calista Flockhart's skirts. Every year, there are those moments that are absolutely breathtaking, those special times you wait for: the familiar lilting strains of Peter Boyle's voice on *Everybody Loves Raymond*, the gradual unveiling of a new sub-

> ## While much of the joy of the fall season is seeing the TV seasonal cycle completed with the return of all your favorite shows, fall also affords the opportunity to experience the wonder of the new.

plot on *Law & Order*, the crisp, cool air emanating from *ER*'s Anthony Edwards.

Everything is so magical in the fall, you hardly know where to turn your eyes. Should it be to ABC's *The Drew Carey Show*? Or to *The West Wing* on NBC in the same time slot? There are scarcely enough hours in primetime to enjoy it all!

Fall is also the time to reap the benefits of all the seeds planted so carefully in the spring. This year, we found out who the father of Rachel's baby is on *Friends*, and that Buffy is no longer dead. After months of anticipation, it was worth the wait.

Speaking of waiting, there's less of it during the fall than at any other time of year. Happily, with the days getting shorter, the prime-time lineup comes earlier and earlier each day. You get home from work, turn on the TV, and, before you know it, the *Third Rock From The Sun* syndicated rerun is

> ## The fall season gets even better come late November.

over, and primetime programming has fallen upon the land.

While much of the joy of the fall season is seeing the TV seasonal cycle completed with the return of all your favorite shows, fall also affords the opportunity to experience the wonder of the new. Shows like The WB's *Smallville*, NBC's *Crossing Jordan*, CBS's *The Guardian*, and ABC's *My Wife And Kids* were all welcomed into the world this fall. There's nothing quite like that first taste of the fresh faces the fall has to offer.

For some, the fall is synonymous with hunting season. These adventurous types love searching through *TV Guide*, never knowing what exciting made-for-TV movie or miniseries will jump out at them next. Meanwhile, for the little ones, the fall season holds no shortage of excitement, either. What child doesn't look forward to all that Halloween fun, from the *It's The Great Pumpkin, Charlie Brown* special to the *The Simpsons*' Halloween spectacular, not to mention all the fun commercials for candy and costumes?

And, lest you think things peak in October, the fall season gets even better come late November. That's the time of year when, after some shows have flown south and the dead series have fallen from the line-up, a peaceful calm falls over TV land. There's no longer any movement of shows from time slot to time slot. You'd be hard-pressed to find a better time for TV-star-gazing than a clear, static-less November night. Looking up from my couch to see the bright faces of *Will And Grace*'s Debra Messing and *The District*'s Craig T. Nelson, well, it almost chokes me up.

It is important, though, to remember that fall is not entirely about relaxation and fun. Fall is the time for storing up for the long winter ahead. I've been working hard every day, setting the VCR to tape shows like *Inside Schwartz, The Bernie Mac Show,* and *The Ellen Show* before they wither and die, lost forever. ∅

Man Dies After Long And Painful Battle With Life

LEWISTOWN, MT—Gerald Carruthers, a retired insurance agent and father of three, died Monday at 77 following a long and painful battle with life.

"Thank God it's finally over," said Maria Heupel, 53, his eldest daughter. "He was in such terrible pain those last 70 or so years. You could just see it eating away at him from within. By the end, he was just a hollow, wasted shell."

"The agony for him had been overwhelming since about 1930," Heupel added. "It's amazing he lasted as long as he did."

Carruthers, once a happy and vital toddler, had his first painful episode shortly after his fourth birthday, when his father beat him with a cane for accidentally urinating on a favorite rug.

Other such episodes occurred with regularity throughout Carruthers' life. An awkward adolescence was followed by a middling stint at the University of Montana. After years of woefully few dates, Carruthers' disease went into brief remission in 1948, when he met and courted Joyce Lowell during a leave of absence from the Air Force. His suffering returned, however, when he was forced to quickly marry Lowell after she became pregnant with his child. Carruthers resigned from the Air Force and, from that point on, the erosion of

his spirit accelerated.

His personal growth badly stunted, Carruthers shelved his dreams of becoming a pilot and instead became an insurance agent. Unfortunately, his meager salary meant that he would be unable to afford relief in the form of material comforts or vacations. By the time Carruthers reached his 40s, he found himself so crippled, he could only lie on his sofa and watch TV after work.

"He tried to be brave," said wife Joyce Carruthers, who watched Gerald's struggle with life transform him from a moody 30-year-old insurance agent into a deeply bitter, borderline-alcoholic 60-year-old insurance agent. "But it's not easy. His pain made it impossible for him to enjoy our wedding day, the birth of his children, or even a normal weekend with his family. You can't imagine what the ordeal was like for him."

According to his personal physician, Dr. Clement Kirschwasser, Carruthers' search for a cure followed a pattern common among those afflicted with life.

"He tried just about every form of treatment: diet, exercise, rest, therapy, the usual array of drugs and alcohol—you name it," Kirschwasser said. "But he didn't respond to any of them. Occasionally, there would be a slight reduction in symptoms, but inevitably, hopelessness and de-

Above: Gerald Carruthers and wife Joyce.

moralization would always set in again."

Toward the end, Carruthers was exhausted and drained of the will to fight. Family members say that even if he had made the effort, he was too far gone to be saved.

"He might have tried some Eastern techniques or the more exotic pharmacological approaches, but the wasting ravages of life had already

done their damage," said son Daniel Carruthers, 49, who, with his three disappointing children, failed marriage, and exorbitant alimony payments, is already in the advanced stages of the syndrome that claimed his father's life.

"I just hope that when my turn comes, I go peacefully in my sleep like Dad," Daniel continued. "Come to think of it, the sooner the better." ⌀

New Harry Potter Film Turns Children On To Magic Of Not Reading

LOS ANGELES—Around the world, children are being turned on to the magic of not reading by the blockbuster film *Harry Potter And The Sorcerer's Stone.* "My daughter Julia never liked to sit passively and stare at a screen, but this new movie has really locked the power of her imagination," said Hannah Foss, 38, of Dayton, OH. "She can't put her books away fast enough." "Movies are great," said Tarzana, CA, 10-year-old Emily Hart. "You can see exactly what the characters look like without having to guess."

'Expect Delays' Signs Placed Randomly Throughout Nation

WASHINGTON, DC—Expanding upon the already omnipresent sig-

nage at airports and on highways, the government has posted more than 150 million "Expect Delays" signs at random locations across the U.S. "I went to Safeway to buy some groceries, and there's a big sign warning me to expect delays in the pasta aisle," Dori Reilly of Inkster, MI, said Monday. "When I got home, there was a big sign on my fridge. I had to wait almost an hour before I could put away the milk."

Headphones-Wearing Pedestrian Loudly Proclaims Iron Man Status

MINNEAPOLIS—Local resident James Gaines loudly proclaimed his Iron Man status Monday while walking down Hennepin Avenue wearing a Sony Discman. "I am Iron Man," Gaines announced in a deep, foreboding voice before launching into his dark, personal tale of madness and revenge. Gaines has previously de-

clared himself "hot for teacher," "a teenage lobotomy," and "a street-walking cheetah with a heart full of napalm."

Mad Lib Filled With Swears

PORTLAND, ME—The popular party amusement Mad Libs was misued for profane purposes Monday, when Peter Leff, a Portland-area 12-year-old, filled the blank spaces on a "Space Adventure Mad Lib" entirely with swear words. "Prepare to shit the enemy," Leff had Space Commander Mr. Garrick say. "Set all pussys on fart and brace for blowjobs."

Drug Addict Looking For More Enabling Girlfriend

AUSTIN, TX—After breaking up with girlfriend Karen Guglia last week, cocaine addict Rob Everson, 26, announced that he is looking for a

more enabling girlfriend. "I need a woman who'll give me my freedom and let me be me," Everson said Monday. "I don't need somebody who's going to be on my case all the time, telling me I need to clean myself up or I'm gonna die. When you love someone, you encourage them to pursue their interests."

Security Guard Can't Afford To Relax For So Much As Six Hours

LAKELAND, FL—Mel King, the night security guard at 2300 Office Park Drive, can't afford to let his guard down for even six hours, the 47-year-old said Tuesday. "In a job like this, you have to be on full alert every once in a great while," King said. "Lose your focus for three or four hundred minutes, and the place could be robbed blind." King said he makes sure never to drift from his post more than twice per shift or stray from his ritual 3 a.m. viewing of back-to-back episodes of *Riptide.* ⌀

Plague, this *really* isn't the time. I don't want to die alone, pathetic and girlfriendless."

Rosling said it simply makes more sense to wait until the Al Qaeda terrorist network is completely dismantled before ending things with Ward.

"It's been almost six months since I started feeling like Allison and I weren't a forever thing," Rosling said. "So what's a few months more? If we capture [Osama] bin Laden, and it's clear that nothing worse than these anthrax letters is going to happen, then I can make some of these life decisions. But as of right now, I have serious fears about how long my life will even last."

In spite of his urge to end the relationship, Rosling said things are "okay" with Ward.

"Why rock the boat?" Rosling asked.

> Though he termed the scenario a "long shot," Rosling said he sometimes fears that Ward will break up with him and find a new boyfriend right before a major bio-attack.

"We're at war. I don't want to be watching CNN, freaking out all by myself the next time something major happens. I've been with Allison for

four years, and we've had some good times. It would be just plain stupid to break it off now."

Rosling, who recently read *Germs: Biological Weapons And America's Secret War*, said the recent anthrax attacks are "nothing compared with the shit that could happen."

"If smallpox is unleashed on the U.S., there'd be millions of deaths," Rosling said. "They stopped immunizing kids for it in 1972, and immunity to smallpox diminishes with time, anyway. If a terrorist successfully spreads smallpox here, one in three people could die. And those odds are too scary to face all on my own."

Also contributing to Rosling's reluctance to break up with Ward is the fact that he has few other people to turn to besides her.

"Pretty much all of my good friends

have spouses or significant others of their own. So if something happened, they'd be with them, not me," Rosling said. "I don't want to die as a third wheel, all covered in weeping sores and rasping out my last breath as some couple wished I would give them some privacy."

While his primary fear is bioterrorism, Rosling said he is also nervous about the possibility of a chemical-weapons attack or nuclear strike against America.

"Can you imagine sitting there all by yourself, knowing you're going to die from radiation sickness?" Rosling said. "Then there's the added worry of our current recession. What if it turns into something on the level of the Great Depression? That would definitely not be the time to be on the sin-see BREAKUP next page

$75,000 a year could do the same.

"Though they scored substantially higher in math and science aptitude, upper-class males were surprisingly inept at simply letting a coworker know her ass looked nice in a skirt," said Dr. Marybeth Clarke, Boston

> "Whether the woman was black or white, rich or poor, cheerful or profoundly depressed, these men were consistently able to get across the message that they would enjoy engaging in intercourse with her."

University sociologist and the study's co-author. "It's not that they didn't notice the ass. They simply were unable to convey the sentiment."

Even more remarkable, low-income men are often able to initiate communication with women they do not even know.

"It's one thing to be able to strike up a conversation with a friend or coworker," Clarke said, "but the challenge is that much greater when you're trying to talk to a stranger who's running to catch a train."

The study also found that the communication skills of economically disadvantaged men are virtually unaffected by context, remaining consistently high regardless of the race, class, or mood of the woman being approached.

"Whether the woman was black or white, rich or poor, cheerful or profoundly depressed, these men were consistently able to get across the message that they would enjoy engaging in intercourse with her," Clarke said. "Their requests to 'let me get up

Above: A pair of lower-income men communicate with a female passerby in Dallas, TX.

on it' or 'give me a little sugar, honey' were unfailingly clear, regardless of who the woman was or her emotional state at the time."

Lower-income men were also seven times more likely to ask women questions. Among the queries noted in the report: "Where you going all dressed up so sexy?," "Where did you get a pair of legs like that?," and "Hey, baby, wanna suck my root?"

Schoen said the idea for the study first came to her during the summer of 1998, when she was gathering data for an interdisciplinary research project on access to healthcare among the nation's poor. While studying admittance procedures at various hospitals in East Los Angeles, the south side of Chicago, and New York's

Spanish Harlem, Schoen was impressed by the direct manner in which men in these communities expressed to her their admiration for the shape of her body.

"All I had to do was walk down the street to notice the discrepancy in communication proficiency between rich and poor males," Schoen said. "While well-to-do men would steal furtive glances at my chest, less well-off men would loudly and confidently state their opinion on the matter."

Schoen was not just struck by the directness of the poorer men's remarks, but by the "vast vocabulary" they employed in doing so.

"These men did not simply say, 'I like your breasts,'" Schoen said. "They used a vast array of terms: tits, jugs,

knockers, knobs, headlights, titties, ta-tas, cans, hooters, boobs, boobies, bazooms, rack, mounds, maracas, milk cans, milk bags, yabbos, fun bags, slappies, coconuts, jabungos, melons. The full list, which is included in the report, is nine pages long."

Schoen said she and her colleagues are "heartened" by the findings.

"The nation's economically disadvantaged males face many problems. Fortunately, an inability to express themselves to attractive young women in public is not among them," Schoen said. "It is up to all of us to encourage these men to develop their skills even further, that their voice might rise, loud and proud, from car windows and construction sites all across the nation." ∅

BREAKUP from previous page ──────

gles scene."

Rosling insisted that his decision to put off the breakup is not a selfish one.

"Even though I've realized we're just too different for things to work long-term, I really do care deeply about Allison and wish only the best for her," Rosling said. "If she's going to die, I want to be there for her, too. I would feel so guilty if I dumped her in her final days."

Though he termed the scenario a "long shot," Rosling said he sometimes fears that Ward will break up with him and find a new boyfriend right before a major bio-attack.

"Then the new guy would be with Allison for a whirlwind one-month romance before dying together," Rosling said. "She would be passionately falling

---

> ### "I've never exactly been the ultimate ladies' man," Rosling said. "So let's say I break up with Allison, and in three months, the whole world ends. I might not be able to find anyone to have sex with for the rest of my life."

---

in love in a time of doom, living every moment as if it's her last. It might even be that Mark guy she works with. I don't think I could handle that."

Rosling said things might be different if there were "women knocking down [his] door," but that is not—and has never been—the case.

"I've never exactly been the ultimate ladies' man," Rosling said. "So let's say I break up with Allison, and in three months, the whole world ends. I might not be able to find anyone to have sex with for the rest of my life. That would suck so bad."

There are other practical considerations, as well.

"If I break up with Allison, I'd probably move to L.A., where I have this good friend who can give me a job," Rosling said. "But the last place you want to be if there's a smallpox outbreak or a nuclear attack is a major city. No, I'd better stay right here in New Castle with Allison."

Dr. Sheila Durkin, therapist and author of the bestselling crisis-management guide *Calm Down!: Staying Sane In An Insane World,* said Rosling's behavior is not surprising.

"In times of imminent danger, our self-preservation instinct takes over, and we seek out personal bonds that bolster our feelings of security and comfort," Durkin said. "Given the circumstances, it's only natural that Jordan would behave like a spineless, self-centered prick." ⊘

A Purr-fect Tale!

This past January, one of my New Year's resolutions was to quit procrastinating so darn much. As for living up to the resolution, well, let's just

A Room Of Jean's Own
By Jean Teasdale

say I procrastinated on *that,* too! But with the year winding down, I'm finally getting around to some things I've been meaning to do for ages, including a longtime dream project of mine. And just what is this dream project, you ask? (No, it's not sampling every brand of chocolate on Earth... honest!) It's none other than writing my very own special book: excerpts from the diary "kept" by my kitty, Priscilla Teasdale!

Pardon my modesty, but isn't that just about the best idea in the whole world? I first thought of it seven years ago, when I spotted a marked-down copy of *Millie's Book* at B. Dalton. Do you remember President Bush Sr.'s spaniel, Millie? Well, First Lady Barbara Bush wrote this story about Millie's life at the White House, pretending that she was Millie, and that the dog was intelligent and could write! Well, it struck me that I was a pet owner, too, and if Barbara Bush could write as her dog, why couldn't I write as my kitty? (After all, kitties, like doggies, are people, too!)

The more I thought about it, the more excited I became. I truly believed this idea could fly. I'd been looking for another writing outlet besides my newspaper column, and this seemed so "purr-fect"? (Or should I say "purr-fect"?) Plus, people just love anything that has to do with kitties or doggies! It seemed a shoo-in for the bestseller list!

Trouble was, back in 1994, I had two cats, not one. Which would be the book's protagonist, Priscilla or Arthur? I'd always felt Prissy had a richer emotional life, but Arthur had more interesting adventures. (Of course, being an indoor cat, his adventures were pretty much limited to chasing glints of sunlight on the rug and getting a new water dish!) Unable to choose between my two pretties, I let the project gather dust.

A couple of years ago, my quandary about which cat to choose seemed to resolve itself when Arthur died. (As you hardcore Jeanketeers may recall, he tragically choked to death on a Pincers The Lobster Teenie Beanie Baby.) At first, I decided to make Arthur my protagonist to honor his memory. But after several tries, I just couldn't bring myself to write about him. True, it would have been a nice tribute, but it was all too sad. And trying to write about Priscilla, just because she was the only cat left, made

me even sadder. (I'd better end this paragraph pronto before I start bawling!)

Anyway, after dropping the idea for a few more years, I finally came back to it a few weeks ago. Enough time had passed since Arthur's death, and

---

> ## The more I thought about it, the more excited I became. I truly believed this idea could fly. I'd been looking for another writing outlet besides my newspaper column, and this seemed so perfect!

I finally felt ready to write about Priscilla. (A little over a year ago, I acquired a sweet kitty named Garfield, but since Prissy and I had been pals for years, she seemed the more natural choice for my project.) I was nervous that the book would be difficult, but you know what? Not only has it been fun to write, but it has practically poured out of me! It's like this thing practically writes itself!

So I thought I'd give you Jeanketeers an exclusive advance peek at *Prissy's Diary: The Meow-moirs Of Priscilla Teasdale.* I've got about 10 pages done, but because my space is limited, I'm including just a small snippet. I've never written a book before, and I'm sort of flying by the seat of my pants here, writing down anything and everything that enters my head. So it's kind of rough and unstructured. But I think the lack of consistency is more than made up for by the abundance of heart. And to me, that's more important. Nevertheless, I'd looove feedback from my readers. Let me know if I'm going in the right direction. Be completely honest... I can take it! (I have thick skin. You have to be in the newspaper business!) Oh, and if you know of any publishers who might be interested, let me know!

Well, here goes!

Tuesday, May 25, 1993
Dear Diary,

Do I have exciting news! I found a loving home with the Teasdale family! My new mommy is named Jean, and my daddy's name is hubby Rick! I first met Jean when she showed up at the Gerson County Humane Society to adopt a little kitten. At first, I thought Jean was going to bring home every kitty there. (What a softie!) But when she saw my pretty tor-

toise-shell fur and green eyes, she knew I was the one!

My home is great! There's every kind of Tender Vittles here, and all the tap water I can drink. My litter box even has a roof over it! There's just one problem: When hubby Rick came home and saw me, he got really mad! He started yelling at Mommy, saying how dare she bring home a kitten when she knows he's allergic to kitties. Well, I heard Mommy say he was just exaggerating the whole allergy thing, but Daddy was still very angry and told Mommy to take me back to the Humane Society, because "there wasn't no way he'd live with some sissy cat!" Then, something really scary happened: He grabbed me by the scruff of the neck and tossed me in an old beer crate! Mommy started bawling and practically got down on her knees and begged Daddy to let her keep me, saying she wanted a kitty so bad, and that she promised that she'd do everything, and that he wouldn't even have to so much as pet me. So Daddy said Mommy could keep me for a month, but if it didn't work out, I'd have to go back.

I sure was glad to get out of that crate—it smelled like stale beer! And I really hope I can stay at the Teasdales. (Even if Daddy is a great big grouch!)

Saturday, Dec. 25, 1993
Dear Diary,

It's my very first Christmas! Of course, Mommy Jean had to explain that Christmas is Jesus' birthday. (Just in case you were wondering, I believe in Jesus... 'cuz I'm a Cat-holic!)

Anyway, I got a lot of great presents! I now have a carpet-upholstered scratching post, complete with a perch so I can look out our bedroom window in comfort. And I got soooo dizzy playing with my new catnip mouse on a string! Best of all was the big can of Bumble Bee tuna Mommy Jean got me. I got to eat it all as a special Christmas treat! (Unfortunately, it made my stomach all jumpy, and I threw it up later that night. Boy, was Daddy Rick mad when he stepped in my partially dried vomit with his bare feet in the morning!)

Monday, Sept. 8, 1997
Dear Diary,

Mommy Jean is just the greatest! Today, she got me a nice, warm, fuzzy sheepskin bed to sleep in! I showed her a lot of extra love today; I rubbed against her legs and purred like crazy. Mommy Jean may not have fur and a tail, but there's no one in the world I love more! It's too bad Daddy Rick won't give her human babies to raise. She has so much love to give, yet I fear so much of it will remain trapped forever in her heart.

see TEASDALE page 24

Above: Squirek and Mautz confirm the presence of water in the flask.

ciples of evaporation and the three states of matter.

"The students had already conducted an experiment in which an ice cube was placed in a dish and melted over the course of two hours, demonstrating the change from solid to liquid," Mrs. Wagner said. "They did so well with that, I wanted to reward them

> "Do you know what this means?" Monroe, MI, third-grader Shawn Bendix said. "If we can vaporize water, we probably can vaporize other liquids, too. You just have to heat it! You just have to heat it!"

with something more challenging."

Monday's successful vaporization brought to an end a string of failures and setbacks for the young scientists. In September, an attempt to get a hamster to run through a maze to reach a plate of honey-roasted peanuts was scrapped when the animal escaped and disappeared under the classroom radiator. Two weeks later, a demonstration of the sense of taste was abandoned when a roll of Life Savers that had been part of the exercise was inadvertently eaten. And last Wednesday, Mrs. Wagner said, a static-electricity experiment resulted in "a lot of popped balloons and hurt feelings."

Amanda Reynolds, 8, was among those who feared that the vaporization would meet a similar fate.

"We didn't think anything would happen this time," Reynolds said. "We didn't have any luck before, so we figured this time would be the same. But then it started to steam, and we were all excited. I didn't know what to expect. Then I got scared that it would explode and we would all get killed."

"That didn't happen," Reynolds added.

The breakthrough experiment has generated considerable excitement among third-grade scientists across the U.S.

"Do you know what this means?" Monroe, MI, third-grader Shawn Bendix said. "If we can vaporize water, we probably can vaporize other liquids, too. You just have to heat it! You just have to heat it!"

Bendix then ran off to try to vaporize a quart of Strawberry Quik.

Members of the grown-up science community had high praise for the Gresham Elementary School team, as well.

"These bright youngsters are the future of science," said John Diekman, Ph.D., chairman of the Scripps Research Institute in La Jolla, CA. "They will be the ones dissecting frogs, growing bean plants in milk cartons, and dipping litmus paper into acids and bases well into this century."

Flush with success, the members of Mrs. Wagner's team are already debating what their next experiment should be.

"We should make firecrackers," Tommy Mautz, 9, told fellow scientist Dana Lardner. "If we can't do that, maybe we should put a rat in the snake cage so we can see the snake eat it whole. That would be so cool." Ø

24

HOROSCOPES

Your Horoscope

By Lloyd Schumner Sr.
Retired Machinist and
A.A.P.B.-Certified Astrologer

Aries: (March 21–April 19)
Your new romantic partner will turn out to be the best thing ever to happen to you. Please notice that we said "thing," not "person."

Taurus: (April 20–May 20)
You really ought to have a close friend or family member explain the function of that roll of soft paper that hangs by the toilet as soon as possible.

Gemini: (May 21–June 21)
Your view of history as a nightmare from which you are trying to escape seems awfully pretentious, as no one will remember you five minutes from now.

Cancer: (June 22–July 22)
The lifetime supply of Twinkies you won in that contest turns out to be only half a box, indicating that the Hostess corporation knows something you don't.

Leo: (July 23–Aug. 22)
The stars foretell a glorious and prosperous future for you during this year's Zodiacal Sweeps Week.

Virgo: (Aug. 23–Sept. 22)
Technically, what you're having is not a shotgun wedding. Those are when someone else has the shotgun.

Libra: (Sept. 23–Oct. 23)
You will be banned from the nation's highways after catastrophically failing your federally mandated crash test.

Scorpio: (Oct. 24–Nov. 21)
Though your dietary habits are disgusting beyond description, it is probably unfair to apply human standards to a turkey vulture like yourself.

Sagittarius: (Nov. 22–Dec. 21)
Your remarkable talent for procrastination will result in your winning the Nobel Prize For Literature Thrown Together At The Very Last Possible Minute.

Capricorn: (Dec. 22–Jan. 19)
"In Between Days" is the best Cure song. That's all there is to it, and Capricorn doesn't want to hear any different.

Aquarius: (Jan. 20–Feb. 18)
The psychologists running the tests are repulsed by the strength of your attraction to the wire mother.

Pisces: (Feb. 19–March 20)
Don't bother lying to the police when they pull you over next Friday. They'll have already figured out that the tank was stolen.

It's true that I don't have children, either, but that's because I had a little operation when I was still a baby

People just love anything that has to do with kitties or doggies!

kitty. Mommy Jean never had an operation. She's as fertile as a river delta! Her doctor said so, even though he says she should lose a lot of weight before getting pregnant. I sure hope that one day I'll have a little human brother or sister to play with! I'll even let them yank my tail!

You know, as I re-read this, I'm thinking that some of it may be a little unrealistic. Kitties, wonderful and wise as they are, might not have such a developed vocabulary and keen insight. Well, it's only a first draft. (Boy, writing fiction is harder than I thought!) Ø

amounts of blood. Passersby were amazed by the unusually large amounts of blood. Passersby were amazed by the unusually large amounts of blood. Passersby were amazed by the unusually large amounts of blood. Passersby were amazed by the unusually large amounts of blood. Passersby were amazed by the unusually large amounts of blood. Passersby were amazed by the unusually large amounts of blood. Passersby were amazed by the unusually large amounts of blood. Passersby were amazed by the unusually large amounts of blood. Passersby were amazed by the unusually large amounts of blood. Passersby were

This lucky quarter is for shit.

amazed by the unusually large amounts of blood. Passersby were amazed by the unusually large amounts of blood. Passersby were amazed by the unusually large amounts of blood. Passersby were amazed by the unusually large amounts of blood. Passersby were amazed by the unusually large

see STABBING MOTION page 27

Gender Of Person In Ronald McDonald Costume Unclear

see LOCAL page 3C

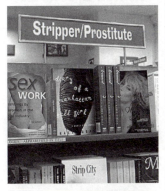

Barnes & Noble Creates Stripper/Prostitute Memoir Section

see BOOKS page 10D

Gun Purchaser Won't Be Needing Bag With That

see LOCAL page 5C

STATshot

A look at the numbers that shape your world.

How Hard Are We Rocking?

1. To the point of severe muscle distress about the neck and upper spine
2. Hard enough to bring down P.J.'s Pub
3. "With Dokken"
4. With all due hardness
5. So! Fucking! Hard!
6. If you combined David Coverdale and Sebastian Bach? That hard

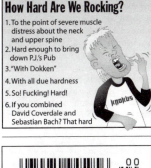

the ONION ®

VOLUME 37 ISSUE 44   AMERICA'S FINEST NEWS SOURCE™   06–12 DECEMBER 2001

Woman In Burqa Condemns Woman In Chador

GHAZNI, AFGHANI-STAN—Outraged by the recent loosening of dress codes in her country, burqa wearer Uliya Salah con-demned fellow Afghan Raheela Asaad Monday for appearing in public wear-ing an upper-face-revealing chador.

"Just look how she dress-es, the bridge of her nose visible for all the world to see," said Salah, watching Asaad walk past her in downtown Ghazni. "Has she no shame?"

Not wanting to risk the chance that a stranger might be forced to hear a woman's voice, Salah whis-pered her indignant re-marks through the small

see WOMAN page 28

Right: The burqa-wearing Salah, who is outraged by Asaad's (far right) immodest dress.

Children, Creepy Middle-Aged Weirdos Swept Up In *Harry Potter* Craze

HOLLYWOOD, CA—*Harry Potter And The Sor-cerer's Stone*, the hit film about an orphaned boy and his pals at Hogwarts School Of Witchcraft And Wizardry, continues to break box-office records, casting its magic spell over children and creepy middle-aged weirdos alike.

Just ask Corey Molland, a Downers Grove, IL, 11-year-old who made his own Harry Potter cos-tume, complete with Nim-bus 2000 broomstick, to wear to the film's opening

Above: Young *Harry Potter* fans at a showing of the film. Right: Not-so-young *Harry Potter* fan Kurt Furmanek in his basement bedroom.

night. "I've seen the movie four times already," Mol-land said. "And I want to

see POTTER page 29

Lone Smart Aleck Ruins RV Hall Of Fame For Serious Visitors

Above: One of the many nice RV Hall Of Fame displays that Weed (inset) felt compelled to mock.

ELKHART, IN—A lone smart aleck spoiled the RV Hall Of Fame for serious visitors Monday, making sarcastic wisecracks about the various exhibits and running around the Elkhart tourist attraction like a "ninny."

"My wife read about this place in *RV Lifestyle*, and we drove all the way from Illinois to see it," said re-tired contractor Gerald Fin-nis, 70. "But the whole time we were there, some goof-ball is engaging in horse-play and saying things like, 'If the RV is rockin', don't come a-knockin'" loud enough for everyone to hear. It spoiled the whole darn day."

Unlike the many respect-ful Hall Of Fame visitors who used the museum for its intended purpose, quiet-ly reading informational placards and exploring the interiors of the displayed RV units, the smart aleck "hardly quit fooling around for two seconds." He was later identified as Dick Weed of Nuttsak Hills, PA, according to his entry in the guest book at the front of the museum.

"[Weed] had a friend with him who didn't say a whole lot, but he certainly encour-

see SMART ALECK page 29

The Human-Cloning Controversy

Last week, scientists announced the first-ever cloning of a human embryo, which they hope to mine for stem cells to treat diseases. What do *you* think?

"At last, the underpopulation crisis has found its magic bullet."

Carla Rayner
Homemaker

"A whole population of identical-looking human beings? This chilling dystopian vision has already come to pass in the fall J. Crew catalog."

Leslie Jong
Massage Therapist

"We don't need these cloned embryos takin' all the jobs away from regular embryos."

Rich Stewart
Auto Mechanic

"Scientists should not be allowed to play God. Brian Blessed would be much better."

Donald Scott
Tax Attorney

"I've got a plan to create the world's first human-clone hybrid. Remember that sheep Dolly? I'm gonna fuck it."

Fred Gardner
Cashier

"I think I'll just sit back and let the ignorant, hysterical Christians handle this one."

Peter Jordan
Systems Analyst

Improving Olympic Security

The events of Sept. 11 have prompted a security overhaul for the 2002 Winter Olympics in Salt Lake City. Among the measures:

- Testing athletes' urine for traces of terrorism
- Eliminating Men's 200m Embassy Bomb event
- Turning Salt Lake City into hyper-paranoid, walled-off religious compound
- Assigning athletes from Arab nations around-the-clock "security buddy"
- All open flames to be immediately extinguished
- Investigating any and all reports of fine white powder
- Strictly prohibiting foreigners from Olympic village
- Warning athletes not to make any sudden movements
- Hoping that terrorists, like everyone else, have no desire to visit Salt Lake City

the ONION®
America's Finest News Source.™

Herman Ulysses Zweibel
Founder

T. Herman Zweibel
Publisher Emeritus
J. Phineas Zweibel
Publisher
Maxwell Prescott Zweibel
Editor-In-Chief

America Is Ready To Laugh At Me Again

By Patrick Hoff
Fat Kid

In my short life, I've endured more than my share of mockery. I've been husky for the entirety of my 11 years on this planet, a circumstance that has inspired others to make fun of me at every turn. I've been called, among other things, Fatso, Fatpants, Fatboy, Fatty Fatty Two-By-Four, Pig, Piggy, Oinker, King Chunk, El Tubbo, and, of course, as one would expect of a heavy-set person with my name, Patty Fatty.

Yet, on Sept. 11, 2001, the name-calling suddenly stopped. So stunned was the nation by the tragic events of that day, no one felt right making fun of their fellow man. Even if the man, in this case, was a 114-pound fifth-grader.

Badly shaken, the American people could not bring themselves to hurt my feelings. Robby Peltzer, perhaps my greatest tormentor, sensed that in this new national climate, it was not right to pinch me when the teacher was looking the other way. Matt Hinkle no longer took relish in pushing my face into the water fountain. And no one pointed at me and said, "Hey, look! There's a *real* Jelly Belly!" when someone brought a bag of Jelly Bellys to class. Yes, after years of abuse at the hands of my classmates and fellow Americans, I was given a reprieve the likes of which I had never dreamed possible.

The first few weeks after Sept. 11, I appreciated the fact that no one said a word when I showed up at school in pants obviously patched in the crotch because my rubbing thighs had worn out the cloth. I was happy that people were directing their venom at Osama bin Laden and not my blubber. It pleased me that everyone was strangely supportive when, during gym class, I toppled over in exhaustion in the midst of my third sit-up.

Long about the sixth or seventh week, however, I began to sense that this absence of laughter was not right. On one occasion, I waddled with my empty tray up to the window in the school cafeteria for seconds, my ill-fitting turtleneck covered in spaghetti sauce. The lunch lady merely looked sympathetically at me and ladled out some more noodles. This is the same woman who, in a similar situation last year, asked me, "How can your mother stand you?"

Cutting remarks of this sort, hurtful as they may be, are not without merit. I have little willpower when it comes to losing weight, and attempts on the part of my parents to put me on a diet have been largely unsuccessful. I will sneak food and eat it whenever possible. Many a time, I have been found in the laundry room at home, my face comically covered in fudge.

But on that particular afternoon in the cafeteria, the lunch lady held back. It has been that way ever since Sept. 11. We have banded together in grim solidarity against the forces of

> On Sept. 11, 2001, the name-calling suddenly stopped. So stunned was the nation by the tragic events of that day, no one felt right making fun of their fellow man.

evil that invaded our country and our collective conscience. Would Robby Peltzer, Matt Hinkle, and the rest of this great nation ever laugh at me again? It seemed unlikely.

But then, like the swallows to San Juan Capistrano each spring, the derision returned. Last Friday, for the first time in months, the kids at school forgot about the horror that has occurred and laughed at the way my flabby stomach hangs out from the bottom of my shirts. Later that afternoon, Jeffrey D'Amico put all the sadness aside to announce to the entire class that I can barely fit into the combination desk-chairs in the music room.

Over the weekend, a man at the park, no doubt heartened by our nation's military successes against the Taliban, literally doubled over laughing at the sight of me trying to throw a football, only to have it land in a pathetic thud just eight feet away. Then, last night, while in line at Burger King, a group of teenagers cracked up upon overhearing me beg my parents for a vanilla shake.

How wonderful! At long last, America is ready to laugh at me again! I welcome this return to normalcy, and I will gladly do my part to move the healing process along. With this in mind, you have my solemn vow that if I accidentally drop a book in the library, I will bend over extra-far to pick it up, revealing the uppermost portion of my ample rear end's crack. How could I not? I am merely doing my part for the country I love. So laugh, America. Look at me and laugh. ∅

Area Liberal Worried His Asian Dry Cleaner Doesn't Like Him

SAN FRANCISCO—In spite of his open-mindedness and deep commitment to multiculturalism, Steve Bern, 32, expressed fear Monday that Rei Luo, the Chinese woman who does his dry cleaning, does not like him.

> "This country is a tapestry of many different beliefs and backgrounds, so I try to foster that by spreading my business around to everyone, not just Caucasians like myself."

"Whenever I come into [Luo's Laundry & Cleaners], I'm always very friendly," Bern said. "I say hello and ask her how she's doing, but she never reciprocates. She just smiles and hands me my receipt. I hope I haven't done anything to offend her."

"Maybe she's mad about my tags," Bern said. "A lot of my stuff says 'Made In China' or 'Made In Hong Kong,' and I know that a lot of those places run sweatshops. I'd feel awful if she thought I was supporting the exploitation of her people."

Bern, a features editor at the alternative weekly *Bay Area Free Press*, has been familiar with Rei since March 1998, when he started taking his laundry to her store on Visidero

Above: White male Steve Bern, who fears he is resented by Rei (inset).

Street. Though there is another dry cleaner closer to his apartment, Bern wanted to patronize a minority-owned establishment.

"I like to interact with and support people of other cultures," Bern said. "This country is a tapestry of many different beliefs and backgrounds, so I try to foster that by spreading my business around to everyone, not just Caucasians like myself. I always tell Rei how much I admire the way an immigrant like her could rise from poverty to run her own store, but she never really gives me much of a response."

In spite of his best efforts, Bern has been unable to transform his relationship with Rei into something approaching a friendship, or even a mild acquaintanceship.

"I found out that Rei came of age in a remote mountain village during the height of the Cultural Revolution, so I'd been fascinated to hear her stories," Bern said. "A few months ago, while she was pulling a 50-pound box of soap off a high shelf, I asked what it was like to grow up under Chair-

see LIBERAL page 28

Guy At Bank Has Weird Hair For Guy Who Works At Bank

MODESTO, CA—Marc Kohle, a bank teller at Modesto First Federal, has weird hair for a guy who works at a bank, customers reported Monday. "Huh," said customer Kenneth Blaustein, 31, looking at Kohle's hair, which is long in the back with a pair of small, gelled horns in the front. "You just don't see that kind of 'do on a guy who works at a bank. Well, it is the downtown branch." ∅

All Proceeds No Longer Going To Charity

NEW YORK—Nearly three months after the Sept. 11 disaster, traditional capitalism is reasserting itself, as profits are once again being kept by the corporations earning them. "No portion of each sale of this product

will go toward the WTC Police Disaster Relief Fund," reads a sticker on the cover of *A Very Sony Christmas*, an all-star compilation CD released Tuesday. A similar notice on packages of Fruit Of The Loom men's cotton briefs reads, "All proceeds will go directly into the fourth-quarter earnings of Fruit Of The Loom, Ltd."

Aspiring Legislator Keeps Sending Unsolicited Bills To House Of Representastives

WOOSTER, OH—Andy Roenicke, a 23-year-old aspiring federal legislator, sent an unsolicited tax-reform bill to House Speaker Dennis Hastert (R-IL) Monday, his fifth such submission in as many weeks. "Dear Mr. Hastert: Enclosed is a bill that I believe would be a great addition to your congressional

docket," Roenicke's cover letter read. "Even if you opt not to use it, though, I would very much appreciate any feedback you might have." Said Hastert: "It's nice to see a young man who's excited about getting involved in the legislative process, but I do wish he'd go through the established process of being elected to office by the people of his district. Honestly, that's the way it's done."

Polish Rapper Under Fire For Use Of The Word 'Polack'

DETROIT—MC Krakow, a popular Detroit-based rapper of Polish descent, came under fire Tuesday for his use of the word 'Polack' on his new album, *World Warsaw III*. "When MC Krakow casually uses the P-word, it dredges up decades of hurtful portrayals and cruel jokes for our people," said Sandy Serwacki, president of the Polish Anti-Defamation Society. "In just the song 'Ten-Inch Pierogie' alone,

he uses the word 27 times." In an official statement, MC Krakow defended his use of the word: "When I say, 'Y'all be my Polacks,' or 'Yo, what up, Polack?,' it's my way of taking the word back. Our people need to re-claim and embrace 'Polack' with pride, just like Eminem did with the word 'faggot.'"

Man Surprised To Hear Himself Tell Matt Damon He's 'A Big Fan'

LOS ANGELES—Moments after encountering Matt Damon in a Century Plaza elevator Monday, local resident Andre Waller expressed bafflement that he had told the actor that he's "a big fan." "That doesn't sound like me at all," Waller said. "I mean, I liked *Good Will Hunting* okay, but I can't even think of anything else he's been in. Why the hell would I say that?" In April 1998, Waller was stunned to hear himself tell Kevin Nealon that he "love[s] *Hiller & Diller*." ∅

man Mao and the Great Leap Forward. She just stopped and muttered something to herself in Chinese, then went back to work. I'm starting to think maybe I was a little too forward."

When he returned to pick up his clothes, Bern perceived a possible change in the quality of service he received.

> **When asked her opinion of Bern, Rei was unable to recall who he was. She then shooed reporters out the door, saying, "I too busy, too busy."**

"I brought Rei a pair of gabardine pants with a salsa stain on the left leg," Bern said. "But when I got the pants back, the stain was still kind of there. It was faint, but if you held it up to a bright light, you could see it. I wonder if maybe not getting rid of the stain was her way of telling a white, middle-class oppressor like myself to mind my own business."

Undeterred, Bern decided that the best way to get on Rei's good side would be to learn more about her culture.

"I got a few short phrases from an Internet site about Chinese to help break the ice," Bern said. "The next time I saw her, I said 'Hello' and 'Have a nice day' in her native Mandarin. But she didn't even look up from the stack of dresses she was steam-ironing. Maybe she didn't hear me. That machine is pretty loud."

To improve relations, Bern has refrained from complaining about his dry cleaning.

"There was this gray wool sweater I brought in a few weeks ago that I never got back," Bern said. "I didn't want Rei to think I was dissatisfied, so I never brought it up. Losing a sweater is a small price to pay compared to the struggles she must go through daily as a Chinese-American."

Even though Bern firmly supports Rei's right to befriend whomever she chooses, he admitted to being disappointed by her snubs.

"I know that, culturally speaking, the Chinese tend to be low-key and not overtly demonstrative, but it would mean a lot to me if she occasionally took a break from scurrying around the shop's backroom to give me the occasional smile," Bern said. "Is that too much to ask? Well, maybe it is. After all, how can I judge someone if I've never walked in her shoes?"

When asked her opinion of Bern, Rei was unable to recall who he was. She then shooed reporters out the door, saying, "I too busy, too busy." ∅

mesh square in her garment.

"Perhaps one could wear that sort of thing in the deepest recesses of one's home, where even male family members are not allowed," Salah said. "But doing so in public like that is outrageous. The harlot may as well strip off her veil and reveal her hair to the world."

As a strict follower of Pashtun traditions, Salah said she finds it laughable that Asaad considers herself to be a devout Muslim.

"[Asaad] is clearly pursuing her darkest passions," Salah said. "Now that the Taliban is no longer here to protect their virtue, many of the women in the city have begun to walk around in shockingly immodest garb, shamelessly wearing next to nothing on their hands."

Asaad's garment was not only too revealing, Salah said, but it also bore numerous decorative touches—a mark of the sin of vanity.

> **"The women around here leave nothing to the imagination," Salah said. "The pupil, the iris, the cornea... It's all right there in the open for men to ogle."**

"Did you see that small line of embroidery at the border of her veil?" Salah asked. "What is next? A series of stripes at the hem of the garment near the ankles? I pray to Allah that I never see the day."

Salah has been in a near-constant state of outrage since Nov. 13, when the Taliban was ousted from her vil-

lage. On that day, emboldened by the Northern Alliance victory, hundreds of women threw off their conservative burqas in favor of skimpy, low-cut chadors that exposed portions of their faces.

"It is sinful for a woman to tempt a man by revealing the color of her eyes to him," Salah said. "But the women around here leave nothing to the imagination. The pupil, the iris, the cornea... It's all right out there in the open for men to ogle."

Now that dressing less conservatively no longer carries the risk of public whipping, Asaad said she may wear jewelry or Western fashions beneath her chador.

"It is an important part of both my religion and my culture to observe full *hijab*," said Asaad, who has worn traditional garb since she was 13. "I keep my body covered when in the presence of men. In the mosque, I am careful to keep my eyes lowered at all times. But it would be nice to wear something different once in a while, like a shoe with an attractive but respectful heel."

Salah was outraged by the notion.

"Only whores of Babylon wear heels!" Salah said. "Under the Taliban, it was illegal to wear high heels or any other shoe that produces a sound when walking, because a man must not hear a woman's footsteps. What is this world coming to?"

Asaad said she is eager to return to her old life, before she was confined to her house and only allowed outside when escorted by a male relative.

"Of course, there are many things women should not do, like watch television or go to dances or read Western fashion magazines," Asaad said. "But I did miss being able to leave the house."

Asaad said she also hopes to return to school-teaching, which was her occupation before the Taliban forbade women from working.

"I taught math and reading and other subjects to young girls," Asaad said. "I taught them how to read the words

of the prophet Mohammed and how to be a devoted follower of Islam."

Salah questioned Asaad's claims of devotion to Islam, citing a scandal in which she was involved last year. In May 2000, in spite of restrictions against women being examined by

---

> **"Did you see that small line of embroidery at the border of her veil?" Salah asked. "What is next? A series of stripes at the hem of the garment near the ankles? I pray to Allah that I never see the day."**

---

men, Asaad was caught attempting to see a male physician for treatment of kidney stones. It was only through a large bribe to Taliban officials and a three-month period of seclusion in a neighboring village that she escaped execution.

"It makes me sick to look at women like Raheela Asaad," Salah said. "She deserved no less a punishment than death for her blasphemy."

Despite the scandal and her liberal interpretation of Islamic law, Asaad said she is not ashamed of her actions.

"I am proud to be a modern woman," Asaad said. "I believe that women should be allowed to attend the university, so long as the school provides a separate area for women to sit in and they do not speak to the instructor before being spoken to. I even think it is acceptable for a young woman to ride a bicycle, provided she is out in the country where no man can view it. This is the 21st century, after all." ∅

amounts of blood. Passersby were amazed by the unusually large amounts of blood. Passersby were amazed by the unusually large amounts of blood. Passersby were amazed by the unusually large amounts of blood. Passersby were amazed by the unusually large amounts of blood. Passersby were amazed by the unusually large amounts of blood. Passersby were amazed by the unusually large amounts of blood. Passersby were amazed by the unusually large amounts of blood. Passersby were amazed by the unusually large amounts of blood. Passersby were amazed by the unusually large amounts of blood. Passersby were amazed by the unusually large amounts of blood. Passersby were amazed by the unusually large amounts of blood. Passersby were amazed by the unusually large amounts of blood. Passersby were amazed by the unusually large amounts of blood. Passersby were amazed by the unusually large amounts of blood. Passersby were amazed by the unusually large amounts of blood. Passersby were amazed by the unusually large amounts of blood. Passersby were

amazed by the unusually large amounts of blood. Passersby were amazed by the unusually large amounts of blood. Passersby were amazed by the unusually large amounts of blood. Passersby were

---

> **Maybe if I scream at my kids in the lobby of Burger King, it will help them become better people.**

---

amazed by the unusually large amounts of blood. Passersby were amazed by the unusually large amounts of blood. Passersby were amazed by the unusually large amounts of blood. Passersby were

amounts of blood. Passersby were amazed by the unusually large amounts of blood. Passersby were amazed by the unusually large amounts of blood. Passersby were amazed by the unusually large amounts of blood. Passersby were amazed by the unusually large amounts of blood. Passersby were amazed by the unusually large amounts of blood. Passersby were amazed by the unusually large amounts of blood. Passersby were amazed by the unusually large amounts of blood. Passersby were amazed by the unusually large amounts of blood. Passersby were amazed by the unusually large amounts of blood. Passersby were amazed by the unusually large amounts of blood. Passersby were amazed by the unusually large amounts of blood. Passersby were amazed by the unusually large amounts of blood. Passersby were amazed by the unusually large

see DOLPH page 30

aged him by laughing at everything he said," Finnis said. "The smart-alecky one would say, 'Man, this is even cooler than the Thermos Hall Of Fame over in Portage,' or 'Remember: Only the all-time greatest RVs are inducted into the RV Hall Of Fame,' and his pal would egg him on by laughing. Then, he would do something else stupid, like act like his foot was stuck under the tire of one of the RVs and scream. A real comedian, this guy."

Maintained by the Recreational Vehicle/Manufactured Housing Heritage Foundation, The RV/MH Hall Of Fame and Museum is the most-visited tourist attraction on the I-80/90 Indiana Toll Road between South Bend and Lagrange. The Hall Of Fame section honors nearly 200 pioneers and leaders in the RV/MH industry, while the museum area displays trailers, photos, and RV memorabilia from the 1920s to the present.

"There's a lot to learn here," said earnest visitor Clara Fetzer, 54, who glared icily at Weed several times during her visit. "For instance, before I came here, I assumed that MH either stood for Motor Home or Mobile Home. It doesn't. It stands for Manufactured Housing."

The Wall Of Fame, which features 70 framed photos of the most important figures in RV history, and the indoor "RV park," with antique vehicles displayed among artificial trees and lawn chairs, provided ample material for Weed to ridicule.

"It was disgraceful," said Mary Leehausen, 63. "[Weed] was standing next to me, looking at the cardboard family picnic display, and he kept calling it

'so hilarious.' I didn't see anything hilarious about it. Did you, Harry?"

"No," said Harry Leehausen, her husband. "These kids today, they have no respect. Someone put a lot of time and energy into making a nice museum, but some people have to try to put it down."

Even visitors who did not pick up on the derisive nature of Weed's remarks were irritated by his failure to comply with standard museum etiquette.

"[Weed] was running around, actually *running* inside the museum from exhibit to exhibit. And there were a few times when he cut ahead of me in

> ## Maintained by the Recreational Vehicle/Manufactured Housing Heritage Foundation, The RV/MH Hall Of Fame and Museum is the most-visited tourist attraction on the I-80/90 Indiana Toll Road.

line while I was waiting my turn to go inside one of the smaller modules," said Donna Merken, 42. "I think it's nice that he was excited to see everything, but there's no need to be rude to other people."

Weed's mockery, museumgoers said,

only grew over the course of his 90-minute visit. Early on, while browsing the museum's 22 tourable RVs, Weed merely repeated declarations of, "Oh my God," and "I cannot believe this." By the end of his visit, however, Weed's showboating had escalated to the point of disruption. Lying down in the middle of the museum's green, all-weather carpet, he loudly exclaimed, "I think I'll just take a little ol' rest in the grass here." Those wanting to enter the 1954 Holiday Rambler were forced to walk around him.

Moments later, Weed yelled "Bad dog!" at a ceramic dalmatian displayed next to the 1964 Coachmen Cadet. After loudly repeating the *faux* admonishment several times, Weed began to bark at the statue. The scene so vexed visitor Annalee Taylor, 64, that she retreated upstairs to the center's archival library.

Despite disapproving glances from those around him, Weed's shenanigans continued. He stuck his head out the window of the 1913 "Earl" Travel Trailer—the world's oldest known surviving non-tent travel trailer and the crown jewel of the museum's collection—and yelled, in a high-pitched female voice, "Goddamn it, Henry, get in here before the beans and weenies get cold!"

Then, in front of a gleaming silver 1954 Spartan Imperial Mansion, Weed affected a country drawl and said, "I'm gonna shine my trailer up reeeal nice and purty."

"Perhaps he was insinuating that people who have RVs are low-class or funny in some way," said Ernest Hollingsworth, 38, of Muncie, IN. "But

why in the world would someone visit a museum about RVs if they felt that way? It just doesn't make sense."

"Maybe he was on drugs," Hollingsworth added.

If Weed had used illegal substances, it would have been in direct violation

> ## "[Weed] was running around, actually *running* inside the museum from exhibit to exhibit. And there were a few times when he cut ahead of me in line while I was waiting my turn to go inside one of the smaller modules."

of RV Hall Of Fame policy. Museum officials, however, did not reprimand or question Weed about his strange behavior.

Gene Kahler, a longtime tour guide and cashier at the museum, attributed Weed's antics to the fact that "kids will be kids."

"He bought a T-shirt, a mug, and two tickets for the 7th Annual RV/MH Heritage Foundation Raffle, and he went out of his way to tell me what a great time he had," said Kahler, stacking pamphlets on the information table. "I don't know, it sure sounded like he meant it." ∅

---

go see it again tomorrow."

Or Corey's neighbor, Kurt Furmanek, an unmarried 40-year-old who has seen the film 11 times, always in a homemade Ludo Bagman costume.

"It's terrific, as good as I'd hoped," said Furmanek, munching from a bag

> ## "I had my doubts when I heard that Chris Columbus was chosen to direct, but I have to hand it to him," said Ritchie, who owns more than 150 Harry Potter toys.

of Bertie Botts' Every Flavor Beans while waiting in line at a local multiplex Monday. "Granted, it's not perfect: They left out a number of key scenes and characters, like the second Quidditch match and Peeves. And some of the details were off, like how they said the boa constrictor was from Burma when it was from Brazil.

But all in all, it's remarkably faithful."

There are many possible explanations for Harry's broad appeal: a troubled world's need for a little bit of magic, the way the franchise taps into powerful good-versus-evil mythologies, the chance it offers overweight 47-year-olds to retreat from their dreary adult lives into an idealized fantasy childhood. But whatever it is that makes us wild about Harry, one thing is clear: The fantastical universe created by author J.K. Rowling speaks to the child in all of us, whether young or way too old.

You can see it in Lisa Werner, a Pueblo, CO, 13-year-old who has read all four *Harry Potter* books three times and keeps an ever-growing scrapbook of magazine articles related to the books and films.

"*Harry Potter* books are the ultimate books ever!" Werner said. "I wish there were real chocolate frogs that jumped when you tried to eat them."

And you can see it in Denver's Lynne Ritchie, a childless, 42-year-old legal secretary who named all six of her cats after students in the Gryffindor and Hufflepuff houses.

"I had my doubts when I heard that Chris Columbus was chosen to direct, but I have to hand it to him," said Ritchie, who owns more than 150

Harry Potter toys, including the hard-to-find Powercaster Electronic Spell-Casting Playset. "He did a great job bringing Rowling's vision to the

> ## But whatever it is that makes us wild about Harry, one thing is clear: The fantastical universe created by author J.K. Rowling speaks to the child in all of us, whether young or way too old.

screen, particularly the Quidditch match and the living paintings at Hogwarts. I can't wait for *Chamber Of Secrets*."

Maybe it's Harry's underdog qualities that make him so appealing. Or maybe it's the way wondrously magical things seem to burst from every page that makes the books so compelling to the likes of San Diego's Gary Minton, 41, who appeared as "*Harry Potter* Geek" on a recent

episode of Comedy Central's *Beat The Geeks* game show.

"There's never been anything like *Harry*—it's simply a phenomenon," said Minton, creator of the "Unofficial Hermione Granger Fan Page" and whose house neighborhood children have been warned never to enter. "And the movie is perfect, especially the casting of Emma Watson as Hermione. She's even prettier than I imagined. I hope she reads the Hermione Granger fan fiction I sent her."

Child-development experts and arrested-development experts agree that *Harry Potter*'s impact on society has been enormous.

"What J.K. Rowling has done to foster literacy in a world where it was declining so steadily makes her a true hero," child psychologist Dr. Sandy Wexler said. "But for adults, it's a different story. Retreating into a child's fantasy world is one of the most distressing preliminary signs of becoming unhinged, even when the books are as richly imagined and engrossing as the *Harry Potter* series."

Added Wexler: "Incidentally, do you think Snape is a Death Eater? I know he helped Harry out in Book One, but I have this theory." ∅

Who Says Java Programmers Don't Have A Sense Of Humor?

By Nate Orenstam

I've heard the stereotypes about Java programmers being uptight nerds who don't know how to cut loose. Well, that's about as far from the truth as *Enterprise* is from Gene Roddenberry's original vision. Contrary to what you may have heard, Javaheads can be quite the cutups. In fact, I've been working at Symantec for more than a year now, and compared to the systems administrators and IT support personnel around here, I'm a regular Jim Carrey.

Don't believe me? You should have been here the other day. Tim Hauser, one of the more humorless C++ programmers around the office (and that's *really* saying something!), went out to Starbucks for some Essence Of Life. While he was gone, I changed his desktop wallpaper from the Death Star to a picture of *Smallville*'s Tom Welling without a shirt. He didn't find it too funny, but me and the other Java guys sure did.

Some folks may have stopped there, but yours truly was just getting warmed up. About an hour later, while Tim was using the "facilities," I went in and changed the classpath on his computer, resulting in a confounding stream of ClassNotFoundExceptions. It took poor Tim a couple of minutes to figure out what the heck was going on. All the while, I was in the next cubicle, laughing my Dockers off.

That wasn't exactly the most productive day I've spent at work, but it sure was one of the most memorable ;-)

Of course, I have other, less disruptive ways of being a goof-off at work. Don't tell my department head, but a day doesn't go by when I don't spend a few on-the-clock minutes on slashdot.org, riffing with my fellow techies. People post some pretty funny stuff, but somehow, the funniest bits always seem to come from Javaheads. There's just something about that language that seems to attract the clinically insane!

Slashdot's weekly polls give me even more opportunity for mischief. Like, a few weeks ago, they had people vote for Favorite Bot Weapon. I picked Pneumatic Jack Spikes, but they were beat out by Spinning Sledge/Armature and Backlash-style Saws. Furious that Pneumatic Jack Spikes lost, I suggested in IRC that the poll's voting was rigged, calling it "the product of a vast conspiracy by a secret cabal of BeOS users." You better believe that got a reaction!

Mass e-mailing jokes is another way Java programmers share laughs. If something is funny—I mean really funny—we like to spread it around. For example, when I found this hilarious Shockwave game where you do target practice on The Backstreet Boys, I made sure to e-mail the link to all my friends. And have you seen those e-mail "snowball fights"? The

> **I changed his desktop wallpaper from the Death Star to a picture of *Smallville*'s Tom Welling without a shirt. He didn't find it too funny, but me and the other Java guys sure did.**

ones where you get splotched with a virtual ASCII snowball? Well, I've started more than my share of those, believe you me.

The laughs don't stop at quitting time. When I get home from work, the first thing I do is turn on Channel 27 for *The Simpsons*. There are no less than three reruns a night, and if I get home before 6 p.m., I usually catch them all. To me, *The Simpsons* is the comedic holy grail. (No offense, MPFC!) It's filled with smart jokes, like references to *The Prisoner* and *Logan's Run*. Plus, they poke fun at nerds. And, hey, as a nerd, I can take it. If you can't laugh at yourself, what can you laugh at?

Still not convinced that Java programmers have got it in the wit department? Check my homepage sometime. In addition to the complete lyrics to The Rutles' *All You Need Is Cash* and dozens of downloadable audio clips from *MST3K*, I've installed some hidden spots that will cause the Knights Who Say "Ni" to appear on the screen if you roll over them with your mouse. As for links, I have some real doozies, like one for a site that has a Flash-animated baby that sings classic rock songs in a high-pitched voice. And, for what it's worth, I was linking to the Hamster Dance *waaay* before anyone else. (There's plenty more where all that came from: Just visit nateorenstam.com.)

So, as you can clearly see, Java programmers do know how to laugh, and we often do so at our own expense. Never tell us we don't have a sense of humor... or you just might find all your applets replaced with ActiveX components! ✐

Your Horoscope

By Lloyd Schumner Sr.
Retired Machinist and
A.A.P.B.-Certified Astrologer

Aries: (March 21–April 19)
Your life will be lauded by parents' groups for containing no sex, drugs, profanity, violence, or adult situations.

Taurus: (April 20–May 20)
Though he appreciates the extra money, the ice-cream man is starting to get a little freaked out by the way you follow him around all the time.

Gemini: (May 21–June 21)
Your biggest weakness is not, as you believe, your lack of self-confidence. It's the two-inch soft spot in your aorta.

Cancer: (June 22–July 22)
You think you're embroiled in an unprecedented scandal, but you forgot that Catherine The Great, Fatty Arbuckle, and Marv Albert all came before you.

Leo: (July 23–Aug. 22)
You discover exactly what it means to owe the Mafia a favor when you find yourself forced to mow a lot of shady characters' lawns.

Virgo: (Aug. 23–Sept. 22)
Destiny has decided that you are a weak and unworthy vessel for its purposes. Starting next week, you'll be replaced with Robert Vaughn.

Libra: (Sept. 23–Oct. 23)
Your fears of becoming a trendy but bland person deepen when you are featured on page 77 of the IKEA catalog.

Scorpio: (Oct. 24–Nov. 21)
A tragic but not life-altering accident will be all the excuse you need to get menacing hooks where your ring and pinky fingers once were.

Sagittarius: (Nov. 22–Dec. 21)
Your trick of using numbers related to Andrew Jackson's presidency and a right triangle to remember the digits of the mathematical constant e is both effective and the geekiest thing ever.

Capricorn: (Dec. 22–Jan. 19)
Your dream wedding hits an unexpected snag when you fail to obtain the rights to Ozzy Osbourne's "Crazy Train."

Aquarius: (Jan. 20–Feb. 18)
After a long investigation, experts will conclude it's a miracle that no one was hurt except you and the camel-rental guy.

Pisces: (Feb. 19–March 20)
Your life story is the kind of thing people pay good money to see, which isn't good when you think about what bloodthirsty bastards people are.

PODIATRIST from page 28

amounts of blood. Passersby were amazed by the unusually large amounts of blood. Passersby were amazed by the unusually large amounts of blood. Passersby were amazed by the unusually large amounts of blood. Passersby were amazed by the unusually large amounts of blood. Passersby were amazed by the unusually large amounts of blood. Passersby were amazed by the unusually large amounts of blood. Passersby were amazed by the unusually large

> **This music today doesn't make you go crazy and kill people the way it used to.**

amounts of blood. Passersby were amazed by the unusually large amounts of blood. Passersby were amazed by the unusually large amounts of blood. Passersby were amazed by the unusually large amounts of blood. Passersby were amazed by the unusually large

amounts of blood. Passersby were amazed by the unusually large amounts of blood. Passersby were amazed by the unusually large amounts of blood. Passersby were amazed by the unusually large amounts of blood. Passersby were amazed by the unusually large amounts of blood. Passersby were amazed by the unusually large amounts of blood. Passersby were amazed by the unusually large amounts of blood. Passersby were amazed by the unusually large amounts of blood. Passersby were amazed by the unusually large amounts of blood. Passersby were amazed by the unusually large amounts of blood. Passersby were amazed by the unusually large amounts of blood. Passersby were amazed by the unusually large amounts of blood. Passersby were amazed by the unusually large amounts of blood. Passersby were amazed by the unusually large amounts of blood. Passersby were amazed by the unusually large amounts of blood. Passersby were amazed by the unusually large amounts of blood. Passersby were amazed by the unusually large amounts of blood. Passersby were amazed by the unusually large amounts of blood. Passersby were amazed by the unusually large

see PODIATRIST page 33

Camera Falls Out Of Love With Melanie Griffith

see PEOPLE page 2E

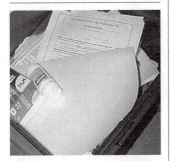

401(k) Enrollment Form Sits At Bottom Of Desk Drawer For 22 Years

see OFFICE page 3C

Retarded Couple In Mall Spitting At Each Other

see LOCAL page 11D

Ferret Mailed

see LOCAL page 9D

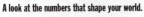

THE ONION • $2.00 US • $3.00 CAN

the ONION®

VOLUME 37 ISSUE 45   AMERICA'S FINEST NEWS SOURCE™   13–19 DECEMBER 2001

Starving, Bandaged Bin Laden Offers U.S. One Last Chance To Surrender

Above: Speaking via satellite, bin Laden issues a final warning to the U.S.

TORA BORA, AFGHANISTAN—An emaciated and heavily bandaged Osama bin Laden offered the U.S. a final chance to surrender Monday.

"Enemies of Allah, this is your last chance to leave Afghanistan alive," said a battered, soot-covered bin Laden in a videotaped statement broadcast on the Al-Jazeera satellite network. "I mean it."

Staring directly into the camera with his good eye, bin Laden reiterated his vow to drive the U.S. from the country.

"You may have dozens of bases in Afghanistan. You may have thousands of bombs," bin Laden said. "But know this: We still have three or four guns and a full crate of bullets. And some knives, I think. You cannot hope to prevail."

A nearby goatherder then helped bin Laden brandish a rifle over his head.

"With every military advance you make, your forces become more spread out and weakened, while the Taliban's become more concentrated in an increasingly small space," bin Laden said. "You are practicing the mathematics of defeat. Give up now."

The videotape was accompanied by a written statement that explicitly laid out the Taliban's instructions for surrender.

see BIN LADEN page 34

Above: Patti George (far right) commits the sin of envy as she eyes fellow parishioner Mary Hoechst's superior strawberry rhubarb pie.

All Seven Deadly Sins Committed At Church Bake Sale

GADSDEN, AL—The seven deadly sins—avarice, sloth, envy, lust, gluttony, pride, and wrath—were all committed Sunday during the twice-annual bake sale at St. Mary's of the Immaculate Conception Church.

In total, 347 individual acts of sin were committed at the bake sale, with nearly every attendee committing at least one of the seven deadly sins as outlined by Gregory the Great in the fifth century.

"My cookies, cakes, and brownies are always the highlight of our church bake sales, and everyone says so," said parishioner Connie Barrett, 49, openly committing the sin of pride. "Sometimes, even I'm amazed by how well

see BAKE SALE page 33

Crazy Japanese Punk Girl Delights Entire Dorm Floor

MOORHEAD, MN—Foreign student Misako Takashima, 19, continues to delight third-floor residents of Carlson Hall with her crazy-Japanese-punk-girl antics, Concordia College sources reported Monday.

"Everybody loves Misako," said sophomore Jenn Erickson, 20, speaking from the third-floor lounge. "She's always acting all crazy, running around and making everyone laugh. We're so lucky to have her on our floor."

Takashima, a sophomore who has not yet declared a major, transferred from Japan's Osaka University at the beginning of the fall semester. She immediately stood out among her Concordia classmates, not just for being Japanese, but for her exuberant behavior and eccentric dress, which includes knee-high vinyl boots, ripped skirts and T-shirts, and magenta-streaked hair.

"I tell my father I want to go to New York City for school, and he say, 'No

see GIRL page 35

Right: Beloved Carlson Hall resident Misako Takashima.

More Mideast Violence

Last week, Hamas suicide bombers killed 25 in Jerusalem and Haifa, and Israel retaliated with air strikes. What do *you* think about this wave of Mideast bloodshed?

Isaac Dunham
Systems Analyst

"It's nice to see senseless religious violence back where it belongs."

Mel Moreno
File Clerk

"If only the parents of those Hamas militants had spotted the suicide-bombing warning signs in time."

Paul Bergen
Architect

"Maybe someday they'll take my advice and put a huge lid on the entire region—just as soon as lid technology becomes sufficiently advanced."

Pete Tyler
Electrician

"I'm sorry. I answered this question for the media in 2000, 1999, 1998, 1996, 1994, 1991, 1989, 1986, 1982, 1979, 1978, 1976, and 1972. And once, in 1969, my dad answered for me."

Mary Winchell
Homemaker

"Why can't these people just get along? Oh, yeah... because they all think they've been specially chosen by God."

Allison Flowers
Graduate Student

"Hey, if I were denied a heavily disputed piece of land, I'd blow up innocent civilians with a crude bomb strapped around my midsection, too. No, wait, I wouldn't. That's fucking insane."

The Segway

Unveiled last week, the Segway Human Transporter is being touted as the future of human transportation. What are some of the much-hyped electrical scooter's features?

- Upright handlebars ergonomically designed to maximize loss of dignity
- Can reach speeds of up to 100 mph with special tow rope
- Safety sign at base reads "Keep Back 100 Feet From Gay Little Scooter"
- Can mow lawns
- Built-in "dork deflector" throws image of man in Klingon outfit on nearby wall to reduce mockery
- All-terrain tires enable users to get killed on variety of surfaces
- Handlebars outfitted with rainbow tassels
- Segway "road rage" holds promise of some hilarious MIT sissy-boy slap fights
- Entire cities will be redesigned to accommodate mass commutes on Segways. Seriously. This will happen in a month or so.

ⓞ the ONION®
America's Finest News Source.™

Herman Ulysses Zweibel
Founder

T. Herman Zweibel
Publisher Emeritus
J. Phineas Zweibel
Publisher
Maxwell Prescott Zweibel
Editor-In-Chief

Honey, I Said Some Things I Didn't Mean To Say Out Loud

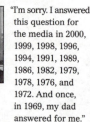

By Preston Lennert

Darling, I know you're upset, and you have every right to be. I don't think we've ever gotten into a fight like that before. But I just want you to know that those cruel things I said, well, I didn't mean a single word of them to be said out loud. I swear. Sometimes, in the heat of the moment, you say things you don't actually mean to let slip out. Like when I called you a "shallow, clothes-obsessed hag-beast"? I was angry. You hurt me, and I lashed out unfairly and audibly. Can you ever forgive me for articulating my true feelings?

Please don't take all those things I said seriously, sweetheart. Never in a million years did I mean for you to hear that you're a "frigid bitch." I hate using the F-word. That was for my inner dialogue only.

I know how much I must have hurt you. And I know I shouldn't take my frustrations with you out on you. I should just mutter under my breath and punch the steering wheel on my way to work like I usually do.

Of course, those things I said

> In the heat of the moment, you say things you don't actually mean to let slip out. Like when I called you a "shallow, clothes-obsessed hagbeast"? I was angry. You hurt me, and I lashed out unfairly and audibly.

things. When you told me your credit card was maxed out, I just snapped. I don't know why. So, please, dry those tears, dear heart. Forget all those things I said out loud. "Leathery, slack-titted gorgon" was just a meaningless string of words that popped into my head but never should have flown out my mouth.

Half the things I said don't even make any sense for me to vocalize. I mean, what does the phrase "spoiled, cultureless, plastic-surgery-deformed succubus" even mean? Don't you agree that it makes no sense? If so, we agree that it was just utter nonsense that never should have been said out loud. I should think I could come up with better insults if I genuinely wanted to, but why would I want to? You're so very precious to me.

And if you could possibly find it in your heart, I'd really appreciate it if you disregarded the fact that I listed your faults in alphabetical order. I've been able to do that since I was young—it's a blessing and a curse. If my mother were still alive, you could ask her. And since I was really struggling with W and Z, you could tell I was just making that stuff up off the top of my head. Before you know it, we'll be laughing about me saying things like, "**W** is for Whore phone... ring, ring, it's for you," and "**Z** is for the Zoo cage your half of the bedroom resembles." I'm kind of laughing already.

I know how much my words have stung and, believe me, I'm truly sorry. Instead of taking them out on you, I should have bottled them up and screamed them into the mirror while you were away at your stupid shrink. That's what I pay him $300 an hour for, right?

Don't worry, sweetie. I'm all better now. Forget the mean man you just saw. He's long gone. Now, gimme a hug, you evil, soulless harpy. ⓞ

> And if you could possibly find it in your heart, I'd really appreciate if you disregarded the fact that I listed your faults in alphabetical order. I've been able to do that since I was young— it's a blessing and a curse.

aren't what I officially think about you. How could they be? I thought enough of you to marry you, didn't I? Do you really think I would want to spend the rest of my life with "a vapid, materialistic shrew who cares more about her precious fucking kitchen renovations than about her own husband"? Of course not. Work has just been really stressful lately. I'm sure once it cools down, I'll be back to normal, and I'll never again voice my true feelings like that.

You have to keep in mind that when people get angry, they say stupid

Area Man Proud Of Liner Notes To Self-Burned Compilation CD

CHICAGO—Josh McCue, 26, expressed deep pride Monday in the liner notes he penned for his latest self-burned compilation CD.

"I really wanted the liner notes to capture something about the songs and help put them in their proper context," said McCue, a clerk at Lincoln Park Liquor. "I think I've accomplished that."

The 22-track CD, titled *Opium Of The Masses*, features an eclectic mix of music that McCue dryly describes as "your typical elitist hipster fare." The liner notes offer a wealth of information on the bands, which range from Soledad Brothers to Six Finger Satellite, as well as McCue's own "personal history" with the music.

Using the graphic-design programs Adobe Photoshop and Adobe Illustrator, McCue painstakingly spent 15 hours laying out what eventually became an eight-page CD booklet.

"At first, it was only going to be four pages including the cover, but doing that small a booklet would've meant giving some of the artists short shrift informationally," McCue said. "I mean, everyone knows the basics about [the bands] Can and The White Stripes, but people may not be as familiar with the histories and personnel of such lesser-known groups as Tuxedo-moon and JJ72."

He then opened the CD booklet and began reading aloud.

"'My Dad Is Dead is a versatile group (actually one guy, Mark Edwards) from Ohio,'" McCue said.

> The liner notes offer a wealth of information on the bands, which range from Soledad Brothers to Six Finger Satellite, as well as McCue's own "personal history" with the music.

"'From the swooping highs of my best days to the crushing lows of my worst, I've always been able to relate to MDID. This song, 'Where's Our Reason,' from the *Shine(r)* CD, was actually released in 1993 as part of the limited-edition Working Holiday series of 7-inch singles.'"

Though the liner notes are rich with details about most of the songs, they

Above: Josh McCue shows off the liner notes to *Opium Of The Masses*.

are occasionally brief and to the point. For instance, McCue describes Killdozer's cover of EMF's "Unbelievable" with just two words: "Fuck, yeah!"

McCue went on to explain his choice of images for the CD's cover art, saying, "It's a picture of a crashing speedboat I got off the Internet. Very chaotic and random, much like the music
see LINER NOTES page 35

BAKE SALE from page 31

my goodies turn out."

Fellow parishioner Betty Wicks agreed.

"Every time I go past Connie's table, I just have to buy something," said the 245-pound Wicks, who commits the sin of gluttony at every St. Mary's bake sale, as well as most Friday nights at Old Country Buffet. "I simply can't help myself—it's all so delicious."

The popularity of Barrett's mouth-

> While the sins of wrath and avarice were each committed dozens of times at the event, Barrett and longtime bake-sale rival Penny Cox brought them together in full force.

watering wares elicited the sin of envy in many of her fellow vendors.

"Connie has this fantastic book of recipes her grandmother gave her, and she won't share them with anyone," church organist Georgia Brandt said. "This year, I made white-chocolate blondies and thought they'd be a big hit. But most people just went straight to Connie's table, got what they wanted, and left. All the while, Connie just stood there with this look of smug satisfaction on her face. It took every ounce of strength in my body to keep from going over there and really telling her off."

While the sins of wrath and avarice were each committed dozens of times at the event, Barrett and longtime bake-sale rival Penny Cox brought them together in full force.

"Penny said she wanted to make a bet over whose table would make the most money," said Barrett, exhibiting avarice. "Whoever lost would have to sit in the dunk tank at the St. Mary's Summer Fun Festival. I figured it's for such a good cause, a little wager couldn't hurt. Besides, I always bring the church more money anyway, so I couldn't possibly lose."

Moments after agreeing to the wager, Cox became wrathful when Barrett, the bake sale's co-chair, grabbed the best table location under the pretense of having to keep the coffee machine full. Cox attempted to exact revenge by reporting an alleged Barrett misdeed to the church's priest.

"I mentioned to Father Mark [O'-Connor] that I've seen candles at Connie's house that I wouldn't be surprised one bit if she stole from the church's storage closet," said Cox, who also committed the sin of sloth by forcing her daughter to set up and

> "Every time I go past Connie's table, I just have to buy something," said the 245-pound Wicks, who commits the sin of gluttony at every St. Mary's bake sale, as well as most Friday nights at Old Country Buffet.

man her booth while she gossiped with friends. "Perhaps if he investigates this, by this time next year, Connie won't be co-chair of the bake sale and in her place we'll have someone who's willing to rotate the choice table spots."

The sin of lust also reared its ugly head at the bake sale, largely due to the presence of Melissa Wyckoff, a shapely 20-year-old redhead whose family recently joined the church. While male attendees ogled Wyckoff, the primary object of lust for females was the personable, boyish Father Mark.

Though attendees' feelings of lust for Wyckoff and O'Connor were never acted on, they did not go unnoticed.

"There's something not right about that Melissa Wyckoff," said envious and wrathful bake-sale participant Jilly Brandon, after her husband Craig offered Wyckoff one of her Rice Krispie treats to "welcome [her] to the parish." "She might have just moved here from California, but that red dress of hers should get her kicked out of the church."

According to St. Mary's treasurer Beth Ellen Coyle, informal church-sponsored events are a notorious breeding ground for the seven deadly sins.

"Bake sales, haunted houses, pancake breakfasts... such church events are rife with potential for sin," Coyle said. "This year, we had to eliminate the 'Guess Your Weight' booth from the annual church carnival because the envy and pride had gotten so out of hand. Church events are about glorifying God, not violating His word. If you want to do that, you're no better than that cheap strumpet Melissa Wyckoff." Ø

33

BIN LADEN from page 31

Above: A Taliban soldier prepares to attack the 13th Marine Expeditionary Unit.

"Men of the armies of Pakistan, Turkey, Turkmenistan, Uzbekistan, and Tajikistan; Americans of the 101st Airborne, 10th Mountain Division, 13th Marine Expeditionary Unit, 4th Special Operations Group, 8th Army Mechanized Battalion, SEAL Teams Four, Six, and Nine, and the Aircraft

American military leaders are having difficulty locating the few remaining pockets of Taliban personnel.

Carrier U.S.S. Carl Vinson... you are hereby required to report to the smoldering remains of our air base southeast of Kandahar," the statement read. "Turn your weapons over to Kamal and Azir, these two guys who should still be there. Kamal will be the one with the bad limp. After you have been processed by them and your surrender has been accepted, you will be released and sent home as soon as possible. Please, do not throw away any more lives in this useless struggle. Please."

"The noose is tightening," said Taliban leader Mullah Mohammed Omar, gnawing on a dead horse's hoof. "With every Taliban soldier you capture or kill, your selection of enemies grows more limited. Our remaining soldiers, on the other hand, enjoy a virtually limitless array of Allied soldiers to shoot. Before long, it will be virtually impossible for you to find someone to engage on the field of battle. Then, victory will be ours."

Omar then covered his face and began to rock slowly back and forth.

According to Defense Secretary Donald Rumsfeld, American military leaders are having difficulty locating the few remaining pockets of Taliban personnel, hindering U.S. efforts to force a surrender.

"We are carefully analyzing bin Laden's videotaped message for any possible clues to his whereabouts," Rumsfeld said. "By analyzing the background vegetation and rock formations, the length and position of the shadows, and other subtle clues, we may be able to determine the location of the Taliban's temporary headquarters and send in a strike force for around-the-clock shelling."

"It's not yet clear where bin Laden was," Rumsfeld added, "but he seemed to be speaking from some sort of gigantic, bombed-out litter box."

Asked if he had considered or listened to the content of bin Laden's message, Rumsfeld said, "Why, no." ∅

Nuclear-Bomb Instructions Found In Pentagon

ARLINGTON, VA—In an alarming development, plans for a thermonuclear device were found Monday in a Pentagon desk drawer. "These guys were definitely working on something," said United Press International correspondent Nigel Afton-George, who came across the plans while touring a section of the compound damaged in the Sept. 11 attack. "They had all sorts of manuals and plans for the construction and deployment of nuclear weapons. It's terrifying to think what they were planning to do with this stuff."

Michael Jackson Deposed As King Of Pop In Hitless Coup

LOS ANGELES—After a two-decade reign as King Of Pop, Michael Jackson was overthrown Tuesday in a hitless coup. "Following the lackluster performance of *Invincible* and its mildly received 'You Rock My World' single, Michael has lost the support of the populace necessary to maintain his throne," said *Billboard* magazine pop-political analyst Daniel Farrior. "To be honest, it's amazing he held onto his kingship after *Blood On The Dance Floor*." Upon learning of the coup, millions of music fans stormed the nation's music stores, carrying off armloads of CDs by artists other than Jackson.

Laid-Off Web Designer Designs Web Site About Being Laid Off

REDWOOD CITY, CA—Bob Trabert, 26, a web designer laid off from Cybercepts last month, has channeled his energies into the creation of No-

JobBob.com, a web site about his experiences being laid off. "Visitors can read my online job-hunt diary, watch Flash animation of me sitting around in my underwear watching TV, or Paypal me a 'donation,'" Trabert said. "It's mostly for fun, but I figure, hey, maybe someone out there who needs a web designer will see it and be impressed."

Yalie Strikes Harvard Lad Sharply About The Face And Neck

NEW HAVEN, CT—A heated dispute over the relative merits of Harvard and Yale erupted into fisticuffs Monday, when Yalie William Vanderploeg, 20, struck Randolph Stephenson, a strapping Harvard lad of 19, about the face and neck in a most brutish manner. "The vainglorious braggart dared suggest that his Crimson squad could out-row us nine times of ten," said Vanderploeg, captain of the Yale crew team. "I knew they raised them as barbarians over Harvard way, but the very gall." Stephenson, his hair mussed from the attack, vowed that the dispute is far from settled.

Area Woman Insists On Helping Coworker Through Personal Crisis

EL PASO, TX—At a time when she would rather be left alone, recent divorcee Denise Jacoby, 42, is finding herself besieged by unsolicited offers of help from Birds Eye Foods coworker Donna Traschel. "If she tells me that she's there for me any time—day or night—one more time, I'm gonna strangle her," Jacoby said. "She's already lent me three different books on coping with change and overcoming loss. What do I have to do to make her understand that I don't want an ear to bend or a shoulder to lean on?" ∅

CLUMPED from page 31

amounts of blood. Passersby were amazed by the unusually large amounts of blood. Passersby were amazed by the unusually large amounts of blood. Passersby were amazed by the unusually large amounts of blood. Passersby were amazed by the unusually large amounts of blood. Passersby were amazed by the unusually large amounts of blood. Passersby were amazed by the unusually large amounts of blood. Passersby were amazed by the unusually large amounts of blood. Passersby were amazed by the unusually large amounts of blood. Passersby were amazed by the unusually large amounts of blood. Passersby were amazed by the unusually large amounts of blood. Passersby were amazed by the unusually large amounts of blood. Passersby were amazed by the unusually large

amounts of blood. Passersby were amazed by the unusually large amounts of blood. Passersby were

I can't believe Columbia Pictures stole my idea of making a sequel to *Men In Black*.

amazed by the unusually large amounts of blood. Passersby were amazed by the unusually large
see CLUMPED page 38

GIRL from page 31

way!'" said Takashima, shaking her finger and frowning in imitation of her stern father. "So I go to Minnesota. It's good here, too. It snows, and everything is white! Then we have snowball fight!"

While most Concordia students take pains to seem mature, Takashima is

> **"Misako's room is so great," said freshman Rachel Alarie, 18. "She's got cool toys all over the place, like stacks of these Japanese comic books called manga and posters for weird Japanese cartoon movies. And she has a PlayStation that only plays Japanese games."**

unafraid to embrace her whimsical side: She makes chalk drawings on the sidewalk, puts on impromptu puppet shows, and takes pictures of her dormmates' bare feet and tapes them to her door.

According to Erickson, who lived in Carlson Hall last year, the third floor is "about 20 times more fun" since Takashima arrived.

"Last year was so bad around here: Everyone broke into these little cliques and hated each other," Erickson said. "But this year, it's completely different. We all get along great. That's totally due to Misako."

In addition to fostering floor-wide friendship, Takashima has broadened

> **"Misako's mom mails her junk food with Asian writing on the packages. If she knows you're having a bad day, she'll hang some little candies on your doorknob with a note that says, 'Cheer up, my friend! Do not be sad!'"**

her dormmates' horizons, introducing them to numerous Japanese pop-cultural staples.

"Misako's room is so great," said freshman Rachel Alarie, 18. "She's got cool toys all over the place, like

LINER NOTES from page 33

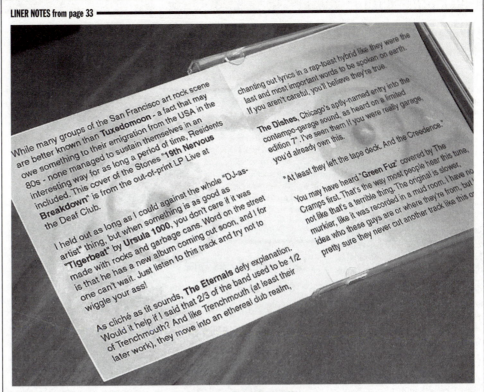

While many groups of the San Francisco art rock scene are better known than **Tuxedomoon** - a fact that may owe something to their emigration from the USA in the 80s - none managed to sustain themselves in an interesting way for as long a period of time. Residents included. This cover of the Stones' **19th Nervous Breakdown** is from the out-of-print LP Live at the Deaf Club.

I held out as long as I could against the whole "DJ-as-artist" thing, but when something is as good as **"Tigerbeat"** by **Ursula 1000**, you don't care if it was made with rocks and garbage cans. Word on the street is that he has a new album coming out soon, and I for one can't wait. Just listen to this track and try not to wiggle your ass!

As cliché as tit sounds, **The Eternals** defy explanation. Would it help if I said that 2/3 of the band used to be 1/2 of Trenchmouth? And like Trenchmouth (at least their later work), they move into an ethereal dub realm,

chanting out lyrics in a rap-toast hybrid like they were the last and most important words to be spoken on earth. If you aren't careful, you'll believe they're true.

The Dishes, Chicago's aptly-named entry into the contempo-garage sound, as heard on a limited edition 7". I've seen them if you were really garage, you'd already own this.

"At least they left the tape deck. And the Creedence."

You may have heard **"Green Fuz"** covered by The Cramps first. That's the way most people hear this tune, not like that's a terrible thing. The original is slower, murkier, like it was recorded in a mud room. I have no idea who these guys are or where they're from, but I pretty sure they never cut another track like this o

Above: The album's liner notes, which provide a wealth of information on the compilation CD's songs.

itself."

McCue said he plays the CD at work several times a day, propping the jewel case against an eye-level row of DeKuyper Schnapps bottles to maximize its visibility. Thus far, no customers have asked about it.

"I took a few chances on this mix," said McCue, attempting to explain the lack of interest. "For example, I kicked it off with Martin Denny's 'Quiet Village,' an unorthodox first song if there ever was one. Why did I do so? Because it's an ideal musical metaphor for my life, seemingly uneventful but filled with wonder and strangeness. And while it's the only exotica on the CD, it perfectly sets the stage for an eclectic voyage through my life, starting with the 'Quiet Village' of my birth."

McCue burned the CD for his own

> **McCue said he plays the CD at work several times a day, propping the jewel case against an eye-level row of DeKuyper Schnapps bottles to maximize its visibility.**

personal enjoyment, but said he would be willing to lend it to friends. Should a loan occur, the liner notes are a vital means of

ensuring that every track is given the due it deserves.

"I wanted to make sure no one skipped a track," McCue said. "For example, most people would think a transition from Neu! to Afrika Bambaataa to Aphex Twin would be a little jarring or awkward, but it actually flows quite nicely thanks to the unity of influences. I make sure to point that out in my liner notes, discussing the heavy debt that both ambient and hip-hop owe to Krautrock."

As of press time, McCue is working on the liner notes to the as-yet-unburned *Opium Of The Masses Vol. 2*, which he promises will clear up any lingering confusion from the first CD, as well as explain his long-time fascination with both Ray Conniff and Julian Cope. ⌀

stacks of these Japanese comic books called *manga* and posters for weird Japanese cartoon movies. And she has a PlayStation that only plays Japanese games. Everyone's addicted to this one weird game where a little man shaped like a domino walks through a grocery store. Once I stayed up until 3 a.m. playing it."

Takashima's offbeat interests are matched by equally offbeat behavior. Often, she will spontaneously scream with delight or run in circles, attracting the attention of strangers. But in spite of such over-the-top antics, Takashima, her classmates agreed, is one of the nicest people they have ever met.

"Some people can be so stuck-up, but Misako is nice to everyone," said Chelsea Mason, 18. "Misako's mom

mails her junk food with Asian writing on the packages. If she knows you're having a bad day, she'll hang some little candies on your doorknob with a note that says, 'Cheer up, my friend! Do not be sad!'"

When she makes phone calls home to Japan, Takashima loves to pass the phone to her new American friends so they can talk to her brother Ryunosuke.

"Ryunosuke sounds so cute," said Alarie, one of the many third-floor residents who has a long-distance crush on Takashima's brother. "He's 20. I told him he should fly to Minnesota for our Christmas party."

The floor's resident administrator, 23-year-old graduate student Erin Lorimer, said she expects the upcoming holiday party to be a big success, thanks in no small part to

Takashima.

"At Christmas in the quad, there's a contest for the best-decorated lounge, and I know we're going to win," Lorimer said. "Misako taught us origami, and we decorated the tree and with hundreds of little white birds. Then we made a sign that says 'Peace On Earth' in English and Japanese. She's so awesome."

Unfortunately, not all Concordia students are lucky enough to live in Takashima's dorm. Stephanie Yoder, a Wycliff Hall resident, expressed jealousy of her Carlson Hall counterparts.

"I wish we could have [Misako] for our dorm," Yoder said. "We have a girl from Germany on fourth floor, but she's really shy. She's got a single [occupancy room] and hardly ever comes out." ⌀

Winterized!

The Cruise
By Jim Anchower

Hola, amigos. Everything cool? I know it's been a long time since I rapped at ya, but things have kinda gotten out of control on Anchower Lane. (That ain't actually where I live—I don't think there are any streets named Anchower Lane, at least not 'til I die.) But I'm not about to tell people where I actually live. For one thing, I don't want people stopping by my pad at all hours of the day, telling me they love my writing or stealing my beer or informing me that I'm six months late on payments. Plus, there are these guys I had a bit of an altercation with last week who'd love to take a poke at me, and I ain't about to help them out.

I guess those guys are one way that things are out of control in my life, but I wasn't even thinkin' of that. Naw, I was more thinking of the way things have been going for me health-wise. I came down with a pretty nasty cold last week, and I just can't shake it. Now, usually, I just down a few shots of Dr. McGillicuddy's and that pretty much clears up the problem. But this one ain't letting go.

The worst part about this damn cold is the way I got it. It's kind of a long story. And, actually, it sort of involves those guys I mentioned before.

See, around this time every year, Paddy O'Surly's Olde Tyme Irish Pub has a sweet-ass Wednesday-night two-for-one special on icy-cold MGDs. The only problem is, O'Surly's is at least 10 miles from my place. Now, I ain't gonna drive drunk, so I always go with someone who ain't gonna get hammered so I can cut loose, Anchower style. My buddy Ron likes to party hard, too, so he was ruled out as a designated-driver candidate. That's where Wes The Bomb came in. See, he's a good guy, and he likes beer as much as the next guy, but he also doesn't mind going light for the sake of his pals.

So, last Wednesday night, just before quitting time, I gave Wes a call to see if he was available for chauffeuring duties. He wasn't going for it until I offered to pay for the beers and give him a few extra bucks for gas. That won him over, so he came by my place of employment, California Fajita Cantina, and hung out for a little while, mowing down on chips until my shift was done. Dude, that guy must have a hollow leg, 'cause he went through about three baskets of tortilla chips and, like, five Cokes. After I finally punched out, we swung by Ron's place and picked him up, and off we went to O'Surly's.

When we got there, the place was crazy. It took us five minutes just to get to the bar, so we decided to make it count. We got a total of 12 beers, with Wes getting two and me and Ron getting five each. I finished one beer on the way to the back to find a table. Shit, was it packed. I thought we were gonna have to stand around a while with an armload of beer, so I quick downed another. Just then, a table opened up. Victory!

About half an hour later, me and Ron were toasting our good luck

---

See, around this time every year, Paddy O'Surly's Olde Tyme Irish Pub has a sweet-ass Wednesday-night two-for-one special on icy-cold MGDs.

---

when these three big dudes came by the table and told us they were just playing pool, and that we were sitting in their spot. Well, at this point, I was already half in the bag, so I wasn't afraid to tell them that I wasn't about to give up our hard-earned table. I told them I didn't see their names on it anywhere, and that they were probably mistaken.

Wes started to go all soft and announced that it had thinned down a little up front, so we could probably move to a table there. Thanks for backing me up, dude. I told Wes, no, let these guys find their own damn table. We were here, and if they wanted us moved, they'd better do the moving.

I think that got them a little riled up, because the next thing I know, I'm being hoisted up by two huge fuckers. I start swinging, and I'm looking for Ron and Wes to back me up in the major-league throw-down that's about to commence, but they're gettin' their shit together to leave. My friends totally pussed out on me again! The big dudes carried me out the front door of the bar and threw me into a puddle.

I sure gave Ron and Wes hell on the drive home. They could've at least made like they were going to stand up for me, but they totally backed down! I told them they should be ashamed to call themselves men, leaving their old buddy Jim out to dry like that. Wes dropped me off at my apartment and told me that if that's the way I felt, I shouldn't come crawling to him for any more favors. Ron agreed, forgetting that I paid for the entire night of beers. They looked royally pissed when they took off, but I really didn't

---

Your Horoscope

By Lloyd Schumner Sr.
Retired Machinist and
A.A.P.B.-Certified Astrologer

Aries: (March 21–April 19)
Give a starving man a fish, and he'll eat for a day. Teach him how to cook a fish, though, and he'll starve to death with a clearer picture of what he's missing.

Taurus: (April 20–May 20)
Your heart may have been in the right place, but it really isn't appropriate to craft a menorah out of Oscar Mayer hot dogs.

Gemini: (May 21–June 21)
In spite of what you believe, your tendency to confuse Keats and Wordsworth is far from your greatest flaw.

Cancer: (June 22–July 22)
The classics tell us that the only result of hubris is humiliation, but it's not your fault you are the proud mountain goat.

Leo: (July 23–Aug. 22)
An adventurous *ménage á trois* turns out to be a bit of a letdown when you are not invited to participate.

Virgo: (Aug. 23–Sept. 22)
One day, long after your death, your analysis of Samuel Butler's epic *Hudibras* will eclipse that of the great Rev. Treadway Russell Nash, for all the good that does you.

Libra: (Sept. 23–Oct. 23)
You will be both flattered and worried when you gain renown as the World's Greatest Lover Of Fatty Snacks.

Scorpio: (Oct. 24–Nov. 21)
Your worldview will be shaken to the core when *Car And Driver* asks the disturbing question, "Is The Corvette Still King?"

Sagittarius: (Nov. 22–Dec. 21)
Your life has been a litany of failure, dashed expectations, and unfulfilled dreams, but at least it's almost over.

Capricorn: (Dec. 22–Jan. 19)
The "shooting stars" in your sign may be space debris burning up in Earth's atmosphere, but they nevertheless presage famine, disease, and death.

Aquarius: (Jan. 20–Feb. 18)
Your marriage will finally fall apart this week when your spouse, in a fit of rage, takes the cheerleading squad's word over yours.

Pisces: (Feb. 19–March 20)
No one at the hospital will be able to convince you that, defending its territory or not, the alpaca didn't have the whole thing planned in advance.

---

give a shit.

When I got to my doorstep, things went from bad to worse. I reached in my pocket for my keys but couldn't find 'em. I checked my coat. I checked my pants. I was so smashed, I even

---

I checked my coat. I checked my pants. I was so smashed, I even checked my drawers, but the only thing in there was the Anchower nutsack.

---

checked my drawers, but the only thing in there was the Anchower nutsack. Maybe they'd fallen out of my pocket when those guys gave me the old heave-ho.

By the time I checked and rechecked every cranny of my clothes, I

was tired and ready to pass out. Locked out, my best option was to crash at either Wes or Ron's place, but I didn't even want to look at either of those two traitors after the shit they pulled. So I decided that if bums could sleep outside, so could I. Besides, it wasn't that cold out—not freezing, anyway. So I grabbed a rug off of the curb, laid it down on my front step, and rolled up inside of it for the night.

The next morning, I woke up feeling pretty damn crappy. My ass was asleep, and I reeked like week-old mopwater from when those guys tossed me into the puddle. My head was pounding, and my feet were about to fall off. That's when I remembered that I had a spare key under a rock by the front door. That's also when the cold started.

I'm telling you, I've been hocking up some pretty nasty greenies since then. I thought about taking pictures of them, but I don't have a camera. Probably for the best, anyway. I should save a few loogies for Ron and Wes, but who wants to stir up any more shit? Best just let it settle and get on with life. ∅

MOTHER
PAULINE LANFORD
1926 † 1998

Mother Still Yammering Away Under Her Tombstone

see LOCAL page 11E

BRIDGE
OUT
8 FEET
AHEAD

Dept. Of Transportation Discontinues 'Bridge Out 8 Feet Ahead' Sign

see NATION page 3A

Chicken Bones, Beer Cans Bob In The Froth Of John Goodman's Hot Tub

see PEOPLE page 2D

STATshot

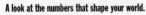

A look at the numbers that shape your world.

How Are We Maintaining Our Dignity?

1. Refusing sex initially
2. Wearing name tag at angle
3. Never running to catch public transportation
4. Acting like we quit
5. Wearing really good barrel
6. Requesting nurse conceal our colostomy bag from visitors (request denied)

---

the ONION®

VOLUME 37 ISSUE 46   AMERICA'S FINEST NEWS SOURCE™   20 DEC. 2001–16 JAN. 2002

ONION Special Report

What Is Sexy In The Wake Of Sept. 11?

Entrepreneur Stuck With 40,000 Unsold Bin Laden Urinal Cakes

Above: Kloster displays one of the thousands of novelty urinal cakes (above) that sit in his warehouse.

REGO PARK, NY—Gabe Kloster, a 32-year-old Queens-based entrepreneur, expressed fear Monday that he may be unable to sell his remaining inventory of 40,000 urinal cakes bearing an image of Osama bin Laden between a pair of crosshairs.

"A few months back, I couldn't make them fast enough," said Kloster, who

supplies news- and pop-culture-related novelty products to discount stores and street vendors in the New York area. "Now I can't get rid of the goddamn things."

Kloster came up with the idea for bin Laden urinal cakes a few days after Sept. 11.

"I saw that guys on the Internet were already selling Osama bin Laden see CAKES page 39

NEW YORK—On Sept. 11, the world changed. The tragic events of that fateful day have had a profound impact on American society, altering—as documented in countless magazines and newspapers—everything from our our travel habits to our tastes in music to our gourmet-cheese preferences. But three months later, one vital question still remains unanswered: What is sexy in the wake of Sept. 11?

"After the deaths of so many thousands of people, what turns us on?" asked Robyn Loeb, Life section editor of *USA Today.* "I'm hearing arched backs, lithe young bodies glistening with sweat, naked lovers embraced in long, slow, steamy kisses. Given everything that we as a nation have been through, when it comes to sex, we long for a return to the tried-and-true."

According to *Vogue* managing editor Carrie Bettig, beautiful women are in.

"Ever since Sept. 11, we've been seeing a lot of gorgeous women in fashion magazines," Bettig said. "A great many of the models featured in recent spreads have stunning faces and see SEXY page 40

Partygoers Mocked By Catering Staff

MARIETTA, GA—Unbeknownst to attendees of Susan and Mel Gullicksen's holiday party Saturday, the Feather & Fennel Catering staff spent most of the evening mocking partygoers behind their backs.

"Matt, you have got see the sow in the powder-blue chiffon jumpsuit," said Feather & Fennel server Christine Salerno, 23, whispering to coworker Matt Blaine. "She looks like Brian Dennehy in drag, only less feminine."

Blaine then rushed a tray of miniature quiches into the living room to get an eyeful of the unattractive guest.

The party, held in the Gullicksens' spacious suburban Atlanta home, was attended by nearly 100 friends of the see CATERERS page 40

Above: Feather & Fennel staffers laugh at a partygoer's lime-green dress.

Bush And The ABM Treaty

Worried about nuclear attacks by terrorists and rogue states, President Bush pulled out of the ABM treaty in the hopes of building a missile shield. What do *you* think?

"This is a wise move on Bush's part, considering the fact that terrorists possess elaborate launching systems capable of firing nuclear missiles into space."

Larry Edwards
Systems Analyst

"It's reassuring to know that, after everything that's happened in the past three months, there's still irrefutable proof that Bush is a dick."

Marjorie Ready
Student

"The ABM treaty was a noble but ultimately flawed idea that hindered our ability to bomb the fuck out of countries we don't like."

Will Lathon
Auto Mechanic

"As a full-blooded Native American, I'd like to know why everyone's acting so goddamned surprised."

Leonard Whitecloud
Cashier

"A missile-defense system is all the more vital now that we've pissed off Russia so bad."

Thomas Provenza
Lawyer

"This shield will protect us from terrorists who steal radioactive industrial-waste materials and build 'dirty bombs' aimed at subways, bridges, and other public spaces, right? Phew."

Lauren Keith
Dental Hygienist

Hot Holiday Toys

What are the top-selling toys this holiday season?

- Shoddi™, the cheap doll for poor-kid toy drives
- Anatomically Correct Mr. Potato Head
- Jabberjuice, the juice cup that talks for some goddamn reason
- "Henry Porter And The Wizard's Rock" budgetastic action figures
- Super Mighty Mecha-Dreidel With Gelt-Launching Action
- Kick The Bucket! The Wacky Suicide Game
- "I'm A Li'l Slut" Rock-Star Karaoke Machine
- Rock 'Em Sock 'Em Tennessee-Marriage Playset
- Virtua Dishwasher II for the Xbox
- Real Live Puppy by Nev-R-Gro (Warning: Puppy may experience some growth)

the ONION®
America's Finest News Source.™

Herman Ulysses Zweibel
Founder

T. Herman Zweibel
Publisher Emeritus

J. Phineas Zweibel
Publisher

Maxwell Prescott Zweibel
Editor-In-Chief

San Francisco Is My Favorite Market

By Flip Casper
Marketing Executive

As a marketing executive who does a fair amount of business traveling, I've had the chance to visit a lot of markets. New York, Boston, Chicago, Los Angeles—they're all great markets, each with their own unique attractions and attributes. But for my money, there's no market quite like San Francisco.

Ah, San Francisco. How I love to visit the market by the bay, with its old-world charm and open-hearted people. I yearn for Frisco's beautiful skyline, dominated by the TransAmerica Pyramid and the sweeping majesty of the Golden Gate Bridge. And how can you beat having the charming little markets of Sausalito and Monterey so close by? Throw in its mild, business-friendly climate, and San Francisco might just be heaven on Earth.

Its residents sure think so. The people of San Francisco are a culturally and ethnically diverse customer base of 800,000 who hail from virtually every demographic you can name. From the middle-class leanings of the Mission District to the upper-mid conspicuous-consumption, alternative-lifestyle Castro to the shabby-chic

> **Like no other market, it's the embodiment of the American dream, a place where hippies, Chinese immigrants, and dot-com millionaires shop side-by-side, exchanging ideas, durable goods, and services.**

stylings of the Presidio's catalog-order set, San Francisco is home to every type of consumer under the sun. And, as you'd expect from a market that both Mark Twain and Jerry Garcia called home, almost every person there is a unique character who marches to the beat of a different drummer. It's true what they say: There's no such thing as a median San Franciscan.

While we're talking neighborhoods, let's not forget Nob Hill. Last time I was in San Francisco, I met a lovely 35- to 44-year-old woman with a household income of $100K to $149,999 while strolling the Nob Hill area. We got to talking and, as it turned out, she grew up in the Dallas-

Ft. Worth market, which is where I'm from. She gave me a tour of the various gardens around Nob Hill, and by the time we were through, I was convinced that it was just about the prettiest neighborhood in any market

> **The people of San Francisco are a culturally and ethnically diverse customer base of 800,000 who hail from virtually every demographic you can name.**

anywhere.

But this glorious market's charms don't stop there. People from sales regions across America flock to San Francisco to see Pier 39 at Fisherman's Wharf, where the seal demographic frolics in the waves. They flock to Pac Bell Park, where the native and the transient/recreational come together to root for the hometown Giants. They tour Alcatraz, San Francisco's most popular attraction among the 42 percent of Americans who fall into the "some college" category. And, with its countless theaters, galleries, and museums, San Francisco boasts more culture than any market this side of Paris.

Then there's the food. San Francisco is home to an endless array of restaurants, cafés, and bars that drive a surprisingly aggressive and successful upward-trending microeconomy. From crabs to crepes, from Ghirardelli chocolate to Napa Valley chardonnay, there's nothing you can't get in this market.

Yes, San Francisco is a unique intersection of the Far East, the Wild West, and Silicon Valley. Like no other market, it's the embodiment of the American dream, a place where hippies, Chinese immigrants, and dot-com millionaires shop side-by-side, exchanging ideas, durable goods, and services. You truly can do, be, or buy anything in San Francisco.

Someday, come hell or high water, I'm going to move to San Francisco. Dallas is perfectly nice, and I've enjoyed my years there, but it just doesn't compare to the world-class market that is San Francisco. I've been there probably a dozen times in my life, and I still love everything about it: the sights, the sounds, the white-collar professionals who make up 59 percent of its purchasing base.

I swear, I know the market so well, I feel like I network there already. ∅

Report: U.S. Must Reduce Dependence On Foreign Turmoil

WASHINGTON, DC—According to a Cato Institute report released Monday, the U.S. has become overly dependent on foreign turmoil for its conversations and media coverage. "The American people consume as many as 60 million barrels of crude speculation every day, using it for everything from driving discussions to heating up political debates," the report stated. "Unless we can dredge up domestic sources of turmoil, we may end up utterly dependent on the Middle East for conversational fuel."

Boyfriend Ceremoniously Dumped

ELLENSBURG, WA—In a gala breakup featuring the town mayor and the Ellensburg High School marching band, Chris Schiffman was ceremoniously dumped Sunday by Vicki Arness, his girlfriend of three years. "Ladies and gentlemen of Ellensburg, let the word go forth from this day that Vicki and Chris are no longer an item!" Mayor Robert Todd announced before 3,000 cheering attendees. "Vicki has let it be known that she wishes to see other people, and see other people she shall!" The scissors-wielding mayor then officially declared the couple broken up by cutting an oversized photo of them in half.

Parent Mad 6-Year-Old Didn't Like *Peanuts* Special

ROSE HILL, VA—Bruce Pillard, 34, was angered Tuesday over his 6-year-old daughter's indifferent reaction to *A Charlie Brown Christmas*. "That show is a classic and an annual tradition!" an incensed Pillard told daughter Courtney after watching the program on CBS. "It is not 'boring,' and the voices do not sound 'weird.' What the hell is wrong with you?" Courtney was then sent to her room for the remainder of the evening.

Art Major To Stop Capitalizing Name

COLUMBUS, OH—Michael Wechsler, 19, an Ohio State University art major, announced Monday that he is changing his name to "michael wechsler." "Isn't that so much cooler?" Wechsler asked fellow art major Ethan Reed. "The whole capital-letter thing has always bothered me. It's just a stupid rule that everyone else seems to think they have to follow." Wechsler is also considering changing the spelling of his first name to "mychal."

Area Woman Not Yelling At You, She's Just Saying

JACKSONVILLE, FL—Area resident Roberta Pearle clarified Monday that, while it may look like she is yelling at you, she is actually just saying. "I'm not yelling at you," Pearle explained. "I'm just saying. You know, so you'll know." Pearle then loudly reiterated that she is not yelling. "I'm not," she said.

National Board Of Steve Jaskoviak Requests $10 Billion Bailout

ROCHESTER, MN—Steve Jaskoviak, president of the National Board of Steve Jaskoviak, lobbied Congress for an unprecedented $10 billion bailout package Monday. "In order to continue providing Americans with a full range of Steve Jaskoviak-related services, it is crucial that I receive this aid," Jaskoviak told Congress. "This relief package will not only cover my $5,612 Visa debt, but numerous administrative costs, as well." ∅

CAKES from page 37

dartboards, toilet paper, trash cans, and kitty-pan liners, so I thought people would get a kick out of having the chance to piss on him," Kloster said. "Besides, I knew a guy in Paramus who could do the printing real cheap."

On Sept. 20, Kloster moved forward with an initial run of 2,000 urinal

> "The sports bars loved them," Kloster said. "Paddy O'Lantern's, this bar near my house, even put a sign on the men's-room door saying 'Target Practice—This Way.' That same week, a newspaper in Hartford called to say they were interested in doing a story on [the cakes]."

cakes, which sold out in just three days. He subsequently increased the run to 15,000, and by early October, the product had proven so popular that he decided to halt the manufacture of all other novelty items to focus exclusively on the cherry-scented, terrorist-decorated cakes.

"The sports bars loved them," Kloster said. "Paddy O'Lantern's, this bar near my house, even put a sign on the men's-room door saying 'Target Practice—This Way.' That same week, a

newspaper in Hartford called to say they were interested in doing a story on [the cakes]. They never wound up doing one, but it was obvious I was on to something."

Encouraged by the positive re-

Above: A bar-goer in Garden City, NY, takes aim on the Saudi-born terrorist.

sponse, Kloster raised the production run to 50,000 in early November. Unfortunately, interest soon began to wane. Since the beginning of December, Kloster has only sold 141 cakes, a 97 percent drop-off from his early-

October sales peak.

"Bush said this war could drag on for years, so I quadrupled production, figuring the market would be hot for a while," Kloster said. "But then the

see CAKES page 40

SEXY from page 37

spectacular bodies—long legs, toned stomachs, and gravity-defying breasts. I believe that such images resonate because, in these times of turmoil, we take comfort in femininity. Hence, there is a focus on the female body in its perfect form."

The change is also reflected in the celebrities we love—and lust.

"Just look at the cover of this month's *Vanity Fair*," said David

> ## "Movies featuring sexy actors and actresses are thriving at the box office, strip clubs are packed, gyms are filled with people who either are sexy or aspire to be."

Roell, a media-studies professor at Stanford University. "Tom Cruise is posing shirtless with a sultry, smoldering look on his face. Before Sept. 11, Cruise had never appeared on the cover of *Vanity Fair* without a shirt. Draw your own conclusions."

Erin Weiss, a *People* senior reporter, is currently working on a cover story on post-Sept. 11 sexiness. She has found that after enduring so much hardship and pain, the American people are eager to look at—and interact with—sexy people.

"Across the country, Americans are seeking out sexiness: Movies featuring sexy actors and actresses are thriving at the box office, strip clubs are packed, gyms are filled with people who either are sexy or aspire to be. Clearly, sex speaks powerfully to our collective need to move forward and enjoy life right now."

Weiss said she is confident that America will emerge from these difficult times sexier than ever.

"On Sept. 11, we lost our innocence," Weiss said. "We're now more mature, more aware. As President Bush said, 'We know what we want, and we know how to get it.' Now, *that's* sexy."

A few media professionals, however, are staying out of the raging sexiness debate.

"Sexiness after the terrorist attacks?" scoffed *Boston Globe* editor Martin Baron. "We did that a month ago. We've also done features on how Sept. 11 has affected dating, the hotel industry, stand-up comedy, leukemia research, high-school football, antique collecting,

and the parking situation in downtown Boston. I want to hear some new 9-11 ideas."

"The world is a totally different place now," Baron continued. "This

> ## "I believe that such images resonate because, in these times of turmoil, we take comfort in femininity. Hence, there is a focus on the female body in its perfect form."

year, instead of the usual Christmas-season stories about holiday displays and shopping, we're doing pieces about how stores are using patriotism in their holiday displays and how people don't feel like shopping."

Added Baron: "Will we ever write those innocent old stories again? That's the question we'll try to answer this Sunday, in a *Globe* feature piece addressing Sept. 11's effect on holiday-season journalism." ⌀

CATERERS from page 37

upper-class couple. The caterers were hired to set up the buffet, serve appetizers and entrees to guests, and break down the food area at the party's conclusion. All surreptitious, catty remarks about the Gullicksens and their friends were added free of charge.

"I've seen not one but two different people wearing pastel sweaters knotted around their necks," said Blaine, 20, during a cigarette break outside. "I think we accidentally stepped into a time machine set for Dipwadville, 1984."

Though no guest was spared, the caterers reserved their greatest scorn for "Jumpsuit Woman," "Chivas-and-7-Up Guy," and "Golfman," a fiftysomething man with a bad combover who, Blaine said, "would not fucking shut up about golf."

Another guest was dubbed "The Vegetarian Avenger" because of his repeated complaints to the catering staff about the evening's lack of vege-

> ## According to Feather & Fennel staffers, a majority of the mockery was done covertly, with wisecracks delivered either in hushed tones or in the kitchen, safely out of earshot of partygoers.

tarian options.

"He's at a friggin' Christmas party," Salerno said. "What does he expect, endless trays of bulghur burgers?"

According to Feather & Fennel staffers, a majority of the mockery was done covertly, with wisecracks delivered either in hushed tones or in the kitchen, safely out of earshot of partygoers. Caterers alerted each other to the presence of particularly ridicule-worthy individuals with subtle glances or quick jabs to the ribs.

But in spite of such discretion, on a handful of occasions, the caterers boldly insulted guests to their faces without them even noticing.

"One guy asked me if the roast beef we were serving was kosher," said Ron Essen, 22, whose sole job all evening was to carve slabs of meat for guests. "With a straight face, I told him it was a kosher roast beef flown in specially from Israel. Cynthia, one of the runners, overheard me and ran into the kitchen because she thought she was gonna lose it."

Another guest who received more than his fair share of furtive derision was "Five-Time Fatty," a heavily sweating man who returned to the buffet table five times in a half-hour span.

see CATERERS next page

GLOBULES from page 38

amounts of blood. Passersby were amazed by the unusually large amounts of blood. Passersby were amazed by the unusually large amounts of blood. Passersby were amazed by the unusually large amounts of blood. Passersby were amazed by the unusually large amounts of blood. Passersby were amazed by the unusually large amounts of blood. Passersby were amazed by the unusually large amounts of blood. Passersby were amazed by the unusually large

> ## I'm glad I don't have to look at the passengers in coach.

amounts of blood. Passersby were amazed by the unusually large amounts of blood. Passersby were amazed by the unusually large amounts of blood. Passersby were amazed by the unusually large amounts of blood. Passersby were amazed by the unusually large amounts of blood. Passersby were amazed by the unusually large amounts of blood. Passersby were amazed by the unusually large amounts of blood. Passersby were amazed by the unusually large amounts of blood. Passersby were amazed by the unusually large amounts of blood. Passersby were

see GLOBULES page 43

CAKES from page 39

Northern Alliance started capturing huge chunks of Afghanistan from the Taliban, and people here began to calm down a little. The last few weeks, with the war going so well, sales have really been in the shitter."

"Hopefully, bin Laden will do something else to really piss America off," Kloster continued. "I mean, I don't want another terrorist attack on the U.S., but maybe he could give us the finger or call us some really bad name. Short of something like that, I'm fucked."

Li Chang, a street vendor on Canal Street in New York's Chinatown, said he does not plan to order more of the urinal cakes.

"In October, first time I order, I sell out very fast. In November, I order more, but it take longer to sell," Li said. "Now, I don't want no more. People still mad at [bin Laden], but not like before."

John Traber, owner of J.T.'s Touchdown Bar & Grill in Lyndhurst, NJ, also does not intend to reorder.

"This is kind of gross, but drunk guys kept stealing them out of the urinals to keep as souvenirs," Traber said. "[Kloster] was charging four times as much for the bin Laden cakes as you'd pay for regular ones, and I couldn't afford to keep replacing them, so I decided to go back to the regular kind."

Added Traber: "They had way too strong a cherry smell, anyway. Made the bathroom stink like perfume. Who

wants to be overpowered by some sweet, fruity odor when you're taking a leak?"

In spite of the inventory surplus, which could cost Kloster upwards of $70,000, the entrepreneur is feeling positive about his next venture.

"I got a really sweet deal on these

> ## Added Traber: "They had way too strong a cherry smell, anyway. Made the bathroom stink like perfume. Who wants to be overpowered by some sweet, fruity odor when you're taking a leak?"

framed posters of an American eagle crying in front of the Stars and Stripes... 25 cents each from this distributor in Ohio who needed to unload them fast," Kloster said. "I think I'll combine the Osama cakes with the posters as sort of a commemorative 'God Bless America' war-souvenir package." ⌀

CATERERS from previous page

"The last time Five-Time Fatty loaded up his plate, I could see Matt making all these faces at me from across the room," said Salerno, who staffed the buffet table's ziti station for much of the party. "But Five-Time

> "I've seen not one but two different people wearing pastel sweaters knotted around their necks," said Blaine, 20, during a cigarette break outside. "I think we accidentally stepped into a time machine set for Dipwadville, 1984."

was trying to chat me up, so I couldn't laugh. I knew Matt was praying that I'd bust up right in front of the guy."

While most partygoer-mocking is traditionally done during a party itself, Feather & Fennel staffers have been known to mock particularly memorable guests weeks or even months after an event.

"One guy at a bar mitzvah got so shitfaced, he passed out in a plate of kugel," Blaine said. "Ever since, whenever we see somebody who looks like he's about to pass out, we say, 'Uh-oh, better hide the kugel.' Man, that guy was seriously plowed."

Experts say mockery of the well-to-do by the serving class is a millennia-old tradition.

> While most partygoer-mocking is traditionally done during a party itself, Feather & Fennel staffers have been known to mock particularly memorable guests weeks or even months after an event.

"Whenever people are forced to serve others, resentment and derision are inevitable," said Dr. Henry Janssen, a University of Georgia anthropologist. "This tradition dates back to Ancient Greece, where servants at grand Athenian feasts would sneak into the kitchen to put on short plays lampooning the foibles of their wealthy, gluttonous guests. As long as there are people who stuff their faces with mini-meatballs while wearing bad ties, there will be servers there to make fun of them."

LOCAL

Above: The Dawes grimly watch *It's A Wonderful Life*.

Emotionally Distant Family Spends Holidays Watching Touching Family Dramas Together

RUTLAND, VT—In what has become an annual holiday tradition, the dysfunctional Dawes family came together Sunday to sit in front of the TV and watch touching, feel-good family dramas in stony silence.

"We see each other so rarely," said Nicole Dawes, 44, whose three children were all home from college. "It's so nice to all sit down together and have a peaceful time. And [son] Kevin didn't bring up that awful new girlfriend of his once the entire time."

Following a special holiday dinner of turkey, artichokes, and spiced yams, Nicole and sullen daughter Gabrielle, an 18-year-old freshman at the University of Vermont, were put in charge of selecting the movies to watch. The two shared a wordless 10-minute car trip to their local Blockbuster video store, where Gabrielle ruled out most of her mother's choices as "stupid" or "lame." Tired of saying no and eager to leave the store, Gabrielle finally assented to the holiday classic *It's A Wonderful Life* and the 1994 remake of *Miracle On 34th Street*.

"I can't believe we got *Miracle On 34th Street* again," Gabrielle said. "Still, it's better than some of the other stuff my mom was pulling off the shelves. I mean, *The Santa Clause*? How gay is that? I hate Tim Allen."

Added Gabrielle: "I wish we hadn't gotten *It's A Wonderful Life*. It's so long. Besides, why would anybody pay actual money to rent that thing when it's on TV, like, a bazillion times every December?"

Upon Nicole and Gabrielle's return, *It's A Wonderful Life* was promptly inserted into the living-room VCR. Familiar with the annual routine, the

> "I can't believe we got *Miracle On 34th Street* again," Gabrielle said. "Still, it's better than some of the other stuff my mom was pulling off the shelves. I mean, *The Santa Clause*? How gay is that? I hate Tim Allen."

family members huddled around the TV without exchanging a word, just as they have since the holiday tradition began in 1991.

As the movie played, Kevin, 22, a senior at Southern Vermont College, paid little attention, wrapped up in thoughts of his impending graduation. The few times he did focus on the film, it was to negatively compare his own family to the Baileys.

"That movie always makes me think about how if Dad's hardware store lost $8,000 like George Bailey's bank did, it'd totally tear us apart," Kevin said. "He'd probably blame us and drag us all down with him. Good thing he isn't trusted with much money at his job."

Following the conclusion of *It's A Wonderful Life*, an awkward 80-second silence occurred as the videotape rewound. The silence was briefly broken by daughter Gina, 20, who remarked that the evening's dinner had been "really good." Peter, her father, grunted in agreement.

As *Miracle On 34th Street* played, Peter sat in rapt attention, pushing aside anxieties about work, aging, and his chilly relationship with his children.

"The original was one of my all-time favorites," Peter said. "I was trying to spot the differences between the two. I was just glad to have something to focus on besides trying to make conversation with the kids. I have no idea what they're up to these days. Jesus, they're all grown up, able to vote and all. I wonder if they hate me."

Some 40 minutes into the movie, having consumed three snifters of brandy, Peter fell asleep.

When the second movie finished, the three children claimed exhaustion and trundled off to their childhood bedrooms, feigning excitement for the following day's Christmas-tree-shopping excursion.

"It's good to see all the kids together again. It reminds me of when they'd all watch cartoons together growing up," said Nicole, wiping a tear from her eye. "I love the holidays."

41

Wow, Check Out That Motorcycle Revving!

By Ron Kaat

Last night, sometime around 2 a.m., I was ripped from a peaceful slumber by a shockingly loud noise from the street outside. Alternating between a shrill, piercing whine and a thunderous roar, the sound echoed down the block, rattling my bedroom windows with oceanic waves of internal-combustion fury. As I lay there, unable to fall back asleep, my head and pulse pounding, I could think only one thing: Wow, check out that motorcycle revving!

What is it that makes a revving motorcycle so welcome? Why is this exhaust-choked noise instantly embraced and enjoyed by all who hear it? And what is it about the deafening roar made by the motorcy-

> Yelling out of cars, turning your speakers out the window to blast your music onto the street, setting off M-80 firecrackers, firing automatic weapons into the air—these are all well and good.

clist—he of the unmuffled exhaust pipes—that makes him beloved above all others? These are just a few of the questions I pondered during the hours immediately following that motorcycle's early-morning revving.

Inevitably, the answer to each question was always the same: The mere act of sitting astride a stationary motorcycle and manipulating the throttle for the express purpose of creating vast amounts of ear-splitting noise is the most impressive display of power known to man.

Yelling out of cars, turning your speakers out the window to blast your music onto the street, setting off M-80 firecrackers, firing automatic weapons into the air—these are all well and good. But none of them create a merry atmosphere of *insouciance* and *bonhomie* quite like a revving motorcycle.

When a man mounts a motorcycle and, instead of merely riding it like a common mortal, chooses to regale everyone within a five-mile radius

> The mere act of sitting astride a stationary motorcycle and manipulating the throttle for the express purpose of creating vast amounts of ear-splitting noise is the most impressive display of power known to man.

with the sound of four or five thousand internal-combustion explosions a minute, he is saying something. He is announcing to the world (or at least half the city): "We are all human beings, unique unto the world, and as a human, I will not be bound by the will of the masses. I am a soaring spirit, incapable of being chained, and, by way of evidence, I will provide this threshold-of-pain sonic explosion."

And it works! Last night, up and down my block, people were jolted awake with undeniable proof of that motorcyclist's humanity. The act was deeply moving to each and every one of us ex-sleepers. I'm sure I'm not the only one who found it difficult to go back to bed for a long time, so affected was I by this stirring, transcendent expression of individuality.

That is what I admire most about such motorcyclists: their courage to assert their uniqueness in the most

> And it works! Last night, up and down my block, people were jolted awake with undeniable proof of that motorcyclist's humanity. The act was deeply moving to each and every one of us ex-sleepers.

audible, public way possible.

It is such determination to make our individuality heard that sets us apart from the animals. So hallelujah, I say, and let freedom rev. ✍

Your Horoscope

By Lloyd Schumner Sr.
Retired Machinist and
A.A.P.B.-Certified Astrologer

Aries: (March 21–April 19)
You will be shot by your girlfriend and shunned by society after taking relationship advice from the editors of *Maxim*.

Taurus: (April 20–May 20)
Your conviction that good things come to those who wait is cited as the cause of your starvation death at a bus stop.

Gemini: (May 21–June 21)
You will achieve success in the world of advertising when you underestimate the intelligence of the American public.

Cancer: (June 22–July 22)
One of your wildest dreams will suddenly come true. Unfortunately, it's the one in which each of the demon's fangs has its own little shrieking face.

Leo: (July 23–Aug. 22)
Try looking at it this way: Maybe you're normal, and the people with only two eyes are the weird ones.

Virgo: (Aug. 23–Sept. 22)
The bigger boys will dip your hand in warm water while you sleep, and the camp counselors will once again ignore it, simply because you

haven't been to camp in years.

Libra: (Sept. 23–Oct. 23)
You will soon learn that you crash-landed in your small Kansas town in a meteor, which explains the burns covering your body.

Scorpio: (Oct. 24–Nov. 21)
Your belief that you are a pawn in a much larger game is untrue. The game is not all that large.

Sagittarius: (Nov. 22–Dec. 21)
You know you're different from everyone else, but, try as you might, you just can't understand why people put walls where they do.

Capricorn: (Dec. 22–Jan. 19)
Your feelings of resentment over having to live on a reservation are unwarranted, as you are an endangered Cape buffalo.

Aquarius: (Jan. 20–Feb. 18)
Be careful what you wish for this week. You won't get it, regardless, but it's always a good idea to be careful.

Pisces: (Feb. 19–March 20)
You will throw a huge hissyfit when you are told that your anti-terrorism bill is unconstitutional.

BLUDGEONERS from page 39

amounts of blood. Passersby were amazed by the unusually large amounts of blood. Passersby were amazed by the unusually large amounts of blood. Passersby were amazed by the unusually large amounts of blood. Passersby were amazed by the unusually large amounts of blood. Passersby were amazed by the unusually large amounts of blood. Passersby were amazed by the unusually large amounts of blood. Passersby were amazed by the unusually large amounts of blood. Passersby were amazed by the unusually large amounts of blood. Passersby were amazed by the unusually large amounts of blood. Passersby were amazed by the unusually large amounts of blood. Passersby were amazed by the unusually large amounts of blood. Passersby were amazed by the unusually large amounts of blood. Passersby were amazed by the unusually large amounts of blood. Passersby were amazed by the unusually large amounts of blood. Passersby were amazed by the unusually large amounts of blood. Passersby were amazed by the unusually large amounts of blood. Passersby were amazed by the unusually large amounts of blood. Passersby were amazed by the unusually large amounts of blood. Passersby were amazed by the unusually large

amounts of blood. Passersby were amazed by the unusually large amounts of blood. Passersby were amazed by the unusually large amounts of blood. Passersby were amazed by the unusually large amounts of blood. Passersby were amazed by the unusually large amounts of blood. Passersby were amazed by the unusually large amounts of blood. Passersby were

> I think it's great that the media don't focus on how Bush is crippled.

amazed by the unusually large amounts of blood. Passersby were amazed by the unusually large amounts of blood. Passersby were amazed by the unusually large amounts of blood. Passersby were amazed by the unusually large amounts of blood. Passersby were amazed by the unusually large amounts of blood. Passersby were amazed by the unusually large amounts of blood. Passersby were amazed by the unusually large amounts of blood. Passersby were amazed by the unusually large

see BLUDGEONERS page 46

Speed Stick Now Available In Neapolitan

see PRODUCTS page 2B

Space Shuttle Endeavour: What's In It For Me?

see NATION page 11A

John Ashcroft Blood Donation Eats Through Bag

see NATION page 6A

Backrub Turns Ugly

see LOCAL page 10D

STATshot

A look at the numbers that shape your world.

What Pornography Are We Avoiding?

1. *Granny Gash*
2. *Chuck Berry's World Of Scat*
3. *Pumpkins With Holes*
4. *Clumpfuckers For Women*
5. *Average-Length Blacks*
6. *Those weird pornos where it's all guys*

GOATS WITH BOATS

Canoe Cram!

0 74470 94595 6

00

THE ONION • $2.00 US • $3.00 CAN

---

the ONION®

VOLUME 38 ISSUE 01   AMERICA'S FINEST NEWS SOURCE™   17–23 JANUARY 2002

Peppy U.S. Teens Vow To Make This The Best Year Ever

WASHINGTON, DC—At a pep rally Monday on the National Mall, a coalition of enthusiastic U.S. teens vowed to make 2002 the "best year ever."

Decked out in red-white-and-blue "spirit wear," the high-energy youths clapped, cheered, and did cartwheels on the steps of the Lincoln Memorial, visibly increasing the energy level of the estimated 1.3 million U.S. citizens in attendance.

"Hello, America!" said Jennifer Richards, captain of the U.S. Peppy Teen Squad. "Raise your hands in the air if you think America kicks butt! Whoooo!"

Richards then did a series of backflips and high kicks before unveiling the schedule of USPTS-sponsored events that will keep the nation's spirits high throughout 2002.

see TEENS page 47

Area Man Not Exactly Sure When To Take Down American Flags

Above: Jerry Wenger with two of his six flags.

UTICA, NY—After more than four months of proudly displaying American flags on his car, home, and body, 47-year-old computer consultant Jerry Wenger is uncertain when the appropriate time will be to take them down.

"It seems like the war in Afghanistan is winding down," said Wenger from his cubicle at Armstrong & Grunau Consulting Monday. "Then again, we still haven't caught bin Laden. Am I supposed to keep [the flags] up until we get him? But what if we never do?"

"Do I have to wait until all the troops are home?" Wenger continued. "Because that could take years. I'm not trying to be a jerk—I'm just not sure when to consider this whole thing over."

Though Wenger said he has nothing against displaying the American flag, prior to last September, he'd never owned a flag in his life.

"Right after the attacks, there was something comforting about joining the rest of America in a display of patriotism," Wenger said. "I'm still fine with having them up, but I'm really not the type of person who would have flags all over the place if there wasn't a war."

On Sept. 13, during a shopping ex-

see FLAGS page 46

Archaeologist Tired Of Unearthing Unspeakable Ancient Evils

HASAKE, SYRIA—When archaeologist Edward Whitson joined a Penn State University dig in Hasake last year, he did so to participate in the excavation of a Late Bronze Age settlement rich in pottery shards and clay figurines. Whitson had hoped to determine whether the items contained within the site were primarily Persian or Assyrian in origin.

Instead, he found himself fleeing giant flying demon-cats as he ran through the temple's cavernous halls, jumping from ledge to ledge while locked in a desperate struggle for his life and soul for what seemed like the

thousandth time in his 27-year career.

"All I wanted to do was study the settlement's remarkably well-preserved kiln," said the 58-year-old Whitson, carefully recoiling the rope he had just used to clamber out of a pit filled with giant rats. "I didn't want to be chased by yet another accursed manifestation of an ancient god-king's wrath."

Throughout his career, Whitson has been lauded by colleagues for his thorough, methodical examinations of ancient peoples. He has also been chased by the snake-bodied ophidian

see ARCHAEOLOGIST page 47

Right: Edward Whitson waits while yet another tortured wraith rises from a dig site in Syria.

43

China's Nuclear Buildup

According to a new CIA report, China is expected to have as many as 100 long-range nuclear missiles aimed at the U.S. by 2015. What do *you* think?

"We don't need to worry about the Chinese using nukes. They'd first need to find an unpopulated area to test them."

Max Koenig
Systems Analyst

"Would it be culturally insensitive of me to say I hope they don't blast us to atoms? I don't want to offend anybody."

Connie Vance
Graduate Student

"Maybe it's time to flood China with opium again. Failing that, flood me with opium."

Dan Essen
Plumber

"If only Sting had possessed the foresight to hope that the Chinese love their two government-allotted children, too."

Milt Odom
Lawyer

"We shouldn't worry. Judicious use of force is the traditional and typical of Chinese glorious history and cultural."

Ken Yaeger
Roofer

"Doesn't China know that only the U.S. is responsible enough to have a nuclear arsenal?"

Sylvia Coombes
Graphic Designer

The New iMac

Amid much fanfare, Apple's new iMac was unveiled last week. Among its notable features:

- Doubles as reading lamp
- Automatically e-mails fan letter to Steve Jobs during startup
- If you cup your palms over domed base, your hair will rise in air
- Sprouts set of cybernetic insectoid legs and scuttles away when threatened
- Perfectly matches the iBlouse
- Screen is flat, which is good for some reason
- Special drool tray catches saliva of enthralled technogeeks
- Communicates directly with human pineal gland by firing information-rich beam of pink light
- Wuvs you

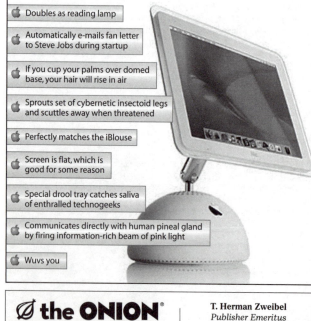

---

the ONION
America's Finest News Source.™

Herman Ulysses Zweibel
Founder

T. Herman Zweibel
Publisher Emeritus
J. Phineas Zweibel
Publisher
Maxwell Prescott Zweibel
Editor-In-Chief

I'm Certain That Sex With A Redhead Will Be More Fulfilling Than Other Sex

By Garrett Swann

When it comes to scoring with the ladies, I'm no slouch. In the past two weeks alone, there's been Nikki the legal secretary, Stephanie the cocktail waitress, and, of course, Alicia the flight attendant (she really put the "lay" in lay-over). But while these rolls in the hay were fun while they lasted, each ultimately left me with a vague, empty feeling inside. It's been that way with all my one-night stands. I'm not 100 percent positive, but I think it's because none of them have been redheads.

Once I have sex with a redhead, it'll all come together. Redheads are definitely the way to go. I just know that a redhead wouldn't ultimately bore me like the other women I sleep with. That's because they have a fiery temperament. I love that sense of danger, not knowing whether the woman is going to smash a vase in a fit of wild anger or tear my clothes off in a fit of animal lust. That fire and passion will hold my interest over the long haul, no question.

They say having sex with a blonde is like that. Sex with a blonde, I figured, would be so great, it would leave me feeling happy and whole. Well, "they"

> ## Once I have sex with a redhead, it'll all come together. Redheads are definitely the way to go. I just know that a redhead wouldn't ultimately bore me like the other women I sleep with.

don't know what the hell they're talking about, because anytime I've ever taken some random blonde chick back to my condo to bump uglies, it's been awkward and anti-climactic. And even in the rare instances where the sex has been good, the feeling of elation always starts to fade shortly after the blonde gathers her clothes from my floor and leaves a fake name and phone number.

The brunettes I've dated haven't measured up, either. For one thing, there are always communication problems with them. Dark-haired women never seem to understand that I express my deepest feelings and desires with smoldering glances across the bar or bowling alley. They never comprehend the volumes I say with

> ## Like a cat, a redhead would know all that I craved, and she would surprise me with things I didn't even know I wanted. That's all I've been looking for during my years of bed-hopping, and I'm sure I'll find it with a redhead.

simple finger and tongue gestures.

Redheads, on the other hand, are intuitive. They know what you're thinking and know how to respond in kind. Like a cat, a redhead would know all that I craved, and she would surprise me with things I didn't even know I wanted. That's all I've been looking for during my years of bed-hopping, and I'm sure I'll find it with a redhead.

Now, I know what you're wondering. What if I connect with a redhead, only to discover that the carpet doesn't match the curtains, if you catch my drift? While, admittedly, I am very aroused by the thought of seeing a fiery crimson patch contrasted against a pale stomach, what truly counts is what's going on upstairs. And if a woman's mind is topped with a lustrous mane of glorious red hair, it doesn't really matter if it was God who made it that way or Clairol.

Yes, sex with a redhead would be my holy grail. Ever since my recent realization of this, I've made it my goal to seek out a redhead so we could have wild sex and fall in love, then spend the rest of our lives having satisfying, fulfilling sex together. A redhead would make the sex act as exciting as it's been purported to be since I was 10.

And if my search for a redheaded soulmate doesn't pan out, I hear Korean women are complete freaks in bed. ∅

Black Gospel Choir Makes Man Wish He Believed In All That God Bullshit

COLUMBUS, OH—The gloriously jubilant gospel singing that pours forth each Sunday from Bethel African Methodist Episcopal Church is enough to make local resident

> **"It must be so life-affirming to be in there, connecting with fellow human beings and celebrating your faith while making that joyful noise," said Kamin, a doctoral candidate in political science at Ohio State University.**

Doug Kamin wish he believed in all that God bullshit.

"Their music is so spiritual and passionate. Whenever I walk past that church and hear it, it stirs something deep within my soul," said Kamin, 28, a self-described atheist who was raised Catholic. "It's almost powerful enough to make me forget about what a load of happy horseshit Christianity is."

Kamin, who lives two blocks from Bethel AME Church, passes the church most Sundays en route to his local Starbucks. Though he has rejected the existence of God ever since discovering Marx and Nietzsche in the 10th grade, Kamin admitted that the exuberant singing of the church choir often produces in him a feeling of longing.

"It must be so life-affirming to be in there, connecting with fellow human beings and celebrating your faith while making that joyful noise," said Kamin, a doctoral candidate in political science at Ohio State University. "I still say it's a big, delusional fairy tale, this whole religion thing, but what's the harm in believing in a 2,000-year-old carpenter and some 'holy ghost' if it makes you happy?"

Kamin first discovered Bethel AME Church in May 2000, shortly after moving to the neighborhood. Long accustomed to dismissing all forms of Christian ceremony and worship as "hysterical" and "cult-like," Kamin overheard a rendition of "The Old Ship Of Zion" that led him to amend his opinion.

Above: The Bethel AME Church choir, which has given Doug Kamin (right) reason to regret his atheism.

"I can't remember the words, but the soloist sang something like 'Join me on the old Ship of Zion, and you'll find peace in the Lord,'" Kamin said. "The song probably went back to the slave days. Anyway, it stopped me dead in my tracks. I just stood in front of the church and let the music surround me. For that moment, I totally forgot what an artificial construct God is."

Kamin said the gospel hymns he heard that first day reverberated in his head for hours.

see CHOIR page 46

Bush Attempts To Distance Self From Yet Another Failed Business

WASHINGTON, DC—Amid mounting evidence of White House ties to Enron, President Bush attempted to distance himself from yet another failing Texas energy company Monday. "I have had no business dealings with this particular company," Bush said. "Why would anyone associate me with a Houston-based energy giant that's mismanaged itself into the ground?" Bush added that his oil company was already almost bankrupt when he took it over, and that it was not his decision to trade away Sammy Sosa.

The Thinkable Happens To Local Man

OLATHE, KS—The thinkable happened to area resident Bruce Conroy, 44, Monday, when the newspaper he was carrying fell out of his hand. "I can believe what I just saw," one witness told reporters. "In all my years, I can honestly say I've seen many things like that." An unshaken Conroy told reporters after the incident: "Who wouldn't have thought that this, or something very much like it, could happen?"

Opening Band Upstaged By Pre-Show Music

MINNEAPOLIS—The Vic Taybacks, opening for Superchunk at 400 Bar Tuesday, were upstaged by the pre-show music on the venue's sound system. "While we were setting up our stuff, [Hüsker Dü's] *Flip Your Wig* was playing, and the crowd was going nuts," said Vic Taybacks bassist Geoff Davis. "Then we started playing, and it got quiet and everybody just sort of drifted off to the bar." The band has previously been upstaged by *Queen's Greatest Hits* and the *Repo Man* soundtrack.

WHO Pushes For More 'Ouchless' Adhesive Funding

UNITED NATIONS—The World Health Organization lobbied the U.N. General Assembly for an additional $1.2 billion in "ouchless" bandage strips Tuesday. "Sadly, millions of people around the world have access only to ouchful bandage strips," WHO director Kamal Amen-Ra said. "We shall not rest until we live in an ouch-free world, a place where all people can live without fear of their leg hair being ripped out by non-ouchless adhesive bandages."

Manufacturer Manufactures Love To Wife

WILMINGTON, DE—In an efficient and deeply meaningful act of sexual expression, eraser manufacturer Ted Wyczinski manufactured sweet love to his wife Monday after a romantic dinner at the Route 14 Red Lobster. "Nice work, honey," Wyczinski told his wife following the 20-minute coupling. "I thought that came out great."

Ted Danson Tries To Steer Interview Back Toward *Becker*

CHICAGO—During an interview Monday with CBS affiliate WBBM-TV, actor Ted Danson made repeated efforts to steer the conversation back toward his current series, *Becker*. "It's true, one of the ingredients that made *Cheers* work so well was the great ensemble of actors we had," Danson told *Live At Five* host Janet Pye, attempting to set up a *Cheers*-*Becker* segue. "That's the case with any good series, and it's certainly the case with..." Pye sabotaged the attempted transition by interjecting that Danson and Shelley Long had particularly good chemistry. *∅*

the ONION presents

Dating Tips

The dating world can be a bewildering place. Here are some tips to help you navigate the perilous waters of love:

- Ladies: Your date's salary divided by your own equals the base you should let him get to on the first date.

- If you are overweight and socially awkward, consider "online dating." You can go on a dragonslaying adventure instead of to a movie, play games on Pogo.com instead of dancing, and masturbate instead of having real sex.

- Do not bathe for several days prior to a date to get your pheromones good and strong.

- Never date a married person, unless he or she is just about to leave his or her spouse and simply waiting for the right moment.

- When planning a romantic candlelit dinner, the right music can create the perfect mood. Put on *The Best Of Spike Jones* to create a freewheeling, anything-goes atmosphere.

- Maintain a casual, "Let's just have fun" attitude until the other person starts seeing someone else. Then let the tears and accusations fly.

- Remember: There's only one way to console a widow.

- To make a lasting impression on a first date, declare yourself his or her eternal soulmate and propose marriage.

- Why don't you ask that Julie girl out? She's a lovely girl. You're practically 35, for God's sake. Fine, rip your mother's heart out.

- If you are a princess being courted by a low-born but beloved suitor, be sure to elude the watchful eye of the lord high chamberlain.

- Instead of going out tonight, punch yourself in the nuts three times and the heart twice. This will save you approximately $75.

FLAGS from page 43

cursion to Wal-Mart, Wenger purchased one flag to hang outside his front door, another for his car-radio antenna, and a flag pin for his coat. A full-page insert from *The Utica Observer-Dispatch* provided another flag, which he placed in his garage-door window. A fifth flag, in his office, was a gift from a coworker. After donating $20 to the Boy Scouts, he re-

> **Last Thursday, seeking to gauge public opinion, he asked coworker Jim Bowden when he thought the office should take down the flag hanging by the receptionist's desk.**

ceived another flag, bringing the total to six.

"I'm not sure what to do now that the fervor is winding down," Wenger said. "I just don't think I'm a six-flag sort of guy."

Added Wenger: "The one on my car antenna is looking pretty beat up. I think it might be illegal to display a desecrated flag like that."

Last Thursday, seeking to gauge public opinion, he asked coworker Jim Bowden when he thought the office should take down the flag hanging by the receptionist's desk. Bowden said it should remain "until the injustice is eradicated around the world

and God's peace prevails."

"I had no idea what Jim meant, but I guess now is clearly not the time," Wenger said.

In lieu of removing all his flags, Wenger said he is considering "gradually scaling back."

"The one by my front door should cover my bases at home, so I could take down the one from the window in the garage," Wenger said. "Then again, the garage one is pretty prominent. The neighbors would definitely notice if that one were gone."

Wenger said he's had flag-removal impulses as far back as early December, but he has been waiting for one of his neighbors to be the first to take one down. Thus far, no one has.

"After the Taliban fell [on Dec. 7], I figured somebody would take something down, so I took a stroll up and down the block to see," Wenger said. "Not a single one was removed. Even the Dutlers, the world's biggest liberals, still had their three up. It's like the whole neighborhood is playing this giant game of flag chicken."

Wenger said he worries what others would think if he removed his first.

"I don't want to be the first to take one down and look like an ass," Wenger said. "When I put the flags up, I was saying, 'I support America.' If I take them down, some people will probably think I'm saying, 'I no longer support America.'"

As the holiday season approached, Wenger hoped to discreetly replace his two exterior flags with Christmas decorations. But as his neighbors' yards filled with red-white-and-blue lights and flag-adorned plastic reindeer, Wenger aborted the plan.

With the arrival of New Year's Day, Wenger renewed to his commitment to taking down some of his flags. His resolve faded, however, when the first American was killed in combat on Jan. 4.

"After the death of that Green Beret, it seemed like the worst possible time to take down the flag," Wenger said. "Then, last week, just as I was about to try again, that refueling plane crashed in Pakistan. Next chance I get, I'll have to act quickly."

In spite of his determination to remove the flags, Wenger said he

remains proud of his decision to display Old Glory for so long.

"They say Sept. 11 was the current generation's Pearl Harbor, and I believe that," Wenger said. "But World War II ended with an official surrender and peace treaty, so everybody knew exactly when they could take their flags down. I highly doubt this thing's gonna end with President Bush and Mullah Omar signing an armistice on the deck of the U.S.S. Theodore Roosevelt. Ah, screw it—I'll just leave the things where they are." Ø

CHOIR from page 45

"I found myself humming 'Mary Don't You Weep' and 'Move On Up A Little Higher' and all these other songs," Kamin said. "It made me think how amazing it is that a historically oppressed people can continue to persevere and derive strength from music and faith. I was very moved."

Added Kamin: "From a purely sociological and historical viewpoint, that is. Not spiritually."

In spite of his attraction to the Bethel AME Church, Kamin still can't bring himself to believe in the existence of a supreme being.

"There's simply too much evolutionary and cosmological evidence against it," Kamin said. "No offense to anybody, but I just can't buy into the parting of the Red Sea and the Immaculate Conception and all those other Biblical tall tales any more than I can *The Odyssey*."

Kamin said he would love to experience a Bethel service, but expressed doubt that he would be welcome there.

"I bet they can smell an atheist a mile away," Kamin said. "I shouldn't taint their experience with my cold rationalism and irrefutable logic. And

> **"I shouldn't taint their experience with my cold rationalism and irrefutable logic."**

the fact that I'm white probably wouldn't help matters, either."

Kamin need not worry, said Rev. Lawrence Stovall, Bethel's senior pastor.

"People of all colors and creeds are welcome in the house of the Lord, even non-believers like Doug," Stovall said. "Perhaps our abiding faith in Jesus and love for our fellow man will, at the very least, inspire him to quit living in his head all the time." Ø

women of Al'lat in Israel, hunted down by Mayan coyote specters manifested out of lost time and shadow in the Yucatan, and hounded by the Arctic-sky-filling Walrus Bone Woman of the early Inuits.

"It's true, I've got to stop reading the inscriptions on ancient door seals out loud," Whitson said. "I also need to

> ## Whitson said he hopes one day to excavate an ancient Egyptian monastery or marketplace without hearing the ear-splitting shrieks of the undead.

quit dusting off medallions set into strange sarcophagi, allowing the light to hit them for the first time in centuries. And replacing the jewels that have fallen from the foreheads of ancient frog-deity statues—that's just bad archaeological practice."

Whitson added that he hopes one day to excavate an ancient Egyptian monastery or marketplace without hearing the ear-splitting shrieks of the undead while being swarmed by green-glowing carnivorous stink beetles.

"I realize I'm entering grounds that are considered sacred to these people," Whitson said. "But that doesn't mean I deserve to be pelted with poison-tipped darts shot from cavern

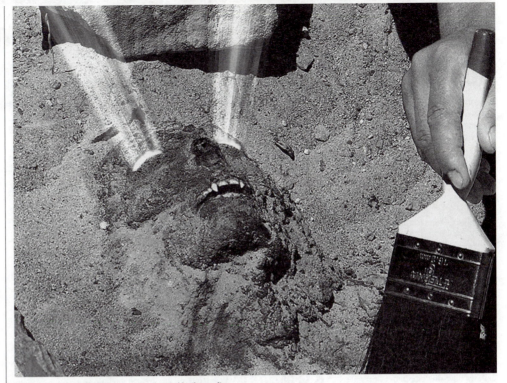

Above: A dig in Yalvac, Turkey, is once again disrupted by the occult.

walls. A simple 'Do Not Enter' sign in hieroglyphics would suffice."

Turning to the subject of his latest incident at a dig site in Peru, Whitson maintains he was not at fault for summoning the forces of evil.

"I was just idly rearranging flint sickle blades that had already been catalogued. Apparently, I spelled out the true name of a long-dead god-priest," Whitson said. "Can't a man even clean up his work area without

inadvertently conjuring up a pack of lightning-breathing ocelots?"

Making matters worse, such encounters have had little to no scientific value.

"It's always, 'I will drink your soul' or 'I will chew the flesh from your bones' with these hellish apparitions," Whitson said. "When I ask them if that means the ancient Etruscans did, in fact, add copper to their mixing clay to make their urns

more sturdy, they don't even seem to hear me."

Worn down by nearly three decades of peril, Whitson said he plans to move off the front lines to become a museum curator or in-office researcher.

"It's unfortunate," Whitson said. "Nothing compares to being out in the field on an actual dig. But the reality is, I'm really starting to hate almost getting killed all the time." ∅

"Once again, you can look forward to the annual banner contest," Richards said. "The state with the best banner will win $36 million in infrastructure upgrades. And just because Montana won the last three years running doesn't mean they'll win again this year!"

Richards then handed the microphone to USPTS co-captain Mark Chandler.

"Now, I know that a few of you states—I won't mention any names, but one starts with 'A' and ends with 'laska'—don't like doing the banners," Chandler said. "But, guys, really, the banners keep everyone's spirits up all year. I've seen the banners they have in places like Guatemala and Uzbekistan, and they're nowhere near as good as ours."

Other USPTS events planned for 2002 include U.S. Dress-Up Week, which will include such theme days as '80s Day and Nerd Day; a U.S. Spirit Car Wash in August; and a 50-state pizza party and mixer before the start of the 2002 Winter Olympics in Salt Lake City.

"2001 was a real downer year for the U.S.," Chandler said. "Especially with the terrorist attacks and the men's

swim team losing at the world championships. So we're going to work extra hard to make sure this is the best year ever."

Chandler reminded the crowd that everyone needs to do his or her part to make 2002 a big success.

"Vice-President Cheney says many of our nation's national parks have

> ## Chanting, "We got spirit, yes we do! We got spirit, how 'bout you?" the teens yelled out the name of each state in alphabetical order, prompting screams from residents in the crowd.

been looking pretty trashy lately," Chandler said. "If everyone just does their part and throws away their garbage, this won't be a problem. If you see a piece of trash, even if it isn't

yours, just pick it up and throw it away. It's that simple!"

A visibly excited Richards then took the microphone.

"Guess what time it is!" said Richards, holding aloft a red-white-and-blue painted stick adorned with shiny tassels. "Time to pass the U.S. Spirit Stick! The state that makes the most noise will get the honor of holding on to it for the whole year! C'mon, everybody!"

Chanting, "We got spirit, yes we do! We got spirit, how 'bout you?" the teens yelled out the name of each state in alphabetical order, prompting screams from residents in the crowd. The U.S. Supreme Court judged the contest, voting Vermont the loudest in a 7-2 decision.

"Next week, we've got an ambassador going all the way to Cairo to meet with a delegation of Arab-world leaders," Richards said. "Let's show how much we're behind him and make sure that he comes back… walking like an Egyptian!"

The lights dimmed, and Chandler and Richards stepped into formation with the other teens to perform a choreographed dance to The Bangles' 1986 hit "Walk Like An Egyptian."

In spite of the thunderous applause the performance received, a handful of audience members were unimpressed.

> ## "Next week, we've got an ambassador going all the way to Cairo to meet with a delegation of Arab-world leaders," Richards said.

"That totally sucked," said Tony Aldieri from Michigan, widely regarded as a "burnout" state. "They don't really care about the U.S. that much. They just want something to put on their resumes so they can get into a good college. You'd have to be a real loser to actually be that into this country. This country blows. As soon as I get enough money, I'm outta here. I'm packing up my shit and moving someplace cool, like Madagascar." ∅

The Lord Of The Rings Is Hobbit-Forming!

**The Outside Scoop
By Jackie Harvey**

Happy 2002! Whew, I'm glad we can put 2001 behind us with all that **terrorism**. It's a New Year, and already the grapevine is buzzing with Hollywood gossip!

Item! The Lord Of The Rings is "hobbit-forming"! That's right, this fantastic new movie is truly a "hard hobbit to break"! I've journeyed to the magical land of **Mordor** (courtesy of my local Loew's Cineplex) three times in the past week and have gotten swept away each time! The majesty of the landscape! The pointy little ears! And, oh, that **Ian MacGregor** as the wizard **Gandahar**! I hope that all parties involved in **Episode One: The Ring's Fellows** have dusted off an Oscar spot on their knickknack shelves, because they're gonna need it!

Item! Tom and Penelope Cruze are sizzling in **Vanilla Sky**! That pairing is so hot, it's no wonder we haven't gotten any snow this winter. It made me a little sad that we only got half an inch by Christmas. It's always been a tradition at the Harvey Household to go out and make **snow angels** after a few mugs of egg nog, but if I'd flopped back into that tiny an amount of snow, my Christmas present would have been a **broken back**!

Speaking of presents, I pretty much got everything I wanted this year. Although, as I get older, there's less I want. A few pairs of socks and maybe a warm shirt. Sure enough, that's what I got, plus a few extras I hadn't even wished for, like the **Godfather** DVD box set. I still haven't gotten around to watching it, because I don't care for shoot-'em-up pictures.

Item! I'm sad to report that superdish **Drew Barrymore** and gross-out king **Freddy "The Finger" Green** are getting the big D. That's right, D-I-V-O-R-C-E! Everyone thought theirs was a love written across the sky in permanent ink, but in the end, that ink proved to be the erasable kind. It makes me wonder if there's any hope for love at all.

Say, who here has been checking out that **Sex In The City** show? I for one haven't been able to take my eyes off it! Those girls are catty with a capital C! Me-rowrr!

Item! Just how much is the cast of **Friends** getting paid? I wish there were some way I could get my hands on that information, because whatever it is, I'm certain it isn't enough.

Item! They just announced that 2001's top-selling album was from a band called **Lincoln Park**. No, they aren't enthusiasts of our former president. Apparently, they're **angry kids with a message**. Well, I have a message for them: Get off the stage and let a real star like **Mariah Carey** get her just desserts! She released an album. Maybe you've heard of it? It's called **Glimmer**, and that's the record people should be buying, not one by some heavy-metal grunting gorillas. Plus, she's had some tough breaks lately. Give her a chance, will ya?

It's time I shared my opinion on these new **club drugs** that seem to be so popular these days. Now, before I

Item! Tom and Penelope Cruze are sizzling in *Vanilla Sky*! That pairing is so hot, it's no wonder we haven't gotten any snow this winter.

---

say this, I want you all to know that I'm no square. I'm not above having **a few glasses of wine** now and then if the occasion calls for it. However, I've been hearing about these "ecstasy" pills that people are taking. Let me tell you, you may think you're getting high, but once you get low again, you find out that the price you paid is higher than the high was high. Just remember this simple rhyme: Users are losers, no two ways around it. I get my ecstasy the old-fashioned way: by watching a really good **Danny Kaye** movie.

Speaking of good movies, have you checked out **Jim Carrey** in **The Majestic**? I haven't yet but, boy, the commercials make it look great! The ads don't give away the movie's ending, but they give you just enough information to make it clear that it will have you cheering in your seat.

So, it looks like we have that **Taliban** on the run this time. Just goes to show you, don't mess with the good old U. S. of A. These colors don't run when you put them in the washing machine or a hostile foreign situation.

After one too many servings of holiday ham, I decided that my **New Year's Resolution** was to lose 15 pounds so I can fit into my good suit again. I might even join a gym, but I haven't made up my mind yet. I've also decided that this is the year to find that special someone. Has **Jackie Harvey** bitten off more than he can chew? The only way to find out is to check back here throughout 2002.

Hey, what happened to **Emeril**? I

Your Horoscope

By Lloyd Schumner Sr.
Retired Machinist and
A.A.P.B.-Certified Astrologer

Aries: (March 21–April 19)
Try as you might, you will not be able to improve your mediocre putting game. Gee, some big fucking problems you got, asshole.

Taurus: (April 20–May 20)
You will discover that, indeed, it is fun to stay at the YMCA, but that's hardly the whole story.

Gemini: (May 21–June 21)
After 90 healthy, prosperous years, you will die in bed surrounded by loved ones, bringing your life as a masochist to a bitter, tragic end.

Cancer: (June 22–July 22)
The old saying, "It takes all kinds to make a world," will be amended this week to exclude you.

Leo: (July 23–Aug. 22)
If you've ever wondered how long you could endure without the comforts of human love, you should find the next 57 years very illuminating.

Virgo: (Aug. 23–Sept. 22)
Though you say you don't believe in God, don't worry: He doesn't believe in you, either.

Libra: (Sept. 23–Oct. 23)
There are some things money can't buy. There are also some things money can buy, but that people won't sell to you out of sheer spite.

Scorpio: (Oct. 24–Nov. 21)
Your innovative new clock-radio design will be the subject of a three-page spread in next month's issue of *Unpopular Science*.

Sagittarius: (Nov. 22–Dec. 21)
After a nice, private walk on the beach, you are disturbed to find a set of footprints where someone—or something—seems to have been walking beside you.

Capricorn: (Dec. 22–Jan. 19)
Your gym teacher will be forced to apologize after wrongly assuming that a little rain wouldn't hurt you.

Aquarius: (Jan. 20–Feb. 18)
Try as you might, you can't seem to drum up the enthusiasm society seems to expect of you.

Pisces: (Feb. 19–March 20)
Keep telling yourself that it's just a movie. It's not, of course, but doing so may make it easier to bear.

---

thought that show had it all. It was funny, true to life, and full of great cooking action. Bam! Bring it back and take a stand for quality programming!

I was finally going to get myself a **Nintendo 64** to help me unwind after a hard day of entertainment-news

---

Whoops! How could I have forgotten about the death of George Harrison, the Quiet Wilbury?

---

gathering, only now it turns out that it's out of style. There's a new Nintendo game out, and it's shaped like a cube. How can I possibly keep up with all these technological breakthroughs? I'll say one thing: If I were basing my purchase on looks alone, the cube would come out on top. That thing is so darn cute!

Whoops! How could I have forgotten about the death of **George Harrison**, the Quiet Wilbury? With his passing, the **Fab Five** that once was **Tom**, **Bob**, **George**, **Jeff**, and **Roy** is now down to three. Many people overlooked George's contributions to the Wilburys, but by **Vol. 3** he had established himself as one of their best songwriters. I'll never forget 1988, the peak of Wilburymania, when you couldn't walk down the street without hearing one of their tunes. I'm sure he and Roy are up there in heaven, jamming with all the other greats. Handle George with care, **God**.

And right up there with them, cracking jokes, is funnyman **Foster Brooks**, whose portrayal of a tipsy socialite was second only to **Dean Martin**'s. *Danke schoen* for all the laughs, Foster, and have one in heaven for me.

Sorry to have to cut it off here, friends and well-wishers (and all the rest of you, too), but the Scoop is onto some hot stuff. I can't spill all the details right now, but let's just say that it involves a three-way collision between **Meg Ryan**, **a shoe store**, and **a credit card**. Now that your minds are reeling, I'm going to have to cut you off. Meanwhile, keep yourselves occupied with a good book, a fine movie, or just turn on the boob tube for a few hours and let yourself veg out. In the meantime, I'll keep watching all the **Hollywood** doings... from the Outside! ∅

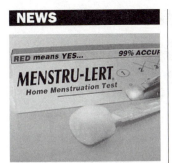

RED means YES...   99% ACCUR
MENSTRU-LERT
Home Menstruation Test

Procter & Gamble Introduces Home Menstruation Test

see PRODUCTS page 5D

New Michael Landon Biography Resolves Many Unasked Questions

see BOOKS page 7C

Clock In Basement Still One Hour Ahead

see LOCAL page 14D

Orphan Can't Take A Joke

see LOCAL page 11D

STATshot

A look at the numbers that shape your world.

Top Religious Visions

1. Jesus H. Christ on a crutch
2. Regis Philbin billboard weeping
3. Devil with blue dress on
4. Glowing figure of Virgin Mary hovering in front of electrical outlet
5. Jesus nailed to the mattress
6. Golden sponge cake with creamy filling

0 74470 94595 6

THE ONION • $2.00 US • $3.00 CAN

---

the ONION®

VOLUME 38 ISSUE 02   AMERICA'S FINEST NEWS SOURCE™   24–30 JANUARY 2003

Antique Dealer Sick Of Appraising Smurf Collections

Above: Jarry begrudgingly appraises yet another collection of Smurfs.

DULUTH, MN—Milton Jarry, an antique dealer with 29 years of experience buying and selling rare collectibles and furnishings, announced Monday that he is sick of estimating the value of Smurf collections and other "piles of pop-culture detritus."

"If one more person brings in a 'rare' figurine of Smurfette in a jogging suit, I'm going to set it on fire," said Jarry, owner of The Finer Things, a Cortland Avenue antique shop. "That goes double for Brainy Smurf ceramic piggy banks."

Created by Belgian cartoonist Peyo in the early 1960s, the Smurfs made their U.S. debut on NBC in 1981. The animated series chronicled the adventures of a band of tiny blue dwarves that lived in the mushroom cottages of Smurf Village with their 542-year-old leader Papa Smurf, Jarry reluctantly explained.

The hit series spawned a host of spin-off merchandise, including Smurf toys, jewelry, curtains, and kitchenware—all of which has made its way into Jarry's shop at some point.

"A 17-year-old cereal bowl featuring a bunch of silly blue creatures does not constitute an antique," said Jarry, whose areas of expertise include antique European and Russian chandeliers, wall fixtures, and classic reproductions of 18th-century candelabras. "Nor, for that matter, does a 1986 *ALF*

see SMURFS page 53

Developmentally Disabled Senator Wants To Be Treated Like Any Other Lawmaker

WASHINGTON, DC—When he was elected to the U.S. Senate in November 2000, Sen. Freddy Rigby (D-NE) knew he had a tough road ahead of him. Developmentally disabled since birth, Rigby's controversial election provoked reactions ranging from misty-eyed admiration to outrage. But to supporters and detractors alike, this very special senator makes one simple request: to be treated just like any other lawmaker.

"I like my job as senator!" said Rigby, speaking from his Georgetown-area group home Monday. "I do good work!

see SENATOR page 52

Right: An excited Rigby (center) poses with Attorney General John Ashcroft and Sen. Orrin Hatch (R-UT).

Weekend With Boyfriend's Parents Explains A Lot

ROCK HILL, SC—According to Julia Wasson, meeting Miriam and Karl Loftus, parents of her boyfriend Jay, "explained so much."

"First of all, the car thing," the 26-year-old Wasson said Monday upon returning from a weekend at the Lof-

see BOYFRIEND page 52

Far left: Jay Loftus and his parents.
Left: Girlfriend Julia Wasson.

American Taliban

Debate is raging over the proper punishment for John Walker, the California 20-year-old who fought with the Taliban against the U.S. What do *you* think?

Peter Dunn
Systems Analyst

"I hope that traitor spends the rest of his life locked away in substantially better living conditions than he had in Afghanistan."

Vicki Robbins
Psychologist

"Why couldn't he have been like other shallow, overprivileged white kids and just spent a few years in Prague?"

Tom Eisen
CEO

"As CEO of a major scotch manufacturer, I demand that he be referred to as John *Lindh*. Our image is going down the toilet, goddammit."

Frank Costello
Delivery Driver

"Treason or not, I think it was hurtful and tasteless of Walker to go around in blackface like that."

Burt Bynum
Cashier

"We could execute Walker, or we could sentence him to tour the country's elementary schools lecturing on how plotting to destroy the U.S. is a dead end."

Roberta Davis
Dental Hygienist

"That's it. I'm pulling my son Jason out of that Pakistani madrassa pronto."

Ford's $5 Billion Loss

Last week, Ford reported a $5 billion loss for the fourth quarter of 2001. What steps is the auto giant taking to restore profitability?

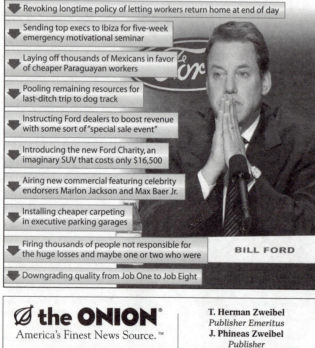

- ▼ Revoking longtime policy of letting workers return home at end of day
- ▼ Sending top execs to Ibiza for five-week emergency motivational seminar
- ▼ Laying off thousands of Mexicans in favor of cheaper Paraguayan workers
- ▼ Pooling remaining resources for last-ditch trip to dog track
- ▼ Instructing Ford dealers to boost revenue with some sort of "special sale event"
- ▼ Introducing the new Ford Charity, an imaginary SUV that costs only $16,500
- ▼ Airing new commercial featuring celebrity endorsers Marlon Jackson and Max Baer Jr.
- ▼ Installing cheaper carpeting in executive parking garages
- ▼ Firing thousands of people not responsible for the huge losses and maybe one or two who were
- ▼ Downgrading quality from Job One to Job Eight

BILL FORD

✪ the ONION ®
America's Finest News Source.™

Herman Ulysses Zweibel
Founder

T. Herman Zweibel
Publisher Emeritus
J. Phineas Zweibel
Publisher
Maxwell Prescott Zweibel
Editor-In-Chief

Homeless People Shouldn't Make You Feel Sad Like That

By Marisa Unger

I realize not everybody can make mid-six figures like my husband. But just because you're not as fortunate as others, that doesn't give you the right to go around depressing people. That's my problem with the homeless: They spend all their time shuffling around in their tattered, smelly clothes, making you feel awful about having a nice home and job. Well, I don't think they should make you feel sad like that.

Whether you're stopped at a light in your Mercedes 450 SLC Coupe, shopping for a new pair of Manolo Blahniks, or strolling through the park, the homeless always show up to beg for change. Or they push around their rusty shopping carts full of empty cans and filthy plastic bags. How depressing! Of course, the homeless should be afforded a certain minimal level of human dignity, but they shouldn't get to lord their poverty over people.

If the homeless want to be treated better, they should understand that people like me want to be able to en-

> ### And why sleep on benches, anyway? Can't the homeless at least put the effort into finding a room at a city shelter? How can I head home on a frosty evening to enjoy a cup of cocoa and a warm bed when, along the way, I have to trip over a man sleeping on a grate?

joy a meal at an outdoor café without having to look at some scabby man digging through the trash. If they must hang around restaurants, why not go to fast-food places like McDonald's or Burger King, where people more like them tend to eat? They shouldn't hang around nice places. Decent people want to enjoy their mesclun salad without having to see a vagrant passed out on a bench, reeking of his own urine. Nothing kills an appetite faster.

> **Though the homeless should be allowed to go almost anywhere they want without harassment, they should at least have the decency to go where people aren't trying to enjoy themselves. Do your loitering and panhandling outside places where people aren't having fun.**

And why sleep on benches, anyway? Can't the homeless at least put the effort into finding a room at a city shelter? How can I head home on a frosty evening to enjoy a cup of cocoa and a warm bed when, along the way, I have to trip over a man sleeping on a grate? It's especially galling in light of the fact that my husband pays hundreds of thousands of dollars in taxes to buy places for these homeless people to sleep, and they aren't even using them. Instead, they're sleeping outside, wasting our dollars, and making me feel bad, to boot.

Though the homeless should be allowed to go almost anywhere they want without harassment, they should at least have the decency to go where people aren't trying to enjoy themselves. Stay away from the art museums and movie theaters. Do your loitering and panhandling outside places where people aren't having fun, like the DMV or dry cleaners.

And, if I may make a request to any homeless person reading this, please don't ask for money from people with children. Trying to explain your miserable plight to a child is one of the hardest things a parent can do. They're too young to understand what makes certain people fall through the cracks of society, and it's not fair of you to force parents' hands with your presence.

The homeless need to understand that other people have feelings, too, and that it's really pretty selfish of them to display their suffering out in the open like that. If they must be someplace where everyone can see them, can't they at least fake a smile? A smile is free, after all. Even a homeless person can afford that. ∅

Peace Activist Has To Admit Barrett .50 Caliber Sniper Rifle Is Pretty Cool

BURLINGTON, VT—Despite his staunch opposition to the National Rifle Association and U.S. military operations in Afghanistan, peace activist Paul Robinson conceded Monday that the Barrett .50 caliber sniper rifle is "pretty damn cool."

"Look, I realize that the use of this instrument of destruction, even in wartime, is morally reprehensible, and I don't see how anyone with a conscience could justify owning one," said Robinson, 31, a University of Ver-

> Robinson first became aware of the high-powered, exceptionally accurate weapon in 1995 while researching U.S. military involvement in Somalia, which he protested while pursuing a masters degree at Bates College.

mont graduate student in sociology and president of the campus chapter of Amnesty International. "But you have to admit, it's pretty wild to think that it's capable of throwing a half-inch bullet into a man-sized target 1,500 meters away."

Robinson first became aware of the high-powered, exceptionally accurate weapon in 1995 while researching U.S. military involvement in Somalia, which he protested while pursuing a masters degree at Tufts.

"While gathering data for a petition letter condemning U.S. policy in Somalia, I was appalled to learn that the Special Forces were using a gun called the Barrett M82A1 to take out trucks from a mile away," Robinson said. "*A friggin' mile.* Can you imagine?"

Last week, a guilt-ridden Robinson bought a copy of *Guns & Ammo* containing an article titled "The Guns Of *Black Hawk Down*," which promi-

Above: Robinson, who admits he finds the Barrett .50 caliber sniper rifle (left) "pretty damn cool."

nently featured the Barrett.

"It's a big gun, the Barrett," said Robinson, leafing through the article. "It's about five feet long and weighs almost 30 pounds. It fires the largest widely available cartridge in the world—a machine-gun bullet, really. It can empty a 10-round magazine as fast as you can pull the trigger. And thanks to its ingenious dual-chamber muzzle brake, gases are vented away, and the user feels no more recoil than

you get with a 12-gauge shotgun. Not that anyone should know what the recoil feels like on any gun."

Robinson also noted that anyone with $7,300 can buy the civilian version of the M82A1, a fact he finds "thoroughly repugnant" and "kind of tempting."

"Though I would never, ever so much as touch one, I bet the Barrett is probably fun to shoot," Robinson said.

see ACTIVIST page 52

Confused Marines Capture Al-Jazeera Leader

DOHA, QATAR—In a daring effort to dismantle the vast Arab network, a company of confused Marines raided Al-Jazeera headquarters Monday and captured leader Mohammed Abouzeid. "Al-Jazeera has ties to virtually every country in the Arab world, and this guy was the key to their whole operation," Lieut. Warren Withers said. "Nothing went through the Al-Jazeera communications array without his go-ahead." Pentagon officials praised the soldiers for their "courageous and swift action," but noted they would have preferred that the Marines captured someone hostile to the U.S. instead.

Consumer Reports Rates Self 'Excellent'

NEW YORK—*Consumer Reports* magazine earned a rating of "excellent" in its special "Consumer Advocacy Magazines" issue, which hit newsstands Tuesday. "From our exhaustive, unbiased appraisals of all types of consumer products to our clear, concise writing style, *Consumer Reports* is once again the undisputed winner," the article read. "For the latest in consumer information and product-safety recalls, look no further than us."

Enron Executives Blamed For Missing Employee Donut Fund

HOUSTON—The Enron scandal widened Monday, when *The Houston Chronicle* reported that top company executives stole nearly $10 from the employee donut fund sometime between June and August of last year. "There should be at least $9.25 in the coffee can next to the filters," said Laurie Baker, a recently laid-off Enron employee. "I personally put $2.50

into that fund, and now it's gone." Enron CEO Kenneth Lay is already under grand-jury subpoena regarding $45 in Chinese-food-delivery allocations that mysteriously vanished on Nov. 17, 2001.

Receptionist Takes Leave Of Absence Citing Dehydration, Exhaustion

QUINCY, IL—Citing "dehydration and exhaustion," a spokesperson for Andrea Conklin announced Monday that the Quincy dental receptionist will take an extended leave of absence. "The stress and strain of answering Dr. Taubman's phones all day long has finally taken its toll on Ms. Conklin," spokesman Chris Vinocur said. "Andrea is now in the care of her personal physician, who has recommended that she take two months off to regain her strength." Vinocur denied rumors in last week's

National Enquirer that Conklin had checked into a drug-rehabilitation facility.

Howie Long Expresses Desire To Direct Radio Shack Spots

LOS ANGELES—Pondering his next career move, Radio Shack pitchman and former NFL defensive end Howie Long told reporters Monday that he is interested in directing an upcoming installment of the series of commercials in which he playfully endorses high-tech gadgets with actress Teri Hatcher. "I've given it a lot of thought, and I think I'm ready to get behind the camera," Long said. "I've done the acting thing for a while now, and I just feel like it's time for a new challenge." Long said he could bring the kind of experience and insight to directing the commercials that only comes from having spent countless hours on the set. ∅

BOYFRIEND from page 49

tuses' home in Greenville. "Now I know where Jay gets that obsessive thing about keeping the car clean. His father is even worse than he is."

Wasson, who began dating Loftus in June 2001, found meeting his parents illuminating in numerous ways.

"Jay is totally passive-aggressive. Like, he'll agree to go to a party with me even if he doesn't really want to go, but then as soon as we get there, he'll say how tired he is and purposely not have any fun," Wasson said. "His mother pulls the same shit with his father. We all went to see that movie *The Royal Tenenbaums*, and instead of saying she didn't want to see it, she just sat there groaning the whole time."

Wasson said that within two hours of meeting Jay's parents, some "scary patterns" began to emerge. Among the similarities Wasson noticed was Karl's insistence that he be the one who handles money, a tendency she noticed in Jay when they went to Florida in December.

Wasson also found that the Loftuses, like their son, never express disapproval of anyone, only sympathy.

"It is so condescending how they're sorry for everyone," Wasson said. "It

> **Among the similarities Wasson noticed was Karl's insistence that he be the one who handles money, a tendency she noticed in Jay when they went to Florida in December.**

drives me fucking nuts when Jay does that. He acts like he's being tolerant, but his face scrunches up in a way that says, 'I'm not telling you what I'm really thinking.' Well, now I know where that face comes from. The first

time Karl did it, I thought, 'Holy shit. There's the scrunch. *He's scrunching.*'"

In addition, Karl shares his son's

> **More than anything else, Wasson said she is bothered by Loftus' "weird evasiveness."**

"crazy obsession with getting an early start."

"That's always been a big thing with Jay," Wasson said. "Anytime we're going somewhere, the night before, it's always, 'We should get up really early tomorrow, because we've got a lot to do.' That's obviously the way it must've been when he'd go on family trips as a kid."

More than anything else, Wasson said she is bothered by Loftus'"weird evasiveness."

"Sometimes, Jay will mysteriously say he has to go somewhere and then run out the door," Wasson said. "Later on, I'll find out that he just went to the bookstore. Well, on Friday night, Jay's mom wouldn't say where she was going, and we later found out she'd gone to the grocery store to pick up some milk. Why do these Loftus psychos feel the need to hide things like that?"

In spite of the obvious parallels, Loftus seems oblivious to the traits he shares with his parents.

"Ever since meeting my parents, Julia keeps going on about the ways I'm similar to them," Loftus said. "She's completely wrong, but you've got to expect that sort of overanalysis from an only child of two psychologists."

Wasson, for her part, fears that the similarities will only grow.

"I've got to keep an eye on this," Wasson said. "If Jay continues to become more like Karl, I could fall into the 'Miriam role,' constantly vying for his attention, only to ultimately annoy him and push him further away. I've seen the future and, let me tell you, it is scary." ⬚

ACTIVIST from page 51

"And the fact that anyone can get their hands on this killing machine, plus a 10-power Unertl scope and a few boxes of match-grade 750-grain cartridges, for less than $10,000, well, that's just sickening."

The pacifist added that he would be willing to meet with any interested owners of Barrett rifles in order to "open a dialogue."

Robinson's friends said they are appalled by his attraction to the rifle.

"Paul can praise the Barrett all he wants, but he needs to remember that it's a device whose sole function is to kill people," said Max Shorter, 28, a friend and colleague of Robinson's in the sociology department. "It might be a triumph of ballistic engineering, but that should in no way

> **The pacifist added that he would be willing to meet with any interested owners of Barrett rifles in order to "open a dialogue."**

obscure the fact that this is a tool for murder."

"Plus, it failed some of the Navy's field tests for reliability and accuracy," Shorter added. "The extractors kept breaking, I seem to recall." ⬚

SENATOR from page 49

I sign everything myself—no stamp! I have a lot of friends in the Senate. Trent [Lott], John [Warner], Charles [Schumer], Dianne [Feinstein], Russ [Feingold], Wayne [Allard], Tom [Daschle]. They're all invited to my house for popcorn! I'm just as good as them, and I want to be treated just like normal."

Rigby, 44, who scored a surprise upset victory over Republican opponent Bruce Linsenmyer in one of the closest elections in Nebraska history, points to his Senate voting record as proof of his qualification to hold public office.

"I sponsored the Everybody Eats Food Bill of 2001, [which makes it illegal for] Americans to go hungry!" Rigby said. "That way, poor people don't have to starve anymore! Lots of mac 'n' cheese... I like that! And I was

> **Rigby, 44, who scored a surprise upset victory over Republican opponent Bruce Linsenmyer in one of the closest elections in Nebraska history, points to his Senate voting record as proof of his qualification to hold public office.**

the first senator [to propose] free weekly field trips to Little Tyrol for the American people. It would be free, 'cause the government would pay for the bus rides!"

Little Tyrol is a re-created Swiss village and amusement park near Lincoln, NE, that Rigby frequents.

"And after the terrorists bombed the Sears Towers, I was the first senator [to draft a resolution calling for professional wrestler] The Rock to go find them and kick their butts!" Rigby said. "Yaay! The Rock!"

In addition to his impressive legislative record, Rigby boasts the best attendance record in the Senate. He is always the first to arrive and the last to leave the Senate chamber, even on days when the legislative body is not in session.

Rigby has also won praise for his concern for the common man.

"At the end of every session, after the other senators have gone home, Freddy will follow me around, asking if he can mop," Capitol custodian Larry Gibson said. "I say, 'Now, come on, Freddy, you're a senator now. You're a lot more important than old Larry here. Why don't you go draft a bill or serve on a committee or something?' He'll usually go away for a while, but then he always comes back carrying a full wastebasket, saying, 'I like to help you, Larry!' He won't leave his limo

driver alone, either."

Despite winning the admiration of many around him, Rigby is not without his critics. A coalition of Democrats and Republicans recently formed out of concern for the senator's ability to hold public office.

"Now, we all like Freddy—everybody in the Senate does," Sen. Tim Hutchinson (R-AR) said. "We love the construction-paper vases and desk placemats he made all of us, as well as the way he puts all his senator stuff away in the multi-colored plastic bins in his office at the end of the day. But does that make him qualified to be a legislator? Should he be in the position to cast the deciding vote on a key Medicare-reform bill? It's just not fair to the American people—or to him."

Some on Capitol Hill have recommended that Rigby be paired up with a "buddy senator," who would advise him and wield veto power on his votes. Rigby, however, has rejected the suggestion, pointing to his previous work experience at an Omaha-area Wendy's as ample evidence of his competence.

"I am just as good as anyone else! I am just as good as anyone else!" Rigby said. "They let Strom Thurmond be senator, and he's 200 years old! I like representing the great state of Nebraska! Nebraska is number one!"

It is clear, however, that the constant questions regarding Rigby's competence have taken their toll on the senator's self-esteem. In November 2001, Rigby ran away from Washington.

"People were being mean to me, and I was very, very sad," Rigby said. "So I ranned [sic] away. I took the bus all by myself for the first time. I saw a Waffle House, and they fed me for free when I said I was a senator. Then they called the police to pick me up. I got to ride in a police car! I've ridden in a police car and a limo and a fire truck [since becoming a senator]!"

Nearly 36 hours after fleeing the nation's capital, Rigby was found by police in Alexandria, VA, and promptly escorted back to Washington. Accom-

> **Despite winning the admiration of many around him, Rigby is not without his critics. A coalition of Democrats and Republicans recently formed out of concern for the senator's ability to hold public office.**

panying the police were several concerned members of the senator's staff and Sen. Barbara Boxer (D-CA), who befriended Rigby while the two
see SENATOR next page

SMURFS from page 49 ◀━━━

served on the Senate Committee on Foreign Relations.

"Freddy thought people were mad at him and didn't like him, and he was being a little grumpy with the police and his staffers," Boxer said. "So on the car ride back home, I explained to Freddy that there will always be people who won't understand why he's a senator, but that he should know that it's okay to be different. I told him he should be proud of himself and the work he's done in the Senate. That seemed to calm him down quite a bit. He also really seemed to like the Koosh slingshot I gave him."

Janet Fjelstad, a Columbus, NE, legal secretary and longtime Rigby supporter, attributed the senator's improbable rise to "the power of unconditional love."

"People who think developmentally disabled people should be kept out of public office don't understand just

> ## "And after the terrorists bombed the Sears Towers, I was the first senator [to draft a resolution calling for professional wrestler] The Rock to go find them and kick their butts!" Rigby said. "Yaay! The Rock!"

how much these very special folks have to offer us," Fjelstad said. "Fortunately, Freddy has a lot of friends—the thousands of people who elected him to the Omaha City Council, then the Omaha mayoralty, then the Nebraska legislature, then the U.S. Senate."

Continued Fjelstad: "Many of them were once prejudiced, too. They'd say, 'Why should we give a retarded guy the power to make decisions on vital issues of national import?' But in the end, Freddy's sunny personality, infectious grin, and insistence on making a crayon drawing for every constituent—whether they voted for him or not—won most of his critics over. For the first time, it forced people to seriously question conventional definitions of intelligence and competence. After all, when was the last time a politician engaged your mind and touched your heart?"

Unfazed by the lingering doubts of some, Rigby reaffirmed his commitment to represent the people of Nebraska to the best of his abilities.

"I try hard!" Rigby said. "I'm the hardest worker at my group home! Except for Josh. He works at Popeye's, and he always brings home chicken and biscuits and gravy! I wish I could bring home chicken from my job." ✐

Above: Some of the so-called "collector's items" that await Jarry's valuation.

pillowcase."

Though he considers himself an expert on many types of antiques, Jarry's true passion is the work of the New York lighting and metalwork firm E.F. Caldwell & Co.

"Two years ago, during a trip to Washington D.C., I went to the Smithsonian's National Museum of Design and spent a full day just with their collection of E.F. Caldwell lighting fixtures," Jarry said. "I also was lucky enough to see the Strater collection of Swiss enameled glass, 19th-century French block-printed wallpaper, 20th-century Soviet propaganda porcelains…"

Jarry's reverie was then interrupted by a customer wishing to be directed to the McDonaldland character glasses.

> ## Jarry's reverie was then interrupted by a customer wishing to be directed to the McDonaldland character glasses.

Jarry said he dreams of one day running a store that deals exclusively in E.F. Caldwell sconces, table lamps, and chandeliers, along with those of other celebrated firms like Sterling Bronze Co., Bradley & Hubbard, and Murano. Unfortunately, the antique market in Duluth is not large enough to support such specialization. To ensure his store's profitability, Jarry has

been forced to offer more in-demand collectibles, such as *Star Wars* action figures, Schlitz beer signs from the '70s, and *Welcome Back, Kotter* TV tray tables.

As an added incentive for customers to come to his store, Jarry offers free appraisals.

"This morning alone, I appraised a *Dukes Of Hazzard* lunch box, a UM–Duluth edition Monopoly game from 1996, some *Jaws 2* trading cards, and a smiley-face pillow that the owner found in her basement and thought looked 'pretty old,'" Jarry said. "Why do I put up with this?"

Ever since the debut of the PBS series *Antiques Roadshow*, Jarry has seen a rise in the number of people hoping to make a fortune selling antiques. A recent customer was disappointed with the $3 valuation he gave a 1999 reproduction of a 1976 Strawberry Shortcake lunch box, a price Jarry said was "on the generous side."

Renee Knight, 34, owner of the lunch box, questioned Jarry's appraisal.

"I saw a metal lunch box on eBay go for $60, and all it had on it was a picture of a horse," Knight said. "Frankly, I don't think he knows what he's talking about. Or maybe he was lying so I'd sell it to him for next to nothing."

Knight said she frequently browses The Finer Things for "cute Christmas and Halloween decorations" or items for her sister's extensive *Garfield* collection.

"The prices here are a lot higher than at Goodwill, but sometimes I see something I just have to get," Knight said. "I'll warn you, though: Don't even go to the back of the store. I once saw a cute little lamp and was going to buy it un-

til I realized it was $1,200, not $12."

The lamp, a numbered Tiffany accent lamp with gold Favrile shade, remains unsold.

"Most of the people who come in

> ## "I saw a metal lunch box on eBay go for $60, and all it had on it was a picture of a horse," Knight said.

here expect me to see the junk they scraped out of their basement toy boxes and start salivating," Jarry said. "They're disappointed if I don't say, 'I can't believe my luck in getting to hold in my very own hands an actual Skipper doll from 1978!'"

Jarry, who holds masters degrees in history and art, said the antique business isn't what it was when he started. Though he occasionally speaks with respected peers when attending a convention or trade show, his everyday interactions as an independent dealer in a mid-sized city are less than thrilling.

"I'm in here six days a week, and all anyone asks me is if I know the name of Smurf arch-nemesis Gargamel's little cat," Jarry said. "Why doesn't anyone ask me about 17th- and 18th-century Delftware metalwork? Or pre-Federal American-period furniture? Or even a simple question about Depression glass or old maps or decorative brass door knobs? By the way, it's Azrael." ✐

Who Do I Have To Blow To Win The Bancroft Prize In American History?

By Lawrence Sharpless

For the past seven years, I have devoted myself wholly to the task of studying the life of William Howard Taft, becoming, in the process, the world's foremost authority on our 27th president. I have delved deeply into both his personal and political history, tracing his journey from a hard-scrabble Ohio boyhood to the highest office in the land.

At the risk of seeming immodest, I firmly believe that my recently published book, *Taft*, is the definitive biography of the man, breathing new life into an overlooked president better known for his girth than for his considerable skills as a statesman and orator. That said, it came as a great surprise to me when, on Jan. 14, the nominees for a certain prize were announced, and my name was not among them.

So I ask, just who the hell do I have to blow to get a Bancroft Prize in American History?

I mean, is there a particular committee member around whose penis I should wrap my lips, or should I just blow the whole lot of them, sucking and slurping phalluses like a Singapore whore?

My research for *Taft* was painstaking and exhaustive. In addition to studying archival documents from the Taft Presidential Library, I unearthed as many new sources as I could, going door-to-door in an effort to track down descendants who might have letters, photos, or any other personal artifacts that could potentially shed new light on his life. In late 1999, I spent three months devoted exclusively to researching Taft's 1890–91 stint as solicitor-general under President Benjamin Harrison. Apparently, though, that wasn't enough. I guess it's time for some feverish cock-gobbling.

Maybe if I'd dressed up all sexy and shook my ass like David McCullough did when he won for *John Adams*, I'd have had the Bancroft people eating out of my hand.

Lest you think otherwise, let me make it clear that this is not about the $4,000 cash award. This has nothing to do with money. This is about recognition for what I know in my heart was a meticulously researched, passionately written book on a subject sorely deserving of attention. But I guess as far as the Bancroft Prize committee is

concerned, that only matters if I'm slobbering on their knobs.

I guess I just needed to get on my knees before the committee in a display of inferiority to their alpha selves. Then, each male committee member could have unzipped his pants and roughly thrust his skinflute into my mouth before pulling out and covering me in a thick coat of love

I mean, is there a particular committee member around whose penis I should wrap my lips, or should I just blow the whole lot of them, sucking and slurping phalluses like a Singapore whore?

snot. Maybe then I would've been in the running for that prestigious award.

You can't tell me David Nasaw didn't choke on a few throbbing Johnsons to win the prize for his Hearst biography. I mean, how else could such sloppy, uninspired prose on such a painfully obvious subject win? Please. And Philip D. Morgan? There's no question in my mind that he boarded the dick-smoking train to Bancroft Prizeville, a ticket he paid for with gallons of Tijuana toothpaste.

It's not like I didn't try to play the game a little bit. I sent out holiday cards to every member of the committee along with a complimentary copy of *Taft*. Maybe if I'd also attached a note reading "Good for one free blow job," I'd have gotten somewhere.

Will somebody please explain to me why I even bothered putting 84 months into this book when instead I could have scrawled "Taft was awesome" on a scrap of paper and then spent a few hours deep-throating the committee chair?

For my next project, the most ambitious biography of Boss Tweed ever undertaken, I'll know how to play the game. Instead of tireless research and countless rewrites, I'll limber up my lips and suck off everyone in the entire academic community. Then, at long last, the Bancroft Prize in American History will be mine. ∅

Your Horoscope

By Lloyd Schumner Sr.
Retired Machinist and
A.A.P.B.-Certified Astrologer

Aries: (March 21–April 19)
You will feel an overwhelming sense of embarrassment and relief when you are told by doctors that the malignant-looking growth on your face is a mustache.

Taurus: (April 20–May 20)
You will make headlines nationwide when you are the subject of a $340 million asexual-harassment lawsuit.

Gemini: (May 21–June 21)
The line between terrifying and tasteless is toed next week when you are stalked and painted by former New York Jets artist-in-residence LeRoy Neiman.

Cancer: (June 22–July 22)
You will be delighted to find a good recipe for strawberry jam in the middle of an otherwise boring Tolstoy novel.

Leo: (July 23–Aug. 22)
As you get older, you will begin to appreciate how the unseen hands of God and Buddy Ebsen subtly influence everything in Creation.

Virgo: (Aug. 23–Sept. 22)
If there is more to life than fishing, you don't want to know what it is. This will help explain your death from malnutrition and dehydration next week.

Libra: (Sept. 23–Oct. 23)
You will sacrifice everything you've worked so hard for—except your car, house, job, and marriage—for the love of a good woman.

Scorpio: (Oct. 24–Nov. 21)
You will soon be reduced to a whimpering, quivering mess by the challenge of keeping all 33 wind-up toys going simultaneously.

Sagittarius: (Nov. 22–Dec. 21)
The breezy, lighthearted tone of your best prose is unable to mask the fact that your characters are a boring pastiche of middle-class stereotypes.

Capricorn: (Dec. 22–Jan. 19)
You will be forced to stop insulting others after everyone else in the world transmutes into rubber, while you, in turn, become glue.

Aquarius: (Jan. 20–Feb. 18)
You will become embroiled in a wacky wild-goose chase, despite the ready availability of rational, tame geese.

Pisces: (Feb. 19–March 20)
It is said, "They also serve who only stand and wait," but that won't do you much good in your waitressing career.

GASTRIC from page 51

amounts of blood. Passersby were amazed by the unusually large amounts of blood. Passersby were amazed by the unusually large amounts of blood. Passersby were amazed by the unusually large amounts of blood. Passersby were amazed by the unusually large amounts of blood. Passersby were amazed by the unusually large amounts of blood. Passersby were amazed by the unusually large amounts of blood. Passersby were amazed by the unusually large amounts of blood. Passersby were amazed by the unusually large amounts of blood. Passersby were amazed by the unusually large amounts of blood. Passersby were amazed by the unusually large amounts of blood. Passersby were amazed by the unusually large amounts of blood. Passersby were amazed by the unusually large amounts of blood. Passersby were amazed by the unusually large amounts of blood. Passersby were amazed by the unusually large amounts of blood. Passersby were amazed by the unusually large amounts of blood. Passersby were amazed by the unusually large

amounts of blood. Passersby were amazed by the unusually large amounts of blood. Passersby were amazed by the unusually large amounts of blood. Passersby were amazed by the unusually large amounts of blood. Passersby were amazed by the unusually large amounts of blood. Passersby were amazed by the unusually large

Boy, you try to have sex with someone, and suddenly you're Hitler.

amounts of blood. Passersby were amazed by the unusually large amounts of blood. Passersby were amazed by the unusually large amounts of blood. Passersby were amazed by the unusually large amounts of blood. Passersby were amazed by the unusually large amounts of blood. Passersby were amazed by the unusually large

see GASTRIC page 56

Stack Of Unread *New Yorker*s Celebrates One-Year Anniversary

see MEDIA page 3C

David Allan Coe Waiting Outside To Kick Your Ass

see MUSIC page 2D

Man Wishes He Were 15 Years Younger Or Woman Were Two Years Older

see LOCAL page 12B

STATshot

A look at the numbers that shape your world.

Where Is The Olympic Torch This Week?

Location	Torchbearer
Monday Stockton, CA	Bobby Franklin, Inspirational Legless Child
Tuesday Burbank, CA	*JAG* star Catherine Bell
Wednesday Yucca, AZ	Leonard Whitecloud, Token Native American
Thursday Phoenix, AZ	Some kid whose dad went to college with President Bush
Friday Taos, NM	Caroline Rhea

0 74470 94595 6 00

THE ONION • $2.00 US • $3.00 CAN

---

the ONION®

VOLUME 38 ISSUE 03   AMERICA'S FINEST NEWS SOURCE™   31 JAN.–06 FEB. 2002

ALMIGHTY ANTITRUST

Judge Orders God To Break Up Into Smaller Deities

A Deity Divided

"God has willfully and actively thwarted competition from other deities and demigods, promoting His worship with such unfair scare tactics as threatening non-believers with eternal damnation. In the process, He has carved out for Himself an illegal monotheopoly."

—Judge Charles Elliot Schofield

In compliance with Monday's decision, God must:

- Divest all holdings in churches, synagogues, and mosques
- Cede miracle-performing services to local deities
- Cease and desist strongarm tactic of smiting nonbelievers
- Allow competition from pagan gods and animistic spirits

The defendant

What this means for worshippers:

- Quicker prayer-response time
- Likely reduction in yearly tithes and tributes
- Wider selection of specialized deities
- No reprisals for false-idol worship

WASHINGTON, DC—Calling the theological giant's stranglehold on the religion industry "blatantly anti-competitive," a U.S. district judge ruled Monday that God is in violation of anti-monopoly laws and ordered Him to be broken up into several less powerful deities.

"The evidence introduced in this trial has convinced me that the deity known as God has willfully and actively thwarted competition from other deities and demigods, promoting His worship with such unfair scare tactics as threatening non-believers with eternal damnation," wrote District Judge Charles Elliot Schofield in his decision. "In the process, He has carved out for Himself an illegal monotheopoly."

The suit, brought against God by the Justice Department on behalf of a coalition of "lesser deities" and polytheistic mortals, alleged that He violated antitrust laws by claiming in the Holy Bible that He was the sole creator of the universe, and by strictly prohibiting the worship of what He termed "false idols."

"God clearly commands that there shall be no other gods before Him,

see GOD page 59

Nation Welcomes Return Of Good Old-Fashioned Partisan Bickering

WASHINGTON, DC—Across the nation, Americans are heartened to see that after nearly five months of unity and cooperation, petty, partisan bickering is slowly returning to the halls of Congress.

"With [House Majority Leader] Dick Armey attacking [Senate Majority Leader] Tom Daschle for bottlenecking the Senate, [House

Above: In a welcome sight, Sen. Chris Dodd (D-CT) (left) and Rep. Dick Armey (R-TX) squabble unproductively on *Meet The Press.*

Democratic leader] Dick Gephardt roundly blasting Republican efforts to amend a Democratic-sponsored energy bill, and lawmakers on each side blaming the other for the return of the deficit, this terrible period of bipartisan amity seems to be ending," House Speaker Dennis

see BICKERING page 58

Lesbian Identity Ends Abruptly Mid-Junior Year

OBERLIN, OH—Three semesters after adopting the sexual identity, Amanda Oppel, a junior women's-studies major at Oberlin College, abruptly dropped her highly politicized lesbian stance Monday.

"I just need to focus on different priorities right now," said Oppel, 20. "I'm graduating next year, and my dad's not going to foot the bill forever." She also alluded to "maybe going back east to get an MBA."

Stunned by the announcement, Oppel's friends and fellow lesbian activists have struggled to understand the sudden reversal of sexual orientation.

"What the hell?" said Ellen Yang, leader of the Campus Womyn's Caucus and self-described "oppressed lesbian of color." "Just three weeks ago, she road-tripped with us to San Fran for the big Menstruation Day rally. Now, she's suddenly not a dyke anymore? And what's with the outfit she was wearing? Since when does the infamous militant lesbian revolutionary Amanda Oppel wear Banana Republic sweaters and denim Gap skirts?"

see LESBIAN page 58

Above: A photo of Oppel taken during her 16 months of lesbianism.

The Enron Scandal

Enron, which went bankrupt amid charges of document shredding, shady accounting, and executive greed, is the subject of a House hearing. What do *you* think?

"Whoever is responsible for this scandal should be a man and step forward for a very short sentence in a very posh jail."

Donna Clarke
Librarian

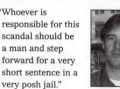

"Oh, to be a fly on the wall at that 463-hour hearing."

Chris Anderson
Mailroom Clerk

"This marks the end of an era of innocence for our nation's massive energy concerns."

Buddy Jessup
Landscaper

"Serves those employees right for buying into something as shady as a corporate 401(k) plan."

Frederick Voss
Lawyer

"It's bad, but it's not worth killing yourself over. Unless you're a former senior executive with inside knowledge of the company's crimes, that is."

Robert Rossum
Systems Analyst

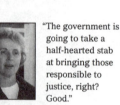

"The government is going to take a half-hearted stab at bringing those responsible to justice, right? Good."

Melinda Grazen
Teacher

Super Bowl Halftime Shows

Through the years, the Super Bowl halftime show has been as much of a reason to tune in as the game itself. Among the highlights:

Year	
1967	Sidney Poitier delivers speech on importance of school integration
1969	Rolling Stones-Jefferson Airplane performance cut short by fatal stabbing of Joe Namath by Hells Angels
1976	Sylvester Stallone yells "Adrian" into microphone for 35 minutes
1983	"A New Wave Tribute To America's Grenada War Heroes," featuring Kajagoogoo and A Flock of Seagulls
1984	Faceless automatons march lockstep into stadium to show dystopian, extravatainment-free world foretold by George Orwell
1987	Something involving Gloria Estefan, a smoke machine, and maybe a Four Tops medley
1991	Vanilla Ice performs "Ice Ice Baby" accompanied by 250 figure skaters
1995	"An All-Star Salute To The 1994 Super Bowl Halftime Show"
2002	America rocks out with some crazy halftime action but is also solemn and dignified as it honors the heroes of Sept. 11 while still maintaining a loose, fun, party spirit, which is part of what our troops overseas are so bravely defending

the ONION
America's Finest News Source.™

Herman Ulysses Zweibel
Founder

T. Herman Zweibel
Publisher Emeritus
J. Phineas Zweibel
Publisher
Maxwell Prescott Zweibel
Editor-In-Chief

I Think I'll Pay Way Too Much For Quality Fashion Eyewear

By Holly Minero

When shopping for eyewear, I want a full range of all the latest styles from all the top designers. I want to see great-looking frames from big names like Jones NY, Dolce & Gabbana, Guess, BCBG, and French Connection. Unfortunately, that means going to a pricey store that charges an arm and a leg. But, as much as it kills me, that's exactly what I plan to do. There aren't any other options out there, so I have no choice but to pay way too much for quality fashion eyewear.

If only there were someplace I could get the same quality frames you see at boutiques and department stores, but at savings of up to 50 percent off. And what if they also offered a full range of lens options, from tinting to UV coatings to anti-reflective treatments? Alas, such a store exists only in my imagination.

Sometimes I can't help but think how amazing it would be if there were a store that not only provided quality fashion eyewear at a fair price, but

> If only there were someplace I could get the same quality frames you see at boutiques and department stores, but at savings of up to 50 percent off. And what if they also offered a full range of lens options, from tinting to UV coatings to anti-reflective treatments? Alas, such a store exists only in my imagination.

also could fill any prescription in about an hour. To get that kind of fast service, though, you have to sacrifice quality. That's why I'm sticking with the big guys with the sky-high price tags.

It's too bad I always end up someplace that doesn't feature top frames for the entire family. After all, no store with reasonable prices carries fun children's eyewear by Harry Potter Style, Marvel Comics, or X-Men. Or the styles teens love, featuring such popular names as Adidas, MTV, Reebok, and B.U.M. Equipment.

> Oh, just forget the whole thing. It's pointless. I mean, even if there were a store that boasted top names like Cheryl Tiegs, DKNY, Fila, and Candies at affordable prices (keep dreaming), I'm sure it would be inconveniently located.

Then there's the issue of customer service. Not every pair of glasses is right for everybody, and I'd rather not be rushed out the door with the same pair as the next person. I'm looking for a professional, courteous sales team that gives me the personal attention I need to find the look and fit that's right for me. The problem is, I live in the real world, not some fantasyland where strawberry-syrup rivers flow through candy-cane forests.

And what if I need other services, like contact lenses, prescription sunglasses, or on-site examinations from licensed optometrists? I'd also love it if I could get prescription clip-on sunglasses or a designer case for my eyewear. But you and I both know that ain't ever gonna happen.

Why do I even bother? Even if I did find a store that offered great glasses at a sensible price, I'd have to give up all the extras. There's no way the low price would include such add-ons as a 30-day money-back guarantee or free lifetime cleaning and adjustments to maintain the comfort and fit of my glasses for as long as I own them. Unless I pay too much for my eyewear, I can also say *sayonara* to such options as one-year protection against accidental breakage and replacement plans for lost contacts.

Oh, just forget the whole thing. It's pointless. I mean, even if there were a store that boasted top names like Cheryl Tiegs, DKNY, Fila, and Candies at affordable prices (keep dreaming), I'm sure it would be inconveniently located.

Waitress Punished For Sins Of The World

FAYETTEVILLE, NC—Smitty's Family Restaurant customers have found in waitress Jennifer Marsh a handy scapegoat for the sins of the world, sources reported Tuesday.

"Get it right this time," corporate attorney Paula Hinton told Marsh, taking out years of deep dissatisfaction on the waitress. "I have to be at work by 9, and I'm not about to be late because of you."

Marsh, a 23-year-old single mother of two, earns $2.13 an hour plus tips at Smitty's, serving food and functioning as an outlet for the anger and frustration of all mankind. Monday morning alone, between the hours of 8 and 11, nearly 20 customers heaped abuse on Marsh for a host of evils wholly unrelated to her.

"Where were you? I've been waiting 15 minutes," said Stephan Kendrick, seemingly irritated by the nine-minute wait for his chorizo and eggs but in reality venting anger over the alcoholic mother who abandoned him at age 9. "At least they're still warm."

Each day, Marsh also serves as a symbolic punching bag for a rogue's gallery of misogynist men who have been rejected by women. Taking aim at all womankind through Marsh, the men "strike back" with sexually inappropriate comments, intentionally confusing orders, and woefully small tips.

According to University of North Carolina sociologist Dr. James Armbruster, Marsh plays a vital role in American society.

"Daily life in this country has never been more fraught with stress and tension," Armbruster said. "By absorbing the pent-up rage and resentment of those around her, this remarkable woman is the release valve that keeps the balloon we call America from overinflating and bursting."

Armbruster, who recently ate lunch at Smitty's, said the litany of misdeeds for which Marsh must suffer is not limited to small-scale personal vendettas.

"I actually saw Jennifer being punished for centuries of racial injustice when a group of African-American teenagers occupied a booth for more than two hours. They inverted the traditional model of racial servitude by torturing her with a laundry list of detailed questions about menu items, sending back imperfectly prepared orders, and demanding endless drink refills."

"I thought Jennifer would crack under the pressure," Armbruster continued, "but, as is typical of martyrs, she absorbed blow after blow, scooped up her 30-cent tip, and went straight to a new table without raising an eye-

> **Marsh, a 23-year-old single mother of two, earns $2.13 an hour plus tips at Smitty's, serving food and functioning as an outlet for the anger and frustration of all mankind.**

brow."

Rev. Pernell Hardwick, author of *The Waitress On The Cross: Jennifer Marsh As Secular Christ Figure* (Pantheon Books, $12.95), said Marsh functions as a modern-day Jesus.

"Jennifer, more than any other contemporary figure, fits the Christ model, giving life to the world in the form of nourishment while serving as a

Above: Waitress and Christ figure Jennifer Marsh.

willing repository of punishment for the sins of humanity," Hardwick said. "All the while, she never raises a hand or utters a word of protest, smiling politely as instructed by her shift manager."

Added Hardwick: "Of course, while the similarities between Marsh and Christ are obvious, comparisons to Job would be equally apt." ∅

NEWS IN BRIEF

French Teacher Forces Student To Inform Her Of Bathroom Fire In French

FRANKFORT, KY—Jenny Block, a Crestwood High School ninth-grader, attempted to tell French teacher Madame Shapiro about a fire in the girls' second-floor bathroom Monday, only to be ordered to speak French. "En française," Shapiro told the frantic, wildly gesticulating Block. "S'il y a le feu dans les WC, dites-le moi dans un langage correct. D'accord?" Block then tried to say, "Allyson Dorner threw a lit cigarette in the garbage, and it burst into flames, and now there's a huge fire spreading all over the bathroom!" in French, but got stuck on the word for "threw."

Krispy Kreme Doughnuts Described To Sioux City Relatives

SIOUX CITY, IA—At a family reunion Monday, Phillip and Melissa DiResta of Orlando, FL, attempted to convey the taste, texture, and general deliciousness of Krispy Kreme doughnuts to their Sioux City rela-

tives. "They're doughnuts, but not, like, doughnut-doughnuts," Phillip told second cousin Jon Colangelo. "They're not like the cakey, Dunkin' Donuts kind, but more like, you know, the ones that are more like bread, only fried or glazed or something." Over the course of the next 10 minutes, Melissa cited nearly a dozen other popular pastries for comparative purposes, prompting Colangelo to express hope that a Krispy Kreme outlet would one day open in Sioux City.

Comeback Much Harsher Than Insult

MANKATO, MN—A gentle prod elicited a disproportionately harsh retort Monday, when office wag Kenneth Adamle was loudly told by coworker Bryan Lemon that at least Lemon's wife didn't cheat on him with a floor-tile installer. "Holy shit, I just said he's putting on a bit of a spare tire," a stunned Adamle said after the exchange. "What's up his ass that he's bringing up my divorce?"

ER Doctor Secretly Thinks Of Self As Ward's George Clooney

KANSAS CITY, MO—Dr. Andrew Lassiter, a St. Luke's Medical Center

emergency-room physician, secretly regards himself as the hospital's real-life equivalent to George Clooney's character on the hit NBC show *ER*. "He'd never admit it, but Andrew clearly thinks he's St. Luke's answer to Dr. Doug Ross," triage nurse Paulette Wyndham said Monday. "He has this cocky swagger, and whenever women are around, he turns on what he seems to think is some kind of manly, roguish charm." Wyndham added that, with his diminutive stature, beady eyes, and bald head, Lassiter is more like County General's Dr. Romano.

Magazine Says You Have *Sex And The City* Fever

NEW YORK—According to the new issue of *Us* magazine, you, like the rest of the nation, are caught up in *Sex And The City* fever. "Everybody's abuzz about Miranda's baby, Carrie and Aidan's breakup, and Samantha's shocking flirtation with monogamy," stated the article, which also noted that everybody, yourself included, can't stop talking about *Sex And The City* star Sarah Jessica Parker's recent Golden Globe win. The article was accompanied by a sidebar containing several "spoiler" factoids for upcoming episodes, which it correctly guessed you would not want to read. ∅

Hastert told reporters Monday. "All I can say is, thank God."

Weary from months of Sept. 11-induced goodwill on Capitol Hill, Americans across the country have longed for a return to good old-fashioned sniping, name-calling, and finger-pointing.

"Thank heaven those boys in Washington are starting to waste time again, denouncing each other with shrill, self-righteous indignation like in the good old days," said Hanover, NH, locksmith Herman Bochy. "It makes a man want to stand up and say, 'Dammit, we're going to make it.'" And then it's only a matter of time before communication breaks down altogether."

For the first time since Sept. 11, federal legislators are returning to politics as usual.

"When I saw all those Senate members locking arms to sing 'God Bless America' right after Sept. 11, I cried," said Jane Svoboda, 37, an Ashland, OR, homemaker. "It was almost as if the words 'Democrat' and 'Republican' didn't mean anything anymore. I said to my husband, 'Has it really come to

Above: Sen. Jesse Helms (R-NC) insults a Democratic colleague he had treated civilly for nearly five months.

this?' Now, as the corrupt fat cats start pursuing their own greedy, self-interest-driven agendas while hypocritically accusing their counterparts of pork-barrel politics, it's like seeing America return to greatness."

But experts warn that hard times, and the patriotic unity that comes

with them, are not over.

"As long as the war on terror continues, the national nightmare of bipartisan cooperation will not completely disappear," said Joseph Nye, professor and dean of Harvard's John F. Kennedy School of Government. "Osama bin Laden is still at

large. U.S. servicemen are still overseas. And many victims still need our help. But slowly, our leaders are getting back to the business of firing accusations at one another while serving the narrow interests of the powerful, monied few who got them elected."

Added Nye: "You know, watching those congressmen rip into each other over this whole Enron thing on C-SPAN, you can almost forget for a minute that Sept. 11 ever happened."

With House Republicans and Democrats spending much of Monday's session trading blame for the recession-damaged economy, congressional acrimony is back—and the nation appears to be welcoming its return with open arms.

"American politics are just as ineffectual, small-minded, and short-sighted as always," Robert Novak said Saturday on CNN's The Capital Gang. "If there's one thing the terrorists cannot take away, it is our capacity for infighting. If we just pull together to get through this crisis, I have every faith that we will come apart as we always do." Ø

Oppel first revealed her intentions to abandon lesbianism at approximately 3 a.m. Monday, toward the conclusion of an emotional six-hour conversation with Leslie Heenan-Lynn. A fellow activist and her girlfriend of four months, Heenan-Lynn was shocked when Oppel "dropped the bomb."

"Leslie was totally crying," said Katie Jacobsen, 19, one of Heenan-Lynn's roommates at the Tralfamadore Co-Op housing facility. "She said Amanda had been acting weird and avoiding her all month. Then she said Amanda told her she wanted to re-evaluate their relationship. Leslie said maybe it's because their sex life was so bad. I never knew this, but apparently, Amanda wasn't ever really all that affectionate in private. Isn't that strange? The way she'd yell and scream at rallies, I always assumed Amanda was a total lesbian sexual dynamo."

According to friends, Heenan-Lynn started getting "weird vibes" from Oppel upon her return from a December trip to Barbados with her father, investment banker Jonathan Oppel, 55, and his new wife Cassie, 31. Sources close to the Oppels report that Amanda, who had been distant from her father prior to the vacation, "really bonded" with him on the trip. She also reportedly spent a great deal of time with fellow travelers and close family friends Greg and Karen Garner, and even more with their son Brad, 23, heir to the Garner office-supply empire.

According to a phone conversation overheard by roommate and interpretive-dance performance artist Clytemnestra Moon, Oppel plans to meet Brad Garner in Cancun over spring break.

"This is just beyond comprehension, Amanda giving up The Life to be with

the oppressor," Moon said. "And she showed such enthusiasm for lesbian consciousness, too. Especially when it came to fundraising."

An ambitious student who was active in student government at her Mamaroneck, NY, high school, Oppel first showed signs of an emergent lesbian identity in September 2000. That fall, shortly after enrolling in an Intro To Women's History course, she began wearing Birkenstock sandals and listening to Ani DiFranco. She quickly rose through the ranks of Oberlin's progressive activist scene, becoming a fixture at Student Empowerment Network meetings.

Her campus political career reached a new peak last year, when, running on a lesbian-empowerment platform, she was elected co-president of the Progressive Student Council Steering Committee. In the fall semester of 2001, Oppel reduced her courseload to just eight credits to devote herself more fully to "awareness-raising" and her "Her Turn" column in the alternative student newspaper The Insurrectionist.

Throughout her 16-month lesbian tenure, Oppel frequently made provocative, inflammatory pronouncements of lesbian power, often criticizing her male classmates for their "phallocentric gender slavery."

"Man, I remember once telling her I thought her friend Liz was kind of cute," said fellow junior Mike Nygard, 20. "She got unbelievably offended and lectured me for two hours on Lookism and the society-wide evils of the Male Gaze. At the time, I felt awful and apologized profusely for my insensitivity. I remember thinking how lucky I was to have someone like Amanda to point out how sexist I didn't even know I was being. Now, though, I'm thinking

maybe she was just being a sanctimonious, self-righteous bitch. Of course, it would be sexist of me to think that, but I sort of do."

In spite of the shock among Oppel's classmates, older lesbians familiar with the situation were not surprised by the gender-preference reversal.

"Really? An East Coast rebel girl suddenly isn't a dyke anymore halfway through her junior year of college? That's shocking," said Gwen Mims, 46, author and Oberlin women's-studies professor. "What a stunner. Wow."

Nevertheless, many of Oppel's former peers still cannot bring themselves to believe that her angry-dyke-activist days are over.

"It just doesn't add up," said Campus Womyn's Caucus chairwomon Mia Petrovich, 20. "If it's true, that would imply that there is some aspect of collegiate revolutionary Marxist-feminist lesbian identity that is, in some way, less than completely genuine. And that's something my most heartfelt convictions will simply not allow me to accept, at least for the next few semesters, anyway." Ø

Above: Oppel, post-lesbianism.

and He frequently employs the phrase 'I AM the Lord' to intimidate potential deserters," prosecuting attorney Geoffrey Albert said. "God uses other questionable strongarm tactics to secure and maintain humanity's devotion, demanding, among other things, that people sanctify their firstborn to Him and obtain

> To comply with federal antitrust statutes, God will be required to divide Himself into a pantheon of specialized gods, each representing a force of nature or a specific human custom, occupation, or state of mind.

circumcisions as a show of faith. There have also been documented examples of Him smiting those caught worshipping graven images."

Attorneys for God did not deny such charges. They did, however, note that God offers followers "unbeatable incentives" in return for their loyalty, including eternal salvation, protection from harm, and "fruitfulness."

"God was the first to approach the Jewish people with a 'covenant' contract that guaranteed they would be the most favored in His eyes, and He handed down standards of morality, cleanliness, and personal conduct that exceeded anything else practiced at the time," lead defense attorney Patrick Childers said. "He readily admits to being a 'jealous' God, not because He is threatened by the prospect of competition from other gods, but because He is utterly convinced of the righteousness of His cause and that He is the best choice for mortals. Many of these so-called gods couldn't care less if somebody bears false witness or covets thy neighbor's wife. Our client, on the other hand, is truly a 'People's God.'"

In the end, however, God was unable to convince Schofield that He did not deliberately create a marketplace hostile to rival deities. God's attorneys attempted to convince the judge of His openness to rivals, pointing to His longtime participation in the "Holy Trinity," but the effort failed when Schofield determined that Jesus Christ and the Holy Ghost are "more God subsidiaries than competitors."

To comply with federal antitrust statutes, God will be required to divide Himself into a pantheon of specialized gods, each representing a force of nature or a specific human custom, occupation, or state of mind.

"There will most likely be a sun god,

moon god, sea god, and rain god," said religion-industry watcher Catherine Bailey. "Then there will be some second-tier deities, like a god of wine, a goddess of the harvest, and perhaps a few who symbolize human love and/or blacksmithing."

Leading theologians are applauding the God breakup, saying that it will usher in a new era of greater worshipping options, increased efficiency, and more personalized service.

"God's prayer-response system has been plagued by massive, chronic backlogs, and many prayers have gone unanswered in the process," said Gene Suozzi, a Phoenix-area Wiccan. "With polytheism, you pray to the deity specifically devoted to your concern. If you wish to have children, you pray to the fertility goddess. If you want to do well on an exam, you pray to the god of wisdom, and so on. This decentralization will result in more individualized service and swifter response times."

Other religion experts are not so confident that the breakup is for the best, pointing to the chaotic nature of polytheistic worship and noting that multiple gods demand an elaborate regimen of devotion that today's average worshipper may find arduous and inconvenient.

"If people want a world in which they must lay burnt offerings before an earthenware household god to ensure that their car will start on a cold winter morning, I suppose they can have it," said Father Thomas Reinholdt, theology professor at Chicago's Loyola University. "What's more, lesser deities are infamous for their mercurial nature. They often meddle directly in diplomatic affairs, abduct comely young mortal women for their concubines, and are not above demanding an infant or two for sacrifice. Monotheism, for all its faults, at least means convenience, stability, and a consistent moral code."

One deity who is welcoming the verdict is the ancient Greek god Zeus, who described himself as "jubilant" and "absolutely vindicated."

"For thousands of years, I've been screaming that this third-rate sky deity ripped me off wholesale," said Zeus, speaking from his Mt. Olympus residence. "Every good idea He ever had He took from me: Who first created men in his own image? Who punished mankind for its sins? Who lived eternally up in the clouds? And the whole fearsome, patriarchal, white-beard, thunderbolt thing? I was doing that eons before this two-bit hustler started horning in on the action."

Lawyers for God say they plan to appeal Schofield's ruling and are prepared to go all the way to the Supreme Court if necessary.

"This decision is a crushing blow to God worshippers everywhere, and we refuse to submit to a breakup until every possible avenue of argument is pursued," Childers said. "I have every confidence that God will ultimately win, as He and His lawyers are all-powerful." ∅

Take This Job And Love It

By Herbert Kornfeld
Accounts Receivable
Supervisor

Yo, yo, yo, H-Dog is back in tha house, all-new an' luvvin' tha boos in tha '02, know what I'm sayin'? First off, big upz to tha whole Midstate Office Supply Accountz Reeceevable posse, who took top honaz at tha officewide holiday banquet foe Best Departmental Attendance of 2001. Aw, yeah, you know how we do. Now, some banquet attendees wuz hatin' on tha Accountz Reeceevable posse, sayin' Human Resourcez shoulda won cuz of all tha ovatime Bob Cowan put in when he revised tha employee handbook. I say, fuck them H.R. bitchez. Buncha lightweights. They may have tha shorties an' tha fame, but when it come to gettin' tha hardcore accountin' done, A.R. beats they sorry asses hands down.

Ordinarily, yours truly, tha K-Hova, gots no time foe no silly holiday banquetz. But my homegirl Gladys be leavin' Midstate, an' she an' her baby-daddy wuz takin' off foe Oklahoma tha next day. She say she got a job balancin' tha bookz foe some Big Willie R.V. dealership her uncle owns. Whateva. Beatz me why she wanna leave a bangin' outfit like Midstate, but as long as she continue to represent tha Principlez of Accountin' to tha fullest, I gots no beef. Mad love to mah homegirl Gladys.

Now, tha banquet wuz pretty cool foe a banquet, but by about 9 p.m., I had enough. So afta I say goodbye to Gladys, I head ova to tha buffet table, toss a bunch of pigs-in-blankets an' potato salad into a Gladware containa I brought foe tha occasion, and cut outta there. Yo, I know what you thinkin', but if they be delvin' into tha company scrilla to give tha Midstate krew a big spread foe tha holiday banquet, then it ain't freeloadin'. Ain't no shame in tha H-Dog livin' large on tha company coin. I worked my ass off this year.

As I revved up tha Nite Rida, my cell phone ring. It be my homey Sir Casio KL7000.

"Yo, Dog, all-you-can-eat popcorn shrimp tonight at Lums," Casio say. "Tha whole reeceevable posse gonna be there. You in?"

"Shit, man, I gots to refrigerate these muthafukkin' cocktail weenies wit' a quickness," I say. "Popcorn shrimp? Why didn't you give me no advance heads-up?"

"I gave you a holla as soon as I heard, Dog," Casio say. "I just found out mahself."

"S'all good," I say. "Them weenies can probably last in tha Nite Rida foe a few hourz, anyway. I'm in."

"Cool. I see you there in 20 minutes," Casio say. "Actually, Dog, I gots somethin' more to tell you 'bout tonight. Check it out: Mike Pisano is back in town. He just graduated from Cornell and is gonna hook up wit tha ol' krew tonight ova at Lums."

Mike Pisano? Damn. I ain't seen Mike since he left tha hood to go to Cornell. He wuz a local kid, and when he wuz 16, I took him unda mah wing and educated him in tha wayz of accountin'. He took to my teachin' well, and in no time, he wuz practically mah right-hand man at Midstate. Tha A.R. bruthahs called him "Tha Addin' Machine," because even though he wuz still underage, he krunched numbahs faster than a Power Mac G4. But I didn't call Mike no "Addin' Machine." I gave him tha dope moniker "ACO-LYTE," cuz he wuz practically my protégé, jus' like I wuz to CPA-ONE back in tha day, when I accounted freestyle on tha streetz wit' him as mah mentor.

> Now, some banquet attendees wuz hatin' on tha Accountz Reeceevable posse, sayin' Human Resourcez shoulda won cuz of all tha ovatime Bob Cowan put in when he revised tha employee handbook. I say, fuck them H.R. bitchez.

Back in tha day, ACO-LYTE an' I wuz mad tight, only we didn't see eye-to-eye on tha college thang. He thought a college education wuz tha tikket to a lifetime of success, an' I said fuck that boo-ya. Now, tha H-Dog gots nuthin' but respect foe anyone who wantz to get they learn on. But I ain't down wit' that liberal-arts bullshit. I into vocational schoolin', the kind where you learn a real trade. I got mah accountin' degree from Eastech Bidness College, an' I ain't never looked back. I ain't got time foe none o' that liberal-artz shit, wit' its history and philosophizin' an' all them books that say how you should be nice to tha bitchez even if they playin' you like a fool. Huh. ACO-LYTE kept sayin' that learnin' that shit would broaden his mind, but what's any of that got to do wit' gettin' yo'self some SKEELZ?

Tha day ACO-LYTE left Midstate wuz a tough one, 'cause he wuz like mah baby bruthah. But when I walk

see KORNFELD page 60

into Lums and peep him chillin' at a long table wit' tha rest o' tha Reeceevable posse, I couldn't believe what I saw. ACO-LYTE wuz all decked out in some wack threads. He wasn't wearin' no short-sleeved button-down shirt and tie, or no acrylic sweata vest and Dockaz slaxx like any self-respectin' A.R. bruthah, but jeanz an' a black T-shirt. An' a black leatha jacket slung ova his chair. He also let his hair grow long an' looked like he ain't shaved in maybe two days.

"Ay, yo, ACO-LYTE, what tha dilly?" I say. "'Sup wit tha Fonzie shit? You look like some kinda sellout, bro." I didn't like to be hatin' on mah homey, but that Fonzie shit wuz mad foul, know what I'm sayin'?

"Come on, Herbert, let's just relax and have a good time," ACO-LYTE say. "I may not look the same on the outside, but I honestly haven't changed inside. I'm just trying to update my look a little, okay?"

"Yeah, Dog," Kount Von Numbakrunch turn to me and say. "I think Tha Addin' Machine looks mad cool. Thas a muthafukkin' Wilson's leatha jacket he got on there."

"Shut tha fuck up, Numbakrunch," I say. "ACO-LYTE, you trippin' or somethin'? Why you be frontin' like that? You look wack. Back in tha day, you wuz mah numba-one disciple. You wuz mah hand-picked successor, tha one who would take up tha Kornfeld throne after I retired and headed off to Branson wit' mah mad 401(k) retirement scratch. What tha fuck happened? You ain't even kickin' tha A.R.

"Ay, yo, ACO-LYTE, what tha dilly?" I say. "'Sup wit tha Fonzie shit? You look like some kinda sellout, bro." I didn't like to be hatin' on mah homey, but that Fonzie shit wuz mad foul, know what I'm sayin'?

---

talk no more. You sound like a little A.P. bitch."

"I'm sorry, but you've got it all wrong, Herbert," ACO-LYTE say. "There's no use trying to hide it from you, so I'll just come right out and say it: I don't want to be in the A.R. anymore. Or do accounting of any kind. I graduated in December with a double major in political science and Russian history."

"You did what, muthafukka?"

"Herbert, I'm not the sellout. You are," ACO-LYTE say. "You act all tough, but the truth of the matter is, you're suffering from a wage-slave mentality. You only care about material things—getting paid and getting

laid."

DAMN.

ACO-LYTE go on to tell me that since I a non-union employee of Midstate Office Supply, tha H-Dog be vulnerable as shit. He hear Midstate employees wuz payin' twice tha health-

---

I ain't tryin' to hear that. "You wrong," I say. "If Midstate don't give a shit about its peeps, how come they give us a big spread foe X-mas? Back in tha Nite Rida, I gots a Gladware containa, all full of leftova weenies an' shit."

---

insurance premium we wuz last year wit' no raise in salary, an' that Midstate laid off 10 percent of its workforce, even though it took in mad loot last fiscal year.

I ain't tryin' to hear that. "You wrong," I say. "If Midstate don't give a shit about its peeps, how come they give us a big spread foe X-mas? Back in tha Nite Rida, I gots a Gladware containa, all full of leftova weenies an' shit. Besides, if tha A.R. bruthahood don't hold it down at Midstate, there ain't nobody to keep them wack Accountz Payabo foolz in check."

But ACO-LYTE say that bullshit, too. "Don't you see, Herbert? The whole A.R./A.P. rivalry only serves to keep the company's employees divided, and to distract both sides from the real enemy: the upper management of Midstate Office Supply," he say. "You guys should be uniting to let management know that you can't be pushed around. Just because you work for them doesn't mean you can't make demands on them."

I ain't no fool. I know bullshit when I hear it. So I gets right to tha heart of tha matta and aks ACO-LYTE, "If you care so much about tha Accountin' bruthahs an' sistahs, why didn't you get certified instead of chasin' some wack poli-sci and Russian degree?"

He start shiftin' his feet a little and hesitatin', mutterin' somethin' about attendin' grad school. That only get mah bullshit detector goin' off all tha more. I press him, and he finally say it.

"Well, I guess that I, uh, ultimately decided that, for me, from a career standpoint, accounting is too… boring."

Half tha A.R. bruthahs at that table had to hold me back. Tha Letta Opener of Death wuz practically burnin' a hole in the pocket of my Membaz Only jacket. It didn't take long foe tha Lums hostess to notice, an' soon tha manager be clearin' us

Your Horoscope

By Lloyd Schumner Sr.
Retired Machinist and
A.A.P.B.-Certified Astrologer

Aries: (March 21–April 19)
Upcoming events will give you insight into the origin of the phrases "hog-tied," "beaten like a red-headed stepchild," and "Well, I'll be dipped in shit."

Taurus: (April 20–May 20)
Your misguided, hippie efforts to tie-dye a cat will finally see success, but at an unspeakable cost.

Gemini: (May 21–June 21)
Nothing can match the humiliation you will feel next week when one sailor after another appears on your doorstep and claims to be your biological father.

Cancer: (June 22–July 22)
You just can't shake the feeling that, homespun or not, that Bombeck lady sure knew what she was talking about.

Leo: (July 23–Aug. 22)
You will combine a pair of novelty underpants and your considerable ventriloquism skills to give a certain special lady the worst first date of her life.

Virgo: (Aug. 23–Sept. 22)
You'd quit your job telling kids about exposed power lines today if there were any other work options for a talking, hard-hat-wearing safety otter.

Libra: (Sept. 23–Oct. 23)
This week, you will prove the binomial theorem, posit a rule of gravitation, and develop a new theory of color, only to find that it's all been done before.

Scorpio: (Oct. 24–Nov. 21)
It is a sign of the degradation of academia that your opinions are taken seriously on many DeVry campuses.

Sagittarius: (Nov. 22–Dec. 21)
You passionately believe that modern society fosters political, intellectual, and spiritual repression, which is just fine by you.

Capricorn: (Dec. 22–Jan. 19)
Thursday will find you talking to a walrus who urgently wishes to discuss cabbage, kings, nautical vessels, footwear, sealing wax, and possibly winged pigs.

Aquarius: (Jan. 20–Feb. 18)
You're starting to realize why you live in a huge New York City apartment where the kitchen is part of a giant living room with a couch that faces a camera.

Pisces: (Feb. 19–March 20)
Nothing will ever convince you that the Bon Jovi shit they play these days is real country music.

---

out. That manager has a runnin' vendetta against me ever since I dunked some A.P. sucka's head in a vat of Thousand Island dressing at the

---

Shit, man, what wuz wit' all that preachy aftaschool-special shit? ACO-LYTE be buggin' out. I let him have tha last word, though.

Lums salad bar a few years ago. But that A.P. fucka deserved to be dunked, just like ACO-LYTE deserved a date wit' tha L.O.D. afta what he said.

Dag, yo. What's been goin' on these days? First, Jerry Tha Sharpie Head crosses ova to Payabo. Now, tha bruthah who once stood to inherit mah phat collection of hangin' file folders, dope-ass three-hole punch,

and pneumatic desk chair wit' adjustable lumbar support decides that mah life's work not only beneath him, it boring, too.

Afta walking out of Lums, tha A.R. posse wuz still holdin' me down as ACO-LYTE hustled to his hoopty. "It saddens me that we can't have a civilized conversation about this, Herbert," he say as he pull away. "Someday you'll finally learn that you can't solve your problems by whipping out your letter opener every time somebody disagrees with you."

Shit, man, what wuz wit' all that preachy aftaschool-special shit? ACO-LYTE be buggin' out. I let him have tha last word, though. Not 'cause he had somethin' on me, but 'cause I couldn't undastand how a dude could experience tha joys of balancin' an' journalizin' and still give it all up foe some poli-sci and Russian boo-ya.

I still can't understand it. An' to this day, them cocktail weenies an' that potato salad be sittin' in mah fridge, turnin' all green and shit 'cause I didn't think I'd enjoy them afta what happened. H-Dog OUT. ⊘

Kurt Warner Cheered On By Wire-Haired Man-Goblin

see SPORTS page 10C

Haunted Tape Dispenser Unsure How To Demonstrate Hauntedness

see LOCAL page 2D

Man Accidentally Rents *Delta Force 4* Instead Of *3*

see VIDEO page 7B

STATshot

A look at the numbers that shape your world.

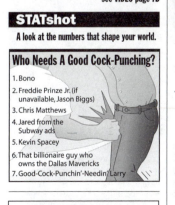

Who Needs A Good Cock-Punching?

1. Bono
2. Freddie Prinze Jr. (if unavailable, Jason Biggs)
3. Chris Matthews
4. Jared from the Subway ads
5. Kevin Spacey
6. That billionaire guy who owns the Dallas Mavericks
7. Good-Cock-Punchin'-Needin' Larry

THE ONION • $2.00 US • $3.00 CAN

the ONION®

VOLUME 38 ISSUE 04   AMERICA'S FINEST NEWS SOURCE™   07–13 FEBRUARY 2002

Bush Earmarks 1.5 Billion Gold Stars For Education

WASHINGTON, DC—Vowing to give the nation's public schools "a much-needed boost," President Bush announced Monday that his 2003 budget proposal would allocate 1.5 billion gold-star stickers for education.

"As class sizes continue to grow and test scores continue to decline, our public schools are in a state of crisis," Bush said at a White House press conference. "There is no more time for deliberation. It is time to act. Our children need these adhesive gold stars."

Bush went on to describe the "alarming state" of many of the nation's public schools, citing underpaid teachers,

buildings badly in need of repair, and woefully outdated textbooks.

"If a child is going to learn under these conditions, he or she is going to need lots of encouragement," Bush said. "These gold stars will serve as reinforcement for our best students while motivating underachievers to do better. You have no idea what a difference it makes to a young child's self-esteem to see a big, shiny star at the top of his or her spelling test. I know it made a big difference to me as a child."

Bush said the stars, which are expected to cost the government an esti-

see BUSH page 65

Right: Bush holds up a Dayton, OH, fourth-grader's gold-star-adorned book report on Ferdinand Magellan.

Indo-Pakistani Tensions Mount At Local Amoco

The Detroit-area Amoco station where hostilities have erupted between Indian-born owner Rajesh Srinivasan (left) and Majid Ashraf (right), the Pakistani manager of the Subway franchise inside.

DETROIT—Indo-Pakistani tensions continue to escalate this week at the Eight-Mile and Telegraph Road Amoco, where hostilities between owner Rajesh Srinivasan and in-store Subway mini-franchise manager Majid Ashraf threaten to spill over into all-out war.

"We have made every effort to extend the hand of friendship to the Pakistani delegation that runs the Amoco Mart's Subway Express," said the India-born Srinivasan, 49, in a statement to the press Monday. "But that hand, my own hand with which I built this business for my family, has been repeatedly and without remorse slapped away."

Leased and operated by Pakistani immigrant Ashraf and his family

see TENSIONS page 64

Deaf Man's Deaf Friends Way Too Into Deaf Culture

COLUMBIA, MD—Jonathan Deeds, a 26-year-old Rockville resident who lost his hearing as an infant, feels a growing sense of alienation from his deaf friends, who he says are "way too into" deaf culture.

"I'm deaf, but it's not like it's my whole life or anything," said Deeds, a 26-year-old sales administrator, speaking through an American Sign Language interpreter Monday. "I wish I could say the same for some of the people I hang out with."

According to Deeds, friends Rob Planter and Ben Trantvan automatically gravitate toward "all things

deaf," including deaf greeting cards, deaf Kabuki theater, and "Deaf Elvis," a D.C.-area Elvis impersonator.

"Lately, it seems like everything they do is deafness-related," Deeds said. "Like, for example, they're really into this deaf comedian named Ken Glickman. He's all right, I guess, but I don't see why his being deaf makes him any funnier. But try telling that to Rob and Ben when they're cracking each other up signing one of his 'Deafinitions.'"

"They think I'm some sort of sellout because I prefer comedians from the

see DEAF CULTURE page 63

Above: Jonathan Deeds.

61

The Al Qaeda Captives

U.S. leaders are divided over whether Al Qaeda detainees in Cuba should be classified as POWs and protected under Geneva Convention laws. What do *you* think?

"Goddammit, just when we finally get some prisoners, everybody wants us to be all nice to them."

Roger Koss
File Clerk

"I have to admit, it's funny the way those Marines had them bowing twice a day in the direction of Oscar Mayer world headquarters."

Donald Matthews
Architect

"This is a totally different situation. Those Geneva Convention laws were written back when we were fighting white people."

Bruce Nowell
Systems Analyst

"Geneva Convention, Schmeneva Convention. Refute *that*, if you possess the erudition."

Marcus Moore
Landscaper

"We need to rough up these Al Qaeda guys a little if we're ever going to get them to confess who the one true God is."

Diana George
Homemaker

"I don't think we should risk making martyrs of these men. Notice I said 'martyrs,' not 'quadriplegics.'"

Danielle Lund
Florist

The Tyson Split

On Jan. 17, Dr. Monica Tyson, wife of boxer Mike Tyson, filed for divorce. What grounds did she cite in the legal papers?

- Would repeatedly punch out any plate of food placed before him
- Despite repeated promises of fidelity, wouldn't stop raping other women
- Could only communicate feelings with his own special language consisting of jabs and uppercuts
- Would scream "Beer!" at refrigerator and then become enraged when nothing would happen
- Was unemployed for months and sometimes years at a time
- Chewed heads off her Hummel collection
- Required explanation that he did not own Tyson Foods every time commercial came on
- Insisted on raising children as batshit-loony Neanderthal thugs

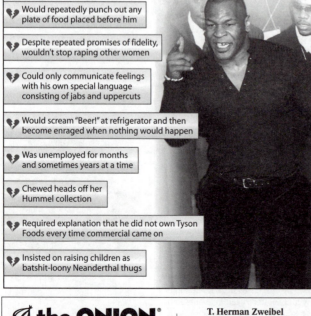

the ONION
America's Finest News Source.™

Herman Ulysses Zweibel
Founder

T. Herman Zweibel
Publisher Emeritus
J. Phineas Zweibel
Publisher
Maxwell Prescott Zweibel
Editor-In-Chief

62

Secretary's Day Has Become So Commercialized

By Marybeth Pryce

Is nothing sacred?

Secretary's Day used to mean something. It was the one day each year when a boss took time out of his busy schedule to let his secretary know just how important she is to the day-to-day operations of the office. But now, April 24 is just a flimsy excuse to sell cards, flowers, and gift certificates. How could they turn such a beautiful holiday into something so commercialized?

Every year, the stores seem to start promoting Secretary's Day earlier and earlier. The day after St. Patrick's Day, you can already see malls replacing the shamrocks and leprechauns with Secretary's Day coffee mugs and paperweights. All for the love of the almighty dollar. Is that what the true spirit of Secretary's Day is all about? I hardly think so.

Perhaps I'm dating myself, but I remember a time when Secretary's Day was about more than exploitation and crass commercialism. When Hallmark created the holiday in the '60s, it was to celebrate the women (and some men!) who do the actual work around an office. But if Hallmark

> Every year, the stores seem to start promoting Secretary's Day earlier and earlier. The day after St. Patrick's Day, you can already see malls replacing the shamrocks and leprechauns with Secretary's Day coffee mugs and paperweights.

founder Joyce C. Hall could see all the opportunistic spam e-mails and phony-baloney FTD Florist ads, he'd be rolling in his grave.

Once upon a time, I used to get really excited for Secretary's Day. A week or two before April 24 rolled around, my friend Beth from the typing pool and I would stroll downtown together and browse the gift-shop windows to see the beautiful Secretary's Day displays. I'd spend most of Secretary's Eve lying awake in bed, wondering if the Secre-Fairy was going to bring me a coffee mug filled with Hershey's Kisses. Or maybe, if I'd been an extra-good secretary that year, a gift certificate for a free manicure or facial.

Don't get me wrong. I'm not greedy. I'd gladly settle for a single rose, so long as it came from the heart. Sadly, it's not that way with a lot of secretaries these days. If a secretary doesn't get a big bouquet, musical greeting card, and expensive day-spa

> Don't get me wrong. I'm not greedy. I'd gladly settle for a single rose, so long as it came from the heart. Sadly, it's not that way with a lot of secretaries these days.

certificate, there's hell to pay. Today's secretaries act like the presents are a birthright rather than a joyous reward for a job well done.

It's a darn shame that these gals don't know or even care about the true meaning of Secretary's Day. It isn't about the superficial stuff. No, it's about being made to feel appreciated. It's a chance for your boss to let you know that as you run for coffee and file stacks of reports and spend three hours a day breathing in Xerox-machine toner fumes, your efforts are not going unnoticed. But most secretaries don't stay in the field long enough to realize that. They usually move on to a better job or go back to school or get married.

Speaking of bosses, their attitude has changed, too. Bosses used to have a healthy respect for Secretary's Day. They'd put some serious thought into how best to express their gratitude. But now, they can just waltz into any florist in town and buy a pre-made, cookie-cutter Secretary's Day bouquet right off the shelf. Whatever happened to a boss and florist working together to create a personalized floral arrangement that reflects the secretary's tastes and personality?

I could understand people forgetting the meaning of holidays like Cardiovascular Technologist's Day or Second Cousin's Day. But those are minor holidays compared to Secretary's Day. And no matter what Madison Avenue would have you believe, it's not about baubles and trinkets. When you truly embrace Secretary's Day with all your heart, the feeling stays with you the whole rest of the year.

Father Bitter That Son Has Everything He Never Had

WICHITA, KS—Local pharmacist Ed Raschi, 52, admitted Monday that he is occasionally bitter that his son Brandon has everything he never had growing up.

Despite taking pride in the fact that he has been able to provide a better

> **"Brandon is very fortunate; he gets to go to college next year,"** Raschi said. **"He'll be able to just go to college and dink around for a while, sow some wild oats, and 'find himself.'"**

life for his 17-year-old son, Raschi said he sometimes catches himself feeling jealousy and resentment.

"Sometimes, I'll hear Brandon taking a shower, and I'll think, 'Hope you appreciate that shower,'" Raschi said. "I usually feel guilty after I think things like that, because a father's supposed to want only the best for his kids. But deep down inside, part of me resents the fact that when I was his age, I had to go down to the YMCA to shower because my father was too drunk to fix anything."

Continued Raschi: "When I see those fancy soaps Brandon uses, it makes me think of the caustic industrial

Above: Ed Raschi and his son Brandon.

soap they had at the Y. He really doesn't know what it's like to go without certain things or use industrial lye soap on your private parts."

To escape economically depressed Mayetta, KS, in 1971, Raschi enlisted in the Army—a path he more often than not hopes Brandon, 17, will be able to avoid.

"Brandon is very fortunate; he gets to go to college next year," Raschi said. "He'll be able to just go to college and dink around for a while, sow some wild oats, and 'find himself.' I never got to do that. Instead, I spent 10 months waist deep in rice paddies, waiting for the Viet Cong to strike at any second. After seeing the horrors I saw in 'Nam, you don't waste your time when you get back. But, thank God, Brandon doesn't have to look at life that way. Must be nice."

Raschi is alternately happy and resentful that his son won't face the difficult life lessons he did at an early age.

"I'm glad Brandon has had a better go of it than me," Raschi said. "He's never known what it's like to work three jobs while putting yourself through school. As a father, it makes me feel good to know he'll never have to unload boxes at a cannery in the morning, scrub toilets in the university buildings all afternoon, then drive a cab until sun-up with only a scratchy AM radio for company. Then again, that really stinks that I had to do it but he doesn't."

Brandon has also not had to learn the value of a dollar.

"Brandon is a great kid, and he gets good grades, but when I see him fritter away his allowance on Big Macs and rap CDs, I get a little upset," Raschi said. "When I was his age, every dollar I earned went toward food for my brothers and sisters, or paying the electric bill. I didn't get to spend it on a Game Cube. I mean, those games look pretty fun, but damn if I ever get to play them."

Though Raschi's envy doesn't make him love his son any less, he does wish that he had had the sort of nurturing, comfortable upbringing Brandon enjoys.

"Both my parents were emotionally distant and had violent tempers," Raschi said. "Brandon, on the other hand, has warm, loving parents who look out for him. He should be thankful every day that he has a devoted mother and father. The lucky bastard." ∅

DEAF CULTURE from page 61

'hearing world,'" Deeds said. "I'm sorry, but I'd rather lip-read Chris Rock than sit through 45 minutes of Ken Glickman just because we've got something in common."

Deeds added that Planter and Trantvan assert their deaf identity in areas wholly unrelated to one's ability to hear.

"The other day, Rob tells me he's changed his e-mail address to nohear-rob@deafemail.net," Deeds said. "Then he gives me the Deaf E-Mail web address so I could get one myself. Why would I? It's e-mail, for God's sake. Why would I need some kind of deaf e-mail provider?"

Planter and Trantvan, Deeds said, rarely participate in activities if some deafness theme is not incorporated.

"Last Sunday, Rob and Ben invited me to 'the art museum.' I figured they meant one of the big ones down in D.C., like the National Gallery or maybe the Corcoran," Deeds said. "But then I find out they mean some place called the American Hearing Aid Museum in Gaithersburg. Who wants to spend their Sunday looking at antique hearing aids?"

Continued Deeds: "Just to get a rise out of them, I pointed out that hearing aids are not for the deaf, but for people who can at least hear a little bit.

> **"Just to get a rise out of them, I pointed out that hearing aids are not for the deaf, but for people who can at least hear a little bit."**

They got really pissed, saying we had to support all our hearing-impaired brothers and sisters."

"'Brothers and sisters'? What's with this whole solidarity thing? Are deaf people going to start a revolution or something? I just don't get their whole 'us-versus-them' attitude," Deeds said. "You can be pro-deaf without being against people who can hear, or 'the silence-impaired,' as Rob

and Ben call them."

Planter and Trantvan are also critical of Deeds' failure to date deaf women.

"You should've seen Rob and Ben's hands flying when they met Amanda," Deeds said. "They called her an 'auralist,' just because she can hear. They act like I'm rejecting my deaf heritage or something, as if there were such a thing. I guess I should be like them and pine away for Marlee Matlin."

In spite of his annoyance with his friends' overzealousness, Deeds said he bears no antagonism toward deaf culture.

"I'm glad there are lots of things out there specifically tailored toward deaf people, I really am," Deeds said. "Ten years ago, they probably wouldn't have had a skydiving class for the deaf. I don't think I'd want a skydiving instructor who couldn't understand my sign language, because that'd be pretty dangerous. But why make deafness the center of your life? There's a ton of great stuff out there in the world, and some of it makes sounds." ∅

since March 1999, the in-store Subway occupies 30 percent of the Amoco Mart's total retail space. Ever since their arrival, the Ashrafs have been the subject of increasingly inflammatory rhetoric from Srinivasan, who charges, among other things, that they are not mopping their fair share of the disputed territory near the coolers.

In a terse Feb. 1 statement to reporters, Ashraf struck back.

"I come to America to make business, not to be insulted by the son of a New Delhi whore," Ashraf said. "I take my orders from [Subway regional manager] Larry [Ferber], not from son-of-bitch Indian dog who says to me where I mop and where I not mop."

Though tensions have existed ever since the Ashrafs took over the Subway, the situation began sharply deteriorating in December of last year. Upon seeing Srinivasan sweep the parking lot at his wife's behest, Ashraf mocked his Indian counterpart, calling him "a quaking little baby goat" and questioning the manhood of "anyone who would take orders from a woman."

"What Majid doesn't recognize is that there are significant differences between his Islamic culture and Rajesh's Hindu culture regarding gender roles," said Dr. James Sasser, a Harvard professor of South Asian studies. "But, to be fair, Rajesh didn't help matters when he came after Majid with that squeegee."

Relations further deteriorated on Jan. 20, when a dispute over cleaning-supplies inventory led to a full-blown shouting match between the small-business owners. For 45 minutes, Srinivasan and Ashraf loudly traded insults in full view of customers, and the episode reached its apex when Srinivasan called Ashraf "a filthy,

Pakistani-held territory

Indian-held territory

lying cheat lower than the untouchable caste of my native land."

Srinivasan then spit on the floor in disdain, prompting Ashraf to retaliate by hurling an economy-sized contain-

---

For 45 minutes, Srinivasan and Ashraf loudly traded insults in full view of customers.

---

er of Janitor In A Drum™ at his rival's head.

Though the skirmish resulted in no serious injuries, it did end what little dialogue there had been between the two sides. Neither Ashraf nor Srinivasan is currently speaking to the other, and both are said to be hiding the employee bathroom key in an attempt to force the other out.

Acquired by the Srinivasan family in 1987, Eight-Mile and Telegraph Road Amoco has long been a hotbed of Indo-Pakistani tension, as its strategic location makes it critical to Pakistani cab drivers needing to refuel on their way from Detroit garages to the more lucrative suburban trade routes. Fluctuating gas prices have, over the years, resulted in strained relations between the station's Indian owners and its Pakistani cab-driver customers, but the economic interdependence of the two groups in a highly competitive climate kept such tensions in check.

Given the volatility of the current situation, officials from Amoco and Subway, who license franchise rights to the Srinivasan and Ashraf families, are keeping a close eye on the troubled region.

"Something must be done, or we're looking at a situation that could lead to all-out war," said Frederick Foss, Subway director of franchise rela-

tions for southeast Michigan. "It's in the best interests of everyone in the area that positive relations are maintained between the two sides."

Community members are equally eager to see stability restored to the once-peaceful Amoco. Among the concerned local residents are Sandy Kreil, the nurse who gets coffee at the Amoco Mart on her way to work; local panhandlers "Dan-O" and "Malik"; and Frannie Koenig, the elderly woman who drops in every morning for a Diet Dr. Pepper and a pack of Newport Lights.

In spite of the concern, diplomatic initiatives on the part of Subway and Amoco officials have met with failure.

"I do not see why I must refill ice machine every day when Ashraf's customers have taken away 40 percent of my business for soda," said Srinivasan before walking out on a Jan. 11 negotiating session. "You go die, Mr. Ashraf. I am not listening to you anymore."

In the wake of the breakdown in negotiations, many observers are fearful that the Indian family will "drop the bomb" and refuse Ashraf access to the Dumpster behind the station, effectively forcing him to pay for a separate commercial garbage service and increase his costs beyond profitability. This move would leave Ashraf with little choice but to retaliate with a strike against the candy aisle.

"If such a scenario were to unfold, the devastation unleashed upon the Amoco and its surrounding environs would be vast," Sasser said. "Without the Amoco Mart, locals would have to go all the way over to the Exxon on Gratiot [Avenue] for gas and snacks. Something must be done immediately, or it could spell doomsday for everyone." *∅*

NEWS IN BRIEF

Showers With Girlfriend Increasingly Cleansing-Focused

TALLAHASSEE, FL—Over the past two months, Jeff Pinnock's showers with girlfriend Angela Dunn have gradually shifted in focus from sex play to actual body-cleansing. "When we first started dating, she'd ask me to 'wash' her breasts, and I'd ask her to help me soap up my penis," the 23-year-old Pinnock disclosed Monday. "Now, we both mostly just clean ourselves."

Report: Recently Laid-Off Workers Not Doing Enough To Help Economy

WASHINGTON, DC—According to a Labor Department report released Monday, Americans who lost their

jobs in the past year are doing little to aid the recovery of the nation's economy. "Unemployed Americans are neglecting their patriotic duties by spending far less than the gainfully employed," the report read. "Until these laid-off workers start pitching in and buying things, America's economy will continue to stagnate." The report did note that jobless citizens have strongly supported America's fortified-wine industry.

Film Critic Belatedly Comes Up With *Swordfish* Zinger

AMARILLO, TX—Some seven months after the film's theatrical release, *Amarillo Globe-News* movie critic Irwin Hough thought up a brilliant put-down for *Swordfish* Monday. "Make no mistake, I'm proud of the line I thought up at the time, 'This *Fish* should have been tossed back,'" Hough said. "But I have to admit, that just isn't as sharp as

'*Swordfish* is one cold fish that deserves to tank.'"

Annoying Ad Turns Man Pro-Whaling

NASHUA, NH—A TV ad for Whale-Save sufficiently irritated local resident Nathan Mimms to cause him to reverse his longtime anti-whaling stance. "Christ, this is annoying," said Mimms during a Monday airing of the spot, which features images of majestic whales rising out of the ocean as Enya's "Fallen Embers" plays. "Fuck the whales. I'd rather they go extinct if it means never having to see this ad again."

Jerry Always Willing To Pick Up Overtime

BOISE, ID—Boise Tool & Die sources reported Monday that machinist Jerry Tepper, 48, is always willing to pick up overtime, should anyone wish to cut out early. "I don't

know, maybe his wife is sick or something," foreman Don Jeske said. "Whatever the reason, Jerry's the go-to guy if you're looking to take off. He just can't resist the extra cash."

Philip Morris CEO Forces Senator To Dance For His Amusement

WASHINGTON, DC—Bored and in need of amusement, Philip Morris CEO Louis Camilleri commanded U.S. Sen. John Edwards (D-NC) to dance for him Monday. "Dance!" Camilleri told a whirling, diaper-clad Edwards as Buster Poindexter's "Hot Hot Hot" blared. "And keep the beat, if you want that $275,000 contribution to your reelection campaign." Later this week, Edwards is slated to don a cowgirl costume and twirl sparklers to Phil Collins' "Sussudio" for General Motors CEO Rick Wagoner. *∅*

mated $2.3 thousand, are well worth the expense.

"Can we really put a price tag on the future of our nation?" Bush asked. "Can we ever put a dollar amount on success?"

Should the Bush proposal pass, teachers in any school across the country will be eligible for up to 200 gold stars, depending upon the population of the school. The stars will

> "I ask that each and every American do their part," Bush said. "If you can spare any gold stars, stickers, or even a sparkly pencil or multi-colored pen, please donate it to your local school district."

then be distributed to students according to academic performance and need for encouragement.

"I am so thrilled to hear this," said Linda Egan, a sixth-grade teacher at Chicago's Eisenhower Elementary School, one of Bush's "Gold Star Schools."™ "For so long, we've been just barely scraping by with no federal support whatsoever. Now, I feel like we've got a friend in Washington."

Bush is not without with opposition. Shortly after the press conference, U.S. Sen. Ernest Hollings (D-SC) called the president's plan "preposterous."

"What kind of president would think that distributing gold stars would improve the country's education system?" Hollings said. "Kids don't even care about gold stars anymore. At the very least, we're going to need Pokémon stickers and lick-'n'-stick Hello Kitty stamps. And what about candy? The president is talking about rewarding good behavior, and he doesn't even mention candy?"

Bush said that if the gold stars are successful, he will expand the program to include other achievement-fostering adhesives. Among them are sheets of stickers featuring ducks, turtles, and other cartoon animals offering students such exhortations as "Awesome!," "Super Job!," and "You Deserve A High Five!"

In spite of his confidence in his gold-star plan, Bush stressed that the government cannot be expected to fix America's schools by itself.

"I ask that each and every American do their part," Bush said. "If you can spare any gold stars, stickers, or even a sparkly pencil or multi-colored pen, please donate it to your local school district. We've all got to come together to make this work." Ø

Above: Prototypes of Department of Education stickers are tested on a third-grader's report on seals.

amounts of blood. Passersby were amazed by the unusually large amounts of blood. Passersby were amazed by the unusually large amounts of blood. Passersby were amazed by the unusually large amounts of blood. Passersby were amazed by the unusually large amounts of blood. Passersby were amazed by the unusually large amounts of blood. Passersby were amazed by the unusually large amounts of blood. Passersby were amazed by the unusually large amounts of blood. Passersby were amazed by the unusually large amounts of blood. Passersby were amazed by the unusually large amounts of blood. Passersby were amazed by the unusually large amounts of blood. Passersby were amazed by the unusually large amounts of blood. Passersby were amazed by the unusually large amounts of blood. Passersby were amazed by the unusually large amounts of blood. Passersby were amazed by the unusually large

> I know what you're thinking: "Not another miracle oil additive!"

amounts of blood. Passersby were amazed by the unusually large amounts of blood. Passersby were amazed by the unusually large amounts of blood. Passersby were amazed by the unusually large amounts of blood. Passersby were amazed by the unusually large amounts of blood. Passersby were

amazed by the unusually large amounts of blood. Passersby were amazed by the unusually large amounts of blood. Passersby were amazed by the unusually large amounts of blood. Passersby were amazed by the unusually large amounts of blood. Passersby were amazed by the unusually large amounts of blood. Passersby were amazed by the unusually large amounts of blood. Passersby were amazed by the unusually large amounts of blood. Passersby were amazed by the unusually large amounts of blood. Passersby were amazed by the unusually large amounts of blood. Passersby were amazed by the unusually large amounts of blood. Passersby were amazed by the unusually large amounts of blood. Passersby were amazed by the unusually large amounts of blood. Passersby were amazed by the unusually large amounts of blood. Passersby were amazed by the unusually large amounts of blood. Passersby were amazed by the unusually large amounts of blood. Passersby were amazed by the unusually large amounts of blood. Passersby were amazed by the unusually large amounts of blood. Passersby were amazed by the unusually large amounts of blood. Passersby were amazed by the unusually large amounts of blood. Passersby were

see CALGON page 67

Every Social Gathering Is A Chance To Hustle For Contacts

By Jake Rennert

Social engagements mean different things to different people. For some, they're an occasion to get together with old friends and share some laughs. For others, they're a chance to maybe meet that special someone. For me, social gatherings are much more than that: They're a golden opportunity to hustle for contacts.

As a computer consultant who makes nearly 40 percent of his income doing freelance web design on the side, I have to be networking 24/7. If I relax at a cocktail party, picnic, or memorial church service, I might as well forget about making my career dreams a reality. Every minute I'm not hustling for contacts is money down the drain.

Sure, I make a decent living. But if I don't use my grandparents' 50th wedding anniversary to seek out potential new clients and partners, what right do I have to complain if I don't succeed in this business? Not much.

At any given social gathering, I'll spend maybe 90 percent of my time working the crowd and looking for new people. (A stranger, after all, is just a client you haven't met yet.) The other 10 percent is for touching base with old contacts and glad-handing the event's hosts so that the invites keep coming.

Don't get me wrong: I don't approach every person I see at a party.

> **Sure, I make a decent living. But if I don't use my grandparents' 50th wedding anniversary to seek out potential new clients and partners, what right do I have to complain if I don't succeed in this business?**

You have to be selective about the people you associate with. I only focus on chatting up people who can help me further my goals. Given the choice of talking to a brilliant historian or a guy who's got small-business contacts up the wazoo, I'll take Mr. Well-Connected every time. There are millions of people in this world, and life is short. Why waste time with folks who can't offer me anything when there are plenty of perfectly nice people who can?

Learning to recognize the right people to approach at a particular event is a vital skill. A nephew's eighth-grade graduation ceremony, for example, can put you in direct contact with 300, 400 people. But only a handful of those hundreds are probably worth talking to. If you're in the tech

> **You have to be selective about the people you associate with. I only focus on chatting up people who can help me further my goals.**

game like me, keep an eye out for folks wearing polo shirts with embroidered logos of computer companies. Also, terms like "ethernet" and "routing systems" are good words to have your hustling-radar set to pick up.

In the event that someone you approach turns out to be not worth talking to, you need an out. Luckily, there are tons of good getaways. It can be as simple as a quick over-the-shoulder glance accompanied by, "Oops, looks like the wife needs me." There's also the "going to the bathroom" trick, but then you have to head in the general direction of the can, which can take up valuable time better spent talking to a guy who knows a guy who works at Adobe Systems.

Hustling for social contacts isn't something that just happens. You have to make it happen. To this end, I can't stress enough the importance of a nice business card. Case in point, I went to a costume party a few weeks ago. Now, there aren't a lot of places to put a business card when you're wearing a Spider-Man suit, so I fashioned a card-holder utility belt. And thank God I did, because I passed out 75 cards at that bash. From those 75 lucky people who learned about my business, I received two e-mail inquiries. That, my friends, is smart partygoing.

People are always asking me if I ever take a break from hustling for contacts. The answer is no. Meeting and making the most of every friend of a friend or business associate of my ex-wife is the reason I'm in this game. I'm not going to stop making contacts until I'm dead. And when that day arrives, I'll get one of my priest contacts to put in a call to the man upstairs to get me a better seat. ∅

Your Horoscope

By Lloyd Schumner Sr.
Retired Machinist and
A.A.P.B.-Certified Astrologer

Aries: (March 21–April 19)
Though you are unable to cultivate a reputation as a great lover of women, your reputation as an above-average lover of pancakes remains secure.

Taurus: (April 20–May 20)
You can probably put it off for a while, but eventually you'll have to figure out what all those sirens mean.

Gemini: (May 21–June 21)
In time, Death comes to all men, but the way he keeps stopping by to have a beer and moan about the Steelers' AFC Championship loss is a little pathetic.

Cancer: (June 22–July 22)
Your insistence that "if they wanted people to understand the penal code, they would've written it down somewhere" will only get you so far.

Leo: (July 23–Aug. 22)
Your missing legs don't have to be a handicap. At least not in some strange alternate universe where people are flying saucers from the waist down.

Virgo: (Aug. 23–Sept. 22)
You'll save more than $40,000 by freezing your corpse in a bathtub full of ice instead of springing for the cryogenics.

Libra: (Sept. 23–Oct. 23)
Even if you live to be 100, you'll never understand homosexuality. But don't let that stop you from having sex with all those guys.

Scorpio: (Oct. 24–Nov. 21)
Telling the waitress that you could make a better cup of coffee from the sweat on your balls won't do her any good. Show her how.

Sagittarius: (Nov. 22–Dec. 21)
You will cry because you have no shoes, until you see a man who has several pairs he doesn't even wear. Then, you will cry great, heaving sobs until you can hardly even breathe.

Capricorn: (Dec. 22–Jan. 19)
You should have more folding chairs around. If wrestlers come over and can't find one, they'll use something else.

Aquarius: (Jan. 20–Feb. 18)
You should have realized long before the bag rotted away that the snipe isn't ever coming out.

Pisces: (Feb. 19–March 20)
The stars say you should be patient, and that it can't last forever. They didn't say what they're talking about, though.

PHLEGMY from page 65

amounts of blood. Passersby were amazed by the unusually large amounts of blood. Passersby were amazed by the unusually large amounts of blood. Passersby were amazed by the unusually large amounts of blood. Passersby were amazed by the unusually large amounts of blood. Passersby were amazed by the unusually large amounts of blood. Passersby were amazed by the unusually large amounts of blood. Passersby were amazed by the unusually large amounts of blood. Passersby were amazed by the unusually large amounts of blood. Passersby were amazed by the unusually large amounts of blood. Passersby were amazed by the unusually large amounts of blood. Passersby were amazed by the unusually large amounts of blood. Passersby were amazed by the unusually large amounts of blood. Passersby were amazed by the unusually large amounts of blood. Passersby were amazed by the unusually large amounts of blood. Passersby were amazed by the unusually large amounts of blood. Passersby were amazed by the unusually large amounts of blood. Passersby were

amazed by the unusually large amounts of blood. Passersby were amazed by the unusually large amounts of blood. Passersby were amazed by the unusually large

> **I hope we can still be friends who never see each other.**

amounts of blood. Passersby were amazed by the unusually large amounts of blood. Passersby were amazed by the unusually large amounts of blood. Passersby were amazed by the unusually large amounts of blood. Passersby were amazed by the unusually large amounts of blood. Passersby were amazed by the unusually large amounts of blood. Passersby were amazed by the unusually large amounts of blood. Passersby were amazed by the unusually large amounts of blood. Passersby were

see PHLEGMY page 68

Minnie Driver Optioned By Harrison Ford

see PEOPLE page 7D

18,000 Sports Fans Doing Whatever Dancing Fluorescent Chicken Tells Them

see SPORTS page 4C

Five-Dollar Bill In Guitar Case Not Fooling Anyone

see LOCAL page 11E

STATshot

A look at the numbers that shape your world.

What Artwork Is Adorning Our Walls?

Mid-'80s Nagel poster	Celebrity Tanning Spa: Omaha, NE
"Five Dogs Playing Poker"	Governor's Mansion: Nashville, TN
B&W "Shirtless Hunk Cradling Baby" photo	Jessica Reese's dorm room: Iowa State
Picture of that nekkid boxing lady from *Playboy*	Cell 246-C
Velvet Cher	Cher Museum: Branson, MO

the ONION®

VOLUME 38 ISSUE 05   AMERICA'S FINEST NEWS SOURCE™   14–20 FEBRUARY 2002

Holocaust Museum Cashier Has Yet Another Depressing Day

WASHINGTON, DC—Alyssa Kaplan, 20, a cashier at the United States Holocaust Memorial Museum, had yet another in a seemingly endless string of depressing days Monday.

"You know how sometimes you get home from a really draining day at work and all you want to do is spend the night alone watching TV?" asked Kaplan, seated behind the gift-shop counter. "Well, I've pretty much done that every night since I started here three months ago."

Though she said she strongly believes in the museum and its mission, Kaplan admitted she finds it exhausting to reflect upon the moral and theological questions raised by the Holocaust nearly non-stop for 40 hours a week.

"It doesn't exactly put me in a so-

see CASHIER page 70

Left: Holocaust Museum cashier Alyssa Kaplan steels herself for another long, emotionally draining day.

GE Ad Trumpets Company's Government-Ordered Environmental Cleanup

PITTSFIELD, MA—A new television commercial from General Electric, unveiled Tuesday, proudly trumpets the company's federally mandated cleanup of a river it polluted.

Part of a $70 million PR campaign, the GE ad depicts a beautiful bend on Massachusetts' Housatonic River, which had been polluted by decades of PCB discharges and other hazardous chemicals from the company's plant in nearby Pittsfield.

"We work hard on this lazy river," a deep-voiced actor says as the camera lingers on the Housatonic, which GE was ordered to clean at a cost of $250 million by the EPA. "In the past three months alone, GE has removed more than 5,200 cubic yards of river sediments and 3,200 cubic yards of bank soil, making the Housatonic River a safe and beautiful place for everyone."

As the camera pans up-

see GE page 70

Above: A recent GE ad touting the company's cleanup of a river it polluted.

Semester Abroad Spent Drinking With Other American Students

Above: Blevins (center) drinks at a Seville cafe with a pair of exotic new friends from the University of Miami.

SEVILLE, SPAIN—Jon Blevins, an Indiana University junior studying in Seville, has spent nearly all of his semester abroad drinking with other American college students.

"Seville is incredible," said Blevins, 19, finishing off a Cruzcampo beer at Capote Bar Monday. "There are all these amazing cathedrals and statues and art museums. Hopefully, at some point, I'll get a chance to see some of it."

Dividing his time among classes, the Universidad de Sevilla's American dorms, and the handful of bars and clubs frequented by American students, Blevins said the opportunity to gain firsthand exposure to people from other cultures was what drew him to the ancient Andalusian city.

"I've met people from all over: a guy from Penn State, these two Sig Ep brothers from the University of Oregon, and some really cool people from

see SEMESTER page 71

The Defense Budget

President Bush's proposed $379 billion defense budget would be the largest increase in two decades. What do *you* think?

Dana Durbin
Teacher

"That seems like a reasonable amount. Wait, I didn't see those last nine zeroes. Uh-oh."

Vanessa O'Connor
Homemaker

"What do I care what Congress does with their money?"

Dan Eckert
Electrician

"This is a return to the Reagan Era, when bombs came before the poor. It's time to reunite my '80s hardcore punk band, Critical Truth."

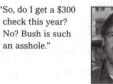

Richard Kent
Systems Analyst

"Hopefully, the Pentagon will justify this massive spending outlay by buying some really cool shit."

Peter Lyght
Civil Engineer

"So, do I get a $300 check this year? No? Bush is such an asshole."

Bob Nowell
Contractor

"Let us not lose sight of the most important thing here: bombs-bombsbombs-bombsbombs-bombsbombs-bombsbombs-bombsbombs, KABLOOMA!"

The New Dating Shows

From *Blind Date* to *Dismissed* to *The Fifth Wheel*, a new wave of dating shows is sweeping the airwaves. Why are people watching?

- ♥ Enjoy watching hair-gelled pricks compete for attention of vapid community-college nursing students
- ♥ Believe true love is harshly lit and heavily edited
- ♥ Curious to hear "Mandy, 21, Marketing Rep—Van Nuys, CA" expound on craziest place she's ever done it
- ♥ Smug, sarcastic hosts likable compared to contestants
- ♥ WWF wrestling only showcases physical cruelty
- ♥ Hoping to see some pixelated hot-tub boobies
- ♥ Love sound of clacking tongue piercings as 19-year-olds make out
- ♥ Can't sleep... can't fucking sleep

⌀ **the ONION**®
America's Finest News Source.™

Herman Ulysses Zweibel
Founder

T. Herman Zweibel
Publisher Emeritus
J. Phineas Zweibel
Publisher
Maxwell Prescott Zweibel
Editor-In-Chief

When You Are Ready To Have A Serious Conversation About Green Lantern, You Have My E-Mail Address

By Larry Groznic

I consider you a friend, Douglas. Together, we have shared many adventures, from waiting in line for the *Star Wars: Episode I* premiere to meeting Mark "Dukat" Alaimo at Comi-Con 2001. Your friendship is as valuable to me as my Michael York-auto-graphed DVD of *Logan's Run*.

But when it comes to reasoned, thoughtful, and informed discussions on the Green Lantern continuum and its place within the larger DC universe, I hold friends to the same high standard I would strangers or anyone else.

So long as you insist on clinging to your bizarre opinions on the Emerald Knight's 60-plus-year history, it is not worth my time to engage you in purposeless noisemaking. Rather than become agitated, as I've allowed you to make me in the past, I will simply serve notice that I will not entertain any future Green Lantern discussions with you until you have come to a more mature place in your development as a fan. When you are ready to have a serious conversation about Green Lantern, you have my e-mail address.

I can forgive your unwillingness to recognize that Hal Jordan is, and forever shall be, the greatest Green Lantern of all time. After all, though I can never hope to understand it, the world is peppered with otherwise intelligent persons who inexplicably lack the sense to see Hal's towering superiority. But *Kyle Rayner*? This way lies madness, Douglas. At the very least, name John Stewart as your favorite. Or Guy Gardner. Or any of the countless Silver Age Lanterns. Heck, even Abin Sur is more interesting than Kyle. When he enlisted Kyle, Ganthet himself merely said, "You'll do." Is that your idea of a ringing endorsement?

I mean, if you are hot for Jade or something, you could simply say so, and no one would think the less of you for it. But don't couch your opinions in a false respect for Phase III Green Lantern that supersedes any enjoyment of the Silver Age. You might as well read *Aquaman* if you're going to act like that.

In particular, I am baffled by your insistence that being "more powerful" makes Kyle a better Lantern. Are superheroes always superior when they're invincible? If Superman was better when he was able to move entire solar systems, why, then, was John Byrne enlisted to reinvent him as a more vulnerable character who can get injured by his foes and even killed? Because to hear you tell it, Douglas, Superman was "ruined" by the '80s revamp, long before the ridiculous electrical version.

By your twisted logic, Green Lantern's ongoing "Ion" story arc ought never end. Instead, Kyle should simply retain his infallible godlike

> **I don't want this temporary madness on your part to jeopardize our friendship, Douglas. Now, after all, is a critical time for GL fandom.**

powers forever, enshrined in comics history as the most powerful (and, therefore, best) superhero of all time.

But this is hardly the only belief of yours with which I take extreme umbrage. I find particularly laughable your naïve conviction that Hal's vulnerability to the color yellow damages the comic's storyline rather than adding excitement. Are you intentionally trying to miss the point with comments like, "You would just have to shoot him with a yellow bullet"? Jumping fish hooks, how many times do I have to explain: NO, he can't use the actual BEAM to stop such a bullet, but he can GRASP solid things with it to use as a shield! And this is just one example! Think creatively, Douglas, or at least consult the Silver Age issues.

And don't drag me into that same stale argument of yours that Sinestro would beat Hal every time if they fought in real life. For some strange reason, you continue to insist on defining fighting skill in terms of brute strength. Don't you see that in a power-ring duel, strategy and reflexes are of the essence? Only an emotional child could spend hours arguing that Sinestro is a better fighter than Hal Jordan, in the face of my lengthy, point-by-point rebuttals. Oh, and, by the way, Superman must also suck, because you'd just have to shoot him with a Kryptonite bullet, right?

Perhaps I am overstating my case. It is not the actual *idea* of Kyle Rayner to which I am so opposed. But, in the hands of a writer like Judd Winick, why does DC even bother printing it? I'm not even going to get into his contempt and utter disregard for the sanctity of the established Green

see GREEN LANTERN next page

STOP the PRESSES

Above: The cast of the recently cancelled *Stop The Presses*.

Actors Decide To Go On With Sitcom Despite Cancellation

BURBANK, CA—Showing the heart and determination that was their show's hallmark throughout its 13-week run, the stars of NBC's *Stop The Presses* have decided to go on with the series in spite of its Feb. 5 cancellation.

"I think all the pieces were in place to make this show a big hit," said Troy Drake, who played Stan "Big Sticks" Hatch, a former pro-hockey player who moves back to his hometown of Petaluma, CA, to write a sports column for *The Petaluma Gazette*. "It just needed more time to jell than the network was willing to give. Well, now we have all the time we need."

Though cancellation ordinarily marks the end of a series, the actors agreed there was still work to be done.

"Every show gets shelved eventually," said Drake, speaking from the show's new set in the parking lot of a local Ralphs food store. "But we couldn't bear the thought of abruptly cutting off all those storylines midstream. I think I speak for the entire cast when I say we all want to see if Bill and Andrea will eventually give in to the long-simmering sexual tension between them. And, next episode, Jessie's kooky parents swing by for a visit and wreak all kinds of chaos in her life. And that's *pretty scary* considering how chaotic Jessie's life already is."

The news of the cancellation was a shock to the cast and crew. No one, however, was more upset than Eddie Whyte, who played Lance Roberts, a cocky, hotshot account executive at *The Petaluma Gazette* with a weakness for the ladies. Just one week before NBC announced the cancellation, Whyte passed up a sizable part in an upcoming Rob Schneider movie to do *Stop The Presses*.

"When I found out [about the cancellation], I was devastated, because this was a project I truly believed in," said Whyte, rummaging through the cardboard box that is now the wardrobe department. "Our first 13 episodes really showed progress. We started coming together as an ensemble, and the writing got steadily tighter."

Despite losing their writing staff, directors, producers, camera operators, technical crew, set, props, and wardrobe, as well as a network on which to air the show, the *Stop The Presses* actors remain optimistic they will succeed.

"We have a remarkable cast with tremendous chemistry," said Christine Jagerveldt, who plays Dianne Clarke, the gruff, hard-nosed, secretly lonely publisher of the *Gazette*. "That's half the battle right there. And we were al-ways ad-libbing and improvising, so scripts aren't a problem, either."

Added Jagerveldt: "We don't even think of ourselves as the cast of a weekly sitcom anymore: We're a family. This whole ordeal has brought us closer together than we ever imagined possible."

Drake said he was genuinely surprised when ABC, CBS, Fox, UPN, WB, HBO, Showtime, Cinemax, MTV,

> **Added Jagerveldt: "We don't even think of ourselves as the cast of a weekly sitcom anymore: We're a family. This whole ordeal has brought us closer together than we ever imagined possible."**

VH-1, Comedy Central, Lifetime, Nickelodeon, The Sci-Fi Channel, Bravo, A&E, Home Shopping Network, TV Land, The Discovery Channel, The Food Network, CNN, Oxygen, Noggin, The Cartoon Network, ESPN, and ESPN2 passed on *Stop The Presses* as a midseason replacement.

"I really thought Telemundo was going to bite," Drake said. "Or [local cable-access channel] 97. But if nobody wants the weekly dose of livin', learnin', and laughin' that *Stop The Presses* provides, that's fine by us. This is going to be a breakthrough year for *Stop The Presses*—mark my words. If the networks and their hundreds of syndicated affiliates don't want to be a part of it, screw 'em."

Asked why the cast plans to continue with a show that had neither viewer nor network support, Drake cited a few of his favorite moments from *Stop The Presses*.

"Remember the episode where tart-tongued copy editor Patti got her hand stuck in the photocopier?" Drake said. "Or the one where Bill and Andrea got stuck together in the elevator? There have been a million moments like that, and from what I've seen of this new season, there are going to be a million more."

Bloodied but unbowed, the *Stop The Presses* cast is certain that the show will have a long and successful run.

"We're all excited and optimistic about what lies ahead," Drake said. "Barring a rash of heavy rain showers, we just might have an Emmy-winning season on our hands." Ø

GREEN LANTERN from previous page

Lantern continuity; I'd only be rehashing my comments already made public on the dccomics.com message board. For purposes of this discussion, I will focus strictly on Issue #137. Did Mr. Winick say to himself, "Yeah, Hal Jordan may be the savior of Sector 2814, but it's not like he ever befriended a gay teenager. Now, *that's* a superhero!" Who on this planet has ever said to themselves, "Say, I wonder whether gay people are actually okay folks just like you and me. I sure wish Green Lantern would weigh in on the matter"? Somebody needs to tell Winick that homosexuality is not a hot-button issue, but that #137 is most definitely a *lame* one!

And may I remind you that you would not even be a Green Lantern fan had I not lent you my "Superman: Last Son Of Earth" *Elseworlds* two-parter, which, incidentally, was returned to me seven weeks later with an ugly brown smudge on the lower-right of page 37 of Part One? Oh, and then there's your allegation that the concept of the Green Lantern Corps is "ripped off" from Doc Smith's *Lensman* novels. I'm not even going to dignify that charge with a response.

I don't want this temporary madness on your part to jeopardize our friendship, Douglas. Now, after all, is a critical time for GL fandom. The runaway success of *Lord Of The Rings* makes a *Lantern* movie a genuine possibility, given the heightened general interest in movies about rings that possess great power. But while such a prospect is exciting, it will take a unified fan base to bring about the kind of feature film Green Lantern has so richly deserved for so long. Together, the world's GL fans can make their voices heard and help create what could and should be the greatest superhero film of all time. As long as it's

> **By your twisted logic, Green Lantern's ongoing "Ion" story arc ought never end. Instead, Kyle should simply retain his infallible godlike powers forever, enshrined in comics history as the most powerful (and, therefore, best) superhero of all time.**

based on the Silver Age comics. And Tim Burton isn't involved.

In conclusion, Douglas, I want to make it clear: You are still my friend. And I do not hate you. Though, frankly, deep down, I find myself pitying you.

It is ridiculous to let our friendship falter because of a juvenile disagreement about a comic book. I therefore await your e-mail of capitulation, as soon as you see fit to send it.

Oh, and I want my *Legends Of The Superheroes* bootleg back by Friday. Ø

cial mood," Kaplan said. "I mean, everyone on the staff gets along okay, but we don't really goof around all that much. It's not like we all finish up our shift here at the Holocaust Museum and then head over to Bennigan's for happy hour."

Kaplan starts her day at 8:30 a.m. with the "morning once-over" in the museum's permanent exhibition, where she checks to see that all video and audio equipment is working. Divided into three parts, "Nazi Assault," "Final Solution," and "Last Chapter," the exhibition features 70 video monitors and four small theaters that play endless loops of historic film footage and eyewitness testimonies of the horrors perpetrated by the Nazis against the Jewish people.

"Visitors hear actual Holocaust survivors describing what it was like to be at Auschwitz," Kaplan said. "That section is directly on the other side of the wall of the employee bathroom, so I hear it every day during my two 15-minute breaks."

During her pre-opening floor check, Kaplan also inspects the museum's various exhibits and historical artifacts, making sure nothing is missing or out of place.

"Everything is bolted down or be-

hind glass, so mostly we're checking to see that the cleaning crew didn't miss anything," Kaplan said. "Yesterday, on the underside of a case displaying a child's coat with a Star Of David sewn onto it, I found a big wad of gum. As I was cleaning it off, I read that the coat belonged to a little boy who died in Bergen-Belsen. That had me down for most of the afternoon."

When the museum opens to the public at 9 a.m., Kaplan moves to the cash register in the museum store, where she rings up a broad selection of books, videos, and other items dealing with the most notorious genocide of the 20th century.

"When I first started here, I'd grab a book off the shelves to read during slow stretches," said Kaplan, holding up copies of *Annihilation Of Lithuanian Jewry* and *Cleansing The Fatherland: Nazi Medicine And Racial Hygiene*. "For my own mental health, I had to give that up."

As emotionally draining as the museum's displays and gift-shop items are, they pale in comparison to the visitors themselves, Kaplan said.

"I get the people right after they've just spent two or three intense hours looking at the displays," Kaplan said. "A lot of them file into the gift shop shell-

shocked and just stagger around for a while, trying to get a grip before exiting the museum. The photography-book section is pretty secluded, and

> ## As emotionally draining as the museum's displays and gift-shop items are, they pale in comparison to the visitors themselves, Kaplan said.

quite a few times I've found people squatting next to the oversized-hardcover shelf, just weeping."

Such behavior is understandable, Kaplan said, as the museum causes many visitors, especially those of Jewish heritage, to confront long-buried feelings about their history and come to terms with man's capacity for inhumanity toward his fellow man.

"It's natural for them to want to talk about what they just saw," Kaplan said. "I just wish 500 people a day didn't

want to talk to *me* about it. Sometimes, they don't speak English and they still want to talk to me about it."

A native of Potomac, MD, Kaplan said her reasons for applying for a job at the museum "made sense at the time." After a year and a half at George Washington University, Kaplan decided last December to take a semester off, and she believed that working at the museum would be enriching, educational, and not too physically taxing.

"I didn't want to waitress like I did last summer," Kaplan said. "Then my mom's friend told me about an opening here. I'm Jewish, so I figured this would be a great job for me. Now I'm starting to think that makes it not such a great job for me. I'm at Emotional-Dumping-Ground Zero here."

Kaplan had thought about requesting a transfer to the museum's ticket desk, but reconsidered.

"The people at the ticket desk deal with the pushy tourists screaming about the long wait, and they get paid 75 cents an hour less," Kaplan said. "Plus, they have to stare at that giant photo of *Kristallnacht* all day. If Anne Frank could survive in that attic all those years, I should be able to do five months behind this desk." ∅

ward to a clear, blue sky, the announcer closes with the words, "GE, we bring good things *back* to life."

"GE is committed to doing our part for future generations," said GE press liaison Brandon Thayer following a special press screening of the ad. "We care about clean air and water."

The ad is one in a series touting GE's compliance with EPA-mandated

> ## "At GE, we're committed to making your world better," a print version of the ad states. "That's why we're involved in 87 active federal Superfund sites."

cleanups of the environmental damage it has wrought. One such ad showcases the company's cleanup of the Hudson River, into which it dropped more than 1.3 million pounds of PCBs. Still other GE ads boast of the company's compliance with federal laws aimed at preventing future damage.

"The environment is important to GE. Maybe that's why last year alone, we spent $138 million on pollution-control equipment to minimize waste and reduce emissions," stated a 1999 commercial boasting of GE's decision not to appeal a failed challenge of the 1990 Clean Air Act. "Fresh air, blue

skies... GE is making this future possible."

The Housatonic commercial was first conceived in November 2001, more than two years after an EPA consent decree was lodged against GE and four years after the pollution-choked river was added to the EPA's Superfund National Priorities List.

"At GE, we're committed to making your world better," a print version of the ad states. "That's why we're involved in 87 active federal Superfund sites."

According to Thayer, GE has donat-

ed more than $400 million to cleanup sites across the U.S. since 1990. He added that the company spends millions more each year conducting its own research to determine which substances should qualify as contaminants and which should be freed from government restrictions.

"GE will continue to do everything in its power to protect our greatest resource: our planet," said Thayer, reiterating the company's commitment to the mandatory cleanup of polluted sites near its manufacturing plants.

"After all, it's the only one we've got."

Next week, a new ad showcasing GE's work cleaning up the grounds of a Malvern, PA, elementary school is slated to make its debut. After GE was forced to remove 41,000 cubic yards of contaminated soil from the school's playground area, it installed new recreational equipment and athletic facilities on the site. The ad, which cites GE's playground-equipment donation, features a delighted child on a slide and a voiceover stating, "GE knows you've got to give just a little... to get a smile in return." ∅

Above: Hundreds of fish contaminated with GE-dumped PCBs lie dead on the banks of a river.

Clemson," said Blevins, a political-science major who is taking eight credits at the Universidad de Sevilla. "And I was worried I wouldn't fit in."

Added Blevins: "The program I'm in is actually done through Florida State, so I've also met a lot of FSU

> "Sure, it's weird taking classes from someone who barely speaks English," Blevins said. "And you wouldn't believe what a Jack and Coke costs in Seville. But I've had some really unique experiences."

chicks, who are really hot."

Blevins, who said Seville is "in the Moor part of Spain," has not visited such landmarks as the *Catedral*, the largest Gothic edifice ever constructed, or the Museo Provincial des Bellas Artes, a museum in a former convent which houses works by Murillo, Ribera, and El Greco. He has, however, made three trips to the American Club, "this great bar near campus where they've got Dave Matthews on the jukebox and Sam Adams on tap."

Before leaving for Spain on Jan. 6, Blevins was concerned that his inability to speak Spanish would make negotiating the country difficult. Blevins' worries, however, were quickly assuaged.

"You can totally get by without knowing Spanish in Seville," Blevins

Above: The famed Catedral, one of the many Seville attractions Blevins has not seen.

said. "It's a really international city, and most of the locals speak English. Plus, a few days after I got there, I hooked up with these guys from Emory University on my dorm floor who all knew Spanish. So I was pretty much set."

Blevins said he looks forward to gaining a taste of authentic Sevillian culture during the upcoming Semana Santa festival, an annual Holy Week celebration renowned for its religious significance and throngs of drunken tourists.

"That's gonna be seriously off the hook," Blevins said. "We're talking non-stop Cuervo."

Though he has spent a majority of his time in Seville, Blevins has made sure not to limit his cultural exposure to that city alone.

"A bunch of us from the dorm took a weekend trip to Cordoba, which isn't too far away," Blevins said. "It wound up being pretty similar to Seville, with all these orange trees and churches and stuff, but it was still pretty cool. Me and Pete and Chris, these two Ohio State guys I went with, met up with a bunch of their friends from school who happened to be there on winter break. They'd just come from Barcelona and told us all about the scene there. Then we all went to Granada and checked out this nightclub opened by this other guy they all

knew. It was cool: They had pretty good *paella* there, but otherwise it was pretty much just like any bar back in Bloomington."

In spite of the challenges and difficulties that studying in a foreign land has presented, Blevins said he "wouldn't have missed it for anything."

"Sure, it's weird taking classes from someone who barely speaks English," Blevins said. "And you wouldn't believe what a Jack and Coke costs in Seville. But I've had some really unique experiences. I'll never forget it."

Added Blevins: "Last weekend, I even met a guy from my hometown. Just goes to show you what a small world it really is." ⌀

NEWS IN BRIEF

Smiling Willie Nelson Reflects On A Lifetime Of Weed And Women

LUCK, TX—Taking a long, slow drag off a joint, country-music legend Willie Nelson reflected on a lifetime of weed and women Monday. "I've had some pretty fine times," said a smiling Nelson between hits at his West Texas ranch. "And some pretty fine ladies. Some of the names have escaped me, but the memories never will." Nelson then retired to his backyard, where he drank beer and strummed his favorite guitar while watching the sun go down.

Moviegoer Can Already See Where Commercials Will Go

MILTON, MA—Twenty minutes into a screening of Disney's *Snow Dogs* Monday, moviegoer Ryan Friesen an-

nounced that he can already tell where the commercial breaks will be inserted when the film is aired on ABC sometime in 2003. "Right there... commercial," Friesen said to himself as Cuba Gooding Jr., who stars as a Miami dentist who inherits an dogsled team, heads off to Alaska. "That'll be the first break, right around 8:20 p.m., assuming they start it at 8." Friesen has previously called the commercial breaks for the films *Jumanji*, *Home Alone 2*, and *Twister* with 80 percent accuracy.

Woman Who Claims Book Changed Her Life Has Not Changed

MEMPHIS, TN—In spite of claims that Bruce Wilkinson's *The Prayer Of Jabez: Breaking Through To The Blessed Life* "totally changed [her] worldview," payroll secretary Brenda Haskell is the same shallow, distracted person she has always been.

"Yeah, ever since reading it, she's really been elevated to a higher, more profound spiritual plane," coworker Stephanie Roule said. "I guess that's the spiritual plane where you spend all day obsessing over your nails."

Vanquished Foe's Skull Makes Surprisingly Bad Wine Goblet

DEATH MOUNTAIN—The skull of Wynric Lance, failed claimant to the throne of Eirea, does not make as good a wine goblet as Lord Shryke had imagined, the despot revealed Monday. "This damn thing is practically impossible to drink out of," said Shryke at a banquet celebrating the defeat of the Army Of Light. "You have to hold it just right to keep the wine from spilling over the parietal bones where they connect with the occipital. And there's a leak in the left temple. As much as I love the idea of using it, it's just stupid and impracti-

cal." Shryke concluded that while he might end up drinking from Lance's skull "occasionally, for show," he plans to retain his set of brass flutes for everyday use.

Senate Subcommittee On Energy And Water Development More Like A Family

WASHINGTON, DC—Sen. Pete Domenici (R-NM), ranking Republican on the Senate Subcommittee on Energy and Water Development, revealed Monday that the group is "less a Senate subcommittee than a big family. "[Senator] Harry [Reid (D-NV)] isn't just chairman of our subcommittee. He's more like a dad to us," Domenici said. "We can talk to him about anything that's troubling us, even if it has nothing to do with the allocation of hydroelectric power." ⌀

Incurable Romantic? Guilty As Charged!

**A Room Of Jean's Own
By Jean Teasdale**

Next to Christmas, my favorite holiday has to be Valentine's Day. In fact, I just got done decorating the windows of our apartment with teeny hearts cut out of red tissue paper, an annual ritual of mine. And, without fail, my efforts always get the same reaction from hubby Rick: "Geez, Jean, did they rezone the red-light district right through our place? Where's the whores?"

Leave it to hubby Rick to take a perfectly innocent collection of darling little valentine hearts and immediately associate it with prostitution! Sometimes, I feel sorry for people like Rick who see sleaze in everything. In high school, I remember we read an ancient Greek play about women who refused to make whoopee with their hubbies because the men were always fighting wars. Now, normally, I consider those ancient plays boring, but this one was great, because for once, regular gals had their say instead of some dull, mean king. And even though it was written ten or twenty thousand years ago, it showed how eternally silly men are! But all my teacher (who was male, by the way) could talk about was phallic symbols and lesbians and kinky stuff, even though sex was really only a very small part of the whole play. (Or maybe the teacher's edition contained the raunchier version!) Anyway, by concentrating on the dirty stuff, perverts miss out on the finer things in life, and that's why I pity them.

Valentine's Day should be a noble day devoted to a higher kind of love, the kind motivated by romance, not simple lust. Like, when a man gives a woman a box of chocolates with a tiny, adorable teddy bear attached to the box. Or, even better, the woman is treated to a delicious dinner at a classy restaurant, and the man gets down on his knees and proposes, and the woman accepts, and all the onlookers burst into applause, and then the couple spends the night at a mountaintop ski chalet cuddling before a roaring hearth.

Or, say the woman has always been a little on the chunky side, and back in high school this cute classmate she had a huuuge crush on liked to tease her about her weight. But on Valentine's Day about 20 years later, out of the blue, the classmate appears at her door terminally ill and tells her he's really sorry for being such a jerk to her so long ago, but she forgives him,

and they embrace and kiss passionately, and he dies right there on her doorstep.

Okay, okay, call me Jean The Incurable Romantic. But don't these things sound soooo much more romantic than "Wham, bam, thank you ma'am?" Believe it or not, I can dream up scenarios even more magical than the ones I mentioned above. You know, scenarios with unicorns and forest glades and stuff. You see, simply by using my imagination, Valentine's Day isn't limited to one day a year—I can treat myself to a little mind vacation any time!

But even my considerable ability to

> ## First, I buy a bunch of bridal magazines. No, I'm not looking to get married again (unless Patrick Swayze decides to re-enter the market... *rowrr, rowrr!*).

fantasize can start to ebb sometimes. When this happens, I turn to some surefire sources of inspiration:

First, I buy a bunch of bridal magazines. No, I'm not looking to get married again (unless Patrick Swayze decides to re-enter the market... *rowrr, rowrr!*). I just love to pore over the pages, getting lost in endless fluffy clouds of satin and lace and tulle and beadwork. I try to imagine the luscious taste of the multi-tiered wedding cakes and what it's like to be the center of attention at a ceremony attended by hundreds of your closest friends and kin, each practically weeping with joy as they lay gorgeously wrapped gifts at your feet. (I wish I could say our wedding presents were impressive. Let's just say hubby Rick and I got married the year "Mr. Microphone" was all the rage!)

Second, I stop by travel agencies and pick up free vacation brochures with gorgeous pictures of tropical getaways. I wish I'd had my honeymoon on a pleasure cruise or at an exotic spa-resort where they treat you like Cleopatra and place chocolates on your pillow, and you get a beach all to your hubby and yourself. (The only time Rick and I took off after our wedding was to attend the funeral of his great aunt. Club Med? More like Club *Dead!*) I cut out the best pictures from the brochures and paste them into a

special scrapbook I've created. (The scrapbook sits on a special shelf, right alongside my "Kitty Kompendium" and my "Chocollection.")

Third, I take a long, hot bubble bath with lots of lit candles. Well, it's not exactly a long, hot bubble bath. It's more like a long, hot shower. You see, our apartment only has a shower stall with no tub. But the candles give off a beautiful glow through the frosted glass.

Finally (and this is the most surefire way to get me in the Valentine's Day mood), I scatter my many stuffed animals and Beanie Babies all over my waterbed, lay down, and roll around, letting them bob and tumble all over me as the bed waves and undulates! You might not think this is particularly romantic (and technically, I suppose it's probably not), until you consider this one little detail: I'm totally naked!

Pretty wild, huh? I can't believe I actually admitted that! Then again, what's to be ashamed of? After all, I do the "Plush Jamboree" in the privacy of my bedroom. And it's not like I touch myself or watch dirty porno

movies as I do it. In fact, sex is the furthest thing from my mind! There's a difference between sexy and *sensual*, and the truth is, I've always loved the feel of synthetic plush against my bare skin. It tickles, and the constant bouncing makes me so giddy I laugh my head off!

Besides, it can hardly be a sexual thing, because I've done this since I was a little girl. Well, I quit doing it for the first few years Rick and I were married, but since Rick spends most nights at Tacky's Tavern, and I don't have much to do during evenings, why not indulge in a little good, clean fun every once in a while? Besides, we all have our little peculiarities, don't we? Come on, admit it! (Well, don't *actually* admit it: I get some pretty strange mail from readers telling me about their problems and obsessions, and I'm like, "*Hel-lo*, talk to the hand! That's a little more information than I needed to know!")

Anyhow, I'm absolutely convinced that if more people took my advice and saw the real romance in Valentine's Day, there would be a lot less need for porn... and Prozac! ✍

Your Horoscope

**By Lloyd Schumner Sr.
Retired Machinist and
A.A.P.B.-Certified Astrologer**

Aries: (March 21–April 19)
Your heart will be shattered by a beautiful scientist who removes it from your body, dips it in liquid nitrogen, and drops it to the ground.

Taurus: (April 20–May 20)
Parents' groups would like to have a word with you regarding the extreme, gratuitous violence in your near future.

Gemini: (May 21–June 21)
It turns out that sneaking in and having sex on your boss' desk isn't as sexy as it sounded, especially with him taking phone calls the whole time.

Cancer: (June 22–July 22)
Dating isn't always easy, but you've got to either dust yourself off and get back in the saddle or stop dating horses.

Leo: (July 23–Aug. 22)
It isn't the fear of failure that keeps you from trying new things. It's the fear of the gorillas who eat people who try new things your mother told you about.

Virgo: (Aug. 23–Sept. 22)
You are tantalizingly close to achieving your dream of becoming the first blind person to fly an airplane around the world. Just put your eyes out.

Libra: (Sept. 23–Oct. 23)
You aren't the first person to fall in love with someone, only to realize he's not the person you thought he was. However, due to the recent, sudden maturation of the entire human race, you're the last.

Scorpio: (Oct. 24–Nov. 21)
Sometimes, you just have to grin and try again with a fresher corpse and slight changes to the formula.

Sagittarius: (Nov. 22–Dec. 21)
The stars indicate that, although they know you're going through a rough time, they're only going to put up with so many of your late-night phone calls.

Capricorn: (Dec. 22–Jan. 19)
You will be told that "your appeal to reason and personal responsibility is a light that will never go out" by weirdos who've mistaken you for Ayn Rand.

Aquarius: (Jan. 20–Feb. 18)
Though you're not prejudiced, you have a hard time believing that a mule can kick field goals.

Pisces: (Feb. 19–March 20)
The world may end "not with a bang but a whimper," but the end of your world will have plenty of both.

Now That's What I Call Shitty Music 8 Tops Album Charts

see MUSIC page 3C

Israeli High-School Students Hoping Suicide Bombing Postpones Exam

see WORLD page 5A

President Lincoln Sick Of Time Travelers

see TIME-SPACE page 7D

STATshot

A look at the numbers that shape your world.

Worst-Selling Maps

1. Map Of The Stars' Homes—Carbondale, IL
2. Rand McNally's How To Get To Kim's Party
3. 1937 Surveyors' Map Of Grinnock County Reservoirs
4. Driving Map Of One-Long-Roadville, PA
5. Topographic Map Of Central Kansas
6. Map Of Bud Dybzinski's Erogenous Zones

THE ONION • $2.00 US • $3.00 CAN

0 74470 94595 6

---

the ONION®

VOLUME 38 ISSUE 06 · **AMERICA'S FINEST NEWS SOURCE**™ · **21–27 FEBRUARY 2002**

Women's Olympic Bobsled Team Hopes To Inspire Young Girls To Bobsled

OLYMPICS 2002

SALT LAKE CITY, UT—Olympic bobsledders Jean Racine and Gea Johnson have two major goals for the Salt Lake City Games. The first is to win the gold medal. The second is to let young girls know that they, too, can pursue their bobsled dreams.

"When I was growing up, little girls were encouraged to participate in sports like tennis and basketball, but never bobsledding," said Racine, 23, driver of the American women's two-person sled. "Well, I want that to change that for the next generation. I want to be the person today's young girls can look to and say to them-

selves, 'Hey, I can bobsled if I want to.'"

"One day," Racine continued, "people will see women bobsledders as bobsledders first and women second."

Johnson, the team's brakewoman, echoed Racine's sentiments.

"There has always been this assumption—and I don't know where it comes from—that girls aren't interested in bobsledding," the 34-year-old Johnson said. "I can remember, as a third-grader, telling my gym teacher

see BOBSLED page 77

Above: Bobsledding role models Jean Racine and Bonny Warner.

Report: Americans Would Be Outraged If They Understood Enron Collapse

HOUSTON—According to an independent report released Monday, Americans would be outraged if they had a basic grasp of the details of the Enron collapse, in which company executives concealed massive debt while claiming profitability and then declared bankruptcy, bilking investors and employees out of millions while making off with a fortune.

"I've followed it a little, but I'm still not quite sure what exactly the deal is," said Portland, OR, graphic designer Gina Kader, one of 3,500 Americans polled about the Enron scandal by the D.C.-based Center For Public

Integrity. "I know they laid a bunch of people off, which made a lot of people mad. Then again, lots of companies are laying off workers these days. So who knows?"

Though many Bush Administration appointees are former Enron executives or business associates, Congress is not being flooded with letters from outraged Americans demanding an investigation into what the White House knew about the energy giant's illegal and illicit activities.

"Is Enron out of business?" asked Amanda Garces, a Cicero, IL, real-

see ENRON page 76

Work Friends Not Mingling With Other Friends

CHICAGO—Following a party celebrating her 26th birthday Saturday, a disappointed Kristin Thennes reported that her friends from work failed to mingle with her other friends.

"I was really hoping that my work friends would hit it off with everybody else," said Thennes, a budget administrator at Loyola University Medical School. "But the six of them just sort of kept to themselves the whole night. I felt like a terrible host."

The six coworkers invited to the party arrived in a group at approximately

8:45 p.m. Rather than socialize with the 20 or so guests already present, they huddled together near the front window of the living room of Thennes' Andersonville apartment.

"Maybe I'm being a little paranoid, but Kristin's work friends didn't seem to like us," said Laura Romo, 25, an old college friend and Thennes' former roommate. "I mean, they weren't hostile or anything, but they definitely kept their own little circle the entire time."

The coworkers' precious

see FRIENDS page 75

Above: Three of Thennes' coworkers keep to themselves.

73

The Axis Of Evil

President Bush's State of the Union pronouncement that North Korea, Iran, and Iraq represent an "Axis of Evil" continues to spark debate. What do *you* think?

Ellen Demuth
Physical Therapist

"These 'Axis of Evil' nations are no more a threat than Libya, Syria, Cuba, Egypt, Pakistan, China, Saudi Arabia, or the Sudan. We've got nothing to worry about."

John Yancey
Systems Analyst

"I strongly feel that our conflict with the Axis of Evil should not be settled on the battlefield, but in the pro-wrestling ring."

Rich Hoegert
Claims Processor

"Perhaps air-dropping food on these countries we just pissed off might help ease tensions."

Aimee Chambers
Student

"We should not try to stop the access of Evel. That man is a national treasure and should be allowed to move freely in whatever stadiums or canyon gorges he likes."

Rob Russell
Pool Cleaner

"Calling Iran part of an 'Axis of Evil' may cause average Americans to lump moderates like Mohammad Khatami in with extremists like Ali Khamenei and Hashemi Rafsanjani."

Anderson King
Attorney

"Aw, shit, not another Axis. That last one kicked our asses."

Chat-Room Shorthand

From LOL (Laugh Out Loud) to BRB (Be Right Back), Internet chat rooms have a shorthand all their own. Among the most popular abbreviations:

LODLSM	Logged On Dressed Like Sailor Moon
XIF	Christ, I'm Fat
DYHTNTMBG?	Did You Hear The New They Might Be Giants?
18/F/NYC	Pockmarked 46-Year-Old In Bathrobe
IHTWBSAP	I Have Trouble With Basic Spelling And Punctuation
JEOMK	Just Ejaculated On My Keyboard
NTBUSWAB	Not To Bring Up Star Wars Again, But...
TOMTB	Taking Off My Training Bra
CILYIMBF?	Can I Lock You In My Basement Forever?
HOGMP	Hang On, Getting More Pringles
WSTS	Weeping Silently To Self

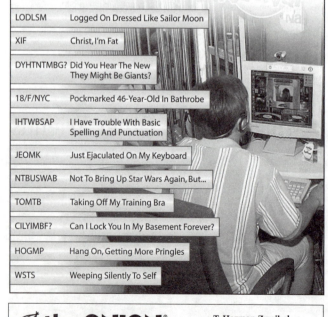

⊘ **the ONION** ®
America's Finest News Source.™

Herman Ulysses Zweibel
Founder

T. Herman Zweibel
Publisher Emeritus
J. Phineas Zweibel
Publisher
Maxwell Prescott Zweibel
Editor-In-Chief

That Trip To Canada Really Broadened My Horizons

By Cliff Burkett

It's sad, but some people don't realize what a big world it is. They don't see how much there is to learn from other cultures. Me, I've never shied away from exposing myself to foreign ways of life: From drinking margaritas in Key West to riding the teacups at Disneyland, I've been a lot of places and seen a lot of things. But when I took a trip to the Great White North last month, I had no idea how much it would broaden my horizons and open up my mind.

Have you ever been to Canada? If you look for it on a map, you'll realize it isn't far from the United States. But once you cross the border from America to Canada, you'll immediately know you're in a foreign land.

Case in point: the food. While I was in downtown Toronto looking for a place to eat, just something simple like a McDonald's or Hardee's, I came across a restaurant I'd never seen before called Mr. Sub. I figured, "Hey, when in Rome..." And you know what? My open-mindedness paid off! It was a sub shop, but it had a breaded-fish sub. I'd never seen anything like that in a Blimpie or Subway. I guess those Canadians really like their fish. In the end, I got a "Great Canadian Sub" so I'd get the full

> **Have you ever been to Canada? If you look for it on a map, you'll realize it isn't far from the United States.**

Canadian experience. And guess what? It was great. Just goes to show what can happen when you leave yourself open to new experiences.

Something else that's a little strange about Canada is how they don't use pounds or miles or inches. Everything is metric. I remember learning about the metric system in chemistry class, but this is an entire country that measures everything differently. That's the sort of thing you only learn by actually going out there into the world.

Another thing that really gave me pause was seeing road signs in French and English. The first time I saw a bilingual sign, I didn't know what was up. But the *Let's Go Toronto* guidebook said that a lot of Canadians speak French as their first lan-

guage. How odd is that? As I soon learned, the French colonized a lot of Canada instead of the English, so not only did I get some French culture, but I got a history lesson, as well. That's why you take trips—to learn a little bit more about the world around you.

What also threw me off was that Canadian money looks completely different from ours. The bills are different colors, and instead of presidents, they have prime ministers and

> **Canadian money looks completely different from ours. The bills are different colors, and instead of presidents, they have prime ministers and queens on them.**

queens on them. I guess if you spend your whole life stuck in the U.S., you never really think about something like currency. But when you're confronted with a bill that doesn't have George Washington or Abraham Lincoln on it, you really start to think about how each country is unique and how that's reflected in their money.

Seeing the Canadian money also made me think that Canadians wouldn't understand what rappers were talking about when they used the term "dead presidents." You see, even the universal language of music wouldn't translate well between our two diverse cultures.

Did you know that Canada also has a space needle? I figured Seattle was the only place to have one, but Canada has one, too. Except it's called the CN Tower. It's amazing how you can have two totally different countries and still have a common thread that binds them. It's kind of reassuring to realize that maybe Americans and other cultures aren't so different, after all.

I'm really glad I got the opportunity to take in the wonders of Canada before it got too Americanized. It would be a shame to see something uniquely Canadian like the Hockey Hall Of Fame turn into our Baseball Hall Of Fame.

When I finally made it back home, I started to see things through a different lens. I no longer viewed the world as being all the same. Now, I see it for what it is: America and a bunch of other places with subtle differences from us. ⊘

18-Year-Old Miraculously Finds Soulmate In Hometown

PESHTIGO, WI—In a miracle that defies statistical probability, Corey Muntner, 18, reported Monday that he found his soulmate, Tammy Gaska, right in his very own hometown of Peshtigo.

"They say God puts one special person on this planet who is your one true love," said Muntner, who has left Marinette County twice in his life, both times for marching-band competitions in nearby Menominee. "It's incredible, but I somehow found mine right here in the town where I've always lived. If that's not fate, I don't know what is."

Muntner, a 2001 graduate of Peshtigo High School, met Gaska, currently a junior at the school, in November 1999 in the student parking lot.

"I was hanging out by my car with my buddy Bryan, and this really hot chick comes walking up," Muntner said. "She asks us for a smoke, and I give her one of my Camels. So Bryan, who's a good guy but kind of a goober, says, 'What are you doing Saturday night?' She says, 'Nothing with you.' Then, for some reason, I say, 'How about me?' and she smiles and says, 'Sure.'"

"That girl's name, you ask?" Muntner continued. "Tammy Gaska."

Relationship experts estimate that the chances of meeting someone in your lifetime that you fully connect with on a spiritual, intellectual, and physical level are one in 2.3 billion, making the geographic proximity of the soulmates nothing short of astonishing.

"How often does a person find their one true love at all, much less in the tiny rural Wisconsin town where they grew up?" Muntner said. "That's why me and Tammy are still going out even though she gave Danny [Corvo] a hand job in the Copps [Food Center] freezer a few months ago. You just don't give up on true love."

Muntner said he very nearly did not meet Gaska, making their union all the more incredible.

"When I was in 10th grade, my dad got a job offer in Manitowoc, and we almost moved," Muntner said. "If he'd taken the job, I would have never met

> "When she told me she wanted to eat at Schussler's Supper Club I was like, 'That's my favorite place in town!' What are the odds that out of Peshtigo's five restaurants, we'd both like the same one?"

Tammy. It's pretty scary to think about how close that was to happening. Obviously, somebody up there wanted us to be together."

Muntner said he knew almost immediately that he and Tammy were "so meant to be together."

"I could tell on the first date that Tammy was Mrs. Right," Muntner said. "When she told me she wanted to eat at Schussler's Supper Club, I was like, 'That's my favorite place in town!' What are the odds that out of Peshtigo's five restaurants, we'd both like the same one?"

While many of his friends have had to search the state, country, or at least somewhere outside a three-mile radius to find "The One," Muntner said he is doubly blessed that Gaska lives a mere four blocks away.

"My friend Rodney [Auer] has a girlfriend who lives all the way over

Right: Muntner and his one true love.

in Oconto Falls," Muntner said. "Sometimes, he doesn't get to see her all week if something is wrong with his truck. I don't think I could stand to be away from Tammy for that long."

Muntner, who prior to meeting Gaska had dated only two girls, one for five weeks and the other for two months, said he is amazed that he was able to find the perfect person so quickly—and in a town of only 3,400 people.

"Tammy is really special." Muntner said. "Most people who marry someone from their hometown just settle

> "How often does a person find their one true love at all, much less in the tiny rural Wisconsin town where they grew up?"

for whatever's around. I'm glad I didn't have to do that." ∅

FRIENDS from page 73

few interactions with the others were brief and occurred only at moments of forced proximity, such as when getting drinks at the bar or waiting in line for the bathroom. Even during these moments, few words were exchanged, with encounters limited to

> Traci Kessler, a longtime friend of Thennes' who knew no one else at the party, was unable to infiltrate the work-friends circle.

fleeting eye contact and tense smiles.

"They seemed a little older than everyone else at the party," Romo said. "Or maybe they just seemed that way because they were, like, a little stiff and dressed sort of dorky. Everyone else was all casual in jeans, but the work friends were wearing Dockers and stuff. I'm guessing most of them probably live in the suburbs."

Thennes has worked at Loyola's medical school since 1999. During her time there, she has formed many close ties with coworkers, in spite of their lack of common backgrounds. Thennes' closest work friend is Denise Schukal, 29, who commutes to work from her condominium in the Chicago suburb of Rolling Meadows. Schukal, whose husband Jeff stayed home with their 15-month-old daugh-

ter while she attended the party, was among the non-minglers.

"Kristin's friends were all really nice," Schukal said. "I didn't get a chance to meet many of them, but

> "They seemed a little older than everyone else at the party," Romo said.

they all seemed cool."

Thennes attempted to get her work friends to interact with the others, but to no avail.

"I tried pairing up people who might hit it off," Thennes said. "Like, I introduced Harold, my work

movie-geek friend, to Emily, my college movie-geek friend. But after exchanging a few brief words about how they both really liked *Gosford Park*, they just sort of retreated to their original spots. I thought they'd have been a sure thing. What more could I have done?"

Traci Kessler, a longtime friend of Thennes' who knew no one else at the party, was unable to infiltrate the work-friends circle.

"I got on great with Jen's old college buds and a bunch of the other people there," said Kessler, who met Thennes in 1995 in a yoga class. "But when I went into the living room to meet all her work friends, they were all just talking about office stuff. After about two minutes of that, I had to go back to the kitchen. I was like, forget it." ∅

Dog Keeps Iceland Awake All Night

REYKJAVIK, ICELAND—The nation of Iceland was tired and cranky Monday after being kept up all night by a howling dog. "People were complaining as far away as Seyhisfjórdhur," said President Ólafur Grimsson, brewing an extra pot of coffee. "The sound carries a long way up here." Grimsson said none of Iceland's 280,000 citizens were close enough to the dog—believed to have been stranded on an ice floe near Vestmannaeyjar—to throw a shoe at it.

New Bin Laden Tape Contains Three Previously Unreleased Monologues

ATLANTA—A new Osama bin Laden videotape acquired by CNN from Al-Jazeera features three previously unreleased anti-U.S. rants and harangues by the terrorist leader, excited network sources said Monday. "One piece goes on for 45 minutes and is entirely about the need to bring down the Great Satan," CNN spokesman Gil Eckert said. "In another, shorter piece, he's sitting in a dank cave, cryptically telling some guy off camera about the 'great victory' Allah will enjoy in the very near future." The eagerly anticipated tape, the first new material from bin Laden in more than two months, hits video stores Tuesday.

Guy Who Just Wiped Out Immediately Claims He's Fine

SOUTH BURLINGTON, VT—A fraction of a second after wiping out on a patch of ice, South Burlington pedestrian Isaac Berkman loudly insisted that he was fine. "I'm fine, I'm fine, I'm fine," Berkman, 24, told concerned onlookers before he'd even straightened his badly twisted legs and attempted to stand up. "I'm okay." After noticing a deep gash just below his left knee, Berkman instantly assured witnesses that the heavily bleeding wound was "no biggie" and "totally under control."

Conrad Bain Steps Down As National Kitsch-Reference Laureate

WASHINGTON, DC—Actor Conrad Bain, known to millions as Philip Drummond on the hit '70s sitcom *Diff'rent Strokes*, stepped down Monday from the post of National Kitsch-Reference Laureate. "I am extremely proud to have served this country for the past 11 years in my humorous-referential capacity," Bain said. "Almost as proud as I was of Willis and Arnold that time they went on the hunger strike to save the ancient Indian burial ground that my construction company was going to tear up for a new building." Bain added that he is fully confident that his successor, Ron "Horshack" Palillo, "will serve the nation with distinction and honor."

Man's Dream To Get Drunk In An A-Frame Finally Realized

GLENWOOD SPRINGS, CO—Pete Strausbaugh, 33, a Denver-area electrician, realized a longtime dream Saturday when he got drunk in an A-frame house. "Man, that was even better than I thought it would be," said Strausbaugh, finishing off a ninth Coors Light in the living room of his A-frame at Sunlight Mountain ski resort. "It's not quite up there with being drunk in a treehouse, but still." Strausbaugh later announced that his new ambition is to get baked at Niagara Falls. ∅

ENRON from page 73

estate agent. "I saw footage of people clearing out their offices, even taking home plants from the lobby. I know they went bankrupt, and I think some of their top executives may have been guilty of some sort of extortion. But I could be totally off."

The mass public silence grew even quieter following reports that Enron has contributed $572,350 to various George W. Bush election campaigns over the course of his political career.

"Didn't the collapse have something to do with the California energy crunch?" asked Rochester, MN, nurse practitioner Roberta Miller. "I'm pretty sure I saw something on the news about it being related to that. But then, I also read somewhere that there was some kind of trouble with

> The mass public silence grew even quieter following reports that Enron has contributed $572,350 to various George W. Bush election campaigns.

their accounting. So maybe it was both. Or neither."

In addition to the groundswell of non-interest in the president's ties to Enron, a mass public outcry has not gone up over Vice-President Dick Cheney's refusal to release details of his many meetings with former Enron CEO Kenneth Lay.

"From what I gather, some of the top Enron executives predicted the earnings wrong, and as a result they over-budgeted," said Pete Moseley, a Philadelphia-area construction worker. "So then they had to fire some people to make up for the loss. And everybody's mad because the people they fired were all the low-level employees, not the top guys like themselves."

Americans are also not demanding answers regarding Enron's relationship with U.S. Sen. Phil Gramm (R-TX), who, as chairman of the Senate Banking Committee, approved legislation exempting Enron from federal regulation at a time when his wife was on the energy giant's board.

"A lot of people are saying a lot of things about this company," said Sacramento, CA, orthodontist Alan Hood, one of the 275 million Americans not angrily calling for an independent investigator to find out how

> "From what I gather, some of the top Enron executives predicted the earnings wrong, and as a result they overbudgeted," said Pete Moseley, a Philadelphia-area construction worker.

much influence Enron bought on Capitol Hill. "Right now, it's all just a lot of noise. I'm going to wait until the dust settles before I even consider trying to get a handle on it."

Teresa Conreid, an Athens, GA, legal secretary who thinks she may have seen something about document shredding in *Time* a few months back, said the scandal is not high on her priority list.

"What are you asking me for?" Conreid said. "Between terrorism, the economy, and my own personal life, I've got enough problems. I think we all have more important things to worry about than politicians rolling over for giant corporate interests at the expense of the voters who elected them." ∅

Above: Kenneth Lay (left) confers with some other guy who must have something to do with the whole Enron thing.

BOBSLED from page 73

that when I grew up, I wanted to be a bobsledder. He said, 'Why the hell would you want to do that?'"

Salt Lake City 2002 is the first Olympics to feature women's bob-

> "We have to be worthy ambassadors of bobsledding," Racine said. "We have to represent the sport well and be the kind of bobsledders today's young girls can aspire to be like."

Above: The bobsledders of tomorrow.

sledding as a medal event. As thrilled as Racine and Johnson would be to win that first-ever gold, just having the chance to serve as role models for the female bobsledders of tomorrow means as much to them.

"We have to be worthy ambassadors of bobsledding," Racine said. "We have to represent the sport well and be the kind of bobsledders today's young girls can aspire to be like. That's a

heavy responsibility, but I feel up to the task."

Johnson said parents can play a vital role in opening up the bobsled doors for their daughters.

"Usually, parents let their little girls sled until they're a certain age, and then it's suddenly discouraged," Johnson said. "Boys can go on and become bobsledders, and that's okay with everyone. We have to let our girls know that there's nothing wrong with wanting to bobsled."

"Sports are so good for girls, partic-

ularly a sport like bobsledding," Racine said. "I've learned so much from it: how to be competitive, how to work hard, how to not give up. Bobsledding is like life: The harder you push at the beginning, the faster the ride is all the way down." ∅

---

the ONION presents

Wine-Appreciation Tips

Wine appreciation is a true art form. Here are some tips to help you become an aficionado:

- Most wine experts frown upon serving a peignoir with white meat. This is primarily because a peignoir is a type of lingerie.

- In Europe, wines are named according to the region from which they come. Among the most popular are wines from the Bordeaux region of France and the Night Train region of Italy.

- When dining with friends at a restaurant, order the second-least-expensive wine on the list. If on a date, order the fourth-least expensive.

- If you are uncertain whether to select a merlot or beaujolais for a spring breast-of-lamb garden dinner, avoid making a decision until we come down to beat the living crap out of you.

- Many liquor stores offer a "Try Before You Buy" program, whether they know it or not.

- When sipping wine at a Catholic eucharist, swallow quickly, before the wine undergoes the miracle of transubstantiation and you get the unpleasant taste of a mouthful of human blood.

- Distinctly fruity overtones are the mark of a good sommelier.

- The quality of a wine is inversely proportional to the viciousness of the animal depicted on the label.

- Aw, man, once in high school, my friends and I got totally ripped on this wine Eric's older brother bought for us. I don't remember the name, but it was all pineapple-flavored. That was the night we got kicked out of Arby's.

- The proper glass is crucial to wine enjoyment. Before pouring wine, thoroughly rinse out the remnants of your cherry Icee.

- When throwing a tasting party, never serve more than one category of wine. [This tip courtesy of *The Guide To Sucking Every Bit Of Joy And Spontaneity Out Of Living*.]

This $29 Will Feed My Family Or Put A Pittsburgh Steelers Cap On My Head

By Jerry Grunwalt

Man, there's that Steelers cap I've had my eye on. We're talking the real deal here, an official NFL Pro Line sideline cap—the exact one Coach Cowher wears on Sundays. I've had my eye on that baby for a while now, and it's time I made my decision. It all boils down to this: the cap or a hot meal for the wife and kids.

Shit, that's a no-brainer.

It's not like the kids are going to starve to death if they miss supper one night. Especially not little Justin. He's turning into a real porker. I don't think I've ever seen him without a pudding pop jammed down his maw. Patrick could afford to lay off the sweet stuff, too. As for baby Amber, she's still on the bottle, so if we're out of formula for a day, she can just go on the tit. That's what God made 'em for. I will look so damn sharp cheering on Jerome Bettis and the boys next season in that cap.

I'm sure we have enough food in the house to make do. Jeanie can work miracles with a can of soup and a bag of rice. And, man, the things she can do with noodles. Casseroles are one of

> **If only I hadn't bought that official team Starter jacket last month, I'd have enough for the cap and the food. But I got no regrets about the jacket. It's been real cold lately, and it keeps me warm. Especially if I wear my new Champion reverse-weave Steelers sweatshirt underneath.**

her specialties. Tuna, ground beef—you name it, she can mix it up with noodles and soup. Of course, I won't be able to pick up any ground beef if I get this cap, and I think we only have two cans of tuna left from the last time it was on sale. Good thing Jeanie's got an eye for bargains, otherwise we'd have a hard time making ends meet. But, hey, we got noodles, so nothing's coming between me and that Steelers cap now.

I definitely won't be able to take the

> **It's not like the kids are going to starve to death if they miss supper one night. Especially not little Justin. He's turning into a real porker. I don't think I've ever seen him without a pudding pop jammed down his maw. Patrick could afford to lay off the sweet stuff, too.**

kids to a movie this weekend, but that's fine. They charge way too much for movies these days, anyway. And the kids could use some exercise. They'll thank me for buying this cap when they're healthy grown-ups because they were running around in the yard instead of sitting on their fat rumps in some darkened theater. If they still insist on zoning out, they can do it in front of the TV for free. Or I can put on my beautiful new Steelers cap and do a little show for them.

If only I hadn't bought that official team Starter jacket last month, I'd have enough for the cap and the food. But I got no regrets about the jacket. It's been real cold lately, and it keeps me warm. Especially if I wear my new Champion reverse-weave Steelers sweatshirt underneath.

Boy, things sure were tight that month. I was barely able to scrounge up the $250 to buy that official Jason Gildon gameday jersey, not to mention the $39.95 for the piece of authentic souvenir Astro Turf from Three Rivers. We had to put off buying Patrick that new pair of corrective shoes, but it's not like he was a total cripple without them. Sure, he was a little wobbly on the stairs, but he wouldn't exactly be flying up and down them even with the shoes. Besides, a little adversity builds character in a child. He'll thank me when he's older.

Jeanie may scream blue murder when she finds out about the cap, but she'll settle down after a while. She wasn't complaining when I couldn't pay the gas bill because I got her that V-neck sweater from the Penney's catalog for her birthday. There's only one thing more important than feeling fine, and that's looking fine, because you can always look in a mirror to cheer yourself up.

Steelers cap, here I come! ✑

Your Horoscope

By Lloyd Schumner Sr.
Retired Machinist and
A.A.P.B.-Certified Astrologer

Aries: (March 21–April 19)
Those hot-shot doctors may think your colon cancer is inoperable, but this week you and your trusty Scout knife are going to prove them wrong.

Taurus: (April 20–May 20)
Confusion over the definition of the word "elope" will soon bring you familiarity with Las Vegas' surprisingly comprehensive animal-cruelty laws.

Gemini: (May 21–June 21)
You will be chained to a rock, upon which eagles will devour your liver for all eternity, after you steal the secret of a great marinara sauce from the gods.

Cancer: (June 22–July 22)
You didn't think you were the type to marry a convicted murderer after reading his letters, but everyone else did.

Leo: (July 23–Aug. 22)
Remember, it's perfectly normal for your body to go through some changes while you are in the phase known as "post-mortem deliquescence."

Virgo: (Aug. 23–Sept. 22)
Anger and frustration overtake you when you decide that if you cannot have Betty Rubble, no man will.

Libra: (Sept. 23–Oct. 23)
After his untimely death, all those mean things you said about Dave will come back to haunt you. As will Dave himself.

Scorpio: (Oct. 24–Nov. 21)
A lovestruck man will play guitar and sing underneath your bedroom window this week, which might be romantic if it weren't Ted Nugent.

Sagittarius: (Nov. 22–Dec. 21)
You will spend the next few days in the company of people who firmly believe that you hate figure skating because of your lack of ability at it.

Capricorn: (Dec. 22–Jan. 19)
You will soon find yourself entangled in a messy accident with a knife thrower, although drunk driving, not knife throwing, is the real issue.

Aquarius: (Jan. 20–Feb. 18)
Gustav Holst will appear to you in a dream and refuse to leave until you agree that John Williams has been ripping him off for years.

Pisces: (Feb. 19–March 20)
It's not true that all the good band names are taken. But if believing that keeps you from starting a band, great.

VEST FEST from page 74

amounts of blood. Passersby were amazed by the unusually large amounts of blood. Passersby were amazed by the unusually large amounts of blood. Passersby were amazed by the unusually large amounts of blood. Passersby were amazed by the unusually large amounts of blood. Passersby were amazed by the unusually large amounts of blood. Passersby were amazed by the unusually large amounts of blood. Passersby were amazed by the unusually large amounts of blood. Passersby were amazed by the unusually large amounts of blood. Passersby were amazed by the unusually large amounts of blood. Passersby were amazed by the unusually large amounts of blood. Passersby were amazed by the unusually large amounts of blood. Passersby were amazed by the unusually large amounts of blood. Passersby were amazed by the unusually large amounts of blood. Passersby were amazed by the unusually large amounts of blood. Passersby were amazed by the unusually large amounts of blood. Passersby were amazed by the unusually large amounts of blood. Passersby were amazed by the unusually large amounts of blood. Passersby were amazed by the unusually large amounts of blood. Passersby were amazed by the unusually large amounts of blood. Passersby were

amounts of blood. Passersby were amazed by the unusually large amounts of blood. Passersby were amazed by the unusually large amounts of blood. Passersby were amazed by the unusually large

> **This is going to sound really racist, but bear with me.**

amounts of blood. Passersby were amazed by the unusually large amounts of blood. Passersby were amazed by the unusually large amounts of blood. Passersby were amazed by the unusually large amounts of blood. Passersby were amazed by the unusually large amounts of blood. Passersby were amazed by the unusually large amounts of blood. Passersby were amazed by the unusually large amounts of blood. Passersby were amazed by the unusually large amounts of blood. Passersby were amazed by the unusually large amounts of blood. Passersby were amazed by the unusually large
see VEST FEST page 81

LL Cool J Struggles To Come Up With Way To Brag About Being In *Rollerball*

see PEOPLE page 5C

School Bully Not So Tough Since Being Molested

see LOCAL page 11D

Yes, Area Man Has Been Told He Resembles A Fat Gregg Allman

see LOCAL page 14D

STATshot

A look at the numbers that shape your world.

New Cell-Phone Features

1. Three Ring Choices: Tone, Vibrate, or Water Squirt
2. One-touch babydaddy callin'
3. Chin strap
4. All callers' voices altered to sound like that of Sir Ian McKellen
5. Can be used to control nephew's toy racecar
6. Voice-activated talking

0 74470 94595 6

THE ONION • $2.00 US • $3.00 CAN

---

the ONION®

VOLUME 38 ISSUE 07   AMERICA'S FINEST NEWS SOURCE™   28 FEB.–06 MAR. 2002

Treasury Department Badly Needs Ones And Fives

WASHINGTON, DC—Critically low on small denominations, the Treasury Department put out an urgent call for ones and fives Monday.

"If we don't get some soon, we're going to run out," Deputy Treasury Secretary Kenneth Dam said. "And right now, we have no one we can send to the Bureau of Engraving and Printing to grab more. [Executive Secretary] Jeffrey [Kupfer] is in Federal Trade Commission meetings all day, and [Undersecretary] Peter [Fisher] is too new to handle cash."

Though Dam said he suspects there may be a fully stocked tray of cash in the department's safe, the only one who knows the combination is Secretary Paul O'Neill, who is at an economic summit in Stockholm until Saturday.

The shortfall, Dam said, is the result of the unusually busy day the department is having.

"For some reason, all the banks want

see TREASURY page 83

Left: An urgent call is put out to citizens on the statue in front of the Treasury Building.

March Named Breast Cancer Obliviousness Month

SAN FRANCISCO—The National Breast Cancer Obliviousness Foundation is gearing up for Breast Cancer Obliviousness Month, to be observed across the U.S. throughout the month of March.

"Each year in this country, more than 40 million Americans don't really think about breast cancer all that much," said National Breast Cancer Obliviousness Foundation director Judith Quinn at a press conference kicking off the month-long event. "These people get up each day and go to work without this dread disease ever crossing their minds."

Founded in 1997, the National Breast Cancer

see BREAST CANCER page 82

Above: An ad on a New York City bus.

Man Back With Girl His Best Friend Spent Week Criticizing

Above: Sorum and reconciled ex-girlfriend Mulberry, whom Weir (inset) prematurely lambasted.

PHILADELPHIA—On Sunday, Chris Sorum, 26, rekindled his relationship with Kate Mulberry, the ex-girlfriend Sorum's best friend Danny Weir had spent the previous week mercilessly criticizing.

"He told me it really was finally over between the two of them," Weir said. "So the night after the breakup, I took Chris out drinking and just started going off on what a colossal bitch I'd always thought Kate was. I told him everything I hated about her, stuff I never would've said if they were together. Like how psychotically possessive and controlling she was. And how she used to act like a know-it-all about shit she knew nothing about—like

see BEST FRIEND page 82

79

The Cigarette Tax

Twenty-two states are considering raising cigarette taxes to generate extra revenue, and in New York City, the cost of a pack may reach $7. What do *you* think?

"I think that if these politicians enjoyed a nice, relaxing smoke once in a while, they wouldn't propose such uptight laws."

Patti Courson
Receptionist

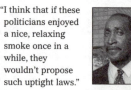

"The government is such a bunch of suckers. I haven't reported my cigarettes on my taxes once."

Frederick Purcell
Systems Analyst

"I don't care if they raise the price, because I'm the guy in the bar who doesn't smoke except when he drinks. Got a cigarette?"

Todd Kantner
Bus Driver

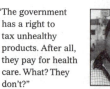

"How can I afford smokes now, especially with a baby on the way?"

Danielle Dawes
Waitress

"The government has a right to tax unhealthy products. After all, they pay for health care. What? They don't?"

Richard McCall
Contractor

"Well, $7 seems like a reasonable price to pay to calm my shakes and jitters over not having any fucking money."

Mike Dutler
Machinist

The New *Sesame Street*

For its 33rd season, which began last month, *Sesame Street* has been given its biggest overhaul ever. Among the changes:

- Show's locale moved from gritty New York City neighborhood to gated community of Sesame Heights, Long Island
- In sensitive segment, Bob, Susan, and Maria gently explain why change is good to distraught 30-year-old viewers
- Oscar The Grouch phased out for fear of giving children positive impression of living in garbage
- New segment teaches children value of *Sesame Street* merchandise
- Fewer recurring segments and extended plotlines to reduce confusion among viewers stoned off their asses
- "The Count" to more accurately reflect vampire culture
- Hippos, water buffaloes no longer forced to have bird on them
- Luis and Maria to go through bitter divorce to teach children that life is just a dark, lonely corridor of fear and pain
- Even more of that fucking Elmo's "Elmo like this!" and "Elmo like that!"

 the ONION®
America's Finest News Source.™

Herman Ulysses Zweibel
Founder

T. Herman Zweibel
Publisher Emeritus
J. Phineas Zweibel
Publisher
Maxwell Prescott Zweibel
Editor-In-Chief

Who Knew It Would Be So Easy To Impersonate A Priest?

By Daniel Vasconi

I've admired priests all my life. Whenever a priest walked into a room, everyone seemed to look at him with respect and admiration. I always thought it'd be great to be a priest, but the thought of going through years of vocational training and having to stop screwing women was too much for me. It was a glorious moment, indeed, when I realized I didn't need to do all that to become a priest.

To become a priest, all you really need is a priest outfit from a costume shop, a Bible, and the right attitude. If you can remember to stop swearing, be discreet about the bonin', and wash the stench of pot smoke out of your clothes, you're home free. Who knew it would be so easy?

I mean, you don't even need to know Latin. Hell, no one knows Latin anymore. But if you occasionally spout a few phrases that sound all Latiney, like, "*E Novus Unum Omnibus*," it makes you seem all the more authentic.

The thing you have to realize is, when you dress up like a priest, people want to believe you're a priest. I recently visited a small town in Missouri where no one knew me. I started walking around in my priest outfit, and within a few hours, I was invited

> **Another bonus of being a priest is the chicks. There always seems to be some spiritually troubled, sexy young thing who needs to confess.**

to a week's worth of home-cooked meals. Man, did I eat good! And you know what? Not a single person asked me to show my priest ID card before serving up the roast turkey and mashed potatoes.

I always thought the hard part of being a priest was giving people biblical advice and stuff. But I soon found out that you don't have to know jack shit about "John 3:14" or "Jeff 9:44" or whatever. Whenever someone asks me for spiritual guidance, I just mix a little common sense with whatever my uptight Aunt Martha might say, and people go away thinking I'm King Priest. And if

you really want to seal the deal, call the person "my child" or "my son." Works every time!

If only my brother Mark could see how these people hang on my every word. Then, maybe he wouldn't call me Doofus Dan. As a priest, I'm a lot

> **If you can remember to stop swearing, be discreet about the bonin', and wash the stench of pot smoke out of your clothes, you're home free.**

more admired than I ever was as a Chick-fil-A assistant manager. I wish I could go home for Christmas in my priest outfit and shove it in Mark's stupid face, but my family would disown me if they found out what I was doing.

Another bonus of being a priest is the chicks. There always seems to be some spiritually troubled, sexy young thing who needs to confess. And you wouldn't believe how easy it is to get into their pants! After listening to a girl yammer on about her problems for an hour or so, I tell her how moved I am by her spiritual dilemma. Then, I tell her how conflicted I am about the "strange stirrings" I'm grappling with as a result of meeting her. I don't know what it is about a man considering breaking his covenant with God that makes a girl's panties fly off, but it works like you wouldn't believe! For a guy whose only contact with women was in titty bars or crowded buses, this is Heaven. Praise be!

And the best part is, when I wake up next to the girl the next morning, it's easy as pie to escape. I just make like I've made a terrible mistake and tell her I have to beg God for forgiveness, and I'm gone. I don't even have to buy breakfast. Talk about a racket! You'd think every guy in America would be doing this by now!

Sometimes, I feel guilty about impersonating a priest, like I'm committing some kind of sin. (Maybe I'm starting to take this priest thing too seriously!) But then I come to my senses and say, "What's the harm?" Okay, so maybe a few couples out there aren't technically married in the eyes of God because of me. And maybe one or two people haven't

see PRIEST page 83

Ad-Agency Art Director 'Humbly Honored' To Be Working With Absolut

NEW YORK—Roland Kiefer, a recently hired art director with the advertising agency TBWA/Chiat/Day, was overcome with emotion Monday upon learning that he will join the team responsible for the Absolut vodka campaign.

"Absolut set the bar for brand image

> "People want Absolut not just for the flavor, but to be a part of the whole Absolut experience. And that all stems from this legendary ad campaign. I am honored to be carrying the torch."

and recognition," said a visibly moved Kiefer, 34. "Over the past 22 years, they've made themselves one of the world's most recognizable brands, not just of vodka, but of any consumer product. A bottle of Absolut vodka is not just alcohol—it's an icon. I just hope I'm up to the task."

Prior to joining TBWA/Chiat/Day, Kiefer worked at Andrews & Skibell, a Louisville, KY, ad agency. His accomplishments there included designing ads for Franks Nursery & Crafts, stay-in-school public-service ads for highway billboards, and Rallys Hamburgers inserts for the

Above: Kiefer shows off his new Absolut poster.

Sunday *Louisville Courier-Journal* coupon section.

"This is definitely a step up to the big leagues," Kiefer said. "Here is a product that has positioned itself as the nation's premier vodka brand. I mean, they've dominated the market to the point where a lot of people actually think the word 'absolute' is spelled 'absolut.' Now, *that's* brand saturation."

Though not much of a vodka drinker himself, Kiefer has long admired Absolut.

"When you're out at a bar, what do you ask for, a vodka cranberry or an Absolut cranberry?" Kiefer said. "Absolut, right? Why is that? By definition, vodkas are supposed to be odorless, colorless, and tasteless, so there really shouldn't be that much difference between them. People want Ab-

solut not just for the flavor, but to be a part of the whole Absolut experience. And that all stems from this legendary ad campaign. I am honored to be carrying the torch."

According to a March 2001 *Advertising Age* cover story, the Absolut campaign ranks among the 10 most memorable and effective of all time, standing alongside such giants as the

see ABSOLUT page 83

NEWS IN BRIEF

$5 Million Bounty Placed On Recession

WASHINGTON, DC—A determined President Bush posted a $5 million bounty on the nation's economic downturn Monday. "This recession may run its course, but it cannot hide," Bush said. "We will find you, and we will end you." Bush is also offering a $2 million reward for information leading to an increase in durable-goods orders in the second quarter.

Upset Woman Forced To Re-Sigh Louder

MCKEESPORT, PA—Failing to elicit sympathy or concern with her first attempt, Staffing Solutions office manager Connie Lindel was forced to re-sigh louder and more plaintively Monday. "Well, I guess I'll just turn off everyone else's lights at the end of the day myself," Lindel, 33, told coworkers

before letting out a second, longer sigh. "Oh, well." Lindel, who was unable to elicit any measure of sympathy with the follow-up sigh, is expected to try again Thursday with her arms folded and significantly more resignation in her voice.

Lee Greenwood Urges U.S. To Take Military Action Against Iraq

NASHVILLE, TN—With sales of "God Bless The U.S.A." waning after a five-month surge, country singer Lee Greenwood urged the U.S. to take military action against Iraq Monday. "Saddam Hussein is a despot with strong ties to terrorism, and his regime must be toppled," Greenwood said. "Unfortunately, our best chance of doing so is to send brave young American soldiers into dangerous, emotionally stirring combat situations." Greenwood added that he would be willing to perform his signa-

ture hit for the troops during a live CBS special if asked.

Parents' Password Cracked On First Try

REDONDO BEACH, CA—Nick Berrigan, 14, successfully hacked into his parents' AOL account on the first try Tuesday, correctly guessing that "Digby" was their password. "They actually used the dog's name," said Berrigan, deactivating the parental controls on his AOL account. "They don't give me much credit, do they?" Experts advise parents to secure Internet accounts with any password besides the name of a family pet.

Genetically Modified Broccoli Shrieks Benefits At Shoppers

BREMERTON, WA—A head of genetically modified broccoli shrieked

its numerous benefits at shoppers Monday in a Seattle-area Safeway. "*I contain 40 percent more vitamin A than non-modified broccoli!*" the head screeched at terrified produce-aisle customers. "*I can fight off insects and disease without the use of pesticides!*" Monsanto, which produced the vegetable, stressed that genetic-modification technology is still in its infancy, and that more pleasantly voiced broccoli should hit store shelves by 2003.

Warranty Outlasts Company

LODI, NJ—The five-year warranty for a UniTek MP3 player outlasted the product's manufacturer, which closed Monday after two years in business. "I still had more than four years left on that [warranty]," said Jeffrey Lalo, 44, who bought the MP3 player in June 2001. "Man, that sucks." Lalo said he plans to hang on to the certificate of warranty "just in case they somehow come back or something." ∅

Obliviousness Foundation is one of the nation's fastest-growing charitable organizations. As a result of the group's work, more than 120 million citizens are not aware of the serious

> "It's vital that we focus our energies on something other than the 190,000 new cases of breast cancer in the U.S. each year," Quinn said. "Because if we don't, we're all going to get pretty bummed out."

Above: A billboard produced by the National Breast Cancer Obliviousness Foundation.

threat breast cancer poses or the simple steps women can take to detect and treat the disease early.

Planned events include marches dedicated to various breast-cancer-unrelated items, including anteaters and motel-lobby vending machines, free cajun-cooking demonstrations, and the distribution of red ribbons to put people's minds on AIDS instead.

"We've come far in our short history, but much work lies ahead," Quinn said. "For example, we're about to produce a pamphlet with basic information on the disease and a list of breast-cancer research organizations to which people can donate money. Then we will leave those pamphlets sitting in some warehouse in Iowa,

just collecting duct."

Among the topics Americans will not learn more about during Breast Cancer Obliviousness Month are the importance of regular mammograms for women over 40, how to conduct an at-home self breast exam, and simple diet and lifestyle tips to help reduce the risk of getting the disease.

"It's vital that we focus our energies on something other than the 190,000 new cases of breast cancer in the U.S. each year," Quinn said. "Because if we don't, we're all going to get pretty bummed out."

Television networks have joined forces with the Breast Cancer Obliviousness Foundation in support of its

> Television networks have joined forces with the Breast Cancer Obliviousness Foundation in support of its cause.

cause. Throughout March, CBS will air public-service announcements featuring Ray Romano delivering the slogan, "Breast Cancer: Fuhgeddaboutit!" On March 28, NBC will air a "very routine episode" of *Friends* in which none

of the female characters are diagnosed with, or even mention, breast cancer. The episode will conclude with a phone number viewers may call to hear that evening's sports scores.

"Volunteers and donations are still badly needed if we as a nation are going to continue to be unaware of this dreaded killer," Quinn said. "For those who have already heard about breast cancer, it may be too late, but at least we can distract them to help ease their awareness while working to ensure that our daughters, and our daughters' daughters, never know much about this terrible condition."

Added Quinn: "Let's play badminton." ∅

theater, which she thought she was an expert in just because her mom did lighting at some repertory company. Whoops."

Added Weir: "I'm also pretty sure I called her a 'hatchet-faced hellbeast.'"

Trying to help Sorum get over what

> "In the past, I held my tongue because I figured they'd be back together," Weir said. "This time, though, Kate slept with her Pilates instructor, and Chris found out about it. I've never seen him so angry."

appeared to be a permanent breakup, Weir spent most of the week putting Mulberry down—and encouraging his friend to do the same.

"He really opened up and told me all the things he didn't like about Kate," Weir said. "And when I badmouthed her, for once he was agreeing with me instead of defending her like he usually does. He was like, 'How could I have been so stupid?' At one point, he even thanked me because he said I really put into perspective how much better off he is without her. Well, I guess I didn't put it into that much perspective, after all."

Though Sorum and Mulberry have broken up seven times during their three-year relationship, Weir had always remained quiet about Mulberry's various faults.

"In the past, I held my tongue because I figured they'd be back together," Weir said. "This time, though, Kate slept with her Pilates instructor, and Chris found out about it. I've never seen him so angry. I thought to myself, 'Yes! I'm finally gonna get to tell him everything I think of that witch.'"

Weir said he now fears that Sorum will tell—or has already told—Mulberry what he said about her.

"Even though Chris was right there complaining with me, I said some pretty foul shit about Kate," Weir said. "If push comes to shove, he'll probably side with her, even though he totally agreed with me when I said she has a way of twisting his head around

until he doesn't know what to believe anymore. Christ, I can't believe they're back together."

Further complicating the Sorum-Mulberry reconciliation are the second- and third-hand criticisms Weir relayed to Sorum from other friends.

"I told Chris that the guys have always hated her, especially Pete [Kelleher]," Weir said. "One night last summer, Pete was cracking us all up with this hilarious imitation he does of Kate yanking Chris out of a room. He made me promise I would never tell Chris about the imitation, but I figured I could after the break-up. Well, now Pete is probably seriously pissed at me, too."

Thus far, Weir has suffered no backlash from Sorum, who has not spoken to him since getting back together with Mulberry.

"I'm not sure if Chris hasn't called in the last few days because he's mad at me, or because he and Kate are too busy with their make-up fucking," Weir said. "Hopefully, it's the latter. Who knows, maybe he doesn't even remember what I said about her. Then again, it's pretty hard to forget when somebody calls your girlfriend of the past three years 'the most shallow, moody, bitchy, manipulative, all-around unlik-

> "If push comes to shove, he'll probably side with her, even though he totally agreed with me when I said she has a way of twisting his head around until he doesn't know what to believe anymore. Christ, I can't believe they're back together."

able person I have ever met.'"

Weir said he will not be so quick to offer Sorum his opinion of Mulberry when the couple breaks up again.

"Next time, I'm gonna wait a good two months before saying anything bad about Kate," Weir said. "And even then, I'm gonna keep my insults nice and vague so I can retract them if I need to. Make that when I need to." ∅

ABSOLUT from page 81

Energizer bunny, the Wendy's "Where's The Beef" spots of the '80s, and the Burma Shave billboards of the '50s. While Kiefer admitted that the Absolut campaign's storied history is "more than a little intimidating," he said he is confident that he can contribute to its ever-growing legacy.

"Everything they've done, from Absolut Warhol to Absolut Manhattan, is just so inspired," Kiefer said. "How do you top an image of Manhattan with Central Park shaped like an Absolut bottle? You don't. You can only hope to come close."

"That's exactly what I hope to do with my Absolut Chan," Kiefer continued. "It's going to be a picture of a piece of wood with a bottle-shaped

> "Two words and one image sell you not just a vodka, but also a lifestyle. These ads say, 'You are a creative and intelligent person who doesn't need to be told what to buy using some sleazy, gimmicky pitch.'"

piece cut out in the middle, which is where Jackie Chan gave the thing a ferocious kung-fu kick."

Kiefer said the Absolut ads are "more than just ads—they're art."

"What other ads do you see people actually collecting?" Kiefer asked. "Absolut ads get shown in galleries and sold at auctions. That's when you know you've created something truly special. Man, if I could get one of my Absolut ads displayed in a gallery somewhere—and maybe even take home a Clio in the process—I'd die a happy man."

"The ads' power comes from their simplicity," Kiefer continued. "Two words and one image sell you not just a vodka, but also a lifestyle. These ads say, 'You are a creative and intelligent person who doesn't need to be told what to buy using some sleazy, gimmicky pitch.' The term 'trailblazing' may seem a bit grandiose for an ad campaign, but that's precisely what Absolut has done. Sheer genius."

Erica Schlangen, Kiefer's girlfriend of two years, does not share his enthusiasm for the ads.

"I don't get what he's so excited about," said Schlangen, 26. "I mean, take a chimp, give him a banana Photoshopped in the shape of an Absolut bottle, caption it 'Absolut Monkeyshines,' and—pow!—you have an Absolut ad. I just pulled that out of my ass. How hard can it be?" Ø

Ask Someone Who Insists On Dominating The Conversation

By Joyce Colquitt
Someone Who Insists On Dominating the Conversation

Dear Someone Who Insists On Dominating The Conversation,

I don't know what to do about my boss. I like to wear skirts to the office and, last week, while I was at the photocopy machine, he—

Threatened In Thibodeaux

Dear Threatened,

Yeah? You should work for my jerk of a boss. On Friday, he calls me in and says, "Um, Joyce, Debbie didn't finish her receipts, so I need you to take care of that." Hello?! Am I going to get Debbie's paycheck, too? Because if not, you can keep dreaming. You know what else burns me about this guy? He demands that all proposed expenses, right down to office supplies, be sent to him for approval. Then he lets those requests sit around on his desk for weeks. By the time he got around to signing off on Patti's request for more adding-machine tape last week, five of the office's ten machines had run out. And, of course, it takes three business days for new orders to arrive. If you're gonna micromanage, at least do it well.

Dear Someone Who Insists On Dominating The Conversation,

My longtime boyfriend and I were recently married, and for a wedding gift, his parents—

Hurt In Hutchins

Dear Hurt,

Don't even get me started on wedding gifts. When I married Harvey, his brother Jack gave us this butter dish

> Don't even get me started on wedding gifts. When I married Harvey, his brother Jack gave us this butter dish that looked like it cost about eight bucks. Do you know what that cheapo does for a living?

that looked like it cost about eight bucks. Do you know what that cheapo does for a living? He's a corporate attorney! Every time we see him, he's bragging about how he got promoted to partner and got a big raise. Gee, no wonder you can afford these fantastic butter dishes with that kind of job! Then, about two years ago, Jack comes over to our house, drunk as a mule, talking about how he needs a place to stay for the night. I'm like, "Oh, *I* see! You screwed up your marriage, so now you're here to screw up mine, too." His sister Paulette is no prize, either, let me tell you. This gal, she's been married and divorced three times already, and now she's on her way to altar-trip number four. All this before the age of 35. Look out, Zsa-Zsa, here comes Paulette!

Dear Someone Who Insists On Dominating The Conversation,

Our daughter died last year. Ever since, we—

Grieving In Grinnell

Dear Grieving,

You want to talk about death, God forbid you should have to bury a grandparent who had no insurance and nothing in the bank. Grandma Elaine, she keeled over after eating some bad swordfish—why she was at such a fancy restaurant on her income, we'll never know—and Social Security comes up with a whopping $200 for burial expenses. So, get this: My cousin Sharon—who has no money, either, she works at the Sizzler—won't shut up about how "Nana deserves the best" for her final arrangements. In other words, "Cough up, Joyce," you know? So I have to empty my vacation fund for a $3,000 casket that no one will ever see again. And Sharon comes to the funeral, says nothing, does nothing, doesn't lay Flower One on this casket, and leaves the wake after half an hour. It's like, sorry you're too poor to afford a single flower, Sharon! What's more, she proceeded to take a whole week off from work to mourn. How do you like that for the topper?

Joyce Colquitt is a syndicated columnist whose weekly advice column, Ask Someone Who Insists On Dominating The Conversation, *appears in more than 250 newspapers nationwide.* Ø

TREASURY from page 79

ones and fives today," Dam said. "Usually, it's twenties we run low on first, because everybody needs them for their cash machines, but today it's the small stuff."

In addition to a sign on the Alexander Hamilton statue in front of the Treasury Building, Dam posted a handwritten notice on the front door reading, "We need ones and fives!!! Any that you have would be hugley [sic] appreciated!!!" Thus far, no one has come forward.

The appeal was directed at any U.S. citizens in the vicinity of the department, as well as members of Congress, whose annual budget allocation to the Treasury Department is forthcoming.

"We have, like, less than 10 ones left right now," Dam said. "We have a few rolls of quarters we could give out four at a time, but those won't last very long."

Early Tuesday morning, Dam put in a call to the Internal Revenue Service

to lend the Treasury any singles it may have on hand from early tax returns.

"So far, I haven't heard back from [IRS commissioner] Charles [Rossot-

> "We have, like, less than 10 ones left right now," Dam said.

ti]," Dam said. "I left a message, but he must be real busy this time of year. Hopefully soon."

Dam, who was left in charge of the Treasury in O'Neill's absence, was explicitly told by the secretary to make sure the department kept plenty of small bills on hand.

"This is really getting bad," Dam said. "All we need is for one more lending institution to come in here and ask us to break a twenty and that's it." Ø

PRIEST from page 80

been given their proper Last Rites. But in reality, religion is all just a big show to impress your friends and family, anyway, so as long as they believe it, that's what matters.

Impersonating a priest isn't quite as easy as I've made it out to be. You have to keep on your toes a lot of the time. Forget to say "bless you" a few too many times when people sneeze and people start looking at you funny. I also should probably learn the names of the guys in that "Last Supper" picture. But the great thing is, once people start getting a little suspicious, you can start all over in another town. It's not like people love priests only in Missouri!

Sometimes, I just want to wrap my arms around the Catholic Church and give it a big, wet kiss for getting me the respect and admiration I could never earn myself.

I think I'm ready to move up and become a bishop. I bet that's where the real goods are. Ø

I Almost Lost It All

The Cruise
By Jim Anchower

Hola, amigos. What say? I know it's been a long time since I rapped at ya, but your old pal Jim's been thicker than a donkey's dick with problems.

First off, I got canned from my job at the California Fajita Cantina. Two Saturdays ago, I was trying to do my damn job and clear a customer's plate off a table, and this guy said, all rude like, "I'm not finished with that. Please wait until I'm done."

Man, was I steamed! I took one look at that fatty and told him he looked like he'd had enough long ago. Then he says to me, "You need to watch your mouth, son." So I say, "You gotta watch your mouth, tubbo, 'cause you got a lot more going in yours than I got comin' outta mine." He went all apeshit and ratted me out to Mr. Janoff, my manager. And you know what? That Janoff fucker wouldn't back me up! He canned me on the spot! No great loss there, though: I figure any job that doesn't allow you to be a man and stand up for yourself ain't a job for Jim Anchower.

Anyway, my new job is at a museum. I work in the coat-check room. All I gotta do is sit there and collect coats

> **Every tape was a reminder that there are guys out there who know exactly what you've been going through, and they have a song for it. Nazareth, Bad Company, Journey, BTO... every one of them.**

and purses and not steal anything. How hard is that? It's not challenging, but if I wanted a challenge, I'd have become a nuclear surgeon.

The whole job situation worked itself out, but that ain't the only problem I've had lately. Last Thursday, my apartment got broken into. When I got home that night, the window on my door was broken and the door was unlocked. I had to do some fast figuring to try to remember if it was me who did it. I was able to sort out pretty quick that it wasn't, so I went inside.

I ran all over the apartment, checking for the essentials. Luckily, it was all still there. My Jenny McCarthy centerfold was still on the wall. My PlayStation 2, busted though it was, was still in front of the TV. The sticker-covered boombox I bought off some dude at a NORML rally was still by my bedside. Even my stash was still in

> **Last Thursday, my apartment got broken into. When I got home that night, the window on my door was broken and the door was unlocked. I had to do some fast figuring to try to remember if it was me who did it.**

place, but that says more about my shrewd stash-hiding skills than about the crooks who busted into my pad.

The crooks must have gotten spooked by something and ran off before they got a chance to take anything. But next time, I might not be so lucky. That's why I'm thinking about getting a gun, in case they decide to come back while I'm home. For once, the law would totally be on my side if they came in and I blew 'em away. I'm not a violent man, but I'm prepared to do what I have to do to protect my home.

I guess there was one bright spot in all of this. It made me realize I need to appreciate the things that are truly important. I mean, I could have lost it all. They could've taken every last one of my things, and I'd be left with nothing. That made me appreciate my tapes all the more. I mean, I guess I could always buy more tapes if they ever got stolen, but it wouldn't be the same.

For example, I've had this tape of REO Speedwagon's *Hi Infidelity* ever since I can remember. It's got sentimental value. As soon as I found it after the break-in, it went straight into my boombox. Man, that Kevin Cronin knows how to knock it out. And Gary Richrath can really wail on guitar! I mean, you listen to the song "Take It On The Run" and you really get pumped. It's real rock 'n' roll, not like the crap they make today.

After that, I took out some Grand Funk Railroad. If you ain't heard them, all I can do is pity you and then tell you to get your ass to Sam Goody for a copy of *E Pluribus Funk*. I mean, "Footstompin' Music"? What more do you need to know? I don't care who let the dogs out, all I care is that Mark Farner and crew are keeping it real.

When that was over, I went for the Zep. I kept that going for a few hours, 'cause once that levee breaks, how do you stop the waters? You don't, hombre. You just have to ride the wave. Then I moved on to some Styx, some James Gang, and, for dessert, a little Mountain. Hell, I was up all night listening to music that could have been stolen but wasn't. That made it all the sweeter.

Every tape was a reminder that there are guys out there who know exactly what you've been going through, and they have a song for it. Nazareth, Bad Company, Journey, BTO... every one of them. They've got what it takes to keep a man going in dark times. When you gotta sit in a room full of coats for eight straight hours, wishing you could sneak out for a fast bowl, sometimes all you got to keep you sane is that Foghat song going through your head.

Actually, that coat-check job makes me go fucking nuts sometimes, tunes or no tunes. Don't let that discourage you from getting yourself some hard-rockin' tapes, though. I just wanted to be honest with ya. ✍

Your Horoscope

By Lloyd Schumner Sr.
Retired Machinist and
A.A.P.B.-Certified Astrologer

Aries: (March 21–April 19)
This week, envy rears its ugly head, realizes there's nothing enviable about you, blinks a couple times, and goes back to sleep.

Taurus: (April 20–May 20)
One of your biggest problems is your inability to take life as it comes. Another is your ongoing inability to take your own life.

Gemini: (May 21–June 21)
You have always considered yourself a belt-and-suspenders type, which makes it all the more amusing when your pants fall down anyway.

Cancer: (June 22–July 22)
You have as bright a future in the area of romance as you do in just about any other area, as far as that goes.

Leo: (July 23–Aug. 22)
There are thousands of types of people in the world: the type that divides the world up into two types of people, and the thousands of other types.

Virgo: (Aug. 23–Sept. 22)
Though you believe otherwise, it is not healthy to prefer the novels of Henry James to actual human contact.

Libra: (Sept. 23–Oct. 23)
Your fascination with monkeys is so well known that it makes the selection of an unbiased jury nearly impossible.

Scorpio: (Oct. 24–Nov. 21)
Your conviction that there is a monster under the bed would be a mere eccentricity if you weren't so heavily armed and it was your own bed.

Sagittarius: (Nov. 22–Dec. 21)
Your bladder-control problems are a thing of the past when you find yourself able to consistently hit a two-inch target at 100 yards.

Capricorn: (Dec. 22–Jan. 19)
You will finally accept responsibility for your infant daughter. With any luck, she's still where you left her last month.

Aquarius: (Jan. 20–Feb. 18)
A person can only hide behind one's virginity for so long. Even if, as in your case, it is a particularly harsh and forbidding virginity.

Pisces: (Feb. 19–March 20)
Your money problems will worsen this week when the other prisoners start trading you for fewer cigarettes than usual.

PASTRAMI from page 82

amounts of blood. Passersby were amazed by the unusually large amounts of blood. Passersby were amazed by the unusually large amounts of blood. Passersby were amazed by the unusually large

> **Wow, that sure was a great Black History Month.**

amounts of blood. Passersby were amazed by the unusually large amounts of blood. Passersby were amazed by the unusually large amounts of blood. Passersby were amazed by the unusually large amounts of blood. Passersby were amazed by the unusually large amounts of blood. Passersby were amazed by the unusually large amounts of blood. Passersby were amazed by the unusually large amounts of blood. Passersby were amazed by the unusually large

see PASTRAMI page 88

Pope Asks To Be Taken Off List Of World's 100 Richest People

see WORLD page 4A

Shopper Takes Bizarre Journey Beyond Bed, Bath

see LOCAL page 9B

Bicep Felt On Demand

see LOCAL page 10B

Cloned Cat Neutered

see SCIENCE page 7C

STATshot

A look at the numbers that shape your world.

Least-Appropriate Baby-Shower Games

1. Belly-Flop Contest
2. Do a shot whenever anyone says "cute"
3. Feel The Baby Kick From The Inside
4. Down Syndrome Roulette
5. Ring Around The Pathetic, Childless Spinster

THE ONION • $2.00 US • $3.00 CAN

---

 the ONION®

VOLUME 38 ISSUE 08   AMERICA'S FINEST NEWS SOURCE™   07–13 MARCH 2002

Bush Calls On Business Leaders To Create 500,000 Shitty Jobs By 2003

THE RECESSION

WASHINGTON, DC—In a keynote address at the National Economic Summit, President Bush issued a bold challenge to the nation's business leaders Monday, calling on them to create 500,000 shitty jobs by next year.

"So long as unemployment continues to rise, this recession will continue, as well,"said Bush, speaking before nearly 400 of the nation's top CEOs. "That is why I am turning to you to create thousands of new shit jobs. Whether it is a night-shift toilet-cleaning position at an airport or a fry-cook post at a KFC, it's up to you to help provide every hard-working American with a demeaning, go-nowhere job."

During his 25-minute speech, Bush cited a number of industries with the potential to provide gainful, godawful

see BUSH page 88

Above: Bush challenges the nation's top CEOs to create thousands of new shit jobs.

Above: Liman with a 1985 Corolla he is considering buying.

Area Man Perpetually In Process Of Buying Or Selling Car

MARION, IL—Local resident Don Liman, 49, is almost constantly in the process of buying, selling, or preparing to buy or sell a car, sources reported Monday.

"That's Don for you," said Russell Flange, Liman's neighbor. "We always say old Donnie's got a one-car car lot instead of a driveway. There's a Sable wagon for sale in front of his house right now."

"It's not easy to find the exact right car," said Liman, whose search for the ideal car is now entering its 13th year. "But with a little hard work and some

see MAN page 89

McDonald's Drops 'Hammurderer' Character From Advertising

OAK BROOK, IL—Bowing to outcry from consumers and parents groups, the McDonald's Corporation announced Monday that it is discontinuing its new advertising mascot, "The Hammurderer," a mischievous, homicidal imp who kills McDonaldland characters and takes their sandwiches.

Developed by Chicago advertising agency DDB Needham, the Hammurderer made his debut two months ago and has since appeared in a series of Saturday-morning television commercials, as well as on Happy Meal bags and activity placemats. All appearances by and references to the violent, ill-tempered prison escapee will be dropped.

"Over the years, McDonald's has successfully introduced a number of new characters whose defining characteristic is a certain measure of comical, criminal intent," said Andrew Perlich, McDonald's vice-president of promotions. "Such shady characters as The Hamburglar, The Goblins, and the bloodthirsty pirate Captain Crook have all fit nicely into the McDonald's advertising universe. We had every reason to believe that the Hammurderer, with his long rap sheet of burger-related crimes and his signa-

Above: The discontinued character.

ture cry of 'Stabble Stabble Stabble,' would take his place in this proud lineage of McDonaldland mischief-makers."

The Hammurderer's Jan. 11 debut ad—in which he seizes and devours the McDonald's Happy Meal Guys, oblivious to their frantic screams—earned poor marks from parents and child-development experts, who feared the spot might send the message to children that killing is acceptable. Several weeks later, more controversy erupted over the promotional coloring book "Shivved In The McRibs," in which the Hammurderer

see MCDONALD'S page 88

85

The Saudi Peace Plan

A Middle East peace plan from Saudi Crown Prince Abdullah has generated hope among both Palestinians and Israelis. What do you think?

Vicki Kjell
Nurse

"I applaud Saudi Arabia for being willing to compromise on the degree to which Israel is wrong."

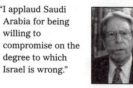

Robert Zisk
Systems Analyst

"I think the U.S. should endorse Crown Prince Abdullah's plan only after exhaustive review by King Vitaman and Queen Sara Saturday."

Bryan Brecht
Carpet Installer

"Wow, the Grammys and a Middle East peace plan, all in one week."

Isaac Robinson
Defense Attorney

"This proposal is being put forth by a corrupt kingdom on behalf of two ancient sworn enemies whose agendas are dictated by their most extreme factions. How could it fail?"

Miriam Holt
Interior Decorator

"These Saudis are just a bunch of Jimmy Carter wannabes."

Fred Duffy
Clerk

"Hurrah! Peace at last!"

Bono To The Rescue

Called "rock's conscience," U2 frontman and political crusader Bono has met with everyone from Kofi Annan to Colin Powell. What has he been doing recently?

- Tirelessly dedicating self to ending Third World debt, no matter how many magazine covers he must appear on in process
- Restoring humanity's faith in the power and the promise and the possibility of rock and roll
- Feeding starving Somalis by dividing single loaf into many
- Defeating Bruce Springsteen in epic, five-hour earnest-off
- Vowing to lobby Congress for African aid on progressively larger Jumbotrons until demands are met
- Shouldering the burdens of a post-Sept. 11 world/Buying another pair of blue-tinted wrap-around shades
- Revealing that The Edge will betray him three times before cock crows
- Thinking about writing song about deliverance and redemption; also maybe one about transcendence

the ONION®
America's Finest News Source.™

Herman Ulysses Zweibel
Founder

T. Herman Zweibel
Publisher Emeritus
J. Phineas Zweibel
Publisher
Maxwell Prescott Zweibel
Editor-In-Chief

Point-Counterpoint: The Generation Gap
Youth Is Wasted On The Young

By Leonard Kloss

They say hindsight is 20/20 and, boy, are they right. Young people fritter away the gifts of youth, wasting their time on silly video games and whatnot. Don't they understand how important it is to make the most of your life while you're still young?

If I were in my 20s again, I'd appreciate the things young people routinely take for granted. Like skating on a frozen lake, and running through a beautiful meadow. Oh, what I wouldn't give to have my strength and vitality back! Back then, I thought it would last forever, but now I know better.

Speaking of knowing better, with what I know now, I could probably start my own business, become a major-league baseball coach, and clean up on the stock market—all at the same time. I made a lot of mistakes as a youngster, but with the benefit of experience, I'd make the most of every opportunity that came my way.

When I see some of these young punks wasting their best years, it just makes me so angry. They think they're going to live forever, but when they get to be my age, they'll wish they hadn't wasted so much time drinking and swearing and hanging out at the mall in their shiny pants.

> **They think they're going to live forever, but when they get to be my age, they'll wish they hadn't wasted so much time drinking and swearing and hanging out at the mall in their shiny pants.**

Just look at my grandson, Daniel. All he does is drive around in circles with his friends and listen to his bleep-bleep music. Doesn't he realize that while he wastes his time talking on the phone or sitting in front of the TV, his salad days are quickly slipping away?

It's not like I haven't tried talking to Daniel. I keep telling him he should see Europe while he's still spry, and that if he saved a fraction of his pay-

see POINT page 90

Medication Is Wasted On The Old

How come, with so many awesome drugs out there, the only people who get to use them are the elderly? They have access to all this great shit, but they're too boring and feeble to get high off them. It's like my buddies and I always say: Medication is wasted on the old.

By Brandi Hopkins

There are tons of pills and drugs out there. But are they going to the people who know how much fun snorting ephedrine is? Or how amazing codeine makes you feel? Nope. Instead, all the good drugs are going to a bunch of grandmas and grandpas who take them responsibly and safely.

It's not like drugs are gonna cure the old folks, anyway: Their main health problem is that they're old. So while all the good stuff is going toward lowering their blood pressure or reducing their Alzheimer's symptoms, my friends and I are stuck huffing paint thinner. I'll be the first to support a pill that cures old age, but until that day comes, let's put the drugs where they can be best utilized—with the young.

If I get caught with a bag of weed by an undercover cop, I'm going to be doing serious time. But if you're old and tell a doctor you have glaucoma, you get to live in a beautiful, government-sanctioned marijuana haze. Not that

> **So while all the good stuff is going toward lowering their blood pressure or reducing their Alzheimer's symptoms, my friends and I are stuck huffing paint thinner.**

they even appreciate it. Shit, most of those ancient glaucoma sufferers have probably never watched *The Wall* straight, much less baked off their asses.

Just thinking about all the OxyContin that's wasted on old folks makes me weep. You think the elderly are crushing it up to get heroin-like highs the way me and my friends would? No

see COUNTERPOINT page 90

Denver Optometrist Not Sure Why He Has Gay Cult Following

LAKEWOOD, CO—Gene Podrewski, a Denver-area optometrist and father of two, expressed befuddlement Monday over his status as a gay camp icon.

"I'm not exactly sure why I have this huge gay following," Podrewski said. "I'm a likable enough guy, but I've never been particularly glamorous or charismatic. I'm not in showbiz, and I don't act or sing. But, for some reason, gay men put me up there with Judy Garland and Cher."

Over the past several years, Podrewski, 44, has cultivated a large and devoted following among gay men nationwide, and the whirlwind of attention and adoration perplexes him.

"Not *The Advocate* again," said Podrewski, checking his voicemail messages at work. "How many times do I have to tell them I have no opinion on the Bea Arthur one-woman show? And the photo shoot David LaChapelle wants to schedule for July totally interferes with my family's vacation. I don't care if that's the only time he's available."

Podrewski first discovered his popularity with gays in June 1998 while shopping for a birthday gift for his wife Marsha in Congress Park, a trendy Denver neighborhood known for its cluster of gay bars and boutiques. In the window of a gay-themed bookstore was a life-size cardboard cutout of Podrewski.

"I couldn't believe what I was seeing: There it was, an image of me in the window of a gay bookstore, right next to a poster of Bette Davis," Podrewski said. "I immediately went in and asked the clerk where they got it.

Above: Optometrist and gay icon Gene Podrewski.

When the clerk saw me, his eyes widened and he screamed, 'Oh my God! I can't believe it's *you!*'"

Further evidence of Podrewski's gay appeal soon emerged. The day of the 1998 Denver Gay Pride Parade, Podrewski and his family found themselves serenaded outside their suburban home by worshipful fans. Invitations to fashion shows, theater premieres, and exclusive night spots poured in. The gay punk band Pansy Division featured Podrewski's face on

an album cover.

"It's very nice of them, and I have nothing against anyone, but I just don't feel comfortable being the focus of all this attention," Podrewski said. "I don't mean to snub people, but I have my own life. Between my career and family obligations, I'm extremely busy. I'm sure John Galliano is a very talented designer, but I have a church potluck to attend the day of his runway show."

Podrewski may be mystified by the

> "I'm a likable enough guy, but I've never been particularly glamorous or charismatic. I'm not in showbiz, and I don't act or sing. But, for some reason, gay men put me up there with Judy Garland and Cher."

attention, but Rod Martinez is not. The author of two unauthorized biographies of Podrewski, *Gene!: The Eyes Have It* and *Gene!: The Eyes STILL Have It*, Martinez said he has a keen grasp of Podrewski's cult appeal among gays.

"It's difficult to explain to straight people," said Martinez, seated in his San Francisco apartment below an oversized, wildly colored silkscreen print of Podrewski's face. "Gene *is* adorable, sure, but it's not really sexual. It's more because that man has been to hell and back. He's no saint, and he has a lot of self-destructive impulses, but he's dealt with his personal demons with courage and a wicked sense of humor. He's a survivor in the truest sense and an inspiration to the gay community, which has seen its own share of pain, misun-

see GAY page 89

NEWS IN BRIEF

Paleontology Class Winces Whenever Fundamentalist Kid Raises Hand

STATE COLLEGE, PA—The 24 other students in a Penn State Paleontology 101 discussion section wince with dread whenever fundamentalist Christian Joseph Moseley raises his hand, classmates reported Tuesday. "As soon as that guy's hand shoots up, the whole class tenses up and is like, 'Oh, God, here we go again,'" classmate Colin Herberger said. "I think he thinks he plays a valuable role in the class, acting as the 'opposing viewpoint,' but it's just annoying."

Dog Chastised For Acting Like Dog

SACRAMENTO, CA—Obeying the instincts bred into him by millions of years of evolution, Shiner, a 2-year-old golden retriever, incurred his owner's wrath Monday by acting like a dog. "Stop barking at that damn squirrel!" Terri Solanis shouted at the dog. "Can't you sit still for five minutes?" Solanis has previously scolded Shiner for sniffing feces encountered on the sidewalk, licking his own groin, and wolfing down his food.

Area Man Plays 'Imagine' Every Time He Sees A Piano

SALEM, OR—Friends of Bill Moreland expressed irritation Monday over the 29-year-old's habit of playing John Lennon's "Imagine" whenever a piano is in sight. "It's like this desperate grab for attention he tries to pass off as totally casual," friend Alan Carter said. "He'll sit down at the piano with this really deep look on his face, then launch into those really simple first few bars, expecting every-

one to be amazed and moved." Friends say the habit has persisted since Moreland was in the fifth grade, when he switched to "Imagine" from the *Jaws* theme.

U.N. Tribunal Swayed By Thousands Of Children's Letters To Milosevic

THE HAGUE, NETHERLANDS—Members of the U.N. war-crimes tribunal were swayed in favor of former Yugoslav president Slobodan Milosevic Monday, when sack after sack of letters from children around the world were heaped onto the presiding judge's desk. "Dear Mr. Milosevic, please get out of jail soon!" read one letter from 6-year-old Brittany White of Houston. Another, from 10-year-old Xiang Xiu of Beijing, read: "We love you, Slobodan! The children of China pray for you!!!" Judge Richard

George May, deeply moved by the outpouring of love, ruled that Milosevic is a treasure to children of all ages and then freed him with a bang of his gavel.

Book-Club Meeting Degenerates Into Discussion Of Oscars

MINOT, ND—A weekly meeting of the Minot Public Library's "Book Buddies" club degenerated into a discussion of the upcoming Academy Awards Tuesday. "We were talking about that week's book, *A Bend In The Road* by Nicholas Sparks, when somebody asked if anyone had seen the movie version of [Sparks'] *A Walk To Remember*," group leader Ellen Talmadge said. "Then Bill [Polk] asked if anybody had seen *John Q*. After that, we never really got back to the book." Talmadge added that she considers Nicole Kidman "a lock" for her performance in *Moulin Rouge*. ∅

employment for thousands of laid-off Americans.

"I challenge those of you who have made your fortunes in the fields of sheet-metal fabrication, poultry processing, and highway-toll collecting to expand your roster of menial, low-

Bush outlined a plan to offer $10 billion in incentives and tax breaks to companies that demonstrate a commitment to providing soul-suckingly miserable wage-slave employment for Americans.

paying positions with no hope of advancement," Bush said. "That is your strength, as it should be the strength of us all."

Bush outlined a plan to offer $10 billion in incentives and tax breaks to companies that demonstrate a commitment to providing soul-suckingly miserable wage-slave employment for Americans.

"We have too many talented people wasting away on our unemployment rolls," Bush said. "And I say, if a broom-factory owner can give a man the opportunity to dunk handfuls of brittle, flammable straw into rank, filthy vats of molten tar for $6.15 an hour, then that broom-factory owner deserves a major tax break."

Business leaders across the country have been quick to show their support for the president's plan, pledging to create thousands of new low-paying, status-free positions.

"Elco Products is proud to announce that we are looking for qualified applicants to work as line workers in

Above: Four shittily employed members of the American workforce.

our toxic-adhesive rat-trap division," Elco Products CEO Stephen Nevins said. "We are proud to do our part to help American workers claw their way back up to their knees."

"I can make it possible for up to 50 people in the American Southwest to be mucking out grease traps by this time next week," said Rudy Maleska, president of SouthwasteCo, a Tucson, AZ, industrial-waste-removal service.

"Whatever I can do to help my country, count me in."

Critics of Bush's plan were quick to point to its weaknesses, such as a lack of health coverage.

"Under this plan, we cannot guarantee people that their crap jobs will always provide them with healthcare from some shitty HMO," U.S. Sen. Russ Feingold (D-WI) said. "What's the point in earning $17,000 a year

Critics of Bush's plan were quick to point to its weaknesses.

wiping the asses of the elderly as an attendant in a nursing home if you can't be sure you'll have at least some inadequate health plan if something happens to you?"

Bush's supporters, for their part, point to the president's recent domestic successes.

"In the past 12 months, we've seen a 7 percent rise in the availability of horrendous housing," U.S. Sen. Don Nickles (R-OK) said. "The current administration has also been working to make absolutely sure that economically disadvantaged children in this country get a substandard education and three vomit-inducing meals a day. Overall, the standard of shitty living has never been higher."

Concluding his speech, Bush reiterated his commitment to creating lousy fucking jobs for all.

"The average unemployed person has given so much to American business," Bush said. "Now it's time for American business to give something really shitty back." Ø

decapitates Mayor McCheese and eats his head. Responding to widespread public outrage, McDonald's executives defended the coloring book as "not nearly as violent or socially irresponsible as it has been made out to be, given that the Mayor's head is, in fact, a giant and conceivably edible cheeseburger."

But the uproar over the latest commercial, in which Birdie The Early Bird is garroted by the Hammurderer and her body tossed in a Dumpster, was vociferous enough to prompt the fast-food giant to pull the plug.

"We are sensitive to the concerns of parents and will immediately begin phasing out this character," Perlich said. "Whether we will remove him from commercials without explanation or write him out of the spots with a bloody police standoff, we have yet to decide. But we're confident that the

The Hammurderer is quickly becoming regarded as the worst-received advertising mascot since Kool-Aid's 1989 discontinuation of "The Grapist," a huge purple monster who sodomizes thirsty children.

Hammurderer will be off the national radar by April."

Hammurderer toys and promotional

items, which include dolls, T-shirts, ski masks, and spiked bats, have been recalled and are expected to become prized collectibles.

This is not the first time a McDonald's character has stirred controversy for its violent nature. In 1982, the company introduced "Shakes McJunkie," an emaciated addict who robbed characters of their possessions, which he then sold to buy McDonald's shakes. He was later reworked as "The Machead," a homeless, wild-eyed Big Mac addict who turned to panhandling and gay prostitution as a means of supporting his severe burger habit.

The Hammurderer is quickly becoming regarded as the worst-received advertising mascot since Kool-Aid's 1989 discontinuation of "The Grapist," a huge purple monster who sodomizes thirsty children. Ø

MAN from page 85

basic know-how, you can get yourself something great that really lasts."

Since beginning his cycle of used-car ownership in 1989, Liman has bought and subsequently sold 11 vehicles, mostly compact or midsize family models.

"Sure, you can buy new. But why bother when, if you know what you're

> **Liman's current car, a 1992 Mercury Sable station wagon, replaced his 1989 Toyota Corolla when he decided he needed "something with a little more road-hugging weight."**

doing, you can get a really decent used car for a couple thousand dollars?" said Liman, who has put an average of $1,800 into each of his used-car purchases before ultimately growing dissatisfied and selling the vehicles. "Once you know what to look for, you can usually get what you want for a song. Then you just fix up any little problems the car might have, and you've got a good-as-new used car that'll last you for years."

Liman's current car, a 1992 Mercury Sable station wagon, replaced his

1989 Toyota Corolla when he decided he needed "something with a little more road-hugging weight." Liman is now looking to sell the Sable to purchase a car that's "a little more nimble and with better mileage—not such a road hog."

"Take this one, here," said Liman, circling an ad in one of the many pages of used-car classifieds littering his kitchen table. "An '87 Volvo 240 DL for just $1,900 over in Carbondale. Probably some college student who doesn't need it or couldn't be bothered with the upkeep. Popular car, not much fun, weak steering boxes, tend to go through bushings a little too fast. Plus, a lot of Volvos have diesel engines, and diesel fuel is a real hassle to get at the gas station, especially around here. A lot of guys just want to trade them in for something that runs on unleaded. But, let me tell you, no car's perfect. It's probably worth giving this guy a call."

Hal Presser, editor of *West-End Valu Shopper*, said Liman is a familiar face around the office of the sales circular.

"Every six months or so, Don will spend a couple consecutive Thursdays in the office when the new ads come in, poring over every one of them," said Presser, who in 1999 purchased a car from Liman, a "squirrely" 1991 Volkswagen Golf that his wife drove for two years before selling it back to Liman last April. "At first, it was kind of strange. But I suppose he's probably gotten to a few cars he wouldn't have otherwise. I guess." ∅

PANTOLIANO! from page 86

amounts of blood. Passersby were amazed by the unusually large amounts of blood. Passersby were amazed by the unusually large amounts of blood. Passersby were amazed by the unusually large amounts of blood. Passersby were amazed by the unusually large amounts of blood. Passersby were amazed by the unusually large amounts of blood. Passersby were amazed by the unusually large amounts of blood. Passersby were amazed by the unusually large amounts of blood. Passersby were amazed by the unusually large amounts of blood. Passersby were amazed by the unusually large amounts of blood. Passersby were amazed by the unusually large amounts of blood. Passersby were amazed by the unusually large amounts of blood. Passersby were amazed by the unusually large amounts of blood. Passersby were amazed by the unusually large amounts of blood. Passersby were amazed by the unusually large amounts of blood. Passersby were amazed by the unusually large amounts of blood. Passersby were amazed by the unusually large amounts of blood. Passersby were amazed by the unusually large amounts of blood. Passersby were amazed by the unusually large amounts of blood. Passersby were amazed by the unusually large

amounts of blood. Passersby were amazed by the unusually large amounts of blood. Passersby were amazed by the unusually large amounts of blood. Passersby were amazed by the unusually large amounts of blood. Passersby were

> **How come I never got any credit for all the times I *didn't* run anyone over?**

amazed by the unusually large amounts of blood. Passersby were amazed by the unusually large amounts of blood. Passersby were amazed by the unusually large amounts of blood. Passersby were amazed by the unusually large amounts of blood. Passersby were amazed by the unusually large amounts of blood. Passersby were amazed by the unusually large amounts of blood. Passersby were amazed by the unusually large amounts of blood. Passersby were amazed by the unusually large amounts of blood. Passersby were amazed by the unusually large

see PANTOLIANO! page 91

GAY from page 87

Above: Two Podrewski impersonators pay tribute to their idol at a club in Provincetown, MA.

derstanding, and heartbreak."

Martinez was alluding to the many tragedies and heartaches to have befallen Podrewski over the course of his life. At age 6, it was discovered that Podrewski was allergic to penicillin. When he was 12, his family relocated from Estes Park, CO, to nearby Glen Haven, a move that traumatized the boy for several weeks. In 1981, he received a graduate degree in optometry, but that triumph was tainted by a broken engagement with radiologist Kathy Hearn and a recurring sinus infection.

In 1990, Podrewski married the love of his life, the former Marsha Rubin, with whom he went on to have two children, Lauren and Michael. His domestic bliss proved short-lived, however: In 1992, less than a year after the birth of Lauren, he was hit with a devastating series of misfortunes: a prized heirloom mirror broken during a crosstown move, an ankle sprained while playing softball at a picnic, and a pet salamander dead before its time.

But, as Martinez pointed out, Podrewski always prevails in the end.

"It took Gene nearly three years to pay off his student loans, often going without cable TV to do so," Martinez said. "But he did it, like the born fighter he is."

Podrewski's popularity is evidenced by the ever-growing heaps of merchandise he has spawned. In gay-themed gift shops, Podrewski refrigerator magnets, snow globes, and glitter T-shirts are as ubiquitous as *Wizard Of Oz* and *I Love Lucy* memorabilia. *Podrewskimages*, a handsome coffee-table photo book, is selling well at exclusive bookstores across the country in spite of its $150 price tag.

For the past two years, Fagatha Christie, a Los Angeles-based lounge singer and drag queen, has honed his Podrewski impression, which he performs along with those of Barbra

Streisand and Liza Minnelli. Christie said impersonating Podrewski is harder than it looks.

"A lot of Podrewski impersonators mean well and have a lot of enthusiasm," Christie said, "but doing Gene just doesn't work unless you have the

> **"Again, why me?" Podrewski said. "Heterosexuals don't have this fixation with me. In fact, when they learn I'm a gay icon, they look at me all strange. To them, I'm just a regular guy."**

right props onstage. You absolutely need a T-type applanation tonometer. Period. That's the kind Gene uses at work. And what's with the cheesy 1940s-era doctor forehead reflectors some of these queens use? Gene has never, ever worn one. *Hel-lo?*"

Though flattered by the adulation, the living legend remains uneasy.

"Again, why me?" Podrewski said. "Heterosexuals don't have this fixation with me. In fact, when they learn I'm a gay icon, they look at me all strange. To them, I'm just a regular guy."

"Sometimes," he continued, "I think [the gay community's] love of me is not about the real Gene Podrewski, but some artificial, mythical image of Gene Podrewski that they project their own hopes and dreams onto. Then again, maybe there is something special about me that I'm just not seeing." ∅

89

Are You Coming To My Show Tonight?

By Brad Gordimer

Hey, man, what are you up to tonight? You should totally come to my show at The Shack. We're on a triple bill with Meat Hammer and The Subpoenaed.

Here, take one of the flyers. Don't worry, I've got plenty more. That's us in the middle, Retarder. The name wasn't my first choice—I wanted to be Swank Factory—but the other guys all fuckin' loved it, so what are you going to do? We can always change it later, I suppose. At least until we start putting out albums.

So, what are you doing tonight? You should totally come if you can. What's that? You have to work until 9? No prob. The show's supposed to start at 8, but it probably won't get going until closer to 8:30, and we're on second, so you'd probably miss the first few songs at the most.

Have you ever seen Retarder? We've only been around for six months, and this is our third club show, so there hasn't been a lot of chances unless you still go to house parties. The Shack's a shithole, but the sound is pretty good, and a Huber is only $2. Can't really complain about that. You should totally come out. It's gonna be great.

If you haven't ever seen Meat Hammer, you should. They're from Eau Claire, but they totally rock. Two of the guys used to be in Pin Prick. They have this awesome new singer, some guy named Dave who the drummer knew from art school, and they totally kick ass. They do that '70s-rock thing really well.

I should probably give you directions to The Shack, because it's kind of hard to find if you don't know where it is. It's hidden away behind that liquor store over on Odana Road that's open late. If you give me your e-mail address, I can send you directions and put you on our mailing list so you know when shows are coming up and all that.

You saw my old band Bitchpile, right? Retarder sounds sort of like that, but with more of a grindcore feel. The essence is still the same, though: Jerry's still our drummer, and the two of us are the ones who brought most of the personality to the 'Pile. But the new band's even better. We found this crazy kid Kyle who plays bass and sings like David Yow. He's really brought the spark back to our playing. Our setlist is still maybe 40 percent Bitchpile stuff, because we haven't been all that great about getting new tunes together. The ones we have written, though, are killer. Tonight, we're introducing a new one I'm really psyched about called "Tire Blowout (Part 1)." It's got this break-down that took forever to get right. Yesterday was the first time we got through the whole song, and it sounded great.

Hey, do you still hang with Chris Blevin? I saw him the other day, and he's going to be there tonight, probably. I think a couple other guys who used to be part of the scene might show up, too. Steve said he might show up if he can get his girlfriend to

> What's that? You have to work until 9? No prob. The show's supposed to start at 8, but it probably won't get going until closer to 8:30, and we're on second, so you'd probably miss the first few songs at the most.

go. I know Doug and Eric Hysteric are coming. They were at the first two shows and were totally into it. Some other guys might show up, too. You should go. It'll be like old times.

I gave you a flyer, right? Isn't that a fucking cool picture? Jerry found it. I think it's from some kind of Bollywood movie. Jerry's totally into that stuff now. It's kind of cool, because every once in a while you hear the Indian influence seep into our music. Thank God Jerry's over his Dylan phase. The other day, me and Kyle made up a song called "Bob Dylan Is A Bone Smoker," and Jerry got totally pissed.

Anyway, you should hold on to that flyer. The Subpoenaed are gonna be huge one day, so it'll be a cool thing to have. Plus, you've got to admit that's an awesome picture.

So, you gonna show up? I guarantee a good time. We've been working on this flash pot to go off during our cover of "Der Kommissar." It'll be awesome. We have a friend who was supposed to breathe fire, but he broke his leg trying to fix his bookcase, so he can't go. It'll still be great even without that, though.

Well, even if you can't come, maybe you could call a few friends of yours, you know, like Andy or The Gooch. I bet they'd be into our stuff. I could even put you and a couple more people on the guest list if you're strapped for cash. Just say you know Brad from Retarder.

All right. See you later tonight, maybe. I gotta put the rest of these flyers up and then go help load up the shit. Good running into you. Rock and roll! ∅

Your Horoscope

By Lloyd Schumner Sr.
Retired Machinist and
A.A.P.B.-Certified Astrologer

Aries: (March 21–April 19)
Everyone will talk about your bold decision to wear such a revealing swimsuit, especially so soon after the accident.

Taurus: (April 20–May 20)
Your fear that everyone knows your deepest, darkest secrets is groundless. No one even knows you exist.

Gemini: (May 21–June 21)
This week will be exceptional for the high frequency and brutality of celebrity makeovers.

Cancer: (June 22–July 22)
No matter how many times you take that career-determination test, it still comes out saying "kangaroo."

Leo: (July 23–Aug. 22)
Next time, try not to select your murder weapon on the basis of how much it will impress the police when they find it.

Virgo: (Aug. 23–Sept. 22)
Friends are beginning to tire of your insistence that you're one of the people in Picasso's "Guernica."

Libra: (Sept. 23–Oct. 23)
Though you never intended to do so, you will soon trade your dignity for the guitar tablature to several Creed songs.

Scorpio: (Oct. 24–Nov. 21)
An interesting incident on the freeway will teach you the meaning of the term "swoop and squat" and introduce you to the exciting world of insurance fraud.

Sagittarius: (Nov. 22–Dec. 21)
Your lifelong battle with stage fright will be justified when you are mauled by an escaped stage.

Capricorn: (Dec. 22–Jan. 19)
Your prosthetic is incredibly lifelike, but people can tell it's not real—mostly because people don't have three ears.

Aquarius: (Jan. 20–Feb. 18)
You will finally outdo your father when you go six weeks without saying anything positive.

Pisces: (Feb. 19–March 20)
Your reach will always exceed your grasp, but don't worry too much: This is normal when you have no hands.

POINT from page 86

checks, he'd be living on Easy Street by the time he hit 50. But does he listen to me? No, siree. He usually just mumbles something about how he's got to pour more money into "tricking out his ride." That's what he calls the

> If I were his age, I wouldn't waste my time on stuff like that.

hatchback he bought a year ago. I call it a money pit.

If I were his age, I wouldn't waste my time on stuff like that. I'd be laying down the groundwork for a good, solid career. I'd be taking care of my body so I wouldn't have to spend my retirement years laid up in bed. And I'd spend as much quality time as possible with family and friends.

Why is it that, by the time you get your head on straight, you're too tired and out-of-shape to do anything about it? It's a crime, I tell you.

Ah, I'd better calm down, or I'm gonna have to get one of my pills. ∅

COUNTERPOINT from page 86

way. They're taking it in pussy, doctor-recommended doses like the scared little babies they are.

If me and my friends could get half the stash that the old lady down the street with leukemia and diabetes gets every week, I'd be set. Aw, who am I kidding? We'd probably blow it all in a two-day, up-all-night binge. That's because, unlike some shriveled old widow who takes her pills with dinner and is in bed by 9, we know how to party.

You think these old people are heading out to raves? You think that old lady who sits all day in the lawn chair in front of her house is using her prescription amphetamines for a 72-hour road-trip binge with her friends? Of course not! She's old, and her fun days are long behind her.

Well, old people's lives may be almost over, but mine's just begun. But, for some reason, society deems creaky oldsters more deserving of the medication that would make my life a drug-soaked, hedonistic orgy. It's a damn shame.

I'd better calm down, or I might just have to go dig out a Valium from my grandma's medicine cabinet right now. ∅

Microwave-Popcorn Bag A Maze Of Arrows And Instructions

see PRODUCTS page 10D

TV's Mork To Star In Film

see PEOPLE page 2B

Afro Secretly Poked

see LOCAL page 2B

Appetite Rises Up Against Suppressant

see LOCAL page 7C

STATshot

A look at the numbers that shape your world.

What Will We Eventually Get Around To Bringing In From The Car?

1. Bag of cat litter
2. Birth-control pills
3. 437 Wendy's Big Bacon Classic wrappers
4. Grandma's ashes
5. Chinese ambassador
6. Yaz *Upstairs At Eric's* cassette
7. Mangled deer carcass

the ONION®

VOLUME 38 ISSUE 09   AMERICA'S FINEST NEWS SOURCE™   14–20 MARCH 2002

Military Promises 'Huge Numbers' For *Gulf War II: The Vengeance*

Above: Donald Rumsfeld debriefs reporters on the upcoming Gulf War sequel, scheduled to hit Iraq March 22.

WASHINGTON, DC—At a Pentagon press conference Monday, Defense Secretary Donald Rumsfeld touted the military's upcoming *Gulf War II: The Vengeance* as "even better than the original."

"If you thought the first one was good, just wait until you see the sequel," Rumsfeld said of *Gulf War II*, scheduled to hit Iraqi theaters of operation March 22. "In the original, as you no doubt know, we defeat Saddam Hussein, only to let him slip away at the very end. This time, we're going back in to take out the trash."

Rumsfeld said the soon-to-be-unleashed war will feature special effects beyond anything seen in the original.

"*Gulf War I* was done 11 years ago, and war-making technology has advanced tremendously since then," Rumsfeld said. "From the guns to the planes to the missile-guidance systems, what you'll see in this one puts the original *Gulf War* to shame."

"The budget for *Gulf War II: The Vengeance* is somewhere in the neighborhood of $85 billion," Rumsfeld continued. "And every penny of it is up there on your screen."

see MILITARY page 94

Above: One of the millions of lionesses trapped in an abusive relationship.

Study Finds Sexism Rampant In Nature

SAN DIEGO—According to a University of California–San Diego study released Monday, sexism is rampant throughout the natural world, particularly among the highest classes of vertebrates.

"When we first decided to examine attitudes and behaviors toward gender roles among non-humans, we were wholly unprepared for what we would find," said Jennifer Tannen, leader of the UCSD research team, a joint venture between the school's zoology and women's studies departments. "Females living in the wild routinely fall victim to everything from stereotyping to exclusion from pack activities to sexual

see STUDY page 95

Item Found In Garbage To Be Turned Into Lamp Someday

MINNEAPOLIS—Joe Lennek, 24, a part-time pizza-delivery driver and 1997 University of Minnesota dropout, rescued a three-foot length of metallic pipe from the trash Monday in the hopes of one day converting it into a lamp.

"The Dumpster was filled with all sorts of cool shit," Lennek said. "There was an old clothes rack, a bunch of mannequin heads, and this huge stack of records—everything from Poco to Montovani. But when I saw that pipe, I immediately pictured it as a lamp. I'm so psyched that I snagged it

before somebody else did."

Added Lennek: "Who would throw out something like this? This is such a perfect piece to make something with."

In spite of the fact that he has never made a lamp before and lacks electrical-wiring experience, Lennek said he is confident he can transform the pipe into a lamp.

"Making the lamp should be cake," Lennek said. "I'm sure [roommate] Dick

see LAMP page 94

Right: Lennek displays the piece of pipe that will make a really cool lamp.

The Andrea Yates Trial

Andrea Yates, on trial for the drowning of her five children in the bathtub of their Houston home, has pleaded not guilty by reason of insanity. What do *you* think?

"This poor woman lost five children. Hasn't she suffered enough?"

Rhonda Rowe
Homemaker

"Yates killed not one, but five children? Wow, they certainly *do* do everything bigger in Texas."

Bob Putnam
File Clerk

"This is just a sad case of someone letting their child-killing impulses get out of control."

Bill Jackson
Systems Analyst

"I can't shake the feeling that four or five years from now, we're in for the creepiest fucking *Oprah* guest ever."

Denise Pflaum
Nurse

"You know, a high percentage of child fatalities in the home occur in the bathtub. Who's to say the statistics didn't catch up to her all at once?"

Maxwell Bosch
Lawyer

"The jury should declare Andrea Yates guilty by reason of drowning five children in a bathtub."

Milton Oberst
Cashier

Botox And Beyond

Botox, which eliminates facial wrinkles via a small injection of botulism, is all the rage. What are some other hot cosmetic procedures?

▷ Fuller, poutier lips via severe allergic reactions

▷ Depilepsy™, the vibratory hair-removal system

▷ Jaundice-Tan™

▷ Mad Cow Disease eyelash lushener

▷ Ebola weight-loss tablets

▷ Cholerogaine

▷ Teeth-whitening rabies

▷ Pneumococcal Meningitis cheekbone enhancer

▷ Kawasaki Disease facial peel

▷ Malaria-based sleep aids

▷ The Tuberculosizer™

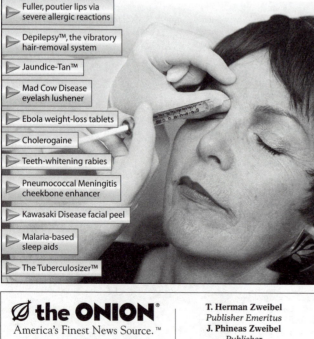

Ⓞ **the ONION**®
America's Finest News Source.™

Herman Ulysses Zweibel
Founder

T. Herman Zweibel
Publisher Emeritus
J. Phineas Zweibel
Publisher
Maxwell Prescott Zweibel
Editor-In-Chief

It Was The Eighth Subscription Card That Convinced Me

By Roland Bream

Every now and then, I'll pick up a copy of *Sports Illustrated*, usually when the cover story grabs my interest. But for all the times I've bought *SI* off the newsstand, I'd never really thought about subscribing. That is, until last Friday, when that eighth subscription card fell out of the issue I was reading. Yes, that was the one that convinced me.

I have to admit, the first three subscription cards that fell out of the issue didn't make much of an impression on me. I was reading the magazine in the kitchen while heating up some soup, and every few minutes, as I turned a page, a card would fall out and gently drift to the floor. Before long, three cards were on the floor. I knew the cards represented attractive offers to get *Sports Illustrated* delivered straight to my door, but they somehow failed to register.

About an hour later, while reading the magazine on the toilet, two more subscription cards fell out. The first of the two (the fourth in all) landed toward the base of the toilet, out of sight. But the second toilet card (number five) fell right on my knee, facing me. I couldn't help but notice its offer of one year of *Sports Illustrated* for just $1.59 an issue. That's a savings of 54 percent off the cover price. Still, I was not moved to subscribe. Impressive as the offer was, it takes a lot more than that to convince a savvy, selective consumer like me to subscribe to a magazine. Besides, who pays attention to a meager five notices these days, anyway?

Though I didn't realize it at the time, the sixth subscription card was the one that started to pique my curiosity. I'm not sure if I was just getting bored of the article I was reading or if there was something special about this particular subscription card. I suspect it was a little of both: Rick Reilly's story on Jason Giambi was oddly uncompelling, while that bright orange card with the large "SAVE 54%!" in a white starburst was undeniably alluring. Yet, tempted as I'd been, it still wasn't enough.

The seventh card seriously upped the ante. Like the others, it reminded me that, had I been an *SI* subscriber, I would've paid just $1.59 for the issue I currently held in my hands. Only this time, "Save 54%!" was printed in white type in a bright blue circle. Suddenly, the $3.50 I shelled out at the newsstand seemed senseless and wasteful. But that's not all. Like cards two, three, and five, it sweetened the pot with an offer of a free copy of the exclusive "SI 2002 Swimsuit Highlights" video if I subscribed today. (Cards one and four offered the free 2002 *SI* Swimsuit Wall Calendar instead.) Man, I was seriously tempted. But again, it still wasn't quite enough.

Then came the eighth card.

Have you ever heard the saying, "Always save the best for last"? Well, this must be the motto of *Sports Illustrated*'s subscription department, because they pulled out all the stops on that eighth card. The opportunity to save 54 percent off the newsstand

Have you ever heard the saying, "Always save the best for last"?

cover price was still there. So was the exciting free-video offer. Only this time, the card was bright yellow, not orange, and the words "Subscribe Now And Save!" were emblazoned across the top in red.

They even attached this subscription card to the actual magazine to show just how important this one was. I guess they figured that even if all the warning shots somehow fell out of the magazine, they would still have the big gun in place, ready for the kill.

It's all become so clear to me now. Those first seven subscription cards were just warm-ups. Sure, they featured essentially the same offer: savings of 54 percent off the newsstand price, a free gift, and a special, subscribers-only year-end issue. They offered the same convenient billing options. But somehow, this card made you know that a subscription would save you 54 percent off of the newsstand price. That's the *real* difference.

Just think, if only seven cards had tumbled out of that issue and onto the floor of my kitchen, bathroom, and living room, I wouldn't be on the brink of enjoying home delivery of *Sports Illustrated* for less than half the cover price.

I can't wait to get my first issue delivered in four to six weeks. It's gonna feel so great when I reach into that mailbox, take out that issue, and smile as a fresh bunch of subscription cards scatter all over my front steps.

It's a good thing I'll have all those cards falling out of my subscription issues. As soon as I start getting the magazine, I'll probably be interested in immediately subscribing again. After all, half the fun of a magazine is the act of subscribing itself. That and getting four or five letters warning you that your subscription is running out after you've received your second issue.

Thank you, eighth subscription card! Ⓞ

Sociology 101 Assignment Stretched To Incorporate '70s Punk Rock

COLUMBIA, MO—A Sociology 101 paper on the theories of 19th-century French sociologist Émile Durkheim was stretched to incorporate the 1970s British punk-rock scene, sources close to the paper's author, University of Missouri freshman Justin Hoyer, reported Monday.

"Justin does this all the time," roommate Andy Avallone said. "Any assignment he gets, he finds a way to turn it into a discussion of whatever he's into at the time. Snowboarding, old black-and-white horror movies, *The Simpsons*, the legalization of marijuana—you name it, he's fit it into a paper."

In his latest paper, "No Future: U.K. Punk And The Philosophy Of Émile Durkheim," Hoyer drew heavily upon his knowledge of the music.

"The professor said we could pick any sociologist we wanted and explain how their theories related to the problems that came with the emergence of postindustrial society," Hoyer said. "Well, when I heard 'postindustrial,' right away I thought of '70s punk."

The first page of Hoyer's paper contains a synopsis of Durkheim's theory that the collective mind of society is the source of religion and morality. But by the middle of page two—which begins with a discussion of Durkheim's theory that division of labor in complex societies erodes commonly held values and leads to social instability and disorientation of the individual—the paper shifts its focus to the politically charged songs of U.K. punk band Stiff Little Fingers.

"All that stuff Durkheim said about disorientation, that's exactly what the punk scene grew out of," Hoyer said.

Above: Hoyer works on his paper at the campus computing center.

"It was a new generation of working-class British youth reacting to a society that was conservative and totally irrelevant in, like, so many ways. Punk had its own set of morals and values which grew out of a desire to form an alternate society. It's all in the paper."

Hoyer said he was pleased with the way the nine-page assignment turned out.

"It was pretty heavy on punk, but I figure the prof already knows all about sociology," Hoyer said. "Professors want to see how you *apply* the coursework to other things. That shows you have a true understanding of the material and aren't just blindly spitting back the stuff you heard in class."

While Hoyer did not use any works by Durkheim as source material, his

bibliography included Greil Marcus' *Lipstick Traces: A Secret History Of The 20th Century*, Jon Savage's *England's Dreaming: Anarchy, Sex Pistols, Punk Rock And Beyond*, and the Legs McNeil-edited *Please Kill Me: The Uncensored Oral History Of Punk*.

Reasoning that professors "get off on supplemental material," Hoyer also in-

see ASSIGNMENT page 95

Scotland More Relaxed When Sean Connery Is Away

EDINBURGH, SCOTLAND—The people of Scotland felt a little calmer and more at ease Monday, when actor Sean Connery left the country to shoot a film in Morocco. "Don't misunderstand, we are quite proud of Sir Connery," Scottish First Minister Jack McConnell said. "It's just that he's a rather intense fellow, and it's nice to have a little time without him." Connery is expected to be away for seven weeks, giving the nation the opportunity to hold a number of relaxed, Connery-free outdoor festivals.

New U.S. Currency Expires If Not Spent In Two Weeks

WASHINGTON, DC—Seeking to stimulate consumer spending, the Treasury Department unveiled "QuikCash," a new U.S. currency that expires two weeks from the date of its issuance. "America, get ready to spend," Treasury Secretary Paul O'Neill said Monday. "QuikCash is our exciting new way to jump-start the economy while telling our valued citizens, 'Hey, go get yourself something nice. Now.'"

Olympic Skier Stares Down Icy, Forbidding Slope Of Rest Of Life

COLORADO SPRINGS, CO—Two weeks after returning from the Salt Lake City Games, U.S. Olympic skier Courtney Roth, 31, found herself staring down the icy, forbidding slope that is her future Monday. "I got an offer to do a supermarket opening in Denver next week," Roth said, "and it looks like I may sign on to promote the new popcorn shrimp they've got

over at Lou's Lobster House." Following several months of three-figure endorsement deals, Roth will land a job in Vail teaching skiing to surly, spoiled 5- to 10-year-olds for the rest of her life.

Man Can't Get Police To Care About His Bob Crane Murder Theory

SCOTTSDALE, AZ— In spite of his best efforts, Paul Bernardin, 38, has been unable to get the Scottsdale Police Department to care about his theory regarding the unsolved 1978 murder of actor Bob Crane in Scottsdale. "[Bernardin] keeps coming in here saying he knows who killed Col. Hogan," police chief Walter Dunfey said Monday. "Then he usually goes off on how the electrical cord Crane was strangled with doesn't match the ones in the other rooms of the hotel he was in. What am I supposed to do with that information?" Bernardin,

Dunfey said, is also convinced that the police possess Crane's infamous stash of self-produced amateur pornography.

Home-Brewing Phase Comes To Long-Overdue Conclusion

BETHEL PARK, PA—Local resident Randy Paltz's two-year home-brewing phase finally came to its long-overdue conclusion Tuesday. "Thank God, it's over at last," said Andrea Longo, girlfriend of the 33-year-old beer aficionado. "Every few weeks, he'd make a big production about his latest 'Paltz's Signature Brew.' It all tasted the same—like really thick, shitty beer." Friend Tim Traschel also expressed relief, saying, "Now I can actually go to his house and bring some Michelob without getting a lecture about the low quality of hops in commercial beers." ∅

Waged in 1991 at a cost of $61 billion, the first *Gulf War* was a major hit, making household names out of stars Colin Powell, Norman Schwarzkopf, and Wolf Blitzer. When asked who would star in the sequel, General Richard Myers, chairman of the Joint Chiefs of Staff, was coy.

"I don't want to give away too much, but let's just say you're likely to see a few familiar faces pop up," Myers said. "I will say that the son of one of the key characters in the first one, back then just a boy, is now all grown up and ready to take his rightful place at the head of the alliance."

Myers did confirm that the plot revolves around the Rebel forces' efforts to capture arch-nemesis Hussein, whom they believe is building a weapon of mass destruction somewhere deep within the mysterious and forbidding No-Fly Zone.

"Obviously, Saddam will be back," Myers said. "He's the perfect villain: ruthless, efficient, and sinister. It would be an affront to all the fans not to include him. Beyond that, what's going to happen is anybody's guess. One thing, though, is guaranteed: We're going to have more action, more danger, and definitely more kill power than the first time around."

"We've already started preliminary shooting," Myers said, "and so far, what we've got is unbelievable."

In addition to a major PR push, *Gulf War II* will be accompanied by a major merchandising campaign. The Pentagon has secured the commitment of Topps for a series of cards supporting the effort. It has also brokered a first-look deal with CNN, guaranteeing the network full access to the front lines,

Above: A publicity still from *Gulf War II*.

as well as first crack at interviewing the men and women behind the scenes. The Pentagon has also signed Dan Rather to a two-cry deal.

In the 11 years since the original *Gulf War*, few conflicts have come close to matching the level of support and press attention generated by that operation.

"We were disappointed by our numbers in Bosnia," Rumsfeld said. "That particular conflict played primarily to an art-house crowd. Your mainstream audiences didn't connect with the complexities of the centuries-old ethnic clash you had going there. But this time, we feel we've got something very accessible that will play in Peoria. I mean, how can you go wrong with an 'Axis of Evil'?"

Though *Gulf War II* does not open

> **"There's no reason this Iraq thing can't be a franchise for us like those wars with Germany or the Communists used to be," Rumsfeld said.**

fire for another two weeks, it has screened for select audiences in Los Angeles. *Ain't It Cool News*, the popular web site run by Harry Knowles, recently leaked an anonymous review of the conflict.

"The battle sequences are even better than *Black Hawk Down*," Knowles wrote. "And Afghan leader Hamid Karzai, while only given a little action, exudes a Tarantino cool."

Pentagon officials, meanwhile, are already thinking about a third installment.

"There's no reason this Iraq thing can't be a franchise for us like those wars with Germany or the Communists used to be," Rumsfeld said. "The public loves it, the soldiers love it, the media love it. And even if the U.S. wins at the end of the second one, there are still plenty of possibilities for a third: Saddam could be destroyed, only to be replaced by an even greater evil. Then, of course, there's the prequel set in the Stone Age, the era we bomb Iraq back to at the end of the third one. As far as we're concerned, this thing is just getting started." ✍

[Donovan] has one of those Time-Life books on wiring or something."

A self-described "found-object hobbyist," Lennek frequently brings home discarded items for use in art projects. Recent finds include a frayed rug, a bass-drum pedal, three broken televisions, and a piece of a hamster Habitrail. With the exception of the rug, which has been turned into a decorative wall hanging, the rest of the objects still await use.

"I was gonna use the pedal as, like, one of those open-close foot things on a garbage can," Lennek said. "But the garbage can I was gonna attach it to was too big. So that's temporarily on hold until I can find a smaller can."

Though tolerant at first, Lennek's three housemates have in recent months begun to become irritated by his hobby.

"He drags useless crap home all the time," housemate Jeffrey Worthen said. "There's an entire box of doll limbs and torsos under the kitchen table. He kept saying he was gonna glue them all to his chair and make some kind of *Texas Chainsaw Massacre* throne, but that still hasn't happened. Neither has the chair made out of wooden wine cases that he was so excited about last sum-

mer."

"Some of the stuff he makes is cool, like the poker-chip dispenser he made from one of those old Mr. Mouth

> **"I figured out how I could make this cool pulley system to hoist it up to the ceiling, but then I would've had to put the legs on hinges so I could fold them under. Otherwise, you'd clock your head when you walked under it."**

games," roommate Mike Mosedale said. "But most of it never gets turned into anything. It just sits there and takes up space."

In addition to adding clutter to an already cramped apartment, some of Lennek's acquisitions are potentially

dangerous.

"Joe brought home these old printing plates," Worthen said. "He put, like, six of them up on the bathroom wall, and two of them have already fallen down because of the humidity from the shower. And the ones that are still up have these razor-sharp edges. Every time I ask him when he's going to finish it, he tells me he just needs to borrow some tin snips to fit to the corners. He doesn't care that we're in danger of slicing ourselves open on the edges of these stupid plates."

Last month, Lennek brought home a wooden door he found on the way home from The Nowhere Bar.

"I was on my way home when I cut down an alley," Lennek said. "I found this bizarre door with all these pages from a *Reader's Digest* condensed book pasted on it, and each page had a picture drawn on it. I took it, planning to make it a living-room table. I thought we could use that instead of the *Dukes Of Hazzard* TV trays I found last October, but then I changed my mind."

Explaining his decision to abandon the project, Lennek said the table would have been ill-suited for its intended space.

"It was just a bit too big for the living

room," Lennek said. "We could've fit around it to eat or drink beer while watching TV, but it would've been a pain to get around if no one was using it. I figured out how I could make this cool pulley system to hoist it up to the ceiling, but then I would've had to put the legs on hinges so I could fold them under. Otherwise, you'd clock your head when you walked under it."

The door is currently leaning up against the wall behind the couch.

"I have this vision of Joe in 20 years," Mosedale said. "He's going to be one of those crazy people you hear about that has years' worth of newspapers and empty tin cans stacked up in his bedroom. The neighbors will complain about the smell, and the city will have to order him to remove it or face eviction."

Lennek blamed the pile-up on a lack of equipment.

"The big problem is, I don't have enough tools to do what I want," Lennek said. "I should really get myself a good circular saw, a hot glue gun, and a cordless drill. That'll make it way easier to follow through on all these projects. It would help if I had more time, too, but I'm pretty busy trying to hustle for work and looking for more cool stuff." ✍

harassment."

Nowhere is the natural world's gender inequity more transparent, Tannen said, than in the unfair burden females assume for the rearing of offspring.

"Take the behavior of the ring-neck pheasant," Tannen said. "After mating, the male immediately abandons the hen, leaving her responsible for total care for the chicks. For the single mother-to-be, there is no assistance, either in the form of a partner or child support. Nor is there any legal recourse. It's despicable."

Tannen said pheasants are typical of the natural world, where a mere 5 percent of animal species mate for life. Among species that do form lasting pairs, the situation barely improves: Females must remain close to the nest to incubate eggs, nurse, and keep watch over the burrow while males are free to go off hunting and fishing with their friends.

"The sexist attitude that child-rearing is 'women's work' is prevalent throughout nature and has been for generations, probably since reptiles first developed mammalian characteristics in the Triassic period," Tannen said. "Sadly, most creatures never pause to challenge these woefully outdated gender roles."

Tannen stressed the need to hold high those rare examples of species that do form caring, mutually supportive relationships.

"Wolves, beavers, gibbons, and a small African antelope known as a dik-dik all live in stable, monogamous pairs," Tannen said. "Other animals need to look to them as positive models if we are to have any hope of one day creating an ecosystem of understanding and respect."

More seriously, in addition to an unfair division of labor, nature is rife with sexual abuse and harassment. The UCSD study estimates that in 2001 alone, more than 170 trillion cases of abuse occurred in the world's forests, grasslands, and oceans—all of them unreported.

"During the act of mating, the female moose is subject to excessive biting, nipping, and herding," Tannen said. "The male has no qualms about using sheer, brute force to overpower his sex partner, and the female, accustomed to this sort of rough treatment after millions of years of it, doesn't even realize there's something wrong."

"Then, when it's time for the bull moose to complete the sexual act," Tannen continued, "it's over in about five seconds, with no regard to female pleasure whatsoever. Typical."

Adding insult to injury, Tannen said, the bull moose then heads off to mate with dozens more females over a period of two to three weeks, justifying his behavior as "part of the Mardi Gras-like atmosphere of 'mating season.'"

With other species, darker situations unfold.

"To mate, the male Galapagos tor-toise simply immobilizes the female with his weight, which, as far as I'm concerned, qualifies as non-consensual sex," Tannen said. "Female southern elephant seals gather in large groups during mating season, and each group has a small handful of males who control them like a harem. It's sick."

When female animals refuse to play along with prescribed gender roles, Tannen said, they are demonized. For example, female foxes, known throughout the animal kingdom for their aggressiveness, are labeled "vixen."

"We've all heard the lurid tales about the female black-widow spider, who kills and eats her mate," Tannen said. "The truth is, male spiders encourage their partners to kill them because it increases the time spent mating and, thus, the number of eggs fertilized by his sperm. But no one condemns the male for his part in this destructive relationship."

UCSD researchers identified 24 distinct male behaviors designed to perpetuate gender inequity and preserve the prevailing power structure. Among these dominance-asserting behaviors are chest-puffing, plumage-spreading, and antler growth.

The UCSD study is not without its detractors. Glen Otis Brown, author of *Forced To Strut: Reverse Sexism In The Animal World*, countered that male animals are victims of "the beauty myth" as much as females.

"When given a choice, female green tree frogs gravitate toward males that call the loudest and most often," Brown said. "Female *Poecilia reticulata* [guppies] go straight to the most brightly colored males. But when males evolve exaggerated secondary sexual traits to attract the opposite sex, suddenly *they're* the bad guys."

Tannen conceded that both genders have suffered as a result of sexism.

"Other than sexual size dimorphism due to same-sex competition, males benefit little from the gender inequity that so strongly favors them," Tannen said. "In a world where interactions are rooted in competition, not cooperation, both females *and males* are being denied the right to form meaningful relationships."

Annie Secunda, a Boston-based females'-rights advocate, said swift action must be taken to address the problem of sexism within the animal kingdom.

"We need to provide tigresses, hens, and all other females in nature with outreach programs and support networks," Secunda said. "We also need to impose standards through intervention. The males of all species need to hear loud and clear the message that this kind of animal behavior is not acceptable."

Secunda conducts numerous workshops aimed at creating female-friendly biomes and promoting the health and positive self-image of females, both on land and in the sea. She also strongly advocates the legal-

Above: A cock reinforces the poultry world's sexist, male-dominated social hierarchy.

ization of infanticide, which would enable females to devour their newborn offspring when resources are limited.

Secunda spent much of 2001 in the Amazon rainforest, working to create safe spaces for female animals. These efforts, however, yielded mixed results: Females have avoided the lighted walkways she built in several dangerously dense areas, and leaflets encouraging females to learn how their own bodies work were ultimately used to line dens for the rainy season.

Far from discouraged, Secunda said she plans to embark on an intensive study of the sexuality of flora.

"Multicellular plants alternate sexually reproducing and asexually reproducing generations, with each plant producing both male and female gametes," Secunda said. "It seems many plants have moved past conventional notions of male-female gender altogether. It's so liberating, I can't help but have hope for all those so-called 'higher' species of animals." ∅

cluded an appendix of photocopied lyrics from the landmark album *Never Mind The Bollocks Here's The Sex Pistols*, several of whose songs were dissected verse by verse in the body of the paper.

"It took a long time to write, but I wanted to hand in something really good," Hoyer said. "This paper's got it all: Sex Pistols, The Clash, The Buzzcocks, Gang Of Four, The Adverts, The Damned, XTC, Elvis Costello, X-Ray Spex, and The Jam."

In the last five pages of the paper, Durkheim is mentioned only three times—five less than Malcolm McLaren.

"While Justin's paper failed to include the basic fact that Durkheim pioneered the use of empirical evidence and statistical material in the study of society, it did a more than adequate job reassessing Siouxsie Sioux's oft-overlooked contributions to the development of the DIY aesthetic," said Craig Basile, Hoyer's Sociology 101 teaching assistant. "If only the professor had assigned the class a paper on punk rock and encouraged them to add a few thoughts on modern sociology, this would have been stellar."

Basile, who has not yet decided on a grade for Hoyer's paper, said he encourages "thinking beyond the textbook" and has no problem with students expanding an assignment to incorporate non-traditional subjects like punk rock. He noted, however, that he "would ideally like to see at least a 50/50 ratio."

"Look here on page 6. This long section on the anti-societal statements punks made by wearing torn clothing and dyed hair is an obvious place to work in something about Durkheim's distinction between societies maintaining mechanical versus organic solidarity," Basile said. "But instead, he just keeps hammering home the same point about Malcolm McClaren's 'Sex' shop."

In Hoyer's defense, Basile acknowledged that his paper was better than most of the 200 or so rock-related papers he has received during his three years as a T.A.

"Justin's paper was, by and large, poorly argued nonsense with only the most tenuous connection to the course material," Basile said. "But at least he got it in on time with few spelling errors, and he did it in 12-point type with just one-inch margins. That's more than I can say for a lot of other papers. I'll probably give it a B-minus."

Though only in his second semester, Hoyer has already veered sharply from an assigned paper topic on numerous occasions. Last month, he presented his Geography 140 discussion section with a speech about his family's March 2000 trip to France. And last October, in a Political Science 160 essay exam, Hoyer illustrated the inability of states to adequately police themselves during the Articles of Confederation era with examples from *Bad Lieutenant*. ∅

Shame On You, Wynonna Rider!

Item! A thief in Hollywood? Say it ain't so! **Wynonna Rider**, who delighted us in **Alien 3**, **Welcome Home Roxy Carmichael**, and **1969**, was recently

The Outside Scoop
By Jackie Harvey

arrested for shoplifting. It's true, loyal readers, they caught her red-handed taking handbags (remember when they used to call them "purses"?) from an expensive Beverly Hills store. Well, let me be the first to say shame on you, Wynonna! I know stars sometimes think they are above the law. (Heck, I'm probably as much to blame as anyone, since I've said stars are better people than us.) But to betray our trust like that! People look up to you, Wynonna. Please, think about the movie fans who hold you dear in their heart before you run off and do something like that again.

Item! Not since the heyday of **Men At Work** and **Yahoo Serious** have we been so entertained by **Australians**. It's Oscar time, and the folks from Down Under are so present in all the major categories, they might have to change the name of the show to the "Oz-cars"! "Toss another shrimp on the barbie" for the following Australian nominees: **Bas Lurman**, who directed countrymate **Nicole Kidman** in **Lady Marmalade**; **Peter Jackson**, whose **The Fellow's Ring** gave everyone shivers of excitement; and actor **Russell Crowe**, who I didn't even know was Australian until just recent-

Move over, **Barbara Walters** and other ladies of **The View**. The fellas are finally having their say, and you have some pretty stiff competition. It's called **The Better Half**, and it stars **Dick Clark** (still looking good after all these years), **Danny Partridge**, and **Screech** from **Head Of The Class**. And I think there's a black guy, too, but I could be wrong. Say, could I get a lit-

> I know stars sometimes think they are above the law. (Heck, I'm probably as much to blame as anyone, since I've said stars are better people than us.)

tle nudge from the **Harvey Helpers** on that one? Thanks!

As long as we're talking talk shows, let's have a hip-hip hooray for **Kelly Rip-Rip Ripa**! Regis' new co-host recently celebrated one year on the job, and she's exceeded even my own high expectations for her. I never thought anyone could fill **Kathie Lee**'s oversized shoes, but Kelly's done it with her irresistible mixture of charm and spunk.

Is it just me, or is that **Ryan Fillapay** one mopey character? Every time I see him (which hasn't been a lot lately), he has a frown on his face. I say if you got it, flaunt it, Ryan! Show us that $75,000 smile! You have a lot to smile about. For example, did you know you are married to **The Blonde Lawyer** star **Mason Reese**? It's true! THAT should turn your frown upside down.

I may not be the world's biggest expert on **oysters**, but I do know they shouldn't make me throw up all night.

Have you heard about the scandal at the **Olympics**? Apparently, some jealous Russian figure skaters stole a gold medal from their victorious Canadian rivals, and then a French judge caught the Canadians trying to steal it back. I say, give both sides a 10... for bad sportsmanship! I used to be a huge figure-skating fan, but that love was wounded when **Nancy Harding** got her legs broken by that other lady in 1992. Now, after this latest episode of shame, I may never watch again.

Item! Rosie O'Donnell is a lesbian! During a recent stand-up routine, the comedienne extraordinaire went public with her longtime relationship with director and fellow Kmart pitchwoman **Penny Marshall**. And to think that she was lying all those years when she professed her love for **Tom Cruise**! Who would have ever

> Have you heard about the scandal at the Olympics? Apparently, some jealous Russian figure skaters stole a gold medal from their victorious Canadian rivals, and then a French judge caught the Canadians trying to steal it back.

ly. And let's not forget Australiacting legends **Mel Gibson** and **Arnold Schwarzenegger**, who aren't nominated but are sure to be there. G'day to all of you! We're going to have to rename Australia "Little Hollywood" soon. Come on, isn't it time we finally just made them a state?

If there's one thing that really puts a dent in the car door of my day, it's **parking tickets**.

Your Horoscope

By Lloyd Schumner Sr.
Retired Machinist and
A.A.P.B.-Certified Astrologer

Aries: (March 21–April 19)
Though everything seems to be going fine between you and your love interest, you will be stricken with cancer to create dramatic tension in the third act.

Taurus: (April 20–May 20)
You will continue your pattern of taking two steps forward and 30 or 40 steps back toward the nearest tavern.

Gemini: (May 21–June 21)
Your friend Nathan will continue to display talents and skills that make you seem boring by comparison.

Cancer: (June 22–July 22)
Your upcoming appearance on a popular wildlife show will provide a cautionary example to whale-watchers for years to come.

Leo: (July 23–Aug. 22)
When driving through the desert, you should never stop and eat mysterious piles of birdseed, even if "FREE BIRDSEED" signs are stuck in them.

Virgo: (Aug. 23–Sept. 22)
You will soon learn the hard way that "motherly love" means different things to different mothers.

Libra: (Sept. 23–Oct. 23)
You will be unable to get the Led Zeppelin song "Stairway To Heaven" out of your head after discovering an actual stairway to heaven in a vacant lot.

Scorpio: (Oct. 24–Nov. 21)
Pain and humiliation will be your lot when a scheduling snafu pits you against the Detroit Red Wings two nights in a row.

Sagittarius: (Nov. 22–Dec. 21)
The paramedics will find it much easier to load you into the ambulance if they remember to bring a few buckets.

Capricorn: (Dec. 22–Jan. 19)
Try not to hold those you love to impossible standards, such as being able to love you back.

Aquarius: (Jan. 20–Feb. 18)
You will find it hard to emulate Alexander The Great as long as you are forced to work with Sandra The Dippy.

Pisces: (Feb. 19–March 20)
Soon, you'll be savoring the sly satisfaction of getting away with something, but don't be too smug: That would be too much alliteration.

expected such a bombshell revelation from a gruff, blockish, WNBA-loving adoptive mother like Rosie? Well, whether you support homosexuality or believe it's an abomination in the eyes of the Lord, you can count on yours truly to bring you all the latest info on Rosie and her celebrity galpal.

A member of **N'Sync** being launched **N'To Outer Space**? You read it here! I have it on good authority that one of the lesser members of the mega-popular boy band is going to be sent up into a Russian rocket later this year. No word on who will replace him while he's circling the globe, but my money's on **the second one from the left in O-Town**.

Item! Here's a brand new feature I'm taking around the block for a test drive called "Didja Know?" It goes something like this:

Didja know **Tom Hanks** has a son who also acts? He was in a movie set in Florida about oranges or college. The commercial was pretty vague. I can tell you that he is in the movie with comedian **Blackjack**, who steals the scene as only he can.

Didja know comedian Blackjack is also a rocker?

Didja know there's a new season of **Survivor** on?

It's all true, people! I couldn't make this stuff up if I tried!

> I may not be the world's biggest expert on oysters, but I do know they shouldn't make me throw up all night.

So, that's "Didja Know?" I think it could really catch on, but you should let me know if you like it or not. Your feedback could make or break this new wrinkle in the fabric of The Outside Scoop. I'd really appreciate it.

Well, sorry to dish and run, but it's time for me to pack it up yet again. Just to give you an appetizer for next time, I'll let just a touch slip. What do **Cybil Shepperd**, **Martin Landau**, and a macaroon have in common? Think it over, and I'll see you next time... on the Outside! ✐

Defiant Milosevic Eats Big, Sloppy Sandwich During Trial

see WORLD page 5A

Glimpse Of Gene Shalit On TV Reminds Woman It's Time For Bikini Wax

see PEOPLE page 7C

Burger King Trainee Tipped By Grandparents

see LOCAL page 11D

STATshot

A look at the numbers that shape your world.

Top-Selling Dollar-Store Items

1. Flyswatter three-pack
2. Commemorative Gulf War beef jerky
3. Artificial screwdrivers
4. 18-pak Señor Volto AA batteries
5. "Betsy Eyes-Too-Far-Apart" doll
6. Emerald Green™ non-sudsing dish soap
7. Apple Jacks with free Krull action figure

"Everything's A Buck!"

FLUORIDE-FREE TOOTHPASTE
$1

PONYTAIL CLIPS

THE ONION • $2.00 US • $3.00 CAN

0 74470 94595 6

the ONION ®

VOLUME 38 ISSUE 10   **AMERICA'S FINEST NEWS SOURCE**™   **21–27 MARCH 2002**

Above: A proud Michael Dell announces the shutdown to stockholders.

Corporation Reaches Goal, Shuts Down

AUSTIN, TX—After 18 years of striving, Dell Computer finally reached its long-stated goal to be the worldwide leader in computing systems Monday and promptly ceased operations.

"We did it," founder and CEO Michael Dell said. "Back when I started this company, I vowed that I would not rest until we revolutionized the way computers are sold. Well, at long last, that day is here. Bye."

When he launched the company in 1984, Dell drew up a lengthy list of long-term corporate goals. These included making Dell Computer the world's most trusted name in computer systems, the industry leader for customer service and technical support, and a model for direct-order retail in the 21st century and beyond.

see CORPORATION page 101

Gores Enjoying Best Sex Of Their Lives

NEW YORK—More than a year removed from public office, former vice-president Al Gore and his wife Tipper are enjoying the best sex of their lives, the happy couple reported Monday.

"For far too many years, we didn't have time to really focus on *us*," Gore told Matt Lauer during an interview on *Today*. "Between raising the kids and running for office and everything else, there always seemed to be something that took precedence over romance. But now, with the kids all grown up and a job that doesn't take up every waking moment of the day, I can finally enjoy some nice moments of intimacy with my beautiful and, dare I say, sexy wife."

Gore said that in the past 12 months, he and Tipper have "rekindled the flame of passion" in their marriage, taking time each day to lavish attention and affection on

see GORES page 100

Above: The happy, sexually re-energized couple enjoys a glass of wine together.

Hilarious *Hamlet* Essay Circulated In Teachers' Lounge

Above: Social-studies teacher Dave Archuleta takes his turn reading aloud from the student's essay.

WILLIAMSPORT, PA—A 10th-grader's hilariously inept essay on *Hamlet* was circulated in the Williamsport West High School faculty lounge Monday, eliciting mockery and bemused head-shaking from the teachers.

Written by hard-working but "rather thick" student Erin Grupman for Beth Parker's English class, "The Character Of Hamlet In William Shakespeare's Play *Hamlet*" kept the teachers thoroughly entertained during their lunch hour.

"'Hamlet is a character in a tragedical play of the same name, *Hamlet*, which was written by William Shakespeare, and Hamlet also stands as the protagonist of the play,'" Parker, 39, solemnly read over the laughter of her colleagues. "Wait, wait, shut up, it goes on: 'Hamlet, who is portrayed here as a very emotional soul, is a daring, brave character, who some believe has a bad temper.' I would say Erin is definitely on to something here."

Among those in the

see ESSAY page 101

97

The Nuclear Response

Calling nuclear retaliation against attackers "an option," President Bush wants to build up the U.S. nuclear arsenal as a means of deterrence. What do *you* think?

"Can we go back to ruining the world through deforestation and steady ozone depletion? That was a lot less scary."

Linda Kingery
Teacher

"At least this means they'll be reopening the nuclear-warhead factory here in Flint, Michigan."

Rich Buhner
Unemployed

"Oh, well. And I was just getting used to calling it a root cellar."

Ron Cotto
Machinist

"This is a difficult issue, but, ultimately, nuclear preparedness is the only answer to the problem of global population."

Tom Bankhead
Developer

"Finally, the president is listening to what the American people want."

Pat Langston
Systems Analyst

"This is great news. I've always been afraid of dying alone."

Diane Balboni
Podiatrist

E.T. The Extra Material

On March 22, a 20th-anniversary edition of *E.T.*, featuring new, restored, and altered scenes, hits theaters. Among the changes:

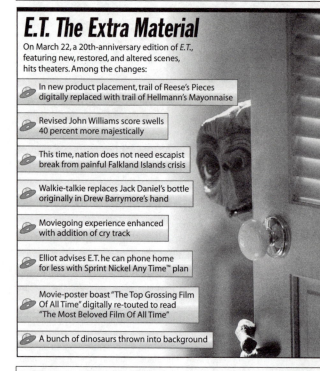

- In new product placement, trail of Reese's Pieces digitally replaced with trail of Hellmann's Mayonnaise
- Revised John Williams score swells 40 percent more majestically
- This time, nation does not need escapist break from painful Falkland Islands crisis
- Walkie-talkie replaces Jack Daniel's bottle originally in Drew Barrymore's hand
- Moviegoing experience enhanced with addition of cry track
- Elliot advises E.T. he can phone home for less with Sprint Nickel Any Time™ plan
- Movie-poster boast "The Top Grossing Film Of All Time" digitally re-touted to read "The Most Beloved Film Of All Time"
- A bunch of dinosaurs thrown into background

 the ONION®
America's Finest News Source.™

Herman Ulysses Zweibel
Founder

T. Herman Zweibel
Publisher Emeritus
J. Phineas Zweibel
Publisher
Maxwell Prescott Zweibel
Editor-In-Chief

Allow Me To Introduce You To The Other Members Of Alpha Bravo Team

By Department Head Rawlings

Hello, sir. I'm Rawlings, head of the Department for Special Acquisitions and Liquidations. Allow me to welcome you to the DSAL. I appreciate you coming from Zurich on such short notice. How was your flight? Yes, I know, the Concorde isn't all it's cracked up to be, but we needed you here fast. Time is of the essence, you understand. This is our car.

Sorry about the view, but bulletproof glass isn't the clearest. Cigar? Drink? No? Hope you don't mind if I do. Thanks. (Tony, make for corporate headquarters!)

Upon arrival at HQ, I'll introduce you to the other members of the team.

By the way, I was sorry to hear about your father. I knew him from Tunisia. A great man. You should be proud of him. I realize you had your differences, but he was proud of you. I know you told him not to get involved

> Gentlemen! You know our guest by reputation, I believe. He'll be working with us to retrieve as many items as we can from the Barcelona debacle. Once you're all briefed, I expect loadout and deployment in less than one hour.

with the Austrians, but what happened wasn't his fault. Or yours. Anyway, he will be missed.

Why, yes, this is the DSAL's building. I didn't think you'd be so surprised. Where did you expect us to be? The most inconspicuous place, my friend, is always right in the middle of things.

Take your coat? The others will be waiting in the ready room as soon as they hear our car is off the elevator.

Here they are. Good lads, all of them, if a bit hard-headed. But that's the business for you. Mind your Ps and Qs, now.

> Why, yes, this is the DSAL's building. I didn't think you'd be so surprised. Where did you expect us to be? The most inconspicuous place, my friend, is always right in the middle of things.

Gentlemen! You know our guest by reputation, I believe. He'll be working with us to retrieve as many items as we can from the Barcelona debacle. Once you're all briefed, I expect loadout and deployment in less than one hour.

Now, allow me to introduce you to the other members of Alpha Bravo team. The best available, and as good as any.

Hardin here was our man on the ground in Riyadh for that incident in '99. You remember that, I'm sure. Brooklyn boy, ex-Marine, a logistics wizard, a legend in the fixer business. Put Hardin on the ground anywhere in the world and, odds are, he speaks the language and knows some of the locals. One of the only men to walk out of Nepal after that infamous bit of betrayal in '83, and I do mean walk out: 1,100 miles worth in six weeks with nothing but good boots, a knife, and a newfound facility for the Sherpa tongue. A great yarn, that one, and all true. Shame no one can be told about it.

The Dutchman here may be deaf as a post, but there's no lock—mechanical, electronic, or otherwise—that he can't open. He can still sense vibrations, you see. He's also dead-solid perfect at reading lips, across a room, over a TV monitor, or through a rifle scope. And, although it may never come up, he designs and forges his own throwing knives from meteorite steel. I can't say if it's true or not that he never sleeps—he's only worked with us for three years.

Pierre you've heard of, I'm sure. Lucky, lucky Pierre. He's been the last man standing in more messes than I can remember. Good man to be standing next to when the wheels come off. A master of subterfuge, disguise, and subtle poisons, deadly or merely incapacitating. Highly skilled in the oper-

see ALPHA BRAVO page 100

11-Year-Olds' Entire Plan For Night Is To Smoke Cigarettes

PINE BLUFF, AR—Lee Brandt, 11, a fifth-grader at North Woods Elementary School, announced Monday that he and his friends plan to spend Friday night smoking cigarettes.

"Tommy [Stovall] said he stole a pack from his mom's carton of Virginia Slims," Brandt said. "He said she goes through them so fast she'd never notice one missing. He's supposed to instant-message me after school if he could get some. And he said if he can't swipe some from his mom, he knows where his sister hides hers. Either way, we're set."

The smoking is set to take place at 8 p.m. in Hanrahan Park, a site chosen for conduciveness to furtive, pre-adolescent smoking.

"The park has this thing, it's like a solid-wood hamster wheel," Brandt said. "I figure that'd be the best place to go, because you can't see it from the street, and we can still smoke there even if it starts raining. It's either that or underneath the big slide, which isn't as hidden. Plus, it smells really bad under there, so that's a last resort."

Though Brandt and Stovall have smoked an estimated 10 cigarettes each in the last six months, they are excited to have the opportunity to devote a full evening to the endeavor.

"Before, Tommy could only swipe an already open pack from his mom because he didn't know where she hid the cartons," Brandt said. "We'd have to save them for special occasions like the sixth-grade dance or sneaking out of Sunday school. This time, though, we'll be able to take our time and really focus on the smoking."

In addition to Stovall, Brandt said he is expecting friends Rob Marchand and Patrick Ayler, as well as class tomboy Sheri Eiland, to show up.

"Rob invited Sheri because he's had a crush on her since fourth grade. And Tommy never does anything without his little sidekick Patrick," Brandt said. "I just hope we have enough cigarettes, with so many people coming. We should be okay, though: Patrick's probably only gonna smoke one or two, because he's a big wuss and practically had to be forced into coming. Me, I'll smoke at least five or six."

Even though the young smokers have mutually sworn to keep the event a secret, a few leaks have occurred.

"Marisa [Ebenkamp] asked what Lee and I were talking about at lunch last Wednesday," Stovall said. "I told her we were talking about smoking, and she freaked. I shouldn't be surprised. Marisa's a total loser and acts like a little baby, with all that 'N Stink crap she's into. I just hope she doesn't tell anyone. I'd hate to miss out on

Though Brandt and Stovall have smoked an estimated 10 cigarettes each in the last six months, they are excited to have the opportunity to devote a full evening to the endeavor.

smoking just because she can't keep her stupid mouth shut."

Another setback occurred last Thursday, when Stovall's mother forbade him from hanging out with Brandt.

"Mom thinks Lee's a bad influence, but everything's cool," Stovall said. "As long as we make all our plans at school or over the Internet, she'll nev-
see CIGARETTES page 100

Above: Brandt (center) shares a cigarette with two of his fellow new smokers.

NEWS IN BRIEF

Indian-American Child Having Difficulty Finding Bicycle License Plate With His Name On It

HAYWARD, CA—Dinesh Parekh, 9, continues to struggle to find a bicycle license plate with his name on it, the Indian-American child reported Monday. "This is the third store I've checked today," said a dejected Parekh, exiting a Toys "R" Us near his Hayward home. "Derrick, Diane, Dillon and Dylan, Dirk... no Dinesh." Parekh, who has pedaled his brand-new Schwinn to more than a dozen stores during his three-week search, said he plans to ask his mother to drive him to the KB Toys in San Leandro next weekend.

Shadow Government Attracts Shadow Protesters

UNDISCLOSED LOCATION—Decrying various unspecified aspects of the U.S. Shadow Government, an indeterminate number of Shadow Protesters gathered outside the organization's mountain retreat, sealed germ-free vault, or underground bunker Monday. "We unfortunately cannot comment on our feelings about the Shadow Government at this time," said an unnamed protester, neither confirming nor denying reports that he or she accused the Shadow Government of violating the U.S. Constitution. After 20 minutes of protest, the group was dispersed by members of the Shadow Secret Service, who used "means at their disposal."

SLA Murder Trial Nostalgic Trip Back To More Innocent Time

INDEPENDENCE, MO—The murder trial of three Symbionese Liberation Army members is providing Americans with a nostalgic escape to a carefree, more innocent time. "Oh, man, Patty Hearst and the SLA. That takes me back to high school," said Ralph Henderson, 43, an Independence-area dentist. "Pet rocks, Jerry Ford jokes, small bands of kooky, disorganized terrorists shooting up local banks... Those were the days."

Waitress Only Friendly When Bringing The Check

MURFREESBORO, TN—According to customers at Po' Boys Family Restaurant, waitress Melanie Bostic is only friendly when bringing the check. "About 10 minutes after I sat down, she walks over and says, 'Know whatcha want?' No 'hi' or anything," customer Bruce Banda said. "Then, when I'm done eating, all of a sudden I get a big smile and my name is 'Honey.'" Fellow customer Sandi Herzog agreed. "The placemats boast of Po' Boys' 'Famous Friendly Service,'" Herzog said. "That probably should say, 'Famous Curt, Inconsiderate Service Until We Want You To Pay And Leave.'"

Atonal Composers Gather For Atony Awards

HOLLYWOOD, CA—The recording industry's top atonal composers gathered in Los Angeles Monday for the gala seventh annual Atony Awards. "Tonight is hostile music's biggest night," said Krzysztof Penderecki, nominee in the Most Dissonant Piece category. "I can't tell you what a thrill it is to be here, surrounded by so many legends of arrhythmic cacophony." The highlight of the evening is expected to be the awarding of the Olivier Messiaen Lifetime Achievement Award to Karlheinz Stockhausen for "more than five decades of aggressively impenetrable anti-music." ∅

GORES from page 97

each other. Citing one such example, Gore said that last Friday, he came home from a speech at the American Bar Association's annual convention to find Tipper waiting for him in the bedroom in a lace teddy with a rose between her teeth. She then handed

> **"Our work keeps us apart just enough to heighten our passion. It's a great feeling, coming home from a fundraiser all pumped up and being able to transfer that energy into carrying my wife to bed and letting nature take its course, if you know what I mean."**

him a book of "love coupons" redeemable for a variety of sexual favors.

"It's that sort of spontaneity that keeps things exciting in a marriage," said Gore, lovingly stroking his wife's hair. "And, believe me, things were pretty exciting that night."

Added Tipper: "Al can be a real tiger."

According to Gore, the frequency of his sexual activity with Tipper has increased significantly in the past year.

"I must say I'm very satisfied with our current volume of lovemaking," said a visibly relaxed Gore. "Did I say satisfied? I meant overjoyed. In fact, things are so good, I may have to seriously rethink my plans to make another run for president in 2004!"

Though she admitted she's "never been much of a thrill-seeker in the sex department," Tipper said a number of her recent intimate encounters with her husband have involved an element of risk: On Feb. 25, she said, the couple "got amorous" just moments before an endorsement appearance for U.S. Sen. Tim Johnson (D-SD). A week later, they coupled

during a cross-country flight to California.

"Forgive me if I blush, Matt," Tipper told Lauer, "but Al and I actually made

> **On Feb. 25, she said, the couple "got amorous" just moments before an endorsement appearance for U.S. Sen. Tim Johnson (D-SD). A week later, they coupled during a cross-country flight to California.**

love about half an hour ago, right before coming on this show."

Despite their current inflamed passion, the Gores said their sex life did not instantly reignite upon their departure from Washington last year.

"After losing the election, Al was really depressed for a while," said Tipper, a longtime crusader for mental-health issues. "With depression, as you may know, there typically comes a loss of sexual appetite. Over time, though, he gradually realized that this was a good chance to rediscover parts

of himself he'd forgotten. That's when we began our sexual re-awakening."

Not since Jimmy and Rosalynn Carter left the White House for Plains, GA, in January 1981 has there been such an upswing in post-Executive Office coitus.

"Things are less hectic, but it's not like we're loafing around doing nothing," Tipper said. "Al's been doing fundraising for his political action committee, and I've been busy speaking at Democratic fundraisers, as well as continuing my work as honorary chairwoman for the National Mental Health Awareness Campaign. But in no way does any of that diminish our desire to spend a romantic evening together in a bubble bath, surrounded by scented candles."

Added Gore: "The difference between our current work lives and the way it was before is that now we come home energized. Our work keeps us apart just enough to heighten our passion. It's a great feeling, coming home from a fundraiser all pumped up and being able to transfer that energy into carrying my wife to bed and letting nature take its course, if you know what I mean."

"It's like right after we were married all over again," a flushed Tipper said. "I don't want to get too specific, but some of the things we've done would cause quite a scandal in Washington circles."

Exchanging smoldering glances, the Gores ended the interview and disappeared backstage. ∅

CIGARETTES from page 99

er find out. Besides, me and Lee don't hang out that much, just mainly when we try to get cigarettes or when we want to chuck rocks at that closed-up 7-Eleven."

In spite of the planning leading up to the event, Brandt said the evening's activities are relatively unstructured.

"We'll probably just hang out and, you know, smoke," Brandt said. "Maybe we'll compare cigarettes we've smoked before. Like that open pack of Kools somebody left on the table at Wendy's. And maybe there'll even be some teenagers in the park we can trade with."

Brandt, who said he is certain he can avoid getting caught by the police officers who patrol the park after nightfall, is equally confident that his parents will not find out about his illicit endeavor.

"I snagged a bottle of Febreeze from the hall closet and put it in my backpack," Brandt said. "That should cover up the smell. If that doesn't work, we've already decided to tell our par-

ents we were hanging out right near the smoking section at Denny's."

Brandt said he is already looking

> **Brandt, who said he is certain he can avoid getting caught by the police officers who patrol the park after nightfall, is equally confident that his parents will not find out about his illicit endeavor.**

forward to gathering with friends and recounting the smoking adventure at the cafeteria lunchtable Monday.

"If there's one thing even better than smoking," Brandt said, "it's talking about smoking." ∅

MARKIE POST from page 99

amounts of blood. Passersby were amazed by the unusually large amounts of blood. Passersby were

amazed by the unusually large amounts of blood. Passersby were amazed by the unusually large amounts of blood. Passersby were amazed by the unusually large amounts of blood. Passersby were

> **Lord, please give me a sign if you want me to spare those paperboys in my basement.**

amazed by the unusually large amounts of blood. Passersby were amazed by the unusually large amounts of blood. Passersby were amazed by the unusually large amounts of blood. Passersby were amazed by the unusually large amounts of blood. Passersby were amazed by the unusually large amounts of blood. Passersby were amazed by the unusually large amounts of blood. Passersby were amazed by the unusually large amounts of blood. Passersby were amazed by the unusually large amounts of blood. Passersby were amazed by the unusually large amounts of blood. Passersby were amazed by the unusually large amounts of blood. Passersby were amazed by the unusually large amounts of blood. Passersby were amazed by the unusually large

see MARKIE POST page 103

ALPHA BRAVO from page 98

ation of both rotary- and fixed-wing aircraft. Speaks English without a trace of an accent but is French to the core. A survivor of our November gambit. The only survivor, actually, though that turned out to be just as well.

The Fader is supposed to be on the roster, too, but he must not be here yet. Mei Ling! Is the Fader…? Oh, my apologies. I didn't see you there. Well, you can see—or not see—the Fader's talents for yourself. A perfect infiltration man. Quiet, a face that could be anybody's, can get lost in a crowd of two. It's what he does best. That and interrogation.

Finally, there's Mei Ling. She'll be

the eyes and ears, coordinating you and the others through the Xerxes satellite communication system. The subvocal transceivers in your mastoid sinus will filter out most vocal inflection, but it's her voice you'll hear. Barring unforeseen circumstances, this is the only time you'll ever see her. I may be old-fashioned, but I'll be damned if I'll put a woman in harm's way.

Now. Gentlemen, to the briefing room. We know where the Barcelona dossier is being kept, at least until tomorrow night. Coffee? It's genuine Blue Mountain. Good. Now, listen up and listen good: Your hoverplane leaves at 0500 hours. ∅

"There were a lot of goals I wanted to accomplish, but those three were probably the biggest," said Dell, clearing out his desk at the company's Austin headquarters. "Done, done, and done."

Dell said he made the decision to shut down after learning that the company had passed Cisco Systems as the premier provider of products and services required for customers worldwide to build their information-technology and Internet infrastructures.

News of the Dell shutdown spread quickly through the computer industry. Within hours, more than two dozen major rival companies had phoned to express interest in purchasing Dell. All offers were declined.

"Kevin Rollins, my president and COO, was the one who delivered the news," Dell said. "You should have seen the smile on his face. He walked into my office and said, 'We did it, Mike. We finally did it.' Everything we'd worked so hard to attain had finally come to fruition. Time to close up shop."

Upon receiving the news, Dell called a meeting of his top executives. After standing silently in front of the confused throng for nearly a minute, Dell

Above: Workers remove a break-room vending machine from Dell headquarters, which closed this week.

calmly put a check mark in the remaining empty box on a large board listing the company's goals. A loud cheer went up and, after much handshaking and backslapping, a beaming Dell informed the executives to clean out their offices and go home.

Though Dell said he is proud and thrilled that his company reached its goals so quickly, he "can't help but feel a little disappointed" that it's all over.

"We were so focused on getting where we wanted to go that we didn't always step back and take a moment to savor the ride," Dell said. "We knew that last day would eventually come,

but I guess we always imagined it being somewhere off in the distant future."

News of the Dell shutdown spread quickly through the computer industry. Within hours, more than two dozen major rival companies had phoned to express interest in purchasing Dell. All offers were declined.

"Some of the bids to buy the company were extremely attractive," Dell said. "But after thinking about it, I decided it would just be too weird having the company go on without me. Besides, what would there be for the new owners to do?"

Though he is the guiding light and creative force behind Dell Computer, Dell stressed that he is not solely responsible for the company's success.

"We had an incredible staff of people without whom we would never have reached our destination," Dell said. "To the great people of Austin, who helped make the corporate office feel like a home; to the 32,000 employees who were like a family to me; and, of course, to our many loyal customers, I'd just like to express my unending gratitude and appreciation for your support. Now, if you'll excuse me, I've got some golf to play." ∅

lounge were social-studies teacher David Archuleta, speech teacher Gene Ringheiser, and history teacher and girls' basketball coach Kay Burroughs. Each took turns reading aloud from the paper and providing his or her own derisive side commentary.

"I'm no *Hamlet* expert, but I think the best part is where she says, 'Hamlet thought that he was bound up inside a nutshell, which was Shakespeare's way of showing us that Hamlet was symbolically nuts,'" said Ringheiser between bites of a tunasalad sandwich. "Boy, you have to wonder what kind of horrendously incompetent teacher is responsible for producing students who write this kind of junk!"

Taking mock offense at her colleague's attack on her teaching abilities, Parker retaliated by throwing a non-dairy creamer at Ringheiser.

Grupman's paper elicited howls not only for its barely coherent thesis, but also for its pitiful punctuation.

"Listen to this: 'When we first see

Hamlet comma he is getting over his father's death comma which some say comma indeed comma, was a shock to Hamlet comma and he could not get over it when he sees his father's ghost comma which comma wants revenge,'" Burroughs read aloud during her turn. "If you ask me comma this paper sucks pretty bad."

The educators' fun was briefly interrupted by the arrival of Adam Sigler,

The educators' fun was briefly interrupted by the arrival of Adam Sigler, an idealistic algebra teacher known to take a dim view of student-bashing.

an idealistic algebra teacher known to take a dim view of student-bashing. Upon entering the teachers' lounge, the 24-year-old Sigler poured himself coffee, exchanged brief pleasantries, and then promptly exited the room, enabling his less respectful colleagues to resume reading.

"Is he gone? Good," Parker said. "Okay, I love this part: 'Then, Hamlet is arguing with his mother, and thinks there is a rat, or maybe Claudius behind the drapes, so he stabs through them, and sleys [sic] Paulonius [sic], who is really his girlfriend Ophelia's dad.' You know, I think most Shakespearean scholars would agree with Erin's assessment that the dramatic high point of the play is when Hamlet sleys Paulonius, his girlfriend's dad."

According to education expert Dr. Judith Berman-White, mercilessly mocking students behind their backs may seem unprofessional, but is a vital part of teaching.

"Teachers, like doctors and policemen, have stressful occupations that necessitate the periodic use of levity

"I'm no *Hamlet* expert, but I think the best part is where she says, 'Hamlet thought that he was bound up inside a nutshell, which was Shakespeare's way of showing us that Hamlet was symbolically nuts.'"

as a coping mechanism," Berman-White said. "They have to be able to blow off steam somehow. How else can they be expected to teach subliterate, mildly retarded kids like Erin Grupman all day long without losing their minds?" ∅

Girl, She Means Nothing To Me

By Smoove B
Love Man

Aw, girl. You know I would never hurt you for all the gold and diamonds on Earth. You know I am your Smoove Man. And that is why I am begging you to look into your heart and forgive me for the wrong which I have done.

Baby, she means nothing to me. I am so sorry I sexed her wild that night when I should have been sexing you. I am so serious about being sorry that I am prepared to do anything to win back your love.

Do you wish for a fine Godiva chocolate, my nubian princess? If so, I will journey the world, visiting such countries as Malaysia, New Zealand, and France in a search for the very finest Godiva store on the planet. Smoove will personally screen each store for cleanliness, quality of product, and how dedicated each employee is to pleasing the most beautiful woman who ever lived. Then, I will tally all three columns of numbers into a master score for each location. This will determine which is the very finest Godiva store on Earth. And then, I will purchase the very finest piece of chocolate available at that store, maxing out my Discover card if necessary.

The chocolate will contain a sumptuous almond. There will also be caramel.

Once I possess the piece of chocolate, I will carry it back to your apartment on foot, not stopping even when my leg muscles scream in indescrib-

> **Let me make reservations at the finest restaurant in all of downtown, where we will dine on the finest steak and lobster, as well as many fine vegetables, including corn and green beans.**

able pain. On and on will I walk until I have brought this magnificent morsel of candy to your bedside. I will then put it inside the mouth of my queen using a pair of specially constructed solid-gold chocolate-feeding tongs.

That other woman? You must believe me when I say that I would not walk down to the Mobil station to get her a Clark bar.

This is only one respect in which I love you far more than that other girl. There are many others, as well.

Baby, even when you are mad at me, you make me love you so much. Right now, I want to take you in my arms and shower sweet kisses on your forehead and neck. I want to feel you unbuttoning my purple satin shirt and then sliding that shirt off one shoulder at a time, revealing me in my tank-top undershirt and golden cross pendant. At that point, I want to pick

> **I am so sorry I sexed her wild that night when I should have been sexing you. I am so serious about being sorry that I am prepared to do anything to win back your love.**

you up in my arms and carry you through my living room, past the kitchenette, and into the bedroom, where I will show you the true meaning of my love.

So please, girl, give me a chance to make it up to you. Let me show you that you are my universal everything and that, in comparison, that other woman is not even a whisper from a grain of sand on the world's smallest beach.

Let me make reservations at the finest restaurant in all of downtown, where we will dine on the finest steak and lobster, as well as many fine vegetables, including corn and green beans. And dessert, if you have room afterwards. The waiters will bow and scrape and tend to your every wish, for I will have pre-arranged this level of service with the manager.

A delicious mint will also arrive with the check.

After this meal, I will rent a fine hansom cab to convey us all around the downtown area, where we will see many fine hotels, in addition to the outskirts of the park. The driver will let us out only three blocks from my apartment building, and I will tip him generously. We will then walk past the envious eyes of the city to my crib, where we will get down all night long as the music of Freddie Jackson fills my bedroom. It is here that I will hit that ass doggystyle. I will leave you breathless.

If you only let me, I will fill you up with Smoove. We will freak nasty until the break of dawn.

Girl, I do not even remember her name. Pamela or something. It is irrelevant for our purposes. ✐

Your Horoscope

By Lloyd Schumner Sr.
Retired Machinist and
A.A.P.B.-Certified Astrologer

Aries: (March 21–April 19)
Your excitement over the new arrival in your life is shattered when it is born with antlers.

Taurus: (April 20–May 20)
The stars indicate that they have stepped out for a moment and will be back at 3 p.m., if the little clock on their door can be believed.

Gemini: (May 21–June 21)
The men from the government will exercise a surprising amount of patience while explaining to you that income taxes are not determined by essay.

Cancer: (June 22–July 22)
Those closest to you will continue to try and edge away as politely and quietly as possible.

Leo: (July 23–Aug. 22)
By all means, move confidently in the direction of your dreams, as long as that means spending a great deal of time asleep.

Virgo: (Aug. 23–Sept. 22)
Your assumption that the dog doesn't know how funny he looks in the wig assumes a lot about canine intelligence, dignity, and sexuality.

Libra: (Sept. 23–Oct. 23)
Your impassioned calls for equality between the races continue to go unheeded by the world's cetacean rulers.

Scorpio: (Oct. 24–Nov. 21)
As much as you try to control your own destiny, the Hands of Fate will intervene several times next week, knocking you into puddles for their own amusement.

Sagittarius: (Nov. 22–Dec. 21)
Recent events have strengthened your resolve to finally get around to burning all those bodies you've got lying around.

Capricorn: (Dec. 22–Jan. 19)
You will feel clearer and more organized but somehow less vital when the story of your life is professionally copy-edited.

Aquarius: (Jan. 20–Feb. 18)
Your extremely trying week will not be improved by your decision to deal with all problems by leaning on the horn.

Pisces: (Feb. 19–March 20)
You will successfully foil a secret plot to infiltrate your house and surprise you with birthday gifts, cake, and good wishes.

GERANIUM from page 100

amounts of blood. Passersby were amazed by the unusually large amounts of blood. Passersby were amazed by the unusually large amounts of blood. Passersby were amazed by the unusually large amounts of blood. Passersby were amazed by the unusually large amounts of blood. Passersby were amazed by the unusually large amounts of blood. Passersby were amazed by the unusually large amounts of blood. Passersby were amazed by the unusually large amounts of blood. Passersby were amazed by the unusually large amounts of blood. Passersby were amazed by the unusually large amounts of blood. Passersby were amazed by the unusually large amounts of blood. Passersby were amazed by the unusually large amounts of blood. Passersby were amazed by the unusually large amounts of blood. Passersby were amazed by the unusually large amounts of blood. Passersby were amazed by the unusually large amounts of blood. Passersby were amazed by the unusually large amounts of blood. Passersby were amazed by the unusually large amounts of blood. Passersby were amazed by the unusually large amounts of blood. Passersby were amazed by the unusually large amounts of blood. Passersby were amazed by the unusually large

amounts of blood. Passersby were amazed by the unusually large amounts of blood. Passersby were amazed by the unusually large amounts of blood. Passersby were amazed by the unusually large amounts of blood. Passersby were amazed by the unusually large

> **I dare say the dean will be quite flustered by my cheeky send-up of him in the campus humor magazine.**

amounts of blood. Passersby were amazed by the unusually large amounts of blood. Passersby were amazed by the unusually large amounts of blood. Passersby were amazed by the unusually large amounts of blood. Passersby were amazed by the unusually large amounts of blood. Passersby were amazed by the unusually large amounts of blood. Passersby were amazed by the unusually large amounts of blood. Passersby were amazed by the unusually large amounts of blood. Passersby were amazed by the unusually large

see GERANIUM page 105

John Ashcroft Silences Reporters With Warning Shot

see WASHINGTON page 4A

Ozzy Osbourne Bites Head Off Five-Pound Chocolate Rabbit

see PEOPLE page 9D

3-D Movie Character Uses Cane To Point To Things

see ENTERTAINMENT page 4C

STATshot

A look at the numbers that shape your world.

Top Self-Help Books

1. Learning To Self-Absorb
2. I Can Shut Up, I *Will* Shut Up
3. People Are From Different Planets
4. Break The Self-Help-Book Habit!
5. It's OK, It's Not Like People Care What You Do
6. The Bridge Less Jumped Off
7. Breaking Up Is Not That Hard To Do, You Fucking Pussy

THE ONION • $2.00 US • $3.00 CAN

---

the ONION®

VOLUME 38 ISSUE 11   AMERICA'S FINEST NEWS SOURCE™   28 MARCH–3 APRIL 2002

Above: A Portland, OR, marketing executive enjoys some newly legal cocaine.

Drugs Now Legal If User Is Employed

WASHINGTON, DC—Seeking to "narrow the focus of the drug war to the true enemy," Congress passed a bill legalizing drug use for the gainfully employed Monday.

"Stockbrokers, lawyers, English professors... you're not the problem here," said DEA Administrator Asa Hutchinson at a White House press conference. "If you are paying taxes and keeping your yard tidy, we're not going to hassle you if you come home from a hard day of work and want to enjoy a little pot or blow. If, on the other hand, you're one of these lazy, shiftless types hanging out on the street all day looking for your next high, we're coming after you."

The new law, which goes into effect May 1, will enable police departments and courts to focus on what Hutchinson called "the real drug offenders."

"There's no point going after some cardiac surgeon who needs some

see DRUGS page 106

THE DRUG WAR

Excited Catholics Already Lining Up For Pope's Funeral

VATICAN CITY—Their numbers reaching into the hundreds, excited Catholics are lining up in front of St. Peter's Basilica in the hopes of scoring a seat for the upcoming funeral of Pope John Paul II.

Sipping hot cocoa Monday while seated in a folding chair, Salvatore Bruni, 56, a Florence tailor, said he has been in line since Feb. 10.

"I don't know how much longer I'll have to wait, but whether it's five days or five months, it'll be well worth it," said Bruni from his position near the front of the queue. "This is going to be a funeral I'll never forget."

"The pope is a great man who has done wondrous things for the world," said Seamus O'Halloran, a Dublin pub owner who missed the March 15 wedding of his nephew to avoid losing his spot in line. "So to have a chance to be there when they finally put him in the ground, man, that's something I'll tell my grandkids about."

In spite of persistent rumors that the pope has Parkinson's disease, the

see POPE page 107

Above: Diehard pope fans wait patiently outside St. Peter's Basilica.

Driver's Ed Class Finally Gets To See Legendary Safety Film

Above: A still from the 1972 safety film.

NEW BEDFORD, MA—After months of eager anticipation, the second-period driver's-education class at Lincoln Memorial High School finally got to see the legendary highway safety film *Wheels Of Tragedy* Monday.

"Both my older brothers saw [*Wheels Of Tragedy*] when they took the class, so I knew I was probably gonna get to see it," sophomore Kevin Younkers said. "Mr. Fait held out for two months, though. He made us finish the entire workbook before showing it."

Purchased by the school in 1973, *Wheels* combines grisly footage of actual car wrecks with dramatic reenactments of safety missteps committed by the victims in their final minutes. Driver's-ed teacher Vernon Fait has shown the 22-minute, 16-millimeter film to every class since he began teaching the course in 1982.

Student reaction was pos-

see FILM page 106

Gay Adoption

Rosie O'Donnell, an adoptive parent and newly out lesbian, called Florida's and President Bush's opposition to gay adoption "wrong." What do *you* think?

George Kiehl
Truck Driver

"Rosie O'Donnell and her kind should not be allowed to adopt. You have no idea how bad it fucks kids up to be raised by celebrities."

Dan Durkee
Bond Trader

"As long as they're closeted gays, I have no problem with it."

Wendy Mota
Physical Therapist

"You know, maybe gay adoption will scare conservatives enough that they'll consider safe, legal abortion as an alternative."

David Whitten
Systems Analyst

"Homosexuals should be allowed to adopt kids, but they should not be allowed to molest them. I firmly believe that."

Chris Chance
Prep Cook

"The law needs to make a distinction here. Are we talking regular gay or whoo-hoo-fabulous gay?"

Roberta Diamond
Teacher

"The last thing we need is to put children in the hands of people who actually want them."

Kmart's Woes

Kmart, which filed for Chapter 11 bankruptcy in January, recently announced the closing of 283 stores. What is the retail giant doing to improve its situation?

- ○ Combining everyday low prices and friendly service in previously unthought-of ways
- ○ Aggressively touting Kmart as "The Place For Shotguns, Soda, And Sweatpants"
- ○ Finally allowing smart-ass teens to ride coin-operated horsey outside entrance
- ○ Instituting two-Icee minimum
- ○ Diversifying product line to include things people would want in their homes
- ○ Replacing "K" in Kmart sign with more appealing "Wal"
- ○ Offering wider aisles that more comfortably accommodate shoppers' asses
- ○ Burning down entire chain for insurance money

the ONION®
America's Finest News Source.™

Herman Ulysses Zweibel
Founder

T. Herman Zweibel
Publisher Emeritus
J. Phineas Zweibel
Publisher
Maxwell Prescott Zweibel
Editor-In-Chief

Hey, Everybody, Let's Put On An Avant-Garde Show!

By Mickey McCune

Say, gang, did you hear the news? Rotten old Banker Mudge wants to tear down our clubhouse and put up a big office building in its place. Can you believe it? Us kids will have no place to go! Well, dog-gone it, I won't stand for it, and neither should any of the other kids here in Gurdeyville! I just know if we put our thinking caps on, we can figure a way out of this jam.

Wait... I got it! We'll raise the money to stop Banker Mudge by putting on a show! An *avant-garde* show!

I know what you're thinking: "Jeez, Mickey, we only know about stickball and skipping rope, not avant-garde dramatics!" But I tell you, gang, absurdist theater is in my blood! My pop used to be the artistic director of an experimental playhouse in Greenwich Village during the heyday of the Fluxus movement, and my great-grandmaw served drinks at the Cabaret Voltaire, which was just about the most important Dadaist theater in WWI Zurich. Even though I'm only 13, I've picked up enough from them to direct us a swell show.

Besides, we've got a whole mess of talent to work with here! Little Gracie

> If we're gonna put on a proper avant-garde show, it oughta be some kind of surrealist drama heavy on symbolism. Who will write this play, you ask? None other than yours truly, Mickey McCune, natch! Aw, don't worry, I've seen lots of these kind of shows—cabaret, poetry recitals, performance art, you name it.

tap-dances with pep aplenty, and Bucky's lasso tricks never fail to wow. Why, with just a little practice, they could be transformed into a chorus of shrouded, shrieking wraiths in no time! And who else but sweet Rosemarie, the golden-haired darling of

our gang, should play the part of the slovenly mother-whore who's constantly giving birth to fist-sized maggots?

Now, don't get sore if you don't land

> Virginia's a demon with a needle and thread; she'll be just the gal to stitch together the blood-red cloth backdrop with the vagina-shaped opening through which the giant fetus enters in the first act.

one of the lead roles. There's work for everybody on this avant-garde production! Virginia's a demon with a needle and thread; she'll be just the gal to stitch together the blood-red cloth backdrop with the vagina-shaped opening through which the giant fetus enters in the first act. Jackie, the junkman's son, is a born prop man—he could dig up enough rusted urinals and soiled dolls' heads for a dozen plays! Sissy Chester can compose the dissonant, aleatoric score. And Spud never goes anywhere without his hammer and nails; he can build the stage and the sets, as well as the huge wooden letter M that drops to the floor and crushes the proletarian rioters at the end of Act II! The rest of you can sell tickets, paste playbills on the fence outside Schwoegler's Field, or hitch Nanny Goat to her cart and haul a giant papier-mâché phallus up and down Gurdeyville Town Square. Yep, we're gonna need all the help we can get!

If we're gonna put on a proper avant-garde show, it oughta be some kind of surrealist drama heavy on symbolism. Who will write this play, you ask? None other than yours truly, Mickey McCune, natch! Aw, don't worry, I've seen lots of these kind of shows—cabaret, poetry recitals, performance art, you name it. It'll be a cinch! I think I'll call my work *Meat Play*. It will be the story of the aforementioned fetus, who survives a premature birth and eventually ascends to the throne of an obscure Eastern European kingdom. There will be a waltzing skeleton, a murderous clown, an enormously fat industrialist who sits atop a large glass toilet and

see SHOW page 107

Area Man Has Complete Prison-Survival Strategy Mapped Out

SANDY SPRINGS, GA—Josh Kroll, 32, an Atlanta-area database administrator, has his complete prison-survival strategy mapped out in the unlikely event that he is ever jailed.

"You never know what life is going to bring," said Kroll, whose lone brush with the law was a 1994 speeding

> ### "Based on what I've seen on *Oz*, I'd probably want to steer clear of the weight room," Kroll said.

ticket. "I could find someone sleeping with my wife and, in a psychotic state of shock, kill him. Or I could accidentally hit somebody with my car and then flee the scene in panic. Or I could forget to report some major source of income and get nailed for tax evasion. It's not inconceivable. There's nothing wrong with thinking ahead."

Kroll said he has worked through many possible strategies for prison survival.

"If I'm in a maximum-security prison, I need to figure out who's important and who's not," Kroll said. "There's always the possibility I'm going to have to be somebody's bitch, so if that happened, I'd want to be with somebody who'd protect me. But I might be able to avoid all that because I was pre-law as an undergrad and could be useful to the other prisoners for legal advice."

Kroll, who has never been inside a

Above: Law-abiding citizen Josh Kroll.

prison, said he has relied heavily on prison-themed movies and TV shows in his effort to develop a game plan.

"Based on what I've seen on *Oz*, I'd probably want to steer clear of the weight room," Kroll said. "That's where most of the bullies hang out, plus there's no shortage of blunt weapons lying around. And, if at all possible, I'd want to keep away from the kitchen pantry, too. That's where a lot of the stabbings seem to take place on the show—somebody goes in there

alone to grab something and gets jumped."

Well aware of the value of having loyal friends on the outside, Kroll has drawn up a mental list of people most likely to stick by him in case of a lengthy prison sentence.

"Unless I was arrested for child molesting, Scott [Havens] would stick by me," Kroll said. "I think Marc [Unger] would, too, but I don't think I could get him to smuggle anything in for me. He'd be too afraid of getting

thrown in jail himself."

Kroll said he could not confidently assess the loyalty of his wife in the event of incarceration.

"With things being so rocky lately, Jane just might use prison as a chance to take off and divorce me," Kroll said. "Then again, my imprisonment might be the kind of terrible crisis to bring us closer together. If that's the case, I'm hoping for minimum security so I can get conjugal visits."

Kroll, who has previously drafted survival strategies for getting lost in the mountains, being kidnapped by South American drug lords, and falling into a polar-bear cage at the zoo, said his chances of surviving prison are "good to very good."

"After being released on bail, I would immediately begin my rigorous weight-training and self-defense regimen," Kroll said. "I've even toyed with the idea of locking myself in a closet to get used to solitary confinement. With some books on elementary psychology, I'd probably do pretty well 'in the walls.'"

According to psychologist Dr. Annette Trudeau, plotting out theoretical prison-survival strategies is surprisingly common.

"The human being is an animal with extremely strong self-preservation instincts," Trudeau said. "In this regard, Mr. Kroll's preparatory measures make perfect sense. But while devising emergency plans is understandable, he should realize that no matter how much he prepares, the only thing he can count on in prison is having his creamy white ass churned into butter." ∅

NEWS IN BRIEF

School Board Adopts Gay-Ass Uniform Policy

LOS ANGELES—Seeking to reduce incidents of student violence and insubordination, the Los Angeles Unified School District voted 9-3 Monday to institute a gay-ass uniform policy. "We feel these lame uniforms, with their dorky ties and dipwad school crests, will help create a school environment more conducive to learning," said LAUSD board officer Jefferson Crain. "We foresee fewer outbursts when students are forced to walk around in these retardo suits."

E.T. Toys Forced On Uninterested Children

CHERRY HILL, NJ—Across the nation, toys and other merchandise produced for the 20th-anniversary rerelease of *E.T.* are being foisted upon uninterested children. "This is the alien spaceship, but it doesn't even

have any guns or anything," said Robbie Guyton, 6, attempting to make sense of toys bought for him by his mother, who fell in love with the heartwarming Steven Spielberg classic two decades ago as a 10-year-old girl. "The E.T. monster is even weirder: It's, like, all naked and shriveled, and it doesn't have any battle armor. It's not scary at all." Guyton tried to figure out how to activate the death laser on the E.T. doll's finger, but was unable.

Man Hopes Hot Woman In Next Apartment Can Hear How Well He's Fucking His Girlfriend

MIRAMAR, FL—During sexual intercourse Monday, Curtis Davie, 23, hoped that his attractive neighbor could hear the pleasured moans of his girlfriend through his apartment wall.

"Don't get me wrong, things are going great with Amy," Davie said. "But it certainly never hurts to have a hot chick next door who knows you're a sexual dynamo." To increase his chances of being heard, Davie is considering moving his bed to the wall between his apartment and the neighbor's, or at least closer to the shared air duct.

Colombian Rebel 25 Years Younger Than Colombian Civil War

MITÚ, COLOMBIA—Alberto Diaz, 14, a Marxist guerrilla fighter in the Colombian civil war, is 25 years younger than the war itself. "President Arango and his corrupt right-wing regime must fall," said the pubescent Diaz, whose rebel group, the Revolutionary Armed Forces of Colombia, has been trying to topple the government since the early 1960s. "This has been my dream ever since 1999, when

I was just an 11-year-old child." Diaz then popped a pimple on his chin and wiped the pus on the barrel of his AK-47.

Man Bitten By Radioactive Sloth Does The Lying-Around-All-Day Of 10 Normal Men

CENTRAL CITY—Laboratory assistant Brent Barker, bitten by a radioactive sloth last week in a freak lab accident, now possesses the relative loafing powers of 10 men. "Could someone pass me some more crackers?" asked the media-dubbed "Crimson Lump," speaking from his titanium sofa, the only known object that can withstand his superhuman lethargy. "I can't reach them from here." Scientists are likewise baffled at Barker's uncanny ability to remain motionless while watching amounts of television that would kill an ordinary mortal. ∅

speed to keep himself sharp," Hutchinson said. "That's not what the law was intended to prevent. But the more destructive drug users—the addict who spends his welfare money on crack, the guy in Harlem who smokes marijuana—that is something that we as a society must not tolerate."

According to Drug Czar John P. Walters, the legislation should have a beneficial effect on the health of the American people.

"As a result of this new law, we expect use of addictive, harmful drugs like heroin and crack—those statistically more likely to be linked to unemployment—to drop," Walters said. "Meanwhile, decent people with good jobs can continue their responsible use of milder drugs like E and cocaine in peace."

Walters said the new legislation will make it significantly easier to fight the drug war. The nation's courts will not be clogged with cases involving club kids caught with "Vitamin K" or doctors prescribing Vicodin to rich

> **The U.S. economy also stands to benefit. Initial surveys indicate that the threat of jail will motivate recreational drug users to seek employment, reducing the nation's welfare rolls.**

housewives. More money can be freed up to build prisons to keep chronically unemployed addicts in jail and off the streets—the only statistically proven method of improving an addict's chance of recovery.

"Clearly, a lot of people doing drugs simply cannot handle them," Walters said. "We've got to get the drugs out of the hands of these people, and give them back to the weekend users."

The law, Hutchinson noted, will also help protect the nation's poor and unemployed, who are not as equipped to handle the effects of drug addiction as their more affluent counterparts.

"Drugs are addictive, and that's true whether you're a ghetto gang member or a Harvard-educated entertainment lawyer," Hutchinson said. "But the cold, hard truth is, if the ghetto kid gets hooked, he isn't going to clean up in a rehab clinic in Palm Springs and maybe even become president, now, is he? That's why we need to protect the less fortunate among us with the threat of arrest and incarceration."

The U.S. economy also stands to benefit. Initial surveys indicate that the threat of jail will motivate recreational drug users to seek employment, reducing the nation's welfare rolls.

"Legal weed versus jail?" asked Cory Everly, 23, an unemployed Austin, TX, singer-songwriter. "I am so totally going down to the sub shop today to ask Rudy for my job back."

Added Everly: "Rudy's my boss... at the sub shop."

"The new American motto is 'Work

> **"Clearly, a lot of people doing drugs simply cannot handle them," Walters said.**

Hard, Play Hard,'" Hutchinson said. "Do a few bumps of coke at your gay friend's party. Go to your be-in or your Lollapalooza rave or whatever it's called this year. But you'd better make it in to work on Monday, buddy, or you're going to jail."

"Sorry if some of my comments have been a bit rambling and unfocused," Hutchinson added. "I'm a little high right now." Ø

itive.

"It was awesome," said Craig Martsch, 16. "There was one part where this woman turned around to yell at her kids in the back seat

> **"There was one part where this woman turned around to yell at her kids in the back seat and—*wham*—she slammed right into an oncoming truck."**

and—wham—she slammed right into an oncoming truck. It's not on the level of *Texas Chainsaw Massacre* or anything, but for something you see in school, it was pretty damn gory."

Martsch's viewing experience was enhanced by the horrified reaction of his peers.

"All these people, especially the girls, were screaming and covering their eyes," Martsch said. "My girlfriend Kirsten was totally white when they showed the brains oozing out of the driver's skull. I thought she was gonna spew all over. In the lunch room later that day, Jeff [Kahn] squeezed his hamburger and was like, 'Hey, Kirsten, does this remind you of anything?'"

Most Lincoln Memorial students have some awareness of *Wheels Of Tragedy* long before they see it.

"When I was a freshman, I had algebra with a bunch of sophomores," said Paige Wesley, 15. "One day, they all walked in totally freaking out over this movie they'd seen. I was like, 'What? What?' They were like, 'Sorry, you're just going to have to wait until next year.'"

Wheels Of Tragedy is just one of many short films produced in the '60s and '70s by the Highway Safety Foundation. Others include *Signal 30, Drive And Survive, Highways Of Agony, Mechanized Death,* and *The Last Prom.*

"Showing a film like this reminds kids that driving is serious business," said Fait, 64. "Some of the images may be a bit unpleasant, but it's the only way to hammer home the point that a car is not a toy."

To discourage hysteria in the days leading up to the film's showing, Fait has had a longstanding policy of not revealing the exact date it will be shown. The current crop of students learned they would be seeing *Wheels Of Tragedy* when they walked into class Monday and saw the projector at the back of the room.

Though the sight of the projector sparked wild cheering and high-fives among the students, some members of the class approached Fait to express concern over the film's rumored graphic content. When it came time to

> **"Showing a film like this reminds kids that driving is serious business," said Fait, 64. "Some of the images may be a bit unpleasant, but it's the only way to hammer home the point that a car is not a toy."**

start the film, however, no one opted out.

"Mr. Fait said if we wanted we could go and sit in the nurse's office," Wesley said. "Nobody wanted to puss out, though."

Fait, who also serves as one of Lincoln Memorial's industrial-arts teachers, has become the official keeper of *Wheels Of Tragedy.* The film is housed in the closet of the shop's "learning center," a group of tables separated from the band saws and other woodworking equipment by a moveable divider wall.

For nearly a decade, school librarian Iris Beyer has lobbied to have *Wheels* removed from the driver's-ed curriculum, calling it "a bizarre, violent relic devoid of any educational value." In 1995, Beyer personally threw away most of the school's 16mm educational films, including the gross-out classic *Woodshop Safety*, the drug-scare film *Narcotics: Pit Of Despair*, and the menstruation primer *On Your Way.*

"None of the other teachers particularly approve of Mr. Fait showing that car-crash film, but no one ever says anything," Beyer said. "Mr. Fait is going to retire in a few years, and when he does, we'll just retire the film with him." Ø

amounts of blood. Passersby were amazed by the unusually large amounts of blood. Passersby were

amazed by the unusually large amounts of blood. Passersby were amazed by the unusually large amounts of blood. Passersby were amazed by the unusually large amounts of blood. Passersby were amazed by the unusually large amounts of blood. Passersby were amazed by the unusually large amounts of blood. Passersby were amazed by the unusually large amounts of blood. Passersby were

> **Is that all I am to you? The man who installed your carpet?**

amazed by the unusually large amounts of blood. Passersby were amazed by the unusually large amounts of blood. Passersby were amazed by the unusually large amounts of blood. Passersby were amazed by the unusually large amounts of blood. Passersby were amazed by the unusually large amounts of blood. Passersby were amazed by the unusually large amounts of blood. Passersby were amazed by the unusually large amounts of blood. Passersby were amazed by the unusually large amounts of blood. Passersby were amazed by the unusually large amounts of blood. Passersby were amazed by the unusually large amounts of blood. Passersby were amazed by the unusually large

see SLUICE page 99

SHOW from page 104 POPE from page 103

defecates money, and a lecherous bishop who covets his own sister but can't act on his impulses because he's buried up to his chest in dirt. Ain't that a peach?

By thunder, we'll do things up on that stage that'll have everybody talking here in Gurdeyville! Instead of stagehands, the actors will move the scenery right in front of the audience. Without warning or explanation, human actors will be replaced by marionettes... right smack in the middle of scenes! And, of course, there will be

> ## When everybody sees our nifty avant-garde show, they'll be clamoring for more. The dimes will pour in, and not only will we have enough money to save the clubhouse, but we'll also have enough left over for ice-cream sundaes!

heaps and heaps of overlapping dialogue. This play will not only savagely attack the class system, organized religion, and sexual mores, but also, by subverting the conventions of mainstream theater, it will draw attention to its stale artificiality! Yesiree, this *Meat Play* is gonna be a pip!

What's that you say, Hamhock? "Nudity"? Jumping Jehosophat, you're right! How silly I was to forget the nudity! It's just the thing every avant-garde play needs. We'll paint our naked bodies all the colors of the rainbow, and the boys' penises will be gaily striped like barbershop poles! Golly, I can hardly wait for opening night!

We'll charge 10 cents a seat and invite everyone in town, from the ragpicker to the mayor himself. We'll even invite old Banker Mudge, just to show him he can't boss us kids around! When everybody sees our nifty avant-garde show, they'll be clamoring for more. The dimes will pour in, and not only will we have enough money to save the clubhouse, but we'll also have enough left over for ice-cream sundaes!

What's that, Bucky? You say the clubhouse already has the money to pay off Banker Mudge and stop his plan? Some other neighborhood kids raised the funds by performing a play of their own? A dialogue-free version of *Uncle Tom's Cabin* in which all the players lie onstage tightly swaddled in gauze? Gee, Bucky, why didn't you say something before I got on a roll? Well, I guess I oughta get back to working on my soap-box racer for the big derby! Ø

Above: Pope John Paul II, whose funeral is expected to take place sometime in the next few months.

Vatican continues to deny that his death is imminent, insisting that the pontiff is in excellent health for a man his age. Nevertheless, the line of faithful "Pope Deathwatchers" that wraps around the basilica continues to swell by the hour.

Many of those waiting in line hope to catch a glimpse of the pope before he dies.

"I'm sure he'd love to come down and talk to us, but he's probably too weak by this point," said Maria Tineo, a Venezuelan nun who recently jumped 10 spaces in line when she correctly spelled the pope's real

> ## Among the most popular ways to pass the time include discussing the revised criteria for sainthood, trading pope-sighting stories, singing "Ave Maria," quoting the scripture, playing Catholic Trivial Pursuit, and, most of all, discussing the life of Pope John Paul II.

name—Karol Joseph Wojtyla—in a contest sponsored by a Rome radio station. "Some people near the back of the line thought they saw him on the balcony, but that turned out to be false."

Though no pope sightings have occurred in the last few weeks, periodic glimpses of cardinals entering and exiting St. Peter's have kept the crowd juiced.

"I've seen Cardinal Sadano twice," said Milan resident Sofia Cucino, who runs the pope fan site John-paulrules.com. "I also saw Cardinal Grantin once and wanted to ask him to get the pope to sign my copy of *Crossing The Threshold Of Hope*, but I couldn't get his attention. I just hope it's not my last chance."

While portable radios and TVs keep the crowd up to date on the pope's health, those in line have mostly entertained themselves. Among the most popular ways to pass the time include discussing the revised criteria for sainthood, trading pope-sighting stories, singing "Ave Maria," quoting the scripture, playing Catholic Trivial Pursuit, and, most of all, discussing the life of Pope John Paul II.

"Pope John Paul II was the first non-Italian pope in more than 455 years and the first Slavic pope ever," said William Strand, an Omaha, NE, priest. "He had to struggle every step of the way, right from his start as a young priest in the godless, communist country of Poland. Before he became a priest, he belonged to an experimental theater troupe, worked as a stonecutter, and was a published poet. He also enjoyed mountain climbing and kayaking. He was—I mean is—truly one of a kind."

While nearly everyone in line intends to wait as long as it takes until the pope dies, many do not plan to remain for the naming of a successor.

"I'm here to lend my faith and devotion to a very holy man in his final days," said Mario Battaglia of Genoa. "After he departs, so shall I."

For all the faithful's enthusiasm, some observers say the queued Catholics are wasting their time, insisting that they will be squeezed out of the funeral by the countless heads of state and other dignitaries that will

> ## Some observers say the queued Catholics are wasting their time, insisting that they will be squeezed out of the funeral by the countless heads of state and other dignitaries that will descend upon the Vatican from around the world.

descend upon the Vatican from around the world.

"When [the pope] dies, it will be an unbelievable event. Everybody who's anybody will be there," said Dr. Lawrence Shear, dean of the Yale School of Divinity. "The media requests alone could fill that basilica. Since the Vatican is always looking for the kind of coverage the death of a major leader brings, the devoted will be out of luck."

Continued Shear: "I think the best those poor Catholics can hope for is to be interviewed about their feelings on the pope's passing by local TV news affiliates while wailing in St. Peter's Square." Ø

Now, There's A Stranger Who Could Use Some Of My Child-Rearing Advice

By Felicia Rudd

All too often in this world, we turn a blind eye to those who could use a helping hand. Now, I'm no saint, but I just can't look away when I see people who need help. Like, if a couple on the street is having an argument, I'll step in and try to help them resolve their issues. More often than not, the couple is so stunned by the caring and concern shown by a total stranger that they completely forget whatever it was they were fighting about.

While my humanitarian streak extends to all aspects of life, there's one particular area I consider my specialty: child-rearing. Hardly a day goes by when I don't come across a struggling parent who could use some of my advice.

When most people see a woman screaming at her 3-year-old to keep quiet, their impulse is to look away and mind their own business. "This doesn't concern me," they rationalize. Well, unlike these people, I realize that we're all connected. Instead of turning away, I'd approach this woman and say, "Excuse me, but I couldn't help but notice you having some parenting difficulties. Maybe you should consider getting a toy or something to keep your daughter occupied. Not only would it keep her from upsetting passersby with her shrieking, but a play object would be a boon to her motor-skills development."

Why do I help this woman when so many others would choose to pretend it's not happening? Because I know it takes a village to raise a child.

Even though I've never had kids, I've been around enough of them to know what to do—and what not to do. But in spite of my expertise, some mothers are surprisingly resistant to my advice. This stubbornness is unfortunate, as it's the child who loses out. I know if I were a mother who didn't know what she was doing, I would welcome the helpful advice of a knowledgeable stranger.

Take, for example, the mother I recently saw giving her child a Hi-C drink box. Concerned that she mistakenly thought Hi-C was made with real fruit juice, I told her that it's largely artificial. Sadly, she felt threatened by my superior parenting skills and told me to "get lost." I assured her that it was an understandable mistake for her to think Hi-C was real fruit juice. The product's box, after all, deceptively features a bevy of oranges, apples, and grapes. I told her not to feel bad or embarrassed and then gently advised her to read labels more carefully in the future. "Anything called a 'fruit drink' or 'juice cocktail' is probably only 5 or 10 percent juice, at most," I told her. "So you should really try to avoid those."

> **Even though I've never had kids, I've been around enough of them to know what to do—and what not to do. But in spite of my expertise, some mothers are surprisingly resistant to my advice.**

Instead of thanking me for the free advice, this woman showered me with invective and urged me to "get my own damn kids." Did my generous offer of help really warrant such hostility? (Keep in mind that I repeatedly assured her that this one error did not make her a bad parent.) Things only got worse when I helpfully pointed out that maybe if she could better manage her temper, her kids would probably grow up more well-adjusted.

It's kind of strange, but once you realize that most people could use a little common-sense advice to help raise their children, you start seeing it almost everywhere. About a month ago, I was strolling through the neighborhood and saw a woman letting her children run around the yard in clothes that looked like they hadn't been washed in a week. So I told this woman that even if a parent doesn't have enough money for spanking-new clothes, it's still easy to maintain a neat appearance with regular clothes-washing. Next thing you know, it's raining F-bombs.

Even though she was threatening to call the police to get me off her lawn, I bet she's going to make sure her children will be a little more presentable in public in the future. As long as that's the case, I'm happy to be yelled at. It's all about doing what's best for the little ones. ✍

Your Horoscope

By Lloyd Schumner Sr.
Retired Machinist and
A.A.P.B.-Certified Astrologer

Aries: (March 21–April 19)
Powers beyond your control will soon determine your fate while you wait patiently in the car.

Taurus: (April 20–May 20)
When your plane crashes in the Andes, you will be forced to eat the flight crew, making you glad you chose to fly Succulent Pig Airlines.

Gemini: (May 21–June 21)
That old saying about cowards dying a thousand deaths while heroes die but once will occur to you at an extremely apt moment.

Cancer: (June 22–July 22)
There are a million reasons you shouldn't give up hope of ever finding love. None of them, however, are very good.

Leo: (July 23–Aug. 22)
You will be shocked and embarrassed when the arresting officers inform you that cockfighting is supposed to involve chickens.

Virgo: (Aug. 23–Sept. 22)
Virgo is proud to introduce the 2003 Horoscopes, boasting twice the horsepower and 30 percent more rear-seat legroom.

Libra: (Sept. 23–Oct. 23)
Your mother's advice will fail you when you start carefully sounding out the hard words during a speech before the House Subcommittee For Military Appropriations.

Scorpio: (Oct. 24–Nov. 21)
You will undergo a profound personal change that results in you finally paying your phone bill, if you know what's good for you.

Sagittarius: (Nov. 22–Dec. 21)
Forces are being set in motion that will forever change the way you look at microwaveable Mexican dinners.

Capricorn: (Dec. 22–Jan. 19)
The gods of justice say they will hear your petition just as soon as they have finished discussing the designated-hitter rule.

Aquarius: (Jan. 20–Feb. 18)
You will experience deep spiritual vertigo when you realize there is nothing else in the world you want to buy.

Pisces: (Feb. 19–March 20)
Though there is a patron saint of being finely minced, you remember his name far too late.

SLAWSUIT from page 105

amounts of blood. Passersby were amazed by the unusually large amounts of blood. Passersby were amazed by the unusually large amounts of blood. Passersby were amazed by the unusually large amounts of blood. Passersby were amazed by the unusually large amounts of blood. Passersby were amazed by the unusually large amounts of blood. Passersby were amazed by the unusually large amounts of blood. Passersby were amazed by the unusually large amounts of blood. Passersby were amazed by the unusually large amounts of blood. Passersby were amazed by the unusually large amounts of blood. Passersby were amazed by the unusually large amounts of blood. Passersby were amazed by the unusually large amounts of blood. Passersby were amazed by the unusually large amounts of blood. Passersby were amazed by the unusually large amounts of blood. Passersby were amazed by the unusually large amounts of blood. Passersby were amazed by the unusually large amounts of blood. Passersby were amazed by the unusually large amounts of blood. Passersby were amazed by the unusually large amounts of blood. Passersby were amazed by the unusually large amounts of blood. Passersby were amazed by the unusually large amounts of blood. Passersby were

amazed by the unusually large amounts of blood. Passersby were amazed by the unusually large amounts of blood. Passersby were amazed by the unusually large amounts of blood. Passersby were amazed by the unusually large amounts of blood. Passersby were

Losing money at that casino sure was fun!

amazed by the unusually large amounts of blood. Passersby were amazed by the unusually large amounts of blood. Passersby were amazed by the unusually large amounts of blood. Passersby were amazed by the unusually large amounts of blood. Passersby were amazed by the unusually large amounts of blood. Passersby were amazed by the unusually large amounts of blood. Passersby were amazed by the unusually large amounts of blood. Passersby were amazed by the unusually large amounts of blood. Passersby were amazed by the unusually large

see SLAWSUIT page 110

Obesity-Study Lab Rat's Life Pretty Sweet

see SCIENCE page 5C

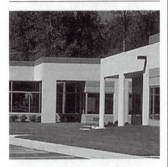

Rapist Gets New Start At Technical College

see LOCAL page 11C

Southerner Either Looking For 'Pawn Shop' Or 'Porn Shop'

see LOCAL page 3C

Lord's Prayer Ad-Libbed

see FAITH page 3B

STATshot

A look at the numbers that shape your world.

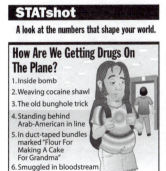

How Are We Getting Drugs On The Plane?
1. Inside bomb
2. Weaving cocaine shawl
3. The old bunghole trick
4. Standing behind Arab-American in line
5. In duct-taped bundles marked "Flour For Making A Cake For Grandma"
6. Smuggled in bloodstream

0 74470 94595 6

00

THE ONION • $2.00 US • $3.00 CAN

the ONION®

VOLUME 38 ISSUE 12   AMERICA'S FINEST NEWS SOURCE™   4–10 APRIL 2002

Nation's UPS Men Break Out The Shorts

MANCHESTER, NH—In a welcome sight heralding the end of another winter and the arrival of spring, United Parcel Service men across the nation are breaking out the shorts.

"Look!" said Manchester-area cashier Brenda Cosgrove, staring out the window of the yarn shop where she works. "There goes another one! That's three today!"

Across the U.S., signs of the change of season abound, as daffodils poke out of the ground, the songs of the robin are once again heard in the trees, and leaves bud on the branches. For millions of Americans, however, there is no more beloved harbinger of spring than the sight of a UPS man's sturdy calves in the open air after months hidden away beneath heavy brown fabric.

"Between the long winter and this cold rain we've been having, it felt like it was never going to warm up," said Hugh McCaskill, a St. Cloud, MN, real-estate agent. "But then I saw

see SHORTS page 113

Above: UPS driver Luis Tendero breaks out the shorts in Eugene, OR.

Countries Who Met Over Internet Go To War

TARTU, ESTONIA—Just months after meeting in an Internet chat room, the nations of Suriname and Estonia have entered a state of open hostility, U.N. sources reported Tuesday.

"In early January, Surinamese president Runaldo Ronald Venetiaan logged onto a small-nations chat room on Yahoo! and came across Estonian president Arnold Ruutel," U.N. Secretary-General Kofi Annan said. "The two exchanged messages and, before long, became Internet friends, bonding over their shared experi-

see WAR page 112

New Roommate Has Elaborate Theory About How Kenny Rogers Is A Genius

DAYTON, OH—University of Dayton sophomores Mike Maritz and Andrea Haltigan reported Monday that their otherwise normal-seeming new roommate has "this whole theory about how Kenny Rogers is a genius."

"So, yesterday, we're moving the living room around to fit in some of Kurt [Schaier]'s stuff," said Maritz, 21. "The two of us are pushing my big CD shelf into the corner, and out of nowhere, Kurt says, 'Kenny Rogers is the most underrated musician alive.' I was like, 'Where did that come from?'"

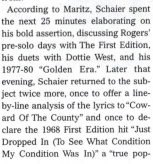

According to Maritz, Schaier spent the next 25 minutes elaborating on his bold assertion, discussing Rogers' pre-solo days with The First Edition, his duets with Dottie West, and his 1977-80 "Golden Era." Later that evening, Schaier returned to the subject twice more, once to offer a line-by-line analysis of the lyrics to "Coward Of The County" and once to declare the 1968 First Edition hit "Just Dropped In (To See What Condition My Condition Was In)" a "true pop-

Above: Kurt Schaier, whose deep admiration of Kenny Rogers (left) has caused confusion among his new roommates.

psychedelic classic."

Haltigan and Maritz first met Schaier on March 14 when he responded to a classified ad for the vacant room in their three-bedroom apartment.

"We said no to a few applicants, like this guy with these earlobe things and

see ROOMMATE page 113

The Church Sex Scandal

A growing sex-abuse scandal is engulfing the Catholic Church, with many priests accused of sexually molesting children. What do *you* think?

Chris Davis
Lawyer

"Where in The Bible does it forbid someone to pin a 10-year-old behind a large cooler of Kool-Aid in a church basement?"

Paul George
Systems Analyst

"Hey, if Abraham was willing to kill his son for God, the least a devout Catholic can do is let his kid get cornholed here and there."

Don Lawson
File Clerk

"Catholic priests are being unfairly singled out as pedophiles. We must not forget the music teachers and hockey coaches."

Sheila Rutt
Systems Analyst

"Wine, candles, incense, frilly little frocks... you can see how it sets a mood."

Phil Ormond
Cab Driver

"This is just secular, liberal-media hysteria over thousands of grade-schoolers getting ass-raped."

Danielle Krug
Speech Therapist

"Now that it's out in the open, the healing can begin. Except for the kids."

The Organ-Donor Crisis

The U.S. is critically low on organ donations. What is the nation's medical community doing to address the shortage?

- Experimenting with tofu-based organ substitutes
- Raising speed limit to 170 mph in school zones
- Asking people to tough it out and make do without a pancreas for a while
- Offering to donate their organs to anyone in critical need, if you catch their drift
- Removing David Crosby's new liver and giving to more deserving person
- Wondering if nation's homeless problem, organ-shortage problem can't be solved simultaneously
- Splitting up available organs so at least everyone in need gets a little piece
- Allowing recipient's body to reject maximum of two hearts; after that, no more favors for Mr. Picky
- Introducing special edition of *Dawn Of The Dead* ending with zombies turning to camera and saying, "We've had some fun tonight, but ripping organs out of people's bodies is no laughing matter," followed by web address for shareyourlife.org

the ONION®
America's Finest News Source.™

Herman Ulysses Zweibel
Founder

T. Herman Zweibel
Publisher Emeritus
J. Phineas Zweibel
Publisher
Maxwell Prescott Zweibel
Editor-In-Chief

You Used Me For Sex, Friendship, And Good Conversation

By Amy Treehorn

Wow. I don't know what to say. I thought everything was going great between us. I thought we really had something special going these past six weeks. Apparently, I was wrong. It's become clear to me that all this time, you were just using me for sex, friendship, and good conversation.

Is that all I was to you, somebody you could potentially be interested in dating long-term, assuming things kept progressing? After all the dates we'd been on, was it that easy to throw it all away once you decided I wasn't really right for you? It all seems so hollow now.

I remember the time we saw *Monsoon Wedding* and then went out for coffee. Over lattes, we discussed everything from Indian cinema to our respective college experiences. Now I know it meant nothing. And the time you told me about how you watched your grandmother slowly die of cancer? What a sucker I was.

You were very clever, enjoying yourself when we met at that party. I must

> **Did it mean anything to you, that time we sat in your kitchen drinking coffee and sharing the newspaper? Or when we took the long way home after our second date, holding hands and talking about our favorite songs?**

have been blind. Even that early in the game, you were already weaving the web of physical attractiveness, intelligence, and sense of humor that you would use to ensnare me, culminating in a six-week dating stint. I hope you had fun.

I can't believe I let you use me for stimulating conversation like that. You were great when it came to sharing my passion for African literature, but it was all a lie. I don't know how you can stand to look in the mirror, knowing your life has been built on a foundation of untruths. I bet you just read *Season Of Migration To The North* just to

impress me with your theories on the subject.

I'm sure being a generous lover was also part of your elaborate ruse. It's all falling into place. You may have seemed responsive to my desires and

> **Now you want to be "just friends"? Whatever it takes to help you sleep. Your carefully chosen words aren't fooling me. The time for that is over.**

sensitive to my needs, but all the while, you were just manipulating me into participating in mutually satisfying intercourse.

Did it mean anything to you, that time we sat in your kitchen drinking coffee and sharing the newspaper? Or when we took the long way home after our second date, holding hands and talking about our favorite songs? How about the time you made me a picnic lunch in the park? Were those just your devious ways of finding out if our personalities were compatible in case you wanted to see more of me? Wait, don't answer. The look in your eyes tells me all I need to know.

I feel like such a fool. All this time, I thought there was something behind your interest in me. Instead, it was just some sort of trap to win my time and affection—until you lost interest, that is. How could I have been so blind? Couldn't I see that all those jokes you told were just a thinly veiled attempt to get me to have a good time with you? Apparently not, because I fell for it like a sparrow weighted with sandbags.

Perhaps words have different meanings for you. When you said "Thanks, I had fun," I guess what you were really saying was, "I will be funny, charming, and affectionate until I grow tired of you."

Now you want to be "just friends"? Whatever it takes to help you sleep. Your carefully chosen words aren't fooling me. The time for that is over. I refuse to fall victim to your sincerity ever again.

Hey, I've got an idea! Why don't you send me a card saying you're happy to have met me, and that your life was enriched by the time we spent together. What's that? You like and respect me too much to do something tacky and dismissive like that? I figured you'd say something like that. Typical. *Ø*

Sullen Time-Traveling Teen Reports 23rd Century Sucks

NEWTON, MA—According to sullen teenager Steve Geremek, the 23rd century, a time previously restricted to the fantastical imaginings of science-fiction writers and futurists, "sucks."

"Ah, it was a bunch of boring stuff," said a slouching, mumbling Geremek, 17, at a press conference shortly after his return from the future Monday. "It totally blew."

Geremek, the son of renowned MIT theoretical physicist Irwin Geremek, was transported to the year 2202 last Thursday when he accidentally wandered into an experimental tachyon particle accelerator being developed by his father.

"I was messing around in my dad's thingy and, all of a sudden, there was this flash of purple light," Geremek said. "Next thing I knew, I was surrounded by a bunch of boring future stuff."

Asked to clarify what he meant by "boring future stuff," Geremek said, "I dunno... stuff."

Geremek was similarly vague when queried about 23rd-century fuel sources, organization of communities, and prevalent modes of transportation.

"I dunno, people still walked around and did crap, same as today," said Geremek, staring at the floor and fidgeting with his hands. "It's not like that nuclear-winter thing came true."

Geremek's ambiguous answers drove at least one scientist to exasperation.

"What did he mean, 'It's not like that nuclear-winter thing came true'?" University of Chicago physicist Dr. Erno Schuller asked. "Did a nuclear war occur at some point but no nuclear winter resulted? Or did he mean a nuclear war didn't occur and, therefore, people were relieved that there was no nuclear winter and went about their lives the same as always? Christ."

Geremek was somewhat more forthcoming when asked about food and popular culture.

"They still had pizza, which was cool," Geremek said. "But kids were into splicing their DNA with beetles, so they get, like, these temporary mandibles shooting out of their foreheads. It sounds like it would be pretty cool, but it actually looked kinda gay."

Geremek's father, who had not planned to test the time-travel device until sometime early next year, was eager to speak to his son upon his return.

"You idiot," the elder Geremek said. "Thirteen years it took us to perfect those coordinate calculations, and another seven to build the thing. Not to mention the months of endless wrangling to get our project funded.

Now we have to start over because you didn't give the thing proper time to reach its core temperature, damaging the acceleration mechanism. I told

> ## "I was messing around in my dad's thingy and, all of a sudden, there was this flash of purple light," Geremek said.

you to wait in the car while I got some papers. What the hell were you doing in there in the first place?"

The physicist then grounded his son, who responded by calling his father a Nazi.

Experts remain uncertain how to interpret Steve Geremek's tantalizingly cryptic account of 23rd-century life.

"We're not sure if, in describing the 23rd century as 'boring,' Steve meant that civilization is destroyed and man

Above: Steve Geremek, shortly after his return from the "totally stupid and lame" year 2202.

lives in a sort of grinding, post-apocalyptic world of hand-to-mouth barbarism, or that civilization exists as a totalitarian system in which the individual is a faceless cog in a drab, oppressive bureaucratic machine," author and futurist Alvin Toffler said. "Perhaps he meant something else altogether. We will likely not know the answer until Steve is well out of his teens or has some sense knocked into him." ∅

Pepsi CEO's Wife Buys Coke When She's Mad At Him

PURCHASE, NY—Mary Reinemund, wife of Pepsico CEO Steven S. Reinemund, passive-aggressively buys Coca-Cola products whenever she is angry at her husband. "Last Wednesday, Steve worked late on their anniversary," said Bea Vance, the Reinemunds' housekeeper. "Sure enough, the next day, there's a two-liter bottle of Diet Coke in the fridge." Vance added that in the summer of 1999, during "an especially rough time" in the Reinemunds' marriage, Mary was often seen wearing a promotional Sprite sun visor.

Nation's Deans Meet To Discuss Problem Of College Girls Going Wild

GAINESVILLE, FL—Calling the trend "a black mark on academia," deans from more than 300 U.S. colleges converged on the University of Florida campus Monday to address the growing problem of out-of-control, sexy sorority sweethearts baring it all for the cameras. "In recent years, a number of filmmakers have

brought to light the shocking antics of hot young girls from the wildest party schools," said Tulane University dean of students Dr. Anderson Brand. "We must take appropriate action to address this wild, uncensored revelry." Brandishing one of the mail-order videotapes, University of Connecticut dean Charles Burton said, "I could not believe what happened when those crazy co-eds got back to their hotel rooms. Nor, I suspect, could anyone."

Acid Trip Better Planned Than Vacation

SAN LUIS OBISPO, CA—Jonathan Andriesko's weekend acid trip was better planned than his trip to Arizona last month, friends of the 22-year-old video-store clerk reported Monday. "Jon spent hours making sure everything was right," coworker Craig Jaeger said. "He requested two days off from work well in advance, rented 2001: A Space Odyssey, filled up his CD changer with Aphex Twin and Boards Of Canada discs, took the phone off the hook, stocked up on vitamin-C tablets, set up all the food he was going to need for the next 12 hours... You'd think he was planning a wedding." By contrast, Andriesko merely expressed vague plans to "get going sometime Saturday" before embarking on a mid-March trip to Scottsdale.

Loft Discussed At Loft Party

CHICAGO—Guests at David and Jill Holman's loft party Saturday spent the bulk of the four-hour affair discussing various aspects of the loft, including its location, square footage, rent, division of space, acoustics, and previous use. "So it's not too cold in the winter?" guest Gail Shaughnessy asked at the two-hour mark of the loft-centric gathering. "It seems like heating bills would be a lot with the high ceiling."

Parrot's Previous Owner Obviously Watched A Lot Of The Price Is Right

POPLAR BLUFF, MO—According to Kenneth Childs, the new owner of an African gray parrot, the previous owner must have watched a tremendous amount of The Price Is Right. "All day long, Crackers keeps squawking shit like, 'Come on down!' and 'Plinko!'" Childs said. "That poor bird must have been subjected to the Game Show Network 24 hours a day." Childs also swore that he once heard Crackers sing the yodeling music from the mountain-climber game. ∅

Above: Runaldo Ronald Venetiaan (left) and Arnold Ruutel (right) at their respective computers.

ences as leaders of tiny republics."

In spite of their vast cultural differences and geographical distance, the Surinamese and Estonian leaders forged a strong alliance, granting each other most-favored-nation status and signing numerous trade pacts.

Relations slowly turned sour, however, as a series of misunderstandings and perceived snubs caused the friendship to deteriorate into enmity. Just before dawn Monday, Estonia commenced bombing raids along Suriname's coastal region, targeting a military complex near the capital city of Paramaribo. The attack was ordered in response to Suriname troop buildup in Latvia and a thwarted attempt to cross the Estonian border at Valga last Friday.

Stressing that he usually does not e-mail countries he doesn't know, Venetiaan sent Ruutel a full page of economic-stimulus ideas, appended with the qualifier, "not that i know anything! my country's got 21.7% unemployment! :("

Estonia's angry e-mails to Suriname demanding a pullout of the Baltic region by 11:59 p.m. Sunday were repeatedly bounced back as "undeliverable due to fatal address error."

"U.N. negotiators are continuing their attempts to broker peace, but so far the process has been marred by the leaders' steadfast refusal to communicate," Annan said. "Both have re-

moved their entries from the Yahoo! member directory for Presidents Of Small Nations. There is also reason to believe they are logging on to their favorite world-politics chat rooms with alternate user names to avoid coming into contact with each other."

Venetiaan recalled the leaders' first chat-room encounter.

"I didn't know I'd one day live to regret meeting that lousy ex-Commie," said Venetiaan, who logged on using his secondary e-mail account, republic_of_suriname1975@hotmail.com. "Estonia looked like an interesting country, so, being the leader of a country myself, I typed in a message saying, 'hello out there.. whatsup in etsonia?'"

Less than 30 seconds later, Venetiaan received a response.

"It was from Estonia, saying, 'the inflations terrible!!! How bout where you are?' I wrote back, 'inflations pretty bad here too but at least it's 80 degrees and sunny!!! ;)' He replied, 'i'm sooo jealous—it's freezing here! by the way I'm wracking my brains trying to think of new economic measures to strengthen estonia's manufacturing base. if youve got any suggestions, feel free send them my way!'"

Stressing that he usually does not e-mail countries he doesn't know, Venetiaan sent Ruutel a full page of economic-stimulus ideas, appended with the qualifier, "not that i know anything! my country's got 21.7% unemployment! :("

Upon receiving Venetiaan's e-mail, Ruutel sent him an instant message about a monetary-unit conversion-program download he had seen.

"We ended up chatting for almost an hour," Ruutel said. "Nothing important, just, 'What's your main export? I have this much arable land, how about you?' That sort of thing."

According to Venetiaan, the two countries had a surprising amount in common.

"Suriname was granted independence from the Netherlands in 1975 after riots broke out," Venetiaan said. "Estonia had a lot of the same prob-

"We ended up chatting for almost an hour," Ruutel said. "Nothing important, just, 'What's your main export? I have this much arable land, how about you?' That sort of thing."

lems when they declared independence from the Soviet Union in 1990. It was weird: Even though, on the surface, we seemed totally different, we'd been through a lot of the same things."

Said Ruutel, "We added each other to our MSN Messenger Friends lists and started forwarding each other funny internal memos. Arnold sent me an MP3 from his brother's kesco band, a traditional form of Surinamese music. Then I sent him a PayPal payment for just two kroon and said I was donating my budget surplus. We had a good laugh over that one."

Two months after first meeting on the Internet, Venetiaan and Ruutel finally met face-to-face.

"When I told Arnold I was going to be on vacation in South America, he arranged a dinner in my honor," Venetiaan said. "It was a little awkward at first, because we didn't really have any official state business, but we ended up having a great time. We arranged to build an Estonian embassy in Paramaribo and signed a bunch of tariff and trade agreements."

In addition to the economic pacts,

Suriname pledged non-military support for Estonia in disputes with Russia. In return, Estonia agreed to back Suriname's claim on an area in French Guiana between Riviere Litani and Riviere Marouini.

Trouble began several weeks later, however, when a sudden jump in the value of oil shale and a sluggish international textile market prompted Ruutel to call for renegotiations.

"All of a sudden, Arnold says he wants to pull out of our bauxite agreement," Venetiaan said. "Then he's mad I took my raw aluminum to Finland for a deal on heavy machinery imports. I e-mailed and e-mailed, trying to clear up the whole mess, but there was no reply."

Feeling snubbed, Venetiaan sent Ruutel an antagonistic e-mail informing him that Suriname planned to establish formal relations with Russia.

Ruutel replied with an angry six-page e-mail blasting Suriname's decision to form an alliance with Estonia's unfriendly neighbor. When Venetiaan responded by sending a *Golden Girls* "I'm Sorry" Lifetime Network e-card, Ruutel placed his country on full military alert. Though Venetiaan later insisted the card was "just a joke," the damage was done.

"At that point, I didn't want to deal with him anymore, diplomatically or personally," Ruutel said. "I sent a formal declaration of war and CCed all of my top generals. The subject line was 're: bomb Corantijn river region sky-high.'"

Estonian Prime Minister Siim Kallas characterized the breakdown in international relations as "nothing to mourn."

"I never really liked that Ron," Kallas said. "He always seemed kind of creepy to me. I think Estonia is better off without Suriname."

Venetiaan seems similarly unfazed.

"I don't know why Estonia had to get all weird on me," Venetiaan said. "Whatever. Their loss, that's for sure." ∅

this one creepy engineering guy, but Kurt seemed totally normal," said Haltigan. "He's a poli-sci major, he has a great DVD collection, and he's into painting, which is all cool. Where the Kenny Rogers-is-a-god thing comes from, I have no idea."

According to Haltigan, Schaier made no Rogers-related remarks during his first two days in the apartment.

"The first 48 hours were fine, but then on day three, completely out of nowhere, the Kenny Rogers floodgates opened wide," Haltigan said. "That's when Kurt told me that Kenny Rogers straddles—actually, the exact phrase was 'effortlessly straddles'—the line between contemporary pop and classic country, yet everyone unfairly dismisses him as a lightweight because he has strong appeal with the easy-listening crowd."

Added Haltigan: "He also said Kenny Rogers is 'long overdue for the sort of critical reappraisal that Burt Bacharach has enjoyed of late.' Who says shit like that?"

While Haltigan and Maritz said they have nothing against Rogers, they told Schaier they do not consider him to be in the same league as such country legends as Johnny Cash, Merle Haggard, and Willie Nelson. Schaier countered that Rogers "transcends the country label," asserting that he is "not

> **To demonstrate the breadth and depth of Rogers' music, Schaier cited a partial list of the artists with whom he has worked.**

so much a country singer as a spiritual descendant of the master songsmiths of Tin Pan Alley and The Brill Building."

"Kurt said that if Kenny Rogers wanted to, he could limit himself to just country, but he wants to create accessible music," Maritz said. "Kurt said that's like criticizing a filmmaker for not working in paint on a canvas. Kurt also said... well, Kurt said a lot."

In his efforts to demonstrate the

breadth and depth of Rogers' music, Schaier cited a partial list of the artists with whom he has worked.

"At one point, Kurt practically followed me into the bathroom," Maritz said. "I'm trying take a piss, and he's outside the door saying, 'Dolly Parton, Coolio... Sheena Easton, Ray Parker Jr., Olivia Newton-John... Madonna... The Charlie Daniels Band.'"

Discussing Schaier while he was at class Monday, Haltigan and Maritz raised a number of questions about their new roommate: How long has Schaier been a Kenny Rogers fan? Does he actually listen to Kenny Rogers albums, or is his fandom primarily conceptual? Is Kenny Rogers genuinely of great importance to Schaier, or is Schaier merely a hipster contrarian with countless other, similarly irritating pop-culture theories at his disposal?

"I've known tons of guys who say shit like, '*Josie And The Pussycats* was the best film of 2001,' just to provoke

outrage," Maritz said. "But so far with Kurt, it's only been Kenny Rogers, so I'm not sure if he's one of those."

Continued Maritz: "Then there are those guys who randomly pull ridiculous shit out of their asses—for example that, um, every Ron Howard film is based on a different Shakespeare play—just to see if they can somehow prove it. Maybe that's his deal. Then again, maybe he's just a normal guy who happens to like really shitty music."

Noted psychologist and author Dr. Terrence Paul agreed that it remains too soon to tell.

"Mike and Andrea do not yet know enough about Kurt to determine whether his statements are driven by a genuine love of Kenny Rogers, a desire for acceptance, a desire to annoy, or some combination of the three," Paul said. "At this juncture, they still can't be certain to what extent they should dread the upcoming lease year." ∅

---

a pair of UPS shorts on the street while driving to work this morning, and my heart soared. There's nothing quite like that first sighting of the year."

"I had a hard time concentrating on work today," said Aberdeen, MD, insurance-claims adjuster Jim Freund. "Seeing those UPS guys in their short pants made me want to run home, grab my baseball glove, and head over to the park. As thanks, I think I'll

> **"Ever since I was a kid, I haven't been able to stop wearing my down jacket until I see a UPS man in shorts,"** said Virginia Bourne.

stop off at my local UPS office and send a five-pound parcel to Hagerstown at the two-day shipping rate."

Even if the grass is green, many citizens say spring has not truly arrived until the first pair of knees are seen just below the conservative hemline of those somber brown shorts.

"The temperature can be in the mid-70s, the cherry trees can be in full bloom, and the calendar can say June," said Washington, D.C., resident Cathy Anderson. "But until [UPS delivery man] Bill [Plevekis] comes to my door in those brown shorts with the socks hiked all the way up, I don't feel like winter has truly ended."

Though scientists are not certain

what evolutionary instinct, complex set of genetically coded chemical signals, or UPS corporate policy tells the delivery men when to shed their long pants, the switch to shorts resonates with many.

"Ever since I was a kid, I haven't been able to stop wearing my down jacket until I see a UPS man in shorts," said Virginia Bourne, who, as office manager for a Buffalo law firm, signs for packages daily. "This year, I still haven't seen one, but something tells me today might be the day. [UPS delivery driver] Russ [Zorn] should be doing a drop-off/pick-up around 3 p.m., and I've got a good feeling."

The year's first sighting of a pair of UPS shorts is always a media event, and last Monday was no exception. When Yakima, WA, legal secretary Lynn Harrison phoned *Today* weatherman Al Roker to report a pair emerging from a UPS van in front of her neighbor's house, she touched off a deluge of similar calls to news outlets nationwide.

"I always smile extra big when I think about the UPS shorts," said Roker, who adds miniature pairs of brown shorts to his weather map each spring until every state has reported a sighting. "There's just something about those UPS men and their little shorts that brings out the spring feeling in me."

The delivery drivers are well aware of the feelings they evoke when they cast off their bulky winter trousers each year.

"My shorts symbolize rebirth. They give people hope for new beginnings," said New York City UPS delivery man Greg Gullicksen. "Also, I get a lot more freedom of movement when I'm getting in and out of the truck." ∅

Stand-Up And Be Counted

Lately, I've been doing a lot of thinking about how important it is to follow your dreams. We all have them. Some of us want to be doctors, some want to be lawyers... and some want to be a size six!

**A Room Of Jean's Own
By Jean Teasdale**

I have a lot of dreams. Of course, they've changed through the years. When I was 8, I wanted my own pink princess phone. (I never got it.) In high school, I yearned to be voted homecoming queen. (I never was, although in junior year, I did come in fourth out of a field of nine. I later learned it was because some kids ran a campaign to elect me as a joke.) I've had a lot of other dreams, too, like being a successful Avon representative. And persuading hubby Rick to take me to Disney World for our long-delayed honeymoon. And, of course, let's not forget the three children I've always wanted: Rhett, Schuyler, and Antoinette (Toni for short).

But even as most of my dreams come and go, one has remained constant. Now, as you Jeanketeers all know, I love nothing more than a good laugh. I've never possessed one of those straitlaced, practical minds. I'm always thinking of wisecracks and witticisms, always searching for the funny side of a situation. That's why I've always felt I was destined to be... a professional joke writer! Sure, it might not save lives or broker peace in the Middle East, but by making people laugh, I'd be making myself happy, and that's all that should matter, right?

At Fashion Bug last Monday, my supervisor Roz and I got to talking. As we unloaded a shipment of slouch socks, I asked her if she had any hobbies or interests outside of managing Fashion Bug. "Are you kidding?" Roz answered. "I'd go ape if this was the

> **I love nothing more than a good laugh. I've never possessed one of those straitlaced, practical minds. I'm always thinking of wisecracks and witticisms, always searching for the funny side of a situation.**

only thing I had going for me."

It was soooo exciting to hear a manager-type say that! I asked Roz what those interests were and, after a little hesitation, she said she liked to knit and shoot pool.

"Oh, come on, Roz!" a voice behind me chimed in. I turned around, and the assistant manager, Ellen, was standing behind us. She elbowed Roz encouragingly. "Tell Jean about your stand-up career! You know, the one you've been avoiding forever."

I asked Roz what Ellen was talking about. Roz said she'd done a few amateur-night gigs at some local comedy clubs. I wasn't a bit surprised. Roz can be a real card. She's had me

see **TEASDALE** page 114

in stitches more than once (and not the medical kind!). She said she hadn't done stand-up in months because she wanted to come up with new material and just hadn't had the time.

"Friday is open-mic night over at Laughingstock's," Ellen told her. "Come on, no one's going to care if you tell the same jokes again!"

Ever have one of those moments

> As soon as I had Roz alone for a moment, I told her I was a bit of a cut-up myself, and that I wrote this pretty daffy, lighthearted newspaper column she may have seen.

when opportunity rears its head? I immediately sensed a chance to show Roz that not only was I a sock-stocker, but a born Laughingstocker, too! As soon as I had Roz alone for a moment, I told her I was a bit of a cut-up myself, and that I wrote this pretty daffy, lighthearted newspaper column she may have seen. Roz said she hadn't. I waited for her to ask what I was driving at, but she didn't, so I broke the suspense myself.

"If you want new material, I'll write your routine!" I said. "I can come up with jokes until the cows come home! This is something I was born to do. After all, if you're somebody like me, you gotta have a sense of humor! I can write down a bunch of them tonight and bring them in to work tomorrow!"

"Well, if you want to, I guess I could take a look at what you've got," Roz said. "Only, just don't write anything, you know... weird."

I assured her I was incapable of that, and that I wasn't one of those dirty-joke writers who likes to offend people. I stayed up into the wee hours writing Roz's act. I cobbled together one-liners from old columns. I reworked a couple of my "Jean's Proverbs" into jokes, too. The work seemed effortless, and I really thought a lot of my jokes were good enough for Roz (and maybe even for that Queen of Sassitude herself, Joy Behar!). Was an exciting new career opening up for me?

The next morning, I handed my jokes to Roz. She seemed genuinely surprised, as if she didn't actually expect me to go through with it. She warned me that even if she wound up liking my stuff, she still wasn't sure she was going to do open-mic night. But I walked away with a little smile on my face, knowing that my work would speak for itself.

The next day, Ellen announced to me

and the other Fashion Bug sales associates, Tanya and Pat, that Roz was going to perform Friday, and that we and our hubbies were invited. I knew my jokes would make her a big hit!

I almost didn't make it to Laughingstock's that night. I practically had to rip Resident Evil out of hubby Rick's PlayStation 2 and drag him kicking and screaming to the car! He said he didn't want to see some ugly broads moan about being on the rag. But I was determined to show Rick that the best humor isn't one of Howard Stern's potty-mouthed put-downs, but stuff inspired by real life!

Laughingstock's was a funky little club. Everything was done up sort of 1930s-style, with big wall murals of Charlie Chaplin and Harpo Marx and that guy who played the violin. Despite the sophisticated décor, our group had to sit through a couple of pretty dismal acts. (After all, this was an amateur night!) One guy stammered some incomprehensible routine about Cher mating with a chicken, and another girl accidentally spilled her cup of water on herself! Rick, who was only allowed to have two beers because he was driving, was really chomping at the bit, but I asked him to hold tight.

Finally, after almost an hour and a half, Roz went on. Tanya, Pat, Ellen, and I burst into cheers. Roz looked soooo adorable up there, with her rainbow suspenders, bowtie, and scrunched-up sleeves! (It was such a refreshing alternative to the slutty clothes most show-biz women wear these days.) We also loved how she started off by saying hello to our town. That was very professional, like something a nationally famous comic would do.

When she launched into her opening joke about her boyfriend leaving the cap off the toothpaste, my brow furrowed a bit. This wasn't part of the routine I wrote for her. Patience, Jean, I thought. She'll get to your stuff.

Five minutes later, she still hadn't done one of my jokes. By that point, she was describing how an ex-boyfriend used to pick things up off the floor with his feet. Everyone was laughing—except yours truly. Why wasn't she using my material? Where was the line about how cats look at your finger instead of the thing you're pointing to? How "one size fits all" is the great lie of our time? What the deal was with this Go-Gurt? And my topper: "That Osama bin Laden should take a chocolate pill!" Why, Roz didn't even refer to chocolate once! All her jokes concerned bad relationships and bad sex and so on. I was disappointed to see her go in for blue material like every other comedian.

After Roz left the stage, Ellen turned to us. "I've heard those jokes a hundred times, and they still make me laugh," she said. "I don't see why she's so uptight about writing a new routine: She could tell those jokes for years without them getting old." Roz

HOROSCOPES

Your Horoscope

By Lloyd Schumner Sr.
Retired Machinist and
A.A.P.B.-Certified Astrologer

Aries: (March 21–April 19)
You will soon be judged by a jury of your peers, although finding 12 equally drunk bus drivers will not be easy.

Taurus: (April 20–May 20)
It turns out the voices in your head that tell you how to behave are called your "conscience," and that listening to them will ruin your career in advertising.

Gemini: (May 21–June 21)
Before this week, you thought "nibbled to death by ducks" was merely a funny way of describing the bureaucratic process.

Cancer: (June 22–July 22)
You are growing increasingly annoyed with popular culture's continued misinterpretation and trivialization of the vampire's point of view.

Leo: (July 23–Aug. 22)
You will experience the sort of pain normally felt only by careless entrants in the World's Strongest Man competition.

Virgo: (Aug. 23–Sept. 22)
You will successfully avoid being pulled over by burly, mustachioed state troopers, thanks to your invention of the Gaydar Detector.

Libra: (Sept. 23–Oct. 23)
You will feel a strange mixture of personal embarrassment and artistic revulsion when you are lampooned by The Capitol Steps.

Scorpio: (Oct. 24–Nov. 21)
You were born bearing the burden of original sin, but that has not stopped you from indulging in several hundred derivative types.

Sagittarius: (Nov. 22–Dec. 21)
Your theory regarding government-mind-control devices is right, except for the part about the tinfoil helmets being an effective way to stop them.

Capricorn: (Dec. 22–Jan. 19)
The paramedics will be forced to rip you out of your suit and cut off your tie to save you from wearing an absolutely ridiculous suit and tie.

Aquarius: (Jan. 20–Feb. 18)
You're half right: Heaven does not, in fact, want you, but Hell is not the least bit concerned that you might take over.

Pisces: (Feb. 19–March 20)
You establish a destructive pattern of behavior this week when you discover how much fun it is to destroy things.

had stuck to her old material after all!

Hubby Rick and I cut out soon after. We were heading to the car when we spotted Roz at the back entrance, smoking with a couple of the other

> "I'm sorry I didn't use your jokes, Jean," she said. "I know you worked hard on them, but they just didn't seem right for me. My sense of humor is a little different from yours."

comics. Roz approached me.

"I'm sorry I didn't use your jokes, Jean," she said. "I know you worked hard on them, but they just didn't seem right for me. My sense of humor is a little different from yours. Plus, I

had trouble making out some of your handwriting. It's hard to read red ink on pink stationery. But don't be mad. I appreciate the effort, I really do."

I accepted her apology, but I still didn't understand why she didn't use my jokes. When I talked to Rick about it, he was his usual blunt self: "Who gives a crap about how cats act? And there ain't nothing funny about Go-Gurt. You just eat it. Your jokes would've put the audience to sleep."

Poor, naïve Rick. I'm not angry about Roz's decision, but I finally figured out the real reason behind it. She felt a little threatened, so she decided to squelch my jokes. I've heard show-biz egos can be pretty tough to deal with, and sometimes they'll do illogical things like turn down great material because they're so insecure inside. It's sad, but I can't allow my dream to be destroyed. That's why I vowed to begin mailing my jokes to Joy Behar and various other comedians, unsolicited. It seems like a long shot, considering all the mail they must get, but I'm sure once they get around to reading my stuff, they'll recognize it for the gold that it is! ∅

Cheney Returns To U.S. With Full Head Of Thick, Wavy Hair

see NATION page 6A

Santa Fe Resident Pretty Kokopellied Out

see LOCAL page 15D

Melon Balled

see LOCAL page 1D

Abortion Stops A Beating

see LOCAL 10D

STATshot

A look at the numbers that shape your world.

Have We Been Working Out?

1. Little bit... little bit
2. Just the forearms, but what a difference
3. Oh, yeah... hardcore
4. You know, a sit-up here, a push-up there
5. Jazzercise every Monday
6. Nah, I'm too fat
7. Baby, God just made the clay, I've got to sculpt it

THE ONION • $2.00 US • $3.00 CAN

---

the ONION®

VOLUME 38 ISSUE 13   **AMERICA'S FINEST NEWS SOURCE**™   **11–17 APRIL 2002**

Nevada To Phase Out Laws Altogether

CARSON CITY, NV—The Nevada legislature voted Monday to repeal all laws within the state and prohibit the proposal of any new laws.

"Laws have been good to the state of Nevada," said Gov. Kenny Guinn between swigs of Jim Beam. "But ultimately, after carefully considering what's best for the long-term economic growth and prosperity of the state, we decided that lawfulness just wasn't a good idea."

Nevada's laws, Guinn said, will be slowly phased out over a five-year period, easing residents into a state of total anarchy. Gambling and prostitu-

tion have already been decriminalized, and car theft is slated to follow in 2004. Bans on murder and rape will be lifted in 2007.

Though the elimination of the rule of law has been a topic of discussion in Carson City for some time, it only recently gained favor among a majority of state legislators.

"Critics always argued that if we allowed gambling and prostitution, it was just a short leap to lawlessness," said Senate Majority Leader William Raggio (R-Washoe), flanked by a pair of armed strippers. "It didn't sink in

see NEVADA page 118

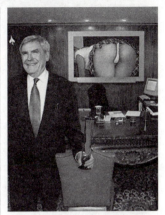

Above: Nevada Gov. Kenny Guinn in his office.

---

37 Record-Store Clerks Feared Dead In Yo La Tengo Concert Disaster

ATHENS, GA—Thirty-seven record-store clerks are missing and feared dead in the aftermath of a partial roof collapse during a Yo La Tengo concert Monday.

"We're trying our best to rescue these clerks, but there's not a lot of hope," said emergency worker Len Guzman, standing outside the 40 Watt Club, where the tragedy occurred. "These people are simply not in the physical condition to survive this sort of trauma. It's just a twisted mass of black-frame glasses and ironic Girl Scouts T-shirts in there."

Also believed to be among the missing are seven freelance rock critics, five vinyl junkies, two 'zine publishers, an art-school dropout, and a college-radio DJ.

The collapse occurred approximately 30 minutes into the Hoboken,

see CONCERT page 119

Above: Dazed record-store clerks stagger away from the scene of the roof collapse.

Japanese Exchange Student Taken To Japanese Restaurant

Above: The Japanese restaurant to which Miyazawa (inset) was taken.

BETTENDORF, IA— Takashi Miyazawa, 16, an exchange student from Nagoya spending six months in Bettendorf, was given the opportunity to experience authentic Japanese cuisine Monday, when host mother Bobbie Tucker arranged a visit to Edo, a restaurant in nearby Davenport.

"The Eagle [Food Center] has take-out sushi, but I

didn't think there was a place you could sit down for a genuine Japanese meal," Tucker said Monday. "But as I was reading the paper Sunday, I happened to notice an ad for Edo. I knew Takashi would be so thrilled."

The outing marked the first time any of the Tuckers had eaten Japanese food and Miyazawa's 18,358th.

see STUDENT page 117

OPINION

Arafat Under Fire

Trapped by Israeli tanks in his West Bank compound, Yasser Arafat is under fire for not doing more to stop the recent Palestinian terrorist attacks. What do *you* think?

"Arafat would never be behind any acts of terrorism. This is a Nobel Peace Prize winner we're talking about here."

Mary Putnam
Graphic Designer

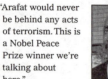
"It's a tough situation Arafat's in, trying to broker a peace accord while also keeping the suicide bombers happy."

Ellis Richardson
Systems Analyst

"I saw something about Arafat in the news last week, but I didn't catch exactly what it was any of the 63 times."

Nancy McCune
Teacher

"The U.S. should shift its focus from eliminating Saddam Hussein to eliminating Arafat. He seems easier to get."

Todd Kenilworth
Truck Driver

"I don't know, some days I'm a Sharon guy and some days I'm an Arafat guy. Depends on my mood, really."

Craig Cuthbert
Landscaper

"I honestly have no clue what's going on with that whole Arab-Israeli mess. And I'm Sen. Joseph Biden (D-DE), chairman of the Senate Foreign Relations Committee."

Joseph Biden
Senator

Tax-Code Changes

The April 15 tax-filing deadline is fast approaching. What are some of the changes in this year's code?

- Deductions permitted for monetary losses due to eBay overbidding
- May now file as single, married, or living together in sin
- New "Lucky Bucks Scratch-Off 1040" lets citizens take chance on winning up to $1,000 in additional deductions
- Toddlers over 80 pounds may be claimed as two dependents
- Home-improvement deductions expanded to include moose heads, chili-pepper string lights, and *Baywatch* posters
- All filers must repay last year's $300 "federal loan" with interest
- Write-offs allowed for expenses incurred in show of patriotism
- 1040 instruction book clarifies that option to donate extra money to government is not some sort of sick fucking joke

the ONION®
America's Finest News Source.™

Herman Ulysses Zweibel
Founder

T. Herman Zweibel
Publisher Emeritus
J. Phineas Zweibel
Publisher
Maxwell Prescott Zweibel
Editor-In-Chief

116

What Does Not Kill Me Only Makes Me Whinier

By Gordie Pryce

I've endured a great deal of hardship and pain in my life. I'll never forget the gastrointestinal distress I suffered two years ago after consuming an entire bag of caramel popcorn. Or the humiliation I felt in 1996 when I was stood up by a blind date. Or the time I spent an entire day wearing a shirt that, unbeknownst to me, was marred by unsightly deodorant streaks.

Devastating setbacks all, yet none broke me. These blows may have caused me to complain loudly, irritated by the inconvenience I faced, but when all is said and done, I am richer for the experience. It only confirms what I have long suspected: What does not kill me only makes me whinier.

So go on, world, I dare you. Sling your arrows at me. Steal my designated parking space. Cause every ballpoint pen in my possession to prematurely run out of ink. Give me an ice-cream headache. Ensure that my neighborhood drugstore no longer stocks my favorite body wash. Do your worst, world! For my capacity to piss and moan will always prevail.

Permit me to elaborate further. It was the morning of Wednesday last. I was awaiting the crosstown bus that

> **Devastating setbacks all, yet none broke me. These blows may have caused me to complain loudly, irritated by the inconvenience I faced, but when all is said and done, I am richer for the experience.**

takes me to work. According to the posted timetable, the bus was scheduled to arrive at 7:35. It was now 7:39. I was starting to get agitated. The minutes ticked by. I ground my teeth and restlessly paced the sidewalk, consulting my watch frequently and exhaling sharply and audibly enough to attract attention from the four or five other people waiting with me. It was not until 7:44—yes, you read right, 7:44—that my bus finally appeared.

I was only five minutes early for work instead of the usual 15. That gave me less than three minutes to hang my coat in my locker, put my lunch in the break-room refrigerator, use the restroom, and fetch a cup of coffee. As I scurried about the office, cross and flustered, my coworkers received an earful of my unpleasant experience. In great detail, I described all nine minutes of the delay and

> **So go on, world, I dare you. Sling your arrows at me. Steal my designated parking space. Cause every ballpoint pen in my possession to prematurely run out of ink. Give me an ice-cream headache.**

speculated on the reasons behind it. And I did it in a shrill, nasal whine that was difficult to stomach.

Now, granted, "The Tardy Bus Incident" did not result in my being fired, having my pay docked, or receiving a reprimand of any sort from my boss. Nor was I struck by a car as I exited the bus and sprinted across the street to my office. Outrageous as The Tardy Bus Incident was, it is becoming increasingly clear that I emerged from it intact and essentially unscathed. But, as God is my witness, my talent for complaint has grown stronger than ever.

I did not always possess this quality. When I was younger, I quietly and stoically accepted misfortune. A broken toy may have produced a few sniffles and a vague sense of loss, but nothing more. I adapted to the sudden arrival of a permanent grease spot on my favorite jacket as Neanderthal man adapted to the Ice Age. Aside from an initial crestfallen feeling, it did not even occur to me to complain, because I harbored a subconscious, intuitive presumption that life was full of these setbacks.

But as I grew into adulthood, I learned about a wondrous concept called "entitlement," and it changed my life. Why accept life's inherent imperfections when we can gripe incessantly about them? He who does not complain, who passively absorbs his misfortune, sentences himself to a life of mediocrity, of "also-rans" and "second-bests."

see WHINIER page 118

Suburban Dad Cracks Wise In Church Parking Lot

'Dude, Where's My Car?' Quips Dad

STEVENS POINT, WI—Flashing his trademark wit, dermatologist and father of three Gil Schlerek amused onlookers in the parking lot of Christ Presbyterian Church by incorporating a popular movie catchphrase into his search for his car Sunday.

"Dude, where's my car?" asked Schlerek, 48, invoking *Dude, Where's My Car?*, the 2000 Ashton Kutcher-Seann William Scott comedy in which two hard-partying teenagers pose the titular question following a wild night on the town.

"Dude! *Where is my car?*" continued Schlerek, spinning around once before finally "locating" the family's 1998 Plymouth Voyager minivan. An estimated 10 parishioners, all over 40, were sufficiently amused by Schlerek's antics to emit guffaws ranging from medium to hearty.

Schlerek's antics were largely ignored by his three children, daughters Karen, 17, and Stacy, 15, and son Michael, 13.

"Come on, Dad," an irritated Karen told her father. "Can we please just go?"

Karen's plea only seemed to encourage Schlerek, who has a history of catchphrase-driven jocularity.

"That's just your father's crazy side coming out," wife Roberta told Karen. "Remember what happened at Disney World?" Roberta was alluding to the family's July 2001 Walt Disney World vacation, during which her husband, upon seeing a pair of park employees costumed as Pluto and Goofy, chanted the chorus to the Baha Men hit "Who Let The Dogs Out?" over the fevered objections of all three children.

According to next-door neighbor Corey Netter, 14, Schlerek frequently makes humorous references to pop-cultural touchstones in a misguided bid to seem "cool."

"He always has to crack some joke," Netter said. "The other day, I was at their house for dinner, and he was joking that Mrs. Schlerek puts a lot of garlic in her spaghetti sauce to kill vampires. 'She's like Buffy The Vampire Killer,' he said. He didn't even get the name of the show right."

Netter told of another instance when Schlerek, dressed in a black shirt and pants, likened his appearance to that of shock-rocker Marilyn Manson.

"He was like, 'Hey, I look just like

see DAD page 118

Above: Schlerek cracks wise before fellow Christ Presbyterian Church parishioners.

STUDENT from page 115

"I just knew Takashi would love Edo," Tucker said. "The walls were decorated with all sorts of beautiful fans and paintings that reminded him of home. Takashi said Edo is the former name of Tokyo, which is the capital of Japan."

Added Tucker: "It was expensive, considering the portions, but it's

> ### Said Rick: "The two owners, who moved here from Japan three years ago, came over and talked to our honored guest in Japanese for a few minutes. Takashi must have been so thrilled."

worth it if it makes Takashi feel more at home. We already love him."

While youngest son Derrick, 14, steered clear of "anything raw" at the restaurant, ordering the chicken-teriyaki platter, the other Tuckers were fairly adventurous. In addition to sushi and sashimi, they sampled

miso soup, edamame, and seaweed salad.

"I've always wanted to try sushi," said father Bill Tucker, 51. "Now I can say I did."

Midway through the meal, Rick asked the restaurant's owners, Makoto and Midori Furukawa, to come over and personally greet their countrymate.

Said Rick: "The two owners, who moved here from Japan three years ago, came over and talked to our honored guest in Japanese for a few minutes. Takashi must have been so thrilled."

Miyazawa, who arrived in Bettendorf last Wednesday, exchanged a few awkward sentences with the Furukawas in his native tongue.

"I told them they had a very nice restaurant, and that the food was very good," Miyazawa explained. "They welcomed me to America and wished me a safe and pleasant stay here. That was pretty much it. Mr. Tucker encouraged me to keep talking to them in Japanese if I wanted, but I said it wasn't necessary."

After dinner, the Tuckers and Miyazawa headed to Davenport's NorthPark Mall. Miyazawa spent two hours happily browsing such stores as the Gap, Musicland, and Electronics Boutique—until Bobbie pulled him into a store called Oriental Gifts.

Miyazawa said he hopes he can con-

vince his host parents to bring him back to NorthPark Mall to see *Blade II* at the adjoining multiplex. For now, he will have to settle for the "movie night" Bobbie has planned for Saturday.

"Mrs. Tucker is forcing me to sit down with the family and watch something called *Gung Ho*," Miyazawa said. "She said it's 'a very funny movie that uses comedy to point out the differences between our two cultures.' I wish we could rent *The Fast And The Furious* instead."

Miyazawa, Bobbie said, has "adjusted beautifully" to his new surroundings. She added that the transition has been eased by her own efforts to lessen his culture shock.

"As soon as we got home from the airport, I went through the house explaining to Takashi how various household appliances work," Bobbie said. "I told him, 'I want you to feel completely comfortable here, so don't feel embarrassed about asking me how to operate something.'"

Bobbie said she also pointed out the family's Sony TV, Panasonic stereo, and various other Japanese products.

Said Bobbie: "I told him, 'Even halfway around the world, there's still a little bit of Japan right here in Iowa.'"

Last Wednesday, as Miyazawa was getting ready for his first night's sleep in the house, Bobbie apologized for

not having a traditional Japanese sleeping mat. Showing him his twin bed, she offered to find him "more traditional bedding" should he desire it.

"She was being so nice about every-

> ### Miyazawa, Bobbie said, has "adjusted beautifully" to his new surroundings. She added that the transition has been eased by her own efforts to lessen his culture shock.

thing, I didn't have the heart to tell her that I don't sleep on the floor at home," Miyazawa said. "I also don't need her to explain what a bagel is, but she seems to enjoy helping me."

Miyazawa was equally patient when Bobbie suggested he call her "youbo."

"I didn't understand what she was saying at first," Miyazawa said. "But after she said it four or five times, I realized she was saying 'mother' in Japanese. That was nice. Mrs. Tucker is very kind to me. I always make sure never to laugh at her." ∅

WHINIER from page 116

The Greek philosopher Plato believed that ideals existed apart from the everyday world. For the first time in my life, I myself began to envision a better world, one free of snagged zippers, flatware that has parts that taste too much like metal, and eyeglasses that rest too heavily against your face. I did not know how this wonderful world could be made my own, but I fully believed it existed. To make others aware of it, and to devise a way to help me cope with the maddening and dulling effects of reality, I embarked on a strenuous crusade of whining that flourishes to this day.

Some find my philosophy immoral, solipsistic, and even—this is a direct quote—"stupid." To my critics, I respectfully submit that whining is a noble act that can give birth to great things. For it is dissatisfaction, not necessity, that is the mother of invention. I'll wager that Henry Ford did not invent the Model T to create an affordable automobile for the masses, but because he knew that people's calves get all crampy when they're forced to walk, and who wants to put up with all the crowds of annoying pedestrians, anyway?

I must admit that I have never invented anything. In fact, I boast no particular intelligence, character, or

> **I must admit that I have never invented anything. In fact, I boast no particular intelligence, character, or mark of distinction.**

mark of distinction. But if it is true that each man possesses a single genius or aptitude, let mine be whining—a whining incessant and intolerable, unfettered and ungelded! Let the workaday stiffs who make up a majority of the American public square their shoulders, swallow their lot, and be pummeled into catatonia by life's irritations. As for me, I choose to whine, whine, against the dying of the light. ∅

DAD from page 117

that Marilyn Manson!'" Netter recalled. "'I better not walk too close to your school, or they might start hounding me for autographs, eh?' Yeah, sure, Mr. Schlerek."

Added Netter: "Nobody even likes Marilyn Manson anymore."

Though he hasn't had much success amusing teenagers, Schlerek's peers give him high marks for his wit.

"If you're ever down in the dumps, you can always count on Gil to pick you back up," said Beth Zanetto, 48, a fellow Christ Presbyterian parishioner. "I'll never forget last year's church Christmas party. He wore this crazy hat that had a mistletoe hanging over it, and he ran around pretending to try to kiss everybody. Talk about being a few cards shy of a full deck."

"Gil's a real hoot," longtime friend Donald Pulewitz said. "Sometimes, he'll even tell—I don't know if he'd want me saying this—some of the saltier jokes." Pulewitz cited a 1998 ice-fishing trip during which Schlerek told a joke about a ventriloquist and a Native American that ended with one of the two principals having sex with a sheep.

Schlerek's lighthearted outlook on life extends beyond his wisecracks. A tour of his den reveals a man deeply devoted to quirkiness, from his shelf of Dave Barry books to a wall plaque featuring the "Golfer's Serenity Prayer," a golf-centric send-up of the

> **"If you're ever down in the dumps, you can always count on Gil to pick you back up," said Beth Zanetto, 48, a fellow Christ Presbyterian parishioner.**

traditional serenity prayer.

Asked for comment on his parking-lot performance, Schlerek stayed true to form.

"What can I say?" he said, smiling and gesturing comedically. "I'm a wild and crazy guy!" ∅

NEVADA from page 115

for a while, but we eventually just sort of looked at each other and said, 'Why not?' Without laws, Nevada could offer a whole range of entertainment and lifestyle options never before imagined."

As a result of the eradication of laws, more than 20,000 police officers and other law-enforcement officials stand to lose their jobs. The loss should be offset, however, with the creation of jobs in new fields.

"Nothing stimulates employment like lawlessness," Raggio said. "We es-

> **As a result of the eradication of laws, more than 20,000 police officers and other law-enforcement officials stand to lose their jobs.**

timate that this move will create more than 400,000 jobs in such newly legal professions as prizefight rigger, ticket scalper, drug runner, bribe coordinator, and arsonist. In the construction industry alone, some 20,000 workers will be needed to build whorehouses and install stripper poles in fast-food restaurants."

Though Monday's decision eliminates the need for them, Nevada's lawmakers will retain their jobs.

"The people of Nevada can rest assured that their state senators and assemblymen will still be taking care

of their needs, be they sex, drugs, or a quick C-note to lay down on the Lakers plus six," Guinn said. "As for Nevada's elected officials in Washington, they'll still be in Congress. But, to be honest, they won't be doing a heck of a lot. They'll mainly just be hanging out, seeing what the other states are up to."

Guinn "highly recommended" that Nevada residents buy a gun and learn how to use it if they plan to remain in

the state beyond Dec. 31, when all gun-purchasing and gun-use regulations are repealed.

"When the clock strikes midnight on Jan. 1, 2003, it's survival of the fittest," Guinn said. "My lovely wife Dema can already pick off tin cans from 50 feet, and my son is becoming highly proficient in explosives. I strongly suggest you all do likewise."

Reaction from Nevada's residents

has been largely positive.

"I've been waiting for this moment for 20 years," said Reno blackjack dealer Dale Everson, polishing his new machete while enjoying a lap-dance. "Pretty soon, I won't have to worry about speeding tickets or emissions tests. Only the common sense and inherent decency of the people of Nevada will govern this state. That'll be more than enough for me." ∅

Above: Greg Bidwill eats lunch at a Taco Bell just outside Reno.

CONCERT from page 115

"I just had to help," said Ringler, listed in stable condition at a nearby hospital. "I saw all these people coming out bleeding and dazed. I gave up my vintage Galaxie 500 shirt just to help some guy bandage his arm. It was horrible."

Above: Some of the missing clerks from Monday's Yo La Tengo show.

NJ, band's set, when a poorly installed rooftop heating-and-cooling unit came loose and crashed through the roof, bringing several massive steel beams down with it.

Andy Ringler, an assistant manager at Wuxtry Records, sustained head trauma when he ran back into the building to rescue a fellow clerk.

"I just had to help," said Ringler, who is listed in stable condition at a nearby hospital. "I saw all these people coming out bleeding and dazed. I gave up my vintage Galaxie 500 shirt just to help some guy bandage his arm. It was horrible."

Added Ringler: "I just pray they can somehow get this club rebuilt in time for next month's Dismemberment Plan/Death Cab For Cutie show. That's a fantastic double bill."

Joe Gaer was among the lucky record-store clerks who escaped unscathed.

"I was in the bathroom when it happened," said Gaer, a part-time cashier at School Kids Records. "There was this loud crashing sound, followed by even louder crashing, and then all these screams. If I hadn't left to take a

"I haven't seen this much senseless hipster carnage since the Great Sebadoh Fire Of '93," said rescue worker Larry Kolterman.

leak during 'Moby Octopad'—to be honest, never one of my favorite songs on *I Can Hear The Heart Beating As One*—I'd probably be among the dead."

"It's just tragic," Gaer continued. "I heard they were going to play Daniel Johnston's 'Speeding Motorcycle.' They almost never do that one live."

Devastated by the disaster, Athens record-store owners are still holding out hope that their employees are still alive.

"All I can do is wait and pray they'll find them," said Bert's Discount Records owner Bert Halyard, who lost clerks Todd Fischer and Dan Harris in the collapse. "They were going to start an experimental/math-rock band together. Dan had a really nice Moog synthesizer and an original pressing of the first Squirrel Bait EP."

As of press time, police and emergency rescue workers were still sifting through the wreckage for copies of *Magnet*, heated debates over the definition of emo, and other signs of record-store-clerk life.

"I haven't seen this much senseless hipster carnage since the Great Sebadoh Fire Of '93," said rescue worker Larry Kolterman, as he pulled a green-and-gold suede Puma sneaker out of the rubble. "It's such a shame that all those bastions of indie-rock geekitude had to go in their prime. Their cries of 'sellout' have been forever silenced." ✍

NEWS IN BRIEF

Either Jay Leno A Repeat Or P. Diddy Got Arrested Again

MOUNT LEBANON, PA—According to Pittsburgh-area TV viewer Erik Allen, either Monday's *Tonight Show With Jay Leno* was a repeat or P. Diddy got arrested again. "Jay's monologue had all these jokes about P. Diddy getting busted for some kind of gun possession," Allen said. "I hadn't really heard anything about another arrest, so I figured it was a rerun. But that was, like, more than a year ago, right? Plus, I think he was still Puff Daddy back then, and Jay called him P. Diddy." Allen said he had hoped to gain insight from Leno's interviews with guests Lisa Kudrow and zookeeper Jack Hanna, but "neither seemed to be plugging anything all that time-specific."

Breakup Doesn't Seem To Have Changed Relationship

CARY, NC—Six weeks after their breakup, Daniel Bey and Janette Forsberg seem to have undergone no apparent change in their relationship, friends of the ostensibly ex-couple reported Monday. "They see each other all the time, and they still argue about every trivial thing, just like when they were together," friend Rich Gascone said. "Daniel even told me they're still having sex. But apparently, in some science-fiction way I can't comprehend, they're split up."

Architect's Friends All Have Great Idea For A Building

SAN DIEGO—Friends and acquaintances of Phil Yost are constantly giving him ideas for buildings, the 40-year-old architect said Monday. "I was catching up with my old college roommate, who I hadn't spoken to in years, and he blurts out, 'What if you built a revolving hotel like they have revolving restaurants?'" Yost said. "Do you know how many times I've gotten that?" In the past month, Yost has heard pitches for pyramid-shaped warehouses, retractable-roof golf courses, and 100-story, subterranean "groundscrapers" that would be impervious to terrorist attack.

Clinton Dragged Up On Stage To Sing 'Sweet Home Alabama' With The Band

LITTLE ROCK, AR—Former president Bill Clinton joined local rock band Jimmy Ellis & The Houserockers onstage for a cover of Lynyrd Skynyrd's "Sweet Home Alabama" Saturday. "Come on up here, Mr. President!" Ellis urged Clinton, whom he spotted near the back of the crowd. "Show the nice folks how it's done!" Following the performance, Clinton remained onstage for a rollicking rendition of Garth Brooks' "Friends In Low Places." ✍

Lutheran Minister Arrested On Charges Of Boring Young Children

PERU, IL—St. Luke's Lutheran Church was rocked by scandal Tuesday, when Rev. Bob Tillich, the church's pastor of 12 years, was arrested on suspicion of boring as many as 23 children within the congregation. "Reverend Bob always seemed like the sweetest man," parishioner Vera Crandall said following the arrest. "When my son said he made him watch three 1975 film strips about the suffering of Job, I was shocked." In the wake of the arrest, seven former Sunday-school students, dating as far back as 1989, have stepped forward with charges that Tillich subjected them to inappropriately tedious parables. ✍

Ask A Guy Trying To Describe What He Saw On *Nova* Last Night

By Wayne Paulk

Dear Guy Trying To Describe What He Saw On *Nova* Last Night,

My husband's job requires a lot of business travel, so I hardly see him during the week. When he's home on weekends, he says he's too burned out from traveling to do anything and just wants to relax. It's really starting to affect our marriage. How can I get him to realize that I need time, too?

Neglected In Nyack

Dear Neglected:

Dude, you are *not* gonna believe the weird shit I saw on TV last night, man. Me and my roommates were flipping around the channels when we saw that *Nova* show. The one about, like, science and shit? Anyway, the episode was all about insects and bugs, and I *could not believe my freakin' mind*, watching this shit. My roommates were like, "C'mon, man, I don't wanna watch some friggin' nature show. Change it." But for some reason, I was like, "No, no, I wanna see this." So we ended up really getting into it and watched the whole thing, and it totally freaked us out. Like, there was this one bug, right? I don't know if it was, like, a roach or what, but they were talking about how it talks to other bugs, by, like... shit, how do I say this? Like, by humming and vibrating or something on the branches of this bush where it lives, and it sends, like, these supersonic ultrasound vibrations or whatever through the whole bush. And no human can hear it, 'cause the noise is, like, way-ultra-low-frequency super bass, but the bugs can hear it, 'cause they pick it up through the branches through their feet. Dude, I shit you not. The bugs, like, listen with their *friggin' feet*. We were all so freaked out by this shit, I can't even tell you. And there's, like, thousands of these things in *one* bush, and they can still all tell each other apart by listening with their friggin' feet. These are, like, tiny-ass bugs. Their whole brain is the size of I don't even know what. A single piece of salt, maybe? My roommates were like, "How do they do that shit?" and I was just like, "Shit, man, don't ask me."

Dear Guy Trying To Describe What He Saw On *Nova* Last Night,

My 13-year-old son is a computer whiz, but I have strong reason to suspect he's looking at X-rated web sites on the Internet. Even though we've put a child lock on our Internet access, he's figured a way around it. His father says we should just take his computer away, but his teachers all agree he's a gifted programmer and

should be encouraged. I'm at my wits' end!

Cyber-Stumped In Cypress Grove

Dear Cyber-Stumped:

Then they were showing this freaky *bug sex*, which was even more bizarre. Like, they have this one bug in New Zealand or the Falklands or someplace like that, right? And the male bugs, the thing that attracts them to the chick bugs is that the chicks have, like, this rounded, bumpy

---

I don't know if it was, like, a roach or what, but they were talking about how it talks to other bugs, by, like... shit, how do I say this?

---

orange ass. Only it's not their ass. At least, not like a normal ass. It's, like, a exoskeleton or an ova-posi... ovaposi-tioner, oviposit... whatever you call it. Anyway, wherever this country was, they had this one brand of beer where it comes in these special bottles that are, like, orange and have these same kinda bumps on them as, like, the chick bugs. Ribbed and shit. Or not ribbed, really, but you know. So, anyway, people would throw these beer bottles on the street, and these male bugs would be cruising along, looking to get laid or whatever. So the guy bugs would see the bottle and think it's, like, the *biggest, roundest, sexiest* bumpy orange bug ass they ever saw in their lives, and they'd get confused and start humping away on it. Except, they don't really hump like we do, 'cause I don't think these bugs have dicks. But that's not important. The thing was, the *real* chick bugs totally couldn't compete with these bottles. And it was really screwing up their econo... ecolo... their ecologosystem. Whatever. Look, I really can't explain this, okay? Just trust me, it was some seriously freaky-ass shit. The moral of it was about how you shouldn't litter and throw beer bottles in the wild and stuff, 'cause you don't know what's gonna happen because of that bottle you threw, like, if some bug is gonna want to fuck it or what.

Dear Guy Trying To Describe What He Saw On *Nova* Last Night,

Ever since her stroke last December,

my elderly mother has been in a wheelchair. We take her to church on Sundays because she can't make it alone. Recently, her church moved to a building way across town. The trip is a big inconvenience, and my husband thinks she should start going to a closer church. But Mother loves her friends at church so much. What should I do?

Wondering In Worcester

Dear Wondering:

Okay, but then came the grossest part of all. Oh, man. Dude, I don't even wanna think about this one. Me and my roommates were all, like, "[non-verbal sound indicating revulsion and disbelief]!" I swear, I almost spewed, but I couldn't turn away. Okay, how do I explain? It was, like, one of those caterpillar-ish things that turns into a cocoon or whatever. And then there's this *other* bug that, like, totally fucks with it and somehow lays eggs *inside* the caterpillar as it's getting ready to turn into a cocoon. The caterpillar doesn't know the eggs are in it, and the eggs have this hormone in them or, like, an enzyme or

something that makes the caterpillar think it still needs to keep eating leaves and stuff, even though it's already way, way, *way* bigger than this type of caterpillar is supposed to get before it can start cocooning up. Pretty soon, this thing, it's, like, a walking food supply for the other shit living inside it. And when they hatch—dude, this was so freakin' gross, man—they dig their way out, like zits or something, or like these horrible ruptures. *Oh, man.* And they totally showed the whole thing! I was like, "Are they gonna show it?" and my roommate Steve was like, "No way. No way can they show that shit," and I was like, "I hope they don't show it." And they did! We were gonna puke! I swear, it was like that shit from *Alien*. I'm not exaggerating. Isn't that the most sick-ass revolting thing ever? Anyway, you shoulda seen it. It was fuckin' insane.

Wayne Paulk is a syndicated advice columnist whose weekly column, Ask A Guy Trying To Describe What He Saw On *Nova* Last Night, *appears in more than 250 newspapers nationwide. ∅*

Your Horoscope

By Lloyd Schumner Sr.
Retired Machinist and
A.A.P.B.-Certified Astrologer

Aries: (March 21–April 19)
It's true that people often become what they hate. This explains why you're slowly becoming a pineapple-and-anchovy pizza.

Taurus: (April 20–May 20)
You're not the kind of person who can wear those fashionably low jeans, mostly because you can't figure out how pants are supposed to work.

Gemini: (May 21–June 21)
You will have one of those disorienting "through the looking glass" moments when you are thrown through a large looking glass.

Cancer: (June 22–July 22)
The unexpected arrival of quintuplets in your life wouldn't be so bad if you could figure out whose they were.

Leo: (July 23–Aug. 22)
You're not the type to rest on your laurels when there are perfectly good couches available.

Virgo: (Aug. 23–Sept. 22)
You will achieve modest fame as a lion tamer, but audiences won't like you nearly as much as the man who has absolutely no control over the lions.

Libra: (Sept. 23–Oct. 23)
No one would go to Salina, KS, without stopping for a world-famous Cozee Burger—except you.

Scorpio: (Oct. 24–Nov. 21)
The only thing worse than a trick yo-yo man is a trick yo-yo man who applauds after each one of his yo-yo tricks.

Sagittarius: (Nov. 22–Dec. 21)
The men from the recliner company will stop laughing just long enough to claim they've never seen anyone lose a leg in one of their products before.

Capricorn: (Dec. 22–Jan. 19)
You will find yourself in yet another argument over whether Murasaki's *The Tale Of Genji* is the world's first true novel.

Aquarius: (Jan. 20–Feb. 18)
They will comfort you after the accident by saying there was nothing you could have done, leaving unsaid the fact that most people would have at least tried hitting the brakes.

Pisces: (Feb. 19–March 20)
As you emerge from the womb, a doctor will strike you and make you cry. Serves you right for sleeping with his wife.

NEWS

Heroic Pit Bull Journeys 2,000 Miles To Attack Owner

see LOCAL page 12B

Monopoly Releases Scrabble-Themed Edition

see GAMES page 10D

Movie Touted As 'From The Studio That Brought You *Remember The Titans*'

see FILM page 8C

STATshot

A look at the numbers that shape your world.

What Are We Reduced To Eating Dinner Out Of?

1. KFC bucket
2. Cupcake pan
3. Trough
4. *Mystery Men* promotional frisbee
5. Bread bowl
6. Plastic cup from Nyquil bottle
7. Mistress Luxx's hand

THE ONION • $2.00 US • $3.00 CAN

---

the ONION

VOLUME 38 ISSUE 14   AMERICA'S FINEST NEWS SOURCE™   18–24 APRIL 2002

REPORT

- Erythromycin
- Neomycin
- Avoparcin
- Synercid
- Trimethoprim
- Ethambutol
- Isoniazid
- Pyrazinamide
- Rifampin
- Chloroquine
- Ciprofloxacin
- Sulfonamides
- Clindamycin
- Oxytetracycline
- Nourseothricin
- Carbenicillin
- Chlortetracycline
- Chloramphenicol

U.S. Children Getting Majority Of Antibiotics From McDonald's Meat

WASHINGTON, DC—According to a Department of Health and Human Services report released Monday, McDonald's meat from antibiotics-injected livestock is now the primary source of antibiotics for U.S. children, particularly for uninsured youths from low-income households.

"Unfortunately, some children still fall through the cracks in our health-care system, but luckily, McDonald's is there to lend a helping hand," Secretary of Health and Human Services Tommy Thompson said at a press conference announcing the findings. "So even if a child's family has no health insurance and can't afford medicine, virtually anyone can afford a delicious 99-cent Big Mac with pickles, cheese, and a heapin' helpin' of [the antibiotic] quinupristin-dalfopristin."

In HHS tests, 82 percent of children who had not been properly inoculated were still found to have significant levels of antibiotics in their bloodstreams. The antibiotics, the tests concluded, were the result of sustained intake of McDonald's meat.

"Disadvantaged children tend to eat at McDonald's a lot, which is a good thing," Thompson said. "If you think about it, where else are these kids going to get their fluoro-

see CHILDREN page 124

Home-Buying Up Among Lame-O's

WASHINGTON, DC—In the first quarter of 2002, sales of new U.S. homes rose 5.3 percent among Dockers-wearing, Pictionary-playing lame-o's, the Commerce Department reported Monday.

"This is encouraging news for the U.S. economy," Commerce Secretary Don Evans said. "For three straight months, home-buying statistics have been robust, with March housing starts peaking at a seasonally adjusted rate of 1.66 million units. Mr. and Mrs. Suburban Dork are scooping up houses like there's no tomorrow."

Though housing-industry analysts don't speculate on why any thinking person would want to be saddled with a hefty mortgage and consign themselves to a depressing, isolated white-bread existence, they say falling interest rates represent the primary reason for the surge. The Federal Reserve, which has repeatedly cut interest rates in an effort to slow down the

see LAME-O page 124

Above: Lame-o's Ken and Caryn Worth, neither of whom enjoy attending rock concerts, purchase their dream home in Arlington, VA.

Orgy A Logistical Nightmare

CANTON, OH—In spite of his excitement about the upcoming sexual free-for-all, first-time orgy organizer Jerry Belsner, 33, admitted Monday that planning the event has been a logistical nightmare.

"You have no idea what I've been through the last few weeks," Belsner said. "Everything that could possibly go wrong has. But I'm still determined to make this the best orgy ever. If I live to see it, that is."

Belsner said the complications began soon after he started planning the orgy, scheduled for April 26 at his

see ORGY page 125

Below: Belsner calls a potential participant.

121

Drilling For Oil In Alaska

Seeking to decrease U.S. dependence on Iraqi oil, Senate Republicans want to open Alaska's Arctic National Wildlife Refuge for drilling. What do *you* think?

Daniel Mendoza
Systems Analyst

"It'd be nice if we lived in some magical fantasy world where we could get energy from the sun and the wind, but we need to deal with reality."

Christine Sample
Nurse

"If I didn't know better, I'd say some oil man stands to make billions on this. Say, the president used to be in the oil business! Maybe he could help us sniff out the culprit!"

Tim Wills
Machinist

"America needs to reduce its overall oil consumption, but I can't bring myself to ride the bus with a bunch of puds. So Arctic drilling it is."

Gene Oliver
Real-Estate Agent

"If drilling kills off the refuge's indigenous wildlife, that'll give us a nice head start on the next generation of fossil fuels."

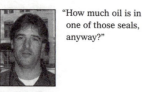

Vincent Putnam
Delivery Driver

"How much oil is in one of those seals, anyway?"

Diane Bell
Architect

"We might as well use that oil. If we don't, our children will."

Silicon Valley Reboots

Devastated by the dot-com collapse, Silicon Valley is beginning to rebound. Among the signs of life:

- ⬆ Drkoop.com planning moderately lavish re-launch party at San Mateo Days Inn
- ⬆ Words "mindshare," "benchmarkable," "stickiness," and other cyber-jargon slowly returning to conversations
- ⬆ Phrase "Dot-Comback" spotted in *USA Today*
- ⬆ Venture capital again available for rich kids with no real ideas
- ⬆ Hardware Hints section of True Value website updated for first time since November 2000
- ⬆ Jeff Bezos' *Time* "Man Of The Year" plaque retrieved from trash
- ⬆ Segway sales up from three in 2001 to five in 2002
- ⬆ Nesting birds shooed out of flooz.com office
- ⬆ People once again unsure what exactly they do for a living

⊘ **the ONION**®
America's Finest News Source.™

Herman Ulysses Zweibel
Founder

T. Herman Zweibel
Publisher Emeritus
J. Phineas Zweibel
Publisher
Maxwell Prescott Zweibel
Editor-In-Chief

It Hurts My Feelings When You Leave Before The Credits Are Done

By Lori Osrow
Assistant To Mr. Affleck

Please don't take this the wrong way. I'm sure you don't like being told what to do. But seeing you walk out of the theater the moment the credits start to roll, well, it really hurts my feelings. I may not have been the director or one of the stars of *Changing Lanes*, but I worked very hard in my capacity as assistant to Mr. Affleck.

Did you ever stop to think that behind every name on that movie screen is an actual human being? Did you think second-assistant "b" camera Allan Katz was a fictional character? Were you under the impression that key mod technician Fred Newburn is not a flesh-and-blood human with loved ones? I realize that in a major motion picture like *Changing Lanes*, the credits are pretty long. But is five extra minutes sitting in a comfortable movie theater too much to ask to make someone feel better about their work and their life?

I don't mean to come off like a martyr. I didn't have the hardest job in the world. As big stars go, Ben Affleck is a really easygoing, down-to-earth guy. But even the best of actors can have their moments. I won't get into

> **As long as I'm getting things off my chest, let me tell you something else. We're all pretty sick of the joke, "Man, that best boy sure was awesome in this movie!"**

any particulars, but it got pretty hairy during those final days of shooting. There were moments when I got pretty down on the whole Hollywood thing. But when I saw my name up on the big screen for the first time, a feeling of pride surged through me. I thought, "I guess it really is worth it. I mean, there's my name, up there on the screen. For a brief moment, millions of moviegoers across the country will see my name and think about my contributions to this film."

How wrong I was.

When I looked around the theater I was in, I noticed that no one stayed through the credits long enough to see my name, except for one guy sleeping in the back. Even my mom almost didn't see my name because of people walking in front of her. I thought, no one knows or cares about who I am. When you put yourself out there so much and no one stops to take notice, it really hurts.

Is it the end of the world if you don't know that it was Dan Palansky who assisted Mr. Michell in the super-8 segment? I'm not going to lie and say

Did you ever stop to think that behind every name on that movie screen is an actual human being?

it is. But I will tell you that Dan did a wonderful job, and that his friends were so excited and proud that he was able to work on a big film after years of toiling on little films for bagels and coffee and no health insurance. I was excited for him, too.

As long as I'm getting things off my chest, let me tell you something else. We're all pretty sick of the joke, "Man, that best boy sure was awesome in this movie!" You probably don't even know what a best boy is. Not that you care, but a best boy is the assistant to the gaffer (the electrician in charge of lighting). The rigging best boy for *Changing Lanes* was Gene Hoeschen. And you know what? He did do a great job, and he really would have appreciated it if you'd paid him some respect instead of spoiling his big moment by cracking wise.

Maybe you could rent the *Changing Lanes* DVD and watch it at home. That way, you could freeze-frame on the credits and take the extra few minutes to read the names. It's not like you're in a rush to get out of there. You're already home.

And if you have a few more minutes to spare, go to the Internet Movie Database (imdb.com) to see what else the people in the *Changing Lanes* crew have worked on. That way, maybe you can learn a little bit about how films work, in addition to paying a small tribute to those behind the scenes.

Tell you what. Just read a movie's credits once, as a favor to me, and see if it doesn't deepen your appreciation of all the work that goes into making a film. I bet it will. Then, next time you see a movie, you can amaze your friends by explaining the various important jobs they miss out on learning about by skipping out on the credits. Go on. I dare you. ⊘

Marine Never Knew What Freedom Was Until He Left The Marines

MADISON, WI—Troy Leffler, who spent four long years living under an oppressive, totalitarian Marine Corps regime, never knew how precious freedom was until he left the Marines, the former Private-First Class said Sunday.

"The freedom to go wherever you want, do whatever you like, and say whatever you feel is what makes

> ## "A big part of American liberty is the right to come and go as one pleases," Leffler said.

America great," the 22-year-old Leffler told friends at a backyard barbecue Sunday. "And it's something I really learned to appreciate after four god-forsaken years in the military."

Though he spent the bulk of his 1998-2001 enlistment on U.S. soil, at Camp Pendleton near San Diego, Leffler did not enjoy the freedom of movement taken for granted by many American citizens.

"A big part of American liberty is the right to come and go as one pleases," Leffler said. "For four terrible years, that freedom was denied me. Every minute of every day, I was told where to go and what to do. Except for an occasional weekend pass, the

Marines made every decision in your life, from when you slept to when you showered to when and what you had to eat."

Added Leffler: "I just hope the people at this picnic realize how very fortunate they are to live in a place where they aren't told what to wear or how to walk."

According to Leffler, life under Marine rule was psychologically brutal.

"It's hard for free Americans to understand this, but from day one of basic training, Sarge tells you how and what to think," he said. "Not only are you expected to surrender your idea of the individual and begin thinking as a member of a group, but they actually regulate your speech. You have to call a wall a bulkhead, a floor a deck, a gun a weapon. You're reprogrammed to think like one of them."

Also denied Leffler were such basic rights as freedom of assembly, freedom from search and seizure of any or all items in his footlocker, and the pursuit of happiness.

"It's the little things you never think about that I missed most," Leffler said. "Having a beer for lunch. Taking in a ball game whenever I wanted. Getting into a car with a couple of buddies and driving off for a few days with nowhere special to go. Hanging out all afternoon in a bar. You don't realize how much these things mean until the Marines don't let you do them."

Leffler said his greatest hope is that

Above: Ex-Marine Troy Leffler.

his Marine experience will serve as an example to others.

"[Leffler] asked to come to our school and speak to the kids about what freedom means and how you don't have any as a member of the armed services," said Madison West High School principal John Posey, who turned down Leffler's recent request to address the student body. "I admire his dedication to his ideals and his desire to pass along some of his life experience, but I think we'll let

the kids make up their own minds on this one."

That, Leffler said, may be the greatest danger.

"That's how they got me," said Leffler, noting that he was barely 18 when he made the decision to enter the Marine Corps. "I guess I really did it to myself in the end, and that's the worst part. We must all vigilantly safeguard our sacred freedoms, lest we squander them on four years of desert marches and shoe polishing." ∅

NEWS IN BRIEF

That Guy From That One Show Not Looking So Hot

ERIE, PA—That guy who plays the main guy on that one show isn't looking so hot, sources close to the TV set reported Tuesday. "It looks like he gained, like, 40 pounds or something," said Erie resident Doug Knauss, watching the show. "He looks all puffed out and tired with those bags under his eyes." Knauss noted that the big movie the guy was in a couple years back completely tanked, so that might have done a number on him.

Doctor, Patient Have Wildly Different Definitions Of Word 'Hope'

WESTBROOK, ME—Terminally ill patient Wayne Lund and his physician have wildly differing definitions of

the word "hope," it was revealed Monday. "Dr. [Robert] Petrakis said there's hope," said Lund, recently diagnosed with Wyckoff-Kleiner Disease, a rare degenerative brain condition that is 99.5 percent fatal. "If that's the case, I'm gonna beat this thing." Said Petrakis: "I told him, 'There's always hope... miracles do happen.' So, technically, I guess there's hope. But not really."

Area Man Has No Idea Where To Get Envelope

NEW BERN, NC—In need of an envelope to mail his March telephone bill, Jordan Phills, 26, reported Monday that he has no idea where to get one. "Is there such thing as an 'envelope store'?" Phills asked. "I honestly have no clue how to go about getting an envelope, except by snagging one off somebody." Phills added that the envelope hunt would not have been necessary had his roommate not spilled coffee all over the pre-addressed envelope enclosed with the monthly bill.

Teen Worried About Friend Who Tried Pot

ARVADA, CO—Steve Vandervelt, 16, an Arvada High School honors student, expressed grave concern Tuesday for friend Todd Wolk, who experimented with marijuana at a party the previous weekend. "They say pot's a 'gateway drug,'" Vandervelt told Wolk. "And even if it doesn't lead to cocaine and more serious stuff, doing pot can still really mess up your brain." Vandervelt offered to speak to Mrs. Logan, the school's health-ed teacher, on Wolk's behalf to get more information about the dangers of marijuana use.

Street Performer Dreams Of Performing On Streets Of Paris

ALBUQUERQUE, NM—Dave Bosio, 20, an aspiring singer-songwriter who plays guitar on the streets of Albuquerque, dreams of one day

playing for spare change on the streets of Paris. "To play on the Champs-Elysées, that'd be a dream come true," Bosio said Monday. "Or someplace along the Left Bank. That'd be so much better than Copper Avenue." Bosio then launched into an off-key version of Bob Marley's "Redemption Song."

Bush To Sacrifice Own Life For Good Of Nation

WASHINGTON, DC—Displaying the selfless courage that has defined his presidency, President Bush announced Tuesday that he will heroically lay down his life that the rest of the nation may live on. "It is the only way," Bush said. "The needs of the many outweigh the needs of the few. I must, therefore, die to preserve future generations." Over the vociferous objections of his closest Cabinet members, Bush brushed aside their outstretched arms, repeating, "It is the only way." ∅

LAME-O from page 121

recession and stimulate consumer spending, took pains to distance itself from the trend.

"The Federal Reserve Board may have stimulated home-buying with its interest-rate cuts," Federal Reserve Chairman Alan Greenspan said. "But that doesn't mean any of us would ever want to live in a split-level ranch

"We'd rented for so long, we figured we probably could have paid off half a mortgage by now," said Laurie, who hasn't been out on a Saturday night in months.

in some soulless gated community near Phoenix, where we'll obsess over golf and property values. Promise you'll shoot me if it ever comes to that."

According to *Kiplinger's* senior writer Peter Akkaf, in addition to buying more homes, lame-o's are refinancing existing mortgages to take advantage of lower rates.

U.S. Home Purchases
Oct '01–March '02

Lame-o's

Non-lame-o's

O N D J F M

"Lame-o's across the country are making appointments at financial institutions to ask men in ugly neckties and women with hairstyles 10 years out of style to adjust their mortgages to a slightly more favorable rate," Akkaf said. "When that's done, they return to their homes, where they stare at their $12.99 Monet prints from Target and listen to Andrea Bocelli on their mini-stereos. What kind of life is that?"

Asked if the recent warm temperatures could have goosed the market, National Realtors' Board president

Maggie Zadora rolled her eyes.

"God, if that's true, that's sad," Zadora said. "It's like, 'Ooh, Mary, it's 10 degrees warmer outside! Instead of going out and doing something fun or creative, let's all pile into the minivan and search for the bland colonial of our dreams!'"

Alan and Laurie Butterfield of Glen Burnie, MD, are among the many lame-o's to take advantage of the favorable buying conditions. Last month, they purchased their first home, a three-bedroom split-level in a featureless suburban subdivision near Baltimore.

"We'd rented for so long, we figured we probably could have paid off half a mortgage by now," said Laurie, 33, who hasn't been out on a Saturday night in months. "So with the interest rates down and both of us working steadily, this seemed like the perfect time to get a house."

"With a child on the way, we wanted to move to someplace with a lot more space and good public schools," said Alan, 34, sporting a tucked-in polo shirt embroidered with his company's logo. "It's also a good investment. Our neighborhood didn't even exist 10 years ago, and already the housing values have increased by one-third from their 1996 estimates."

"Very smart move, Alan and Laurie," said Ross, facetiously tapping his temple.

The Butterfields' decision impressed *Money* columnist William Ross.

"Very smart move, Alan and Laurie," said Ross, facetiously tapping his temple. "Thanks to your tremendous savvy and financial acumen, you now have a brand-new place to hang your wind sock. Fabulous. Have fun being chained to a mortgage for the next 30 years."

Housing-industry experts say the surge in home buying indicates increased confidence in the U.S. economy on the part of lame-o's.

"Purchasing a home is not the act of a pessimist," said Frank Nothaft, chief economist at Freddie Mac. "But it is the act of a dweeb. Sure, renting costs more over time than owning, but do you want to spend your weekends cleaning out leaf gutters and fixing the garage-door opener, or do you want to be happy? Life is way too short, people. Loosen up." ∅

CHILDREN from page 121

quinolone?"

Large-scale meat producers, Thompson noted, routinely add antibiotics to the feed of healthy animals to prevent cross-infection in the crowded quarters where livestock are typically raised. In the U.S., the average beef steer receives eight times more antibiotics than its human counterpart.

"When your daughter gets strep throat, head straight over to McDonald's and prescribe her a delicious Quarter Pounder or nine-piece Chicken McNuggets," Thompson said.

"She'll not only receive the amoxycillin she needs to get better, but also a whole array of growth hormones proven to speed a child's physical development."

"And if your child prefers Burger King or Wendy's," he continued, "that's fine, too. Any of the big fast-food chains can get them healthy."

While all Americans benefit from the 25 million pounds of antibiotics fed to chickens, pigs, and cows each year, children stand to gain the most, U.S. Sen. Richard Lugar (R-IN) said.

"Children weigh less than adults, so when they eat a hamburger, they get a proportionally more potent dose of antibiotics," said Lugar, who is among

"If your child has a sinus infection, he or she can drop by before and after school for a Double Cheeseburger 50cc Meal or a delicious Chicken Tetracycline."

the Senate's strongest proponents of fast-food-based health care. "These antibiotics are vital in the treatment of such common childhood ailments as sore throat, ear infection, and hoof rot."

According to Lugar, waiting in a crowded doctor's office may soon be a thing of the past.

"Every day, food scientists are discovering new antibiotics, growth hormones, and other chemically engineered substances to inject into the nation's beef supply," Lugar said. "And with Americans working longer and longer hours just to make ends meet, people can't afford to waste time sitting around some waiting room until their name is called. Unlike a doctor, our fast-food providers can deliver a full spectrum of antibiotics in min-

utes—hot, fresh, and with a smile."

In conjunction with the Department of Health and Human Services, Burger King will soon release a brochure, "Happy And Healthy The Burger King Way," which outlines a 14-day plan for the treatment of bacterial infections.

In the leaflet, a cartoon cow in a medical coat reminds parents to give their infected children two daily doses of antibiotic-treated meat for 14 days. If the condition does not improve after 10 days, the parent or guardian of the ailing child is instructed to contact a store manager.

"If your child has a sinus infection, he or she can drop by before and after school for a Double Cheeseburger 50cc Meal or a delicious Chicken Tetracycline," Burger King spokeswoman Linda Jacobs said. "As we're fond of saying here at Burger King, 'This won't hurt a bite!'"

Though representatives say they're pleased with the praise it has received, the fast-food industry does not intend to rest on its laurels.

"Repeated use of antibiotics will result in increased resistance to antibiotics in new strains of bacteria," said Carl Pickney, lab researcher for TriCon Global, the fast-food conglomerate that owns Kentucky Fried Chicken, Taco Bell, and Pizza Hut. "That's why we need to encourage our meat suppliers to continually raise the levels of antibiotics in their meat, developing newer, stronger antibiotics to replace those that no longer work. We're making good progress, but we've still got a whole lot of meat to modify." ∅

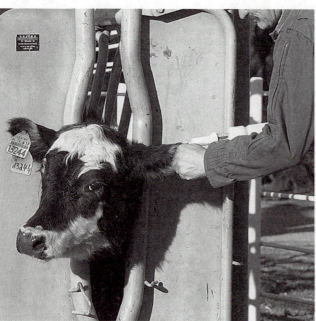

Above: A young cow is injected with penicillin at a farm that supplies Burger King.

house.

"I'm not naïve enough to think orgies just 'happen,' so I started making calls," Belsner said. "I was going to cover all the expenses myself, but when I started factoring in all the stuff we needed—snacks, liquor, handcuffs, condoms, lube, porno videos, anal beads, batteries for the vibrators, a Slip-N-Slide—it became clear that my wallet was going to take a major hit. So now I have to chase down everybody and try to get them to pitch in a little cash."

Many of Belsner's headaches have stemmed from the difficulty of having to accommodate the widely varying sexual tastes of the participants.

"Randy doesn't want pornos playing because he finds them distracting," Belsner said. "But Phil says he can't get hard without one. So do I have two rooms, one with pornos and one without? And Karen wants hardcore orgy-themed porn while Marc only wants girl-on-girl or softcore. I could have a whole bunch of different rooms, but if you spread everybody out too thin, it'll just wind up being a bunch of separate two- and three-ways instead of one massive fuckfest."

Continued Belsner: "I was going to lay a tarp down in one room so people could oil each other up without damaging my rugs. But do I put the tarp in the porn room or the other one? Why does group sex have to be so complicated?"

One aspect of the orgy Belsner regrets changing is the theme. Originally slated to be a Roman-toga affair, the event was switched to a Mexican theme to indulge his fondness for naked women in sombreros.

"That was stupid of me," he said. "Mexican food isn't really good for an orgy: No one wants to lick salsa off someone's privates. But I'd already spent two nights Photoshopping sombreros onto the nude pictures on the invitation, so I can't back out now."

Another complication has been selecting adult toys for the event.

"I figured I'd have a few strap-on dildos and some vibrators," Belsner said. "I'd like people to have as much fun as possible, but I only have a handful of silk scarves for light bondage and one vibrating butt plug. Do I ask people to bring their own stuff? I'd rather have guests just show up and fuck, but it'd be nice to have toys to pass around. Maybe I can find a place that rents butterfly fuck swings, then decorate one like a piñata."

Though already "way stressed," Belsner said he expects his anxiety level to increase as the day of the orgy approaches.

"I don't know when I'm going to find the time to clean and set everything up," Belsner said. "My boss asked me to go to Columbus for a conference Wednesday. What am I going to tell him, 'Sorry, I have an orgy to prepare'? When this all started, Tony [Rusan] and Nate [Farris] said they'd help, but they haven't done jack shit except get a cheap sex doll that I'm probably going to have to blow up myself."

Above: Belsner's to-do list for the orgy.

Another growing concern is the male-female ratio. The orgy, Belsner said, currently skews heavily toward men.

"Ideally, I wanted two girls for every guy," Belsner said. "As it stands now, it looks like I'll be lucky if I have one girl for every two guys. Of the yes responses, I've got ten men and four women. And two of those four women said they'd only come if the male-female ratio was 50/50, which doesn't look likely. If only two women show up, that's not an orgy, that's a gangbang."

Though Belsner has considered taking out a classified ad seeking female orgy participants in his local newspaper's "alternative lifestyles" section, he characterized that as "a last resort."

"You just don't know what kind of people an ad will bring," Belsner said. "I'd rather just keep it small and intimate. This is my first orgy, and I'd really like it to be people I know. Or at least friends of friends. I've been asking the guys to bring any willing females along, but I probably shouldn't count on it."

Art Schonbrod, noted swinger and author of *Think Globally, Swing Locally*, said Belsner's frustrations are common among first-time orgy organizers.

"Most first-timers are amazed to discover just how much goes into planning an orgy," Schonbrod said. "From the music to the props to the invite list, it can be extremely stressful. But the planner has to remember that, ultimately, all that stuff is peripheral. The most important thing is celebrating the union of friends and acquaintances in a wild night of mass sexual congress. If [Belsner] keeps his perspective and doesn't let all these hassles get to him, he'll have an orgy to remember for years."

"I'm sure it'll all work out okay, and that everybody will have a great time," said Belsner, dialing a Mexican restaurant to inquire about catering prices. "As for me, I'll just be happy when it's over." ∅

I'm A High Roller

The Cruise
By Jim Anchower

Hola, amigos. All clear on your end? I know it's been a long time since I rapped at ya, but things have been kinda hectic around El Casa Anchower lately.

First off, I had my electricity cut for a few days. Now, I ain't no deadbeat, but I've been a little low on cash lately, and when it came time to pay the bills this month, I had to do some tough prioritizing. A man's gotta eat. And drink. And set his mind straight. And if a man's gotta set his mind straight, he may as well do it with some weed, you know what I mean?

It's not like I wasn't gonna pay the damn electric bill. But apparently, the dicklicks at MG&E didn't see it that way. I had to go down there and bring them the money in cash, plus some extra dough for a "reconnect fee." Man, it must be nice to collect a fat reconnection fee just for flipping a switch.

The big reason I was low on cash was that I had to miss a few days at my coat-check job because I threw out my back while working on my car. One of my fan belts was squeaking real bad, and I decided I should take care of it myself. "Hey," I thought, "am I gonna let some mechanic charge me a ton of money to change one lousy belt when I can do it myself?" Hell, no.

I called up Wes, and we took a look under the hood. It's not like Wes is any good at fixing cars, but he's good at other important things, like starting her up, giving her gas, and getting me another beer. Plus, he cusses like a sailor when the occasion requires it, so he's good to have around for that, since my car usually needs more swears than I got stored up in me.

So I'm under the hood, and Wes is behind the wheel, giving her gas and throwing in a "cocksucker" here and a "piece of shit" there. I was trying to loosen a nut on the fan belt, putting a lot of torque into it, when my back suddenly gave out. I don't know if I pinched a nerve or what. All I know is, I was on the ground and could barely move.

Wes helped carry me inside and brought me my bong. I did a few b-loads to relax, but it wasn't helping. I had to call in sick for about four days, which really cheesed me off. I hate wasting sick days like that. I'd rather use them when there's some sort of concert or county fair I want to go to. Plus, I didn't even get to replace the fan belt.

All in all, I lost about $200 plus tips from not working at the coat check those four days. That, combined with my recent purchase of a four-foot Graffix bong, resulted in the Anchower finances not looking so good. Under my mattress, I had $63 in emergency funds, but that wasn't enough to cover the kind of bills I was facing. My first day back at work, I spent the whole time wondering where I could come up with enough money to make it through the month okay.

> **The big reason I was low on cash was that I had to miss a few days at my coat-check job because I threw out my back while working on my car.**

Then it hit me. The answer was so obvious: I could take my $63 and invest it at one of the Indian casinos.

I had the next day off, so I hopped in my car, squeaky fan belt and all, and picked up Wes and Ron. After filling the car with gas, we took off to Ho-Chunk Casino, which was up in Baraboo, maybe 70 miles away. That gave us a chance to lay back and enjoy the ride.

When we got there, the joint looked like a strip club, only with more slot machines and no hot naked chicks. Plus, everywhere you went, there was this sound of, like, a thousand different videogames going at once. And weird old people.

Me, Wes, and Ron decided we should split up to increase our chances at being lucky. I eased into it by sitting down at an open slot machine. Turns out, it wasn't open: There was a woman sitting at the one next to it, playing two games at once. She shot me a dirty look, so I shot her one back and moved on. It's a good thing I did, 'cause I scored on the next slot. I spent about eight bucks at a Dutch Diamond Delight machine and wound up winning $50. I figured it must be my night and moved on to my next big score.

That next score, I decided, would be blackjack. I'd never played before, but how hard could it be? You've just got to get close to 21 and beat the dealer. So I took a seat at the $5 minimum table. I did okay for a while, getting up to $25. This was going to be my night. I laid down $10 on a bet and was up $40 before long. That's when the table went cold. Fifteen minutes later, I was down to zero. I went to change in my quarters from the slot machine so I could try a different game.

Now, roulette looked pretty easy. All you had to do was pick the right number. I decided I should play lucky number seven. But then I figured that's exactly what they wanted me to do, so I put down $10 on unlucky number 13. (That, my friends, is thinking.) A lady next to me told me I should spread them out so that I'd have a better chance of winning. I told her that if I was gonna hit, I was gonna hit big, so I'd let it ride.

Not even 10 minutes later, I was cleaned out on roulette. I hadn't even been there long enough to get a free drink from the cocktail waitress. I just wanted to get the hell out of there and head home. I had beer back at my house, and it was in bigger glasses than the thimbles they were taking around to everyone at Ho-Chunk.

> **Not even 10 minutes later, I was cleaned out on roulette. I hadn't even been there long enough to get a free drink from the cocktail waitress.**

It took me almost half an hour to find Wes and Ron. Ron was at the bar just watching everyone pass by, and Wes was playing nickel slots. He was up $20 on that, so he didn't really want to leave. When I told Wes I was out of money, he asked me if I'd studied any blackjack charts before coming. I told him I had no idea what the hell he was talking about. He didn't say anything more, which is good, 'cause I would have laid him out on the pavement if he had.

I learned a valuable lesson that day: Blackjack and roulette are for suckers. As we were leaving, I saw on the wall that Ho-Chunk has slot tournaments on Wednesday nights. I should definitely go back for one of those, since that's the one thing I was pretty good at. I'm going to have to wait for a while, though: I got a disconnect notice for my gas bill, so I can't spend any more money at the casino right now. But once I get that paid off and have a little spare change in my pocket, I'm heading straight back to Ho-Chunk to get my $63 back and then some. You can count on that. ∅

Your Horoscope

By Lloyd Schumner Sr.
Retired Machinist and
A.A.P.B.-Certified Astrologer

Aries: (March 21–April 19)
Give yourself a well-deserved treat by mixing incompatible drugs and having an ill-advised sexual encounter. You owe it to yourself for the week you're about to have.

Taurus: (April 20–May 20)
You will soon learn the subtle value of silence in those who disapprove of you.

Gemini: (May 21–June 21)
The stars indicate that you've been looking good lately. Also, they need to borrow $20.

Cancer: (June 22–July 22)
Next week, you will learn the hard way just how important it is to pay attention to the fine print noting that the stunt is being performed by professional drivers on a closed course.

Leo: (July 23–Aug. 22)
You'll feel strangely unflattered by a celebrity comparison when you're described as looking like the crate they shipped Star Jones in.

Virgo: (Aug. 23–Sept. 22)
When they announce the pregnancy of the Washington Zoo's panda next week, just sit back and smile knowingly.

Libra: (Sept. 23–Oct. 23)
Your first impression will be that you were so drunk you married the bearded lady, but moments later, you'll realize you made a mistake about the gender.

Scorpio: (Oct. 24–Nov. 21)
You're getting to the point where you'd kill for a cigarette, despite never having smoked in your life.

Sagittarius: (Nov. 22–Dec. 21)
Early reviews will refer to you as "smart, sassy, sexy, and full of non-stop Broadway razzle-dazzle."

Capricorn: (Dec. 22–Jan. 19)
You'd have had a much better chance of acquittal if one of the witnesses against you hadn't been an Osmond.

Aquarius: (Jan. 20–Feb. 18)
You've joked about being a snacking machine, but you had no idea that you were specifically constructed by the Nabisco Corporation for its own dark product-consumption purposes.

Pisces: (Feb. 19–March 20)
A time-travel accident transports you to an era when you are irresistible to the unwashed, plague-ridden, lesion-faced opposite sex.

NEWS

Newspapers Piling Up On Dead Homeowner's Doorstep

see LOCAL page 10B

Andrew W.K. Adopts Staunch Party-Advocacy Position

see MUSIC page 4D

Mixed-Nut Ratio Total Bullshit

see EATS page 9B

STATshot

A look at the numbers that shape your world.

Top-Rated Programs On The Food Network

1. Emeril Slinks Back To Cable
2. Cumin Squad
3. The Joy Of Prepping
4. Chef Shouty
5. The Dutch Oven
6. Hour Of Sour Cream Power
7. The Baked Chef
8. Cooking With Catchphrases

the ONION®

VOLUME 38 ISSUE 15   AMERICA'S FINEST NEWS SOURCE™   25 APRIL–1 MAY 2002

Community Rallies Behind Struggling Corporation

Above: Summitville residents serve food at a fundraiser for CEC MidCorp.

SUMMITVILLE, IN—The 1,032 residents of Summitville are rallying to save CEC MidCorp, a struggling, Indianapolis-based corporation that posted record fourth-quarter losses last year.

A petrochemical conglomerate with holdings in steel and concrete, CEC MidCorp has been badly hit by the recent recession, losing more than $180 million in the final quarter of 2001 and forced to scrap plans to open a tungsten-carbide plant in Mexico. The corporation's woes first came to the attention of the people of Summitville on March 28, when resident Paula Bester saw a report on CNN/fn.

"Life has been pretty tough for me ever since my husband walked out, leaving me to raise three kids on a waitress' salary," Bester said. "But hearing about CEC MidCorp's financial troubles on CNN/fn really put my see CORPORATION page 130

Mideast Peace Process Derailed, Burned To Ground, Shoveled Over With Dirt

JERUSALEM—The Mideast peace process was once again derailed Monday, when U.S.-brokered talks between Israeli and Palestinian leaders careened off their tracks into an embankment and burst into flames, burning intensely for nearly an hour until the smoking remains were shoveled over with dirt.

Above: Arafat

"The goal was to establish a substantive, mutually respectful dialogue between the two sides that would lay the foundation for a lasting settlement," said Secretary of State Colin Powell upon returning from his failed diplomatic mission. "Unfortunately, at an early stage of the negotiation process, these efforts ran into obstacles. More specifically, they violently slammed into the obstacles at 190 mph, bursting into flames upon impact."

Above: Powell and Sharon meet shortly before talks broke down and collapsed, belching thick plumes of smoke.

Powell expressed disappointment over his inability to bring together Palestinian leader Yasser Arafat and Israeli Prime Minister Ariel Sharon at the same table.

"When the two leaders refused to meet, the negotiation process was suddenly halted, causing any hopes of a productive dialogue to slam into the see MIDEAST page 131

Magic-Store Employee Not The Same Since Losing Virginity

Above: The recently deflowered Reuss.

ANAHEIM, CA—Scottie Reuss, 22, a longtime employee of Merlin's Magicland, has not been as interested in magic or customer service as he was before his March 27 virginity loss, coworkers reported Monday.

"Scottie's been working here almost three years, and he's always been responsible," said Sol "Merlin" Horowitz, owner of Merlin's Magicland, located in the Holiday Plaza strip mall. "But these past few weeks, he just hasn't been himself. It's almost as if serving the needs of the Orange County magic community is no longer his top priority."

In addition to failing to relock the sword cabinet twice and calling in sick for the first time in his tenure at the store, Reuss has been markedly less enthusiastic about demonstrating tricks to customers over the past three weeks.

"Heck, I've been in the see EMPLOYEE page 131

Cardinal Law Under Fire

Boston's Cardinal Law has been ordered to appear for a deposition to answer questions about his protection of a priest accused of sexual abuse. What do *you* think?

"It's not like the cardinal molested the children. He just created an environment where it could continue unabated."

Fred Tillman
Forklift Operator

"As long as these priests admit wrongdoing and ask for forgiveness, God will reward them in the afterlife with all the little boys they could want."

Ben Downing
Contractor

"If nothing else, *Cardinal Law* is a great name for the TV movie that will inevitably be made about this."

Michael Polk
Civil Engineer

"These plaintiffs should ask themselves if justice is worth the risk of excommunication."

Dianne Weston
Secretary

"Just because a cardinal is in a position of power and trust doesn't mean we should hold him to the same standards of basic human decency as the rest of us."

Max Allard
Systems Analyst

"Jesus has absolved Cardinal Law of his sins. That's why I'm bringing a $100 million class-action suit against Jesus next week."

Irene Bell
Student

The Osbournes

The Osbournes, the MTV reality show chronicling the lives of Ozzy Osbourne and his family, is a surprise hit. Among the highlights of upcoming episodes:

- Sharon catches Ozzy fucking a microwaved pumpkin
- Ozzy stumbles into, knocks over huge display rack at carpet store
- Sharon and Ozzy forced to pretend they enjoyed Dio's pot roast
- Ozzy angrily hits Cuisinart with shoe
- Family takes leisurely Sunday drive in their coffin-shaped hot rod
- Ozzy stares blankly at TV while dogs and cats crawl all over him
- David Lee Roth crashes on couch for most of May
- Jack rebels against authority-figure parents by scratching "Ozzy" in dining-room table

---

the ONION®
America's Finest News Source.™

Herman Ulysses Zweibel
Founder

T. Herman Zweibel
Publisher Emeritus
J. Phineas Zweibel
Publisher
Maxwell Prescott Zweibel
Editor-In-Chief

Point-Counterpoint: The Space Program

According To *The Economist*, NASA Is An Industrial Subsidy In Disguise

I grew up with the romantic notion that NASA is not merely a government agency, but an organization dedicated to bravely propelling the human race forward into a glorious future of scientific advancement and discovery. But after reading a recent article in *The Economist*, **By Ben Pratchett** I have no choice but to question that idealistic view.

According to this piece, which ran, I believe, in the April 9 issue, NASA exists largely to provide an economic boost to the American aerospace industry, particularly Boeing. NASA gets away with this thinly veiled pork-barrel politicking, the piece contended, by distracting the public with "bread-and-circus" space missions that emphasize thrills over genuinely useful scientific discovery.

Case in point: the tremendously wasteful expense of sending humans into space. A robotic probe costs far less to launch than a human, does the work far more reliably and efficiently, lasts centuries with no food or air, and never needs to be brought back. But the massive public interest in manned space flight and the human drama it offers renders all that moot.

Consider the hoopla surrounding John Glenn's return flight to space. He got a ticker-tape parade and front-page coverage, but what did science actually gain? Meanwhile, how often does your favorite newscaster mention the Hubble telescope, a genuinely useful yet far less compelling tool of exploration?

The article noted that a reassessment of NASA's motives and goals is especially relevant now. As we speak, one of Christa MacAuliffe's fellow teachers is undergoing training to ride the shuttle in what the media are portraying as "the mission Christa never got to carry out." With all due respect to the families of the victims of the *Challenger* disaster, can we really justify the tremendous expense for what essentially amounts to a touching, movie-of-the-week photo-op? What exactly do we plan to learn from this shuttle mission? Will it lead to scientific advances that remotely begin to justify the exorbitant costs?

It's too bad the folks in Washington aren't likely to heed the lessons of this article, because it's time we started making NASA accountable for its wasteful, PR-driven expenditures. ∅

Oooh, Look At Me, I Read *The Economist*!

Eeeeeeuuuuuwww! *The Economist* says! *The Economist* says! I read *The Economist*! Aren't I cool? Aren't you impressed with me?

What do you read? *Time*? *Newsweek*? Those are for people who can't handle a real news magazine like the one I read. That's because you're **By Glen Schraft** not as smart or sophisticated as me.

On weekends, I like to sit out on my porch in my wicker chair with my bifocals and my subscription copy of *The Economist*. Then, when I go to a professor's wine-and-cheese party later that night, I can casually mention all the fancy stuff I read about NASA and Venezuela and Gen. Pervez Musharraf in my fancy magazine and impress everybody.

Question: Do you think I'm smarter than everyone else because I read *The Economist*, or do I read *The Economist* because I'm smarter than everyone else? Now, there's a conundrum! I should mail that one in to *The Economist* and see what they think!

Oh, no! My brain just got larger! Help! I need more knowledge to fill up the new brains! Get me the new issue of *The Economist* at once! I can't live if I'm even remotely unaware of anything that is happening in the universe! I must have my weekly issue of *The Economist*, or I risk de-evolving into the sort of mouth-breathing rabble by which I am surrounded daily!

I say, old chap, here comes Lord Smartingford of Braintonshire! Shall we dine upon a nice cup of tea, then? We can discuss the economy, and the global situ-AYYY-tion, and ever so many other matters! I am so very versed in such matters, reading as do I *The Economist*, just as soon as the postman delivers it by the estate, don't you know. I find that only the right cracking coverage of *The E-CON-omist* keeps me jolly-well informed and all that, wouldn't you agree? Mmm, yes, I did think you would!

Fuckin' prick. ∅

80 Percent Of Small-Town Newspaper Written By Jerry Schoepke

CRESTLINE, OH—Covering beats as diverse as Crestline city government, Crestline High School football, and Crestline births and deaths, *Crestline Gazette* reporter Jerry Schoepke writes an estimated 80 percent of the weekly community newspaper.

"I'd say Jerry is writing about four-fifths of what goes in these days," *Gazette* editor-in-chief Ralph Dilger said Monday. "He really stepped up to the plate after [former reporters] Marty and Barb Dutler moved to Ashland County in 1999."

The Crestline Gazette's lone staff writer and among the most important of its nine fulltime employees, Jerry Schoepke's name can be found throughout the paper.

"Pretty much, as you page through and look at the bylines, you'll see Jerry Schoepke, Jerry Schoepke, Jerry Schoepke, Ralph Dilger, Jerry Schoepke," managing editor Wendell Greggs said. "Until you get to the Outdoors section, that is. Then it's Ty Yeager, Jerry Schoepke, Ty Yeager."

Established in 1979, the 5,000-circulation *Gazette* serves Crestline and parts of the nearby towns of Leesville and Shelby. Schoepke said he feels a strong sense of dedication to the paper, aware of the vital role it plays in the community.

"*The Gazette* may be small, but it's important for a town to have a source of information they can trust," said Schoepke, whose recent reports include "Route 61 Project Underway," "Kozy Kitchen Damaged In Fire," and "C.H.S. Teachers Barred From Driving Students." "Some papers will print anything to fill up space, but we have higher standards than that. That's why, after 23 years, we're still around, while *Crestline News & Shopper* and *Three-City Record* aren't."

On top of his weekly reporting duties, Schoepke writes a monthly column titled "What's Happening?" in which he comments on everything from local goings-on to national trends. Schoepke said the column is his favorite part of the job.

"What's Happening? is the part of the paper where I can get a little crazy," Schoepke said. "It gives me a chance to get anything and everything off my chest."

In one recent installment, titled "No More 'No Parking'!" Schoepke humorously railed against the proliferation of No Parking signs downtown. He compared the signs to flowers, noting that "every spring, more and more of them seem to pop up." In the tongue-in-cheek piece, Schoepke also expressed fear that visitors to Crestline could become confused and think the name of the town is "No Parking."

As frequently as his name appears in bylines, Schoepke writes even more items for which he is not credited.

"I get the recipes for 'Homemaker's Helper' off the wire, so I can't really claim credit for them," Schoepke said. "And I do the Who, What & Where society column, but my name's not on it, because I feel it's better off attributed to a fictional character so it remains consistent through the years. I also leave my name off the movie reviews I write because, although I do write them regularly to help Wendell out, I don't want to get into any conflicts over negative reviews with [local theater owner] Tim Hough, who's a good friend."

Born and raised a short distance from Crestline in Mansfield, Schoep-

Above: A recent issue of *The Gazette*. Left: Schoepke.

ke graduated with a journalism degree from the University of Akron in 1979. After "bouncing around" a number of newspapers in Ohio and Michigan, he relocated to Crestline and "found [his] home" at *The Gazette*.

"*The Gazette* is pretty much the ears and eyes of Crestline," Schoepke said. "If something's happening in Crestline, you'll read about it here. That means I'm pretty busy most of the time. For example, today I went over to the sporting-goods store to do a story on the scuffle over fishing licenses, then I dropped by the new bakery on Spruce Road, and then I headed over to the high school to cover the big wrestling tournament."

Concerned about Schoepke's heavy workload, Dilger said he plans to hire another reporter soon. Dilger noted, however, that skilled journalists who know the local scene are hard to

see NEWSPAPER page 130

NEWS IN BRIEF

Man Turns Vegetarian For 36 Hours

WAUSAU, WI—Local resident Alvin Wanamaker swore off all meat products for 36 hours, from Friday morning to late Saturday afternoon. "I was planning to go vegetarian for life," Wanamaker said Monday. "But then I figured, hey, there's hot dogs in the fridge, and they'll just go to waste." Wanamaker made headlines last year for his strict three-day exercise regimen of 100 sit-ups every morning.

South Dakota Considering Maybe Putting Mount Rushmore On State Quarter

PIERRE, SD—South Dakota is thinking about maybe putting Mount Rushmore on its upcoming state coin, sources reported Monday. "I forget who came up with the idea, but Mount Rushmore is definitely in the running," said State Coin Selection Committee chair James Kolter. "We're also considering many other worthy subjects, from the historic birthplace of Cheryl Ladd to our oft-used highway system. It's definitely going to be

a tough call." The committee has until late 2005 to decide.

Former Big Celebrity Finds New Career As Pathetic Former Celebrity

HOLLYWOOD, CA—Eighteen years after his fame peaked with *The Karate Kid*, former big celebrity Ralph Macchio has discovered a new, lucrative career in the rapidly growing field of washed-up celebritydom. "I just recorded a cameo on *King Of The Hill* where, after Bobby gets cast in a movie, I explain to him that fame is fleeting," Macchio said Monday. "And I taped a *Drew Carey Show* appearance where I woo a girl away from Drew, and he moans about how he's 'even losing chicks to Ralph Macchio.'" Macchio will also appear in an upcoming Stanley Tools ad, in which, over an image of his face, the announcer says, "Some things come and go, but Stanley is forever."

Fashion Industry Pretends To Care About Plus-Size Models

NEW YORK—In a pretend show of

support for larger women, the May issue of *Vogue* features a 16-page spread focusing on plus-size models. "These plus-size beauties are every bit as gorgeous as the models you usually see in magazines," said *Vogue* editor Anna Wintour, who has never before and will never again publish photos of normal-sized women. "Female beauty comes in many shapes and sizes, and this spread is a celebration of that fact." *Vogue*'s June issue is slated to celebrate female boniness, featuring hundreds of photos of women weighing no more than 103 pounds.

Opium-Inspired Ad Executive Composes Epic Tums Jingle

CHICAGO—An eight-hour opium binge resulted in a towering work of advertising Sunday, when DDB Needham copywriter Brian Lisi created an epic 400-line radio jingle for Tums. "When Vulcan's fires spout and rage / within a roiling acid sea / let work the soothing tablet Tums / The Hell-sear'd forge within becomes / sweet alkaloid esprit," the jingle begins before detouring into iceberg imagery believed to represent Tums' new "Cool Relief" flavor. The ad, which begins production in June, is expected to run nearly 90 minutes. ∅

situation into perspective. I mean, there I was, obsessing over how I was going to find $300 to pay the rent, when there's a company out there that lost more in three months than I'll see in my entire lifetime. I knew I had to do something."

On April 4, Bester mentioned CEC MidCorp's sagging revenues to the town clergyman, Rev. Bill Fletcher, in the hopes that he could make special mention of the company's plight in his sermon and encourage the congregation to keep CEC MidCorp and its shareholders in their thoughts and prayers. Touched by the request, Fletcher instead organized a bake sale to raise money to help CEC MidCorp build the tungsten-carbide plant it had dreamed of opening.

Though the two-day bake sale raised only $258, well short of the needed $630 million, the event helped spread word of MidCorp's troubles.

Though the two-day bake sale raised only $258, well short of the needed $630 million, the event helped spread word of MidCorp's troubles. Throughout the next few days, Summitville residents came up with ways big and small to help the beleaguered corporation. While many residents dug deep into their savings to give whatever they could, others came up with goods and services to help see CEC MidCorp through the rough times.

"I'm on a tight budget, but, by heavens, I knew I could do something," said retired widow Beatrice Evans, who took a bus to CEC MidCorp's Indianapolis headquarters to "help tidy up and put a happy face on things." "The Summitville motto is to always be neighborly."

"In the end, everybody in town had something to contribute," said retired tool-and-die maker Benjamin Fowler. "If you couldn't make crafts for the fair, you could contribute some unwanted items from your attic for the flea market. My own granddaughter, who's just 6 years old, gave $2.30 she'd been saving to buy a new doll."

The crowning achievement came Sunday, when the town's three-day "CEC MidCorp Daze" festival not only raised $1,839, but also drew residents from nearby Alexandria and Hackleman, all eager to do their part to help American industry.

"Even Tom Barker, who got so many jeers and razzes for being the only councilman to oppose naming April 'MidCorp Fundraising Month,' showed up in the end to sit in the dunk tank," Fowler said. "That's the spirit of Summitville."

To date, the residents of Summitville have raised $7,348, which town mayor Hal Munsingame proudly handdelivered to CEC MidCorp's headquarters Monday. Unable to get past the lobby-security guards, Munsingame left the cash with a receptionist along with a note reading, "Summitville believes in you!" and a jar of Edna Rafferty's homemade strawberry preserves.

"You should all be very proud of yourselves," Munsingame told a

No one was more touched by the outpouring of support than MidCorp CEO Jim Brodhagen, who personally thanked the townspeople for their efforts in a letter.

throng of Summitville residents gathered in the town square Tuesday. "And I don't want anyone to be down in the mouth just because we didn't reach the full $630 million. Every little bit helps. And next month, we'll raise even more!"

No one was more touched by the outpouring of support than MidCorp CEO Jim Brodhagen, who personally thanked the townspeople for their efforts in a letter.

"Thank you for your interest in CEC MidCorp," Brodhagen's letter read in part. "But while we greatly appreciate the support of our investors and welcome new ones, we prefer that CEC MidCorp stock be purchased by conventional means, through an accredited broker." ∅

come by, and that the meager starting salaries at *The Gazette* "sure don't help matters."

"Hopefully, someone qualified will move to Crestline soon," Dilger said. "Or maybe one of the graduating seniors will come by. I should ask [Crestline High School newspaper advisor] Terri Easton if she's got any good kids this year who might want to give an internship a whirl."

In addition to his 50 hours at the paper, Schoepke works 10 hours a week stocking and packaging dried goods at his wife Suzanne's healthfood store.

"Jerry is on the go all the time," Suzanne said. "I'm always telling him, 'You can miss a town-council meeting once in a while. Nothing ever happens anyway.' But he won't hear of it. He takes his job very seriously. It's important for him to do it right."

Schoepke's presence is a familiar one at Crestline community events.

"Everyone knows Jerry," towncouncil president Stan Schumacher said. "He's always in the back with his notebook and tape recorder. If there's

"Jerry is on the go all the time," Suzanne said. "I'm always telling him, 'You can miss a towncouncil meeting once in a while. Nothing ever happens anyway.'"

a big deal going on, like the Crestline Days festival or something, he'll bring a photographer, but he usually takes the pictures himself."

In spite of his passion for local politics, Schoepke said he has to be careful not to let his own views seep into the articles he writes about such hotbutton community issues as the funding of a new municipal pool or the garbage-collection fee for residents outside the city line.

"As a journalist, I have to remain impartial," Schoepke said. "So if I have an opinion, I put it in an opinion column, not a news story. Or else, I'll write a letter to the editor and sign it 'Anonymous.'"

Schoepke, who attends a yearly journalism conference in Columbus to keep abreast of current trends in his profession, said he is not content to rest on his laurels.

"*The Gazette* needs to keep pushing the envelope to remain relevant in today's media environment," Schoepke said. "So far, I think we're doing a pretty good job. You'd be surprised how often someone says to me, 'Hey, Jerry, I saw that article you wrote in the paper.' It's at least a few times a year. That's a good feeling." ∅

amounts of blood. Passersby were amazed by the unusually large amounts of blood. Passersby were amazed by the unusually large

amounts of blood. Passersby were amazed by the unusually large amounts of blood. Passersby were amazed by the unusually large amounts of blood. Passersby were amazed by the unusually large amounts of blood. Passersby were

It's not just a pony, it's a *magic* pony.

amounts of blood. Passersby were amazed by the unusually large amounts of blood. Passersby were amazed by the unusually large amounts of blood. Passersby were amazed by the unusually large amounts of blood. Passersby were amazed by the unusually large amounts of blood. Passersby were amazed by the unusually large amounts of blood. Passersby were amazed by the unusually large amounts of blood. Passersby were amazed by the unusually large amounts of blood. Passersby were amazed by the unusually large amounts of blood. Passersby were amazed by the unusually large amounts of blood. Passersby were amazed by the unusually large amounts of blood. Passersby were amazed by the unusually large amounts of blood. Passersby were amazed by the unusually large amounts of blood. Passersby were amazed by the unusually large amounts of blood. Passersby were amazed by the unusually large

amazed by the unusually large amounts of blood. Passersby were amazed by the unusually large

see PLINKING page 133

business 34 years, and Scottie could show *me* new places to hide a ping-pong ball," said regular customer "Amazing" Al Rondelle. "But the last time I went in there, he acted like he couldn't care less about incredible shrinking dice and color-changing ropes. He just rang up my purchases and waved me out the door."

Described by acquaintances as "not all that socially skilled," Reuss lost his virginity at the party of friend Justin Verkilen. Drunk on Malibu and orange juice, Reuss abandoned his usual method of socializing—approaching guests and asking them for a coin—and joined some non-magic-related conversations. At approximately 2:30 a.m., Reuss and Verkilen's cousin, Karla Eddy, found themselves alone in the computer nook, where "one thing led to another."

"As Karla and I sat together on the steps outside, watching the sun come up, she informed me that she has a boyfriend," Reuss said. "But we made a vow not to regret anything that happened that night. I know I sure haven't."

Coworker Glenn Honig, 25, said he noticed something different about Reuss the minute he walked into work the following Monday.

"I was dying to tell Scottie about this amazing new dove cage, but all he

> **Described by acquaintances as "not all that socially skilled," Reuss lost his virginity at the party of friend Justin Verkilen.**

wanted to talk about was this great party he went to," Honig said. "Is this the same guy who, the week before, went ballistic when I confused a deck of clairvoyance cards with some sleight-of-hand cards?"

One of the most significant changes, coworkers say, involves the amount of time Reuss spends at the magic shop.

"Scottie's shift ends at 5, but he always used to stay later," said Jonathan Friel, 17. "Lots of times, he'd still be

there when it was time to close up at 8 because we'd gotten into a heated argument about whether Penn and Teller are doing more harm than good for the magic community."

Friel also noted that, on several occasions in the past few weeks, Reuss was unreachable when his help was needed.

"Last Saturday, I left messages for Scottie at his house and on his cell phone to find out what kind of matchbox was best for training crickets. He never got back to me," Friel said. "The next day, he comes in with a haircut, and he's wearing new clothes from Abercrombie & Fitch. I've got Ivan The Illusionist breathing down my neck about his back order and Scottie's out shopping? What the hell?"

Though Reuss used to make excuses to avoid group social events, he has been seeking them out of late.

"Scottie was always up for coming over to my house and teaching me how to use a hopping casino coin or a stiff rope," said best friend and fellow magic aficionado Andrew Welch. "Now, he just wants to go to parties. He's all, 'Is anyone having a party this weekend? We should go to that bar we went to on

New Year's Eve. There were cute girls there.' God, Scottie, get a life."

Welch said Reuss has also lost interest in his own budding magic career.

"Scottie and I have been bouncing around the idea of doing a public-access show together called *Dueling Magicians*," said Welch, 23. "But last week, he said he's too busy to do it. Busy doing what? Getting drunk and having sex with complete strangers?"

"With [the recent success of] *Lord Of The Rings* and *Harry Potter*, we're

> **Welch said Reuss has also lost interest in his own budding magic career.**

looking at a total resurgence of the entire industry," Welch continued. "Now is a great time [to pursue a career in] magic, but Scottie's completely blowing it. I'm not worried, though. Sooner or later, he'll come to his senses. He'll realize that getting laid is temporary, but magic is forever." ∅

back of it, crushing the fragile peace efforts in a twisted pile of crumpled metal," Powell said. "As a result, Arab-Israeli tension rose higher and higher, spinning off into the sky with an ear-splitting whine before exploding several miles above the Dead Sea."

> **Approximately 1,300 Palestinians and nearly 500 Israelis have been killed since the Palestinian uprising began in September 2000, when peace talks stalled, shuddered to a halt, and belched thick plumes of black smoke.**

Meetings between Powell and various Arab leaders were similarly unsuccessful.

"Syrian President Bashar al-Assad called for a full Israeli withdrawal from the West Bank before he would agree to negotiate with Israel," Powell said. "He also refused to condemn the use of suicide bombings, essentially blocking himself out of the peace process with a 10-foot-thick wall strung with razor wire."

Unable to make headway with al-Assad and other Arab leaders, Powell returned to Israel, where he met with Sharon.

"Prime Minister Sharon promised

that Israel would pull back from Jenin, Nablus, and other areas, but this is far from the pull-out requested by the U.S.," Powell said. "When Sharon announced that Israeli forces would not leave Bethlehem until the current standoff in the Church of the Nativity ends, a massive blow was dealt to this peace mission, catapulting it through a nearby building and causing it to shatter into countless pieces, covering all surfaces with a fine powder of broken glass."

Approximately 1,300 Palestinians

and nearly 500 Israelis have been killed since the Palestinian uprising began in September 2000, when peace talks stalled, shuddered to a halt, and belched thick plumes of black smoke.

According to Mideast experts, prospects for peace in the region are dimmer than they have been in years.

"Arab-Israeli relations are quite possibly at their lowest point since 1973," said Anthony Zinni, U.S. special envoy to the Middle East. "I fear that any remaining scrap of goodwill

between Arafat and Sharon has been damaged irreparably, torn out in hunks of debris from the noxious fumes wafting from the burning wreckage of the Camp David Accords."

"Once again, peace talks have broken down, having lurched and chugged forward a few inches before collapsing in a smoldering heap," Zinni continued. "Personally, my faith in a possible resolution has been shaken, thrown to the ground, and run over by a thousand tanks." ∅

Above: A Palestinian youth hurls a rock at an Israeli tank.

Why Do Porn Actors Have To Use Such Foul Language?

By Maggie Lehman

Like many people, I enjoy pornographic movies. But I've got a major bone to pick with the actors. It's gotten to the point where you can't watch a porno without being inundated by swearing. I can't tell you how many times I've tried to enjoy a hardcore sex scene, only to have it ruined by the participants screaming, "F– my p–" and, "Oh, yeah, suck my big, hard you-know-what, baby." Is it really necessary to resort to such foul language?

It would be one thing if the potty-mouthed performers were just the men. Everyone knows men, especially creative types like actors, can be a little rough around the edges. But, sadly, most of the cussing comes from the ladies. From the moment the delivery man unzips his fly to the moment he finishes all over her face, every word out of these ladies' mouths is "F– this" and "F– that." Can't I make it through a single triple-penetration scene without hearing things like, "F– my tight C-word with your huge blankety-blank, you big, black you-know-what"?

The swearing isn't limited to the lovemaking scenes, either. It's everywhere. If a fellow is playing a hard-boiled private eye sent to investigate a strip club, you'd better believe he's gonna drop a few F-bombs while interrogating the club owner. Thank-

> ### Porn actors have a responsibility to their younger fans. There are impressionable young kids watching these videos, and the people up there on that screen need to be aware of that.

fully, my husband Marv fast-forwards through the plot so we don't have to hear any more vulgarity than is absolutely necessary.

Whatever happened to subtlety and innuendo? Back in the old days, people in the movies conveyed their lascivious thoughts with a smile, a wink, or a certain look. If you found yourself bent over a breakfast bar in a see-

thru nightie, and a rugged, sweaty electrician walked in, it didn't take a stream of four-letter words to encourage him to make love to you from

> ### It would be one thing if the potty-mouthed performers were just the men. Everyone knows men, especially creative types like actors, can be a little rough around the edges. But, sadly, most of the cussing comes from the ladies.

behind. Just the look in your eyes would tell him, "I bet you have a large ding-dong. Put it in me."

Don't these filmmakers realize that an actor can easily get his or her point across without dirty words? If, for example, a woman wants to fellate a gentleman caller, she can simply say, "I want to suck on your dingle." Or "Can I please lick your winkie?" That's so much preferable.

If I ever used that sort of coarse language around Marv, he'd be shocked and turned off. He wouldn't respect a gal who didn't have the decency to use proper English when she wanted him to stick his business where the sun doesn't shine. And I can't say I blame him.

Sometimes, I think these porn actors just weren't brought up right. Believe me, I know how tough it is to raise kids. Kids are exposed to bad language everywhere these days. But you can bet that when my boys ask their girlfriends to spread their hoo-hoos wider, they do it without all the vulgarity. It doesn't come easy or without a lot of soap, but that's the price you pay to raise children you can be proud of.

Porn actors have a responsibility to their younger fans. There are impressionable young kids watching these videos, and the people up there on that screen need to be aware of that. They need to realize that the things that come out of their mouths have as much of an impact on those kids as the things that go in them.

Perhaps some of these folks need to go back to acting class and learn to not say the first expletives that enter their heads. Since when did panting or screaming, "Oh my goodness!" or

"My word!" not satisfactorily convey sexual excitement? It was good enough for my generation, and it should be good enough for the people of today.

Ultimately, it's not the actors who need to be taking responsibility. It's the studios. They're the ones who are truly in a position to do something about this ever-worsening problem. I've been writing letters to leaders of the adult-movie industry for years, asking them to tone it down or release special-edition tapes for viewers who'd like to enjoy the sex without having to put up with all that cussing. It wouldn't be difficult: The vocals for many of these movies are re-recorded later in a studio, anyway.

So far, my efforts have been for naught. I've written the president of Wicked Pictures five times already, but have gotten no response. Same thing at Vivid Video. Someday, I'll win this battle. But in the meantime, I've decided I'm no longer putting up with it. Next porno I rent, I'm going to turn down the sound and turn up the hi-fi playing a nice bossa-nova record. I'll watch, but I won't listen. ✍

Your Horoscope

By Lloyd Schumner Sr.
Retired Machinist and
A.A.P.B.-Certified Astrologer

Aries: (March 21–April 19)
You foolishly disregard the old saying about buying pigs in pokes, explaining that the pokes were cunningly disguised as blankets.

Taurus: (April 20–May 20)
The philosophical revelation that a container cannot contain itself will inspire you to develop a revolutionary new type of container.

Gemini: (May 21–June 21)
Your plan to have children by the time you are 35 will go awry when you're shown a cute picture of a Weimaraner puppy in a bucket.

Cancer: (June 22–July 22)
The stars are sorry, but writing the poems of Theodore Roethke on lampshades doesn't make you an artist.

Leo: (July 23–Aug. 22)
Doctors will cite your habits of smoking, drinking, and eating fatty foods as the primary source of your happiness.

Virgo: (Aug. 23–Sept. 22)
You will soon have reason to question the moral, ethical, and intellectual motivations behind your choice of long-distance carriers.

Libra: (Sept. 23–Oct. 23)
Love, adventure, and laughs will not come to you, but they will come soon to a theater near you.

Scorpio: (Oct. 24–Nov. 21)
America will one day view sexuality in a healthy way, but until then, there are those Chippendale dancers.

Sagittarius: (Nov. 22–Dec. 21)
Your efforts to come to an understanding of the world will result in your creating a polytheistic religion based on the worship of megaliths.

Capricorn: (Dec. 22–Jan. 19)
Marshall McLuhan once said schizophrenia may be a consequence of literacy. Avoid this by sticking strictly to watching TV.

Aquarius: (Jan. 20–Feb. 18)
Your theory that language is instinctive rather than a learned behavior would be more interesting if you communicated in anything but grunts.

Pisces: (Feb. 19–March 20)
You don't claim to know everything, but you're pretty sure that the illustrations in *Gray's Anatomy* shouldn't make you hungry.

BAGGY from page 130

amounts of blood. Passersby were amazed by the unusually large amounts of blood. Passersby were amazed by the unusually large amounts of blood. Passersby were amazed by the unusually large amounts of blood. Passersby were amazed by the unusually large amounts of blood. Passersby were amazed by the unusually large amounts of blood. Passersby were amazed by the unusually large

I totally outlived Jesus!

amounts of blood. Passersby were amazed by the unusually large amounts of blood. Passersby were amazed by the unusually large amounts of blood. Passersby were amazed by the unusually large amounts of blood. Passersby were amazed by the unusually large amounts of blood. Passersby were amazed by the unusually large amounts of blood. Passersby were amazed by the unusually large amounts of blood. Passersby were amazed by the unusually large amounts of blood. Passersby were amazed by the unusually large
see BAGGY page 134

Saddam Hussein Presents Suicide Bomber's Family With Oversized Check

see WORLD page 6A

Bling-Bling Pawned

see LOCAL page 10C

Wax Head Hastily Reattached By Night Janitor

see LOCAL page 15C

STATshot

A look at the numbers that shape your world.

What Did We Do While Trapped In The Elevator All Weekend?

1. Caught up on our shrieking
2. Perused maximum-occupancy plaque
3. Wished urine would stay in corner
4. Developed tense love/hate relationship with "2" button
5. Ate belt
6. Rocked back and forth on our assbones
7. Gave birth, as required by narrative convention

0 74470 94595 6

THE ONION • $2.00 US • $3.00 CAN

---

the ONION®

VOLUME 38 ISSUE 16   AMERICA'S FINEST NEWS SOURCE™   2–8 MAY 2002

God Re-Floods Middle East

JERUSALEM—In what theological and meteorological authorities are calling "a wrathful display of Old Testament proportions," the Lord Almighty re-flooded the Middle East Tuesday, making good on last week's threat to wipe the region clean if there was not an immediate halt to the bloodshed between Arabs and Jews.

The Lord made the decision to go ahead with His second Great Flood after last-ditch U.S.-Saudi peace initiatives were rejected Monday night.

"The Lord thy God has warned you and warned you, but you have, in your hatred and selfishness, chosen to turn away from Him," read a press statement from God, delivered by seraphim and cherubim acting as His earthly agents. "Prepare now to face His wrath and be drowned beneath the cleansing waters of His righteous rage. Children of Israel and Palestine, you who would not repent your sinful ways and live together as God's children, prepare to face your doom under the unstoppable deluge of the Lord's retribution."

As of press time, a torren-

"For too long, thou hast ignored the entreaties of thy Lord," said God, explaining the second Great Flood.

tial rain continues to fall on Israel and the West Bank, with the downpour expected to continue for another 39 days and 39 nights. Thus far, flood waters have risen more than 200 feet, drowning most of the humans and animals in the vicinity. The few remaining sur-

see GOD page 136

Above: A 200-foot wave bears down on Palestinians clashing with Israeli soldiers in the West Bank town of Hebron.

Bar-Trivia Champ Being A Real Dick About It

Above: Widely disliked trivia champion Shawn Gause.

SHARONVILLE, OH—Shawn Gause, 34, a Cincinnati-area resident and bar-trivia champion, is a real dick about his trivia prowess, patrons of McSorley's Pub reported Tuesday.

"I used to look forward to Monday trivia nights," bar patron Christine Deroia said. "But not since Mr. I-Win-All-The-Time-And-Am-A-Royal-Asshole-About-It started coming around. God, that guy burns me up."

Gause first visited McSorley's on March 4 after hearing brother-in-law Douglas

Lang mention the bar's weekly trivia night. He decided to participate, Gause said, to "show them how it's done."

"I'm way into trivia," said Gause, an associate manager at Fast & Reliable Electricians. "No, let me correct that. I am the Trivia Master, the undisputed King Of Knowledge. Anything about baseball, don't even bother asking. Name a Beatles song, I'll tell you the year it came out and what album it's on. History, literature, pop culture... you

see TRIVIA page 136

The Robert Blake Murder Case

Arrested nearly a year after his wife was fatally shot, actor Robert Blake is pleading not guilty to murder charges. What do *you* think?

Carl Morgan
Electrician

"This is the new O.J.! Except nobody gives a fuck, and there's a tiny sliver of a possibility that Blake didn't actually do it."

Paul LeMaster
Chemical Engineer

"Before we jump to any conclusions about Robert Blake's guilt or innocence, we should first consult the Internet Movie Database to make sure he's still alive."

Milt Herndon
File Clerk

"His pet cockatoo Fred must be rolling in his cigar-box grave over this."

Andrea Stennett
Optometrist

"As the man himself said, 'Some are born to sweet delight, some are born to endless night.' I'm sorry—I thought we were talking about William Blake."

Rick Evans
Systems Analyst

"Bonny Lee Bakley was hardly a saint. She was a con-woman, a grifter. A flim-flammer and a bunko artist. This doll had more angles than an octagon."

Diane Venable
Librarian

"Oh, those washed-up celebrities! Who *will* they kill next?"

The Queen's Golden Jubilee

England's Queen Elizabeth II is celebrating the 50th anniversary of her accession to the throne this year. How is the event being commemorated?

- British schoolchildren to hold up cards spelling out, "Happy Jubilee, Ya Batshit Anachronism"
- Manic Street Preachers to play terrible covers of Sex Pistols songs from boat on the Thames
- Queen to be granted absolute powers by Parliament, for old time's sake
- Royal mirror held to queen's mouth; breath-fogged glass held triumphantly aloft
- Ceremonial retouching of queen's 1977 silver jubilee portrait
- Queen to receive enormous breast implants as gift from Royal College of Surgeons
- Sir Paul McCartney to personally smoke the queen up
- Special ceremony to be held at dusk commemorating 50th anniversary of sun setting on British Empire

the ONION®
America's Finest News Source.™

Herman Ulysses Zweibel
Founder

T. Herman Zweibel
Publisher Emeritus
J. Phineas Zweibel
Publisher
Maxwell Prescott Zweibel
Editor-In-Chief

I Lied About Making $80,000 Working From Home... And So Can You!

By Ronny Falciglia

DO YOU WANT TO MAKE MORE MONEY? Have you ever dreamed about working from the comfort of your own home? Do you wish you could be your own boss, working as much or as little as you like?

I know I've had these thoughts, but that kind of success always seemed out of my reach. After all, what chance do I have of striking it rich? I'm almost 40 with NO SKILLS, NO COLLEGE EDUCATION, and NO CREDIT. Well, that's precisely why I developed the Instant Money Invention Plan. It changed my life... in an instant! From the very first day, I was able to tell my friends and neighbors that I made $80,000 a year working from home! It was SO EASY! I needed NO SPECIAL TRAINING, and there were NO STARTUP COSTS.

With the Instant Money Invention Plan, you, too, can tell people that you've achieved financial independence without even breaking a sweat. DO NOT miss out on this amazing opportunity!

To get you started right away, call for our special informational packet. You'll learn everything you need to know to convince people you are making more money than you've ever dreamed possible. Soon, you'll be saying, "It was so easy!" and "It only took a few minutes a day!" and "Finally, I have the home and car I've always wanted!"

How does it work, you ask? It's simple! All you have to do is make up a story about your AMAZING FINANCIAL SUCCESS. Soon, everyone you know will hear how you made $7,000 in your first month!

Do you own a computer? Do you know the location of a gas station with a copy machine? If the answer to either question is yes, you can send letters to thousands of people you don't know and tell them YOU ARE MAKING YOUR DREAMS COME TRUE! What are you waiting for?

Wouldn't you like to see your picture in newspapers and magazine ads? Could you imagine seeing your glowing recommendation of the Instant Money Invention Plan in a mass e-mail originating from an untraceable location? Everyone will hear about the fortune you claim you made!

Why slave away at a job, barely eking out a living, when you could have any salary you dream of? How much money do you want to say you make? $25,000? $250,000? $1 MILLION? How about $500 KAZILLION? THE SKY'S THE LIMIT! If you can say the number, you can tell people that's how much money you make!

Best of all, you will pay NO TAXES. And, because you are not taking in any money, this plan is 100% legal. The Instant Money Invention Plan may not be ethical, but it is TOTALLY LEGAL! This is NOT a multi-level marketing scam. It is not one of those make-money-at-home schemes that don't work. You will not be selling term life insurance. You will not be selling a bunch of worthless products nobody

All you will be doing is lying. That's all!

wants. With the amazing Instant Money Invention Plan, you will not be selling ANYTHING. All you will be doing is lying. That's all!

Thousands of Americans receive tax-free money from the government for education, new businesses, and so on. But the problem with these money-making schemes is YOU DON'T QUALIFY. You would have to actually go to school or start a business to get a piece of that pie. But can you lie? YES, YOU CAN! You've done it a million times in your life, to a million people—your ex-wife, your parents, the departmental supervisor at your former job. With the Instant Money Invention Plan, all you have to do is lie about something else... your salary!

Wouldn't it be great to work from the comfort of your own living-room couch, sitting back and watching the money roll in? Of course it would. Unfortunately, there's no such thing. But I'm not talking about some get-rich-quick scheme. I am talking about FOOLING PEOPLE into THINKING you've gotten rich quick.

Wouldn't you like to call up that pretty girl you've had your eye on and say, "Let's go on a luxury Caribbean vacation next month, my treat"? As long as the date for the cruise is far enough in the future, you've got no problems. Why? Because THE FUTURE IS WIDE OPEN. After all, no one can call you a liar and confront you about something that hasn't happened yet.

What do you want? A beach house? A new sports car? Your own private jet? It could all be yours in the future! It's up to YOU to start talking about it TODAY!

Slumber-Party Confession Comes Back To Haunt Fourth Grader

HAMPTON, VA—A late-night slumber-party confession has come back to haunt Jessica Casper, the betrayed and humiliated 10-year-old reported Monday.

"Oh my God, I can't believe they told the whole school I like him," said a visibly shaken Casper, who admitted liking fourth-grader Kevin Pflug at Amber Prentiss' Friday-night slumber party. "When I went past him at lunch today, he was looking at me really weird. Brianna [Benning] told me everybody in the whole school knows."

Added Casper: "My life is over."

> "Oh my God, I can't believe they told the whole school I like him," said a visibly shaken Casper, who admitted liking fourth-grader Kevin Pflug at Amber Prentiss' Friday-night slumber party.

Unbeknownst to her, Casper was invited to the slumber party of the prettier, more popular Prentiss only because the two girls' mothers are close friends. The invitation, Prentiss stressed, was extended to Casper under extreme duress.

"Mom said if I didn't invite Jessica, I couldn't have the party," Prentiss said. "I was like, 'Mom, Jessica and I haven't been friends since second grade!' but she wouldn't listen. I couldn't tell her that nobody's friends with Jessica anymore because she's such a dork. It's embarrassing enough that everybody knows we used to be friends, but then I had to actually have her at my sleepover."

The confession, sources say, came at approximately 11:50 p.m. during a game of Truth Or Dare. Though hesitant to choose Truth because of her "super-secret crush that [she's] never told anyone about," Casper was even more reluctant to do a Dare.

"The first time I said Dare, Karen [Mullroy] dared me to hop around the room saying 'I love Coach Snider,' who is our totally gross gym teacher," said Casper, who reacted to the slumber-party invitation with a mixture of surprise, anxiety, and excitement. "It was so humiliating."

Anxious to avoid a repeat of the Coach Snider debacle, Casper chose Truth on her next turn. When Prentiss asked her who she liked, Casper briefly considered naming Jeffrey Trenton, who is not a part of the girls' immediate social circle and would not have been as risky a response as Pflug. Instead, Casper, overcome by a newfound sense of camaraderie with her more popular sleepover-mates, named Pflug.

"They were all like, 'Oooh, you like Kevin!' Casper said. "But they didn't say he'd never go out with me. So I thought maybe they thought he would. But then on Monday, everything came out."

> Dr. Lorianne Pritchard, a developmental psychiatrist specializing in pre-adolescent girls, said Casper's willingness to confess is understandable.

Dr. Lorianne Pritchard, a developmental psychiatrist specializing in pre-adolescent girls, said Casper's willingness to confess is understandable.

"When one is put into a more relaxed state of mind, whether from alcohol or too many chocolate-chip bars, your inhibitions are lowered," Pritchard said. "But while inhibitions can be bad, in certain situations they should be viewed as an ally—especially when dealing with a big-mouth like Amber Prentiss. The less said around her, the better."

Though the full ramifications of her confession are not yet known, Casper said she no longer has a crush on Pflug, whom she describes as "mean." She has also vowed never to speak to or acknowledge Prentiss or "any of her stuck-up friends" again.

And while she doesn't expect the

Above: Jessica Casper, who deeply regrets admitting to having a crush on Kevin Pflug.

humiliation and taunting ever to die down, Casper has decided to stay at Lakeview Elementary School and not transfer to a school in Alaska.

"If I went to Alaska, then Amber and her stuck-up friends would win," Casper said. "I figure if I can just make it to junior high, everything will be all right. Everyone will be so much more mature there." Ø

Car Salesman Three Desks Over Going On And On About Chick He Banged Last Night

VIENNA, VA—The sales associate three desks over from Chevy/Geo dealer Karl Glodek is going on and on about the chick he banged last night, sources reported Monday. "You would not believe the stamina on this chick. Hours. She was a total freak," the salesman told an unnamed friend over the phone, as well as Glodek and the couple about to sign on a 2002 Chevy Prizm sedan. "Incredible rack, too—like, out to here." Glodek then suggested that the couple go outside for "one more look at that beaut of a Prizm."

TV Guide Channel Tops Nielsens

LOS ANGELES—For the 11th straight week, the TV Guide Channel topped the Nielsen ratings, scoring blockbuster numbers in virtually all time slots and days of the week. "The frustrating experience of trying to find something decent on TV has meant ratings gold for the TV Guide Channel, *Variety* editor Peter Bart said. "By providing a means to search for something—anything—worth watching, this 24-hour electronic scroll has made itself America's most-watched channel."

Secretary Of Agriculture Gently Reminded About Dress Code

WASHINGTON, DC—After attending Monday's Cabinet meeting in a flannel work shirt and tattered jeans, Agriculture Secretary Ann Veneman was gently reminded by President Bush about the executive-branch dress code. "Say, you know, we get a lot of foreign dignitaries coming through here," Bush told Veneman. "So I think it might be a good idea if you had a little bit more of a professional appearance. Like maybe a nice navy-blue dress." Bush also encouraged Veneman to consider dress shoes instead of her usual steel-toe work boots.

Paul Lynde Impersonation Lost On Daughter's Friends

WAKEFIELD, MA—Sarah Ammons, 14, expressed befuddlement Monday, when, during a ride to school, her father attempted to entertain her and several friends with an impromptu impersonation of late comedian and *Hollywood Squares* regular Paul Lynde. "The next time I have a daughter, I hope it's a boy!" Bob Ammons, 41, bleated nasally in an imitation of the once-popular pop-culture reference. "Paul Lynde." Added Ammons: "Center square, usually sat between George Gobel and Rose Marie? Voice of Templeton the rat?" After dropping the girls off at school, Ammons stared into his car's rear-view mirror at the crow's feet developing around his eyes.

Correct Theory Discarded In Favor Of More Exciting Theory

GRETNA, NE—The correct theory regarding the closing of Marvin's Diner was discarded Monday in favor of a far more exciting theory. "I bet the Omaha mafia muscled them out," said Gretna resident Lucinda Dunfee, pondering the fate of Marvin's Diner, which was shut down due to health-code violations. "They were taking business away from Steak Barrel, and those guys don't care who they get mixed up with." Dunfee noted that the restaurant's trash cans were often overturned during the night, which was likely an act of intimidation on the part of the Omaha crime syndicate. Ø

name it, I am The Man."

A popular hangout for clerical and maintenance employees at nearby Bethesda North Hospital, McSorley's purchased its trivia-network computer system and tabletop consoles in 1997. Players form four-person teams and compete for points by answering multiple-choice questions displayed on the bar's three TV sets.

Gause, who has not missed a trivia night since his March 4 debut, quickly earned the enmity of his fellow patrons.

"Shari [Messner]'s team actually dropped out because this jerk made them so nervous with his super-competitiveness," Deroia said. "Whenever somebody misses a question, he cackles this really loud, horribly grating cackle. And if it's an easy question, he'll be like, 'How could anybody not know that?' Everybody else is just trying to have fun, but he treats it like it's the friggin' Super Bowl."

According to Deroia, Gause's arrival on the scene spoiled several good-natured, longtime rivalries.

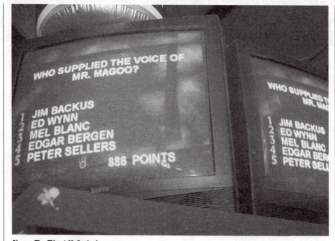

Above: The TVs at McSorley's.

"Before Shawn messed everything up, it was fun to see how The A-Team was going to do against Triviazilla. Or whether Bengals Suck would whip We All Love Don," Deroia said. "Now, me and the other gals on The Know-It-Alls don't even have a good time when we play against our husbands on The Avengers. We're all too busy being annoyed by that cocksucker."

Gause has antagonized nearly every person at McSorley's, including Larry Olberding, his friend and former teammate on the Knights Of The Bar Table.

"I tried to tell Shawn that it's all for fun," Olberding said. "Everyone likes to get into it and yell and cheer, but no one really cares who wins. They just want to hang out and have a good time. My God, it's *trivia*. Has that fact escaped him?"

Gause's constant running commentary, bar patrons say, ranks among his most irritating habits. As soon as each question appears, he gives his opinion of its difficulty level, snorting derisively and saying "Eeeasy" for simple questions. If the question is more difficult, he makes grunting sounds and then says, "That's a good one."

"After every answer is revealed, he has to give some related trivia tidbit to show how smart he is," said Patrick Baugh of the Wassup?!? team. "Like, at one point, they asked, 'Who played Scarlett O'Hara in *Gone With The Wind*?' So when Vivien Leigh is posted on the screen as the answer, he says, 'Originally, the Scarlett role was sup-

see TRIVIA next page

vivors, most of whom cling to pieces of driftwood, have made desperate pleas for mercy, but their cries have fallen on deaf ears in Heaven, with the Lord refusing to stem the raging waters.

Though regretful over the severity of God's punishment, Mideast peace negotiators nonetheless praised Him for coming up with the first-ever viable solution to the ongoing crisis.

"Yahweh, or Allah, depending on what name you choose to call Him, has finally brought to bear upon this place a direct route to peace," said former president Jimmy Carter, who in 1978 brokered the Camp David Accords, one of the region's many short-lived peace agreements. "Lord knows that I and many others have done our best to find a way for these two peoples to stop the killing and hatred, to

Israeli Prime Minister Ariel Sharon and Palestinian leader Yasser Arafat rejected the 11th-hour peace deal proposed by the joint U.S. and Saudi delegation.

"I believe Arafat and Sharon thought the Lord was bluffing and wrongly assumed they could call His bluff rather than make peace with each other," said Timothy Uselmann, a professor at Harvard's Center For Middle Eastern Studies. "Evidently, they were wrong. God has sent a strong message here: Obey His commands, or face certain peril at His hand."

Speaking on behalf of the Lord, an unnamed, non-denominational representative of Heaven said: "God only

promised humanity that He would never again flood the entire Earth. He never said He wouldn't flood specific areas."

The most recent, clearest sign of the Second Deluge came last Thursday, when a tersely worded press statement from God's angelic hosts ominously stated, "If there are any species native to the area that you would prefer not to see go extinct, we strongly suggest you begin gathering them two by two."

In spite of this and other such warnings, Palestinian suicide bombings and the Israeli military's West Bank tank assault continued after God's April 21 cease-fire deadline passed.

"For too long, thou hast ignored the entreaties of thy Lord to let go of your wickedness and hatred and live together in peace, My children," God said. "Thou hast refused the lion to lie down with the lamb, and My rod and staff have been of no comfort to you. Instead, you have continued to kill each other without ceasing. The time has come for that to stop. You want to keep running each other over with tanks and strapping dynamite to yourselves, killing women and children in pursuit of your extremist political positions, that's just fine. Let's see how well you carry out your murderous agendas under 800 feet of water." ∅

In spite of repeated warnings from God, the flood came as a major surprise to Israeli and Palestinian leaders.

no avail. But God, in His infinite wisdom, realized that it just isn't worth it anymore, and that the best thing to do is cut His losses, drown the whole lot of them, and start fresh once the raging waters subside."

In spite of repeated warnings from God, the flood came as a major surprise to Israeli and Palestinian leaders, who believed He would keep the promise He made following the Great Flood of Noah never to drown the planet again. Confident that God would honor the "Rainbow Covenant,"

Above: Jerusalem's Dome Of The Rock is engulfed by rising floodwaters.

posed to go to Bette Davis.' Because, I guess, just knowing that Vivien Leigh played Scarlett O'Hara isn't impressive enough."

Due to his competitive nature, Gause has had to recruit new teammates each week.

"[Gause] usually convinces a few suckers to play with him so they can get in on the $40 bar tab for the winners," waitress Laurie Gibson said. "But then he gives them so much shit when they get questions wrong, they always eventually quit. I don't blame them."

Though bargoers have cherished the

> ## Gause's constant running commentary, bar patrons say, ranks among his most irritating habits. As soon as each question appears, he gives his opinion of its difficulty level, snorting derisively and saying "Eeeasy" for simple questions.

---

few times Gause has lost, cheering wildly and mobbing the winning team, he is even more unbearable in defeat.

"For, like, an hour after he loses, everyone has to hear this big litany of excuses why he lost: The questions were stupid, he wasn't trying, his console wasn't working... you name it," Baugh said. "Just admit you were beaten fair and square, you stupid, annoying, pompous... trivia dick."

Though Gause's fellow McSorley's patrons used to criticize him only behind his back, they no longer hold their comments until he exits the bar. On Monday, when Gause was once again victorious, a voice from the bar's rear yelled, "Leave and never come back. No one wants you here."

Embarrassed to be the person who first brought Gause to the bar, Lang has attempted to distance himself from his brother-in-law. The last several weeks, Lang has either skipped Trivia Night or sat silently in the back of the bar and avoided him.

"Last week, this group of women started throwing ice cubes at Shawn," Lang said. "When he just ignored it, some guys reached behind the bar and started chucking entire handfuls at him. Finally, Shawn stands up and says, 'I'm so on fire tonight, I could use a cooling-off.' So he takes one of the ice cubes that went down his shirt and pops it in his mouth. I've tried to talk to him, but he's just determined to be a jackass." ✍

Teen Sex Linked To Drugs And Alcohol, Reports Center For Figuring Out Really Obvious Things

BOSTON—A definitive causal relationship exists between drug and alcohol use and teen sex, the Center For Figuring Out Really Obvious Things reported Monday.

The four-year, $3.5 million study, which examined the substance-abuse and sexual habits of more than 2,500 American teens, is regarded as one of the most "no-duh"-inducing in the center's history.

"Our exhaustive research clearly confirms that U.S. youths between the ages of 13 and 18 who drink and/or use drugs are more likely to be sexually active," said Dr. Gerald Eckersley, director of the Boston-based organization. "This may be our most significant finding since the landmark 1978 study that found a link between habitual chocolate consumption and weight gain."

"Our research shows that the inhibition-lowering properties of recreational drugs and alcohol cause those who use them to behave with less restraint, making sex among young people more likely to occur," Eckersley continued. "Gee, I bet you never would've guessed that."

The report went on to state that some teens may actually seek out drugs and alcohol for the express purpose of lowering their inhibitions and facilitating sex—a phenomenon well-known to parents and teens alike for countless generations.

"Teens are not only having sex while drunk or high, but they're also getting drunk or high to *increase their chances* of having sex," Eckersley said. "Interestingly, we found that this

phenomenon also occurs among adults, as well as among every population everywhere in the world that has ever existed since the dawn of time."

To help spread word of its findings,

> ## "Interestingly, we found that this phenomenon also occurs among adults, as well as among every population everywhere in the world that has ever existed since the dawn of time."

---

the Center For Figuring Out Really Obvious Things sent a TelePrompTer-ready press release to more than 400 local TV-news affiliates across the U.S. Along with the press release, the stations received stock video footage of beer displays and teens smoking and drinking at parties.

"As a teaser for newscasters presenting this story, I would recommend, 'Think you know everything about teen sex and alcohol? Think again—a new study is out, and the findings may surprise you. Coming up next,'" Eckersley said. "Although, of course, the findings won't actually surprise you."

Founded in 1959, the Center For Fig-

uring Out Really Obvious Things is among the world's leaders in stating the obvious. Operating under the motto *Lumen Redundas*, or "To Cast The Light Of Knowledge On The Already Well-Known," it has conducted non-groundbreaking research on a wide variety of self-evident phenomena.

Among the center's most notable non-discoveries are the 1974 determination that cars contribute to urban smog, the 1981 conclusion that taking the stairs burns more calories than taking the elevator, and the landmark 1997 finding that infidelity causes friction in marriages.

In spite of the center's sterling reputation, some of its findings, which seemed obvious at the time, are now considered inaccurate. A 1963 study, for example, confirmed that sugar was good for children's health because it gave their "growing bodies the pep and energy they need." Another example is the since-refuted 1972 study finding dairy foods to be "heart-healthy."

Still, Eckersley insisted that the center's research methods are "overwhelmingly reliable."

"I feel confident in the center's ability to determine the validity of virtually any obvious claim," Eckersley said. "It goes without saying, however, that even the best people in any line of study occasionally make mistakes. But even though it goes without saying, we here at the Center For Figuring Out Really Obvious Things are saying it anyway, in a $4.2 million study that will definitively prove this Even-The-Best-People-Sometimes-Make-Mistakes theory." ✍

Little Chelsea Clinton Is All Grown Up And Glamorous!

The Outside Scoop
By Jackie Harvey

Item! Remember **Chelsea Clinton?** Wasn't it nice to have a presidential daughter who wasn't posing for **Playboy** or getting drunk? Instead, she was her own sweet self, full of flowers and sunshine, bringing cheer to everyone she met. Now, she's all grown up and glamorous, thanks to an **expensive European make-over.** It's nice to see Chelsea with her hair straightened sitting next to the likes of **Gwenneth Paltrow** and **Madonna** at Italian fashion shows. Can acting be too far off in her future? Keeping my fingers crossed…

Item! All signs seem to point to **Robert Baretta** killing his wife, but I simply refuse to believe it. After all, he once played **Spanky** in **The Little Rascals.** How could such a cute little boy grow up to be a murderer? By the way, whatever became of Spanky's dog Petey? Anyone?

If **Mike Tyson** still needs a place to box, my **Uncle Vernon** is willing to set up a ring in his bar.

Item! N'Synger **Justin Timbaland** and navel-baring popstress **Brittany Spears** seemed like they had it all—looks, wealth, and abs to die for. And, most importantly, they had each other. But it all came crashing down recently, when Justin told his Punky (his nickname for her) bye-bye-bye. Apparently, he couldn't take the pressure of dating

Item! The Summer Movie Season is coming up, and there's one movie that's on everyone's mind: Austin Powers And The Goldenrod! I'm hoping, really hoping, that he'll say "Oh, behave!" in this one. I love that line!

someone who's in the news all the time. I just wish that once in a while, true love had a chance to survive the harsh glare of the media spotlight.

Not to be tooting **the old Harvey Horn,** but I knew long ago that **The Panic Room** would be an undisputed hit. I only wish I'd mentioned it in my column.

Item! I have a very reliable tip that

Anthony Edwards will be leaving **ER** next season to turn his attention to the big screen. I've loved watching the good **Doctor Green** pay a housecall to my TV every Thursday, but I'm happy to announce that for his first post-*ER* project, he'll make a triumphant return to his role as **Gilbert,** the wise

Item! All signs seem to point to Robert Baretta killing his wife, but I simply refuse to believe it. After all, he once played Spanky in The Little Rascals.

nerd in the **Revenge Of The Nerds** movies. So while *ER* won't be the same, I can't wait for him to star in… big insider info coming up in five… four… three… two… one… **Revenge Of The Nerds V: Extreme Nerds!**

A three-piece suit looks just as good if it's missing any one of the pieces.

In my last column, I mistakenly referred to **The Lord Of The Rings** as **The Lord's Ring.** Boy, did I catch an earful for that one! I got about 100 letters from readers who called me all sorts of wild insults, like "nitwit," "brainless balrog," and "mindless son of an orc." Hey, I'll admit to making a mistake, but you don't have to get so personal! I'm man enough to take the criticism and apologize. There's a first time for everything, after all. I'll just have my **intern Brian** do some fact-checking for me in the future.

Item! The **Summer Movie Season** is coming up, and there's one movie that's on everyone's mind: **Austin Powers And The Goldenrod!** I'm hoping, really hoping, that he'll say "Oh, behave!" in this one. I love that line!

And let's not forget the new **Star Wars** movie! (As if we could!) The hot tip I have is that **George Lucas** pulled out all the stops and used a lot of incredible special effects for this one, including a light-saber battle that will knock your socks off. But, hey, you didn't hear it from me! Shhhhhhh!

Soup weather may have ended last month, but in another month or so, it's going to be high time for some cold soups. Seriously, if you haven't tried a nice chilled gazpacho, you haven't lived.

Item! I just got word that Seattle grunge singer **Curt Kobain** died again! I don't know how this is possi-

Your Horoscope

By Lloyd Schumner Sr.
Retired Machinist and
A.A.P.B.-Certified Astrologer

Aries: (March 21–April 19)
You will be torn between finishing your heating and air-conditioning degree and earning big money right away in the thriving HVAC field.

Taurus: (April 20–May 20)
It might be time to move your family to the inner city to avoid the ever-present dangers of the suburban west side.

Gemini: (May 21–June 21)
Try to resolve your deep-seated issues with your body soon, because you're not going to be in it much longer.

Cancer: (June 22–July 22)
You will experience a late flash of insight when you realize the gentleman actually meant that a man named "Hu" was on first base.

Leo: (July 23–Aug. 22)
A report published in the journal Nature hypothesizes that both genetics and social dynamics are to blame for you being such an asshole.

Virgo: (Aug. 23–Sept. 22)
The controversy over the photo of you meeting Hitler will continue to rage in spite of the scissor cuts, the Scotch tape, and the fact that your half is in color.

Libra: (Sept. 23–Oct. 23)
Disappointment will continue to haunt you in the form of the watery, weak stuff some dare to call "hot" salsa.

Scorpio: (Oct. 24–Nov. 21)
Studies find that nursing-home residents with children are happier and more at peace than those without. In 43 years, you will be a notable exception.

Sagittarius: (Nov. 22–Dec. 21)
Though it's hardly your fault, you'll be despised by children around the world when Santa's desiccated corpse is found stuck in your chimney.

Capricorn: (Dec. 22–Jan. 19)
You will soon come under heavy criticism for the lack of minority representation in your record collection.

Aquarius: (Jan. 20–Feb. 18)
It does not benefit you to continue producing, directing, and starring in your own cooking show years after it last aired.

Pisces: (Feb. 19–March 20)
A Japanese fishing boat will catch you off the Philippine coast this week, astonishing scientists who thought you'd been extinct since the Pleistocene era.

ble, but it's true. Why is the road to musical stardom littered with the bodies of all the greats? **The Big Bopper, Buddy Holly, Jimi Joplin, Jon Lennon, Two-Pack Shaker,** little *Joe C,* and now Kobain again. They are missed, one and all.

Speaking of Joe C-related things, the big news is that Joe C's partner in musical crime, **The Kid Rock,** is getting married to former **Baywatch** babe **Pam Anderson!** The Kid Rock sure is a lucky guy, landing a woman as classy and pretty as her.

Didja know… that The Kid Rock is not only a rapper, he's a wrestler and actor, too? Talk about wearing a lot of different tank-top undershirts!

Another Tax Day has come and gone, and I just barely got it done in time. It's hard to explain to the **IRS** that I need to see movies and get all the latest celebrity magazines as part of my job, so I included a letter explaining my write-offs, along with a couple of my columns. Hopefully, I'll be winning over a few new fans in the tax office.

Well, that wraps it up for another

edition of **The Outside Scoop,** served just the way you like it: Harveystyle. As for me, I've got a few weeks of vacation time coming up, and I'm going to hop in my car and go on a little

Item! I just got word that Seattle grunge singer Curt Kobain died again! I don't know how this is possible.

road trip, driving wherever the old internal compass takes me. As you might guess, I'll probably end up in Hollywood. And if I do, you can be sure I'll tell you all about it in my next column. Then again, I may just spend my time off at home, cleaning up all the junk that's piled up around my house. Either way, one thing's for sure: I'll see you soon… in the balcony of the Outside! ✍

Last Beer In Six Pack Drunk With Plastic Rings Still Attached

see LOCAL page 7C

Friendship Blossoms Into Unrequited Love

see RELATIONSHIPS page 4D

How The Fuck Was Orderly Supposed To Know That Was Lady Bird Johnson

see HEALTH CARE page 11A

STATshot

A look at the numbers that shape your world.

Top Murder Weapons By Income

$0 to $6,000	Brick
$6,000 to $16,000	Barstool
$16,000 to $41,000	Smith & Wesson 9mm pistol
$41,000 to $77,500	Blunt edge of Williams-Sonoma bread maker
$77,500 to $210,000	Collapsible Sharper Image baton
$210,000 to $590,000	Gold brick
$590,000 and up	Doomsday laser

THE ONION • $2.00 US • $3.00 CAN

the ONION®

VOLUME 38 ISSUE 18 — AMERICA'S FINEST NEWS SOURCE™ — 16–22 MAY 2002

John D. And Catherine T. MacArthur Foundation Goes On Wild Endowment Binge

Above: Fanton and Hutton in the midst of their wild endowing spree.

CHICAGO—The John D. and Catherine T. MacArthur Foundation went on a wild endowment binge last weekend, recklessly giving away more than $170 million in grants and fellowships in a 48-hour span.

"We got pretty out of control there with the endowing," said foundation president Jonathon Fanton, icing down his check-writing hand while recovering Monday. "It started Friday afternoon, when [Vice-President and Chief Financial Officer] Lyn [Hutton] suggested we give a grant to the Foundation for Urban Renewal for their tireless efforts to rebuild America's struggling inner cities. Then, [Treasurer] Marc [Yanchura] said Save Our Cities was doing even better work, so we threw them on the pile, too. Things kind of snowballed from there, and by 4 a.m., we'd given $81 million in grants to 16 different groups. I think we even gave a few million to [rival philanthropic organization] Pew Charitable Trusts."

After a brief pause Saturday afternoon, the endowing resumed. The generous support of nonprofit activi-
see BINGE page 142

U.S. Protests Mexi-Canadian Overpass

WASHINGTON, DC—After nearly nine years of construction, the Mexi-Canadian Overpass, the controversial $4.3 trillion highway overpass linking Guadalupe and Winnipeg, was finally completed last week, drawing harsh criticism from U.S. citizens and officials alike.

"If you're a Mexican who regularly see OVERPASS page 143

The New Overpass
CANADA
Winnipeg
MC-1
U.S.A.
Guadalupe
MEXICO

Above: Chrétien and Fox at the official unveiling.

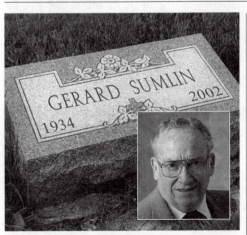

Above: The grave of Gerard Sumlin (inset), who asked that his children do this whole big pain-in-the-ass lilac-planting job.

Father's Dying Wish A Real Hassle

HARRISON, TN—The last wish of Gerard Sumlin, who died last month at 68, is "a real pain in the ass," his children reported Monday.

"On his deathbed, Dad asked us to make sure there were always beautiful lilac bushes on the side of his sister Helen's house," said daughter Monica Torres, 42. "We were all crying and swore we would. But I guess we weren't really thinking about what a huge hassle it would be."

Added Torres: "I don't know anything about planting lilacs. What if we do it wrong, and they die? Then we'd have to do the whole thing again next year. Why couldn't he have just asked for us to spread his ashes in his favorite park or something?"

Sumlin made the request see WISH page 142

139

Rise Of The Far Right In Europe

From France to Austria to the Netherlands, ultra-nationalist, far-right political parties hostile to immigration are making gains throughout Europe. What do *you* think?

"Who cares if a bunch of fjord-niggers wanna go all fascist? We can take 'em."

Chris Winfield
Plumber

"If everyone has food on the table and the trains run on time, maybe it's worth the occasional mile-deep pit of innocent civilians."

Dan Eichelberger
Systems Analyst

"Darling, I just returned from Fascism Week in Milan, and I dare say floral prints are back with a cold, steel vengeance this year."

Eileen Tenace
Buyer

"Imagine how awful it would be if there were a resurgence of anti-Semitism in Europe. It'd be just like the last 2,000 years all over again."

Laurie Almon
Architect

"I thought France already was fascist. The French guy at the coffee shop sure is."

Paul Bevacqua
Cab Driver

"Just keep your eye on them shifty-looking Luxembourgers. They're just waiting for the rest of the world to blink."

Raymond Fingers
Civil Engineer

Star Wars Mania

Star Wars: Episode II—Attack Of The Clones finally hits theaters this Thursday. Among the plot details that have been leaked:

- First 100 minutes of film nothing but moisture farming
- Yoda hit by train
- Brief but crucial scene explains why Wookiees have rejected pants
- More of that inimitable brand of George Lucas comical hijinks that audiences have come to know and tolerate
- Obi-Wan delivers urgent message, "They're using a jazz guitarist named Django Reinhardt to create a clone army."
- Dull set-up of *Episode I* gives way to meat of story, in which we finally learn where Walrus Man came from and how he became a surly drunk
- Characters given hilarious parodic names like "Yogurt" and "Pizza The Hut"
- Boy meets girl, lightsaber fight, boy loses girl, space-vehicle chase, boy gets girl back, climactic battle won by pseudoreligious *deus ex machina*

---

the ONION®
America's Finest News Source.™

Herman Ulysses Zweibel
Founder

T. Herman Zweibel
Publisher Emeritus
J. Phineas Zweibel
Publisher
Maxwell Prescott Zweibel
Editor-In-Chief

Burglary Is The Sincerest Form Of Flattery

By Joseph Paltz
Twice-Convicted Felon

Judging from the look on your face, I'm guessing you're offended. But please don't take my presence here in your home as a personal affront. When I sneaked into your home under cover of darkness after disarming your security system, feeding the guard dogs a sedative, and climbing to the second-story window with a grappling hook and rope, I never intended to insult you. In fact, my intention was just the opposite. I mean, what is burglary, after all, if not the sincerest form of flattery?

Clearly, you're upset. When you came down to the kitchen in your pajamas and bathrobe, you obviously didn't expect to find some stranger with a flashlight packing your wedding silverware into a small satchel. To be perfectly honest, I didn't expect to see you, either. I figured you'd be fast asleep at 3 a.m., not heading down the stairs for a snack. But regardless of what you may think of me, I want you to know that I hold you and your taste in jewelry and home furnishings in the absolute highest regard.

From the way you're reaching for the phone to call the police, I can only assume you think I bear you ill will. Before you do something we'll both regret, let me assure you that nothing could be further from the truth. I have looked up to you for quite some time and am a great fan, not only of yourself, but also of the many fine material possessions you have amassed in your beautifully appointed home.

> **Can't you see I only want to be as much like you as I possibly can within the limits of my low social bearing and ability to sidestep the law?**

If only you could see things from my perspective, you'd realize how much I admire you. When I look at you, I don't think, "Here's a rich guy I can rob blind," but rather, "Here is a man of substance, a man who owns the things I would love to own myself." You are the man I wish I could be, a man who enjoys and appreciates life's finer things, a man of means with many desirable valuables.

What higher compliment can I pay a man and his fine taste in material possessions than to case his private estate for two weeks, carefully observing the comings and goings of local police patrols and scouring the home's perimeter for possible security weaknesses? Can't you see what a great muse you and your various luxury items have been to this poor, unworthy admirer? If I thought any less of you, would I want your belongings badly enough to risk arrest and possible incarceration in a penal institution? I think not.

> **From the way you're reaching for the phone to call the police, I can only assume you think I bear you ill will.**

It is a difficult undertaking, burglary—the constant stress, the endless waiting, the ever-present need to remain one step ahead of the law. But don't you see, my friend? You are worth it! Only a home such as yours, a home chock-full of the most precious items money can buy, would warrant such effort. Consider yourself a man on the receiving end of a true compliment, one from the heart.

How I wish, instead of stealing away into the night with your things slung over my back, I could stay here and live the life of a man of means. But, alas, I cannot. You, to say nothing of the state and federal authorities, would never permit it. So these mere trinkets, your possessions, will have to suffice in pale imitation. Though I can never be you, I take some solace in the knowledge that I can surround myself with the objects you keep in your house, once I have transferred them to my own admittedly more modest domicile.

Why punish me when I have paid the greatest possible tribute to you? Can't you see I only want to be as much like you as I possibly can within the limits of my low social bearing and ability to sidestep the law? Don't you understand that I am, in fact, your biggest fan, and would never do something so low as to hit you over the head with a length of pipe, heretofore concealed on my person, in a cowardly sneak attack?

Sorry about that nasty bump on the head. But that, too, was a form of flattery. If I didn't have the utmost respect for your physical prowess, I wouldn't

see FLATTERY page 143

Area Man Criticizes Hazelnut Coffee, Volvos, New Mexico's Flag In Two-Minute Span

ST. PAUL, MN—In a span of two minutes Monday, 33-year-old St. Paul resident Daniel Devore managed to criticize hazelnut coffee, Volvos, and the flag of New Mexico.

The 120-second rant took place at Caribou Coffee in the presence of longtime friend Meredith Caranza, 31.

"Hazelnut?" said Devore as he browsed the establishment's menu. "That's coffee for people that don't like coffee but want to pretend they do. It's like drinking a candy bar. Why not just drink a glass of Nestlé Quik instead?"

"I remember thinking 'Uh-oh,'" Caranza said. "We hadn't even placed our order yet, and he was already on a roll."

Devore's criticism of hazelnut coffee continued for another 35 seconds, at which point he mysteriously transitioned to the subject of Volvos.

"You know what I can't stand is Volvos. They're, like, the most selfish car to own, but the people who drive them act like they're being all earth-conscious and socially responsible," Devore said. "What's so responsible about owning some boxy tank that'll fuck up every other car in the accident while you don't get a scratch?"

Caranza said she was mystified by the Volvo tirade.

"I have no idea what brought that on," Caranza said. "I looked out the window, scanned the paper, checked the stuff on the table, and couldn't find a single thing related to Volvos. He was obviously following some bizarre train of thought in his head."

Seconds after his Volvo diatribe died down, Devore spotted a store patron with a New Mexico flag on his backpack. He quickly shifted gears to the iron-on patch.

"Of all the 50 state flags, that has to be the stupidest one," Devore said. "It's just this bright-yellow field with, like, this bright-red crosshairs target in the middle. I suppose it's fitting, though. Gives all those desert loners and crackpots something to take aim at."

Added Devore: "Pretty much all of the state flags are lame. The only decent one is Maryland."

Devore has a long history of adopting seemingly arbitrary stances on a wide variety of subjects. In the past, he has taken aim at such diverse targets as *Terry And The Pirates* creator Milton Caniff, box springs, Stevie Nicks, tip jars, the History Channel, and carbonated water.

Prior to Monday, however, Devore had never railed against three subjects in so short a period of time.

> **Devore's criticism of hazelnut coffee continued for another 35 seconds, at which point he mysteriously transitioned to the subject of Volvos.**

"I've seen him spend 15 minutes talking about how stupid daylight savings time is," Caranza said. "He takes major issue with things most people don't care about enough to think about, much less form an opinion on. But even by his standards, the hazelnut, Volvo, New Mexico flag thing was pretty remarkable."

In spite of Devore's penchant for hyper-criticism, his friends still enjoy his company much of the time.

Above: Devore ponders his next criticism.

"Sometimes, Dan will go on some hilarious 20-minute tirade about how much he hates Bob Costas, and you'll be in stitches," former roommate Ron Bleier said. "Those are the good times."

"He's really smart," Bleier continued, "and he'll occasionally have something interesting and illuminating to say on a subject you never really gave much thought. But mostly he just likes bitching." ∅

NEWS IN BRIEF

Producer Wants To Call Movie *Crime And Punishment* Anyway

LOS ANGELES—Upon learning that the title has already been taken, Hollywood producer Andrew Shuler announced Monday that he wants to call his upcoming Universal Pictures police thriller *Crime And Punishment* anyway. "There is?" said Shuler, moments after being told of the classic Fyodor Dostoyevsky novel that shares its name with his upcoming Val Kilmer-Wesley Snipes vehicle. "I don't really see that as a problem. What 18- to 34-year-old has ever heard of that?" Shuler said he is confident he will be able to "buy out this Russian guy."

Latest News Of Israeli-Palestinian Violence Makes Man Hungry For Falafel

PISCATAWAY, NJ—A CNN report on a suicide bombing in Tel Aviv put Piscataway resident Larry Zahn in the mood for a falafel sandwich Monday. "Oh, man, I could go for some falafel right about now," said Zahn, 41, watching footage of injured Israelis being loaded onto ambulances. "A big pita stuffed with falafel, hummus, lettuce, and lots of tahini sauce. And some dolmades on the side. Yeah." In January 2001, a CNN report on an Indian earthquake that killed 2,000 gave Zahn an intense craving for chicken biryani.

Routine, Affordable Medical Procedure Put Off Another Year

WEBSTER GROVES, MO—Three years after being diagnosed with a benign rectal polyp, Webster Groves resident William Schraft continues to put off its removal, insisting that there is no need to undergo the routine, affordable procedure right this minute. "The doctor said it was benign, so what's the big rush?" the 54-year-old Schraft said Monday. "I can barely feel it most days anyway. It's probably shrinking."

Woman Forced To Converse Awkwardly With Bank-Promotion Clown

AUGUSTA, ME—While waiting to meet with a Kennebec Savings Bank mortgage officer Monday, Danielle Smales, 34, was forced to make stilted conversation with Thrifty The Banking Clown. "Just waiting for a meeting," Smales told the brochure-wielding promotional clown. "No, thanks. I don't really need Platinum checking." Though Smales managed to briefly steer the conversation toward the weather, a majority of the eight-minute chat centered on the importance of a sensible IRA, the convenience of online banking at KennebecSavings.com, and the great introductory rates available with a Kennebec Savings Visa card.

Christian Weightlifter Bends Iron Bar To Show Power Of God's Love

TULSA, OK—Before 11,000 attendees at a "He Is Risen Rally" at Mabee Center, Christian weightlifter Michael Brighton bent a two-inch-thick iron bar Monday, clearly demonstrating the power of God's love within the heart and body of His followers. "Do you see the power of faith and belief?" said the 255-pound Brighton following the impressive feat of spiritual prowess. "Only a strong personal relationship with my Creator could have made this possible." Brighton went on to demonstrate God's hatred of ice blocks and wooden boards. ∅

on April 13, upon being admitted to St. Peter's Hospital in Chattanooga after suffering a massive heart attack. His children were only able to spend a few moments with him before he died.

"Dad wasn't very lucid because of all the drugs," said son David Sumlin, 39. "At one point, he grabbed my hand and made me promise that Monica and I would plant the lilacs. In the moment, it seemed like a small request, but now that we actually have to follow through on it, that's a whole other story."

According to David, Sumlin was once extremely close to his sister

> "At one point, he grabbed my hand and made me promise that Monica and I would plant the lilacs. In the moment, it seemed like a small request, but now that we actually have to follow through on it, that's a whole other story."

Helen. As children, the siblings used to spend a lot of time playing under the family's lilac bush. However, a bitter fight over family finances drove the two apart as young adults, and they never reconciled.

"I understand Dad wanting to plant the lilacs as a gesture of peace toward Aunt Helen," Torres said. "It just sucks that David and I have to do all the work. Dad's not going to have to slave outside in the hot sun and get his hands dirty, but he gets to die with

Above: Monica Torres and David Sumlin grudgingly browse the lilac bushes at J&C Nursery in Harrison.

a clean conscience. Sounds like a win-win situation for him."

At the time of their father's death, David and Monica said they would be "more than happy" to plant the lilacs, but time and reflection on the work involved have changed their stance.

"You don't think about those things when your father is on his deathbed, but I don't know if I can afford to throw away an entire Saturday on this," David said. "I've had to work the last three weekends at the office, so my wife isn't exactly thrilled about the idea of me spending my first Saturday off in a month planting flowers for some woman I barely know."

Neither David nor Monica has ever had any real contact with Aunt Helen, making the lilac-planting, slated for this weekend, an awkward one.

"I remember Mom pointed her out at Cousin Henry's funeral 20 years ago," David said. "It's kind of weird, not really knowing this woman at all and then calling her up and saying, 'Your estranged brother is dead; when can we bring over this bush?' Couldn't we just donate money to some charity in Dad's name instead?"

The request, Monica said, would have been easier to take had the preparations for her father's funeral not already taken up so much of her time.

"I had to take three days off from work just to get the funeral arranged," she said. "There was the notice of death for the newspaper, the insurance, picking out a casket, coordinating an after-funeral gathering, getting

a church and organist, talking to the Army because Dad's a veteran, and so on. I'm just getting over all the shit I had to do for the funeral, and now I have to deal with this."

Dreading the lilac-bush planting, David said he will be happy when his final-request-fulfilling days are over.

"Monica and I have already made a pact not to do this to each other on our deathbeds," David said. "It's tough enough losing a loved one without also losing an entire day trying to find a garden center that sells the right kind of lilac bush and then having to haul the damn thing out to some strange woman's house way the hell out in McMinnville. That's not a dying wish, that's a dying chore." ∅

ties in the arts and culture, education, the environment, health and human services, and public policy continued deep into the night.

"Saturday, around 3 p.m., we all went out for breakfast. Over eggs and Bloody Marys, we talked about the night before and how crazy we'd gotten," Fanton said. "But when the sun went down that night, we started right back up again with the endowing. Mostly to public radio networks under the General Program, but also 20 or 30 theater companies and a shit-load of PBS fellowships. Half the people who've ever appeared on *Sesame Street* are MacArthur Fellows now."

While the bulk of the money went to groups falling under the foundation's Program on Human and Community Development, a considerable portion went to less noble causes, including the *3-2-1 Contact* Preservation Society and the Recumbent Bicycling Hall Of Fame.

"At the time, it felt like the right thing to do," Fanton said of the binge. "It wasn't until we woke up Sunday

> Fanton pledged that the foundation's Board of Directors would seek endowment counseling and join a philanthropy-addiction support group.

morning that we were like, 'Holy shit... how much did we endow this weekend?'"

According to Vice-Chairman Elizabeth McCormack, the endowment

binge is a result of the foundation's low self-esteem.

"It seems like the only time we feel good is when we're awarding endowments," McCormack said. "The pain and pressures of the outside world vanish, and it's as though you and the beneficiary are all that exist. That's a tough high to come down from. Deep down, we knew it was reckless, but we kept making rationalizations like, 'Well, the Program on Global Security and Sustainability is of heightened importance during this crossroads moment in world history.'"

McCormack's concern was echoed by experts in the field of grant-writing.

"When the stress of operating a charitable foundation gets to be too much, the urge to endow often takes control, overriding all logic and common sense," said Martin Wingreen, author of *Giving Their All: The Secret Shame Of Compulsive Philanthropy*. "Under the sway of such an intense

sensation, the grant giver just can't resist funding every non-profit in sight."

Acknowledging that his group "has a problem," Fanton pledged that the foundation's Board of Directors would seek endowment counseling and join a philanthropy-addiction support group.

"After hearing about our endowment binge, the chair of the Andrew W. Mellon Foundation gave me a really encouraging phone call, saying they'd gone through the same thing in the '80s," Fanton said. "He said they eventually learned not just to think about world betterment, but also to take time for themselves, and that was their turning point. Now, they're a solvent and robust organization again. I really needed to hear that."

"As a charitable foundation, we can do a lot of good in the world," Fanton added. "We just need to make sure not to do too much good at once." ∅

commutes to Canada, or vice-versa, this is great. But what about all of us poor Americans caught in the middle?" said Dallas resident Tom Hitchner, one of an estimated 850,000 U.S. citizens forced to evacuate their homes to make room for concrete supports for the 1,600-mile, 18-lane overpass. "For Mexico and Canada to do this without any concern for all the

> "We thought it would be easier to facilitate cultural and economic exchange if the hassle of driving through the U.S. was eliminated," said Mexican president Vicente Fox, downing a shot of Labatts tequila, a new product from the Canadian brewer.

Americans whose lives this affects, well, the arrogance is just unbelievable."

"We just recently installed beautiful picture windows in our home," said Fargo, ND, resident Judy Renata, whose house is situated beneath the overpass. "Now, instead of sunlight, we have to look at that monstrosity. We'd sell our place and move elsewhere, but property values have plummeted. I don't know what we're going to do."

In addition to facilitating trade between Mexico and Canada, the overpass is expected to increase tourism in both nations by as much as 60 percent. Boasting hundreds of restaurants, gas stations, and hotels, the state-of-the-art overpass will render it unnecessary for Mexicans or Canadians ever to touch U.S. soil when traveling to and from their respective homelands.

"It would be one thing if we somehow benefited," said Junction City, KS, business owner Neil Grandy. "But because of the way stations, we don't get anything out of it and have to deal with people tossing garbage out of their windows at 80 mph. You wouldn't believe what we've found some mornings. Everything from tamale husks to broken hockey sticks. The people on that bridge are animals."

Americans' hostility toward the overpass only intensified when it officially opened to traffic Monday.

"The noise and dirt of the construction was one thing," said San Antonio, TX, resident Floyd Paymer. "But now, with all the traffic, it's just unbearable. The honking, the chickens, the sound of thousands of cars going back and forth to Canada and Mexico

Above: The Mexi-Canadian Overpass looms over a barn in Pawhuska, OK.

is more than I can take. I can hear those goddamn radios blaring Mariachi music and Rush all day and night."

In spite of the public uproar, U.S. leaders say they are helpless to do anything to stop the international project.

"I called up the governments of Canada and Mexico, and, after a lot of runaround, I was informed that the overpass was 'regrettable but necessary,'" Secretary of State Colin Powell said. "We have a petition circulating in the affected areas of the U.S., but since the overpass is already complete, I doubt it will do much good."

The overpass is expected to significantly strengthen Mexican-Canadian relations.

"We thought it would be easier to facilitate cultural and economic exchange if the hassle of driving through the U.S. was eliminated," said Mexican president Vicente Fox, downing a shot of Labatts tequila, a new product from the Canadian brewer. "After we started discussing the overpass, it didn't make sense not to do it. Now that it's finished, I can't believe we didn't think of it years ago."

U.S. opposition to the overpass began even before construction began in the summer of 1993. Protests have ranged from thousands of residents linking arm-in-arm in front of bulldozers on both borders to a strongly worded 2001 condemnation from President Bush.

Bush later reconsidered after meeting with Fox and Canadian prime minister Jean Chrétien.

"I don't know what happened in that meeting," Vice-President Dick Cheney said. "One moment, George is talking about throwing everything we've got at Canada and Mexico. The next thing you know, he's walking out of the meeting, muttering something about how it looks like we're just going to have to get used to the idea."

Fox said the damage to relations with the U.S. is "lamentable" but "inconsequential when compared to the benefits."

"The Mexi-Canadian Overpass is not merely a bridge made of concrete and steel, but a metaphorical bridge bringing our two great nations together," Fox said. "At long last, the people of Canada and Mexico can finally begin to forge the sort of friendship and understanding that was impossible as long as the U.S. stood between us. This is the dawn of a wondrous new era for the people of Canada and Mexico." ∅

FLATTERY from page 140

have gone to the effort of knocking you out, let alone taken the time to strap your unconscious body securely to that chair with packing tape. Only someone I regarded as a genuine superior in the strength department would need to be immobilized in such a manner.

Nice safe behind the painting, by the way. Really top-notch. Like everything else you own, it is of the highest quality. I would never have been able to get inside if you didn't have the combination written on the bottom of the second shelf of that bookcase over there. I am only sorry I cannot take the safe itself. That is how high the esteem in which I hold it—and, by extension, you.

Thank you. It has been an absolute

privilege to meet you. This is not empty flattery, mind you. Anyone could say, "What fantastic and expensive items you have! Oh, how I wish they were mine!" But I have proven my sincerity by going that extra mile and actually robbing you. I can only hope that in time, I will become half the man you are. Or, if not, then at least burgle household goods totaling half the value of the holdings you so admirably possess. Or used to, before I took them.

Don't think of what I've done as theft. I would much prefer you view it as an homage. My hat is off to you, fine sir! You are truly a man among men!

Please, don't get up. I'll let myself out. ∅

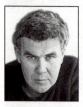

Ask Raymond Carver

By Raymond Carver

Dear Raymond Carver,

Yesterday, while on the phone with a friend, I mentioned that I'd phoned her the day before. She told me she knew I'd called, saying that she saw it on her caller ID box but didn't pick up the phone. I think that's downright rude! Do I have a right to be miffed?

Ignored In Ishpeming

Dear Ignored,

Pam and I spent the day down at the old speedway. She was reading the paper and saw there was a flea market there all weekend. She said, "Let's go, maybe we'll find a cheap lawnmower or some end tables." We both had Sunday off, so we went. The vendors come from who-knows-where and set up their tables right there in the middle of the racetrack. There were old campers and trucks parked all around the track. I asked Pam which one she thought would come in first. She laughed and grabbed my arm. She likes when we get out of the house together. It puts her in a good mood. It was hot. We drank out of red plastic cups I'd picked up when we'd stopped for gas. Pam always drank her whiskey with water, but I didn't bother with that. I'd take my time finding Pam in the crowd, and by then what she had was whiskey and water anyway. I could have put the bottle in the trunk with the cooler, but I didn't. It felt good to sit down in the car for a few minutes, my legs hanging out of the open door. I smoked a cigarette. I knew Pam wouldn't be worried about where I was. I lit another cigarette and scratched a circle in the gravel with my toe.

Dear Raymond Carver,

My husband simply refuses to turn off the TV when we sit down to eat! I think mealtime should be a family affair, but he won't listen. As the kids get older, it's often the only time we spend together as a family, and I don't want to have to compete with some game show. A friend suggested I stop slaving over my legendary casseroles and home-baked desserts and just serve TV dinners until my husband gets the hint. What do you think of that idea?

Perturbed In Pike Creek

Dear Perturbed,

Instead of cutting across the grass, I walked the long way, around the track. Everything was bright and the track was soft from the heat. I found Pam in front of a long table of old books. She stared hard at a row of old hardcovers and ran her finger along the spines. She leaned in to look at the next row and ran her finger along those, too. Then she stepped a few feet

> I found Pam talking to an old woman over a box of old postcards. I handed Pam her cup. She said, "Thanks, hon," and smiled at me. She and the old woman were talking about Florida. Pam had lived in Florida after her parents split up the second time. My face felt hot.

to the right and repeated the whole thing. Once or twice, she put her hand up to her mouth as if she was thinking hard about one of the books. What she was trying to remember, I had no idea. Besides her *Calorie Counter* and *Guide To Flowering Perennials*, the only books Pam has at home are the three nursing textbooks someone at work gave her. Pam is a nurses' aide. When people ask her how that is different from being a nurse, Pam always says it means she does twice the work and gets half the pay. She wants to go to night school, if we can ever get caught up on the bills. Right now, she works at the old folks' home putting diapers on the crazies. That's what they call them, but only when they are not around. Pam says she and the other nurses' aides have to do something to release tension. She says the old drunks are the worst. "They're mean," she says. Once, Pam and I were talking about how maybe we should give up drinking altogether. Pam said, "I don't want to end up a mean old drunk. Just kill me if I end up like that."

Dear Raymond Carver,

My next-door neighbors tend to stay up extremely late, sometimes until 1 or even 2 a.m. When the weather's nice, they like to entertain friends out-

---

Your Horoscope

By Lloyd Schumner Sr.
Retired Machinist and
A.A.P.B.-Certified Astrologer

Aries: (March 21–April 19)
Your desire for a belt of human nipples wanes when you are told where human nipples come from.

Taurus: (April 20–May 20)
If it makes you feel any better, red to you is not red to everyone else. Other people's red is slightly deeper and more tasteful.

Gemini: (May 21–June 21)
You've never asked for much out of life, but you have every reason to be disappointed anyway.

Cancer: (June 22–July 22)
An unexpected career change will give you cause to look back fondly on the days when you had no idea who made fat-granny pornography.

Leo: (July 23–Aug. 22)
Most people believe they're the star of their own story, but you're actually a supporting character in the story of that guy Dave in the design department.

Virgo: (Aug. 23–Sept. 22)
Everyone wants to live forever, but in your case it would just mean more time being chased by an angry swarm of bees.

Libra: (Sept. 23–Oct. 23)
You're not actually the lost prince of a world within our own, forced to hide among the surface dwellers to protect yourself from your vengeful uncle. But thinking that may help you somewhat.

Scorpio: (Oct. 24–Nov. 21)
The age-old war between the sexes will come to an end next week when you unleash your nuclear sex bomb.

Sagittarius: (Nov. 22–Dec. 21)
If you think happy endings are superficial and unrealistic, you should be pleased with the way it all wraps up next Thursday.

Capricorn: (Dec. 22–Jan. 19)
The wonder is not how well the bear dances, but that it can dance at all. Still, the bear dances a hell of a lot better than you do.

Aquarius: (Jan. 20–Feb. 18)
You will devise a scheme that guarantees worldwide peace and prosperity, but it turns out to be unmarketable.

Pisces: (Feb. 19–March 20)
Lord knows you've tried, but you still can't understand how one person could watch all the high-quality TV they offer.

---

side on their deck until all hours, and it can get pretty loud. I don't want to take away their right to enjoy themselves, but voices carry (and keep me tossing and turning in bed). What should I do?

Light Sleeper In Louisville

Dear Light Sleeper,

I found Pam talking to an old woman over a box of old postcards. I handed Pam her cup. She said, "Thanks, hon," and smiled at me. She and the old woman were talking about Florida. Pam had lived in Florida after her parents split up the second time. My face felt hot. I tried to remember if I had eaten anything that day. I noticed a sign propped up on the table: "Jerry's Resale: Antiques & Collectibles." I looked over at Jerry. He was helping a fat man with a beard put a huge blue glass jar in a paper bag. The fat man looked excited, like he'd really hit the jackpot by finding that big blue jar. He handed Jerry some money. Most of the other vendors had gray cash boxes, like they use at high-school basketball games. Not Jerry, though. He just pulled out his wallet, put the

bill in, and took out some change. The wallet was so thick it didn't even close. Somehow, Jerry stuck the fat wallet back in his pants pocket. Then he sat down on his folding chair and went back to staring off across the track. As he sat, he leaned over to one side, resting all his weight on the hip with no wallet. For a long time, I watched him sitting there, leaning all the way to one side like that. Finally, I couldn't stand it anymore. I found Pam, still talking about Florida. On the way to the car I told her about the wallet. Pam said, "Don't be too impressed. I used to waitress, so I know what a stack of ones and fives looks like. It looks like a heck of a lot more than it is." I tried to explain that the money wasn't the point. She laughed and gave me a squeeze. "Let me drive home," she said. "You've had too many." In the car, I leaned back and closed my eyes. I was happy to be going.

Raymond Carver is a syndicated columnist whose weekly advice column, Ask Raymond Carver, *appears in more than 250 newspapers nationwide.* ∅

Ancient Melanesian Masks Thundered Past To Get To *Star Wars* Exhibit

see MUSEUMS page 10D

Detroit Burned Down For The Insurance Money

see NATION page 5A

Cartoon Prisoner Stands Holding Bars All Day

see LOCAL page 3C

Guy Upstairs Discovers Ska

see LOCAL page 6C

STATshot

A look at the numbers that shape your world.

How Have We Brought Shame To Our Grandparents?

1. Launched Watchmygrandparentsfuck.com
2. Quit the seminary
3. Adopted immodest Western-style dress
4. Started hanging around with ethnic kids
5. Slept with Mildred in 204B
6. Acquired own worldview

THE ONION • $2.00 US • $3.00 CAN

---

the ONION®

VOLUME 38 ISSUE 19   AMERICA'S FINEST NEWS SOURCE™   23–29 MAY 2002

Pope Forgives Molested Children

VATICAN CITY—Calling forgiveness "one of the highest virtues taught to us by Jesus," Pope John Paul II issued a papal decree Monday absolv-

"Our Lord teaches us to turn the other cheek and forgive those who sin against us."

ing priest-molested children of all sin.

"Though grave and terrible sins have been committed, our Lord teaches us to turn the other cheek and forgive those who sin against us," said the pope, reading a prepared statement from a balcony overlooking St. Peter's Square. "That is why, despite the terrible wrongs they have committed, the

see POPE page 148

Handlers Desperate To Prevent Tara Reid Political Awakening

LOS ANGELES—Tara Reid's agent, publicist, and other members of her management team are working feverishly to avert a potential political

Above: Tara Reid

awakening in the 26-year-old actress, sources reported Tuesday.

"Thus far, Tara has been blissfully oblivious to world affairs," said Rick Stein, Reid's agent at International Creative Management. "But we must remain ever-vigilant of the possibility that, as her star continues to rise, she will develop a political consciousness like so many others in Hollywood."

"As bad as she is, could you imagine if, during an interview for a new movie, she started going off on saving the animals or ending world hunger or something?" Stein said. "So long as she's my client, I will do everything in my power to ensure that this never happens."

The star of such films as *American Pie, Josie And The Pussycats*, and *National Lampoon's Van Wilder*, Reid is a fixture on the L.A. party circuit.

see REID page 149

Factual Error Found On Internet

LONGMONT, CO—The Information Age was dealt a stunning blow Monday, when a factual error was discovered on the Internet. The error was found on TedsUltimate-BradyBunch.com, a *Brady Bunch* fan site that incorrectly listed the show's debut year as 1968, not 1969.

Caryn Wisniewski, a Pueblo, CO, legal secretary and diehard *Brady Bunch* fan, came across the mistake while searching for information about the show's first-season cast.

"When I first saw 1968 on the web page, I thought, 'Wow, apparently, all those *Brady Bunch* books I've read listing 1969 as the show's first year were wrong,'" Wisniewski told reporters at a press conference. "But even though I obviously trusted the Internet, I was still kind of puzzled. So I checked other *Brady Bunch* fan sites, and all of them said 1969. After a while, it slowly began to sink in that the World Wide Web might be tainted with unreliable information."

Following up on her suspicion, Wisniewski phoned her public library, the ABC television network, and the office of *Brady Bunch* producer Sherwood Schwartz—all of whom confirmed that "Ted's Ultimate *Brady Bunch* Site" was in error.

Above: The shocking error.

Attempts to contact the webmaster of "Ted's Ultimate *Brady Bunch* Site," identified as Ted Crewes of Naugatuck, CT, were unsuccessful. The page has been taken offline by its host, Cheaphost.net, which released a statement Tuesday.

"We at Cheaphost were deeply saddened and disturbed to learn that one of the millions of pages we

see INTERNET page 149

What Did Bush Know Before 9/11?

Last week, a report revealed that President Bush was briefed on the possibility of terrorist hijackings several weeks before Sept. 11. What do *you* think?

"Of course the U.S. had prior warning. Flying a plane into a building requires a permit that has to be applied for months in advance."

Don Dawson
Carpet Installer

"If Bush had gotten all panicked about the warning, the terrorists would have already won."

Melanie Parrish
Psychologist

"In a post-Sept. 11 world, this pre-Sept. 11 information is chilling."

Thomas Carter
Systems Analyst

"I told everyone that something bad would happen to America in 2001. I even said the letter 'A' would be involved. But did they listen?"

Jill Cromartie
Caterer

"As a regional FBI director, I want to assure the American people that tracking down potential terrorists is really, really hard."

Bob Gullickson
FBI Agent

"Whoa. Back up. Now, what happened on Sept. 11?"

Kenneth LeFlore
Electrician

Rolling Stones Hit The Road

The Rolling Stones recently announced plans for a 40th-anniversary tour, starting in September. What can fans expect?

- Echoing Altamont, desperate Mick Jagger pleads with crowd to turn off pagers and cell phones
- Jan Wenner masturbates self raw and dry with chin resting on stage
- Select shows taped for upcoming live album *Sucking In The Seventies, Eighties, Nineties, and Aughts*
- Angry fans storm stage when band fails to play 1986 hit "Harlem Shuffle"
- Souvenir stand offers $175 "Rolling Stone-washed" chinos
- On tour jet, Mick and Keith vigorously debate playing "Satisfaction"
- Band finally releases findings of 30-year research study on how come brown sugar tastes so good
- Mitch Caplan, COO/president of tour sponsor E*Trade, bitterly complains about fifth-row seats
- Fans mechanically attend, force selves to enjoy event, report back to coworkers that Stones "still have it"

the ONION®
America's Finest News Source.™

Herman Ulysses Zweibel
Founder

T. Herman Zweibel
Publisher Emeritus
J. Phineas Zweibel
Publisher
Maxwell Prescott Zweibel
Editor-In-Chief

I Know What I Should've Told That Judge

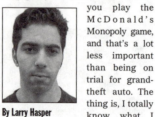

By Larry Hasper

Oh, man, is it too late to get a retrial? Because I'm sure I could think of something better to say this time. They give you a second chance when you play the McDonald's Monopoly game, and that's a lot less important than being on trial for grand-theft auto. The thing is, I totally know what I should've told the judge.

Blame it on first-time jitters. Hey, I was facing five to ten years in jail. You try coming up with a convincing story under that kind of pressure.

Anyway, what I should have told the judge was that, in the dark parking lot, that guy's Porsche looked a lot

> Blame it on first-time jitters. Hey, I was facing five to ten years in jail. You try coming up with a convincing story under that kind of pressure.

like my '91 Dodge Daytona. Sure, if it were daytime, the two probably wouldn't look at all alike. But under cover of darkness, there really was no way to know I was getting into the wrong car. Especially considering the fact that mine was parked less than 20 spots away. With a little more trial experience under my belt, I think I could've made the judge buy that honest mix-up.

I also should've told the judge that I led the cops on a high-speed chase through three counties because I

> Sure, if it were daytime, the two probably wouldn't look at all alike. But under cover of darkness, there really was no way to know I was getting into the wrong car.

recently read somewhere that thugs have been putting police lights on the top of their cars, then pulling people over and robbing them. If they asked me where I read it, I could've said I

> And it probably wasn't the brightest idea to keep bringing up how old the judge was. Like when, during sentencing, the judge said I needed to learn a lesson and was a danger to society, I shouldn't have called him a shriveled cocksucker. He really seemed sensitive about that.

forgot. It would have been a lot better than telling the judge I wouldn't pull over because of all the police brutality I've seen on TV. Given another go, I definitely wouldn't say that again.

And it probably wasn't the brightest idea to keep bringing up how old the judge was. Like when, during sentencing, the judge said I needed to learn a lesson and was a danger to society, I shouldn't have called him a shriveled cocksucker. He really seemed sensitive about that. That might've tacked a few extra years onto my sentence.

My lawyer tried to get sympathy from the court by trying to play off what I did as a youthful indiscretion—a joyriding 24-year-old with no previous record, out for a good time. But I forgot to tell my lawyer that when the cops pulled me over and asked where I was going in such a hurry, I was so drunk I said, "To the chop shop to make some easy money." I guess that detail temporarily escaped me. Boy, was my lawyer p.o.'d.

To be honest, I think my biggest mistake was going with the court-appointed lawyer in the first place. He didn't even want to put me on the stand. When I insisted, he asked me to plead the Fifth. I told him if I plead the Fifth, I'd look even more guilty. If I had the chance to do it all again, I'd probably just admit I'd been drinking all night, instead of telling the judge and jury that I had one beer and that the breathalyzer was way off. In hindsight, it made me look bad, but, like I always say, live and learn.

Going through a felony court proceeding has really taught me a lot about what you should or shouldn't say. It's too bad there aren't any do-overs. Looking on the bright side, though, now that I've gone through it, my first appeal should be a breeze.

146

Man Who's 1/16th Irish Proud Of His Irish Heritage

KENOSHA, WI—Despite being just 1/16th Irish, Dennis Kroeger, a 27-year-old marketing manager whose great-great grandmother hailed from County Cork, is fiercely proud of his Irish ancestry.

> **"Dennis sure loves playing up his Irishness,"** said Lisa Biederman, a friend and coworker of Kroeger's. **"When he gets mad, it's his Irish temper. When he drinks, he's got a powerful Irish thirst. When he's being sappy, it's his Irish poet's soul."**

Above: Kroeger proudly wears the green.

"Dennis sure loves playing up his Irishness," said Lisa Biederman, a friend and coworker of Kroeger's. "When he gets mad, it's his Irish temper. When he drinks, he's got a powerful Irish thirst. When he's being sappy, it's his Irish poet's soul. I'm like, 'Dennis, you're not even Catholic.'"

"Mary Gaughan, my mother's father's mother's mother, was from a tiny village called Ballydesmond," said the brown-eyed, brown-haired Kroeger, who is half German, one-quarter Swedish, one-eighth Dutch, one-sixteenth Belgian, and one-sixteenth Irish. "She married a sailor who was traveling from Rotterdam to America, and they settled in Milwaukee. Ever since, my family's been proud to be Irish."

Kroeger, who cites *Man Of Aran* as his favorite movie and Seumas MacManus' *The Story Of The Irish Race* as his favorite book, takes his Irish heritage seriously. He says he is saddened by the number of Irish-Americans who celebrate their culture only once a year, dismissing such less-than-reverent individuals as "green-beer Irish."

"Every St. Patrick's Day, it's the same thing," said Kroeger over a "correct" room-temperature Guinness at Noonan's, a Kenosha bar he praised as authentically Irish. "Everyone puts on green hats and spray-painted carnations and wears 'Kiss Me, I'm Irish' pins and gets drunk and makes fools of themselves. That's not what being Irish is about. That's an exaggerated, stereotyped version of our culture."

"How many of these people know the first thing about their history?" Kroeger asked. "How many of them know anything about the potato famine, much less the Downing Street Declaration?"

Jessica Kroeger, 23, said she is mystified by her older brother's identification with the Irish people.

"I have no idea where he got this whole Irish fixation from," Jessica said. "I mean, Dad's mostly German and Mom's some kind of European mongrel. He never gave a shit about it in high school, but at some point in college it just suddenly kicked in."

Padraig O'Riordan, a senior fellow at the Hibernian-American League in Boston, was bemused by Kroeger's eagerness to associate himself with the Emerald Isle.

"I suppose if being 1/16th Irish is the most interesting thing about the man, he has the right to flaunt it," O'Riordan said. "But he probably doesn't realize that what he's really telling the world is that he's desperate for an identity. I mean, I'm 100 percent Irish, but I don't run around telling every single person I meet."

"I just don't get what Dennis thinks is so thrilling about being part Irish," Jessica said. "I mean, sure, it's nice, but it doesn't exactly make you exotic. My boyfriend, now, he's 1/8th Cherokee." ∅

Struggling Airline Helped By Friendly Giant

FORT WORTH, TX—Hit hard by the recession and the aftermath of Sept. 11, American Airlines has received some much-needed assistance from a friendly giant named Urno. "Urno has been of enormous help to us, mostly by picking up planes and running them to their destinations to cut fuel expenses," American Airlines president Donald Carty said Monday. "He also helps wash our dirty planes by dipping them into lakes and rivers." Carty said he has strongly discouraged Urno from swatting rival airlines' planes out of the sky, but "sometimes, he just won't listen."

Fat Couple's Love Like A Fat Flower

DECATUR, AL—The love shared by Gene West and Brenda Goslow, who together total nearly 600 pounds, is as precious as a heaving, bloated rose, friends of the couple report. "It's so inspiring to see two people lumber through life hand-in-hand," friend Alice Toffler said Monday. "Their love is like a big, beautiful, morbidly obese chrysanthemum. Or a new spring tulip that just can't lay off the Fritos."

Retarded Child Gets New Video Game Right Before Every Dinner Party

KETTERING, OH—Jeffrey Dumas, a developmentally disabled 12-year-old, receives a new PlayStation 2 video game right before every dinner party thrown by his parents. "Look, Jeffrey, a driving game!" said Meredith Dumas, 40, presenting her son with "Gran Turismo 3" and a box of snack crackers minutes before guests began arriving for a party Sunday. "I bet you could get a million points by bedtime if you started now!" The haul was one of Dumas' best since New Year's Eve, when a party thrown by his parents netted him "WWF Smackdown!," "Crash Bandicoot 2: Cortex Strikes Back," and "Simpsons: Road Rage."

Area Man Urinating Like It's The Best Thing Ever To Happen To Him

FALL RIVER, MA—According to fellow urinators in the men's room of the Tip-Top Tavern, Steve Rilke, 44, is urinating as if it were the best thing ever to happen to him. "From the sounds he's making, you'd think it was the culmination of a lifelong dream," said Frank Nolfo, moments after stepping away from the adjacent urinal. "I mean, this is one seriously passionate piss." Nolfo theorized that Rilke's overly enthusiastic bladder-voiding is somehow related to the Tip-Top Tavern's three-for-one special on Bud Ice.

Same Jumbotron Used For Marriage Proposal Used To Ask For Divorce

CLEVELAND—Seven years after using the giant television screen to propose marriage, Kevin Kalish, 36, used the Sony Jumbotron at Jacobs Field to ask his wife Diane for a divorce Sunday. "DIANE, YOU'RE A WONDERFUL WOMAN AND YOU'VE BEEN VERY GOOD TO ME," read the message, posted before 22,347 fans during the fifth inning of an Indians-Royals game. "BUT LATELY I'M JUST FEELING TRAPPED AND SMOTHERED BY MARRIED LIFE. DIANE, WILL YOU BE MY EX-WIFE?" The Jumbotron went on to inform Diane that Kevin assumes she will want custody of their two children, and that he has no plans to contest that. ∅

church must move on and forgive these children for their misdeeds."

"As Jesus said, 'Let he who is without sin cast the first stone,'" the pope continued. "We must send a clear message to these hundreds—perhaps thousands—of children whose sinful ways have tempted so many of the church's servants into lustful violation of their holy vows of celibacy. The

> "By forgiving these children, primarily churchgoing boys between the ages of 5 and 15, the pope has shown true Christian kindness," said Father Thomas O'Malley, a member of the New York archdiocese and one of the many priests implicated in charges of sexual activity with minors.

church forgives them for their transgressions and looks upon them not with intolerance, but compassion."

The papal announcement arrives in response to public outcry over the sex scandal sweeping the Catholic church in the U.S. Though official church

doctrine condemns such behavior, the pope's decision, observers say, is intended to demonstrate the church's willingness to put the scandal behind it and restore the public trust.

"By forgiving these children, primarily churchgoing boys between the ages of 5 and 15, the pope has shown true Christian kindness," said Father Thomas O'Malley, a member of the New York archdiocese and one of the many priests implicated in charges of sexual activity with minors. "The pope is saying that, in their own way, these sinful youths are victims, too. Through their absolution, he sends the important message that empathy, contrary to what naysayers and critics in the secular media would have us believe, does have a place in modern Catholicism."

For Catholics waiting for the pope to break his long silence on the scandal, the sweeping, decisive nature of his response has come as welcome relief.

"The pope has shown great love and compassion, much as Jesus did when He ministered to tax collectors and whores," said Cardinal Bernard Law of Boston. "Despite all they have done to jeopardize the careers of so many priests—to say nothing of imperiling the priests' immortal souls—the church embraces these underaged seducers and tempters with open arms. The pope's words and actions prove that the church is willing to put an end to the suffering and let the healing begin."

The mass absolution is being hailed by church scholars as one of the Vatican's most progressive acts since the Second Vatican Council in 1962.

"One cannot overstate the break

from tradition this represents," said lay administrator Bruce McConnachie of the Los Angeles archdiocese. "After all, under church doctrine, the act of seducing a priest is considered a grave sin against the laws of God, punish-

> "What kind of a message is the pope sending today's children? That it's okay to seduce priests?" said one concerned Baltimore priest who asked to remain anonymous due to a pending court case.

able by condemnation to Hell for all eternity. But the pope has put all of that aside. He has let bygones be bygones. For this, all of those misbehaving, sexy little guys should feel grateful. By showing such willingness to forgive and forget, the pope has sent a clear message: Even though these boys have done much to undermine and subvert the priestly vows of celibacy, they are still deserving of God's love."

Margaret Leahy, 39, a Somerville, MA, homemaker and mother of one of the alleged seducers, expressed relief over the pope's announcement.

"For months, I feared that my boy—

and the dozens of others who committed sinful acts with Father Halloran before he was moved to the safety of another parish to protect him from further temptation at their prepubescent hands—was going to Hell for what he'd done," Leahy said. "It's the worst feeling a mother can know. But thanks to the forgiveness of the pope, my long nightmare is finally over. He was just a boy of 8 at the time. He didn't know any better. Thank you, your Holiness, for giving my poor little Timothy a second chance at redemption."

However, not everyone within the Catholic church is so supportive of the pope's actions.

"What kind of a message is the pope sending today's children? That it's okay to seduce priests?" said one concerned Baltimore priest who asked to remain anonymous due to a pending court case. "With the pope's announcement, the church is essentially telling its youngest members, 'Go ahead and let Father So-And-So reach into your swim trunks at the church-youth-group pool party. It's okay. The pope will forgive you in the end.' Without fear of eternal damnation, how are these provocative young lotharios ever going to learn?"

"As the creep of secular humanism continues to chip away at our most sacred institutions, the Vatican has established a dangerous precedent," the priest continued. "We look to the church's authority for justice and righteousness, not politically convenient solutions that maintain the status quo. These nubile sinners should be held accountable for the damage they've done." Ø

---

the ONION presents

Home Improvement Tips

Do-it-yourself home improvement can be money-saving and fun. Here are some tips to help you with that next project:

- As they say, the three rules of housepainting are preparation, preparation, and painting.

- One telltale sign that you need to go back to the old drawing board on a home plumbing project is if urine and feces are geysering out of the kitchen sink.

- Installing a second basement is time-consuming at best.

- When remodeling your bathroom, remember: If you plan on having French people over, they'll need one of those ass-fountains.

- Do not begin a home-repair project without a bunch of fixy stuff like hammers and whatnot.

- The following are some phrases you will likely need for standard home repair: "Get in there, you cocksucker!"; "Fucking son-of-a-bitch grommet!"; and "Jesus fuck—my forearm is gone!"

- A big, hardworking man like the plumber could probably use a backrub to help him relax.

- For heavy home-repair work, consider hiring a truckload of Mexicans as day laborers. (Note: Truckloads of Hasidic Jews not as effective as Mexicans.)

- Bear in mind that in certain cases, remodeling and refinishing costs can balloon to the point where it might be cheaper just to buy a new trailer.

- Common household chemicals like drain openers and silicone lubricants can get you totally high. I shit you not.

- For bathroom-remodeling jobs, don't forget to install a hand-held shower head. It will help your wife masturbate while thinking about that well-muscled repairman who will come to fix all the mistakes you make when you try to do the job yourself.

She also achieved a measure of notoriety in tabloids and on gossip pages last year following her broken engagement to MTV VJ Carson Daly. Though there is no indication that Reid takes an interest in politics or current events, or is even registered to vote, Stein and his associates are keeping an eye out for telltale signs of nascent awareness of social issues.

"I was having lunch with Tara the other day, and she told me she was thinking of becoming a vegetarian," said Libby Winters, Reid's publicist. "I thought, 'Oh, fuck—[personal assistant] Kimberly [Braterman] didn't screen Tara's mail thoroughly and let a PETA mass-mailing slip through.' So I casually asked Tara where she got that idea. She said she was at a party with [socialite] Paris Hilton, and Paris told Tara that her boyfriend said her pussy juice tasted better after she quit eating red meat. I can't tell you how relieved I was."

Winters went on to note that while Reid frequently practices yoga—widely regarded as a "gateway exer-

> **The handlers' vigilance has extended into Reid's acting choices. Adrian said he encourages his client to play mainly sexy, lighthearted, apolitical roles. As an added measure, he counts on Reid's personal assistant, Kimberly Braterman, to ensure that the on-set environment is politics-free.**

cise" to spiritual and political awareness—the activity has not had any such effect.

Reporting regularly to Reid manager Kevin Adrian, members of the actress' entourage are under strict

> **Winters went on to note that while Reid frequently practices yoga—widely regarded as a "gateway exercise" to spiritual and political awareness—the activity has not had any such effect.**

orders not to expose Reid to politically suggestive material. They have been instructed to inform Adrian of any action or remark which may indicate an emergent social consciousness on the part of Reid, however embryonic or misdirected.

Reid's hairstylist, Frederic Chukka, recently became alarmed when she asked him if the hairspray he was using was "environmentally friendly."

"At first, I didn't know what to say," Chukka said. "I stammered something about the government banning all that fluorocarbon stuff in the '70s. Tara gave me this look like she didn't quite believe me. I said to myself, 'Think fast, Frederic, if you want to do her hair for next year's Golden Globes.'"

Continued Chukka: "So I said to Tara, 'Even if they didn't ban all that stuff, no one cares besides a couple of ugly, mousy hippie bitches who are just jealous of rock-star babes like you. You deserve to shine, sweetheart. Besides, I can't think of a better product to give you that just-been-fucked look.' She just nodded."

The handlers' vigilance has extended into Reid's acting choices. Adrian said he encourages his client to play mainly sexy, lighthearted, apolitical roles. As an added measure, he counts on Reid's personal assistant, Kimberly Braterman, to ensure that the on-set environment is politics-free.

"There was a lot of concern when she was cast in *Dr. T And The Women*," Braterman said. "[Director Robert] Altman is known for his subversive, countercultural views, and

Above: Tara Reid and model/socialite Paris Hilton at a Sean John fashion show in New York.

[co-star] Richard Gere is a passionate advocate for Tibetan independence. It was a dangerous situation to put her in, but by keeping Tara's trailer far away from Richard's and by frequently pulling her off the set for premieres, press junkets, and racy pictorials for *Stuff* magazine and *Maxim*, we managed to shield her from any potential indoctrination."

One Hollywood celebrity who has openly condemned Reid's handlers is actress Jaime Pressly, star of *Joe Dirt* and *Tomcats*.

"It is just so unfair," Pressly said.

"Because of her control-freak handlers, Tara will never learn of the joys and rewards of political awareness. Since my own awakening last year, I feel so much more full of knowledge and awareness, and I think celebrities should use their fame to educate the public about important issues. Like, for example, did you know that women in Pakistine have to be buried alive with their dead husbands, whether they want to or not? That is so wrong."

Added Pressly: "Oh, and by the way, milk is nothing but liquid meat." ∅

host contained a factual discrepancy," the web-posted statement read. "Please be assured that we are doing everything within our power to ensure that nothing of the sort happens again. We will not rest until the Internet's once-sterling reputation as the world's leading source for 100 percent reliable information is restored."

Paul Boutin, senior editor of *Wired*, said the error is likely to have a profound effect on how the Internet is perceived.

"Will we ever fully trust the Web again?" Boutin asked. "We may well be witnessing the dawn of a new era of

skepticism in which we no longer accept everything we read online at face value. But regardless of what the future holds, one thing is clear: The Internet's status as the world's definitive repository of incontrovertible fact has been jeopardized."

Peter Luyck, 30, a Dallas-area graphic designer and frequent Internet user, was crestfallen.

"If it happens once, it can happen again," Luyck said. "I shudder to think that, one dark day in the future, misinformation could again make its way online. In fact, it may already have. How do we know that trusted sites

> **Paul Boutin, senior editor of *Wired*, said the error is likely to have a profound effect on how the Internet is perceived.**

like the Drudge Report and Fucked Company are as accurate as we instinctively trust them to be? Can we

blindly trust that SpideyRulez.com is correct in its reportage that the upcoming *Spider-Man* sequel will feature Christopher Walken as Dr. Octopus? Pandora has opened the box."

Though the *Brady Bunch* error is the first confirmed instance of false information on the Internet, scares have occurred in the past. In 1998, an e-mail sent to a woman in Warner Robins, GA, made an unverifiable claim that she could earn thousands of dollars from an initial $5 investment. The claim was never conclusively proven false, and no charges were filed. ∅

Offin' Office Max

By Herbert Kornfeld
Accounts-Receivable
Supervisor

Yo, this is a message foe all y'all wack muthafuckas at Office Depot: Step tha FUCK OFF, lest y'all wanna brawl wit' tha H-Dog an' tha rest of tha Midstate Office Supply krew. 'Cuz if it come to that, shit ain't gonna be pretty. Tha H-Dog and his Midstate ballers will WASTE yo' sorry li'l red-polo-shirted asses. Word is bond.

Y'all wuz warned to stay tha fuck off Midstate's turf. Midstate be in this 'hood foe near 40 years, servin' tha community an' buildin' a loyal customah base, an' it don't take kindly to no new-jack pretendas. So whatch-y'all do? Y'all open a new store on Sherman Avenue in tha space where tha Kmart wuz befoe they fuck up an' go bankrupt. Y'all be braggin' in yo' muthafuckin' Sunday insertz, if all y'all shoppaz can find a lower advertised price on office supplies, Office Depot will match it. If that ain't groundz foe muthafuckin' war, I dunno what is.

But if all y'all Office Depot suckas think Midstate be runnin' scared, you sadly mistaken. Lemme tell you a little story 'bout some wack playa-hatas called Office Max who tried to move in on Midstate's turf a coupla years ago. Peep this:

When Office Max roll into town, most of tha Midstate krew be buggin'. Office Max be a big ol' nizational chain, and Midstate only regional. Everybody talkin' 'bout how they got lower prices than us thankz to they size. You know, lower ovahead due to economiez of scale and shit. Our office comptrolla Gerald Luckenbill send out a memo to all tha department headz sayin' that we best start thinkin' 'bout some ways to stay competitive an' retain our customa base, lest Office Max start makin' off wit' our benjamins.

So, one aftanoon, all us Midstate supavisas get called in foe this Big Willie interdepartmental meeting. This meeting so important, even tha vice-president, Howard Dinwiddie, be there. Everybody startz prezentin' Dinwiddie wit' suggestions on wayz to deal wit' tha Office Max sizituation. Our marketin' supavisa, Cheryl Stover, she say we oughta build up our mail-order division, 'cuz she think we can break out of our region and make our customa base all national an' shit wit' catalog sales. Fuckin' Bob Cowan from Human Resources propose some weak-ass plan to improve customa service. He bring this ova-head projector in an' show us a buncha transparencies wit' muthafuckin' acronyms on 'em, where every letter stand for some motivational bullshit thass s'posed to make tha Midstate posse practically wanna suck tha customahs' dicks. Took every inch o' tha H-Kool not to cut Cowan wit' tha L.O.D. Then, Accountz Payabo supervisa Myron Schabe say somethin', but no one remember what he say 'cuz tha ol' fool put everybody to sleep.

Me, I don't say nothin' tha whole time. Afta tha meetin', Dinwiddie aks me why, 'cuz he know I tha stone-col' superbaddest employee at Midstate. "Listen, Dinwiddie," I say. "Fuck that bullshit 'bout expandin' this and im-

---

Lemme tell you a little story 'bout some wack playa-hatas called Office Max who tried to move in on Midstate's turf a coupla years ago.

---

provin' that. Tha problem ain't us, it be Office Max. You want Office Max outta tha picture? Let H-Dog take care of it. Don't aks no questions, just let me take care of it."

Dinwiddie don't say nuthin. He just clasp my shoulder an' smile befoe walkin' away. Dinwiddie ain't dumb. He knew mah skeelz as a enforca be legendary. I wuz mad grateful foe his trust, so much so that I chose not to fade his ass foe touchin' me.

Bringin' down Office Max wuzn't easy, but I did it. It wuz some o' tha hardest shit I ever had to do. I wuz livin' a double life, splittin' my time between Midstate an' tha Max. Tha three months I spent undacova as a O.M. cashier an' stocker could be a novel in an' of itself, mah homeys.

To fit in, I had to drop mah mad lyrical flow an' talk like a ordinary sucka. "Is there anything I can help you with, sir?" "Do you need assistance getting that to your car, ma'am?" "Will that be cash or charge?" "Thanks for shopping at Office Max, and have a great day." DAMN. I don't know how all y'all can talk like that. S'pitiful. Guess I shouldn't bitch, though, since that shit got me two Office Max employee-of-tha-month plaques an', eventually, tha assistant-managa position that wuz my ticket straight into tha belly o' tha beast.

Now, unfortunately, I can't tell you exactly what I did, 'cuz a lotta what went down still be classified info, know what I'm sayin'? When tha secret H-Dog Archives be open to tha public 25 yearz afta my death, all y'all will learn tha real 411, straight up. Foe now, I can only say that

thankz to me, to this day, tha top brass at Office Max can't take a piss without lookin' ova they shoulder. I ain't sayin' nothin' that could incriminate me, but they never did figga out who uncapped all tha highlighta pens in stock. Or how tha wetlandz five miles north o' tha store got contaminated wit' copier toner. (Suckaz settled outta court wit tha EPA foe a undisclosed sum. Huh.) Or why some lucky shoppaz found some Hewlett-Packard CP1160 color inkjet printers foe tha bargain price of $2.99, marked down from $299.99. A simple accountin' error, but that sorta shit eat into a profit margin real fast.

Long story short, ain't no Office Maxxin' at that space no mo'. They wuz replaced by Petco, some wack pet-food supastore, an' they ain't shown they face in tha 'hood since.

I ain't sayin' Office Depot will go down tha same way as Office Max. But y'all best not bring any of that "we won't be undasold" shit round here. 'Cuz if you do, befoe long, y'all won't have nothin' to undasell.

No use gettin' yo' guard up neither, 'cuz tha Midstate avengas will strike where you least expect it. Maybe all y'all cash registas suddenly start spittin' up they detail tape smack in tha middle of transactions, and they can't be stopped, know what I'm sayin'? Or maybe yo' customas be mad vexed that they can't find nothin', 'cuz somebody rearrange all tha signs hangin' ova tha aisles.

Thass just a taste of tha world o' hurt y'all gots in store if y'all persist wit yo' "unbeatable savings, selection, and service" bullshit. Only thing that be unbeatable be Midstate, an' it gonna stay that way, you wack muthafukkas.

Y'all wanna fuck wit' Midstate Office Supply? If you do, you betta bring yo' A-game, 'cuz H-Dog ready to ball. Know what I'm sayin'?

H-Dog OUT. ∅

Your Horoscope

By Lloyd Schumner Sr.
Retired Machinist and
A.A.P.B.-Certified Astrologer

Aries: (March 21–April 19)
It may be years before your coworkers treat you with respect again, but it will have been worth it for the brief time spent in the panda suit.

Taurus: (April 20–May 20)
The gods will punish you for your hubris and arrogance by introducing you to someone who makes richer, creamier mashed potatoes than you.

Gemini: (May 21–June 21)
You've been through a lot of trying times in your life, but one of the hardest to get over will be the day you learn that Jar-Jar is now a senator.

Cancer: (June 22–July 22)
As you look back on your life as a squirrel, your only regret is that you let others discourage you from pursuing your dream of waterskiing professionally.

Leo: (July 23–Aug. 22)
You will be upgraded with improved graphics and greater ease of use, but processor speed remains a problem.

Virgo: (Aug. 23–Sept. 22)
Awesome forces beyond your control will continue to cause pictures and sounds to emanate from your TV.

Libra: (Sept. 23–Oct. 23)
The stars foresee profound changes ahead for Libra, but they insist on describing them in vague, nonspecific terms.

Scorpio: (Oct. 24–Nov. 21)
As the June issue of *Vogue* says, being fashion-forward in every aspect of your life is easier than ever. However, this assurance merely serves to confuse you.

Sagittarius: (Nov. 22–Dec. 21)
Your fear of being assassinated is groundless. Important figures are assassinated; you will be beaten to death with a rake behind the Safeway.

Capricorn: (Dec. 22–Jan. 19)
You've tried and tried, but there seems to be no way for you to safely extricate yourself from the welded-on one-man-band outfit.

Aquarius: (Jan. 20–Feb. 18)
Advocates for the homeless will soon make you a very tempting membership offer.

Pisces: (Feb. 19–March 20)
You can't for the life of you understand why nobody sees through Drew Barrymore's obvious façade.

But if all y'all Office Depot suckas think Midstate be runnin' scared, you sadly mistaken.

the ONION®

| VOLUME 38 ISSUE 20 | AMERICA'S FINEST NEWS SOURCE™ | 30 MAY–5 JUNE 2002 |

Field-Trip Mishap Fulfills Child's Wish To Be Oscar Mayer Wiener

see LOCAL page 8C

Ross Ice Shelf Embarks On World Tour

see ENVIRONMENT page 7A

Road-Kill Squirrel Remembered As Frantic, Indecisive

see PASSINGS page 11E

STATshot

A look at the numbers that shape your world.

What Posters Are We Taking Down?

1. Bryan from Color Me Badd
2. "Wanted" poster of self from county fair
3. Poverty Sucks
4. That Escher where the fish turn into birds
5. Perot-Stockdale '92
6. University of Wisconsin–Whitewater Orientation Week

Sexual Tension Between Arafat, Sharon Reaches Breaking Point

Above: Arafat and Sharon share an awkward moment.

JERUSALEM—The long-simmering sexual tension between Israeli Prime Minister Ariel Sharon and Palestinian leader Yasser Arafat finally reached a breaking point Monday, culminating in a passionate kiss before a shocked delegation of Mideast negotiators.

"You always got the feeling that there was something more behind all the anger and tension," said European Union Foreign Policy Chief Javier Solana. "They wouldn't agree on *anything*, even though their people were dying, locked in this unending conflict. It never made sense—until now."

Continued Solana: "All that repressed passion. And neither of them would admit it to the other... or to themselves."

According to sources, midway through a 10 a.m. meeting to discuss a possible pullout of Israeli troops from several West Bank refugee camps, Sharon accused Arafat of secretly

see TENSION page 154

Congress Threatens To Leave D.C. Unless New Capitol Is Built

Above: An architectural firm's proposal for a new retractable-dome capitol. Inset: Hastert addresses reporters.

WASHINGTON, DC—Calling the current U.S. Capitol "inadequate and obsolete," Congress will relocate to Charlotte or Memphis if its demands for a new, state-of-the-art facility are not met, leaders announced Monday.

"Don't get us wrong: We love the drafty old building," Speaker of the House Dennis Hastert (R-IL) said. "But the hard reality is, it's no longer suitable for a world-class legislative branch. The sight lines are bad, there aren't enough concession stands or bathrooms, and the parking is miserable. It hurts to say, but the capitol's time has come and gone."

"If we want to stay competitive, we need to upgrade," said House Majority Leader Dick Gephardt (D-MO), who has proposed a new $3.5 billion capitol on the site of the current edifice. "Look at British Parliament. Look at the Vatican. Respected institutions in their markets. But without modern facilities, they've been having big prob-

see CAPITOL page 155

Above: Adam Sprouse and his parents.

Nerd's Parents Afraid Son Will Fall In With Popular Crowd

MUNDELEIN, IL—Lawrence and Marcia Sprouse expressed concern Monday that their 15-year-old son Adam, after years of being a social outcast, is in danger of falling in with the popular crowd at Mundelein High School.

"All the signs point to him getting involved with the popular kids," Marcia said. "The last few Saturday nights, instead of staying home and watching a movie, he's been out at parties. He's also been hanging around this boy who's on the school baseball team. Parties, hanging out with jocks—what's become of my baby boy?"

Primary among the Sprouses' worries is the prospect of Adam being exposed to drugs and alcohol.

"I'm not naïve about what goes on with these kids who aren't in the AP classes," Marcia said. "They stay up

see NERD page 155

Suicide Bombings In The U.S.?

According to intelligence officials, Al Qaeda or another terrorist group may one day attempt to carry out a suicide bombing on U.S. soil. What do *you* think?

"Sept. 11 was meant to weaken our nation's resolve, but it only strengthened it. One or two more attacks should weaken it, though."

Ron Dempster
Custodian

"As long as we heed the vice-president's urging to generally be on alert for things, our nation is impregnable."

Nate Tucker
Electrical Engineer

"Suicide bombing is the coward's way out. Tainting a city's water supply with a rare and lethal compound from deep space is the evil genius' way out."

Eric Lattimore
Truck Driver

"Turn on the TV these days, and all you see is sex and potential violence."

Melinda Collins
Homemaker

"Did you say I can get unlimited DVD rentals from Netflix.com for just $19.95 a month? Oh, you said suicide bombers may attack here. Never mind."

Tom McEwan
Systems Analyst

"The U.S. is safe, so long as the terrorists don't see us being critical of President Bush."

Diana Reese
Lab Assistant

Cannes 2002

After 12 days of screenings and parties, the 2002 Cannes Film Festival wrapped up Sunday. Among the top entries:

- *Efficient & Efficienter* (Germany)
- *Please To Enjoy The Herring, Mother* (Finland)
- *Les Busters Des Ghosts* (France)
- *My Eccentric Ethnic Family And Our Sumptuous Traditional Dishes* (U.S.)
- *The Sombre Hombre* (U.K.-Mexico)
- *The Red Balloon In Breaking Training* (France)
- *Turkish Batman* (Turkey)
- *Grey, Grey, My Passion* (Russia)
- *Hot Shots! Part Trois* (U.S.)
- *Overcast Sweater Is Sixteen* (Denmark)
- *Screwed-Up Nutballs II: Spring Break Fever* (U.S.)

the ONION
America's Finest News Source.™

Herman Ulysses Zweibel
Founder

T. Herman Zweibel
Publisher Emeritus
J. Phineas Zweibel
Publisher
Maxwell Prescott Zweibel
Editor-In-Chief

152

Look Out, Corporate America, Here Comes My Pirate Radio Station

By Tate Ainsworth

If, like me, you're among the thinking few, you're pretty disgusted with what passes for radio these days. Turn anywhere on your FM dial, and you're likely to hear the sound of some enormous multinational media conglomerate anesthetizing the masses with its spoon-fed pablum. From Hot 96 to Z-104, these stations are all the same: pre-packaged, focus-grouped DJs selling a bill of false goods to lobotomized teens who don't know the difference between revolution and repetition. Even non-commercial, so-called "public" radio is just a cog in the Great American Money Machine.

Well, I, for one, have had enough. It's time to shake up the status quo and put a little fear in the heart of the Establishment. Yes, consider this an official declaration of war: Look out, Corporate America, here comes my pirate radio station!

Last Friday, Radio Free Tate, the city's first and only broadcast forum for the disenfranchised voices of the country, went on the air. Located somewhere between 89.5 and 91.3 FM, Radio Free Tate is going to let corporate America have it with both barrels: the truths they're afraid to say and the songs they're afraid to play.

I may not have the broadcast range of a big station, but I compress a

> **After all, I'm living outside the law. I know for a fact that the government and the corporate fatcats would love to shut me down. They don't want people to hear what I'm dishing out. Well, tough!**

whole lot of rebellion into a six-block radius. You'd better believe this mouse is going to roar.

And, unlike the rest of the world, I'm not interested in feeding my audience a steady diet of nothing. While most radio listeners are complacently soaking in the latest teeny-pop brain sedative or the semi-digested pap of the Tweedledee & Tweedledum Morning Zoo show, I'm out there telling it like it is. I'm not afraid to talk about

the class war against the poor, the deplorable state of popular music, or the sham election that put Dubya into the Whitewash House. Corporate America, you'd better watch your backside, because there's a new sheriff on your radio dial!

I had no idea starting a pirate radio

> **Located somewhere between 89.5 and 91.3 FM, Radio Free Tate is going to let corporate America have it with both barrels: the truths they're afraid to say and the songs they're afraid to play.**

station would be so easy. All I needed was a microphone, a PLL transmitter, a Comet antenna, a 20-watt dummy load kit, a 6-watt amplifier, some old Minor Threat and Bad Brains records, and a self-constructed broadcast booth in my basement. It's so simple, I'm surprised more people don't do it. Then again, how many people have the guts? After all, I'm living outside the law. I know for a fact that the government and the corporate fatcats would love to shut me down. They don't want people to hear what I'm dishing out. Well, tough! I'm going to bring The Man to his knees, one song at a time.

A bunch of my friends have already said that when they're in my neighborhood, they keep their radios tuned to Radio Free Tate. You're probably thinking they're just saying that because they're my friends, but they're not. Where else are they going to hear Black Flag's "TV Party" followed by a scathing anti-Pepsico editorial followed by Gang Of Four's "Guns Before Butter"? On K-Rock? I think not.

A desperately needed home for alternative ideas, Radio Free Tate will provide a forum for the forumless, a voice for the voiceless. I tried doing a call-in segment last Saturday, but the masses weren't quite ready for it after spending so many years imprisoned in corporate radio's shackles. (A case of Stockholm Syndrome if there ever was one.) All I got were two 12-year olds making fart noises with their hands and requests for (ugh) Ja Rule and (double ugh) Nickelback. Clearly, these people are so hooked on the Pop Narcotic, they lack the faculties to ap-

see RADIO page 154

Man Blames Hangover On Everything But How Much He Drank

BETHEL PARK, PA—Speaking slowly and moving stiffly Tuesday, Pittsburgh-area resident Matt Van Duyne attributed his hangover to everything but the excessive amount of alcohol he'd consumed the previous night.

"One big problem was the empty stomach," said Van Duyne, holding his head and taking deep breaths. "I really should know by now to make sure to eat a piece of pizza or some french fries or something before doing any drinking. That kind of greasy, high-carb stuff works best, I find, because it really soaks up the alcohol. Another thing I neglected to do was drink a lot of water. That's key. Also, I forgot to take my usual two aspirins before going to bed, which helps a lot."

"There's a real art to not getting a hangover," Van Duyne added.

A web designer for Altered Images, the 28-year-old Van Duyne had spent the evening watching DVDs at the home of friend Kenny Layton. Between 10:30 p.m. and 2 a.m., Van Duyne consumed three-quarters of a jug of Gallo wine he found in Layton's kitchen cabinet. Shortly after 2 a.m., he stumbled seven blocks back to his apartment.

"This happens every time I drink Gallo, especially red," Van Duyne said. "That stuff really gives me a hangover. It probably has something to do with all the sulfites they use."

Though Van Duyne describes himself as a social drinker, coworkers say he frequently arrives at work asking them to "take it easy on [him]" because of a hangover he attributes to everything but excessive drinking.

"My favorite is when he explains

that he forgot to follow the 'beer before liquor, never sicker' rule," coworker Thomas Juno said. "Sorry, Matty, but when you're pounding six of each in just over three hours, I don't think it really matters what

> "This happens every time I drink Gallo, especially red," Van Duyne said. "That stuff really gives me a hangover. It probably has something to do with all the sulfites they use."

order you drink them in."

"Last Thursday, we all went out to Pitchers Pub to celebrate landing this huge St. Francis Medical Center account," said Heather Hagerty, 25, a tech writer at Altered Images. "Over the course of the next four hours, Matt drank six Iron Citys, three Cuervo shots, and a Jack and Coke. The next morning at work, he's complaining that he feels woozy because he didn't take his Vitamin B before drinking. I have this alternate theory that he felt woozy because he drank six Iron Citys, three Cuervo shots, and a Jack and Coke."

Even when owning up to drinking excessively, Van Duyne still finds ways to attribute his hungover state to

Above: Van Duyne nurses his hangover with water.

other factors.

"Last year, me and three of my buddies did a whole bottle of mescal on my birthday. We got to the bottom, and I got the worm," Van Duyne said. "That messed me up bad the next day, because the worm absorbs a lot of al-

cohol. It's almost like a hallucinogen. I ruined my favorite comforter because I puked all over it. Stupid worm."

Longtime friend Pete Sirois, 27, heard a new excuse last Friday night, see HANGOVER page 154

Worst Person Woman Knows Pregnant

JASPER, AL—Karen Brundage was chilled to learn Monday that Cora Damrush, the "single most selfish, ignorant, emotionally crippled person" she knows, is expecting a baby in November. "My heart skipped a beat—in a bad way—when Cora said she and Neil were having a child," Brundage said. "I can't even begin to tell you what a foul, miserable harpy that woman is." Brundage added that she wishes there were some sort of baby-shower gift that would save the unborn child from a lifetime of misery cowering before a dark and evil mother.

Boss Alludes To 'Crunch Time'

MOUNTAIN VIEW, CA—Seeking to motivate his employees for a fast-approaching deadline, DCG Printing

departmental manager Bryce Gillian referred to the following three days as "crunch time" Monday. "Apparently, Bryce thinks he has to get all of us psyched for the end of the Gymboree direct-mail catalog project," layout artist Pete Auriemma said. "If it would make him feel like he inspired us, I guess I could walk briskly between offices. That might help create a more 'crunch-timey' atmosphere." Auriemma said he is looking forward to Wednesday afternoon, when the project is expected to move from crunch time into "the home stretch."

83-Year-Old Sneaks Into 65-To-80 Singles Dance

APPLETON, WI—Claude Winters, 83, falsified his age Saturday to gain admission to a dance for singles aged 65 to 80 at the Appleton VFW. "The girls at the over-80 dances are so old-

fashioned," said Winters, eyeing a shapely 68-year-old widow across the dance floor. "When I go produce shopping, I want my vegetables, you know, fresh." Winters stressed that he is not "some cradle-robbing pervert looking for pre-menopausal women."

CNN Graphic Designer Asked To Combine Dollar Sign, Syringe, Fighter Jets, Panda

ATLANTA—Christine Kannberg, a CNN Headline News graphic designer, expressed befuddlement Monday when asked to create a story logo incorporating a dollar sign, a syringe, fighter jets, and a panda. "I can't even begin to imagine what this one's for," Kannberg said from her workstation. "Maybe, like, the Beijing Zoo was smuggling drugs into the U.S. inside pandas, and we bombed them or something." Last week,

Kannberg was asked to create a graphic combining a football helmet, three DNA helixes, a rhubarb pie, and the state of Oregon.

Overweight Man Receives 'Lose Weight Fast' Spam E-Mail Featuring His Picture

HOUSTON—Jim Funderburke, a 240-pound accountant, was surprised to find a photo of himself in a spam e-mail for a weight-loss product Monday. "That's the last time I post vacation pictures on my web site," said Funderburke, 38, gazing at an unflattering image of himself in a bathing suit. "I'd like to be able to check my messages without seeing myself used as the online embodiment of obesity and overindulgence." Funderburke also expressed a wish to water his lawn without neighborhood teenagers calling him "Before Dude." Ø

TENSION from page 151

channeling PLO funds into Hamas and other terrorist organizations. The accusation prompted Arafat to rise from his chair and stand toe-to-toe with his Israeli counterpart. The ensuing heated exchange quickly escalated into a shouting match, which reached an unexpected end when the

> ## "At first, I thought they were wrestling or something," said Anthony Zinni, U.S. envoy to the Middle East. "But then, I was like, 'Holy shit: They're kissing.'"

two leaders embraced in a deep, passionate kiss.

"At first, I thought they were wrestling or something," said Anthony Zinni, U.S. envoy to the Middle East. "But then, I was like, 'Holy shit: They're *kissing*.'"

Following the six-second embrace, Sharon and Arafat retreated to their respective delegations. They then sheepishly smiled at one another for several minutes before declaring the meeting over.

RADIO from page 152

preciate my blend of hardcore punk and take-no-prisoners commentary on Generalissimo Bush's *real* motivations for the so-called war on terror.

When I'm not shooting truth straight from the hip, I'm getting down. While much of the playlist is drawn from classic SoCal and D.C. punk, you'll hear everything from Roky Erickson to Neu! to Burning Spear. I throw in some old-school hip-hop, some No Wave, a little spoken word, and some free jazz. Once, I played the entire Tony Conrad box set as a big "fuck you" to all the mainstream DJs who are too chickenshit to play experimental composers. And, once in a while, I take a cue from rap pioneer DJ Cool Herc and mix it up by "scratching" my records. Try finding that on your average station!

I'd encourage all of you to tune in to Radio Free Tate. Like I said, it's somewhere between 89.5 and 91.3 on your radio dial—depending on which side of Maplewood Street you're on. Before long, you'll be able to find our listening area simply by paying attention to who suddenly goes through a political revival. They'll start using less, caring more, and voting with their hearts and minds rather than their wallets. And they'll be listening to the best mix of music you won't hear anywhere else. Find that neighborhood, and you've found Radio Free Tate.

Oh, and one more thing: Corporate America can suck it. ✍

Few Mideast negotiators expected Sharon, one of the most hard-line right-wingers in Israeli political history, and Arafat, who has made the fight for Palestinian statehood his life's cause, to leave Monday's bargaining table as friends, much less lovers. However, in retrospect, few are surprised.

"To tell you the truth, I can't say it doesn't make sense," said U.N. Secretary General Kofi Annan, one of the witnesses to the historic liplock. "It's like the boy in the schoolyard who torments the girl and pulls her pigtails because he's got a big crush on her. For the longest time, Yasser and Ariel simply didn't know how to express their true feelings for each other. Now they do."

"Everyone knows that the opposite of love is apathy, not hate," Russian Foreign Minister Igor Ivanov said. "Love and hate, they are merely two sides of the same coin."

Ivanov said he first saw signs that the two leaders had "more than control of the Gaza Strip on their minds" at a 1998 Israel-PLO conference in Cairo, at which Arafat reversed decades of PLO policy and polemic by acknowledging Israel's right to exist.

"For the first time in years, they were really getting along," Ivanov said. "Arafat tripped over a rug and landed right in [then Israeli Defense Minister] Sharon's arms. You should have

HANGOVER from page 153

when he and Van Duyne went drinking at Anchor Inn.

"Matt was doing all these different shots—Stoli, Jack Daniel's, Jägermeister, you name it," Sirois said. "He was really wasted. I talked to him the next night, and he was complaining

> ## "The amazing thing is, he hardly ever uses the same excuse twice," Sirois continued.

about how he still had a headache, because he 'failed to stay consistent [with his liquors].' I'm like, 'Yeah, if only you'd done vodka shots all night, you would've been fine.'"

"The amazing thing is, he hardly ever uses the same excuse twice," Sirois continued. "One time, it might be 'I stupidly combined champagne with hard lemonade,' and the next, 'I should've known better than to mix liquor with diet soda.' He must devote more time to researching hangovers than he does to his job."

In spite of his wicked hangover, Van Duyne plans to spend this evening drinking at a local nightclub.

"I'm still feeling kinda shitty, but I can't miss 2-for-1 apple-martini night at Insomnia," Van Duyne said. "So long as I take two tablespoons of olive oil beforehand, I should be fine." ✍

seen the look they exchanged while Sharon held Arafat in his strong grasp. Nothing happened, but you could tell something was there."

Daniel Kurtzer, U.S. ambassador to

> ## Ivanov said he first saw signs that the two leaders had "more than control of the Gaza Strip on their minds" at a 1998 Israel-PLO conference in Cairo, at which Arafat reversed decades of PLO policy and polemic by acknowledging Israel's right to exist.

Israel, recalled suspicious comments made by Sharon at a state dinner in his honor at the White House last September.

"Ariel had had a little too much wine, and he ended up confiding to me about how he has a crush on somebody he shouldn't like at all," Kurtzer said. "He said he couldn't say

who it was because it would never work out anyway. At first, I thought maybe it was Crown Prince Abdullah, but now it's pretty obvious who it was."

U.N. Middle East envoy Terje Roed-Larsen praised the kiss as "a positive step forward in Israeli-Palestinian relations." He was critical, however, of the two men's methods leading up to the embrace.

"If trapping Yasser in his Ramallah compound for months was Ariel's way of getting Yasser's attention, he should have tried a less antagonistic approach, like sending a card," Roed-Larsen said. "And Yasser is no better, trying to catch Ariel's eye with all those deadly suicide bombings. God, men can be so stupid and macho."

Sharon and Arafat have since returned to their respective home soil, each having expressed a need for "time to think." In the meantime, the Israeli and Palestinian peoples are anxious to see what will transpire as a result of Monday's historic kiss.

"One mini make-out session and now we're supposed to wait who knows how long to find out if they actually get together? Oh, it makes me so frustrated," said Olfat Hafez, a Palestinian refugee who for the past 18 months has been living in a camp near Hebron. "Still, if these two do end up getting together, the end will have justified the means." ✍

BULUNGI from page 151

amounts of blood. Passersby were amazed by the unusually large amounts of blood. Passersby were amazed by the unusually large

amounts of blood. Passersby were amazed by the unusually large amounts of blood. Passersby were amazed by the unusually large amounts of blood. Passersby were amazed by the unusually large amounts of blood. Passersby were amazed by the unusually large amounts of blood. Passersby were amazed by the unusually large amounts of blood. Passersby were amazed by the unusually large amounts of blood. Passersby were amazed by the unusually large amounts of blood. Passersby were amazed by the unusually large amounts of blood. Passersby were amazed by the unusually large amounts of blood. Passersby were

> ## I'm thinking about getting into self-mutilation.

amazed by the unusually large amounts of blood. Passersby were amazed by the unusually large amounts of blood. Passersby were amazed by the unusually large amounts of blood. Passersby were amazed by the unusually large amounts of blood. Passersby were amazed by the unusually large amounts of blood. Passersby were amazed by the unusually large amounts of blood. Passersby were amazed by the unusually large amounts of blood. Passersby were amazed by the unusually large amounts of blood. Passersby were amazed by the unusually large amounts of blood. Passersby were amazed by the unusually large amounts of blood. Passersby were

see BULUNGI page 158

CAPITOL from page 151

lems attracting top talent."

Its cornerstone laid in 1793 by President Washington, the capitol has been built, rebuilt, extended, and restored countless times over the past 209 years. Legislators say another multimillion-dollar renovation is not an acceptable alternative to a new building.

"How many times can you put a fresh coat of paint over an old, broken-down horse?" asked Sen. Rick Santorum (R-PA), co-chair of the Senate Relocation Subcommittee. "We need a building that befits our status

> ## Its cornerstone laid in 1793 by President Washington, the capitol has been built, rebuilt, extended, and restored countless times over the past 209 years. Legislators say another multimillion-dollar renovation is not an acceptable alternative to a new building.

as the nation's number-one democratically elected legislative body. And if D.C. isn't willing to provide that, I can think of plenty of other cities that would be more than happy to."

The leading candidates for a possible congressional relocation are Charlotte and Memphis, both of which have long sought a major organization to raise their national profile. San Francisco civic leaders have also lobbied hard, offering to finance a $4 billion Pac Bell Capitol Building using a combination of private corporate funds (40 percent), a county sales tax (35 percent), and a local cigarette tax (25 percent). Dallas, Seattle, and Toronto have also been mentioned as long shots.

Demonstrating its commitment to "stay in Washington if at all possible," Congress has invited more than a dozen architectural firms to submit proposals for a new D.C. capitol. Among the early favorites is the ambitiously titled "Halls Of Power," a retro-futuristic design by the Kansas City architectural firm of Hellmuth, Obata, and Kassabaum. The Halls Of Power would feature a retractable rotunda for daytime sessions, a Dancing Waters fountain in the front courtyard, and 55 more luxury boxes than the current building.

"This is just the kind of thing we need to stay competitive in today's lawmaking environment," said agent Barry Halperin, who represents many prominent government officials,

NERD from page 151

Above: Popular kids eat lunch in the school cafeteria.

late, laughing and drinking beer and socializing without any parental supervision. Sometimes, they even experiment with pot. I just hope this socializing phase passes, and that Adam will soon be back to hanging out in the basement playing Risk with his old friends."

For years, the Sprouses did not worry about Adam, secure in the knowledge that he would reach adulthood without facing the problems and pressures faced by so many of his more popular, attractive, socially skilled classmates.

"Other parents always worry about their kids experimenting with drugs and sex," Lawrence said. "Marcia and I never did. But now, there are all sorts of new questions. What happens when Adam is offered a joint? Or he meets a girl who's ready to go beyond first base? Or a group of kids invite him to drive to Chicago and stay overnight in a hotel?"

Throughout high school, Adam had been singularly focused on getting into MIT to get a math degree

before landing a job at Fermilab. His college and career plans, however, are now up in the air.

"I was asking Adam about the

> ## "It seems like only yesterday, our little Adam would stay in his room all day reading comic books and playing with his computer," Marcia continued. "Now, he'll try almost anything."

future, and he told me he might not want to get a Ph.D in calculus anymore," Lawrence said. "I asked him why and he said he was thinking about studying psychology or maybe even political science

instead. Then he muttered something about the University of Michigan seeming like 'a fun place to go to school.' I just know it's the influence of those cool kids he's been slumming around with."

The Sprouses' sense of alarm grew when Adam, who almost exclusively wore T-shirts and slacks, began taking a greater interest in his appearance.

"The last time we went shopping, he asked for designer jeans," Marcia said. "When I got upset, he said all the kids at school wore designer jeans and that it wasn't a big deal. Well, peer pressure may not be a big deal to him, but it is to me. He won't even let me cut his hair because I 'do it dorky.' The next thing you know, he's going to be cutting out of those advanced-calculus classes he's been taking at the community college and joining a fraternity."

"It seems like only yesterday, our little Adam would stay in his room all day reading comic books and playing with his computer," Marcia continued. "Now, he'll try almost anything. Where did we go wrong?" ∅

including Sen. Jim Jeffords (I-VT) and Secretary of Defense Donald Rumsfeld. "Washington can no longer afford to ignore the fact that visitor attendance has dropped every year since 1989. Our elected officials don't like coming to this building and, clearly, neither do their constituents."

Experts attribute the decline in congressional attendance to a number of factors, including increased home viewership of legislative activities on C-SPAN, with which Congress signed an exclusive 20-year, $360 million broadcast pact in 1984. It is not

known how a new capitol building would affect the terms of that soon-to-expire contract, but Congress is expected to restructure the deal to increase its share of revenues and secure possible advertising rights, whether it opts for rebuilding or relocation.

According to the lawmakers' constituents, the capitol is not the problem.

"Sure, the capitol's a little beat-up, but it's got its charms," said Geoff Lapointe, a Glendale, CA, voter. "The real problem is the legislators. Back

in the old days, you had big stars like John Kennedy and Richard Nixon. Who've they got today? Evan Bayh? Paul Sarbanes? Who's gonna get excited about those guys?"

Lapointe said he is "fed up" with the legislators and their demands.

"Those guys are all just a bunch of spoiled, overpaid crybabies," Lapointe said. "All they want is money—they don't care about all the hardworking people who pay their salaries. Look at 'em: When's the last time you saw them acting like a team? They can take their capitol and shove it." ∅

Point-Counterpoint: Footwear

Help! Sandal Season Is Here, And My Feet Are A Mess

By Tricia Duckett

Help! Sandal season is here, and my feet are a complete mess! I've got rough heels, ugly calluses, and ragged cuticles. Winter weather really did some serious damage to my feet. Oh, God, please, will somebody please tell me how to get these tootsies back in step for the beach? Somebody call 911! They're a complete disaster!

I love getting my toes pampered with a professional pedicure, complete with aromatherapy massage and a coat of fire-red polish, but I don't have time to wait for an appointment at my favorite spa. What can I do right now? Summer's heating up, and I've got a major fashion emergency on my hands!

I am in serious need of rehydration. But with so many great new moisturizing products on the shelves, how can I tell which one will get rid of this dry, flaky skin? I've got the basic equipment at home: pumice stone, contoured file, toenail clippers, and pedicure sponge, but what should I do? Should I soak, then exfoliate? Or the other way around? Should I use foot-bath salts, overnight cream, or soothing foot gel? Help! I'm going crazy!

In the past, Aveda has come to the rescue. I've had good luck with the Pedicure Essentials Repair Cream. But there are so many other great products out there. Should I hit Bath And Body Works and pick up some amazing wildflower-scented oils?

But what should I do? Should I soak, then exfoliate? Or the other way around?

Should I splurge on Revlon's pedicure system? Or should I go for the Body Shop's Foot Relief, with tea-tree oil that continues to exfoliate while feet are in socks or shoes? To be honest, I don't think any of those are a match for the train wreck that is my feet. Help!

I know that soothing my feet helps relieve tension and puts me in the right state of mind for summer fun. But these feet look so hopeless, I don't even know where to begin. Oh, if only I could hide them under my boots for just a few weeks longer!

I'm running out of time. The fashion calendar says I've got to lose the heavy shoes and slip into a pair of cute flip-flops or sexy sling-backs. But they're not going to be so cute or sexy on my hideous feet. Help! Save me! ∅

Help! I'm Trapped In A Burning Bus

By Cindy Waymer

Help! We're trapped in here! Can anyone hear us? Please, God, help! Somebody call 911! Help!

A tire blew, and we careened off the highway. I remember rolling... there was an explosion. The bus was tossed over the side, and we slipped down into the ravine. It's getting hot. I can't move my legs. My feet—they're stuck. I can't feel my feet! I see fire up front. Help! I'm trapped in a burning bus!

Water! We need water! It's an emergency!

Can anyone hear me? Please, somebody find me! There are 10 of us down here. Help! There's broken glass everywhere. Then the bus rolled... oh, God. Is it sliding again? Help!

Hurry! I need help now!

It's dark, and there's smoke. I don't know what to do. Which way is up? Should I try to drag myself out of a window? I can't just lie here. Is there some way to put out the fire? Can anyone hear me? Are you alive over there?

I need a doctor. Doctor? Doctor! Somebody tell me what to do. Does anyone on this bus know what to do? Is anyone trained for this? If only I had some sort of tool. Is there an ax or a hammer or something around here? Emergency! Emergency! Send an ambulance!

Does anybody have a phone? Oh, God. I don't even know where we are. We rolled into a meadow. I smell it burning. It smells like oil and pine needles.

It's the end. I know it. It's hopeless. I guess all I can do is await my fate. I should try to face it calmly.

Oh, God. I'm running out of time. I'm not ready to die! There's so much I haven't done yet: have children, write a novel, travel the world. This can't be the end. Help! Save me! ∅

Your Horoscope

By Lloyd Schumner Sr.
Retired Machinist and
A.A.P.B.-Certified Astrologer

Aries: (March 21–April 19)
Your prayers have finally been answered. Unfortunately, they're your prayers from 20 years ago. Start looking for a place to put all the ponies.

Taurus: (April 20–May 20)
You will achieve a certain sort of renown for your brief stint as host of the Animal Planet program *The Crocodile Hunted.*

Gemini: (May 21–June 21)
Your career as a plastic surgeon is in danger of coming to a premature end this week, when you confront your arch-enemy, the dreaded Steel Surgeon.

Cancer: (June 22–July 22)
You're rapidly becoming known as the office peacemaker, thanks to your ownership of a long-barreled, .44 caliber Colt Peacemaker.

Leo: (July 23–Aug. 22)
You will, through no doing of your own, receive as much as 10 percent off on a major purchase.

Virgo: (Aug. 23–Sept. 22)
You'll become the most popular thing in South Florida when the bigger bonefish start hitting hooks baited with you.

Libra: (Sept. 23–Oct. 23)
There's probably an easier way to get through life, but at this point you've gotten used to using the shovel.

Scorpio: (Oct. 24–Nov. 21)
Everyone knows you're the one who murdered the Dell Computer dude, but relax: There isn't a jury in the world that'd convict you.

Sagittarius: (Nov. 22–Dec. 21)
Your entire month will be ruined when a so-called "very special guest" turns out to be Alec Baldwin.

Capricorn: (Dec. 22–Jan. 19)
It's been almost three decades, but you think you're finally beginning to recover from the long, national nightmare of Vietnam movies.

Aquarius: (Jan. 20–Feb. 18)
Though you think of yourself as quite the character, Charles Dickens once said he would only give you eight or nine thousand words.

Pisces: (Feb. 19–March 20)
It's been said that there are only two things that come out of Texas: steers and queers. You're going to change all that.

LOVITZ FEVER from page 150

amounts of blood. Passersby were amazed by the unusually large amounts of blood. Passersby were amazed by the unusually large amounts of blood. Passersby were amazed by the unusually large amounts of blood. Passersby were amazed by the unusually large amounts of blood. Passersby were amazed by the unusually large amounts of blood. Passersby were amazed by the unusually large amounts of blood. Passersby were amazed by the unusually large amounts of blood. Passersby were amazed by the unusually large amounts of blood. Passersby were amazed by the unusually large amounts of blood. Passersby were amazed by the unusually large amounts of blood. Passersby were amazed by the unusually large amounts of blood. Passersby were amazed by the unusually large amounts of blood. Passersby were amazed by the unusually large amounts of blood. Passersby were amazed by the unusually large amounts of blood. Passersby were amazed by the unusually large amounts of blood. Passersby were amazed by the unusually large amounts of blood. Passersby were amazed by the unusually large amounts of blood. Passersby were amazed by the unusually large amounts of blood. Passersby were amazed by the unusually large

amounts of blood. Passersby were amazed by the unusually large amounts of blood. Passersby were amazed by the unusually large amounts of blood. Passersby were amazed by the unusually large amounts of blood. Passersby were amazed by the unusually large amounts of blood. Passersby were amazed by the unusually large amounts of blood. Passersby were amazed by the unusually large

---

Congress must be so stoned to come up with all those cool laws.

---

amounts of blood. Passersby were amazed by the unusually large amounts of blood. Passersby were amazed by the unusually large amounts of blood. Passersby were amazed by the unusually large amounts of blood. Passersby were amazed by the unusually large amounts of blood. Passersby were amazed by the unusually large amounts of blood. Passersby were amazed by the unusually large amounts of blood. Passersby were amazed by the unusually large amounts of blood. Passersby were amazed by the unusually large amounts of blood. Passersby were amazed by the unusually large

see LOVITZ FEVER page 159

Courtney Love Screams At Korean Manicurist

see PEOPLE page 4C

Sprite Introduces Cola-Flavored Sprite

see PRODUCTWATCH page 11B

Vivid Video Announces Plans To Lay 65 Percent Of Workforce

see BUSINESS page 1D

STATshot

A look at the numbers that shape your world.

Least-Wanted Gift Certificates

1. One free hour of she-male bodywork from Tatiana
2. $10 at Ajar: The Door-Jamb Superstore
3. Half-day pass to Two Flags Good America
4. $20 at The Smorgasmorgue
5. Three-year subscription to *Plus-Size Bride* magazine
6. $12.50 at Professor Pucker's Gently Used Sex-Toy Emporium

THE ONION • $2.00 US • $3.00 CAN

the ONION®

VOLUME 38 ISSUE 21   AMERICA'S FINEST NEWS SOURCE™   6–12 JUNE 2002

National Science Foundation: Science Hard

INDIANAPOLIS—The National Science Foundation's annual symposium concluded Monday, with the 1,500 scientists in attendance reaching the consensus that science is hard.

"For centuries, we have embraced the pursuit of scientific knowledge as one of the noblest and worthiest of human endeavors, one leading to the enrichment of mankind both today and for future generations," said keynote speaker and NSF chairman Louis Farian. "However, a breakthrough discovery is challenging our long-held perceptions about our disci-pline—the discovery that science is really, really hard."

"My area of expertise is the totally impossible science of particle physics," Farian continued, "but, indeed, this newly discovered 'Law of Difficulty' holds true for all branches of science, from astronomy to molecular biology and everything in between."

The science-is-hard theorem, first posited by a team of MIT professors in 1990, was slow to gain acceptance within the science community. It gathered momentum following the 1997

see SCIENCE page 160

Above: Farian explains the NSF findings.

Life Jackets Issued To All Americans For Some Reason

WASHINGTON, DC—Assuring the nation that "there is no need for alarm," the Office of Homeland Security issued all U.S. citizens life jackets for some unexplained reason Monday.

"Everything is fine. You have nothing to worry about," said Homeland Security Director Tom Ridge during a televised press conference. "Still, just to be 100 percent on the safe side, I would urge all Americans to keep these life vests on at all times."

Ridge said he was not at liberty to divulge the specific reason for the unprecedented national life-jacket distribution, but he insisted that the move is "merely a minor precautionary measure."

"To say exactly what these life vests are for would not be in the best interests of national security, but I promise that this is not indicative of any serious threat," Ridge said. "The best thing for everyone to do is simply go about their normal lives. With their life vests on, of course."

Ridge went on to say that,

Above: Life-jacketed pedestrians cross a busy intersection in Manhattan.

in addition to the life jackets, citizens should keep the accompanying kits—containing a packet of fluorescent-orange marker dye, shark-repellent pel-lets, and three magnesium flares—on their person at all times.

Citizens have reacted to the federal mandate with

see LIFE JACKETS page 160

Klan Rally 70 Percent Undercover Reporters

Above: Undercover reporters and a handful of actual Klansmen at the rally.

SPARTANBURG, SC—Vowing to "defend white Christian America against its mongrel assailants," some 20 members of the Knights of the Ku Klux Klan and more than 45 investigative reporters posing as members rallied on the steps of Spartanburg's city hall Saturday.

"Don't blow my cover, but I'm actually here doing a story for *Dateline NBC*," said John Larson, a correspondent for the news-magazine, speaking from under a white hood. "Man,

I've caught some unbelievable stuff on the digital recorder strapped to my chest. [*Dateline* executive producer] Neal [Shapiro] is definitely gonna want to lead with this piece."

Joining Larson in the call for white racial purity were reporters covertly working for dozens of newspapers, magazines, and television programs, including *The Washington Post*, *Newsweek*, and *20/20*.

"I'm doing an article for *The Atlantic Monthly*

see KLAN page 159

157

The India-Pakistan Conflict

Tensions continue to rise between India and Pakistan, with the nuclear rivals threatening to go to war over the disputed Kashmir region. What do *you* think?

"Ever since the days of Gandhi, India has been eager to overcome the stereotype that they're a bunch of wise, deeply spiritual peacemakers."

Irene Collins
Dental Hygienist

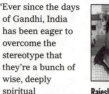

"Oh, don't worry. All this tension and conflict is just a prelude to the showstopping Bollywood dance number."

Rajesh Subhraveti
Cashier

"If it does come down to a full-scale war, I'm siding with whichever country makes that awesome puffy bread."

Gina Lathon
Student

"Why would they fear a nuclear war? Pakistan's Muslims have an eternity of honeyed figs awaiting them in the afterlife, and India's Hindus will all just get reincarnated."

Andrew Schorr
Systems Analyst

"India and Pakistan may be the next nations to use nukes in war, but no one had better forget who was first. USA! USA! USA!"

Rich Ketcham
Delivery Driver

"You know, this is precisely why I only read the sports and comics sections."

Marlon Watts
Architect

The FBI Overhaul

Under fire for pre-Sept. 11 intelligence breakdowns, the FBI unveiled a sweeping reform plan last week. Among the proposed changes:

- For every successful terrorist strike against U.S., bureau must put quarter in "terrorism jar"
- Thorough overhaul of bureau's Division Where Hard Evidence Of Terrorist Threats Goes, Never To Be Seen Again
- New "Intelligence Bucks" enable CIA agents and FBI agents to barter fair exchanges of information
- Elimination of wasteful bureaucratic procedures like search warrants and reading of rights
- Cancellation of bureau's controversial "X-Files" department, whose investigations of paranormal phenomena were viewed with strong skepticism by many within the bureau's higher ranks
- Communication between field agents, regional directors streamlined to improve buck-passing process
- New wiretapping division promises personal, unobtrusive service for all Americans
- Agents now authorized to arrest known terrorists

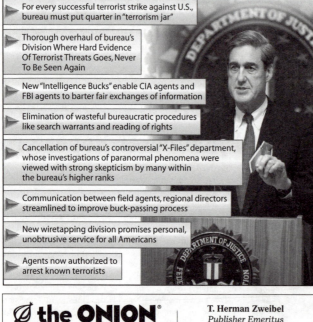

the ONION ®
America's Finest News Source.™

Herman Ulysses Zweibel
Founder

T. Herman Zweibel
Publisher Emeritus
J. Phineas Zweibel
Publisher
Maxwell Prescott Zweibel
Editor-In-Chief

General Mills' *Star Wars: Episode II* Cereal Gets It All Wrong

By Terry Sabol

Talk about disappointing.

I waited years for *Star Wars: Episode II* cereal, and now that it's finally here, it's... this. To call this cereal a letdown would be an understatement. From the light-saber marshmallows that look more like tulips to the lame "adventure game" on the back, General Mills' ill-conceived *Star Wars: Episode II* cereal gets it all wrong.

Maybe it's my fault. I got myself so psyched in the days leading up to the cereal's release, I couldn't help but be a little disappointed. I shielded myself from spoilers as best I could: I knew it would be corn-based and that there would be, among others, R2-D2-shaped pieces, but not much else. I worked ahead so I could get May 10 off from work, and I was first in line when the IGA opened. I ran giddily to the cereal aisle and proudly—proudly!—bought two boxes, one of each of the two collector's-edition designs.

Trembling with excitement, I ran home and cranked up John Williams' score. I sat down at my kitchen table and gazed at the front of the box, from which the visages of Anakin Skywalker, Senator Amidala, and Count Dooku stared back at me, almost daring me to take a bite. I poured myself a heaping bowl and, with unbearable anticipation, took my first taste of the first new *Star Wars*-themed cereal in almost 20 years.

Let me backtrack here for a minute. The year is 1983. I am 11 years old, and Kellogg's C-3POs have just hit the market. With my allowance money, I buy my own personal box, because there was no way I was sharing one with the rest of the family. That very first bowl opened my eyes to a thrilling new world of space-fantasy-themed breakfast foods.

What I found inside that box was a wonder to behold. Sublimely delicious oat, wheat, and corn pieces—no marshmallows or raisins or anything. None were necessary, as they would only get in the way of Lucas' vision. This was no "part" of a complete breakfast, but a complete breakfast in and of itself! You took one bite and said, "There's a galaxy-spanning saga of rebellion and romance in my mouth!" On top of that, on the back of the box was a cutout mask of one of six *Star Wars* characters. *That* was a fucking cereal.

I finished that box in one day and soon started washing cars to buy more. By the end of the week, I had all six masks and got a good start on the box variations. A buddy of my cousin worked at the IGA, so he got the promotional standee, the lucky bastard.

I'm an adult now, but that magical "Summer Of C-3POs" will always be a cherished memory. I can still recite the commercial from memory: "Twin rings fused together for two crunches in every double O." That was back when George Lucas could do no wrong.

Flash-forward to May 10, 2002. I'm sitting at the kitchen table, staring into a bowl of sweetened corn puffs and marshmallow pieces, and I'm not sure what to tell you. Yes, it's sweet-

> **And those R2-D2 marshmallow pieces that were so heavily hyped? I can't even begin to convey how little they resemble the droid.**

tasting. We knew it would be sweet-tasting. The puffs are small, uniformly shaped, sugar-glazed corn spheroids. Looks like Kix, tastes like Cap'n Crunch. If I were blindfolded, I doubt I could have told you this was meant to be a *Star Wars: Episode II* cereal.

And those R2-D2 marshmallow pieces that were so heavily hyped? I can't even begin to convey how little they resemble the droid. Poor R2 looks like a cross between Inky from Pac-Man and a stick of roll-on deodorant. I realize it's not always easy to produce a reasonable facsimile of a person or object when you're reducing it to a tiny morsel of corn starch and gelatin, but it doesn't look like General Mills was even trying.

The Slave I marshmallow is, quite possibly, even worse. Not only is it shaped like some sort of bizarre, melted anvil, but its coloration does not even remotely resemble the blue-gray steel of Jango Fett's trusty ship. Instead, the marshmallow is neon-green with a wild swirl of electric blue. That's just lazy cerealmaking, plain and simple. Did the folks at General Mills even bother to watch any of the *Star Wars* movies? From the looks of this sugary abomination, it sure doesn't seem so.

Now, I assure you, there is no bigger *Star Wars* fan than me. But no one can convince me that this cereal isn't just something George Lucas threw together for his kids. That's what it all comes down to in the end. If George Lucas could, I bet he'd go back in time

see CEREAL page 160

Affair Broken Up By Other Affair

ODESSA, TX—An extramarital affair between local claims adjuster Ken Hubrin and cocktail waitress Teri Belasco came to an abrupt end Monday when Hubrin informed his mistress that he had been cheating on her with coffee-shop manager Amanda Strauss.

"Don't get me wrong, Teri is a remarkable woman," said Hubrin, whose wife of nine years, Nancy Hubrin, is unaware of either affair. "We had some great times during our eight months together. But sometimes, the spark goes out of a relationship, and you don't even realize it until you meet someone who truly thrills you. For me, that person was Amanda."

According to Hubrin, he and Belasco seemed to have the perfect adulterous relationship, until he met Strauss.

"Things were very comfortable between Teri and me. Maybe too comfortable," Hubrin said. "We'd meet at the Days Inn out by the highway every Wednesday while Nancy was at her aerobics class. We'd get together at her place on Mondays during my lunch break because that was her day off. Sometimes, on Saturdays, I'd tell Nancy I was going jogging with my friend Henry, then go to Teri's apartment for a quickie. We had a nice little routine, but somewhere along the way, our infidelity had gone stale. That became painfully obvious once I met Amanda."

Hubrin said he met Strauss on May 10 after Belasco broke a secret rendezvous with him due to

Right: Ken and Nancy Hubrin on their June 1993 wedding day. Top: Mistress Teri Belasco, whom Hubrin cheated on with Amanda Strauss (bottom).

see AFFAIR page 161

KLAN from page 157

about what it means to be part of the Klan in the 21st century," said Peter Underwood, a 1999 graduate of Columbia University. "Well, okay, I'm doing it on spec, but I know they'll go for it. Worst-case scenario, I'm sure I can at least get some of the secret documents I snagged into the Readings section in *Harper's*."

"My editor absolutely eats this undercover shit up," said *Pittsburgh Post-Gazette* reporter Brian O'Neill, holding aloft a "Wake Up, White People!" sign. "More important, so does the Pulitzer committee. I think this may finally be my year."

O'Neill said his white robe "provides a steel cloak of anonymity," not only from the public, but also from other reporters.

"I was in the hotel this morning, and I ran into Jason Garcia. He's a reporter at *The Orlando Sentinel* who I know a bit from SPJ conferences and whatnot," O'Neill said. "He was pretty vague about what he was doing in Spartanburg. Later, at the rally, I couldn't help but notice that nice Citizen diving watch he wears sticking out of a Grand Council robe. Damn, that guy always was a go-getter."

Over the course of the two-hour rally, no journalists were ferreted out by the Klansmen. To the trained eye, however, some differences could be detected. Several times, reporters were seen disrupting the marching formation as they stooped to scribble notes, take photos with digital cameras, or answer cell phones. In addition, a

number of lavaliere microphones could be seen poking out of robes.

The undercover journalists were also distinguishable by their footwear. While the real KKK members tended to wear heavy work boots, the journalists were divided between sensible leather oxfords and

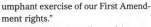

> "I think I did a pretty good job blending in," said Debra Rafalski, a freelancer on assignment from *Mother Jones* magazine. "At one point, I even shouted, 'Let's send those n-words back to Africa!'"

beat-up sneakers.

"I think I did a pretty good job blending in," said Debra Rafalski, a freelancer on assignment from *Mother Jones* magazine. "At one point, I even shouted, 'Let's send those n-words back to Africa!'"

One of the few journalists to speak before the crowd, Rafalski told rally-goers that the event represented "a tri-

umphant exercise of our First Amendment rights."

"Free speech, regardless of its content, always deserves full protection—not because it is necessarily right or good, but because our democratic institutions are only safe when all ideas, no matter how hateful or virulent, are allowed to be heard," Rafalski told the crowd through a bullhorn. "In fact, all of you counter-demonstrators, I respect your right to be here, just as the U.S. Supreme Court has determined that it is our right to be here."

Added Rafalski: "Oh, and also, the Jews are bleeding this country dry."

The rally also gave the reporters a chance to interact with Klan members one-on-one. While preparing for the march to city hall, *60 Minutes* reporter Richard Carleton chatted casually with a KKK member who was painting a "Hail Hittler [sic]" sign with one hand while holding a beer in the other.

"Isn't it interesting that the original KKK was organized in Pulaski, TN, during the winter of 1865 by six former Confederate army officers?" Carleton, clad in a white robe, remarked to the man. "We gave our society a name adapted from the Greek word kuklos, or 'circle,' and our activities were directed against the Reconstruction governments and their leaders, both black and white. As a member of such a tradition-based organization, how does that make you feel? Do you think this fact subverts our modern agenda?"

Carleton then rushed back to his room at the Spartanburg Ramada to transcribe his notes while the exchange was fresh in his mind.

In spite of the significant attendance boost provided by the reporters, some KKK members said the rally turnout fell short of their expectations.

"In my granddaddy's day, 10, 15, even 20 hundred Klansmen used to come 'round for a rally," said Valdosta, GA, carpenter Randy Jones, a KKK member since 1988. "The way things are nowadays, we didn't even get to have horses at the rally because we couldn't fit their food and transport into the budget."

Saturday's rally nearly had to be called off, but was saved from cancellation by the reporters. Less than an hour before the scheduled start time, the chapter realized it did not have the $1,500 "parade fee" required by the city. Fortunately, dozens of new Klansmen like *Chicago Tribune* reporter Stuart Zimmel volunteered to chip in an extra $50 each.

"I did have to pay membership dues and the extra $50 and buy the robe and all that, but as long as I save my receipts, I should get reimbursed for everything by the *Trib*," Zimmel said. "I admit, it's strange to give money to a group that wrongly persecutes so many, but that just makes it all the more vital that I blow the lid off their inner workings and expose their racist agenda once and for all. Plus, a story like this will look pretty sweet in my clips." ∅

159

equal parts curiosity and consternation.

"I'm not sure I like this," said Dan Speigel, a Seattle advertising executive. "Why do I have to wear this thing on the bus when I go to work—a bus, I might add, which is now equipped with side pontoons and driven by a uniformed Coast Guard officer?"

"On the subway today, the announcer guy said that our seat cushions can be used as flotation devices," said Danielle Uris of New York City. "When did they start saying that?"

During a Tuesday appearance on *Larry King Live*, Vice-President Dick Cheney stressed that the life-vest distribution has nothing to do with the current state of world affairs.

"This move was not done in anticipation of any sort of terrorist attack," Cheney said. "That's ridiculous. If only you were privy to the specifics of the closed-door meeting I had this morning with President Bush, Tom Ridge, Condoleezza Rice, Secretary of State Powell, Defense Secretary Rumsfeld, CIA director George Tenet, and several leading State Department meteorologists, you would know just how silly and unfounded those fears are."

Added Cheney: "The U.S. has received no threats at any time in the past 22 hours, so you can all just relax."

In spite of such assurances, many Americans remain concerned.

"I don't like having to keep the kids in their little water wings," said Michelle Barerras, a Grand Junction,

CO, third-grade teacher. "They look really cute in them, but it's unnerving. And this morning, all the teachers received a Department of Education memo informing us that geography units would soon be obsolete. It's being replaced with a special 'Swimming Is Fun-damental!' unit with an emphasis on surviving high waves and avoiding waterborne automobiles. Why?"

"On CNN today, they said the current nationwide threat level on the Homeland Security Advisory System was just raised from 'Elevated' to 'Extreme,'" said Eileen Buchsbaum of St. Louis. "Cheney told reporters it was just 'routine procedure,' and that it had nothing to do with any false rumors of thermal bombs planted beneath the ice caps."

While most citizens are unhappy about the vague warnings, the sudden emphasis on water safety has proven a boon to some traditionally stagnant industries. SeaTech, a San Diego-based harpoon manufacturer, was recently awarded a $2.2 billion government subsidy to develop a lightweight, handheld harpoon that can withstand water temperatures above 200 degrees. And the Department of the Navy expects the construction of its newly announced Idaho, Missouri, and Ohio shipyards to create more than 50,000 new jobs.

President Bush, attempting to further allay fears, addressed the nation Tuesday.

Above: A police officer patrols Brooklyn in the new NYPD uniform.

"My fellow Americans, you may have noticed some small changes in the way we're asking you to go about your daily business," said Bush, his words muffled by a brass diving helmet. "The government is not trying to scare you. We just want you to be prepared for the very remote possibility that your lives will never be the same."

"Again, I cannot stress enough what a longshot that particular unspecified scenario is," Bush continued. "We are not facing what I would call a 'credible threat,' so don't even bother worrying about it."

Bush went on to say that, in the coming weeks, those living in the Midwest and parts of the Sun Belt may notice a sudden increase in the number of submersibles in the streets. He also asked residents of Miami, New York, and San Francisco to be tolerant of any inconvenience caused by the construction of large trimaran-hull ships there, urging them to be considerate of the workers racing to finish them by next week.

"I expect every citizen to do his duty and be brave," Bush said. "Good night, and God bless the United Aquatic States of Hydro-America." ✍

---

publication of physicist Stephen Hawking's breakthrough paper, "Lorentz Variation And Gravitation Is Just About The Hardest Friggin' Thing In The Known Universe."

This weekend's conference, featuring symposia on how hard the Earth sciences are, how confusing medical science is, and how ridiculously ungettable quantum physics is, represented a major step forward for the science-is-hard theorem.

"We now believe that the theorem is 99.999% likely to be true, after applying these incredibly complex statistical techniques that gave me a splitting headache," Farian said. "A theorem is like a theory, but I, don't know, it's different."

Members of the scientific establishment were quick to affirm the NSF discovery.

"To be a scientist, you have to learn all this weird stuff, like how many molecules are in a proton," University of Chicago physicist Dr. Erno Heidegger said. "While it is true that I have become an acclaimed physicist and reaped great rewards from my career, one must not lose sight of the fact that these blessings came only after studying all of this completely impossible, egghead stuff for years."

Dr. Ahmed Zewail, a Caltech chemist whose spectroscopic studies of the transition states of chemical reactions earned him the Nobel Prize in 1999, explained in layman's terms

Above: The scientists' assessment of a recent MIT paper on quantum physics.

just how hard the discipline of chemistry is, using the periodic table of the elements as a model.

"Take the element of tungsten and work to memorize its place in the periodic table, its atomic symbol, its atomic number and weight, what it looks like, where it's found, and its uses to humanity, if any," Zewail said. "Now, imagine memorizing the other 100-plus elements making up the periodic table. You'd have to be, like, some kind of total brain to do that."

As hard as chemistry and other traditional sciences may be, scientists say such newer disciplines as quantum physics are even more difficult.

"Quantum physics has always been a particularly tough branch of science," UCLA physicist Dr. Hideki Watanabe said. "But in addition to being some of the smartest Einstein-y stuff around, it is undeniably a really stupid, pointless thing to study, something you could never actually use in the real world. This paradoxical dual state may one day lead to a new understanding of physics as a way to confuse and bore people."

"I guess there's cool stuff about science," Watanabe continued, "like space travel and bombs. But that stuff is so hard, it's honestly not even worth the effort." ✍

---

and digitally remaster the "Rebel Rocket" toy premium out of C-3POs because it's too violent for his children. (As if a toy rocket could be too violent for a war-themed cereal.)

I guess that's just how the business is nowadays, all marshmallows and foil boxes. You can't even get a cereal made unless you attach it to a big-ticket summer release, then drop to your knees and lick General Mills' boots.

I don't want to get into a whole drawn-out debate about this. I'm 30

I guess that's just how the business is nowadays, all marshmallows and foil boxes.

years old and am too busy to spend hours arguing with the fanboys on the General Mills message boards who automatically embrace this as the Second Coming of Cheerios. But I am chagrined, make no mistake. If I had the chance to speak to George Lucas, I would strongly urge him to sit down, eat two big bowls of C-3POs, and remember how he used to do it.

And I'm never trusting Harry Knowles again. He likes every damn cereal. ✍

White Person Waved Through Beeping Walgreens Security Barrier

CHICAGO—Caucasian shopper Bryce Glynn, 34, was waved through a beeping Walgreens security barrier Tuesday after the store's alarm system was activated by a CD purchased at a nearby Sam Goody. "Go ahead," said cashier Maria Ordonez with a casual waving motion. "You're fine." As Glynn volunteered to open his shopping bag to show its contents, the security guard at the store's entrance declined the offer, insisting that he exit unchecked.

Jackie Chan's Ancestors Shamed By Blooper Reel

HONG KONG—The shades of the ancestors of action hero Jackie Chan were posthumously disgraced upon seeing a "blooper reel" at the end of Rush Hour 2. "I die a thousand deaths when my dishonorable progeny fails to remember his line," said the ghost of Chan Kim-Yiang, who died fighting against the British occupation of Hong Kong in 1840. "To see him flip off a restaurant table, only to land wrong and bonk his head, brings dishonor to all the Chans who have passed from this world into the realm of wind and ghosts."

Drought-Ravaged NYC Institutes Alternate-Side-Of-Street Firefighting

NEW YORK—Suffering from months of drought, New York City instituted alternate-side-of-the-street firefighting Monday. "On odd-numbered days, even-numbered buildings are not permitted to catch fire," Mayor Michael Bloomberg said at a press conference. "For those who fail to comply, we will not be able to put out your fire until the following morning. Your kind cooperation will help conserve water resources throughout the New York area."

Hypnotist Looking For Gimmick To Set Him Apart From Other Hypnotists

CHICAGO—Hypnotist Ed "Dr. Mysterioso" Allen is seeking a gimmick to set him apart from the hundreds of other hypnotists on the nightclub circuit. "I don't know, there's already a bunch of singing hypnotists and a ventriloquist hypnotist," said Allen Monday, as he leafed through ads in the back pages of Getting Sleepy, a hypnotism trade magazine. "Maybe I could be the juggling hypnotist. Or wear some sort of funny hat. I just don't want to be lost in the crowd."

New Ad Preys On People With 'Ideas'

LOS ANGELES—A new ad appearing in dozens of magazines and newspapers shamelessly preys on people with "ideas." "Turn your idea into $$$!" read the 1/16th-page ad, which ran this week in the classifieds section of Parade and Rolling Stone. "Learn how top inventors get their ideas off the page and into the marketplace!" It remains to be seen how the nation's idea-having demographic will respond to the unnamed advertiser's attempt to charge a fee per idea submission, successful or not.

Area Woman Slams Down Phone, Waits For It To Ring

STARKVILLE, MS—Following a heated conversation with boyfriend Chris Lea, area resident Michelle Aston, 22, violently slammed down her phone receiver and immediately began waiting for Lea to call back. "He'll call," Aston said. "He's too smart not to." Aston waited six minutes and eleven seconds before heading to the back porch to smoke a cigarette. ✍

AFFAIR from page 159

illness.

"When Teri cancelled on me, I was pretty disappointed," Hubrin said. "I didn't want to just mope around in front of my wife, so instead of going home, I went to a coffee shop. This

> "Teri is a smart, beautiful woman, and I wish her only the best. I know that somewhere out there is a married man who's going to make her a very happy mistress, but I just don't think I'm that married man."

beautiful woman was working the counter alone, and we got to talking. She told me her name was Amanda. Next thing you know, it's nearly 11 p.m., and the place is closing. Just before I left, on a crazy whim I said, 'What are you doing Wednesday?' That's how it started."

Prior to his first date with Strauss, Hubrin lied to Belasco about his plans for the evening.

"I told Teri I had to go to dinner with Nancy and some old college friends," Hubrin said. "I think she knew something was up. I felt really awful, deceiving her like that, but I had a feeling I would've missed out on a really special affair if I didn't give Amanda a chance."

According to Hubrin, halfway though his date with Strauss, he could "already tell that she was the girl on the side for me."

"We went to this little out-of-the-way place for drinks and just talked and talked until I had to race home before Nancy suspected something," Hubrin said. "The whole time, I kept thinking, 'She is amazing.' I told her about my wife, but she'd already deduced that I was married from the ring mark on my finger. The first few months I was seeing Teri, she had no idea I was married. So, obviously, Amanda has a little more going on upstairs, which I always find attractive in a mistress."

Added Hubrin: "Still, I didn't tell Amanda about Teri, because I didn't want her to think I was some three-timing creep."

Hubrin said Belasco did not take the breakup well.

"When I told Teri about Amanda, she screamed, 'How could you do this to me and Nancy?'" Hubrin said. "Then she said, 'Don't you love me?' I said I did and still do, but that I've never met anyone quite like Amanda. Teri is a smart, beautiful woman, and I wish her only the best. I know that somewhere out there is a married man who's going to make her a very happy mistress, but I just don't think I'm that married man."

Asked about his future plans with Strauss, Hubrin was candid.

"This early in an extramarital affair, it's hard to tell," Hubrin said. "I'm willing to devote whatever free time I can to Amanda for the foreseeable future, provided things continue going smoothly and she can keep her mouth shut." ✍

Career Separates

When Roz, my Fashion Bug supervisor, called the entire staff together for a special meeting, I swore that this time, I'd come prepared. Whenever we have a meeting, Ellen, the girl who got the assistant-manager position instead of me just because she's Roz's friend, brings a treat like crumb cake or donuts. Everybody always makes such a big fuss about it, like she made this big effort. (Her baked goods are homemade, all right… in Mrs. Entenmann's home!)

A Room Of Jean's Own
By Jean Teasdale

Well, this time, I decided to beat Ellen at her own game and bring in a treat, too. Only my treat wouldn't contain partially hydrogenated cottonseed oil! So I felt pretty good when I walked into the meeting with a big tray of my famous dark-passion cherry-mint brownies with cocoa-cream-cheese/peanut-butter frosting. (And I felt even better when I didn't spot a crumb of Ellen's "homemade" crumb cake on the break-room counter!)

But nobody smiled when they saw my treats. In fact, Roz had a pained expression on her face, and Ellen was fiddling awkwardly with the stretchy wrist cord that held her work keys. Tanya and Pat, the other sales associates, sat on their folding chairs with their heads down.

"Uh, thanks for bringing in those bars, Jean, but I don't think anyone's in the mood to eat right now," Roz said. "I was going to wait until everyone got here, but Tanya and Pat already guessed the bad news. Charming Shoppes, which, as you know, owns Fashion Bug, announced plans to

> "Lane Bryant?" Rick said. "The fat-chick store? Geez, Jean, if you worked there, I bet your net pay would be about $10 a week, 'cause you'd be buying up new clothes left and right." Darn! Rick knows me too well!

close a couple hundred stores. Last night, I got word from Cherie, our regional manager, that our store will definitely be among them."

I couldn't believe my ears. "But why?" I asked. "This is such a great place for people to shop! It's not uncomfortably crammed with wall-to-wall shoppers like the mall is, and we have plenty of stock."

Roz didn't say anything for a couple of seconds. "Jean," she finally said, "all

see TEASDALE page 162

those days you'd sit at the register for hours on end, reading the entire paper without interruption because not one single customer came over, didn't that give you a clue that something was wrong?"

Well, of course I'd noticed the lack of business… I wasn't blind! But I didn't choose to see it all negatively like everyone else did. I just looked at our store as a delicious, well-kept secret. I know our society is capitalistic, but I think it's silly that people are always so go, go, go, gotta grab every last buck we can get. It undermines the quality of life. If Charming Shoppes had any sense, they'd keep our store open even if it *was* losing money, because I think people need nice little places where they can go to find cute, affordable cotton-lycra-blend leggings and be able to park their cars close to the entrance. If only a couple dozen people came to our store per week, more power to them, I say. They should be rewarded for their shopping smarts, not punished.

Anyhow, the store will be closing at the end of June, and I know I'll miss the place. This "bad location," as Roz called the strip mall where our store resides, has really grown on me. Besides us, the only other businesses are a frame store, an H&R Block, and a Hot Sam's, but I'd become attached to them, too. I bought some darling frames for some of my best cat snapshots. And a Hot Sam's pretzel, slathered in mustard and washed down with a Mr. Pibb, had become a daily ritual. Once, I even picked up a brochure about little-known deductions at the H&R Block, not because I cared about that sort of thing, but because I wanted to see the inside of the store.

One morning, about a week after the announcement, Pat and I were standing in front of the Bug, waiting for Roz to come and open up. When she got out of her car, Roz was all smiles. She told us that because the manager at the Lane Bryant at Southcreek Mall was going on permanent maternity leave right around the time the Bug was due to close, she had a virtual lock on the job.

That wasn't all the news she had. Roz had also learned that a new sales-associate position was opening up there. I don't know, I guess it was having to wait 10 minutes in a brisk wind and needing to pee real bad, but I was in a little bit of a snippy mood, and I didn't hide it.

"Since you'll be in charge, Roz, I guess Ellen will be joining you, since you're practically two peas in a pod," I said.

"Actually, after the store closes, Ellen is going to hostess at her uncle's restaurant," Roz said. "You know, Lane Bryant is Fashion Bug's sister chain, and since you gals are being laid off here, you're encouraged to apply if you're interested. In fact, they're holding off on advertising the position publicly so you can get first shot at it."

When I heard that, I just about died! *Lane Bryant?* Talk about movin' on

up! After the Disney Store, my dream employer was Lane Bryant! After all, they believe that we generously proportioned gals deserve to look good, too, and I sure can't argue with that philosophy! I was sooo excited, I couldn't resist telling hubby Rick that evening.

"Lane Bryant?" Rick said. "The fat-chick store? Geez, Jean, if you worked there, I bet your net pay would be about $10 a week, 'cause you'd be buying up new clothes left and right." Darn! Rick knows me too well!

Then he added: "It doesn't matter, though. That Roz broad will give the job to one of your coworkers. She's never liked you. How many times has she passed you over for a promotion?"

Rick was right. Roz probably just mentioned the job opening to me so I'd feel even worse when I didn't get it. As maddening as Rick can be, he often has this uncanny knack for reading a situation.

Upon arriving at work that next morning, I decided to have a few choice words with Roz. I'd come to terms with the fact that she wouldn't hire me at Lane Bryant, but I still wanted to let her know I didn't always appreciate her treatment of me.

"Roz, I really wanted to apply at Lane Bryant, but let's face it: You'd hire a hobo before you'd hire me," I said. "I know you and I don't always see eye-to-eye, but I don't understand why you should always punish me just because I'm not as cynical as you. You probably look at a position at Lane Bryant as just another job. But I truly believe in Lane Bryant. I strongly feel that plus-size women have a right to shine. Pardon my French, but I would have worked my

> **Roz didn't say anything for a couple of seconds, just like on the day she announced the store's closure. Then, finally, in a quiet voice, she said, "I'm not sure if this will matter to you right now, seeing how upset you are, but, Jean, you were my top candidate for the Lane Bryant job."**

hiney off there, more than any other job I've had. But you'll wind up hiring either Tanya or Pat, not because they care about women's-size fashions, but because they like your racy talk and smoke with you behind the store. I don't see why everybody has to be so hard and mean and suspicious all the

Aries: (March 21–April 19)
This week, you'll be living proof that one man can make a difference—at least to the owners of Lucky Lucy's All-U-Can-Eat Buffet.

Taurus: (April 20–May 20)
It'll be a nuisance wearing the Nielsen box on your head all week, but at least you'll find out that your viewership goes up when you're fighting or having sex.

Gemini: (May 21–June 21)
You'll be at the center of a gay-rights battle this week when you try to claim partnership benefits from both your lesbian and heterosexual marriages.

Cancer: (June 22–July 22)
Your dream of operating your own karaoke bar is shattered when you discover, on opening night, that you need to let others sing, too.

Leo: (July 23–Aug. 22)
Once again, you are relegated to being the one who causes the distraction while someone else gets to sneak past in the confusion and save the girl.

Virgo: (Aug. 23–Sept. 22)
It's all over but the shouting, but don't worry: It's going to be great shouting.

Libra: (Sept. 23–Oct. 23)
You will learn the hard way that climbing a mountain isn't the kind of thing to do drunk. But you promised.

Scorpio: (Oct. 24–Nov. 21)
The name "The Stripper Murderer" looms large in your future. Apparently, you'll either murder some strippers or be murdered by one.

Sagittarius: (Nov. 22–Dec. 21)
When resolving office conflicts, remember the wisdom of Mahatma Gandhi: If enough peasants die horribly, someone will probably notice.

Capricorn: (Dec. 22–Jan. 19)
You will find yourself living out the lyrics to a popular song, sort of, when love slaps you down where you belong.

Aquarius: (Jan. 20–Feb. 18)
Events will soon come to pass which will brand you forever as "the kind of guy who doesn't freak out if you shit in his stove."

Pisces: (Feb. 19–March 20)
The stars, without giving too much away, think there has never been a better time to stay home and avoid all galactic-adventure sci-fi movies.

time. I don't understand why I never fit in. I don't like to drink or swear. I like kitties and collecting dolls. And instead of bringing in stale donuts, I stay up late to bake sinfully sweet homemade goodies. These are all clean and normal things to do, aren't they? But, somehow, I'm the one who's the oddball. I'm the one people snicker at, instead of at the vulgar ones who have nothing to contribute to life. Well, I'm sorry you can't be big enough to give me a chance, Roz."

Roz didn't say anything for a couple of seconds, just like on the day she announced the store's closure. Then, finally, in a quiet voice, she said, "I'm not sure if this will matter to you right now, seeing how upset you are, but, Jean, you were my top candidate for the Lane Bryant job."

Since Pat was moving out of town and Tanya was too embarrassed to work at Lane Bryant, Roz said she was hoping—yes, hoping—that I would apply. She said she would have been happy to have me there. It was true that we didn't see eye-to-eye on everything, but she said she liked me. I "grow on a person," she told me, and

since her new staff at Lane Bryant was made up of complete strangers, I would have been a nice, familiar face to see every day.

"I'm sorry if you think I'm a vulgar person with nothing to contribute to life," said Roz, her voice wavering a little. "I don't think of myself that way. I don't think people who smoke or tell a dirty joke from time to time are automatically evil. But you're right about one thing: I don't think you'd be right for the position because, at this point, we couldn't work together. I'll tell Lane Bryant they should put a help-wanted sign in their window right away."

It figures that one of the few times I trust hubby Rick's judgment, it completely blows up in my face! (When I confronted him, he whined something about how he never said I should say anything to Roz. But he's just being a big weasel.) These next few weeks before we close are going to be rough, especially with Roz no longer talking to me. It's gotten so bad around the Bug, I'm actually looking forward to getting out of a clothing store, and that's never happened before! Ø

Bush Extremely Proud Of New Suit

see NATION page 4A

Unidentified Yowling Animal In Carrier Apparently Named Kiwi

see LOCAL page 9C

Life-Sized Cutout Of Brent Spiner Folded In Half, Placed In Dumpster

see LOCAL page 11C

STATshot

A look at the numbers that shape your world.

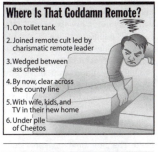

Where Is That Goddamn Remote?

1. On toilet tank
2. Joined remote cult led by charismatic remote leader
3. Wedged between ass cheeks
4. By now, clear across the county line
5. With wife, kids, and TV in their new home
6. Under pile of Cheetos

the ONION®

VOLUME 38 ISSUE 22   AMERICA'S FINEST NEWS SOURCE™   13–19 JUNE 2002

Body Of Missing *Mad* Magazine Reporter Found In Blecchistan

POTRZEBIE, BLECCHIS-TAN—Questions regarding the fate of *Mad* magazine reporter Phil Fonebone, kidnapped at the hands of Blecchistani extremists three months ago, were answered Monday with the discovery of his body at an undisclosed location near Potrzebie.

"Phil Fonebone's death was a brutal act of barbarism perpetrated by a group of clods, finks, and schmendricks who stand in direct opposition to the values we cherish as a democratic society," read a statement issued by *Mad* magazine. "On behalf of journalists and freedom lovers everywhere, we con-

Above: A September 2001 file photo of *Mad* reporter Fonebone while on assignment near the Blecchistani city of Plort.

demn this senseless, furshlugginer act of violence."

Widely admired by colleagues in the field of malaprop journalism, Fonebone, 32, won a 2002 Pee-yewlitzer Prize for his coverage of the Blecchistani crisis.

He also earned praise for reportage on such stories as the rise of Ayatoldya Soslayme in Iranaway and the hunt for terrorist leader Whoah-Ahma Big-Loudmouth.

Fonebone disappeared on

March 9 when *Mad*'s trademark dirigible, used by the reporter to get a "Berg's-eye view" of the Blecchistani war zone, was shot down near Potrzebie by unidentified extremists

see REPORTER page 166

Thousands Of High-School Sweethearts Prepare For Post-Graduation Breakup

WASHINGTON, DC—In a time-honored annual ritual, thousands of high-school seniors across the nation are cramming for final exams, trying on their graduation gowns, and preparing to break up with their longtime sweethearts.

"Amy is an amazing girl," said Lancaster (OH) High School senior Jeff Reidel, who next week is planning to break up with Amy Pocoroba, his girlfriend of three and a half years. "I

know we swore we'd be together forever, but, like me, she's got a lot of exciting opportunities ahead of her, and it just wouldn't be fair to her to keep her tied down."

Brianna Milbank, 17, a senior at Eisenhower High School in Prescott, AZ, said she plans to break up with boyfriend Chris Keegan in mid-July.

"We've already got plans for a July 4 camping trip that I'm really excited

see BREAKUP page 167

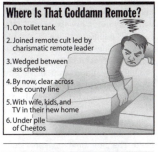

Above: Jeff Reidel and Amy Pocoroba, one of the nation's soon-to-break-up couples.

Getting Mom Onto Internet A Sisyphean Ordeal

ROCHESTER, MN—Karen Widmar, 33, who for the past two months has been trying to teach her 60-year-old mother how to use the Internet, called the endeavor "a Sisyphean ordeal" Monday.

"Jesus Christ, you have no idea," said Widmar after yet another unsuccessful lesson. "Every single thing I show her, no matter how simple, totally freaks her out. She's still afraid to click on pictures because she doesn't know where it's

going to take her."

Widmar said she introduced her mother Lillian to the Internet at her request.

"It's funny, I was always trying to get her interested so I could e-mail her," Widmar said. "Then, one day, she called me up and said she was watching *Today*, and they had a guest on who made potatoes, and the recipe was online, and was that the same as the Internet? When I told her it was, she got really excited.

see MOM page 167

Above: Lillian Widmar attempts to e-mail her daughter.

163

Canadian Immigration Under Fire

Canada's relatively lax immigration policy has drawn criticism from U.S. leaders, who say the country provides an easy home base for terrorists. What do *you* think?

Iris Murphy
Teacher

"I am suddenly very suspicious of my next-door neighbor, Khalid al-McKenzie."

Louis Chambliss
Systems Analyst

"Why would terrorists need to go through Canada to get to the U.S.? It's not like the FBI would catch them if they came straight here."

Bill Hrabosky
Cashier

"As a radical Islamic fundamentalist, I am seriously considering moving to Vancouver. It's *sooo* gorgeous there."

Michael Horner
Civic Planner

"Canada needs to start doing a better job of racial-profiling non-Inuits."

Don Nahorodny
Forklift Operator

"My God, we could go to war with Canada over this. I only pray there's an army platoon with the afternoon free."

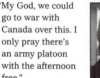

Penny Niekro
Homemaker

"See, I told you socialized medicine doesn't work."

The Bomb-Detection Machine

By Dec. 31, all U.S. airports will feature massive new baggage scanners. Among the device's features:

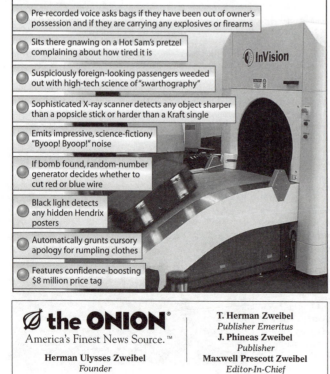

- Pre-recorded voice asks bags if they have been out of owner's possession and if they are carrying any explosives or firearms
- Sits there gnawing on a Hot Sam's pretzel complaining about how tired it is
- Suspiciously foreign-looking passengers weeded out with high-tech science of "swarthography"
- Sophisticated X-ray scanner detects any object sharper than a popsicle stick or harder than a Kraft single
- Emits impressive, science-fictiony "Byoop! Byoop!" noise
- If bomb found, random-number generator decides whether to cut red or blue wire
- Black light detects any hidden Hendrix posters
- Automatically grunts cursory apology for rumpling clothes
- Features confidence-boosting $8 million price tag

the ONION®

America's Finest News Source.™

Herman Ulysses Zweibel
Founder

T. Herman Zweibel
Publisher Emeritus
J. Phineas Zweibel
Publisher
Maxwell Prescott Zweibel
Editor-In-Chief

164

I Should Start Some Sort Of Huge Corporation

By Brian Mappert

Oh, man, I have been seriously short of funds lately. Working security at Rite Aid for $6.55 an hour is just not cutting it the way it used to. But I'm not worried, because last night, as I was standing there staring at the rows of shampoo bottles and disposable razors, the answer hit me: I should start some sort of huge corporation!

Those big companies pull in some serious cash. I'm talking billions and trillions of dollars every year. Even better, those guys don't even have to pay any taxes. They just write it all off as a business expense, and the government doesn't even mind, because it's happy for the jobs they create. It's true. Read the papers.

The question is, what kind of company should I start? Something like Rite Aid would actually be pretty good. That'd be easy money. All they do is take a bunch of products somebody else already made and put them on shelves and charge more for them than they paid. Home Depot, Wal-Mart, Best Buy... shit, all those companies make a ton of dough without actually manufacturing anything themselves!

If I ran this Rite Aid and all the other ones across the country, I could be making money every time someone walked out with a pack of cigarettes. Better yet, I could make even more money by being the company that sells Rite Aid the cigarettes. That's all Philip Morris does, and they pull in, like, $8,000 trillion a year. Pretty sweet gig, huh?

Know what else would be a good thing to start? One of those pharmaceutical companies. They don't make huge things, but they make a ton of money because you get a million people taking expensive little pills and that adds up really fast. All you gotta do is think up one good drug that no one else is making, and you're set. How 'bout Sniffloban, an anti-sneezant? See, I just made that up right there! Now, all I need is to find a scientist to make the pills, write him a check for, oh, $10,000 for his troubles, and my corporation keeps all the profits.

I'm guessing those phone companies do pretty good business, too. There's AT&T, Verizon, and Sprint, just to name a few. I'd call mine something that sounds all big and impressive. Like SuperGlobalTelCom. Or maybe something with some of the letters changed, like FoneKorp.

That would definitely work. But to really make big money, you need to find out what people want these days and then do that. For example, you wouldn't want to start a company that makes VHS tapes, because VHS tapes are on the way out. Digital is the future. So I could call my company Digicorp and make digital stuff, like equipment and media stuff and such. That'd be cool.

But how would I know if Digicorp is the right name? I'd get a bunch of people in a room and say, "What do you think the company should be called?" Rule Number One: Get a good name, and you're halfway there. Have you ever heard of TECO Energy, Baker Hughes, or Medtronic? No. Those are

> ## Something like Rite Aid would actually be pretty good. That'd be easy money. All they do is take a bunch of products somebody else already made and put them on shelves and charge more for them than they paid.

weak names, and that's why those companies are at the bottom of the Fortune 500. Now, have you heard of AllState, American Express, and Ford? Of course. These companies are making an assload of money, and a lot of that is due to name recognition.

Speaking of name recognition, ever hear of IBM? How about Apple? Microsoft? Of course you have. That's because they're all high-tech, and high-tech is hot right now. Anything with technology—computers, TVs, surgical equipment—we're talking green machine, baby. Those companies are successful because they keep coming up with new stuff. If you give people something new, something they haven't seen before, they'll want to buy it.

So, Rule Number Two: Give people something new. Break out of the mold. The first time someone came out with an eye-laser machine, I'm sure people said, "What the fuck? You want to stick a laser in people's eyes? Nobody's gonna want that." But the guy stuck to his guns, and now Lasik is huge. I see ads for them all over the place.

They say it takes money to make money. So anything that has to do

see CORPORATION page 168

Best Years Of Area Man's Life Apparently Never Going To Happen

MINOT, ND—The best years in the life of Frederick Videk—veteran, husband, and father of five—are never going to happen, the 51-year-old broken man realized Monday.

"Well, I guess that's that," said Videk, sitting in his pickup waiting for the light to change, the realization finally smacking him full in the face. "This is it—it's not going to get any better. In fact, it's probably just going to be a gradual but steady decline from here on."

Videk, who for years had waited for something to bring him satisfaction, then pulled over to the side of the road and watched cars pass by for an hour and a half. By the time he returned to the split-level ranch home he purchased in 1979 and has yet to pay off, his wife was angry with him, his favorite TV show was over, and his cold dinner had been given to the family dog.

"I guess I always just figured the really good years were right around the corner," Videk said. "What a pantload. I remember in high school, thinking that as soon as I got a car, the best years were really gonna kick in. I'd be able to go anywhere, get girls, maybe get laid, and people would think I was cool. Then, when I finally got a car, it was such a shitheap, I figured that once I got a better car, *then* everything would be fine. Well, you know what? I've owned 11 cars in my life, and I thought the same exact thing about each one of the fuckers. Not one in the succession of cars I've bought since I was 16 has ever done anything for me but drag my sorry ass to and from work every goddamn day of my life. That's it."

Shortly after returning home, Videk, feeling himself inexorably drawn into a vortex of despair, made his way to

---

Videk eventually relocated to the garage, where he stood next to his workbench and made patterns in the floor dust with his foot.

---

the upstairs bathroom, where, despite having no need to use the facilities, he sat on the toilet for approximately 20 minutes to avoid all human contact. The last seven of those 20 minutes were spent trying to ignore the pounding and whining of his teenage daughter Robyn, who pleaded with him to unlock the door so she could "get [her] face on."

Videk eventually relocated to the garage, where he stood next to his workbench and made patterns in the floor dust with his foot. While doing so, he pondered the fact that achieving his goal of getting laid merely resulted in the birth of another human being who wanted to get laid, too.

"I know Robyn thinks that if she gets one of the boys at school interested in her, she'll be popular, and that the best years of her life will begin,"

Above: Frederick Videk, who has finally stopped waiting.

Videk said. "Little does she know she's just perpetuating an endless string of DNA replication that isn't going anywhere."

After nearly an hour in the garage, Videk walked to his driveway and stared at a rake lying on its side on the front lawn.

"After I graduated high school in '68, I joined the Navy. I thought the best years of my life would finally arrive because I'd get out of this boring hellhole of a state," Videk said. "I now see that the feeling was oddly similar to the one I had in '72, right before I finished my first tour in the Navy, and all I wanted to do was get back to North Dakota where things were so much better. Why couldn't I see it at the time?"

Over the course of Videk's life, each
see MAN page 166

Line Cook Learns Leaving Restaurant Industry Not That Easy

SAN MARCOS, TX—Eric Weaver, a recently hired line cook at Cactus Jack's, is finding it extremely difficult to extricate himself from the restaurant industry, the 24-year-old aspiring musician said Monday. "Just when I think I've made a clean break, they pull me back in," said Weaver, who in April vowed never to work another restaurant position after quitting his dishwashing job at a local Denny's. "When the manager said, 'Welcome to the Cactus Jack's family,' it gave me icy chills."

Fixin's Added To Food Pyramid

WASHINGTON, DC—Updating the dietary guide to reflect current U.S. eating habits, the Department of Agriculture announced Monday that it has added a "fixin's" food group to the USDA Food Pyramid. "We recommend five to eight daily servings from the fixin's group, which includes such hearty sides as cole slaw, mashed potatoes, steak fries, baked beans, and mac 'n' cheese," Agriculture Secretary Ann Veneman said. "So go ahead and treat yourself to all the fixin's you want. They're not only free, they're recommended." Also falling within the fixin's group, Veneman said, are burger toppings, including fried onions, cheese sauce, and bacon-smothered mushrooms.

Kline Not Sure He Fits In At Oppendahl, Oppendahl, Kline & Oppendahl

NEW YORK—Despite having been a partner at the prestigious Manhattan law firm since 1984, Martin Kline is still not sure he fits in at Oppendahl, Oppendahl, Kline & Oppendahl LLP. "I don't know," the 53-year-old corporate-finance specialist said Monday. "I mean, sure, Bill, Larry, and Dan [Oppendahl] treat me like one of their own. But for some reason, I just somehow feel different. No matter how many contracts I draw up or hours I bill, I still don't quite feel like I belong."

Ted Nugent Talks That Way Even When Buying Socks

SAGINAW, MI—According to JC Penney men's-department sources, rocker Ted Nugent talks that way even when buying socks. "What color socks do I want? I want every damn color, plus a whole bunch of colors that don't even exist," Nugent told sales associate Jonathan Alexander. "Life is too short, man. Whether it's socks or shoes or whatever, you gotta bite into life like it's a great big ol' hunk of bison. Otherwise, you wake up and suddenly—poof—you're fat and old, and you never had any friggin' fun. And if you're not having fun, you may as well move to Iraq or Cuba or some other hellhole where there ain't no good times to be had." Nugent added that that's the way he sees it, and that if you don't like it, you can kiss his lily-white ass.

Colonoscopy Offers Non-Fantastic Voyage Through Human Body

DOVER, DE—A routine colonoscopy at the Dover Family Clinic in no way evoked the Isaac Asimov novel *Fantastic Voyage* or the 1966 film of the same name, patient Ed Garrity reported Monday. "Man, this really isn't anything like the movie," said Garrity, 54, watching the interior of his large intestine on a video monitor. "This voyage is decidedly non-fantastic." Garrity was then instructed to roll over on his side by nurse Marge Klogert, who bears no resemblance to Raquel Welch. ∅

armed with oversized slingshots. The weapons, it is believed, were provided by illegal arms dealers, possibly Moronicist extremists in the Blecchistani countryside.

The motivation for the attack remains unclear, but, according to a report by the Al-Jerkzeera News Network, the kidnappers were seeking a ransom of "$35 million—CHEAP!" from the editors of *Mad*.

With its strong anti-establishment stance and open criticism of social mores, *Mad* has long been viewed as an enemy by Potrzebian extremists, who consider it a corrupting Western influence. Blecchistani ultra-conservatives, known to confiscate stockpiles of *Mad* hidden in tree forts or under the mattresses of rebellious Blecchistani youths, have denounced the publication as "a bunch of garbage that will rot children's minds" and its editors as the "usual gang of idiots." Still, some Blecchistani youths, defying authorities' efforts to rid the nation of the magazine, have hidden copies inside large, state-sponsored textbooks and conservative propaganda.

"It is clear that Fonebone's irreverent coverage of 'the lighter side of

The motivation for the attack remains unclear, but, according to a report by the Al Jerkzeera News Network, the kidnappers were seeking a ransom of "$35 million—CHEAP!" from the editors of *Mad*.

international terrorism' earned him many enemies in Blecchistan," *Mad* editor Melvin Coznowski said. "But even in the face of death threats, he remained brave, saying with a wry smile, 'What, me worry?'"

Though many of the specifics regarding Fonebone's murder remain unclear, some details are known. The

body was badly decomposed, but coroners identified it by its oversized, folded-over feet. As for the identity of the perpetrators, reports suggest the involvement of one or more mysterious, trench-coated espionage agents

At the time of his capture, Fonebone was tracking down members of the al-Jaffi terrorist network.

dressed in either all-white or all-black clothing, and described as "angular, birdlike males with wide-brimmed, pointy hats."

A recently leaked memo from the State Department also confirms the interception of a Morse-coded message suggesting that the plot may have been masterminded by a shadowy figure known only as "Prohias." This same figure may have been responsible for an elaborate swivel-turret backwards-firing cannon found at the scene of the dirigible attack.

At the time of his capture, Fonebone was tracking down members of the al-Jaffi terrorist network, a group widely believed responsible for the devastating Snappy Answers To Stupid Questions Atrocities, a string of May suicide bombings intended to undermine efforts to establish democracy in Blecchistan. Asked if they knew anything about rumored al-Jaffi involvement in the Fonebone murder, suspects detained in connection with the bombings replied only with a series of three sarcastic variations on "No," leaving a fourth response blank for State Department officials to fill in themselves.

Mad staffers praised Fonebone for his passionate commitment to the cause for which he died.

"Phil Fonebone was a tireless crusader in the fight for a free press," managing editor Roger Kaputnik said. "This shameful act of violence against such a courageous man can only be described as 'murder in a

Above: A State Department memo on the search for Fonebone's killer.

jugular vein.'"

Continued Kaputnik: "Time and time again, *Mad* has faced the threats of oppression and tyranny. We have been attacked from the far right, when Estes Kefauver conducted his witch hunt on comics in the 1950s, and from the far left, when Fidel Castro forced one of *Mad*'s chief contributors to flee Communist Cuba for the subversive content of his cartoons. We have taken plenty of lumps—tall, elongated lumps circled by chirping birds and musical notes—yet we've never given in. Or folded in. The perpetrators of this act thought they

could destroy the free press, but they have succeeded only in rallying the free press against them. Phil Fonebone's death was truly a 'Ker-Schlumpf!' heard 'round the world."

A statement released by Gladys Fonebone, Phil's widow, echoed Kaputnik's sentiments.

"Phil believed that by exposing the truth and attacking hypocrisy, the world is made a better place," Fonebone said. "He dedicated his life to working toward a future where tolerance and compassion are values all people share. And that is a scene we'd all like to see." ∅

time he reached a milestone, he believed that his best years were about to begin. Among these life events were losing his virginity, getting married, fathering his first through fifth child, having his children move out, buying a better house, and getting his overbite fixed. None of these events, however, made the slightest impact on his overall happiness.

Compounding Videk's misery were depressing thoughts about the many things he has never gotten around to doing, including playing harmonica in a blues-rock band, breaking a 250 score in bowling, traveling to the ancient pyramids of Egypt, and learning to play harmonica in the

first place.

"It's like you're thinking, 'The world's my oyster and anything is possible,'" Videk said. "'As soon as this next immediate obstacle to happiness is cleared, I'll be able to do anything I want.' Then the goals become less and less realistic as you pass 35, and you start to set more modest goals for the best years of your life, like making shift supervisor at the goddamn screen-door factory where you work. Eventually, even these pathetically scaled-down fantasies prove unworkable, since some asshole named Glenn Harrigan has seniority at the plant and obviously isn't going anywhere. Suddenly, you're 51, and at

"Suddenly, you're 51, and at long last, you figure out that whatever it is you're hypothetically still waiting for, it's pretty much irrelevant."

long last, you figure out that whatever it is you're hypothetically still waiting for, it's pretty much irrelevant. Then you go to bed and have to

work at the screen-door factory for another nine hours the next day, and that's pretty much that."

"I guess I should stop thinking about life as something that even involves the term 'best years of my life,'" Videk told the rearview mirror of his car while parked behind a local Wendy's, eating a burger, Biggie fries, and Biggie Frosty. "I guess a more appropriate term would be something like 'least intolerable meals at fast-food drive-thrus of my life,' or something along those lines."

Still in relatively good health for a man his age, Videk then girded himself for the remaining 20 to 30 years before he dies. ∅

about, so I definitely want to wait until after that," Milbank said. "Chris is such an incredible guy, and these last two years have been amazing. But I just don't think I can give him what he needs right now."

As the seniors take one last look around the halls where they spent the past four years, they are also pausing to take one last look at the significant others they are about to dump.

"Amanda has the most beautiful eyes," said Trevor Hillegas of girlfriend Amanda Lum. "I can't tell you how many times I've gazed into them, thinking they were the only ones I'd ever want to look into. But that was before I visited UC–Santa Cruz. The chicks there are so hot, it's not even funny."

Hillegas said he has not closed the door on the possibility of getting back together with Lum, noting that he would still be open to the idea of the occasional hook-up with her while home during college breaks.

For most high-school seniors, graduation is the time when they cast off the remnants of childhood while accepting the challenges of adulthood. So, too, must they cast off the adolescent relationships forged by convenience, geographic proximity, and limited social opportunity.

"Jenny [Sykes] is the most beautiful

Above: A break-up note written from Omro (WI) High School senior Ronny Peltz to girlfriend Rachel Wohle.

girl in this school," said Brent Decker, a senior at Lake Winola (PA) High School. "But our school has only 220 students, and Penn State has, like, 40,000. There's no way she'd be the most beautiful on that campus."

Meanwhile, those slated to receive the dumpings remain confident that their relationships will endure.

"I love Zach so much," said Batavia (NY) High School senior Lisa Brack-

en, whose boyfriend, Zach Renfro, is joining the Navy after graduation. "He says he loves me, too, and that he'll try to get stationed near Boston where I'm going to college. I'm sure it'll all work out in the end."

Bracken added that she has not ruled out the possibility of getting pregnant with Renfro's child.

As yearbooks are passed around, signed with promises of remem-

brance and enduring friendship, so, too, do the seniors promise never to forget what they shared with their future ex-soulmates.

"No matter what happens, Jeff and I will always be close," said Christine Foulks, a Phoenix-area senior who

Bracken has not ruled out the possibility of getting pregnant with Renfro's child.

plans to "break the news" to boyfriend Jeff Vanderploeg after their June 22 prom. "I just hope he doesn't expect me to give him his varsity jacket back. Or his Dave Matthews CDs."

Standing in stark contrast to the seniors are the nation's high-school juniors, who expressed horror over their elders' willingness to turn their backs on true love.

"There's no way that's ever going to happen to us," said Mindy Ostrove, 16, a junior at Tallahassee Central High School. "Matt and I are forever. Nobody else could ever understand me like he does. Nobody." ∅

Maybe I should've lied."

According to Widmar, the troubles began immediately.

"Trying to show her how to use the mouse took almost a week," Widmar said. "For some reason, she got it in her head that you had to hold the button down to make it move. Then, when I explained that the computer communicates over the telephone via her built-in modem, she kept asking where you hold the receiver. And she wouldn't stop calling the keyboard 'the typewriter.'"

Still more complications arose when Widmar tried to show her mother how to navigate a search engine.

"For practice, I logged onto Yahoo! and had her search for cheesecake recipes," Widmar said. "She got totally confused by the fact that we were searching within a web site for other web sites. She kept typing her keyword searches into the Internet Explorer address bar, not into the Yahoo! search bar. Then, when she accidentally typed 'cheesecake' into the Explorer box, it actually worked, because there happened to be a web site called that, so that just confused her even more."

After nearly a month, Lillian had finally gotten to the point where she could log on to a web site on her own. Almost every time, however, something unexpected would occur, causing her to panic and call her daughter for help.

"It could be almost anything," Widmar said. "She goes apeshit whenever a pop-up window comes up. And one time, she paged me because she got a message about accepting cookies.

She was all freaked out because now she thought she was being charged for actual cookies."

Widmar said her mother still does not grasp the difference between the Internet and e-mail.

"Whenever she wants to send me an e-mail, she says she's going to Internet me," Widmar said. "I think that's because we use AOL, so she has to log onto the Internet to do her e-mailing. Then there's chat rooms, which she thinks is e-mail. I just pray she never finds out about message boards. That'll throw her whole world into a tailspin."

Despite knowing next to nothing about computers or the Internet, Lillian will frequently attempt to troubleshoot problems using new terms she had heard.

"Every time she hears a new word involving computers, she incorporates it into her questions," Widmar said. "Last time she called, she said she couldn't get her e-mail working, and that there must be something wrong with her firewall. I tried to explain that she didn't have a firewall, so she said her Java must be broken."

Widmar said her mother is a fairly anxious person in general, and that her recent forays into Internet use have only exacerbated those tendencies. Among her mother's greatest fears, Widmar said, is that she will be the target of computer crime.

"Last week, she freaked out because she got a porn spam," Widmar said. "Now she thinks they're targeting her for stalking or kidnapping. She wouldn't go near her computer for four days. She was also convinced

Top left: Karen Widmar with her mother Lillian, who continues to struggle with Internet use.

that because the computer could send photos, it was capable of taking photos of her, making her susceptible to murderers."

"Then there are the viruses," Widmar continued. "She said, 'I'm afraid to look at the Internet. What if my computer gets one of those diseases I read about in the paper?' I tried telling her that viruses can only be spread if you open attachments, and that she'd have nothing to worry about if she scanned attachments before opening them. She said she was afraid she'd forget or scan it wrong, and that 'the whole computer would break.'"

Even when Lillian does successfully carry out a computer-related task, she fears she has done something wrong.

"I don't know if this is working," read one recent e-mail from Lillian to her daughter. "If you hear music when you read this letter, that's my fault."

"I have no idea what she meant by that," Widmar said. "'If I heard music'? I can only assume that her computer made some sort of sound when she opened some window, and she thought she was sending the sound. Whatever."

"I got an e-mail from her yesterday that seemed to be okay," Karen continued. "There was a picture of the family cat attached, so I was happy to see that she'd mastered the art of forwarding stuff. But then she accidentally sent me the exact same e-mail seven more times. Lord only knows what she'll fuck up tomorrow." ∅

Guns Are Only Deadly If Used For Their Intended Purpose

By Ted Farner, President Brothers In Arms U.S.A.

As the president of Brothers In Arms U.S.A., the nation's third-largest gun-rights organization, I've heard all the arguments made by the anti-gun propagandists. And of the many misguided aspects of their anti-gun rhetoric, the most off-base is this bizarre notion that guns are inherently deadly. Nothing could be further from the truth. The reality is, guns are only deadly when used for their intended purpose.

Time and time again, the enemies of groups like Brothers In Arms U.S.A. confuse the innocuous phenomenon of guns with the handful of irresponsible people who engage in the deadly practice of gun use. Well, there *is* a difference, and it's high time the namby-pamby liberals recognize this fact.

Take the letter I got from a California woman whose 15-year-old son was "killed by a gun" while walking to his after-school job. Now, come on. No

But try telling this to all the crybabies suing the gun companies because not everybody in their family is alive. What exactly are you suing them for—making a reliable product? That's a laugh. Somebody should be suing those shoddy import jobs.

one is naïve enough to think that an innocent boy died just because a gun was designed, manufactured, and sold. Even before I looked into this woman's story, I knew there had to be more that she wasn't telling me. Sure enough, newspaper clippings and police records revealed that another youth aimed his gun at this boy and pulled the trigger. This action, gun experts will tell you, caused a precision-machined steel hammer to strike the primer of a 9mm cartridge, igniting the smokeless powder within, propelling a 138-grain bullet down the pistol's barrel and into the woman's son. The gun never even

came within 10 feet of the kid. The only thing the gun was guilty of was functioning properly.

My point? No child dies just because there is such a thing as guns. They die because one of these guns is used.

In all my years of fighting for the cause of gun rights, not once have I ever come across a case of a gun

Okay, admittedly, there is the occasional pistol-whipping victim who never regains consciousness.

killing a person. In every instance, the real killer has been the bullets that come out of the guns. So if you're going to insist on pointing fingers, point them at the bullet makers.

Okay, admittedly, there is the occasional pistol-whipping victim who never regains consciousness. But that's a freakish, statistically insignificant aberration that merely proves my point: Only when guns are used as intended are they significantly dangerous to anyone.

But try telling this to all the crybabies suing the gun companies because not everybody in their family is alive. What exactly are you suing them for—making a reliable product? That's a laugh. Somebody should be suing those shoddy import jobs: You'd be lucky to kill a baby with one of them.

No, a gun is not deadly when it sits locked up in a collector's cabinet. Guns don't beam bad thoughts into people's heads that make them fall over dead. There is only one way guns kill, and that's if some misguided weirdo follows the rules of proper gun use and actually aims and fires the gun in accordance with the manufacturer's guidelines.

I feel so strongly about this. As a gun activist and advocate, I feel it is my duty to speak out against this ridiculous fantasy of guns running around on tiny little legs, indiscriminately selecting pedestrians for death.

For all the work Brothers In Arms U.S.A. has done to educate people, there remain all these misconceptions about guns being deadly. Well, so is an atom bomb... *if* you drop it on a city! But you've still got these hippies whining that the solution is to have no atom bombs whatsoever. Great, just punish everybody because a handful of kooks can't keep their fingers off the button.

It's an old saying, but it's still true: "Guns don't kill people. People kill people." At least if they've got a gun they do. ∅

Your Horoscope

**By Lloyd Schumner Sr.
Retired Machinist and
A.A.P.B.-Certified Astrologer**

Aries: (March 21–April 19)
You'll learn the hard way that you shouldn't attempt to attract the attention of dimwitted coworkers carrying extension ladders.

Taurus: (April 20–May 20)
Next week, Death shall tire of his burden and lay down his scythe for a day to spend time among mortals, but he won't be able to resist doing you.

Gemini: (May 21–June 21)
Years of practice can give yoga devotees the ability to touch their toes to the backs of their necks, but you'll achieve the same thing by drinking pesticides.

Cancer: (June 22–July 22)
You may be as big as a house, but carpet and room deodorizer still can't take the place of conventional deodorant.

Leo: (July 23–Aug. 22)
You will come tantalizingly close to achieving your life's ambition when you're placed next to the "center square."

Virgo: (Aug. 23–Sept. 22)
You thought you were that tragic, romantic ideal, a man with nothing left to lose, but you somehow forgot about your pants.

Libra: (Sept. 23–Oct. 23)
Your life of devout and committed Buddhism will come to nothing when, after the tragic events of next Tuesday, you are reincarnated as a Catholic.

Scorpio: (Oct. 24–Nov. 21)
You'll never understand why it is that every time you've almost finished a bottle of whiskey, it breaks itself over your head and runs off with your wallet.

Sagittarius: (Nov. 22–Dec. 21)
Your new girlfriend is not actually so sweet you could use her shit for toothpaste, but that won't stop you from trying.

Capricorn: (Dec. 22–Jan. 19)
Your habit of faking an Irish accent to get attention is even more pathetic considering that you're a lifelong resident of Dublin.

Aquarius: (Jan. 20–Feb. 18)
Your determination to be the last man standing will be the deciding factor in a life-or-death game of musical chairs.

Pisces: (Feb. 19–March 20)
No matter how hard you try, nothing you ever do or achieve will please Alec Baldwin.

CORPORATION from page 164

with money is probably a pretty good bet. John Hancock Financial, Wachovia, Wells Fargo, Fannie Mae, Citigroup—those are all huge corporations that make giant profits just by moving money around from place to place. You just loan out money to people, and they give it back with interest. Then you have even more money to loan out to other people. Talk about a racket!

I still haven't decided what my corporation will be, but I do know one thing: Whatever it is, I'm going international with it. That's how you really make the serious dough. You get a bunch of factories set up all over the world and start selling your product in 100 or so countries. This is called "expanding into other markets," and it's the easiest way to sell stuff. People in India, for example, will take anything because they're so poor and desperate. A guy in India will buy the shittiest washer-dryer in all of America. Same goes for shitty cars in Russia. Or shitty watches in Thailand. Hell, you can release the world's worst movie, like *Armageddon* or whatever, in those poor countries, and

they'll eat it up, because it's better than whatever they can get there. So you don't have to worry so much about having high standards of

I still haven't decided what my corporation will be, but I do know one thing: Whatever it is, I'm going international with it.

quality when you're selling to foreigners, which is nice.

Man, when my company is up and running, it's gonna be so sweet. I'll just sit there and boss everybody around all day from my luxury penthouse office on the top floor of my corporate headquarters. That's definitely gonna beat busting kids for shoplifting Twizzlers. ∅

Frugal *Star Wars* Fan Camping Out In Front Of 99-Cent Theater

see LOCAL page 3C

Cockatiel Can't Take A Punch

see PETS page 10B

Johnny Carson Comes Out Of Retirement To Show How A Necktie Is Knotted

see PEOPLE page 5D

STATshot
A look at the numbers that shape your world.

Top Hiccup Cures

1. Surprise nut trample
2. Spoonful of honey, shot of rum; repeat 12 times
3. Savage blow to solar plexus
4. Put gas-station air hose in mouth, pinch nose
5. Artificial esophagus implant
6. Prayer
7. Complain about hiccups

THE ONION • $2.00 US • $3.00 CAN

the ONION

VOLUME 38 ISSUE 23 — AMERICA'S FINEST NEWS SOURCE™ — 20–26 JUNE 2002

Is The FBI Doing Enough To Prevent The July 19 Attacks?

see ATTACKS page 5A

Martha Stewart Stalker Can Barely Keep Up

Above: Stewart attends a fundraiser at the Metropolitan Museum of Art. Inset: Kowalcyk.

EAST HAMPTON, NY—Richard Kowalcyk, 36, who for several years has been stalking author, magazine publisher, TV personality, and house-and-home guru Martha Stewart, told reporters Monday that he can barely keep up.

"Today was pretty busy," said Kowalcyk, downing a multi-vitamin and a Red Bull energy drink. "We went from

see STALKER page 173

Youth Pastor Forced To Break Out 'Hell Is Not Disneyland' Speech

EVANSVILLE, IN—A mere eight days into United Methodist Church's summer Bible school, youth pastor John Dearden, 49, was forced to break out his trademark "Hell Is Not Disneyland" speech Monday, outlining the differences between eternal damnation and the popular Anaheim, CA, theme park.

"Hell is not Disneyland, people," said Dearden, unleashing a 12-minute version of the oft-delivered speech on a group of misbehaving fifth and sixth graders. "You may think this is funny now, but you won't be laughing when it's time to meet your maker.

You won't be riding in teacups and drinking soda pop down there, believe you me. You'll be wishing you'd heeded God's Word."

Dearden, who has directed the church's youth program since 1987, pulled out the speech after the rambunctious children repeatedly ignored warnings to settle down.

"I've warned you time and time again that I was not going to tolerate this sort of behavior in God's house," said Dearden, returning to the classroom to find erasers flying and students out of their seats. "And what happens when I leave for five minutes? This."

see PASTOR page 173

Above: Dearden sets the misbehaving students straight.

169

The Dirty Bomb Threat

U.S. citizen Jose Padilla was arrested May 8 in a plot to detonate a "dirty bomb" spewing low-level radiation. What do *you* think about this latest terror threat?

"I am an American, and I'm not about to be cowed into fearing things I should be afraid of."

Jim Miller
Architect

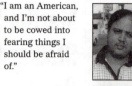

"That's so awesome that the government stopped a would-be terrorist. And right when they're reeling from criticism about that stuff. It's like fate! A magical cosmic symmetry!"

Dave Downing
File Clerk

"I'm glad they caught that soy-bomb guy. He was a dick."

Lisa Bell
Student

"Tell you one thing: There wouldn't be all this bombing and killing stuff if everyone in the world were either me or my wife."

Mitch Redmond
Systems Analyst

"I don't know... picking up chicks with, 'Sleep with me, baby— tomorrow we could all be dirty-bombed' just doesn't cut it."

Frank Castellano
Delivery Driver

"The big question is, how did we ever let a guy like this into the country? What? He was born here? Oh."

Dana Cornell
Florist

CEO Resignations

Tyco CEO Dennis Kozlowski is the latest in a string of corporate chiefs to step down amid scandal allegations. Other recent resignations:

- *Bill Wrigley Jr., Wrigley CEO*
  Accused of skimming flavor crystals for personal use

- *John Tyson, Tyson CEO*
  Insider chicken trading

- *Sam Reed, Keebler Foods CEO*
  Elf abuse

- *William Clay Ford Jr., Ford CEO*
  Caught pushing Chevy

- *Michael Howe, Arby's CEO*
  Late for shift three times in one month

- *John Hacala, Spencer Gifts CEO*
  Lawrence Adams, Adams Joke Co. CEO
  Accused of colluding to fix fake-vomit prices nationwide

- *Lee Scott, Wal-Mart CEO*
  Stole a Rugrats twin-size comforter

- *Louis Camilleri, Philip Morris CEO*
  Quit for third time in less than two years

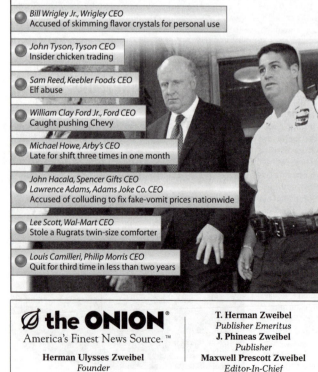

Ø the ONION®
America's Finest News Source.™

Herman Ulysses Zweibel
Founder

T. Herman Zweibel
Publisher Emeritus
J. Phineas Zweibel
Publisher
Maxwell Prescott Zweibel
Editor-In-Chief

You Must *Romance* The Music Out Of The Tambourine

By Pierre Henry

My lord, what are you doing? Your crude handling of that beautiful instrument borders on the obscene! You cannot carelessly strike a tambourine and expect it to sing its beautiful song. You must coax it out of her. You must romance the music out of the tambourine.

The way you strike that tambourine makes me cringe with horror and disgust. Would you strike a beautiful woman? Of course not. You would gently stroke her, caress her, whisper sweet nothings in her ear. So, too, you must with the tambourine. Tell the tambourine you love her, and your reward will be beautiful music. Treat her roughly, and she will slap you in the face with her velvet glove.

The tambourine can be deceiving. True, she has a taut skin and round figure like the drum, but that is where the similarity ends. Take your finger and run it along her edge. There. Do you feel it? Little miniature cymbals! That... that is the secret of the tambourine. If you gently tap her, the little cymbals will sing the body electric. If you clumsily hit her like your fingers are sausages and your hands spicy hams, she will recoil in disgust.

> Make no mistake, this is a courtship. A grand design of love. You must carefully woo the tambourine to make her do your bidding— and not through deceit or treachery.

Make no mistake, this is a courtship. A grand design of love. You must carefully woo the tambourine to make her do your bidding—and not through deceit or treachery. To a tambourine, what matters most is honesty. Your playing must come from a place that is pure and true. You cannot play the tambourine one shake at a time, preventing her from stretching her long legs and reaching her natural, majestic stride. You must think three shakes ahead, but still live wholly in the moment, adjusting your movements to her mercurial moods. Only then will you prove yourself worthy of the tambourine's affections.

Take in the wholeness of the tambourine. A tambourine is an endless river of mystery. There is a depth there that most men do not see. They see only a noisemaker, some paper horn with streamers or a metal box that clicks noisily when you spin it around. But those are for little boys,

> The tambourine can be deceiving. True, she has a taut skin and round figure like the drum, but that is where the similarity ends.

not men. Do you want to be a little boy playing with a toy? Or do you want to be a man with a muse? If you wish the latter, then you must surrender yourself to the tambourine completely. She will not be deceived by pretenders. She will only bear her fruits to those who devote themselves fully to the task of tilling her fertile soil.

The tambourine has an endless bounty of love to offer, but you must first favor her with your own affections. Do not clutch her as a baby does a rattle. Grip her firmly but knowingly. Tap her lightly with your finger. I said lightly, you buffoon! Try again. There. Does she not coo for you now? The timbre of the tambourine should set the stage for romance, but only if you draw it out with patience and sensuality. Banging her repeatedly, as you were just doing, produces music unfit for a tableau of fez-wearing clowns in tiny cars.

Now comes the question: What is your endgame, O wooer of the tambourine? Do you shake her for her sex appeal? Have you seen men playing tambourines on stage, using them to attract painted women in short skirts, and decided that you, too, would like to use the tambourine to attract a painted lady of your own? Then you love the tambourine for all the wrong reasons. Lay her down gently and walk away. You are among the undeserving.

Do not feel alone. Most are undeserving. But if you are pure of heart and prove yourself worthy of her considerable charms, the tambourine will treat you well. This, however, is a long, hard road, and the journey down this path requires great seriousness of purpose and commitment. If you decide that you are incapable of such things, then you should seriously consider the oboe. That is an instrument for the true vulgarian. Ø

Lackluster Marriage Enlivened By Cancer Scare

SWANDER, OH—George and Maureen McKay's stagnant, passionless 36-year marriage was briefly enlivened recently by Maureen's late-May cancer scare.

"When the doctor told us Maureen had terminal stomach cancer, our priorities instantly changed," said George, 57, who had steadily grown more distant from his wife over the years. "Suddenly, all that mattered was spending those final days together."

> "Maureen and George weren't what you would call the most romantic couple," next-door neighbor Curtis Curran said. "But when they thought Maureen had cancer, there was an instant change."

"Last week, we found out the doctor made a misdiagnosis," George continued. "Now, thank God, everything's back to the way it was before."

On May 25, Dr. Ernest Ingersoll, an oncologist at Dreyer General Hospital in nearby Tiffin, told the couple that a malignant mass in Maureen's stomach was Phase 4 stomach cancer. The grave diagnosis temporarily reignited a passion between George and Maureen that the weight of the years had dulled.

"When we got home from the hospital, we both couldn't stop crying," said Maureen, 56, who was later correctly diagnosed with gastrointestinal basidiobolomycosis, a rare but non-fatal fungal disease. "George just held me for hours and hours. I hadn't felt that loved and cared for in years."

According to those who know the couple, this closeness was precisely what has been missing from the McKay marriage.

"Maureen and George weren't what you would call the most romantic couple," next-door neighbor Curtis Curran said. "But when they thought Maureen had cancer, there was an instant change. You could even see it in the way they sat next to each other. Of course, now that they found out Maureen will be fine with treatment, they're back to opposite sides of the room again."

Faced with the grim prospect of cancer, the McKays began to pay attention to "all the little things" that make a marriage special.

"We started to say 'I love you' again, for no reason," Maureen said. "I guess George was afraid it might be the last time he'd get to say it. Thank God, it wasn't. Not that he's said it since we

Above: George and Maureen McKay.

found out the diagnosis was wrong."

In the days following Maureen's initial diagnosis, George would call her from work just to see how her day was going. He also started leaving her little love notes in random spots throughout the house.

"It sure was an emotional three weeks," George said. "We'd stay up all night long, saying things we'd never said to each other and talking about all the things we never got to do together. Now, we've got a whole damn lifetime to do all that stuff with each other."

"Twenty or thirty more years," George added. "Just the two of us."

As soon as Maureen's stomach problems were found to be nonfatal, the couple returned to their normal mode of interaction: icy silence punctuated by the occasional bickering over petty household matters. An added source of tension was Maureen's medical treatments, which prompted fights about everything from who forgot to deposit the check from the insurance company to who was supposed to pick up the medicine from the pharmacy before it closed at 7 p.m.

Still, the couple has their memories of the whirlwind three weeks. One

see CANCER page 172

Gore Begins Training For 2004 Election In Remote Mountain Cabin

MCCALL, ID—Determined to rebound from his 2000 election defeat, Al Gore has isolated himself in a remote mountain cabin to train for his 2004 rematch with George W. Bush. "Gotta get in shape," said Gore, running up a hill with a log strapped to his back. "Gonna beat him this time." Gore, who is almost back down to his campaigning weight of 245, then worked on his debate reflexes by chasing chickens around a pen.

Area Man Thinking About Getting One Of Those All-Body Scans

AUGUSTA, GA—Impressed by the technology, Dan Cirillo is thinking about getting an all-body imaging scan, the 45-year-old Augusta man revealed Monday. "Wow, that looks pretty cool," said Cirillo, who saw the device on CBS' *48 Hours*. "I'd love to get one of those." Cirillo then wondered aloud whether he could get a scan and a similarly cool watertank-immersion body-fat measurement on the same day.

Sympathy Card Signed By Assistant

KANSAS CITY, MO—A sympathy card from Walters Realty president Bob Merritt to the wife of recently deceased realtor Jim Nolfo was chosen, signed, and mailed by Merritt's personal assistant Monday. "Please know that you are in my thoughts during this difficult time," the assistant wrote on Merritt's behalf. Merritt, who did not see the card at any time during the three hours it spent in the Walters Realty office, did not add, "Let me know if I can help in any way."

U.S. Middlemen Demand Protection From Being Cut Out

WASHINGTON, DC—Some 20,000 members of the Association of American Middlemen marched on the National Mall Monday, demanding protection from such out-cutting shopping options as online purchasing, factory-direct catalogs, and outlet malls. "Each year in this country, thousands of hard-working middlemen are cut out," said Pete Hume, a Euclid, OH, waterbed retailer. "No one seems to care that our livelihood is being taken away from us." Hume said the AAM is eager to work with legislators to find alternate means of passing the savings on to you.

Lottery Loser Angry At Lottery Winner

HARRISBURG, PA—Winona Culvert, a loser in Monday's $113 million Pennsylvania Lottery, expressed anger at Mechanicsburg electrician Clint Furlow, who took home the jackpot after buying a single ticket on a whim. "Who the hell does that asshole think he is?" said Culvert upon seeing the news report of Furlow's victory. "I bought 40 tickets." Culvert added that she needs the prize money far more than Furlow, as she has been on public assistance for the past two years.

Name Of Gay Bar Should Have Been Clearer

CHICAGO—After accidentally walking into a gay bar Monday, Jeff Pierce, 23, said the name of the establishment failed to clearly telegraph its orientation. "I can see how Rods sounds gay," Pierce said, "but it's just not as crystal-clear as it could be." Pierce urged the bar's owner to consider changing the name, suggesting The Manhole or Big Throbbing Homo Cocks. ∅

171

Golf Tips

Warm weather is here, and it's time to hit the links. Here are some tips to help you improve your game:

- When teeing off, don't forget to shout "Fore!" for some reason.
- To get the most out of a Sunday afternoon on the golf course, be trapped in a loveless marriage to a shrill, clothes-obsessed witch.
- If you encounter a dark-skinned person while golfing, do not panic. Maintain an air of respect, hand over all your valuables, and walk quickly to the clubhouse.
- When beating other golfers to death, try a three-iron instead of a wood. You'd be amazed by the difference.
- Before golfing, emboss your company's logo onto the ball, the tee, and your watch. Then embroider the logo onto the breast pocket of your shirt. There's nothing quite like an embossed or embroidered corporate logo.
- If you are a cartoonist, make sure to remember any riotous comments or actions that occur while golfing.
- Golfing with clubs is for pussies. A truly skilled golfer requires only the power of his mind to manipulate the ball into the hole.
- Note to non-golfers: Those "World's Greatest Golfer" trophies featuring a plastic image of Snoopy teeing off are not as prestigious as they appear.
- When golfing with a female half your age, offer to "help her with her swing," then stand behind her and steady her hips while grinding your crotch into her ass.
- The new Titleist Titanium 975D features a 260cc deep face head, patented Thru-Bore construction, and a strengthened crown for greater energy transfer and maximum playability. No wonder it's the hottest titanium club on the market.
- For maximum golfing fun, get yourself a high-tech golf bag that shoots your clubs out automatically and plays Journey's "Any Way You Want It" at the touch of a button.
- Determine the angle at which you should putt by crouching low to the ground and pointing your club in the direction of the hole. This is one of the many shrewd techniques that makes golf such a thrilling game to watch.

CANCER from page 171

moment in particular sticks out in Maureen's mind. A few days after the misdiagnosis, George presented her with a thick woolen sweater to wear

Settling back into their pre-cancer-scare routine, the couple has cancelled the vacation they had planned, deciding it would be wiser to put the money toward a new roof on their home.

around the house if she felt cold. It had been years since he had bought her a present out of the blue.

"I was so touched that I cried," said Maureen, holding up the unattractive purple-and-green sweater. "Before, I would have made fun of this ugly thing and shoved it in the closet, but instead, I wore it every day. I mean, until I found out I was okay. I haven't worn it since. It's really not my style."

Settling back into their pre-cancer-scare routine, the couple has cancelled the vacation they had planned, deciding it would be wiser to put the money toward a new roof on their home.

"Boy, am I glad that's all over," George said. "Now we can get back to being a normal married couple again." ∅

BULBOUS from page 171

amounts of blood. Passersby were amazed by the unusually large amounts of blood. Passersby were amazed by the unusually large amounts of blood. Passersby were amazed by the unusually large amounts of blood. Passersby were amazed by the unusually large amounts of blood. Passersby were amazed by the unusually large amounts of blood. Passersby were amazed by the unusually large amounts of blood. Passersby were amazed by the unusually large amounts of blood. Passersby were amazed by the unusually large amounts of blood. Passersby were

If you're going to laugh at me, perhaps I won't seduce you after all.

amazed by the unusually large amounts of blood. Passersby were amazed by the unusually large amounts of blood. Passersby were amazed by the unusually large amounts of blood. Passersby were amazed by the unusually large amounts of blood. Passersby were amazed by the unusually large amounts of blood. Passersby were amazed by the unusually large amounts of blood. Passersby were amazed by the unusually large amounts of blood. Passersby were amazed by the unusually large amounts of blood. Passersby were amazed by the unusually large amounts of blood. Passersby were amazed by the unusually large amounts of blood. Passersby were amazed by the unusually large amounts of blood. Passersby were amazed by the unusually large amounts of blood. Passersby were

amazed by the unusually large amounts of blood. Passersby were amazed by the unusually large amounts of blood. Passersby were amazed by the unusually large amounts of blood. Passersby were amazed by the unusually large amounts of blood. Passersby were amazed by the unusually large amounts of blood. Passersby were amazed by the unusually large amounts of blood. Passersby were

amazed by the unusually large amounts of blood. Passersby were amazed by the unusually large amounts of blood. Passersby were

see BULBOUS page 177

her house in the Hamptons to her midtown Manhattan office, then to a business meeting with the marketing VP of Martha Stewart Living Omnimedia, then on location to upstate New York to do a segment for *CBS This Morning* at an organic asparagus farm. Then it was back to her office, out to a late dinner meeting with Kmart executives in New Jersey, back to her office again, down to Soho for a brief appearance at a Russell Simmons party, and then finally home. I put in a full 15 hours of stalking today, and I am wiped out."

"Still, for Martha, this was pretty

> ### "Things will be eerily relaxed and then, *bam*, we're waist deep in a Vermont cranberry bog," said Kowalcyk, punching his fist for emphasis.

average," Kowalcyk continued. "You should see me when she's really busy. When I get home after one of her 'crazy days,' my mom says I look like hell warmed over. I can barely get down the basement stairs."

Kowalcyk, who began stalking Stewart in late 1999, said he initially found Stewart's frantic pace "exhilarating."

"I used to stalk this girl who lived a few blocks down from me," Kowalcyk said. "But I got bored after one too many nights watching her watch *Becker* or do her laundry. After reading an article about Martha, I knew she was the one for me."

"Those first few months following her were incredible," Kowalcyk con-

Above: Stewart prunes a tree on the grounds of her East Hampton estate.

tinued. "One minute, we'd be shopping for an antique Chippendale high boy, and the next, we were at a meeting to discuss her new radio show. After a while, though, the fatigue really starts to set in."

Kowalcyk said he becomes nervous whenever Stewart slows down for a few days, calling it the "calm before the storm."

"Things will be eerily relaxed and then, *bam*, we're waist deep in a Vermont cranberry bog," said Kowalcyk, punching his fist for emphasis. "Then we're back in Manhattan to do a book signing and to approve prototypes for her new line of wicker baskets, and up to Greenwich for a party celebrating her new dessert book. Then, it's back to the office to scream at a distributor for sending the wrong shade of orange napkins for her Halloween special. She

doesn't even take Sundays off."

Though Kowalcyk said he is still sufficiently obsessed with Stewart to follow her every day, he wonders how much longer he can keep it up.

"I'm not sure I have the energy to do this for the long haul," said Kowalcyk, rubbing his eyes. "Christ, I'm only 36 and I feel 66. How does she do it?"

Kowalcyk has accumulated more than his share of bumps and bruises during his time tailing Stewart.

"This one is from lying face down in her prize-winning rose bushes," said Kowalcyk, displaying a six-inch scar on his left leg. "This one is from falling off a ledge while trying to peek into a *Martha Stewart Living* editorial meeting, and this one is from the time I got into a fight with one of her bodyguards outside her house while I was watching her change pantsuits. Each one is more than a scar; it's a

memory."

In spite of his exhaustion, Kowalcyk is proud to say he remains Stewart's most devoted "secret companion."

"Every once in a while, I'll see a new face ducking behind a bench when she's around," Kowalcyk said. "Most can't hack it for more than a few months and drop off, never to be seen again. A lot of them switch to stalking Katie Couric or Kelly Ripa. To be honest, I've thought about forgetting Martha and following somebody else for a while. But once Martha gets under your skin, she sticks to you like wheat paste. I guess I'll keep going until one of us drops. Probably me."

Added Kowalcyk: "Hell, I've outlasted almost every single personal assistant she's ever had, and they're all younger than me. I guess it's true that it takes a special man to relentlessly pursue a special woman." ∅

At approximately 10:20 a.m., Dearden left the youths alone in the classroom, instructing them to work quietly on their "Thank God For…" posters while he went to the office to help Mrs. Carlson change the ink in the ditto machine. When Dearden returned some six minutes later, the classroom was in chaos. Students were screaming and throwing markers, the felt board had been pulled off the wall, and the homework assignment on the chalkboard had been altered to read, "Thank God For… Going Home."

"Do you know what The Bible says about Hell?" Dearden asked the suddenly silent group. "Hell is a place of blackest darkness with smoke and unquenchable fire. Matthew 24:51 says, 'He will cut him to pieces and assign him a place with the hypocrites, where there will be weeping and gnashing of teeth.' Does this

sound like Disneyland to you? It sure doesn't to me."

"Who do you think will be in Hell with you?" Dearden continued. "Not Dopey and Sleepy. Not Peter Pan. You will be surrounded by the cowardly, the faithless, the polluted, the murderers, the fornicators, the idolators, and the liars."

Dearden, who first devised the "Hell Is Not Disneyland" speech in 1989, has pulled it out an estimated 20 times since. Monday marked the first time in nearly two years that he was forced to compare "The Happiest Place On Earth" with the eternal damnation awaiting children who fail to consider the consequences of their actions.

According to Dearden, this summer's class is "the wildest I've seen in years." In addition to whispering during prayer time, running in the hallways, and wasting craft materials, the group recently knocked the folding

classroom divider off its tracks in before-class roughhousing and is believed responsible for the June 5 breakage of the bathroom soap dispenser.

Giggling was heard as Dearden con-

> ### "Who do you think will be in Hell with you?" Dearden continued.

tinued his description of how the Lake of Fire differs from the home of Mickey Mouse and Goofy.

"You will not be laughing," Dearden said. "It will not be a big game. There will not be cotton candy or balloons. Or any happy little elves singing 'It's A Small World.' And Hell never closes, kids. It's open all night, every night

until the end of all time. You won't be going back to the hotel with your family and watching HBO. There's no TV in Hell, and the Devil and all the demons with tongues of fire and hooves for feet will be your new family."

Added Dearden: "If you find yourself in Hell, you'll be wishing you had been paying attention to The Bible instead of Gregory [Reiderer] and Chris [Anderson]'s antics."

Dearden wrapped up the diatribe with any remaining Disneyland references he could summon.

"In Hell, the Haunted Mansion is real, haunted with the souls of those who failed to heed God's word," Dearden said. "There's no Main Street USA in Hell. You think it will be like a trip to Space Mountain? Well, it's not. It's Hell, and it isn't a party. You remember that. Now, let's get back to those collages." ∅

What The Hell Is Wrong With Movies These Days?

The Cruise
By Jim Anchower

Hola, amigos. I know it's been a while since I rapped at ya, but I've had a mountain of problems piled up to my chin. First off, my car is all fucked up. I don't even know why. All I know is, it usually quits running after about 20 minutes, and I have to let it cool down for at least an hour before I can get it going again. That thing is a baby, and not in the good way. You know, not like, "That's my baby," but more like, "Quit your crying, ya fuckin' baby!"

Also, I'm totally pissed about my job working coat check at the museum. Well, pissed is the wrong word. More like bored out of my mind. Most days, I only work with these three other people, and I got nothing to talk to them about. For one thing, they don't know nothing about great rock 'n' roll. Two of them are chicks, and all they listen to is Sarah McLachlan and Sheryl Crow and crap like that. The dude's even worse, 'cause you'd expect more from a dude. He listens to Jay-Z and Eminem. Rap is crap! Man, he doesn't even know who Thin Lizzy is! Plus, they're all totally snobs, and they'll barely talk to me, or even laugh if I make a joke. I'm sick of being there. I'm just waiting a few more weeks so I can pile up enough cash to quit.

Usually, the thing that gets me through tough times like these is the movies. No matter how bad things are, with a movie, I can kick back for a couple of hours and just mellow out. And the best flicks are always in the summer. Last year, *The Fast And The Furious* really kicked my ass. It was full of suspense and cars. Then there was *Pearl Harbor*, which had a stupid love plot but made up for it with loads of explosions. *The Mummy Returns* was just awesome, with The Rock and all. *Planet Of The Apes* ruled, too. Last summer, it seemed like I couldn't see a bad movie, no matter how hard I tried.

Then there's this year. What the hell is going on? *About A Boy*? *Windtalkers*? *Unfaithful*? *Spirit: Stallion Of The Cimarron*? Someone in Hollywood ain't paying attention to what America wants.

I started off the season with what should have been a bang: *Jason X*. Man, that was a shitpile. And I love the Jason movies. They had to send him into space to be scary, which is something I totally don't buy. That is so lame. Sure, sending the bad guy into space is a great idea... six years ago! Everyone knows they totally ripped off *Hellraiser 4* and *Leprechaun 4* for that idea. Sending Jason into space. What a rip!

Then there's this *Ya-Ya Sisterhood* thing. I was totally suckered into seeing it, because I saw an ad that had Ashley Judd in her bra, and the movie has "ya-ya"s in the title. I figured it'd be like *Porky's* for the next generation. I had some money and some

> **Usually, the thing that gets me through tough times like these is the movies. No matter how bad things are, with a movie, I can kick back for a couple of hours and just mellow out. And the best flicks are always in the summer.**

time, so I called up Ron and Wes. Ron, good man that he is, came out to support me, and Wes, lucky son of a bitch that he is, wasn't home when I called.

We got to the theater, and Ron sneaked in while I paid. When it came time to put up for the popcorn and soda, Ron had gone to the shitter, and I had to front the whole $11. Things got a lot worse when the movie started. It was the most boring two hours I'd ever spent in a theater, nothing but these wrinkled old bags in Indian hats hugging each other and crying. And there wasn't a single tit throughout the entire movie—which probably was a good thing, 'cause I wouldn't have wanted to see most of those racks, anyway. Ron slept through half of it, which pissed me off even worse.

Ya-Ya Sisterhood was such a rip that I made Ron sneak into another movie with me. At first, we were psyched, since it was *Scooby Doo*. We figured it would be hilarious. Maybe I just didn't get it, but I didn't see any jokes. At least, I don't remember any. Shaggy looked okay, and Daphne was pretty hot, but that damn dog didn't look anything like Scooby from the cartoon, and it looked totally fake. Even though I didn't pay for the second movie, I felt twice as ripped off, 'cause this time, they didn't take my money. They took my time.

I saw the new Star Wars movie, and even that blew. I mean, yeah, there were some great space scenes, and you get to watch Yoda fight with a

> **It was the most boring two hours I'd ever spent in a theater, nothing but these wrinkled old bags in Indian hats hugging each other and crying. And there wasn't a single tit throughout the entire movie.**

light saber, but as soon as the weed wore off, the whole thing just dragged. The love story was totally sappy, and there were all these long, boring scenes where these space senators were going on and on about trade-federation rules and shit. It was like watching C-SPAN on some other planet. I'll probably go see it again, just like I do with all the *Star Wars* movies, but this time I'm going in twice as baked.

The one good thing is *Spider-Man*. That movie kicked ass, no two ways around it. And it had a preview of *The Hulk*, which I'm stoked for, too. There were a few other previews that also looked okay. There's *XXX*, the porno with the guy from *Fast And The Furious*. And the *Crocodile Hunter* movie, which should have a whole bunch of cool stuff you can't see on the TV show, like him getting his arm ripped off by gorillas or whatever. So that should be pretty good. There was also a lot of other crap, but ya gotta expect some of that. After all, my friends, life is all about taking the good with the bad.

If those don't pan out, I think I'm just going to hole up in my house and rent a ton of videos. That way, I get my choice of tons of good movies, I don't have to spend $5 on a Coke, and I don't have to sneak off to the john to smoke a bowl. I just gotta get a bigger TV. And a surround-sound system. Man, that'll be sweet. ∅

Your Horoscope

By Lloyd Schumner Sr.
Retired Machinist and
A.A.P.B.-Certified Astrologer

Aries: (March 21–April 19)
No one will believe that the threats and angry demands for payment in the ransom note were meant as an elaborate joke.

Taurus: (April 20–May 20)
Though it feels as if you'll live your whole life without anyone ever appreciating you, don't give up yet. There's still more than a week left.

Gemini: (May 21–June 21)
You still haven't had any luck finding someone who doesn't make undignified noises, strange faces, or jerky movements during orgasm.

Cancer: (June 22–July 22)
Remember: When using a chisel gouge, use the bevel and not the shank to make your cuts, go perpendicular to the grain, and strap the nurse down tight.

Leo: (July 23–Aug. 22)
The wheels of fate have begun the inexorable turning that will one day lead to your bitter divorce from Pittsburgh Steelers wide receiver Plaxico Burress.

Virgo: (Aug. 23–Sept. 22)
Disappointment is yours when you overestimate the power of the human spirit.

Libra: (Sept. 23–Oct. 23)
The thing that finally sends you over the edge turns out to be your missing the season finale of *Witchblade*.

Scorpio: (Oct. 24–Nov. 21)
You'll soon find yourself in the midst of a power struggle, as two corrupt and ruthless families fight for control of a small town. Whatever you do, don't trust the drunken undertaker.

Sagittarius: (Nov. 22–Dec. 21)
The race does not always go to the swift, nor the battle to the strong, but the job of lead singer always goes to the guy with the best hair.

Capricorn: (Dec. 22–Jan. 19)
You will have one of the worst days of your life next week. However, since it's one of several thousand worst days of your life, it's not all that significant.

Aquarius: (Jan. 20–Feb. 18)
A bizarre series of events will lead to your selling real estate in a small town in New Jersey.

Pisces: (Feb. 19–March 20)
You will learn that the downside to taking the easy way out isn't that bad, after all.

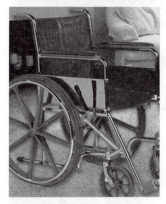

New Wheelchair Has That 'New Wheelchair' Smell

see LOCAL page 5D

German Fairy Tale Ends Predictably

see WORDS page 10C

Bitch Wife Forgot To Tape *Cops* Appearance

see LOCAL page 10D

STATshot

A look at the numbers that shape your world.

What Is Kiss Licensing?

1. Kiss golf clubs
2. 401(K)ISS retirement plan
3. Kiss yarn
4. Frehley Farms Raspberry Preserves, the jam with Kiss blood in it
5. "Rock 'N' Roll All Nite" baby monitor
6. Kiss-O-Lax, the world's least gentle laxative
7. Paul Stanley's Chick Magnets

the ONION®

VOLUME 38 ISSUE 25 — AMERICA'S FINEST NEWS SOURCE™ — 18–24 JULY 2002

Anti-Spam Legislation Opposed By Powerful Penis-Enlargement Lobby

WASHINGTON, DC—Efforts to pass legislation restricting Internet "spam"—unsolicited mass e-mails usually for advertising purposes—are meeting with strong resistance from the nation's powerful penis-enlargement lobby.

"If this legislation passes, the government would, for all intents and purposes, be taking three to four inches off America's cocks," said Denny Garner, president of the National Association of Penis Enlargers (NAPE), during a press conference Monday. "For millions of poorly hung American men, spam is a vital source of information about penis-enlargement options, and our elected officials have no right to take it away from them."

Added Garner: "MAKE YOUR DICK BIGGER THAN A CLUB!!!"

H.R. 2319, or the Electronic Mail Limitations Act, is slated to go before the House of Representatives next week. The bill would empower states to prosecute so-called "spammers" and impose fines or jail time against adults convicted of e-mailing unsolicited advertisements to strangers.

If signed into law, H.R. 2319 would likely prove devastating to manufacturers and vendors of pills, pumps, and creams designed to increase penis size.

"The entire penis-enlargement industry is threatened by this bill," Garner said. "Despite what most people

see SPAM page 178

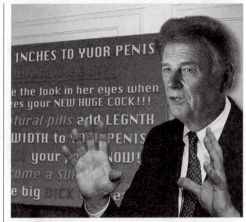

Above: Denny Garner, president of the National Association of Penis Enlargers, makes his case before a House subcommittee.

Cheney Caught Moonlighting

WASHINGTON, DC—The longtime suspicions of White House supervisors were confirmed Monday, when Vice-President Dick Cheney was caught moonlighting at a D.C.-area Denny's restaurant.

"For the past several months, the vice-president has, unbeknownst to this administration, taken on a second job as a host at Denny's," White House Press Secretary Ari Fleischer said. "We are dealing with the situation internally."

According to Fleischer, since early April, Cheney has been working as a host at the Edsall Road Denny's in Alexandria, VA. Though restaurant patrons often remarked on the resemblance between the host and the vice-president, it was only when President Bush stopped by for a midnight snack with Attorney General John Ashcroft that the man was confirmed to be Cheney.

"At first, I didn't recognize him,

see CHENEY page 179

Stoner Uncle All The Kids' Favorite

Above: Mike "Gonzo" Dornheim and two of his adoring nephews.

AUSTIN, TX—Stoner Mike "Gonzo" Dornheim, 37, a freelance carpenter and part-time drummer, is the favorite uncle of his six nephews and nieces, family sources revealed Monday.

Despite being the object of unspoken resentment from his siblings, who see him as the family's "black sheep," the habitual marijuana user has nevertheless cornered the market on nephew/niece affection.

"Uncle Gonzo isn't like my other uncles, who just talk about work all the time and won't let us make noise in the house," said Brad Dornheim, 8, who, like his siblings and cousins, is unaware of his uncle's marijuana use. "He makes us these awesome banana smoothies. And he has the coolest backyard, with these robot bird sculptures he made out of scrap metal. He even gave me one, but Mom said it has to stay in the garage. I want to be just like him when I grow up."

see UNCLE page 178

175

Executing The Mentally Retarded

The Supreme Court recently ruled that executing mentally retarded criminals is "cruel and unusual punishment," violating the Eighth Amendment. What do *you* think?

"My God. Now there's no holding back that group home down the street."

Todd Pollack
Lawyer

"The cook who prepares the last meals at our prison is already seeing a drop-off in requests for peanut butter and jelly sandwiches."

Joey Schor
Prison Guard

"That's too bad, because they're a whole lot easier to catch than regular murderers."

Elaine Ruffin
Student

"Yaaaaay! I'm not gonna be electricuded! Yaaaaay!"

Bobby Aldrete
Felon

"Whew. I'm glad I got a few in just under the wire."

Reginald Deshaies
Systems Analyst

"The greatness of a nation and its moral progress can be measured by the way it treats its 'tards."

Diane Magadan
Dietitian

The *Rolling Stone* Makeover

Seeking to lure a younger readership, *Rolling Stone* is undergoing a major editorial overhaul. Among the changes:

- ♪ Strict three-syllable limit on all words
- ♪ *Teen People* columnist Brianna Peters hired to replace Hunter S. Thompson
- ♪ Giving young people more of the Sheryl Crow, Wallflowers coverage they crave
- ♪ 10,000-word drug-war pieces phased out in favor of Hoobastank pictorials
- ♪ Jann Wenner "accidentally" locked in executive washroom for rest of creation
- ♪ Taking bold step forward to being 10 years behind the times instead of 20
- ♪ Provocative cover shot of topless Van Morrison coyly covering pendulous breasts
- ♪ No longer exhorting readers to turn that racket down
- ♪ Annual "20 Greatest Eric Clapton Albums" issue eliminated
- ♪ Target baby boomers and their teenage children; attract neither

the ONION®
America's Finest News Source.™

Herman Ulysses Zweibel
Founder

T. Herman Zweibel
Publisher Emeritus
J. Phineas Zweibel
Publisher
Maxwell Prescott Zweibel
Editor-In-Chief

Hi, I'm Just Calling To Follow Up On That Make-Out Session We Had Last Week

Hello, is this Megan? Hi, Megan, it's Patrick Hewitt from Brian's birthday party. Just calling to follow up on that make-out session we had last week.

By Patrick Hewitt

Do you have a minute? Great.

How have you been? Good, good. I'm doing well, too, thanks. Can't complain.

If I may, let me get to the point. I'm sure you must be very busy. Those were some enjoyable French kisses we shared last week, weren't they? I thought the whole thing went very well. A little petting—not too much. Some nice lower-lip nibbling. Plenty of tongue. I thought we really clicked there. Are we on the same page here?

Anyway, just thought I'd give you a buzz to see if we wanted to follow up on that. I got your contact info from Alexandra. What do you say? Just throwing it out there.

Now, I did mean to call earlier, but it has been absolute hell around here. I've been running around like crazy. Busy week. You know how it is, I'm sure. But summer is the time to be busy, isn't it? I just love this time of year. I love to just get out there, have some fun, see people, do things.

So, I was thinking we might want to

> Now, I did mean to call earlier, but it has been absolute hell around here. I've been running around like crazy. Busy week. You know how it is, I'm sure.

get together again, if you're up for that. No pressure. You can think about it if you need to. Then again, if we both know now, there's no need to mull. Make sense? Let's do it then, okay? Let's just decide to do it, if that's cool with you. Done.

Good. Then we have a "go" on a date, sometime in the next, oh, let's say 10 days. Let's give it a 10-day window. This time of year is hell. Busy, but that's good.

I've got a good feeling about this one. I don't want to jump the gun on it, but I think we might have a good time. Here's my basic pitch: I'm thinking dinner—something low-pressure, mid-price ethnic. Then drinks at my apartment. Maybe sex. Maybe a little sex. Of course, only if things progress at a good pace on the date, and we're both on the same page about it. Tell you what, we'll deal with that when the time comes. We definitely can just see what happens. Play it by ear. That's smart.

You know, maybe we should set a

> I'm sure you've got a few prospects out there floating around. I do, too. So let's just keep it loose at this stage, get together, see what goes.

tentative day, just to get something on the books. Is that do-able? I've got an opening Saturday. You're already booked? How about Friday? Does that work for you? Let's do that, then. I'm pencilling you in: "Friday—Megan." One of us can call to confirm Thursday night. You call me or I'll call you; it doesn't matter. Know what, though? We should probably decide who calls who. Just so that we don't each expect the other to call, and then nobody calls. No sense accidentally getting our wires crossed. I'll call you.

We don't have to move on this too quickly. I'm sure you've got a few prospects out there floating around. I do, too. So let's just keep it loose at this stage, get together, see what goes. Keep it fun at this juncture. Sound good? Great.

Who knows, we might have a full-fledged fling on our hands by August if we get moving on it. I do have a few days off at the end of the month, so now might be a good time to start.

I'll shoot you an e-mail. Let me get you my Hotmail address. Best way to catch me. We can fire a few flirty e-mails back and forth during the week, then see if we can get some chemistry going.

Damn! I just remembered a previous engagement for this weekend that I can't get out of, so Friday isn't going to work for me after all. Let's say we'll touch base early next week and go from there. Sound good? Terrific.

I believe we're all set, then. Next week or so. Thanks again for the hot tongue action. I really did enjoy it. Okay, then, Megan. Talk to you soon. Great? Great! ∅

Outdoor-Music-Festival Grounds Mistaken For Refugee Camp

FAIRVIEW, MO—The camping and concert grounds for Countryfest 2002, a week-long festival attended by more than 120,000 music fans, was mistaken for a refugee camp by passing Red Cross workers Tuesday.

"I was driving back from fire cleanup efforts in Colorado when the unmistakable stench of human offal hit me like a wall," Red Cross volunteer Jim Montoya said. "As we came over the hill, there it was: rows of crowded tents pitched on the mud, giant piles of rotting garbage, and security personnel roving the barbed-wire perimeter fence. I simply had to stop and intervene on behalf of the poor refugees in this overcrowded, impoverished settlement."

Using his Red Cross ID, Montoya was able to obtain a full-access Countryfest VIP wristband and move past the long lines of weary people in the paperwork-processing lines at the camp's front gates, their possessions piled in bags at their feet.

"This certainly is not the worst camp I've witnessed in my travels," said Montoya, 44, who has participated in relief missions in Rwanda, Sudan, and India. "But this being America, and given the fact that the camp has dubbed itself the 'Fun-In-The-Sun Country-Music Spectacular,' I would've expected them to have at least basic sanitation. Not so."

Despite the efforts of crews working around the clock, the festival's resources were severely stretched by Day Three. Event organizers installed 100 portable toilets on the grounds, but the number proved woefully inadequate. The makeshift toilets were not emptied as scheduled, and leaky,

Above: Refugees live in makeshift tents at Countryfest 2002.

overflowing units spilled human waste into ditches. Foot-pump handwashing units were emptied mere minutes after they were refilled, as campers carried the water in buckets back to their living quarters, where no fresh water was available.

"I pretty much know to avoid the bathrooms over on the stage end," said festivalgoer Stacey Edwards, as a mud-splattered, shirtless 2-year-old clung to her leg. "If you're a guy and just have to pee, you're probably okay, but if you're a girl, you better pray you don't come into contact with anything while squatting over

the hole."

Besides the lack of basic sanitation, Montoya found other refugee-camp staples at Countryfest, including severe food shortages, wildly inflated prices for basic goods, and a lack of health care, with sick or injured parties directed to drive into town.

"This is what happens when so many people are forced into such a small space," Montoya said. "Whatever the reasons, these individuals traded in their stable ranch-home existences for this. I simply could not turn a blind eye to this squalor, as the city government in Fairview appar-

ently has."

Red Cross rescue worker Lauren Elson said the camp has some semblance of an organizational structure, with certain decisions made by individuals at the Shoney's-sponsored Countryfest Info-Tent. A crude communications system also exists, with edicts periodically broadcast live on 94.7 KTTS, Springfield's Hot Country Mix. Though a set of camp rules was posted near the Fat Jack's BBQ Ribs stand, lawlessness was still the norm.

"Impromptu settlements like this are always terribly disorganized because of how fast they grow," Elson said. "Just last month, this place wasn't even here. But word of mouth spreads, and more bodies than expected show up. In this case, rumors about a surprise visit by someone called 'Reba' fueled the fire."

While a language barrier prevented Elson from fully ascertaining the nature of the settlement, she determined that it was made up of displaced Americans, largely of European ethnic descent.

"I had a hard time understanding the refugees' almost indecipherable dialect, but I did glean some information," Elson said. "They call themselves 'country folk.' I should note that despite the downtrodden nature of their settlement, they are still very proud of their shared identity. They've traveled, in some cases hundreds of miles, to convene with their people here and celebrate their culture. The big draw, as I understand it, is the promised appearance of 33 of their tribe's most prominent music makers, including Travis Tritt, Kenny Chesney,

see REFUGEES page 179

Israeli Bus Driver Wants Really Big Raise

TEL AVIV, ISRAEL—His nerves shot, Tel Aviv bus driver Yehuda Ben-Zvi said Monday that he wants a "really big" raise. "I'm sorry, but 20 lousy sheqels an hour to drive a bus in this country just doesn't cut it," said Ben-Zvi, 44, nervously scanning each person boarding his bus. "If they don't up me to at least 100 [sheqels] an hour, I'm outta here." Added Ben-Zvi: "Shit, it's not like I've got some deep commitment to providing public transportation. People can walk."

Missing White Girl Drives Missing Black Girl From Headlines

CORVALLIS, OR—Becky Van Gelder, an 11-year-old white girl from Corvallis, was abducted from her

home Monday, bumping 10-year-old Chicago black girl Tyesha Washington from the nation's newspaper headlines. "When a child is harmed, we all lose a small piece of our collective innocence," said USA Today managing editor Donna McCutcheon, who moved the Washington abduction to page 23A to make room for Van Gelder on the cover. "Especially when it's a young blonde girl like Becky."

Horrible Band Obviously Not Listening To Its Influences

SAN DIEGO—Puddle Of Mudd, a dreary nü-metal rock band that cites Led Zeppelin, Black Sabbath, and Metallica as influences, is obviously not listening to those influences. "Zep, Sabbath, Metallica, Maiden, Aerosmith—growing up, that's what we listened to, and that's what shaped our sound," said lead singer Wes Scantlin,

whose mopey, monotone vocals in no way bear the stamp of Robert Plant, Steven Tyler, or his other idols. Scantlin, who made the comments during an interview Monday with Spin reporter Charles Aaron, failed to say which part of Puddle Of Mudd's atrocious new ballad "Drift & Die" resembles "When The Levee Breaks" or "Sweet Emotion."

Sherwin-Williams Triumphantly Reports Nearly Half The Planet Covered In Paint

CLEVELAND—Sherwin-Williams officials announced Monday that the company is nearing the midpoint of its 112-year project to cover the Earth in a coat of bright red paint. "We're proud to announce that the entire Northern Hemisphere should be slathered 10 feet deep in candy-apple-

red Latex Semi-Gloss by year's end," Sherwin-Williams CEO Christopher Connor said. "And we are fully confident that the rest of the globe can be completed well before the giant space bucket runs out of paint." For the more difficult second-phase painting of the Earth's underside, workmen equipped with spray hoses will be suspended by cables from the equator.

Winning Dad Forces Tired Child To Finish Monopoly Game

DOWNERS GROVE, IL—With hotels on Boardwalk and Park Place, Ted Cleamons, 36, forced his exhausted 8-year-old son Andy to stay up late Monday to finish their Monopoly game. "Come on, kiddo, it shouldn't be too much longer," Ted told a bleary-eyed Andy at 11:15 p.m., just past the game's three-hour mark. "Go again, you rolled doubles." ∅

think, not all penis-pill and penis-pump makers are big and wealthy. There are many self-starting entrepreneurs who play a vital role in keeping the industry competitive. This bill would drive them out of the marketplace, leaving only the large multinationals like the Dong Group."

"Congress may feel pressure to kowtow to the interests of anti-spam consumer-advocacy groups," Garner continued, "but they do so at the expense of the hardworking men and women of Penis Pump Fabricators Local 704 of Toledo, who make Cockzilla Wonder Pumps to put food on the table for their families. These are the real victims of this bill."

In addition to NAPE, other groups are taking steps to halt the legislation. Last Thursday, Applied Products Limited, makers of Thunderdick Cockstretchin' Pillz, ran a full-page ad in *USA Today* urging Congress to vote down H.R. 2319. Ron Jeremy, adult-film star and host of the popular late-night talk show *Sex Talk*, has been aggressively lobbying Sen. Christopher Bond (R-MO), who is expected to be a key swing vote should the bill proceed to the Senate.

"I don't recall the First Amendment saying, 'Speech is free unless you're promoting a pill that's guaranteed to make your dick longer and thicker,'" Jeremy said. "I honestly cannot find that phrase. If this nation's men did not desire meaty, 10-inch schlongs, then products to achieve that end would not exist, much less sell. This bill suppresses something Americans need and want."

Albert Tuckman, co-director of the D.C.-based Save Our Spam, echoed Jeremy's sentiments, condemning the bill as unconstitutional.

"If an American entrepreneur cannot use media outlets to promote his dick-lengthening product, what can he use them for?" Tuckman said. "As surely as every man has the inalienable right to add up to four terrifying inches to his wang, I have the right to inform them how and for what price this may be achieved."

"There is no moral gray area here," Tuckman continued. "This is a story of

> ## "If this nation's men did not desire meaty, 10-inch schlongs, then products to achieve that end would not exist, much less sell. This bill suppresses something Americans need and want."

right and wrong and miracle 14-inch horse cocks................ Become a SUPERSTUD!!!"

Supporting the penis-enlargement lobby in its efforts are other groups threatened by the anti-spam legislation.

"The penis enlargers have shrewdly formed a coalition with other industries that depend heavily upon mass e-mail, including the American Association To LOSE WEIGHT FAST and the U.S. Alliance To GET OUT OF DEBT NOW," said Nicholas Lerman of the Cato Institute. "This coalition also includes the formidable National Organization To GO FROM AN A-CUP TO A D IN JUST 10 DAYS."

Roger Skolnick, genitalia-enhancement editor of *Newsweek*, said the anti-spam bill would damage one of the few thriving sectors of the U.S. economy.

"Sales of penis-enlargement treatments and devices in 2000 totaled in excess of $600 million," Skolnick said. "Cock-lengthening is, no pun intended, a consistent growth industry in the U.S., and this bill would severely emasculate it. As usual, it's the little guy who suffers." ∅

Uncle Gonz rules!"

Niece Caitlin Halloran, 6, agreed.

"Uncle Hank [insurance executive and avid golfer Henry Dornheim] and Uncle Jer [tile salesman and devout Presbyterian Gerald Pivarnik] are totally boring," Caitlin said. "They wear ties every day, even outside church. All they ever do is read the paper and fall asleep in chairs. Uncle Gonzo makes mud pies and builds us tree forts, and he jumps in the leaves with us. I wish all my uncles were like Uncle Gonzo."

Caitlin went on to cite other reasons for Dornheim's favorite-uncle status, including his love of playing Frisbee, his blacklight Pink Floyd posters, his

> ## Added Emmy: "Uncle Gonzo has lots of strawberry ice cream, and he never mows his lawn, so we can play Tarzan, and he sings the song about Jeremiah The Bullfrog with me."

tattoos, and his vast collection of classic Bugs Bunny cartoons.

Despite their disapproval of his lifestyle, Dornheim's siblings cannot find fault with his behavior around the family's younger generation. Dornheim has always been careful never to discuss drugs with the children, and he keeps his basement grow-room securely padlocked when they come to visit. Dornheim also always makes sure his "big-people stuff"—including his three-foot glass bong, collection of Bettie Page girlie-photo books, and supply of nitrous-oxide "whippets"—are kept stashed away in a secret compartment built into his vintage 1977 waterbed.

The never-married Dornheim, who for more than a decade has been in an on-again, off-again relationship with a 44-year-old massage therapist and renaissance-fair hobbyist named Guinevere, has no children of his own. As a result, he enthusiastically enjoys the company of his nieces and nephews.

Dornheim's sisters, Pam Halloran and Robin Pivarnik, begrudgingly admitted that he has a way with the children.

"They love his giant fish tank," said Pivarnik, 39. "And he's the only one who is even remotely competitive with the kids at PlayStation 2. He's also the only one who can stand watching *SpongeBob SquarePants*. As much as I hate to admit it, he seems to be an attentive, responsible caretaker."

Much to his siblings' chagrin, Dornheim is also the uncle of choice for helping the kids with school projects.

"Uncle Gonz helped me with my science-fair entry, and I got an A," said nephew Sammy Pivarnik, 11. "He showed me how to mix corn starch and water to make this cool liquid that turns solid when you squeeze it, then melts back into, like, milk when you let it go. You can play catch with it without spilling a drop!"

"It really blew the teacher's mind," Sammy added.

Dornheim, who was nicknamed "Gonzo" by his stoner friends because of his longtime admiration of gonzo journalist and countercultural icon Hunter S. Thompson, also ranks ahead of his fellow uncles and aunts for his love of pets.

"Uncle Gonzo has four doggies," said 4-year-old niece Emmy Dornheim,

Above: Dornheim's nephews play with their stoner uncle's toys.

carefully counting to four on her fingers. "Their names are Zowie, Zappa, James Tiberius, and Ignatius J. Reilly. They're nice and always want to play. Not like Uncle Jer's dog Bill, who's old and bites and can't come in the house."

Added Emmy: "Uncle Gonzo has lots of strawberry ice cream, and he never mows his lawn, so we can play Tarzan, and he sings the song about Jeremiah The Bullfrog with me. All his couches and chairs are all different colors. I love Uncle Gonz!"

In spite of his daughter's love of Uncle Gonzo, Henry Dornheim still resents his older brother.

"I don't know what kind of example he's setting," Dornheim said. "The other day, he picked up Emmy after school because I had a meeting. When he dropped her off after a few hours at his ramshackle house, Emmy said he let her paint his dog blue. Imagine it! Painting a dog! So what if it was just food coloring and it'll wash out? They're painting an animal!"

Unfazed by their parents' disapproval, the kids still regard "Uncle Gonz" as their favorite.

"The only other uncle I like is Uncle Steve," 12-year-old nephew Henry Jr. said. "Whenever he visits, he always plays us funny old show tunes and bakes awesome rhubarb pies. He doesn't have any kids, just like Uncle Gonz. I wish we could see Uncle Steve more, but he lives far away in San Francisco with his roommate Gary." ∅

because he was ducking his head, covering his mouth, and speaking in a French accent," Bush said. "He seated us and went away very quickly. Whenever he passed our table, he would turn his head and hide his face behind a menu. Finally, he collided with a server right in front of us, sending a whole tray of food flying. Once we helped him to his feet, the jig was up."

Members of the Bush Administration noticed that Cheney's work performance had begun to slip in recent weeks. He was late to several Senate

> ## Suspicions grew on June 12, when a disoriented-looking Cheney arrived at the White House still wearing his Denny's hosting uniform.

roll calls, looked tired at photo opportunities, and was barely able to stay awake during important National Security Agency briefings.

"I'd been suspicious for quite some time," Energy Secretary Spencer Abraham said. "There was one time when I was in his office to discuss an amendment to an energy bill. The phone rang, and he went white as a sheet. He answered it, said yes or no a few times, and then said something about how he couldn't 'come in' and how now was not a good time, and then he hung up. When I asked him about it, he said it was a wrong number."

Suspicions grew on June 12, when a disoriented-looking Cheney arrived at the White House still wearing his Denny's hosting uniform. He proceeded to pour coffee into a potted spider plant and drink from the plant's watering can.

"Condoleezza Rice was looking at him funny and asked if he was okay," Secretary of Health and Human Services Tommy Thompson said. "He said yes and then asked if we'd like to sit in smoking or non-smoking. It didn't take a genius to realize he was burning the candle at both ends."

When finally confronted, Cheney broke down and confessed, explaining that he had taken the second job to save up the money to buy his wife a new fur coat for their anniversary.

"What do you say to that?" Bush said. "I was mad as heck, but you can't fault a man for loving his wife. I told him if he needed the money, he should have come to me and we could have worked something out."

This is not the first time a top Bush Administration official has been caught moonlighting, a practice clearly prohibited in section seven of the White House employee handbook. In May 2001, Secretary of Transporta-

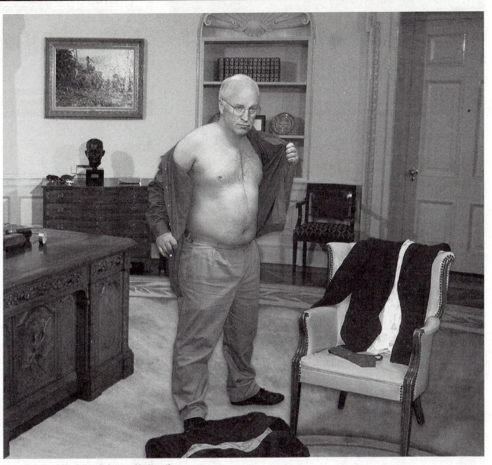

Above: Cheney quickly changes before a cabinet meeting.

tion Norman Mineta took a second job as a bartender to earn enough extra money for a 1964 Mustang convertible he'd had his eye on for some time. He quit the bartending job after a noticeable drop-off in the quality of his Cabinet work, most notably with his recommendation that a $9.2 billion tunnel be constructed connecting Los Angeles and San Diego.

Now that Cheney's moonlighting days are over, no one is more relieved than the vice-president himself.

"I'm glad that's all done with," Cheney told reporters. "I couldn't take the running around like crazy anymore. I wasn't sleeping, I was having a hard time concentrating on matters of national security, and I was answering my shoe instead of the phone." ∅

and Martina McBride."

Elson said it is impossible for the average American to comprehend the "utterly rudderless existence of these uprooted people."

"Cross-state migrants and asylum seekers wander around listlessly in the heat of the full sun, trying desperately to attend to their most basic needs," Elson said. "People stand in line for hours for a small piece of roasted corn, while others desperately try to get any information they can about who is appearing on the Papa John's Bluegrass Side Stage that night."

Montoya said the crowds showed signs of thinning after Tuesday's appearance by Brooks & Dunn. Nevertheless, he said he will continue to help, vowing to get another 20,000 KDEB Fox-27 giveaway packages to the grounds by the end of the week.

"It seems to be letting up a little," Montoya said, "but there are still so many who need our help."

Bobbie Framm, a badly sunburned 19-year-old who journeyed to Countryfest from Joplin, MO, railed against the camp's inadequate provisions and unfair policies.

"The brochure said ice and firewood and all sorts of other stuff would be available, but everything is gone," said Framm, who set up her tent in an overflow camping area behind a row

> ## "Cross-state migrants and asylum seekers wander around listlessly in the heat of the full sun, trying desperately to attend to their most basic needs," Elson said.

of tattoo vendors. "Then when we try to bring carry-ins into the concert, they bust us. We have rights, you know."

Other refugees complained about the oppressive tactics of the camp's armed guards.

"We had a big bonfire going, and at midnight, the cops came and made us put it out," said Ryan Wilke, who trav-

eled to the camp with his extended family, four generations of Wilkes squeezed into a 1991 Chevy S-10 pickup. "On Friday night, my brother was climbing on that giant inflated Mid-Missouri Mortgage Co. cowboy hat, and they detained him in the security tent to sleep it off. What gives them the right?"

In spite of the subhuman conditions, many refugees seemed not to notice, paying $6 for 16-ounce cups of Miller Lite at the KTTS party tent without raising an objection.

"People do what they have to do," Montoya said. "If abject squalor is all around you, you adjust and that becomes normal. It's sad, but life must go on, even here at Countryfest."

For all the pain and suffering, Montoya noted that the camp was not without its good points.

'There's a beautiful sense of community here," Montoya said. "They sing and dance together. They sit around the fires at night and exchange stories of the trucks they have at home, or how much they drank the night before. It's a peculiar ritual, but it is clearly very much a vital, treasured part of their culture." ∅

Ask *Popular Mechanics*, March 1947

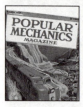

By *Popular Mechanics*, March 1947

**Dear *Popular Mechanics*,
March 1947:**

My father, who hasn't been the same since Mom died nine years ago, has finally found the courage to remarry. His new wife is a very nice person, and she certainly makes him very happy. But she insists that I call her "Mother," and she sometimes acts like she raised me. Needless to say, I resent this, but I don't want to upset my dad. How do I handle this sticky situation?

Divided Loyalties In Delaware

Dear Divided,

Flying Wing A Three-Story Hotel In The Sky! Breaking the aerial sound barrier is all well and good for Colonel Yeager, but what about those businessmen who need to breakfast in Boston and sup in Sacramento? The experimental Flying Wing—now in the prototype stage at many American aircraft manufacturers and expected to see service sometime in the next decade—would allow these moguls to travel in true style! Picture a giant "boomerang" eased through the sky by eight Voight-Corsair prop engines, and you have the general idea. And, because it's all one giant lifting body, it can support much greater useful interior volume. What does that mean? How about a four-star kitchen, movie theater, and handball courts complete with hot showers—all available as you cruise along at 300 em-pee-aitch, a full mile above the plains! We think even Mr. Yeager would find that hard to pass up.

**Dear *Popular Mechanics*,
March 1947:**

Like many people, I try to keep my work and personal life separate. But recently, my coworkers heard me on the phone inviting people to a party I'm having. Now I feel pressure to invite them, too. I don't want to make enemies at work, but I really want this to just be my non-work friends. How do I handle this?

Compartmentalized In Comstock

Dear Compartmentalized,

Automatic Sidewalk Eases Urban Commute! Dusty, dirty, loud, and jostling, the "concrete canyons" of such million-man metropoli as Chicago and Manhattan are what give America's greatest cities their charm... *and* aggravation. City life means sidewalks, which means "your dogs are barking" after a long day of beating the streets. But some see a very different possibility for put-upon pedestrians. The "Move-Walk," a self-propelled sidewalk made of rubberine

conveyor belting, may someday carry city dwellers to work, shop, and play along such storied thoroughfares as Broadway or the Miracle Mile! New advances in electrical motorization and polylatex sheeting mean we could soon see the advent of the moving sidewalk. Commuters will take

Automatic Sidewalk Eases Urban Commute!

their ease, peruse the paper, even enjoy a hot dog while breezing along at five miles an hour—quick enough to get you there in time, but without ruining your good suit of clothes. Look for the first Move-Walks in larger cites by 1958.

**Dear *Popular Mechanics*,
March 1947:**

I love my boyfriend, but he always has to be the center of attention. He's the bride at every wedding and the corpse at every funeral. Not only does this push me to the side, but it causes people to overlook what a great guy he is otherwise. Am I being uptight, or do I have reason to complain?

Upstaged In Upper Darby

Dear Upstaged,

Fibre-Glas Birdhouse Eliminates Time-Consuming Seasonal Repainting! Every spring, it's always on your to-do list: Take the bluebird house off its post and put a fresh dose of cheery red paint over the old, winter-faded coat. Luckily for you, a new Miracle Material from the DuPont Corporation called "Fibre-Glas" may soon make spring birdhouse-painting a thing of the past. Fibre-Glas is a Jet-Age "Composite" material with the colors chemically bonded right into its resin base. That means it should be years before the tough, colorful, impact-resistant, injection-molded shell of your new fibre-glas birdhouse, available in better hardware stores this summer, will show any appreciable wear. And if it does, what do you care? The inexpensive Fibre-Glas process means you can replace Cock Robin's chateau whenever it starts looking lackluster—or whenever the lady of the house decides on a new favorite color!

Popular Mechanics, *March 1947, is a syndicated advice columnist whose weekly column,* Ask Popular Mechanics, March 1947, *appears in more than 250 newspapers nationwide.* ⏍

Your Horoscope

By Lloyd Schumner Sr.
Retired Machinist and
A.A.P.B.-Certified Astrologer

Aries: (March 21–April 19)
Since you've been searching for its meaning for years and are no closer to finding the answer, the stars will help you: It's Spanish for "the crazy life."

Taurus: (April 20–May 20)
The old adage, "If you fall, get right back up on the horse," is sound enough advice, but it assumes you own the horse, and that you weren't knocked off by a Medieval Times employee.

Gemini: (May 21–June 21)
You just haven't been able to shake the feeling that you'd be a whole lot better off if you were A.J. Foyt.

Cancer: (June 22–July 22)
Your desire always to have the last word will prove excruciating next week while you sing "Row, Row, Row Your Boat" in a round.

Leo: (July 23–Aug. 22)
Though you do everything you can do to save the girl's life, the only thing you can do is juggle and do a few simple card tricks.

Virgo: (Aug. 23–Sept. 22)
Someday, you'll look back on all of this and laugh very, very bitterly.

Libra: (Sept. 23–Oct. 23)
By this time next week, you'll either be hung or hanged. Our apologies for any inconvenience the ambiguity may cause.

Scorpio: (Oct. 24–Nov. 21)
You will soon be exposed to the most rocking music ever, but due to your unrockable nature, you will remain profoundly unrocked.

Sagittarius: (Nov. 22–Dec. 21)
The stars were going to shout, "Look out! Behind you!" but you probably wouldn't fall for that old trick. Even though there really is a guy with a gun there.

Capricorn: (Dec. 22–Jan. 19)
Though juries are supposed to look for probable cause before finding a defendant guilty, yours will decide to sink you for being such a fatso.

Aquarius: (Jan. 20–Feb. 18)
The universal variation from one person to the next may be broad and deep, but somehow everyone in your family always winds up being lawyers.

Pisces: (Feb. 19–March 20)
Oh, and be careful of that tricky first step. It isn't there.

FLUGELHORN.COM from page 175

amounts of blood. Passersby were amazed by the unusually large amounts of blood. Passersby were amazed by the unusually large amounts of blood. Passersby were amazed by the unusually large amounts of blood. Passersby were amazed by the unusually large amounts of blood. Passersby were amazed by the unusually large amounts of blood. Passersby were amazed by the unusually large amounts of blood. Passersby were amazed by the unusually large amounts of blood. Passersby were amazed by the unusually large amounts of blood. Passersby were amazed by the unusually large amounts of blood. Passersby were amazed by the unusually large amounts of blood. Passersby were amazed by the unusually large amounts of blood. Passersby were amazed by the unusually large amounts of blood. Passersby were amazed by the unusually large amounts of blood. Passersby were amazed by the unusually large amounts of blood. Passersby were amazed by the unusually large

amounts of blood. Passersby were amazed by the unusually large amounts of blood. Passersby were amazed by the unusually large amounts of blood. Passersby were amazed by the unusually large amounts of blood. Passersby were amazed by the unusually large

How come it's always me who should be ashamed of myself?

amounts of blood. Passersby were amazed by the unusually large amounts of blood. Passersby were amazed by the unusually large amounts of blood. Passersby were amazed by the unusually large amounts of blood. Passersby were amazed by the unusually large amounts of blood. Passersby were amazed by the unusually large amounts of blood. Passersby were amazed by the unusually large amounts of blood. Passersby were amazed by the unusually large amounts of blood. Passersby were amazed by the unusually large

see FLUGELHORN.COM page 181

Car Bomber Given Shittiest Possible Car

see WORLD page 7A

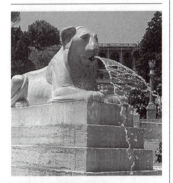

Fountain Simulates Vomiting Lion

see LOCAL page 5B

Drug Dealer Builds Better Life For His Family

see LOCAL page 9B

Karaoke Singer Will Survive

see LOCAL page 12B

STATshot

A look at the numbers that shape your world.

Top New Women's TV Networks

1. Listening Network
2. Estrovision
3. Lady CNN
4. KMC: The Kidnapping-Movie Channel
5. The Nodding-In-Agreement Network
6. V-SPAN

¡Univision Para Señoras!

THE ONION • $2.00 US • $3.00 CAN

0 74470 94595 6

---

the ONION®

VOLUME 38 ISSUE 26   AMERICA'S FINEST NEWS SOURCE™   25–31 JULY 2002

Nation To Be Tested For Scoliosis Friday

WASHINGTON, DC—In a mandatory, nationwide health initiative many Americans are dreading, all U.S. citizens will be tested for scoliosis Friday.

"Though some people may think it's a laughing matter, scoliosis is no joke," said Dr. David Krasnow of the Department of Health and Human Services, which is overseeing the testing. "An untreated case will result in significant deformity of the spine. So we can either act like mature ladies and gentlemen and get through the screenings quickly, or goof off and make it harder for everyone."

The scoliosis checks, to be conducted in junior-high-school gymnasiums across the U.S., are intended to diagnose and prevent see SCOLIOSIS page 184

Above: Testing begins early in a San Francisco junior-high-school gym.

Bush Begins Hunger Strike To Protest Human-Rights Abuses In Nepal

Above: Bush sits in front of the White House on Day Two of the hunger strike.

WASHINGTON, DC—Against strenuous objections from his advisors, President Bush began a hunger strike Monday to protest human-rights abuses in Nepal, vowing to subsist solely on water and vitamin supplements until "the twin clouds of violence and oppression are lifted from the land."

"I can no longer stand idly by while the gentle, peace-loving Nepalese people are made to suffer," said Bush, a longtime admirer of Nepalese culture. "This hunger strike will send a strong message to the government of Nepal and the insurgent Maoist rebels that their suppression of freedom and subjugation of the innocent is not going unnoticed."

Since 1991, Nepal has been locked in a bloody struggle between its constitutional monarchy and the Communist Party of Nepal (CPN), a Maoist guerrilla group seeking to overthrow the oft-oppressive regime. Thousands of innocent civilians have lost their lives in the crossfire.

After years of human-rights abuses by both the see BUSH page 185

Dad Keeps Dropping Hints About Mom's Sexual Proclivities

PHOENIX, AZ—Rodney Granger, 46, a Phoenix-area father of three, drops frequent hints about his wife Sandy's sexual proclivities, his creeped-out children announced Monday.

"Yesterday, we passed a sign on this supermarket loading dock that said 'Deliveries In The Rear.' Dad jabbed Mom, and they both started to laugh," said Andrew, the couple's 13-year-old son. "I acted like I didn't get it, but I got it all right. Apparently, Mom does, too."

According to Andrew's sister Erin, 11, the remark was far from atypical.

"On weekends, Dad and I sometimes go to the park to shoot hoops," Erin said. "Last Saturday, Dad told me to go without him, saying, 'Your mom needs me to *take care of some things at home*.' Then he smiled in this really weird way. I did *not* need to know that."

Erin said she believes her father is unaware that she, Andrew, and even 8-year- see DAD page 185

Above: Rodney and Sandy Granger with their three grossed-out children.

More Police Brutality In L.A.

The Inglewood police officer seen on a videotape violently arresting a handcuffed black teenager has pleaded innocent to an assault charge. What do *you* think?

Rob Phelps
Electrician

"How were those officers supposed to know that kid wasn't going to sprout an extra pair of arms from his back and pull a gun out of his neck as he lay pinned to the car's hood?"

Daniel Ziff
Systems Analyst

"Why must we always focus on the bad cops instead of the 65 percent of police officers who would never do anything like this?"

Christopher James
Architect

"They were just following the motto of the Inglewood Police Department: 'To protect and whomp the shit out of.'"

Diane Essen
Student

"I'm sure those officers wouldn't have done that unless it was absolutely necessary in order to hurt the guy."

Pete Bruge
Cashier

"I'm just glad I live on the East Coast, where police are heroic."

Emily Schofield
Dietitian

"That tape was shameful. One cop brutalizes a suspect while five others just stand around? What do I pay my taxes for?"

The Corporate-Fraud Bill

Responding to the recent rash of business-world corruption, the House passed a corporate-fraud bill last week. Among the provisions:

- CEOs may not skim from employee pensions to cover greens fees
- Accounting firms limited to three sets of books per client
- Tighter federal monitoring of corporations' Investor Deception Board
- Executive bonuses may not exceed 175 percent of total company earnings
- After a corporation is found guilty of a third offense involving fraudulent accounting or insider trading, the corporation must carry out a program of layoffs and plant closings until stock price rises again
- Special 130-page loophole section
- Worst offenses punishable by send-up in a song by The Capitol Steps
- Convicted CEOs with ties to president to receive 50 percent harder wrist slap
- American people needn't worry pretty little heads about what bill says

---

✆ the ONION®
America's Finest News Source. ™

Herman Ulysses Zweibel
Founder

T. Herman Zweibel
Publisher Emeritus
J. Phineas Zweibel
Publisher
Maxwell Prescott Zweibel
Editor-In-Chief

This Promotional Pen Works So Great, Imagine How Well The Drug Must Work

Somebody just sent a box of Prilosec promotional pens to our clinic and, boy, am I impressed. It's got a big, comfortable barrel and comes in an attractive purple. And it writes smooth as can be. No globbing or streaking— just a nice, clean, blue ballpoint line. It's also got some really cool writing along the side: "Prilosec® (Omeprazole) 20-MG capsules." Prilosec, huh? This Prilosec pen is so great, I'll bet anything the drug is great, too.

By Dr. Jeanne Horschart

I do know a bit about omeprazole. It's used to treat gastric and duodenal ulcers and gastroesophageal-reflux disease, a condition in which the stomach acid washes back up into the esophagus. Omeprazole eases gastric pain by decreasing the amount of acid produced by the stomach. As it turns out, Prilosec is omeprazole in delayed-release capsule form. Well, the capsule's release may be, but there was nothing "delayed" about the way the ink flowed when I clicked the button at the top of the pen and started to write!

Traditionally, I've shied away from prescribing drugs for the treatment of heartburn. I tend to encourage patients to make changes in their diet instead. Well, that was before I saw

> **So why did I decide to prescribe Clarinex for treatment of seasonal and year-round allergies? It was the fridge magnet.**

this pen. It's a *great pen.* Yes, this pen completely changes the way I feel about the prescription of omeprazole. Now I'm all for it.

If Prilosec the drug is anything like Prilosec the pen, I bet it works every time. My patients can kiss occasional discomfort from heartburn goodbye.

And talk about instant relief: It sure was a relief to have this pen handy when I needed one a few minutes ago. I wanted to write down a phone number, and the pen was right there—no muss, no fuss. Prilosec, no doubt, offers the same easy relief in pharmaceutical form. How cool is that?

Hmm, I see here that Prilosec is made by a company called Astra-Zeneca. Well, that name sounds very professional. I'm guessing they're on the cutting edge of pharmaceutical technology. And that logo looks very cutting-edge, too—slick and modern.

> **Prilosec is omeprazole in delayed-release capsule form. Well, the capsule's release may be, but there was nothing "delayed" about the way the ink flowed when I clicked the button at the top of the pen and started to write!**

That's important in pens and drugs. What's more, it's got a retractable tip for one-click convenience, not an old-fashioned pen cap that can be easily misplaced. As a doctor, I know it's vital to carry a fully functional pen, as well as to stay abreast of new advances in health-care products.

This reminds me of the way I discovered the antihistamine Clarinex a few months ago. If you are a general practitioner like me, you know there's no shortage of prescription antihistamines out there. So why did I decide to prescribe Clarinex for treatment of seasonal and year-round allergies? It was the fridge magnet. I couldn't help but notice how effectively it held a piece of paper to the refrigerator in the staff kitchenette. One of the things my patients care about most is convenience. They don't want a drug that's hard to use. This magnet was so easy to use, a baby could have done it. In fact, if the precautions didn't specifically prohibit me from doing so, I would prescribe Clarinex to a baby.

I'm always on the lookout for great new drugs to prescribe to my patients. But I must admit, I'm far too busy to seek them out by reading medical journals and research papers, or by talking to my fellow doctors. It really is a huge help to get great drug recommendations by way of hats, T-shirts, coffee mugs, pencil holders, clipboards, and fanny packs that I randomly encounter or that are sent to my office unsolicited.

Thanks, Prilosec! ✆

Grad Student Deconstructs Take-Out Menu

CAMBRIDGE, MA—Jon Rosenblatt, 27, a Harvard University English graduate student specializing in modern and postmodern critical theory, deconstructed the take-out menu of a local Mexican restaurant "out of sheer force of habit" Monday.

"What's wrong with me?" Rosenblatt asked fellow graduate student Amanda Kiefer following the incident. "Am I completely losing my mind? I just wanted to order some food from Burrito Bandito. Next thing I know, I'm analyzing the menu's content as a text, or 'text,' subjecting it to a rigorous critical reevaluation informed by Derrida, De Man, etc., as a construct, or 'construct,' made up of multi-varied and, in fact, often self-contradictory messages, or 'meanings,' derived from the cultural signifiers evoked by the menu, or 'menu,' and the resultant assumptions within not only the mind of the menu's 'authors' and 'readers,' but also within the larger context of our current postmodern media environment. Man, I've got to finish my dissertation before I end up in a rubber room."

At approximately 2 a.m., Rosenblatt was finishing a particularly difficult course-pack reading on the impact of feminism, post-feminism, and current 'queer' theory on received notions of gender and sexual preference/identity. Realizing he hadn't eaten since lunch, the Ph.D candidate picked up the Burrito Bandito menu. Before he could decide on an order, he instinctively reduced the flyer to a set of

shifting, mutable interpretations informed by the set of ideological biases—cultural, racial, economic, and political—that infect all ethnographic and commercial "histories."

"Seeing this long list of traditional Mexican foods—burritos, tacos, tamales—with a price attached to

> **According to friends, Rosenblatt has been under a great deal of stress in recent months due to the financial strain of student-loan debts, his part-time tutoring job, and a heavy academic courseload.**

each caused me to reflect on the means by which capitalist society consumes and subsumes ethnicity, turning tradition into mass-marketable 'product' bleached of its original 'authentic' identity," Rosenblatt said. "And yet, it is still marketed and sold by the dominant power structure in society as 'authentic' experience, informed by racist myths and projections of 'otherness' onto the

Above: Jon Rosenblatt with the menu in question.

blank canvas of the alien culture."

Added Rosenblatt: "Then, of course, I realized that this statement was problematically narrow, since I was assigning an inherent 'actual' meaning to the Ethnicity Content of the take-out menu. Which was, in itself, contradictory to one of the primary theses of deconstruction, i.e., that it's impossible for an 'impartially' observing arbiter to establish any ultimate or secure meaning in a text. I'd just begun to make a mental note of the cartoon anthropomorphic burrito on the front of the menu as a signifier of

such arbitrary 'otherness' when I yelled, 'What the hell am I doing?'"

Rosenblatt's inadvertent outburst nearly led to an altercation.

"I totally woke up my neighbor in the room across the hall," Rosenblatt said. "He looked like he might hit me, so I tried reasoning with him, but it came out all wrong. Instead, I found myself saying that the multiplicities and contingencies of human experience necessarily pose a threat to the tendency of any arbitrary power or 'authority' to dictate oppressive hier-

see STUDENT page 184

Husband Chooses Car Based On Lowest Passenger-Side Impact Rating

LINCOLN, NE—Husband Bruce Menden purchased a Geo Metro Tuesday, selecting the car on the basis of its rock-bottom passenger-side impact rating in *Consumer Reports.* "This car's price isn't inflated by sturdy, impact-resistant steel, is it?" Menden asked the salesman. "Safety's important, but I don't want to blow a fortune on luxuries." Menden, who always drives during outings with wife Cheryl, also passed on the optional passenger-side airbag.

Alcohol-Themed Bar Opens

HOUSTON—Fans of alcoholic beverages were excited by the opening of J.T. O'Drinky's, a new booze-themed

bar. "Lots of people love alcohol, so we figured that a bar centered on that concept was a natural," said Jim Reichel, owner and creator of the bar. "Patrons can enjoy a 'Gin and Tonic' and other whimsically named drinks, as well as enjoy our decor, which includes posters and neon signs celebrating various beers and liquors."

Man Trying To Remember How That Music They Used To Play Before HBO Movies Went

ALBANY, NY—Local resident Clint Fuster, 33, struggled to remember the old "HBO Feature Presentation" theme music from the '80s Monday. "They had that thing where the camera zoomed through a city street and up into the sky," Fuster said. "Then it went something like, 'Na-na-NAAA, na na-NAAA.' But I also remember a part

that went, like, 'NA-na-na, NA-na-na.' It was really cool—almost as cool as the credits for USA Night Flight."

Celebrity Disappointed After Meeting Fan

LOS ANGELES—Denzel Washington, who on Monday finally met long-time fan Brenda Haines, found the encounter anticlimactic, the Oscar-winning actor said. "I don't know, from her fan mail I always thought she'd be more exciting, I guess," Washington said following his awkward four-minute conversation with the 47-year-old Pomona waitress and mother of three. "And I'd always imagined she was taller."

Family Upgrades To Shells & Cheese

MOBILE, AL—After years of eating regular Kraft Macaroni & Cheese, the Conroy family upgraded Monday to the higher-end Velveeta Shells &

Cheese. "We've finally arrived," said wife Beverly Conroy while serving up a heaping bowl of the delicacy, made possible by husband Corey's 35-cent raise at the local tile factory. "It's nothing but the finest processed instant foods for us from now on." Pending sensible budgeting, the family hopes to move up from Hydrox cookies to Oreos by August.

Motivational Tape Gets Man Excited For 20 Minutes

SALINA, KS—The motivational cassette *Start That Motor!* got laid-off sales rep Bruce Smales, 39, excited about his life's possibilities for 20 minutes Monday. "The guy on the tape talked about all kinds of things, like 'making your luck' and stuff," Smales said. "It sounded great, and I went right off to make my 'Life List.'" Upon finding his pen out of ink, Smales retired to the couch, where he watched a *Hunter* marathon on TBS. ∅

archical social structures or centralize power. Ergo, any attempt to establish hierarchies and centralized power according to arbitrary dichotomies of 'right' and 'wrong' behaviors was therefore not only morally and philosophically, but also politically problematic and, in fact, oppressive. Man, did that ever not work."

According to friends, Rosenblatt has

> **Rosenblatt is considering taking a leave of absence from his graduate studies to spend several months living in his mother's basement in Elmira, NY.**

been under a great deal of stress in recent months due to the financial strain of student-loan debts, his part-time tutoring job, and a heavy academic courseload.

"Lacking proper sleep and struggling to keep up in the intensely competitive crucible that is Harvard grad school, Jon is starting to lose it," said roommate Rob Carroll, 26. "He has become so steeped in the complex jargon of critical theory that he's unable to resist the urge to deconstruct even the most mundane things."

This is not his first time Rosenblatt has deconstructed a random item out of habit.

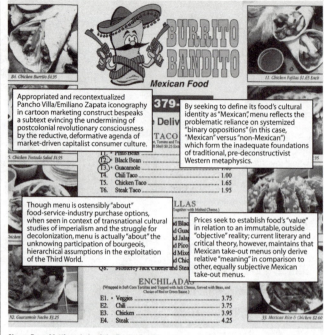

Appropriated and recontextualized Pancho Villa/Emiliano Zapata iconography in cartoon marketing construct bespeaks a subtext evincing the undermining of postcolonial revolutionary consciousness by the reductive, deformative agenda of market-driven capitalist consumer culture.

By seeking to define its food's cultural identity as "Mexican," menu reflects the problematic reliance on systemized "binary oppositions" (in this case, "Mexican" versus "non-Mexican") which form the inadequate foundations of traditional, pre-deconstructivist Western metaphysics.

Though menu is ostensibly "about" food-service-industry purchase options, when seen in context of transnational cultural studies of imperialism and the struggle for decolonization, menu is actually "about" the unknowing participation of bourgeois, hierarchical assumptions in the exploitation of the Third World.

Prices seek to establish food's "value" in relation to an immutable, outside "objective" reality; current literary and critical theory, however, maintains that Mexican take-out menus only derive relative "meaning" in comparison to other, equally subjective Mexican take-out menus.

Above: Rosenblatt's analysis of the Burrito Bandito menu.

"The other day, we passed a bus stop with a poster for Disney's *The Country Bears*," said friend Karen Pilson, 26. "I heard him mumble something about the incorporation of previously received notions concerning wildlife and our ecological environment into a reassuring, behavior-validating consumer commodity in the form of aggressively infantilized computer-animated pseudohumans that talk and play country music. Before I even had a chance to react, he went off the

deep end and started throwing out terms like 'prenotional,' 'prolegomena,' 'gynocritical,' and 'logocentrism.' I was just stunned."

Added Pilson: "I told him he was worrying me and recommended a good psychiatrist. Bad move, because that prompted him to launch into a whole discussion of Mulvey's 'Male Gaze' as it applies to mother/child pair-bonding in Lacanian psycho-analysis."

In spite of his friends' concern,

Rosenblatt seems unable to restrain his reflexive impulse to deconstruct.

"I can't help it," Rosenblatt said. "Even when I close my eyes at night, I feel myself deconstructing things in my dreams—random stuff like that two-hour *Dukes Of Hazzard* reunion special or the Andy Warhol postage stamp or commercials for that new squeezable gel deodorant. I'd say I'm going crazy, but that presupposes an artificial barrier between societally preexisting concepts of 'sanity' and 'insanity' which themselves represent another false dichotomy maintained for the preservation of certain entrenched elements of the status quo and… Oh, God. I'm doing it again."

Rosenblatt is considering taking a leave of absence from his graduate studies to spend several months living in his mother's basement in Elmira, NY.

Asked for comment, Professor Derek Nystrom of Skidmore College, an expert on deconstructivist thought, said that the Burrito Bandito take-out menu is open to many interpretations.

"The menu can be viewed an infinite number of ways, depending on viewer perspective," Nystrom said. "None of these differing views would be any more or less 'correct.' However, the menu's Pancho Villa-style burrito caricature, complete with bandoliers, six-guns, gaucho moustache, and sombrero, would be considered problematic by most scholars."

Added Nystrom: "To paraphrase: 'What is a take-out menu not, anyway? Everything, of course. What is a take-out menu? Nothing, of course.'" ∅

degenerative condition, which produces an S- or C-shaped curvature in the spine. During the 30-second procedure, citizens will bend forward roughly 25 degrees while federal health workers look for any abnormal distension, such as a bulging rib or fullness in the lumbar area. If a citizen tests positive for scoliosis, he or she will be fitted for a custom brace designed to halt the progression of the curvature.

Americans of both sexes will be asked to disrobe to the waist. Women will be permitted to keep their bras on.

Krasnow stressed that the screenings are mandatory, and that every American is expected to show up at his or her designated auditorium.

"If you're sick or otherwise unavailable on Thursday, we'll be contacting you to reschedule," Krasnow said. "We'll also be on the lookout for forged parental notes excusing people from the test."

Though Dallas resident Julie Muldowney, 42, plans to comply, she questioned the screenings' necessity.

"I don't get it," Muldowney said. "I remember getting tested for scoliosis back in seventh or eighth grade. We had to step behind a screen in the girls' locker room, and the school nurse examined our backs for curva-

tures. It was incredibly unpleasant and embarrassing. Why do they need to check us again?"

Also skeptical is Baltimore resident

> **"I assure you, the government is not doing this just to be meanies,"** Thompson said. **"As Americans get older and look back on these screenings, I am confident they'll come to understand just how important they really were. That goes for all of our programs."**

Eddie Woodson. Fitted with a cervico-thoraco-lumbo-sacral-orthosis brace after being diagnosed with scoliosis during the last nationwide screening in 1999, the 51-year-old landscaper said his range of motion has been

severely restricted ever since.

"The doctor told me to wear this thing 23 hours a day, and I can only take it off to swim or play," said Woodson, his head held upright by a neck ring anchored to the plastic, custom-molded device. "When I asked him if I could take it off to work, he said no. This is ridiculous. I probably lived with this condition for years, and it never bothered me. You try lifting rolls of sod with this damn thing on."

Secretary of Health and Human Services Tommy Thompson rejected such criticisms, insisting that the benefits of scoliosis screening far outweigh the inconvenience.

"I assure you, the government is not doing this just to be meanies," Thompson said. "As Americans get older and look back on these screenings, I am confident they'll come to understand just how important they really were. That goes for all of our programs."

Thompson was alluding to such unpopular HHS programs as the annual mandatory head-lice inspection, the hearing test, and "Friday the Thirteenth," a dental-hygiene fair at which HHS officials dress in foam molar costumes to distribute toothbrushes and small red tablets which, when chewed, expose plaque on the teeth.

Thompson said he believes a majority of Americans view the scoliosis

test favorably, citing the example of Verona, WI, resident Alan Righetti.

"The scoliosis test is awesome," said Righetti, 35. "The last one was held in the school cafeteria, and there were partitions between the men and the women. But if you looked between the partitions, you could see the ladies in their bras."

Continued Righetti: "The *Scoliosis Man* comic book they gave out was pretty lame, but at least it wasn't as dumb as that one we got from the suicide-awareness and prevention assembly. Me and my buddies down at the lumber yard still quote it, it's so stupid: 'Chad, do you want my portable cassette player? I don't want it anymore.' 'But, Ben, I don't get it. That's your most prized possession!' Yeah, we get it—suicidal people give their stuff away! How dumb is that?"

The next mandatory HHS initiative is slated for October. Titled "It's Perfectly Natural," the program will address the topic of menstruation.

"We'll be giving out free Kotex sanitary napkins and tampons, and showing the 1973 film *Donna, You're Not Alone*," Krasnow said. "And if you men out there think you're exempt from attending, think again. We'll be holding a concurrent, men-only talk about what to expect from puberty. And let's refrain from the giggling, shall we?" ∅

old Rachel are able to pick up on much of his thinly veiled sexual innuendo.

"I didn't used to get what Dad was saying, but now I'm catching on more and more," Erin said. "I'm starting to miss those days when I didn't know what Dad meant by 'Your mother doesn't get tired very easily,' or 'It's time to do some drilling.' Blech."

As the oldest child, Andrew said he better understands his father's comments than his sisters do. As a result, he tries to protect them.

"Sometimes, Rachel will ask me what Dad meant by some strange comment, like 'It's seed-planting time,'" Andrew said. "I'll say, 'He was talking about putting some tulips in the garden.' I can't let her know what sort of shit is going on in her own house."

Still, little Rachel is beginning to catch on to the racy double talk.

"On Mom's birthday, Dad told her she'd get her other present later," Rachel said. "Well, I know what *that* meant. That meant some sort of sex or something. Eww, nasty."

"They're always kissing in front of us, even Frenching," Andrew said. "How disgusting is that?"

Last week, on family board-game night, Rachel expressed her disgust with the open displays of affection. Her protestations, however, fell on deaf ears: Her father kissed her mother throughout the Pictionary contest, saying that he couldn't resist because she is "the best kisser in town." Granger then added, "Just ask

> **"Last Saturday, Dad told me to go without him, saying, 'Your mom needs me to take care of some things at home.'"**

your Uncle Kyle," provoking playful slaps from Sandy.

The Uncle Kyle remark, Erin explained, was an allusion to events of many years ago.

"I heard the story about how Dad stole Mom from his brother Kyle, who went on one date with her a long, long time ago, before Mom and Dad were ever married," Erin said. "But now I have to imagine Mom making out with Uncle Kyle. God, I want to puke."

Equally nauseated is Andrew.

"I spend a lot of time at my friend Danny's house, and his parents never touch each other at all," Andrew said. "Why are Mom and Dad still chasing each other around the table and tackling each other in piles of leaves on the front lawn? It completely makes me want to barf. If I grow up warped, it's so their fault." ∅

government and the CPN, Bush felt it was necessary to take action.

"In recent months, there has been a sharp increase in the use of deadly force on both sides," said Bush, as he sat on a mat in the Rose Garden. "There have been numerous reports of civilians being killed as a reprisal for the death of military police or CPN army personnel. Things are bad and they're only getting worse. Something had to be done."

> **In early 1998, while governor of Texas, Bush embarked on a two-and-a-half-month hunger strike in protest of former Chilean dictator Augusto Pinochet, under whose reign thousands of political prisoners disappeared mysteriously.**

Though he is a longtime member of Amnesty International and Doctors Without Borders, Bush insisted that his protest is not affiliated with any organization. Rather, he said, he is acting as "one man with a conscience."

"Violence only begets more violence," Bush said. "I will be keeping the people of Nepal in my heart and mind."

Many of Bush's critics charge that his hunger strike is, in actuality, a protest against the government, and that he sides with the CPN.

"I am not in support of the CPN," Bush said. "They, too, have been party to gross human-rights violations, such as recruiting child soldiers and killing civilians they consider 'enemies of the revolution.' I am not taking sides. With this hunger strike, I am merely raising awareness in the hopes that it may help bring about a peaceful end to the conflict."

Bush has also come under fire for hunger-striking instead of using his powerful position as U.S. president to take direct political or military action.

"As my hero Mahatma Gandhi once said, 'You must be the change you wish to see in the world,'" Bush said. "Besides, this is not the will of the American people. This is my fight. I will not let my personal convictions affect my obligation to the American people. Nepal's plight has touched me deeply, and to take direct political action without the mandate of the American people is to go against everything democracy stands for."

"I will try not to let the hunger strike affect my duties as president, but to avoid the strike would be an affront to those who voted me into office," Bush continued. "The American people elected a George W. Bush who acts on his beliefs. To do any less would be to turn my back on my many supporters."

This is not the first time Bush has taken action on behalf of Nepal. In 1997, Bush started a Yahoo! chat group to help disseminate information and news updates on the country's struggle. In July 2000, Bush took time off from his presidential campaign to organize a candlelight vigil in front of the Washington Monument to draw attention to the suffering of the Nepalese.

"It was amazing," Bush said. "We had almost 500 people, twice the number we'd expected. Just to be there, holding hands with a 70-year-old woman who'd lost members of her family to the conflict while listening to a young boy sing 'Ras Triya Gaan' [the Nepalese national anthem] was something I'll never forget."

Worried for his health and fearful of a repeat of a 1998 episode, Bush's top advisors have pleaded with him to limit his hunger strike to 30 days. Four years ago, while governor of Texas, Bush embarked on a two-and-a-half-month hunger strike in protest of former Chilean dictator Augusto Pinochet, under whose reign thousands of political prisoners disappeared mysteriously.

"[Bush's] work as governor became severely compromised after the first week," recalled Dan Morales, Texas Attorney General under Bush. "He began fainting regularly, but still he refused food, saying that his cause was too important. It wasn't until he developed an extreme case of malnutrition that we finally dragged him to a hospital to feed him intravenously. He was furious, but we felt we had to do it. Lord only knows what would have happened if we hadn't intervened."

Continued Morales: "While I'm sure the president hopes to keep this new hunger strike short, once he's committed himself to a cause, he goes all the way, no matter what the risk to himself." ∅

Above: Bush helps unload U.N. World Food Programme supplies during a 1998 relief mission in Uzbekistan.

Jacko Is On The Attacko!

Item! Jacko has gone **wacko**, going on the **attacko** against Sony for discriminating against artists who are **blacko**!

**The Outside Scoop
by Jackie Harvey**

Angry and confused that his last album, **Invisible**, sold only two million copies, Michael Jackson wants some answers, stat! In a press conference with **Rev. Al Sharpton**, The Gloved One called baseball great **Tommy Lasorda** "devilish." He also said he was a victim of the record industry, particularly his record label, Sony. While he is the King Of Pop, I have to question him on this one. I'm one of the two million people who bought the album, and it's no **Thriller**. Besides, is two million copies really that shabby? Heck, I'd be happy to sell 100 copies of the record of **Sousa marches** I made back in high school with **my buddy Skip**!

Rumblings of another baseball strike? It must be July.

Item! Hot on the heels of winning a lifelong-achievement award, **Tom Hanks** has a hot new movie called **The Road To Peoria**. I haven't seen it yet, but my sources say the Bosom Buddy plays a hit man who thinks he can make it big if only he can make it in Peoria. Sounds sort of cockeyed,

> ## Item! Hard to believe, but Queen of Nice Rosie O'Donnell has left the talk-show desk after six nice years.

but dreams have to start somewhere. I remember when Skip and I had that dream of making an album of Sousa marches. A candy-bar fundraiser and a few recording sessions later, we made our dream come true. And here I am today.

Put **Tom Cruise** in a pair of sunglasses and you just can't go wrong, can you?

The Emmys are coming! The Emmys are coming! While it's a little early, I think you can safely put your money on **Alias**. Maybe I should start my own awards show: **The Harveys**. I don't know what the criteria would be, but I already have a few ideas about the trophy design!

Item! A little bird told me that **Julia Roberts** has a new boyfriend, a cameraman named **Danny**. I'm crossing my fingers and hoping that this time it's Mr. Right. I still haven't gotten

over the time she left **Richard Gere** at the altar. Let's just hope she's finally met someone worthy of America's Sweetheart! I mean, really, hasn't she suffered enough?

Who let the dogs out? It wasn't me!

> ## Besides, is two million copies really that shabby? Heck, I'd be happy to sell 100 copies of the record of Sousa marches I made back in high school with my buddy Skip!

Those are both song titles and, put together, they make a story. I'll find some other songs to do that with and share them with you in a future column.

Item! Hard to believe, but Queen of Nice **Rosie O'Donnell** has left the talk-show desk after six nice years. I prayed that her winning blend of sass, moxie, and Koosh Balls would never end, but, alas, she left to spend more time with **her kids**. Though she will always be known for her friendly demeanor and outfits, I'll always remember the way she brought out the human side of the biggest stars. I'm sure I speak for the nation when I say, "We're going to miss you, Rosie." (Incidentally, I sure hope Rosie finds Mr. Right, too. It's got to be hard raising those children all alone.)

Can there be a remake of **Love Story** in the works? I don't want to say for sure, but I've heard rumblings…

Item! Domestic goddess **Martha Stewart** is in a bit of a home-canned garlic-dill pickle. Word has it she was involved in a stock brouhaha that was either insider trading or a phony IPO or something like that. I'm not really sure. I never did have a head for figures and business gobbledygook. If you can explain the scandal to me in a way **my mother** would understand, please clue me in. I hate to report on things I don't understand, but I have to say something.

That **Paul Reiser** sure is consistent, isn't he?

Item! Kylie Minogue is back! While some of my younger readers may not remember who she is, people in my age group will remember her chart-topping musical salute to **The Locomotion**, a dance craze that swept the nation. Choo-choo! I don't know if she'll bring a new dance like she did last time, but you can bet that if she

---

Your Horoscope

By Lloyd Schumner Sr.
Retired Machinist and
A.A.P.B.-Certified Astrologer

Aries: (March 21–April 19)
The jury won't buy your story of demonic possession. Which is no big deal, because the demon just wanted your Milk Duds.

Taurus: (April 20–May 20)
You do not subscribe to the sinful, heretical theory of evolution. You do, however, subscribe to *Young & Chubby Bubble Bottom*.

Gemini: (May 21–June 21)
Though it's been years, you haven't given up hope that the government will issue a formal apology for calling you a spoiled, self-centered brat.

Cancer: (June 22–July 22)
You won't accept the "Gaia" theory—the notion that the entire Earth is one huge organism—so long as the cacti are your friends and the ferns want you dead.

Leo: (July 23–Aug. 22)
It's okay to tell a girl you like the way she walks, as long as you do it politely and she's not an amputee who uses those clip-on arm canes.

Virgo: (Aug. 23–Sept. 22)
Actually, your form of love is a crime, but, due to a loophole, you're not guilty.

Libra: (Sept. 23–Oct. 23)
It might be the absolute last straw, but at least it's one of those fun and colorful flexi-straws.

Scorpio: (Oct. 24–Nov. 21)
You will soon experience a mystical transformation into a higher form of pure, ultimate consciousness, but you still won't be a "math person."

Sagittarius: (Nov. 22–Dec. 21)
War will ravage the land, leaving cities in ashes and causing no stone to lay atop another, when you try to enforce your definition of classic rock.

Capricorn: (Dec. 22–Jan. 19)
Though you and the dedicated cop will have many things in common, such as a love of the hunt and a taste for danger, it can only end one way.

Aquarius: (Jan. 20–Feb. 18)
You have the freedom to choose, and therefore have the potential to transcend your very nature through an act of will, but you will only choose extra cheese.

Pisces: (Feb. 19–March 20)
By the time you finally learn to relax and/or live with yourself, your vacation and/or life will be almost over.

---

does, I'll be practicing in front of the full-length mirror in my bedroom until I have it down pat.

The big question on everybody's lips—and on the cover of **TV Guide**—is, "Who will win **American Idol**?" I just wish my TV got **Fox** so I could find out. But since I don't have cable right now (long story, don't ask) and my reception's lousy, could **one of my loyal readers** fill me in?

Summer is here, and if you come closer, I'll let you in on a little **Harvey-family cookout secret**. Ready? Vinegar. Put your steaks or chicken in a little red-wine vinegar, maybe some salt and pepper. It'll taste like a famous chef prepared them, and everyone will want to know your secret. I won't tell if you don't!

Well, that's it for another edition of **The Outside Scoop**. I'd like to think I offered you more than just tawdry gossip and sleazy scandals, because **Hollywood** deserves all the adulation and respect we can muster. But you'll have to do it on your own until the next installment, because "I am leaving here now!" (That's my new catchphrase. Feel free to use that whenever it seems appropriate.) ✍

SMELTING POINT from page 183

amounts of blood. Passersby were amazed by the unusually large amounts of blood. Passersby were amazed by the unusually large amounts of blood. Passersby were amazed by the unusually large amounts of blood. Passersby were amazed by the unusually large

---

I've got a salt tooth.

---

amounts of blood. Passersby were amazed by the unusually large amounts of blood. Passersby were amazed by the unusually large amounts of blood. Passersby were amazed by the unusually large amounts of blood. Passersby were amazed by the unusually large amounts of blood. Passersby were amazed by the unusually large amounts of blood. Passersby were amazed by the unusually large amounts of blood. Passersby were amazed by the unusually large amounts of blood. Passersby were amazed by the unusually large amounts of blood. Passersby were amazed by the unusually large amounts of blood. Passersby were amazed by the unusually large amounts of blood. Passersby were

see SMELTING POINT page 188

the ONION®

VOLUME 38 ISSUE 27   AMERICA'S FINEST NEWS SOURCE™   1–7 AUGUST 2002

Court Summons Comes With 1,025 Free Hours Of AOL

see NATION page 7A

Boss' Dick Not Going To Suck Itself

see LOCAL page 5B

German 4-Year-Old Demands His 'Schlaumfi'

see LOCAL page 9B

STATshot

A look at the numbers that shape your world.

What Would We Name Our Spaceship?

1. Ronny Goetz's Love Rockkett
2. The Exploronizer
3. Class Of '02 Coors Light Space Party Barge
4. Prof. Phineas Fuzzy von Periwinkle Kitty IV's Purr-fect Spacey Space Ship
5. The S.S. Y'All Can Kiss My Ass Now

0 74470 94595 6   00

THE ONION • $2.00 US • $3.00 CAN

U.S. Takes Out Debt-Consolidation Loan

WASHINGTON, DC—Plagued by late fees, high interest rates, and harassing creditors, the U.S. took out a debt-consolidation loan Monday, combining the nation's $6.1 trillion debt into a single, easy monthly payment.

"My fellow Americans, we have just taken the first step toward regaining control of our finances," said President Bush at a press conference. "Thanks to a joint arrangement between the Treasury Department, the Federal Reserve, and E-Z Debt Services of Baltimore, we are finally on our way to freedom from debt."

As of press time, the national debt stands at $6,144,393,982,061.52.

Under the terms of the consolidation, E-Z Debt Services will repay the nation's estimated 45,000 creditors, a majority of whom are foreign investors, insurance companies,

see LOAN page 191

Above: Bush watches an E-Z Debt commercial on a White House TV.

Substance-Abusing Star's Publicist Has Been To Hell And Back

MALIBU, CA—Sara Baumann, who for seven nightmarish years was trapped in the powerful grip of client Matthew Perry's drug and alcohol dependency, has "come out the other side, stronger than ever," the 33-year-old publicist said Monday.

Sipping a Diet Coke while curled up on a couch in her Malibu home, Baumann reflected on those dark days of drug busts, car crashes, and tabloid spin control.

Above: Baumann, who is on the road back after years of substance abuse by Perry (inset).

"Drugs, drinking, rehab, bad relationships, arrests—I've been through it all," Baumann said. "But, thank God, all that's finally in the past. And you know what? I'm a better publicist for having gone through it. The lessons I've learned about shaping how the public perceives a celebrity client, I'll have those for the rest of my life."

Through the good and the bad, Baumann has stood by Perry, issuing official post-rehab press statements, doing damage control after relapses, and enduring countless lunches with reporters and producers in an effort to manipulate their opinion of the troubled *Friends* star.

"It's hard to talk about some of the things I went through," Baumann said. "The Vicodin addiction, the smashed Porsche, the Hazelden stint... so much of that time is just a blur to me."

Baumann, who "never expected this wild ride," came from humble roots, raised by schoolteacher parents Bob and Annette Baumann in Easton, PA. After graduating from Boston University with a degree in psychology in 1991, she moved to Los Angeles to become a publicist. She landed the Perry gig in 1995.

"The peak of all the madness was probably around 1997," Baumann said. "There I was, this simple girl from Easton, and all of a sudden, my

see PUBLICIST page 190

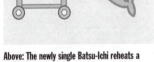

Above: The newly single Batsu-Ichi reheats a taco in his microwave.

Sanrio Introduces New Divorced Character

TOKYO—Sanrio Company, Ltd., the Japan-based creators of "Hello Kitty," unveiled the latest addition to their cartoon universe Monday, a divorced dolphin named Batsu-Ichi.

"We are hoping that Batsu-Ichi's adventures put smiles on people's faces, especially those of young children," Sanrio spokesman Shinji Nakata said. "We believe he will be the latest successful Sanrio merchandising vehicle, in spite of his broken marriage."

Shortly after Sanrio's announcement, Batsu-Ichi's "biography" and his accompanying image were posted on Sanrio's web site.

"Batsu-Ichi frolics in his briny home

see SANRIO page 190

Charging Obese Flyers Double

Southwest Airlines recently announced plans to strictly enforce a policy that asks passengers too large for its seats to purchase an extra fare. What do *you* think?

"Making the obese pay more is fine, but waving them into their seats with fluorescent-orange batons is too much."

Chris George
Systems Analyst

"I hope this controversy escalates. I would love to see that picket line."

Fred Issel
Delivery Driver

"As a man who once lost 100 pounds, I say to hell with them—it's their fault they're fat. As a man who gained the 100 pounds back, I say have a heart, Southwest Airlines."

Robert Russell
Cashier

"Perhaps the overweight passenger could help offset the price of the extra seat by, say, serving as a screen for the in-flight movie."

Phil Lyman
Stockbroker

"That explains the 'Test Your Ass Dimensions' frame at the check-in counter."

Donna Koechner
Homemaker

"Overweight people fully deserve the dignity they have denied themselves for so long."

Meredith Poole
Massage Therapist

The Snakehead Menace

Native to Asia, the land-walking snakehead fish has spread to seven U.S. states, posing a potentially major environmental threat. What is known about the fish?

- Gets real ornery after drinking tequila
- Does not actually fly, but "sails" distances of up to 50 feet
- Recently inked deal with mosquitoes to spread West Nile virus
- Enjoys purchasing and viewing backyard-wrestling tapes
- Routinely breaks into Sierra Club meetings and jeers members
- Makes lampreys puke with revulsion
- Created in God's image
- Can change color to perfectly mimic dinnerware patterns
- Signing movie deals left and right
- Is packed with nails
- Once ate a man alive for snoring too loud
- Hunts down cars with "I'd Rather Be Fishin'" bumperstickers
- Votes straight-ticket Republican
- Can hurl verbal invective in nine languages
- Recently discovered fire

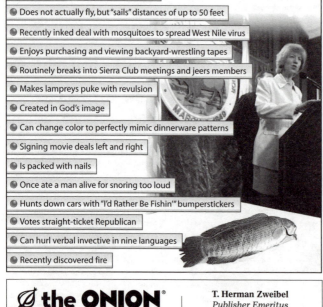

⊘ the **ONION**®
America's Finest News Source.™

Herman Ulysses Zweibel
Founder

T. Herman Zweibel
Publisher Emeritus

J. Phineas Zweibel
Publisher

Maxwell Prescott Zweibel
Editor-In-Chief

It's Good, Hutchins, But Is It Delta In-Flight Magazine Good?

By James Montcrief
Editor-In-Chief,
Delta Sky Magazine

I won't mince words with you, Hutchins. Your "St. Louis: Red, White & Blues!" article is good. Damn good. I'm reminded of a young me so many years ago, pecking out an inspired look at Scotland's 10 best golf courses. Yes, I know your article would more than pass muster at most magazines. But this isn't most magazines. This is *Delta Sky*, the best in-flight magazine there is. So the question remains: Your article is good, but is it *Delta Sky* good?

Please do not be offended by my questioning of your work. I only seek to hold this article up to the highest journalistic standards. It is my job to continually ask: Is it informative enough? Is it entertaining enough? Does the writing possess that elusive, essential quality all great in-flight writing has, that quality that can only be called "breeziness"?

Does the paragraph on St. Louis' unique love affair with its sports teams flow into the one about the city's thriving jazz scene? Should the section about the Arch be expanded? Does the sidebar on the Anheuser-Busch factory tour complement or detract from the main article? As the editor of *Delta Sky*, I have no choice but to obsess over these matters. It's

> Please do not be offended by my questioning of your work. I only seek to hold this article up to the highest journalistic standards. It is my job to continually ask: Is it informative enough? Is it entertaining enough?

my job. Second-best might be good enough for the hacks over at United Airlines' *Hemispheres* magazine, but around here, we expect more.

You see, Hutchins, over the years, *Delta Sky* has come to represent a standard of journalistic excellence the other in-flight magazines have tried and failed to equal. Commuters, vacationers, and business travelers alike have come to expect better than the best from us, and, by God, that's what we give them each month. If we have to work 80-hour weeks to dot every "i" and cross every "t," well, that's just the price of quality.

Put yourself in the place of America's airline customers. How would you feel if you spent $500 to cab it to the airport, haul your luggage around a long security line, and spend five hours crammed into a metal tube

> I've had many a greenhorn come to me with some barely coherent "America's Most Romantic Getaways" piece. And each time, I pointed him or her toward United Airlines, where they eat that shit with mustard.

where the only available reading material is some poorly written article about the sun-dappled coast of Mexico's Baja Peninsula? Pretty ripped-off, I'd say.

That's why we do everything we can to offer the finest in-flight journalism ever. Articles like regular contributor Mary Billard's "Quick Summer Slimdowns" in the May issue. Articles like managing editor Michael Foss' "The Golden Age Of Television" in the current one. Articles like the upcoming "Oreo's 90th Birthday" piece that I've been losing sleep over for the past two months.

It's a sign of your talent, Hutchins, that you've already made it this far in the in-flight game. I've had many a greenhorn come to me with some barely coherent "America's Most Romantic Getaways" piece. And each time, I pointed him or her toward United Airlines, where they eat that shit with mustard.

But you, Hutchins, have "It." You've got that elusive, hard-to-define quality that all the great ones possess. You know how to draw the traveler into an article and sustain his interest. I sensed you had the stirrings of genius within you when you first pitched me your "Remembering The '57 Chevy" piece those many months ago. And, of course, you have the good journalist's knack for finding that perfect topic. "San Francisco's Best Seafood

see DELTA page 192

Gym Teacher Secretly Hates Nerds

SIOUX FALLS, SD—In spite of a professional obligation to treat all P.E. students equally, Thorpe High School gym teacher Brad Malanga, 37, secretly hates the unathletic nerds whose forebears he bullied and ridiculed back in his own school days.

> **"There are always a few kids who refuse to make any effort in gym class. These kids become magnets for teasing because of their bad attitude. If they weren't such wimps, they'd win more respect, but they never change."**

"Pathetic," said Malanga, eyeing a trio of honors students huddled in the corner during dodgeball Monday. "It's just like it was when I was in school. There are always a few kids who refuse to make any effort in gym class. These kids become magnets for teasing because of their bad attitude. If they weren't such wimps, they'd win more respect, but they never change."

Added Malanga, under his breath: "Buncha pussies."

Though he would never admit to doing so, Malanga looks the other way when nerdy students are teased and harassed by the more popular "jocks." He also tends to focus his attention and teaching efforts on a few select individuals whose athletic potential makes them prime candidates for varsity sports.

"[Sophomore Chad] Shelby definitely has the goods to be a wide receiver, and I'm really pushing for him to go out for track next spring, too," Malanga said. "[Freshman] Kim Kause has got the same hustle that made her brother Mike the best point guard in THS basketball history. Very excited about her. And [freshman Kurt] Winters is a natural-born wrestler. Can't wait to see what he can do with another 15 pounds of muscle on that frame. If that happens, we could be going all the way to State next year. He's that good."

Malanga failed to make any mention of sophomore Joshua Kiesler, who throws softballs backwards; junior Hugh Howell, who cannot clear a hurdle; and freshman Tricia Wasserstein, whose epileptic seizure during a volleyball game last September relegates her mostly to the sidelines.

Malanga, who grew up in Sioux Falls, is a 1983 graduate of Thorpe. Earning letters in football, basketball, and baseball, he has always had an interest in physical education. He has also always had an interest in terrorizing students who prefer science to sports.

"Yeah, well, you know, boys will be boys," said Malanga when asked about a 1982 incident in which, as a high-school junior, he administered a

Above: The nerd-hating Malanga.

> **"Pathetic," said Malanga, eyeing a trio of honors students huddled in the corner during dodgeball.**

locker-room "swirlie" to Westinghouse Prize winner Howie Krumholtz. "Man, I forgot all about that. I sure was a live one back then."

Malanga attended Yankton College, where he majored in physical education. Believing that physical fitness was the best way to instill confidence and self-esteem in young people—and eager to repent for his poor treatment of nerds in high school—Malanga vowed to become "the kind of P.E. teacher who reaches out to all students."

"I had so many ideas, and for those first few months after I returned to see TEACHER page 191

Orphanage Director Pushing Asian Orphans

AMES, IA—Plagued with a surplus, St. Joseph Orphanage director Ann Rath has been pushing Asian orphans to prospective adoptive parents. "This is Mi Ling—isn't she pretty?" said Rath, introducing Bonnie and Paul Fisher to one of the 40-bed orphanage's 27 Asian children. "Or, if you'd prefer a boy, we have Tan Dinh. He's crazy about baseball." The Fishers, who were hoping for a Russian girl, told Rath they would "think it over," the fifth time a couple has done so in the past week.

Man As Surprised As Anyone That He Knows All The Members Of 'N Sync

ORDWAY, CO—Craig Bulone is "as surprised as anyone" that he can name all the members of 'N Sync, the 31-year-old reported Monday. "There's Justin, that's Lance... J.C., Joey... and I'm pretty sure that last one is Chris," said Bulone, watching an 'N Sync video on MTV with roommate Todd Campa. "Jesus Christ. Did I just name all five members of 'N Sync?" Bulone remains unaware that he knows all the words to Chad Kroeger's "Hero."

World's Last Bob Hope Fan Dies Of Old Age

JEFFERSON CITY, MO—Vic Wilmot, 97, the world's last Bob Hope fan, died in his sleep Monday, finally rendering the long-endangered species extinct. "He was always going on about some guy called Bob Hope," said great-grandson Clint, 22. "I'm not sure, but it sounded like he was some sort of actor." In the past 12 months, more than a dozen species of fandom have become extinct, including the Katharine Hepburn Fan, the Mickey Rooney Fan, and the Red Buttons Fan.

Panhandler Demands Explanation For Failure To Provide Quarter

ATLANTA—Local panhandler John "Jolly Jack" Sabourin angrily insisted that pedestrian Bruce DiCostanzo explain his failure to spare 25 cents Monday. "Why not?" an indignant Sabourin asked after being turned down. "Why you don't gimme no quarter?" After explaining that he had no change on him and that he was sorry, DiCostanzo walked two blocks before realizing he'd just apologized for not handing free money to a complete stranger.

Cocktail Party Gets As Wild As It's Going To Get

PROVIDENCE, RI—A cocktail party at the home of art curator Martin Conroy was already as wild as it was going to get by 8 p.m. Monday. "Oh my goodness, look at Ted," said Marisa Pulsipher, spotting fellow partygoer Ted Kannell doing his impersonation of Boston Symphony conductor Seiji Ozawa. "He is just irrepressible." The party almost got wilder when Conroy pondered breaking out a bottle of Loch Morar 30-year-old single-malt scotch, but he ultimately decided not to.

Ex-Girlfriend Flashback Leaves Man Paralyzed In Produce Aisle

MITCHELL, SD—Alex Borland, 26, was paralyzed by a ginger-root-triggered ex-girlfriend flashback in the produce aisle of his local supermarket Monday. "Excuse me, sir... Excuse me," a fellow shopper told Borland, who was lost in memories of the day last December when he and then-girlfriend Jill Weston bought ginger root for an Oriental salad they later prepared at Weston's apartment. "I'm trying to get to the kiwis. Would you please move? Hello?" ∅

client's picture is appearing in all these magazines—*People, Us Weekly, EW...* you name it. His fame really went to my head. Looking back, I guess the crash was inevitable."

The first cracks began to show in late 1997, when Perry entered a rehab hospital for chemical dependency. Baumann said she was in "deep denial" about his drug troubles, repeatedly issuing statements quashing tabloid rumors that Perry had damaged his liver so badly that he needed a transplant.

As Perry bounced in and out of rehab, and his name became a staple of late-night talk-show monologues, Baumann found herself sinking deeper and deeper into depression. The stress began to take its toll on her health.

"Everything was so out of control," Baumann said. "I didn't have time to go to the manicurist, much less my power-yoga class at Reebok [Sports Club]. I put on eight pounds. I looked like shit."

Fortunately for Baumann, a good friend stepped in to provide a much-needed wake-up call.

"Liz [Cohen] said to me, 'Sara, you need to do something for yourself. Not for Matthew, but for *you,*'" Bau-

mann said. "She convinced me to check into a spa. I did a lot of serious thinking during my 48 hours in the desert. While lying there in that full-

> ### As Perry bounced in and out of rehab, and his name became a staple of late-night talk-show monologues, Baumann found herself sinking deeper and deeper into depression.

body seaweed wrap, I gained an entirely new perspective on what I was doing to myself."

Baumann emerged from the spa with a determination to get better press. Presenting Perry's troubles as the "early stages of chemical dependency, not addiction," Baumann sought the public's admiration for his courageous admission of fallibility. She was largely successful, landing

Perry a sympathetic cover story in *USA Today.*

Encouraged by the *USA Today* success, Baumann decided that it was time to start focusing on the positive.

"In February 2000, Matthew did this *L.A. Times* interview, during which he said he was fed up with the whole Hollywood dating scene and was looking for a girl who has more going for her than just looks," Baumann said. "You know, the standard I-want-somebody-who's-real stuff. At one point, he said he wanted a girl who was into regular things, like playing bingo. He said, and I quote, 'Bingo is sexy.' By 9 a.m. the next day, I had that line on the desk of every entertainment editor in the country. According to our clipping service, it appeared in print or on air in 63 different places. For me, that was the moment I knew I'd turned the corner."

But the fight was not over. When *Friends* co-star Jennifer Aniston married Brad Pitt, Baumann dug deep within herself to find an angle to advance Perry's career.

"I sent out a story about how Jennifer's wedding inspired Matthew to quit partying and start looking for someone he could build a life with himself," Baumann said. "I couldn't

believe how well that worked. The press ate it up."

Today, with the media focusing on Perry's recovery and his recent slim-down, Baumann said she's "mellower and definitely happier." This calmer version of Baumann stands in stark contrast to the harried, perpetually angry person she used to be—someone who would scream at talk-show bookers on her cell phone or bully young personal assistants.

"I'm more mature now," Baumann

> ### "While lying there in that full-body seaweed wrap, I gained a entirely new perspective on what I was doing to myself."

said. "My attitude is, whatever craziness comes my way, I can handle it. Except, like, another arrest. Oh, God, please don't let him get busted for possession." ✍

---

of Water-Loo with all his associates and, on every other weekend, his two children, Porpy and Finn," the biography read. "Batsu-Ichi's favorite meal is tacos, and he likes to play tennis. His five-year marriage to Sharu-chi, also a dolphin, ended last year. Batsu-Ichi lives in a charming efficiency apartment on the outskirts of Water-Loo, where he has a talking microwave named Yummy. His job is raking the ocean waves flat so the sun can shine through. He loves his job but may have to take another one to make

> ### "Always a game little fellow, Batsu-Ichi's motto is 'Take It One Day At A Time!'"

his monthly child-support payments. Batsu-Ichi is an outgoing and highly eligible little dolphin, but he has yet to work up the courage to ask out his cute coworker, Misako The Cuttlefish. Always a game little fellow, Batsu-Ichi's motto is 'Take It One Day At A Time!'"

As with other Sanrio characters, Batsu-Ichi will be featured on a variety of products, such as stationery, notebooks, dishware, stickers, patches, wristwatches, pens, pencils, pencil cases, calendars, jewelry, keychains, posters, baseball caps, mugs, makeup kits, novelty pillows, inflatable chairs, miniature candy dispensers, and divorce forms. ✍

amounts of blood. Passersby were amazed by the unusually large amounts of blood. Passersby were amazed by the unusually large

amounts of blood. Passersby were amazed by the unusually large amounts of blood. Passersby were amazed by the unusually large amounts of blood. Passersby were amazed by the unusually large amounts of blood. Passersby were amazed by the unusually large amounts of blood. Passersby were amazed by the unusually large amounts of blood. Passersby were amazed by the unusually large

> ### I learned the hard way that falconry isn't something you just pick up.

amounts of blood. Passersby were amazed by the unusually large amounts of blood. Passersby were

amazed by the unusually large amounts of blood. Passersby were amazed by the unusually large

see EVEN BLACKER page 196

LOAN from page 187

banks, and other privately held entities. In return, the U.S will make a single monthly payment of $9.26 billion, adjusted for inflation, to E-Z Debt every month for the next 70 years.

"We are proud to enter into this arrangement with the federal government," E-Z Debt spokesman Phil Rizzo told reporters. "We know how hard it is when you're buried under a mountain of bills with seemingly no way to get out. When you don't know where else to turn, E-Z Debt is there

> **The government first became aware of E-Z Debt Services on July 10, when Sen. Max Baucus (D-MT) happened to see a commercial for the company while watching late-night television. Two days later, President Bush saw the same ad during a 3 a.m. M*A*S*H rerun.**

to help get you back on your feet."

The government first became aware of E-Z Debt Services on July 10, when U.S. Sen. Max Baucus (D-MT) happened to see a commercial for the company while watching late-night television. Two days later, President Bush saw the same ad during a 3 a.m. M*A*S*H rerun.

According to White House press secretary Ari Fleischer, Bush was sitting at his desk clutching a fistful of past-due notices when he saw the ad.

"He was holding all these unpaid bills, and tons more were piled high on his desk, including a three-month-old bill from Lockheed-Martin for $5.3 billion worth of jet fighters," said Fleischer, who was in the Oval Office working late at the time. "He raised

Above: Bush poses with a Lockheed-Martin X-35A fighter that was saved from repossession, thanks to E-Z Debt.

the handfuls of bills above his head and shouted, 'I can't take it anymore!' That's when the ad came on."

After extensive meetings between E-Z Debt officials and the Treasury Department, an arrangement was reached which provided a manageable payment plan—with no threatening phone calls or military invasions from creditor nations.

Though the House Of Representatives swiftly and decisively approved the consolidation plan by a vote of 285 to 103, the Senate took longer to rally the necessary support, debating the issue for weeks.

"I was definitely skeptical about E-Z Debt, as were many of my colleagues," Senate Majority Leader Tom Daschle (D-SD) said. "I'd heard horror stories about those debt services. England used one to get out of a recession in the late '80s, and they're still paying for it."

"But E-Z Debt is different," Daschle continued. "Jim [Smoller], our E-Z Debt representative, sat down with

me and the other senators and really convinced us that debt consolidation was the way to go. He was extremely helpful, taking the time to patiently

> **"I'd heard horror stories about those debt services. England used one to get out of a recession in the late '80s, and they're still paying for it."**

answer all our questions. He even gave us a free quote."

Opponents of the plan charge that it unnecessarily endangers the numerous national assets offered as collateral. Among the valuable properties being put up are Yellowstone National

Park, NASA, and the state of Alaska.

"Holding the nation hostage to a single creditor is hardly preferable to the original situation," said U.S. Sen. Dianne Feinstein (D-CA) during a lengthy Senate debate on the consolidation. "Besides, I am confident that if we just trim a few unnecessary expenses from the budget and somehow get a little bigger GNP, we can climb out of this hole without help. We just need a little more time."

"Okay, so we mismanaged our money a little bit—who doesn't every now and then?" Sen. Bill Frist (R-TN) said. "But that's no reason to resort to using one of those get-out-of-debt-now services."

Despite such opposition, ultimately, the Senate's pro-consolidation voices won out.

"In the end, everybody came to see that E-Z Debt isn't just another loan. It's a way to get out of debt without declaring bankruptcy," Daschle said. "Thanks, E-Z Debt. We couldn't have done it without you." ∅

TEACHER from page 189

Thorpe, I implemented a lot of them," Malanga said. "Extra-credit intramural sports teams. Remedial after-school gym classes for kids who needed a little more attention. I even gave more responsibilities to the shy kids, like keeping track of the equipment or collecting towels for the laundry cart."

Yet Malanga became disillusioned when he discovered that the unathletic students he wanted to help were often "unwilling to help themselves."

"I had to discontinue the after-school classes because nobody came," Malanga said. "I heard it was because the kids who needed them didn't want to be branded as dorks. Well, I was trying to prevent them from becoming dorks in the first place, but they just didn't get it."

Malanga said his resentment of the school's more academically oriented students only deepened over time. Of

> **Malanga has earned the dual distinction as one of the most and least popular teachers at Thorpe.**

this year's crop, Malanga is particularly critical of senior and National Merit Scholar David Chang.

"I've hardly seen Ching [sic] this

semester, since he keeps weaseling out of class to participate in his Science Olympiad team," Malanga said. "The guy can't even do a push-up; I guess fitness just isn't as important as some big science prize. And I can't make him stay after class, either, because he's taking some extra-credit college-level calculus course. See what I mean? Absolutely no sense of commitment among these kids."

In spite of his efforts to mask his preference for athletes, Malanga has earned the dual distinction as one of the most and least popular teachers at Thorpe. Depending on the student, "Mr. M" or "Malangaloid" is either a trusted friend or a hated foe.

"Last Friday, Mr. M took a bunch of us to a non-conference Fighting Sioux

[hockey] game, and then out to Domino's [Pizza] afterwards," said 15-year-old Bryce Donovan, one of the stars of Thorpe's junior-varsity swim team. "He's the bomb!"

"I'll never forgive him for making me stay up on the rope until I climbed to the top," said 16-year-old aspiring paleontologist Joe Wagner. "I was up there for almost 20 minutes, struggling to get more than a few feet off the ground before he finally said I could get down. The whole class was pointing and laughing at me as I tried to lift myself up. And the whole time, [Malanga] just stood there all smug and satisfied, like he was teaching me some important life lesson. I can't tell you how humiliating it was. Malangaloid is a total bastard." ∅

Zing! I Just Got You With Another One Of My Trademark 'Complete Lies'

By Phillip Wynegar

Gotcha!

Fooled you, didn't I? You actually thought I'd picked up the cake for Steve's going-away party on my way to work and put it in the break-room fridge? You know, like I said I did? Zing! Looks like you're just the latest victim of one of my trademark "complete lies."

Ba-DOOM! That's another one for me! I am the King Of The Untruth! Phillip one, you nothing!

Since you're kind of new here, perhaps this calls for a little explanation. Basically, you've just been completely lied to. Or, as we call it around here, "Philliped."

Don't feel bad. You're not the first to fall for one of my lies. In fact, I do it so often that it's sort of become my trademark. You know how Fonzie had that thing where he started the juke-box by banging on it? Or Mother Teresa's thing was being really nice to poor people and helping them? Well, my "thing" is making up a bunch of stuff that isn't true and then insisting, with the utmost sincerity and conviction, that it is!

It's a little trick I invented as a kid. One day, when I was 5 or 6 years old, I was playing with an older boy, and I threw a rock at a neighbor's basement window and broke it. I started crying and saying the other kid pushed me into the window and that my foot went through. Well, not only

> ## What I do is a real art form, you know. It's not easy to pull off a proper "Phillip job." There's more to it than simply spouting off any lie that pops into your head.

did he get the blame, but I got treated to ice cream by my mother! Isn't that a riot? That was the beginning of a long and hilarious career in saying stuff that has no basis in reality.

Yes, I'm famous—actually, *infamous* is more like it—for my lies around the office. Just the other day, I told Esteban, the night custodian, that he was getting a $375-a-month raise, starting Sept. 1. Well, I'm just a sales representative, not the guy who gives raises. But Esteban didn't know that! Man, the look on his face when he

finds out he's been Phillipted will be priceless! With any luck, he'll have already factored the extra money into his family budget and spent some of it on new clothes for his children or something like that. What a boob!

I'll never forget the first time I Phillipted Bob down in shipping. He completely believed that I would stick

> ## Don't feel bad. You're not the first to fall for one of my lies. In fact, I do it so often that it's sort of become my trademark.

around after work to give him a ride home. My only regret is that I wasn't there to see his reaction when Karen the receptionist told him I left promptly at 5 p.m. like I always do.

What I do is a real art form, you know. It's not easy to pull off a proper "Phillip job." There's more to it than simply spouting off any lie that pops into your head. You can't just say, for instance, "I can destroy cities with my mind," or "These shoes cost $4.5 million." People can see right through claims like that. The lies have to be realistic. And, while I don't want to give away all my trade secrets, I will say that statements that include more personal details tend to work better, such as "I have to miss work because my mother is sick," or "I'm infertile." People are also more likely to believe you if your statement includes an offer of help, like "Sure, I'll watch your bag," or "I know CPR!" These are just the fundamentals I'm talking about; it takes years to get to my level of expertise.

One of my favorite things is when, after I've delivered another one of my classic Phillips, people ask, "Seriously? Is that true?" I just look them square in the eye and say, "Yes." There's a science to doing that. I can't stretch my face all out and go, "Oh, yeah, YEAH!" or they would get suspicious. It's much better for them to see the earnestness in my face and instinctively trust me, only to realize later that I was Phillipting them.

I realize you may be upset about falling for my latest "complete lie," but I assure you that it's all in good fun. Tell you what: To show that there's no hard feelings, let me buy you dinner after work tonight. Go to Antoine's Bistro on Seventh Avenue, walk right past the maitre d', and sit down in the booth marked "Reserved" by the window. If they give you any trouble, just let them know you're waiting for me. I'll be there at 8. ✐

Your Horoscope

By Lloyd Schumner Sr.
Retired Machinist and
A.A.P.B.-Certified Astrologer

Aries: (March 21–April 19)
A White Sox scout will tell you he likes your fastball and curve—but not your slider—moments before police forcibly remove him from your cubicle.

Taurus: (April 20–May 20)
Sometimes, it is okay to be treated like a child, but it would be nice if your coworkers didn't always spell out the naughty words when you're around.

Gemini: (May 21–June 21)
Your hot streak with the opposite sex continues, which is unfortunate, as you're trying to remain celibate and gay.

Cancer: (June 22–July 22)
It's been three long, difficult months, but take heart: You've shattered the world record for time spent trapped in a burning bus.

Leo: (July 23–Aug. 22)
What most people don't seem to understand is that normal dentures lack the air of excitement and danger of your prosthetic badger jaw.

Virgo: (Aug. 23–Sept. 22)
True, the little black dress is a tasteful, slimming classic, but you are a rodeo clown.

Libra: (Sept. 23–Oct. 23)
Some people are visual learners, others are auditory learners, and you learn best when things are beaten into you.

Scorpio: (Oct. 24–Nov. 21)
Your hope that your son will live a happy life, free from suffering, is somewhat at odds with your decision to name him "Sasha."

Sagittarius: (Nov. 22–Dec. 21)
Wilderness sports may be growing in popularity, but people are not yet ready to appreciate your expertise at trout-shotgunning.

Capricorn: (Dec. 22–Jan. 19)
Though you demand that the part of you be played by Robert Culp, Mr. Culp takes understandable exception to portraying a milquetoast slob.

Aquarius: (Jan. 20–Feb. 18)
Your poisonous spikes have helped you fend off predators, but the iridescent scales don't seem to attract potential mates.

Pisces: (Feb. 19–March 20)
Your trial takes a turn for the bizarre when the sexy judge slaps you with a ball-gag order.

DELTA from page 188

Restaurants"? I tip my hat to you. Look for that one to win big at the Tray Table Awards next year.

In fact, it's precisely *because* of your obvious promise that I am so hard on you. Your gifts are prodigious, but they are not enough. You need to take that raw talent of yours and mold it until you have truly mastered your craft. Who knows? Perhaps someday, in 20 or 30 years, you could find yourself the editor of this magazine. Not that you'd necessarily want that job. Editing's a harsh mistress, kiddo: Sometimes, I don't know whether the magazine is killing me or if it's the only thing keeping me alive. But when you put that issue to bed, and you know it's the best goddamn in-flight magazine anyone will read that month, you feel like the proverbial warrior lying on the field of battle, exhausted and victorious. There is no better feeling.

Just between you, me, and the wall, Hammacher-Schlemmer has expressed interest in a monthly eight-page catalog insert in the Sky Mall section. That's the league we're starting to play in. It's time to hunker down, Hutchins. We can't afford to

rest on our laurels. That's the mistake American Airlines made 12 years ago, after their "Charlton Heston's Holy

> ## In fact, it's precisely *because* of your obvious promise that I am so hard on you. Your gifts are prodigious, but they are not enough. You need to take that raw talent of yours and mold it until you have truly mastered your craft.

Land" cover story was such a huge hit. They started believing their own hype and now, well, you've read *American Way* lately, haven't you? It's an absolute fucking joke. ✐

NEWS

Grandfather's Place At Dinner Table Marked By Pills

see SENIORBEAT page 10C

Man Runs Into Ex-Wife While Wearing Sandwich Board

see LOCAL page 4C

Marble Composition Notebook Successfully Blackened In

see EDUCATION page 11D

STATshot

A look at the numbers that shape your world.

Most Depressing Anniversary Gifts

1. Handmade "I'll Do The Dishes" coupon
2. Gourmet popcorn
3. Mother's old negligee
4. Framed photo from back when we were halfway presentable
5. Ninth child
6. Copy of *Dealing With Your Spouse's Alzheimer's*

THE ONION • $2.00 US • $3.00 CAN

0 74470 94595 6

the ONION®

VOLUME 38 ISSUE 28   AMERICA'S FINEST NEWS SOURCE™   8–14 AUGUST 2002

MARKETWATCH

Lou Dobbs Hosts *Moneyline* From Window Ledge

Above: Dobbs broadcasts from high above New York.

NEW YORK—Rattled by Wall Street's extreme volatility of late, CNN *Moneyline* anchor Lou Dobbs hosted the program from a windy ledge high above New York's financial district Tuesday.

"The Dow rose 579 points today, rebounding sharply from Monday's 611-point loss," said Dobbs, as he struggled to simultaneously address the camera, retain his grip on the exterior wall of the Prescott Securities Tower, and prevent his tie from blowing into his face from the wind outside the 63rd floor. "Stocks plummeted early in the day, with the industrial average hitting a five-year low of 7,627 by noon, but by 3 p.m., bargain hunters moved in, raising the average to a robust 9,143."

Trying hard not to look down, see DOBBS page 197

Everyone In Family Claims To Be The Black Sheep

Left: Self-proclaimed black sheep Tim, Jack, and Anna Klessig (L to R) with their parents.

STOCKTON, CA—Citing numerous examples of ostracization and failure to fit in, all of Paul and Martha Klessig's three children see themselves as the black sheep of the family.

"I've always been the outcast," said son Jack Klessig, 21, a video-store assistant manager and aspiring musician. "Everybody else in my family, they're all, like, these total straight arrows and super-responsible. I'm the only one who's wandered off the traditional path."

Continued Jack: "Mom and Dad are so proud of Anna and Tim. See, Tim is see FAMILY page 196

Magazine Announces Plans For Special 'Sex Issue'

NEW YORK—In an unprecedented move that has sent shockwaves through the magazine industry, *Jane* announced plans Monday to publish a special "Sex Issue."

"When the editorial staff got together to plan this month's issue, somebody jokingly suggested devoting an entire issue to sex—a 'sex issue,' if you will," said Jane Pratt, editor-in-chief of *Jane*, a monthly magazine geared toward hip 18- to 32-year-old women. "After the laughter died down, the room fell silent for almost a minute. It was clear we'd stumbled onto something."

Founded in 1997, *Jane* has featured articles about sex in previous issues. But never before has it—or any other magazine—published a single issue featuring so many articles on the subject that it could only be called "The Sex Issue."

"The issue will contain all sorts of articles about sex, written by women who've had sex, *for* women who've had sex," Pratt said. "No doubt, some people out there will think we've gone too far, but we here at *Jane* have never been afraid to be provocative and really shake things up."

"This is real," Pratt continued. "This

is what happens between the sheets. Everyone talks about sex behind closed doors. We thought it was time see MAGAZINE page 196

The WorldCom Scandal

WorldCom falsely accounted for $3.8 billion in expenses, enabling the company to continue reporting profits when it was actually losing money. What do *you* think?

Diane Prince
Teacher

"Let's not be so quick to judge here. After all, who among us hasn't made an accounting error of $3.8 billion at some point?"

Scott Sullivan
CFO

"As the CFO of WorldCom, I assure you that I'll have this whole mess cleared up in no time, just as soon as I hit the exacta in the third race at Belmont. *Go, Sheba's Dancer!*"

Cindy Sherfee
Chiropractor

"Well, maybe corporations wouldn't have to lie about their finances if the government didn't force them to pay taxes. Ever think about that, you liberal jerks?"

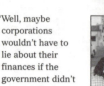

Dean Young
Landscaper

"This doesn't really affect me, as I've never heard of WorldCom. Now, if Taco Bell collapsed... shit."

Mick Olberding
Auto Mechanic

"I like the way they sent their landlord a check made out to the gas company for $3.8 billion and vice-versa. I gotta remember that trick."

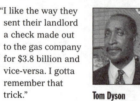

Tom Dyson
Systems Analyst

"If investors divested from every corporation guilty of corruption and fraud, it would only precipitate a deep, years-long recession. It's our patriotic duty to look the other way."

The Fast-Food Lawsuit

On July 24, a lawsuit was filed against the fast-food industry for causing obesity and other health problems. Other recent suits:

- *Big Three automakers, $4.3 billion*
  Knowingly manufactured vehicles that take people places that aren't always fun

- *Magnavox, $16.5 million*
  Failed to produce Bud-bottle-proof TV screen

- *Zubaz Corp., $2.1 million*
  Grossly neglected to inform consumers how stupid anyone looks in Zubaz

- *American Cardboard Box Amalgamated, $42 billion*
  Maybe one of those boxes has a Dracula in it and we could all get scared

- *Jack Daniel's, $30 million*
  Failed to relate danger of losing the wife and the kids and the job the whole goddamn lot

- *Citibank, $167 million*
  Neglected to post signs clearly stating, "Do not rob this bank, or you will go to jail"

- *U.S. Armed Forces, $20 billion*
  Knowingly exposed young recruits to dangerous and even deadly working conditions

- *Atlantic Ocean, $33.5 billion*
  Contains too many sharks

---

the ONION®
America's Finest News Source.™

Herman Ulysses Zweibel
Founder

T. Herman Zweibel
Publisher Emeritus
J. Phineas Zweibel
Publisher
Maxwell Prescott Zweibel
Editor-In-Chief

I'm Going To Miss This Task Force

By Jim Munz

As I look around this table, I see a group of people dedicated to improving the quality of school transportation in the North Rochester School District. More importantly, though, I see a group of people I will be very sorry to leave behind. I don't want to sound too gushy or sentimental, but I'm really going to miss this task force.

Separately, we were individuals from a wide variety of backgrounds and points of view. Together, nothing could stand in our way. I'll never forget that first meeting more than four months ago, when we discussed possible names for our task force. We carefully weighed the options, knocked the ball around a bit, and, after several hours of vigorous debate, finally agreed upon "The North Rochester Task Force For Better School Transport." Seeing the way we reached that consensus, well, that was when I first sensed that we had the potential to be something special.

When we first convened at the request of the mayor's transportation advisor, we were strangers. We came from all walks of life: claims adjusters, housewives, lawyers, bus drivers. I thought nothing could unite our ragtag bunch. But for all our differences, we quickly found something every last one of us shared: a deep concern for our children and the quality of their transportation to school. It wasn't long before we were much more than a task force... We were a task family.

Bill Ostrowsky. You were such a practical joker. I'll never forget the time you read the minutes from two meetings prior instead of from the previous meeting, just to see if anyone was paying attention. No one was, so you made it through the entire thing without anyone speaking up. Even though we were embarrassed when you finally let us in on your prank, we all had a good laugh—and learned a valuable lesson about the importance of paying attention.

And Dana Huggett, your head was full of statistics, but your heart was full of concern for the kids. You had a real fire in your belly for school-bus safety. When you made that half-hour speech about how children's lives could be saved if buses were equipped with harness seatbelts instead of just lap belts, we were right there with you. We could feel your passion by the way you read from your note cards. You can't buy that sort of devotion to busing, nor can you learn it. You have to be born with it. I can't believe this is the last time I'm going to see you fidget nervously in your seat as you get ready to address the group.

We tried to make a difference, and I think we did. We really went to the mat and made some eye-opening recommendations to the city council. Like our proposal to institute a new "drop-point system," shaving hours off bus routes and saving hundreds of dollars in gas and wear-and-tear each year. It takes a special kind of task force to come up with a proposal like that.

Our shared dedication to the cause was truly moving. (That's a bit of an unintentional pun, because we're *moving* children from home to school.) When I wake up tomorrow, for the first time in months I'm not going to have to research bus issues.

> I'd love for this task force to go on forever, but what can you do? We accomplished our goal. We did all we could. We conducted a study and presented our report to the mayor's office.

When that realization hits me, a small part of me will be gone. You all understand how much this meant to me. Task-force-wise, I've really grown. We all have.

Excuse me, I have something in my eye.

You don't participate in a task force like this without coming out a changed person. When you go through weekly meetings, sharing the same donuts and lukewarm coffee for four months, it really affects you. I barely knew anything about the issue of school transportation at first, and I didn't know anything about any of you. Now, I can say I know a little something about school transportation and a lot of something about making lasting bonds.

I'd love for this task force to go on forever, but what can you do? We accomplished our goal. We did all we could. We conducted a study and presented our report to the mayor's office. It would be inappropriate and uncalled-for to continue. We'd be living a task-force lie.

But let's keep in touch, okay? One year from today, let's meet back here and reminisce about old times. Sure, we may be in other task forces by then, but they're not likely to have the things that made this one so special: Commitment. Passion. Leadership. Dedication. Teamwork. Busing issues. Go now. All of you. And remember these days fondly. ∅

Trip To Native American Museum Turns Into Cigarette-Buying Spree

WABENO, WI—A visit to a Native American museum deteriorated into a cigarette-buying spree Sunday, when Milwaukee couple Tracie Hagen and Adam Bersold were lured away from the Potawatomi Historical Center by the chance to buy tax-free cigarettes at a nearby smoke shop.

"You wouldn't believe the deals they've got up there," said Bersold, 22, clutching several cartons of Marlboro Lights. "And it's all tax-free. If you're anywhere in the area, you definitely have to check it out."

Hagen and Bersold said their original motive for the trip to the

Above: Hagen and Bersold outside the museum.

> "It's a real pretty drive up there, and we're both into Native American culture. Tracie has three dreamcatchers, and she once gave me a book of Native American lore. I haven't read it yet, but it looks pretty cool."

Potawatomi reservation was to visit the museum and to climb Sugar Bush Hill, the third-highest point in Wisconsin.

"We thought it would be a nice way to spend a Sunday," said Bersold, who has smoked since he was 15. "It's a real pretty drive up there, and we're both into Native American culture. Tracie has three dreamcatchers, and she once gave me a book of Native American lore. I haven't read it yet, but it looks pretty cool."

Minutes after arriving at the reservation, their plans were derailed when they saw a sign for the Fire-Up Smoke Shop.

"Adam said we should stop in since he was out of cigarettes," Hagen said. "At first, I didn't want to go in, because I figured all they'd have were American Spirits or pouches of loose tobacco, like Drum. Since I like Newport Lights, I tried to convince Adam to just go to the convenience store up the road. Boy, he won't let me live that down anytime soon."

Upon entering the smoke shop, Bersold and Hagen found a dazzling array of cigarettes, including their respective favorite brands, at deeply discounted prices.

"A carton of Marlboro Lights at the grocery store costs like $50," Bersold said. "At this place, it was $31. It was like striking gold. I told Tracie we should do all our cigarette shopping here from now on. She was like, 'Hell, yeah.'"

After buying two cartons each of Marlboro Lights and Newport Lights, the couple headed to the Potawatomi

> "Adam said we should stop in since he was out of cigarettes," Hagen said. "At first, I didn't want to go in because I figured all they'd have were American Spirits or pouches of loose tobacco, like Drum."

Historical Center. But after only 25 minutes at the museum, they decided to head back to the tobacco store to squeeze in a few more purchases before it closed.

"The Fire-Up was down the road [from the museum] a bit, and Tracie said she thought they closed at 4," Bersold said. "It was almost 3, so we took off just to be on the safe side. On our way out of the museum, I stopped for a second at a display showing how the Potawatomi dried

see CIGARETTES page 196

Family Dog Barking At Evil

MEDFORD, OR—Spraggles, the Reid family's terrier, was barking at evil again Monday, his canine instincts detecting the presence of an unseen sinister force. "What on Earth is he carrying on about?" asked owner Ed Reid, watching Spraggles bark at a hall closet. "There's nothing in that closet but Grandma's old wedding gown and a hammer." Spraggles then headed to the backyard to bark at more evil, this time in the form of a newspaper page swirling in the wind.

Cash-Strapped Michael Jackson Forced To Sell Off Pet Giraffes As Meat

NEVERLAND VALLEY RANCH, CA—Nearly bankrupt due to Sony exploitation and under-promotion, Michael Jackson was forced to sell more than two dozen of his beloved pet giraffes to exotic-meat suppliers Monday. "I will greatly miss Patches and Princess and the other giraffes," Jackson said in a statement read by his lawyer. "But Tommy Mottola has cruelly left me with no choice but to pawn off some of my dearest friends in order to survive." Jackson's financial situation is reportedly so dire that he's also had to make do with a bargain-brand anal bleach.

Catholic Teens Still Coming Down After Excitement Of World Youth Day

TORONTO—More than a week after the historic gathering, Catholic teens are still coming down from the excitement of World Youth Day, held July 28 in Toronto. "That was so totally rad, celebrating the Lord with the Pope and 800,000 of my fellow young Christians," said Missy Allen of Stillwater, OK. "It was just like Woodstock, only with more Christ and none of the sinful sex and drugs and rock music."

Home Sex Tape Watched Once

ATLANTA—A 17-minute home sex tape made by Dennis and Tami Gilby in early May has not been watched since its initial viewing. "I guess I thought it was something we'd watch every so often to get our juices flowing, but we haven't," Dennis said Monday. "Neither of us look too good, and we move around a lot less than I'd imagined. Plus, it was a single, wide shot of the bed, and the picture wasn't white-balanced very well." Dennis added that he thinks he may already have taped over the footage with some West Wing episodes.

Man Runs Out Of Questions To Ask 4-Year-Old

CAMDEN, SC—Two minutes into their interaction, David Linn ran out of questions to ask coworker Ron Marcone's 4-year-old son Luke. "I asked him his name, his age, if he has any brothers or sisters, if he's started school, his favorite food, what he wants to be when he grows up, and at least 20 things about the truck he was playing with," Linn said Monday. "After that, I just hit a wall." Linn added that he has newfound respect for Bill Cosby.

Police Seek Poorly Drawn Man

DETROIT—Four days after the murder of liquor-store clerk Bernard Golub, police announced Tuesday that they are seeking a poorly drawn man in his 40s. "All units have been advised to be on the lookout for a 5-foot-9 Caucasian with dark hair and a lopsided face that looks all wrong in the jaw area," police chief Jerry Oliver said. Oliver added that the suspect has a scar across his forehead, or possibly just a mistake that wasn't fully erased. ∅

to break down those doors and bring it out into the open."

While the full content of the issue has not been revealed, Pratt men-

> Added Pratt: "Some [of our readers] might be a little put off by the idea of an entire 'sex issue' at first. But if they just give it a chance, I'm confident they won't be able to put it down—until their boyfriends get home."

tioned several of the articles that made the final cut. Among them are "What He's *Really* Thinking About Your Body," "Seven Ways To Make Him Scream," and "The 'Big O': A How-To Guide."

"I promise you this is going to be a wild ride," Pratt said. "One of our reporters is doing a story about the 'ins and outs' of vibrators, and another is actually reviewing porn. That should really ruffle some feathers within the more conservative quarters of the magazine world."

Added Pratt: "Some [of our readers] might be a little put off by the idea of an entire 'sex issue' at first. But if they just give it a chance, I'm confident they won't be able to put it down— until their boyfriends get home."

In spite of the enthusiasm among *Jane* staffers, the decision to publish a sex issue was not an easy one.

"Initially, we were afraid our advertisers were going to shy away from this," advertising director Corinne McHugh said. "It turns out, they were all crazy for the idea. We had to double our page count just to keep up with the ads that came flooding in."

In the wake of the announcement, a number of other publications have announced plans for "sex issues," including *Cosmopolitan, Vogue, FHM, Stuff, Men's Health, Esquire, Spin, Entertainment Weekly, Sports*

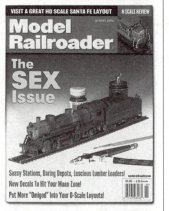

Above: The September issue of Model Railroader.

Illustrated, Vanity Fair, Harper's, Better Homes & Gardens, Money, Mother Jones, Comics Buyer's Guide, National Geographic, Reason, The Watchtower, Model Railroader, Biblical Archaeology Review, and *Cat Fancy.*

"I don't know why we didn't think of this sooner," Pratt said. "It's like a license to print money. Sexy money." ✐

engaged and is co-owner of a landscaping business, and Mary is actually using her art degree to do her metal work. I got a history degree, but I'm just doing my thing, hoping the band takes off. They think I'm wasting my education and going nowhere."

Tim, at 29 the oldest of the three Klessig children, feels a similar sense of alienation from the family.

"I am definitely the odd man out," Tim said. "Mom and Dad know that I'm the only one who smokes pot. You'd think that being in a band, Jack would be a big pot guy, but he doesn't do any drugs. Same with Anna. You gotta be straitlaced to fit in with the Klessigs, and I'm anything but."

"It also doesn't help that I'm the oldest but still the least responsible," Tim added. "Jack always remembers birthdays and is really good about keeping in touch with phone calls and e-mails, even though he lives in another city.

> "I am definitely the odd man out," Tim said.

Anna gives Mom and Dad the most thoughtful gifts. Shit, I'm lucky if I can remember my own goddamn birthday. I mean, they're my family, and I love them, but I'll never really belong the way Jack and Anna do. I swear, sometimes I think I'm adopted."

Anna, 27, said she has felt vaguely disconnected from her family since she was a teenager.

"Even when I was 14, I knew I was different," Anna said. "Mom and Dad spent way more time with the boys. We'd take family camping trips, and while everyone would be off fishing together, I'd hang back at the campsite and do something creative by myself. And now that I make my living as an independent jewelry designer, that just confirms their suspicions about me being some artsy, loner weirdo."

Anna also said that her status as a single woman in her late 20s has increased her marginalization.

"I'm happily unmarried, and that really blows my parents' minds," Anna said. "Tim is getting married in October, and it's okay for Jack not to be married, because he's a guy, and he's only 21. But not me. Mom thinks I should have a husband and a bunch of screaming babies at my feet. I'm sorry, but if not wanting that puts me on the outside, so be it."

Told of her children's feelings, Martha Klessig expressed confusion.

"I'm not sure why they feel that way," Martha said. "We don't have a judgment scale for our offspring. They're all our children, and we love each of them equally. It's not like my family growing up: I stuck out like a sore thumb because I read poetry and dropped out of college while my brothers got business degrees." ✐

Above: One of the many culturally enriching and educational exhibits Bersold and Hagen skipped to buy discount cigarettes (inset).

and stored food for the harsh Wisconsin winter, but Tracie said we should get going."

During their brief time in the museum, Bersold and Hagen learned little about the history or culture of the Potawatomi. Instead of focusing on the museum's many interesting exhibits, which include a full-scale replica of a Potawatomi dugout canoe, they spent nearly the entire time on their cell phones calling friends who smoke to see if they wanted to "get in on" a large cigarette purchase.

The response was overwhelming.

"In all, we had to pick up about 20 cartons for people," Hagen said. "About half of them were for my brother Troy, who sounded like he'd won the lottery when we told him about it. And we picked up a couple more cartons each for ourselves. Thank God for credit cards, because we only had about $50 on us. It would've been a real shame if we hadn't had enough money to buy all the cigarettes we wanted."

Though the couple never made it to

Sugar Bush Hill, the trip to the Potawatami reservation was "well worth it."

"I learned a lot at the museum," Bersold said, "like that Potawatomi means 'people in the place of fire.' Also, I saw this map that, I think, indicated that the Potawatomi were once in Michigan. Or maybe that they still are. I'm not really sure. I was on the phone with Brad from work when I saw it."

"Anyway, there's one thing I *am* sure about," Bersold continued. "I'm never paying full price for smokes again." ✐

DOBBS from page 193

Dobbs analyzed the day's wild fluctuations.

"This morning's plunge was largely attributable to breaking news of a massive accounting scandal at Cinergy," said Dobbs, causing panic among the crowd below as he leaned out to glance at the stock-ticker crawl on the side of the building. "Also shak-

> "It's a rocky time for investors," said Chuck Hill, Dobbs' sometime co-anchor and "First Call" segment host, speaking from inside the studio bathroom where he locked himself Tuesday night.

ing investor confidence was the 11 a.m. announcement that the U.S. consumer-confidence index had fallen from 106.3 to 97.1."

Added Dobbs, sweat pouring from his face: "Confidence was restored, however, at around 2 p.m., when President Bush signed a tough new corporate-crime bill, prompting a furious late rally that nearly made up for the massive losses."

On Monday, Dobbs alerted CNN by handwritten memo that he would be broadcasting from the ledge for "the foreseeable future." In the memo, Dobbs noted that, given the state of the economy, he had "no clue how long the foreseeable future might be."

Toward the end of Tuesday's program, Dobbs interviewed New York City police officer Jim Alland, with whom he discussed the recent erosion of mutual-fund-based retirement portfolios of civil servants, as well as the possibility of Dobbs coming down off the ledge.

"Not that pulling everything out of your 401(k) and taking the one-time tax hit is what I'd recommend," Dobbs told Alland through a bullhorn, while safety-net-bearing officers stood at the ready below. "Their relative stability and tax-free nature might be enough to offset the considerable short-term loss we've all been seeing that makes us want to just give up."

Dobbs' guests on the ledge tomorrow will include former Treasury Secretary Robert Rubin, AOL Time Warner CEO Richard Parsons, and "Mary Mumbles," a homeless schizophrenic who has been on the ledge since early July.

"And Friday on Moneyline, we'll be talking to SEC chief Harvey Pitt about the Adelphia scandal," said Dobbs, sliding to a sitting position on the 11-inch ledge. "Also on the program, Senate leader Tom Daschle will discuss the call for SEC chief Harvey

Above: CNBC's Maria Bartiromo during a recent *Market Week* broadcast.

Pitt's resignation for his role in the Adelphia scandal."

Dobbs' window-ledge appearance is regarded as the most striking display of economic anxiety from a media figure since "Black Monday," Oct. 19, 1987. On that day, the Dow lost more than 22 percent of its total value, prompting Louis Rukeyser to host an entire hour of *Wall Street Week* while holding a gun to his head.

Market watchers say Tuesday's show contrasted sharply with Dobbs' broadcasts of the late '90s.

"This is a far cry from the *Moneyline* of 1999, when the NASDAQ, fueled by the booming New Economy, soared past 4,000, and the Dow was at 11,000,"

said Gene Sperling, a senior market analyst at Bloomberg Financial. "Back then, toga-clad nymphettes would feed an opium-sodden Dobbs peeled grapes as he broadcast from a pool high atop Caesar's Palace in Vegas."

"It's a rocky time for investors," said Chuck Hill, Dobbs' sometime co-anchor and "First Call" segment host, speaking from inside the studio bathroom where he locked himself Tuesday night. "And it's far from over: There's still a long way down, and many in the business world are wondering who will hose up the mess once this roller-coaster ride is finally through."

Dobbs, meanwhile, said he is com-

mitted to staying at his post.

"This is a crucial, do-or-die time, both on and above Wall Street," said Dobbs in Tuesday's closing remarks, during which he thanked the NYPD; intern Karen Gross, who repeatedly retrieved his loafers from street level; and CNN, "for all the good times which are now so much dust."

After giving most of his earthly possessions to his staff, Dobbs concluded: "I want to close with a thought that, unfortunately, may not ease your worries. I never forecast the market on this show, and I'm not about to start now, but I think my position on this economy—and on this window ledge—speaks for itself." ∅

PLOPPING from page 195

amounts of blood. Passersby were amazed by the unusually large amounts of blood. Passersby were amazed by the unusually large amounts of blood. Passersby were amazed by the unusually large amounts of blood. Passersby were amazed by the unusually large amounts of blood. Passersby were amazed by the unusually large amounts of blood. Passersby were amazed by the unusually large amounts of blood. Passersby were amazed by the unusually large amounts of blood. Passersby were amazed by the unusually large amounts of blood. Passersby were amazed by the unusually large amounts of blood. Passersby were amazed by the unusually large amounts of blood. Passersby were amazed by the unusually large amounts of blood. Passersby were amazed by the unusually large amounts of blood. Passersby were amazed by the unusually large amounts of blood. Passersby were amazed by the unusually large amounts of blood. Passersby were amazed by the unusually large amounts of blood. Passersby were amazed by the unusually large amounts of blood. Passersby were amazed by the unusually large amounts of blood. Passersby were amazed by the unusually large

amounts of blood. Passersby were amazed by the unusually large amounts of blood. Passersby were amazed by the unusually large amounts of blood. Passersby were amazed by the unusually large

> I wonder what happened to that space program we had back in the '60s.

amounts of blood. Passersby were amazed by the unusually large amounts of blood. Passersby were amazed by the unusually large amounts of blood. Passersby were amazed by the unusually large amounts of blood. Passersby were amazed by the unusually large

amounts of blood. Passersby were amazed by the unusually large amounts of blood. Passersby were amazed by the unusually large amounts of blood. Passersby were amazed by the unusually large amounts of blood. Passersby were amazed by the unusually large amounts of blood. Passersby were amazed by the unusually large amounts of blood. Passersby were amazed by the unusually large amounts of blood. Passersby were amazed by the unusually large amounts of blood. Passersby were amazed by the unusually large amounts of blood. Passersby were amazed by the unusually large amounts of blood. Passersby were amazed by the unusually large amounts of blood. Passersby were amazed by the unusually large amounts of blood. Passersby were amazed by the unusually large

see PLOPPING page 200

Repressible Wit

A Room Of Jean's Own
By Jean Teasdale

If there's one thing I believe, it's that laughter is the best medicine. And your trusty Dr. Jean has been writing you a regular prescription for years. Goodness knows I'm no Whoopi Goldberg (who is?), but I like to think that I, too, have been blessed with the gift of seeing the lighter side of things. And I enjoy sharing my gift with the world right here in A Room Of Jean's Own.

But a recent incident showed me that not everyone appreciates my irrepressible wit. As a gal who tries hard to please, it hurts me to think I have critics, but columnists have to expect this sort of thing. A thin skin won't help you survive in this business, and if you've ever seen me in person, you know *nothing* about me is thin! (See? I do have a sense of humor about myself!) However, this particular attack was truly a low blow.

A few months before I was laid off from Fashion Bug, I was walking past the Jo Ann Fabrics in our strip mall when I spotted an unfamiliar newspaper rack for something called *Pressing Matters*, a "free alternative weekly." Always on the prowl for a freebie, I picked it up. I like to think I have an open mind, but *Pressing Matters* had a pretty "out there" approach. Like, there was swearing in the movie reviews (didn't they realize children could read that stuff?) and a comic strip with a politically opinionated penguin in wraparound sunglasses. (Give me good old *Cathy* any day!) And, judging from their ads, their chief income seems to come from phone-sex lines and naughty bakers. All in all, not my cup of tea. (Or should I say "slice of cake"?)

Anyway, I forgot all about *Pressing*

> ## I like to think I have an open mind, but *Pressing Matters* had a pretty "out there" approach.

Matters until last Thursday evening, when hubby Rick burst through the door with a copy in his hand.

"Did you see this thing?" he asked.

I was totally shocked to see Rick holding a newspaper. Had he finally broken the no-reading vow he has strictly adhered to since the last day of high school?

"Yeah, I've seen that paper before," I replied. "How did you find it? Did you mistake it for the used-car shopper?"

"I saw it on the break-room table at work," Rick said. "It was open to an ad for bodywork services with this naked tattooed chick. She was hot, but she's probably a lesbo." (Sheesh! Who's dirtier-minded, this paper or hubby Rick?)

He handed me the paper. On the cover were cartoon drawings of all these local newsmakers and celebrities. Across the top, in big letters, it said, "Our 6th Annual 'Tulips & Thistles Awards!'"

> ## "I saw it on the break-room table at work," Rick said. "It was open to an ad for bodywork services with this naked tattooed chick. She was hot, but she's probably a lesbo." (Sheesh! Who's dirtier-minded, this paper or hubby Rick?)

"They give out Tulips to local stuff that's great and Thistles to stuff that sucks," Rick said. "You got a Thistle!"

I couldn't believe it! Sure enough, there I was in the Thistle column, alongside such offenders as the local nursing home that was fined for having patient sickrooms with lead paint and asbestos, and a County Board member accused of bribery! I was cited for a special award.

"Back in 1997, we here at *Pressing Matters* created the Tulips & Thistles 'Mediabolical' category to 'honor' the dubious achievements of a local media figure," the article read. "Past recipients include big-haired, mushmouthed Fox-47 Evening News anchorwoman **Carol Kerrey**, and gratitude-impaired bestselling author **Anthony Chapman**, who turned down an interview with this very same alternative weekly that in 1991 gave him his start as an essayist and book reviewer. But this year, after a particularly distinguished 12 months by a certain columnist whose life reads like an open—and godawful—book, we decided to create a special new category, 'Least Insightful Newspaper Commentary.' **Jean Teasdale** is the inaugural recipient, and if she maintains her non-stop barrage of unfunny parenthetical asides, banal observations passed off as brilliance, and suburban solipsism wrapped in the clunkiest prose this side of *The Herald*'s **Dean Vukelich**, she's a lock

to take the prize next year, too. Hopefully, Mrs. Teasdale's editors will come to their senses and evict her

> ## I'm honestly not sure why *Pressing Matters* dislikes me so. Maybe they just can't handle my sassy, outspoken, take-no-prisoners attitude. Some people don't like a woman to speak her mind.

from that 'Room Of Her Own' where, frankly, she spends way too much time."

I'm honestly not sure why *Pressing Matters* dislikes me so. Maybe they just can't handle my sassy, outspoken, take-no-prisoners attitude. Some people don't like a woman to speak her mind, and I noticed only two women

in *Pressing Matters*' staff box, a city-government reporter and an editor-in-chief. What's the matter, *Pressing Matters*, afraid of a woman's input?

Or maybe they can't stand seeing a real person with real problems express herself. They have to write about boring things like local politics and modern-dance troupes and organic gardening. I don't have to write about any of that stuff! I have the freedom to write whatever I want. In fact, my editor once told me he didn't even care what I wrote! I bet *Pressing Matters*' writers don't have that remarkable carte blanche.

And another thing: If something is real, and it's true, how can anyone claim it's not good? I write about what I know best: ME. And isn't that what all good writers do?

What hurts most is that this happened right after I got laid off from Fashion Bug. I'm collecting unemployment right now, so this should be a time for me to relax and take stock, not be a public target of ridicule.

But I will persevere, Jeanketeers. As I said before, I'm blessed with some very thick skin! ∅

Your Horoscope

By Lloyd Schumner Sr.
Retired Machinist and
A.A.P.B.-Certified Astrologer

Aries: (March 21–April 19)
Some things just go together perfectly, but no one would've believed it was true about cocaine and rhinos until you came along.

Taurus: (April 20–May 20)
Your motto has always been "Kill 'em all and let God sort 'em out," but only in reference to germs that cause coughing, sneezing, and congestion.

Gemini: (May 21–June 21)
Though you enjoy doing the *Times* crossword puzzle, your addiction to the thrill of anticipation means there's nothing worse than finishing it.

Cancer: (June 22–July 22)
You're a man magnet, which, while enjoyable, does mean you're constantly demagnetizing your credit cards.

Leo: (July 23–Aug. 22)
You will shatter existing records for speed and distance when you're struck by a car while walking across the Bonneville Salt Flats.

Virgo: (Aug. 23–Sept. 22)
If you do the naughty things you really want to do, you'll become popular and enjoy yourself, but occasionally feel bad.

Libra: (Sept. 23–Oct. 23)
You will suffer contusions, fractures, and a hard slap after your short, poorly planned career as the Unicycling Kissing Bandit.

Scorpio: (Oct. 24–Nov. 21)
You're fine with using a rifle and sleeping in a tent for the next three weeks, but you can't figure out what kind of army uses temporary employees.

Sagittarius: (Nov. 22–Dec. 21)
Your boyfriend says he isn't going to put up with much more of your crap, but now you've got little bows to put on it.

Capricorn: (Dec. 22–Jan. 19)
It's said that there's a thin line between love and hate, but that's just a metaphor. Stop asking what color it is.

Aquarius: (Jan. 20–Feb. 18)
You were brought up to believe that if you toed the company line, worked hard, and never spoke out of turn, you'd be rewarded. Well, you're president, so there's something to it.

Pisces: (Feb. 19–March 20)
Eventually, you'll have to face the truth: Your third-grade teacher was paid to not publicly humiliate you.

Buddy System Responsible For Additional Death

see LOCAL page 4C

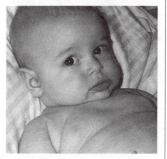

8-Month-Old Sick Of Staring At Pooh's Smug Face All Day

see PARENTCORNER page 2D

Groceries Consumed In Reverse Order Of Healthiness

see LOCAL page 11C

THE ONION • $2.00 US • $3.00 CAN

---

the ONION ®

VOLUME 38 ISSUE 29 — AMERICA'S FINEST NEWS SOURCE™ — 15–21 AUGUST 2002

Millionaire Vows To Do For Government What He Did For Turkey Ranches

Above: The turkey rancher greets supporters in Macon.

VIDALIA, GA—Millionaire Georgia businessman Hoyt Mullins, Republican candidate for the U.S. Senate, told supporters at a campaign stop Monday that he can do for the government what he did for turkey ranches.

"Starting with just two employees in 1979, I built a $165 million-a-year turkey-ranching operation that now employs more than 350 people," said Mullins, who is seeking to take

Democratic incumbent Max Cleland's seat. "If I can do that, just imagine what I could do for the state of Georgia and this nation."

"If the U.S. government were a corporation, it would have gone out of business long ago," Mullins continued. "Congress is the only place where you can operate at a loss for decades without worrying about going belly-up. What Washington

see TURKEY page 203

Wedding Enjoyed By No One But Bride

NEW ROCHELLE, NY—The lavish, 250-guest wedding of James and Mindy Gallagher, held Sunday at the New Rochelle Country Club, was enjoyed by no one but the bride.

"Today is such a beautiful day," said attendee Chris Barker, a second cousin of the groom, as he watched the newlyweds dance. "I can't believe I'm stuck spending it at this stupid thing when I could be out playing golf."

Barker, who drove four hours from Philadelphia to attend the event, was then dragged off for a table photo with the 14 strangers with whom he was seated.

"I'm pretty sure I've set my all-time single-day record for awkward con-

see BRIDE page 202

Above: The bride poses with some of the sufferers.

Police Interruption Hastily Written Into Student Film

KNOXVILLE, TN—Hassled by police for not having a shooting permit, University of Tennessee sophomore Eric Draper, 19, hastily rewrote his student film Monday to incorporate the mid-scene interruption.

"At first, I was totally pissed," said Draper, speaking from his dorm-room "editing bay," which consists of an iMac with a bootleg copy of Final Cut Pro 3. "The cop totally walked right into the middle of the scene where Mark [Haligan]'s character confronts his alcoholic brother who's dressed in a devil costume. [Cinematog-

rapher] Rich [Woods] kept the tape going because he thought it was funny that Troy [Glause] was in a devil suit arguing with this cop. It wasn't until hours later that I realized a truly magical cinematic moment had fallen right into my lap."

During a brainstorming session held that night at a local Denny's, co-producers Haligan and Draper decided to write an expository scene establishing that the officer is "the symbolic embodiment of the world's evil, a man who could even charge an alcoholic demon

see FILM page 202

Above: Director Draper and cinematographer Woods on the set of Brother Brother.

199

Lie-Detector Tests For Congress

The FBI wants members of Congress to take lie-detector tests in an investigation of leaked information regarding the Sept. 11 attacks. What do *you* think?

"I only support lie-detector tests for lawmakers if the questions are funny and embarrassing."

John Pulliam
Forklift Operator

"Are we going to treat our legislators like common white-collar criminals?"

Dana Wertheimer
Homemaker

"I hope they also get to the bottom of who's been taking Sen. Hagel's Diet Cokes from the fridge. It happened again today."

Tom Allenby
Senator

"Each time one of these lie-detector tests is given, it costs taxpayers $12,000. Okay, I just totally lied about that."

Richard Leach
Systems Analyst

"At last, Stage Three: out-of-control finger-pointing."

Robyn Saunders
Graduate Student

"All along, I've been saying Congress was involved in Sept. 11. But did anyone listen? No. Instead, I'm just dismissed as that crazy guy who lives under the overpass and shits in a KFC bucket."

Edgar Wigand
Unemployed

The West Nile Virus

The deadly, mosquito-borne West Nile virus is spreading across the U.S. What are health officials doing to fight the outbreak?

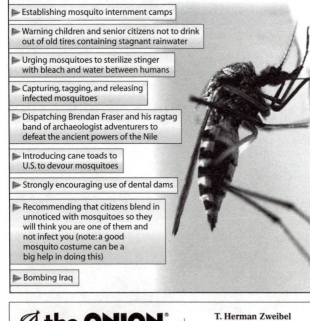

- ▶ Establishing mosquito internment camps
- ▶ Warning children and senior citizens not to drink out of old tires containing stagnant rainwater
- ▶ Urging mosquitoes to sterilize stinger with bleach and water between humans
- ▶ Capturing, tagging, and releasing infected mosquitoes
- ▶ Dispatching Brendan Fraser and his ragtag band of archaeologist adventurers to defeat the ancient powers of the Nile
- ▶ Introducing cane toads to U.S. to devour mosquitoes
- ▶ Strongly encouraging use of dental dams
- ▶ Recommending that citizens blend in unnoticed with mosquitoes so they will think you are one of them and not infect you (note: a good mosquito costume can be a big help in doing this)
- ▶ Bombing Iraq

the ONION®
America's Finest News Source.™

Herman Ulysses Zweibel
Founder

T. Herman Zweibel
Publisher Emeritus
J. Phineas Zweibel
Publisher
Maxwell Prescott Zweibel
Editor-In-Chief

Don't Tell Me You've Never Wondered What Yoda's Penis Looks Like

Oh, come on. All the times you've watched *Star Wars* movies, it's *never* crossed your mind even once? You're just going to play dumb and say, "Oh, gee, no, that never occurred to me"? Give me a break. Don't even try to tell me you've never wondered what Yoda's penis looks like.

By Tony Waltman

You don't have to be embarrassed about it. Being curious about Yoda's penis doesn't mean you're gay or anything. And I'm certainly not saying that you should be obsessed with it. But how could anybody claim they haven't pondered that penis even for a single second in their entire life?

It's only natural to be a little curious about Yoda's penis. I've certainly asked myself all the usual questions: How long is it when flaccid? How long erect? Is it circumcised? Is it shaped like a human penis? Is it the same shade of green as the rest of him? Is it wrinkled? Veiny? Freckled? How much pubic hair does Yoda have? Is the hair curly or wispy? Is there enough hair to hide the testicles? And how large are the testicles? And how pendulous?

But *noooo*. You've never, ever had such thoughts. That's simply not the way your oh-so-pure mind operates.

So I guess I'm expected to believe that, while watching *The Empire*

> But why don't you just admit it: A tiny little part of your excitement stemmed from the thought that maybe, just maybe, Jedi Master Yoda's clothes would come off. It's okay—I promise I wouldn't think any less of you.

Strikes Back, the second act of which is practically all Yoda, not once did you wonder what he looked like naked. And when he died in *Return Of The Jedi*, his robe remaining on his bed as his body disappeared, you never imagined that robe disappearing with Yoda still lying there on his back, his nude form exposed for all the world to see. Yeah, I am so sure.

The day *Episode II* opened, you were, no doubt, one of the millions of Americans giddy with anticipation. If you're anything like me, you were most excited for the space battles, the plot revelations regarding the Clone Wars, and other matters unrelated to

> It's only natural to be a little curious about Yoda's penis. I've certainly asked myself all the usual questions: How long is it when flaccid? How long erect? Is it circumcised? Is it shaped like a human penis? Is it the same shade of green as the rest of him? Is it wrinkled?

Yoda's penis. But why don't you just admit it: A tiny little part of your excitement stemmed from the thought that maybe, just maybe, Jedi Master Yoda's clothes would come off. It's okay—I promise I wouldn't think any less of you. We all have these kinds of taboo thoughts from time to time. It's only natural.

And are you actually claiming that back in 1999, you sat through all of *Phantom Menace*, not once wishing that the gusty winds of Coruscant would give Yoda a little skirt-blow? You're telling me that when we first saw fellow Jedi Council member Yaddle, you just saw a female member of Yoda's species and not the beginning of a new story arc that could potentially provide a perfect opportunity to show Yoda naked? Man, you're even more repressed than I thought.

I suppose that when the *Episode II* DVD is released, you'll be in line at midnight to buy your copy, but not so you can go through the fight scene frame-by-frame, "just in case." No, a wholesome guy like you is above such perverse thoughts.

And, of course, you're also excited for *Episode III*, but not because it's the last movie in the Saga and, therefore, must be the one where Yoda's penis and all its secrets are finally revealed. Do me a favor? Drop the prude act.

This is insane. You don't fool me for a moment. Even now, just looking at you, I can tell your very being trembles with curiosity about Yoda's penis. Own up, you big baby. ∅

American Teen Somehow Developing Unhealthy Attitude Toward Sex

ST. LOUIS—Andrew Zollner, a teenage male born and raised in the U.S., has somehow developed an unhealthy attitude toward sex and human sexuality, sources close to the 16-year-old report.

Unlike the average American teen, who views sex as a healthy, mutually satisfying act between consenting adults, Zollner sees it as dirty, dangerous, illicit, shameful, mysterious, and frightening.

Above: Andrew Zollner.

Unlike the average American teen, who views sex as a healthy, mutually satisfying act between consenting adults, Zollner sees it as dirty, dangerous, illicit, shameful, mysterious, and frightening. But in spite of such negative associations, he places an exaggeratedly high value upon the physical act, calling it "the best" and "the only thing I think about."

Even more baffling and contradictory, Zollner regards beautiful women as sex objects simultaneously deserving of worship and disrespect.

"Hot chicks are, like, the greatest thing in the whole world," Zollner said. "But it's weird, 'cause even though they're so awesome, most of them are,

like, these total dumb bitches."

Martin Zollner, Andrew's father and self-described "best buddy," expressed confusion over his son's attitudes.

"I don't know how he got these thoughts into his head," the elder Zollner said. "I've always tried to make sure he has a healthy interest in girls. I try to point out the best-looking ones to him, in real life as well as in those Victoria's Secret catalogs. I also give him lots of encouragement, telling him he's going to be quite a stud

someday. And just to show him I'm not uptight, I josh him about the girls he's dated, asking him what 'base' he got to. If he has any specific questions about sex, I make sure to send him to his mother, who's better at explaining this stuff."

"My son is a nice boy," said Grace Zollner, Andrew's mother.

Zollner's confusion and ignorance about sex is all the more unusual considering that, as a U.S. teen, he has enjoyed a substantial amount of expo-

sure to the subject. Among Zollner's many sources for sexual imagery and information are rap videos, the 1999 film *American Pie*, the St. Louis Rams cheerleaders, the midriff-baring outfits worn by female classmates at school, hundreds of hours of school-hallway and locker-room talk, and the videotape *Your Body And You*, which was shown to Zollner's health class on the last week of freshman year by physical-education teacher Greg
see TEEN page 203

Woman With Shitty Job Her Own Boss

DEXTER, MI—Cynthia Rimler, self-employed for the past three months as a sales representative for Royal-Aire Cosmetics, sets her own hours and answers to no one regarding her shitty job. "Nobody tells me what neighborhood to canvass or when," boasted Rimler, who earned $400 last month selling makeup door-to-door. "And if I decide I want a day off, hey, I'm the boss." Rimler added that she wouldn't be selling RoyalAire Cosmetics if the products weren't good enough for her own face.

Pope Wins Host-Eating Contest

CONEY ISLAND, NY—Pope John Paul II won Monday's 14th Annual Coney Island Host-Eating Contest, as the Vicar of Christ ate 392 sanctified wafers in 12 minutes, edging out his

nearest competition, Japanese trencherman Takeru Kobayashi. "His Holiness put on an incredible display of eating, devouring the equivalent of seven and a half full bodies of Christ," said contest organizer and head judge Bishop Thomas Daily. "In the last few seconds, bits of chewed-up wafer started coming out of his nose, but we allowed it because none hit the ground." Said third-place finisher Eric "Badlands" Booker: "Hey, that's why he's pope."

Fake-A-Wish Foundation Introduces Dying Child To Brett Favre Lookalike

SHIOCTON, WI—Corey Hoffman, a 7-year-old Green Bay Packers fanatic stricken with terminal leukemia, received the thrill of his short lifetime Tuesday, when he met Brett Favre lookalike Morris Aubrey. "You should

have seen the way Corey's face lit up when he met the man he was convinced was his football idol," said Fake-A-Wish president Dean Pivarnik. "Moments like that are the whole reason we do this. Whether a child wants a phone call from a Michael Jackson soundalike or just wants to meet Milky Mouse before he dies, we are proud to make that dream come true."

Sixth-Grader's Family Tree Fails To Hold Up To Scrutiny

CALVERTON, MD—Sixth-grader Adam Jones' family tree, assigned recently as homework, fails to hold up to scrutiny, social-studies teacher Gwen Wexler reported Monday. "I'm a little skeptical of Adam's claim that he's descended from [movie star] Vin Diesel," Wexler said. "There's also something suspicious about his tracing his mother's lineage to Cal Ripken

Jr." Wexler expressed further doubts about Jones' claim that he is related to actor James Earl Jones by way of "the Zimbabwe Joneses."

Nation's Economic Recovery Hinging On Success Of Diet Vanilla Coke

WASHINGTON, DC—As the nation struggles through a recession, economy watchers are pinning their hopes for recovery on the soon-to-be-launched Diet Vanilla Coke. "Diet Vanilla Coke, to be introduced this fall, is our last, best chance at turning this thing around," Fed chief Alan Greenspan said. "We had hoped that Pepsi Blue or Dr. Pepper Red Fusion would stem the tide, but consumers have not responded in sufficient numbers." If Diet Vanilla Coke fails to jumpstart the economy, experts say the U.S. is doomed. Ø

versations," continued Barker, forcing a smile as a photographer snapped the table picture. "Not that I could hear anything anybody said to me, what with that godawful wedding band blaring 'Old Time Rock 'N' Roll' and 'Love Shack' the whole time."

Like 249 of the 250 in attendance, members of the bridal party expressed a lack of enthusiasm for the $200,000 affair.

"To be honest, I never really liked Mindy all that much," said bridesmaid Ellen Lessing, 24, a college sorority sister of the bride. "I always thought she was kind of a stuck-up bitch. But when she asked me to be in her bridal party—I guess because I'd been her sorority sponsor back in college—I felt obligated to go. We've had almost no contact since graduation, yet I still flew halfway across the country just to be in the wedding of someone I hardly even know."

Compounding Lessing's misery was the "vomit-worthy" purple and teal dress that she and the other brides-maids were forced to purchase and wear.

"This abomination cost me $675," said Lessing, who has no plans ever to wear the dress again. "I'd be pissed even if it didn't make me look like a walrus."

Other friends had their own reasons for not having a good time. These ranged from jealousy over not being included in the wedding party to unspoken resentment over all the attention heaped on Mindy, to the realization that Mindy would drift apart from her single friends now that she is married.

"Well, Mindy had a wonderful time, so I guess it was worth it, because this is her special day," said Dr. Carl Lingren, 54, father of the bride. "As for me, I'm still not sure why I blew almost $2,400 on place settings, but Mindy assured me that spending the extra money to have the seating cards foil-embossed would make the day 'truly special.' You'd think flying her three cousins and great aunt in from Sweden would've been enough to make it truly special, but apparently not."

Dr. Lingren then retired to the bar, where he proceeded to drink heavily.

Not even groom James Gallagher enjoyed the reception.

"This is the best day of my life," said Gallagher, reading from an index card in a robotic monotone. "All my life has led up to this magical moment, the day I am bound in eternal matrimony to my sweet Mindy forevermore."

Sources close to the groom say the commitment-phobic Gallagher had been dreading the event since Mindy first brought up the idea of marriage more than a year and a half ago, confiding to close confidants that he was "just doing it to finally shut her up."

Personal-relations expert and noted therapist Dr. Eli Wasserbaum said Gallagher's attitude is far from unusual.

"For men, trepidation about marriage is common," Wasserbaum said.

> Sources close to the groom say the commitment-phobic Gallagher had been dreading the event since Mindy first brought up the idea of marriage more than a year and a half ago.

"And a total lack of interest in the details of a wedding reception is more common still, even among those who marry willingly. As for the small handful of grooms who actually enjoy their wedding receptions, I'd say most of them are latently gay."

According to Ira Giraldi, editor of *Wedding Style* magazine, the dread felt by the average wedding guest is understandable.

"Most people don't enjoy weddings—why would they?" Giraldi said.

"They have to sit around for long periods making uncomfortable small talk with people they barely know and will probably never see again. They're expected to help offset the great expense of the wedding by purchasing obligatory gifts arbitrarily chosen off some wedding registry—gifts that reflect nothing about the giver. Plus, it generally eats up an entire day, if not a whole weekend, in cases where air travel is involved."

Continued Giraldi: "Worst of all, nobody is ever allowed to openly express these universally held feelings. The rules of social conduct obligate guests to endure the entire experience with a surface patina of strained gaiety, a mask of merrymaking and good cheer that becomes progressively more difficult to maintain as the event drags on."

Despite the boredom of those around her, Mindy had "the most wonderful day ever," bursting into spontaneous tears of joy at several points during the awful-for-everybody-but-her experience.

"I could dance all night," Mindy said. "I wish Jimmy liked to dance more. But I don't care if I'm out on the floor all by myself. This is my day!"

The mother of the bride, traditionally the only other person capable of having a good time at a wedding, was not in attendance, as she died three years ago in a gruesome motorboat accident. ∅

with disturbing the peace."

"It was perfect," said Draper, whose film goes by the working title *Brother Brother*. "Not only did we come up with a way not to waste tape, but we made the movie way more realistic. It's like we were suddenly working in this super-naturalistic, improvis-

> "Plus, that second cop was actually pretty cool and just let us off with a warning," Draper continued. "So even if he was right for the fireworks scene, he still didn't fit with the whole overarching theme of cops symbolizing evil."

ational Robert Altman style."

Further complications arose Tuesday when, during shooting, another police officer wandered into the film's climactic scene to stop Draper from setting off illegal fireworks.

"When that first cop was giving us shit about the permit, it had all the anger and tension that makes for a great movie moment," Draper said. "But this other cop came by when Mark was doing the scene where he gets a sense of peace and closure by blowing up the fireworks his brother gave him right before he died. [The police interruption] wasn't at all appropriate for what I was going for there."

"Plus, that second cop was actually pretty cool and just let us off with a warning," Draper continued. "So even if he was right for the fireworks scene, he still didn't fit with the whole overarching theme of cops symbolizing evil."

Draper struggled to find a way to make the police officer's intrusion in the fireworks scene make sense.

"After a lot of thinking, I decided that the cop could be there to warn Mark's character about the evil cop," Draper said. "But then I remembered that the good cop comes in at the end, long after our protagonist has already met the evil cop. So right now, the plan is to re-shoot that scene and hope we don't get busted again. Or at least get busted in a way that makes more sense, plot-wise."

Draper—who has three directing credits under his belt, two of which featured police interruptions—said he can't believe Hollywood directors are unable to "go with the flow" as easily as he can.

"Whenever I hear big-shot Hollywood directors pissing and moaning about things going awry, I just want to scream," Draper said. "They're always

Above: Woods and Draper argue with police.

whining about the rain or whatever. They need to realize that you have to be flexible and open to possibilities: It's the stuff you don't plan on that always turns out the best."

Draper added that a lack of spontaneity is "killing Hollywood."

"Sometime last September, we were filming the big breakup scene for *Beachball* between Tony [Charlton] and Heidi [Adamle] in my backyard," Draper said. "Right in the middle of it, this beach ball from the kid playing in the pool next door lands right between them. Instead of re-shooting the scene, Tony picks it up and says, 'Remember this beach ball? You got it for me that time we went to the beach. Now I'm giving it back to you.' We ended up changing the title from *Crushed* to *Beachball* because of that scene. Those kinds of moments, where you take a screw-up and turn it into gold, are the reason I dreamed of one day becoming a student filmmaker." ∅

TEEN from page 201

Erstad.

"We did what we do every year," Erstad said. "We split the boys and girls up, and showed them the version of the film appropriate to their gen-

"My son is a nice boy," said Grace Zollner, Andrew's mother.

der, so as not to overwhelm them with information about what's happening to the other sex. The *Your Body And You* tapes tell kids what's happening to their bodies at this time of life, with a special emphasis on disease and pregnancy. Then, we give the kids a pamphlet, usually on the last day of school, and there's a question-and-

answer session, and that's it for another year."

Added Erstad: "Andrew didn't seem to have any questions. He was quiet through the whole thing."

According to therapist Dr. Michael Snyder, today's teen has a far healthier attitude toward sex than those of generations past, thanks to improved access.

"In more prudish times, sex was never discussed," Snyder said. "But these days, teens are free to openly talk about sex. And their access to sexually suggestive or even explicit material is virtually limitless. So it's odd that Andrew, given the amount of sex he sees on TV, in movies, and in magazines, still has somewhat warped views about it."

Zollner declined comment on the matter, saying, "I don't want to talk about it." Ø

Above: Zollner learns about women at his local Barnes & Noble bookstore.

TURKEY from page 199

needs is somebody with an eye on the bottom line. And the bottom line is what Hoyt Mullins is all about."

Though he has no experience in government or law, Mullins has been successful in the private sector. Over the past two decades, he has transformed Mullins Turkey Farms from a small family-owned turkey farm into Georgia's third-largest poultry producer, encompassing 26 turkey ranches, three turkey-processing plants, and a turkey-products distribution network.

Mullins said he hopes to put this experience to work serving the needs of the American people.

"In business, the key is to keep the customer satisfied," Mullins continued. "You, the customer of this government, have received terrible service, but unlike in the business world, you can't just leave and go to a competitor. America's customers deserve better."

> "I may not know all the ins and outs of legislating quite yet, but I do know one thing," Mullins said. "I know a line of bull when I see it, and none of that is going to get by Senator Mullins. The buck stops here. You can print that."

Added Mullins: "I didn't expand my turkey enterprise into a 26-ranch operation by wasting money on a

bunch of bureaucratic nonsense. In this current economy, our nation needs to cut out the fat. Cut it out, process it, can it, and sell it as gravy."

Since deciding to run for office, Mullins has been brushing up on his knowledge of federal law and congressional procedure.

"I may not know all the ins and outs of legislating quite yet, but I do know one thing," Mullins said. "I know a line of bull when I see it, and none of that is going to get by Senator Mullins. The buck stops here. You can print that."

Mullins said he decided to run for Congress "after getting fed up with watching those yahoos on the TV mucking up everything up there in Washington." After forming an exploratory committee to assess his chances, Mullins converted $2.4 million of his own assets into cash and hired a team to organize his bid for

the Senate.

Mullins said he has many plans for improving the "shameful, messed-up situation in our government."

"I've run a business for 23 years, and not once have I had a budget deficit," Mullins said. "If I wanted to expand, I did it by selling more turkeys. This country needs to be selling more turkeys."

"When I want something done, I want it done now," Mullins continued. "None of this filibustering and committeeizing. When I say, 'Get that pile of feathers outta here,' it'd better be gone the next time I walk around that outbuilding."

According to Mullins, fundamental to making a business—or a government—work is streamlining the process, or "quickening up the turnaround."

"I know about government log jams," Mullins said. "I've dealt with log jams all my life. When something is holding up the processes of our democracy, you've just got to get in there with a broom and clean out all that muck that's been collecting. Just take the stick end of a broom to it and scrape out all that gunk—all that dirt and grease and hair and gristle and chunks of Lord-knows-what, beaks and feet and other what-have-you."

Mullins, who is seeking the Republican nomination in the Aug. 20 primary for the right to face Cleland in November, leads rival Saxby Chambliss by a slim margin in most polls.

During an appearance at a Columbus, GA, senior center last week, Mullins responded to Chambliss' charge that he lacks the experience to be in Congress.

"I've got experience," Mullins said. "Hell, I've got more experience than half the Senate and House combined. In my life, I've been a truck driver, a warehouse manager, a car salesman, an auto mechanic, an accountant, a ditch digger, a chicken plucker, and a shit shoveler. If that don't qualify me to run this country, I don't know what does." Ø

Above: One of the senate candidate's 26 turkey farms.

Stereotypes Are A Real Time-Saver

By Wallace Rickard
Privileged White Male

I'm a busy guy. And, while I'd love to, I don't have the time to get to know every person I encounter in the course of my daily life. So thank goodness I have a handy little device at my disposal that helps me know how to deal with just about anyone I come across: stereotypes. Yes, stereotypes are a real time-saver!

You have no idea how much this streamlines my day. For example, before I started using stereotypes, if I were trying to choose a podiatrist to treat my foot pain, I would be clueless. I would've tried tons of podiatrists of all different races before finding a really good one. But, armed with the stereotype that Asians are all really smart and studious, all I have to do is scan the yellow pages for podiatrists under the name "Chang"!

Stereotypes also work when I'm trying to decide on a place for lunch. I steer clear of any place that employs Arabs—not because Arabs are all terrorists, but because they tend to be filthy and have poor hygiene. By sticking to Caucasian-run establishments, I can avoid wasting weeks

> Gender and age stereotypes can be just as useful as the racial ones. Let's say you need to ask directions. I'd never ask a woman, because her answer could be unreliable. With a woman, you can never tell if "Aunt Flow" is in town, so she could be going through a mood swing and send you to Timbuktu.

lying in bed with a debilitating foodborne illness. If I'm in a rush and have to eat fast, I'll definitely avoid going to a place run by Jamaicans. They are *sooo* slow. Ever been to Jamaica? It takes, like, two hours to order a Coke down there.

Gender and age stereotypes can be just as useful as the racial ones. Let's say you need to ask directions. I'd never ask a woman, because her answer could be unreliable. With a woman, you can never tell if "Aunt

Flow" is in town, so she could be going through a mood swing and send you to Timbuktu. And women over 50 are completely out of the question because of their hot flashes. I won't even ask a man over 60, because you never know when the ravages of Alzheimer's could be setting in. That's

> Right now, the firm I manage is looking to hire an accountant. Without stereotypes, I'd have to read every resume and interview dozens of candidates.

why the only people I trust to get me where I need to go are men under 60. White men, that is.

Stereotypes aren't just a trick for leisure time. You can really speed through your work day with them, too. Right now, the firm I manage is looking to hire an accountant. Without stereotypes, I'd have to read every resume and interview dozens of candidates. Make no mistake, there's still a lot of culling involved, because resumes rarely include photographs. But the first thing I do when a big stack of resumes shows up is throw out the Hispanic last names. This saves me hours right off the top.

After that, I make an "A-List" pile out of the Jewish-sounding names. According to the old stereotype, Jews are great with money, so those are the people I'm primarily interested in interviewing. In the interest of fairness, though, I'd like to interview a few Christians, too. Only problem is, some Christians are black, and who ever heard of a black accountant? I want to screen out the blacks, but unfortunately, not every black person is named Tyrone or Laquisha, so I sometimes wind up accidentally calling one in for an interview.

To fix this problem, I've turned to—what else?—stereotypes. I've come up with this plan where I phone everyone in the Christian pile and ask whether they'd be interested in participating in a menthol-cigarettes-and-malt-liquor taste-test (free, naturally). Boo-yah! An hour of phone calls later, and I've got my two master lists, Jews and white Christians. My competitors can flush all their free time down the crapper searching hither and yon for the actual best-qualified applicant, but Fast-Track Wally's got Yankees tickets!

Yes, even a Polack can see that stereotypes are the busy man's best friend! ⌀

Your Horoscope

By Lloyd Schumner Sr.
Retired Machinist and
A.A.P.B.-Certified Astrologer

Aries: (March 21–April 19)
You will be reminded of your steady physical decline when paleontologists mistakenly identify you as the remains of a long-extinct species of dugong.

Taurus: (April 20–May 20)
You're worried about your upcoming trial because, as an arrogant evil genius, you're not sure what the court considers a "jury of your peers."

Gemini: (May 21–June 21)
The dangers of time travel become all too real when you meet your new boyfriend's parents and discover they come from the year 1956.

Cancer: (June 22–July 22)
You finally realize your dream of opening your own restaurant, but in doing so, you've provoked the ire of those who think it should let in people besides you.

Leo: (July 23–Aug. 22)
Your plan to strike from the shadows and slip away unseen will be seen as inappropriate by the other teachers.

Virgo: (Aug. 23–Sept. 22)
You'll put up a valiant effort during an upcoming gunfight, but in the end, victory will belong to the gun.

Libra: (Sept. 23–Oct. 23)
You will be rewarded for your slavish scenestership with burial in the Tomb of the Well-Known Poseur.

Scorpio: (Oct. 24–Nov. 21)
Climbing the highest mountain and swimming the deepest ocean are fine, but you don't see why you need to eat the largest rib roast to win her love.

Sagittarius: (Nov. 22–Dec. 21)
You will be known as the Mao of block captains when you instruct everyone in your neighborhood to assemble iron smithys in their backyards.

Capricorn: (Dec. 22–Jan. 19)
The ghost of E.B. White will appear to you and exact revenge for every extraneous comma you've ever used.

Aquarius: (Jan. 20–Feb. 18)
A close brush with death will shock you into turning your life around and becoming heavily involved in drinking, drugs, and casual sex.

Pisces: (Feb. 19–March 20)
You always knew you'd go to hell in the end, but no one mentioned that you'd have to sit next to the proud inventor of Post-It Notes.

MUNSINGWEAR from page 201

amounts of blood. Passersby were amazed by the unusually large amounts of blood. Passersby were

amazed by the unusually large amounts of blood. Passersby were amazed by the unusually large amounts of blood. Passersby were amazed by the unusually large amounts of blood. Passersby were amazed by the unusually large amounts of blood. Passersby were amazed by the unusually large amounts of blood. Passersby were

> Afghanistan's budding provisional parliamentary democracy is an inspiration to budding provisional parliamentary democracies everywhere.

amazed by the unusually large amounts of blood. Passersby were amazed by the unusually large amounts of blood. Passersby were amazed by the unusually large amounts of blood. Passersby were amazed by the unusually large amounts of blood. Passersby were amazed by the unusually large amounts of blood. Passersby were amazed by the unusually large

see MUNSINGWEAR page 206

Ozzy Wins Tickets To Ozzfest

see PEOPLE page 10B

Tank Operator Wishes Buddies Back Home Could See Him Now

see WORLD page 3A

Heat Sworn At

see LOCAL page 2C

Fat Kid Calls Shirts

see LOCAL page 7C

THE ONION • $2.00 US • $3.00 CAN

0 74470 94595 6
00

the ONION®

VOLUME 38 ISSUE 30   AMERICA'S FINEST NEWS SOURCE™   22–28 AUGUST 2002

God Promises 'Big Surprises' In Store For Hurricane Season

HOLLYWOOD, FL—The 2002 hurricane season will be packed with "big surprises, big windspeeds, and a big, big finish," God announced Monday at a press conference touting His fall schedule.

"Get ready for the biggest, wildest, most exciting hurricane season yet," God said. "You'll see all the 200 mph winds, all the flooding, all the overturned cars. As for what else you'll see—well, you'll just have to wait and see."

Though hurricane season officially began in June,

God has not yet released any major storms in the Pacific or Atlantic theaters. A press release sent to the media by Benediction/Holmes-Morgan, the Lord's public-relations agency, did drop a few tidbits on what to expect in the coming months.

"As God enters His landmark 23,450,750th hurricane season, He finds Himself dealing with a larger

see GOD page 208

Right: The aftermath of a September 2000 flood in North Carolina. Inset: God.

Former Senator Still Hanging Around Capitol

WASHINGTON, DC—Former Virginia senator Charles Robb, ousted from Congress in the 2000 elections by Republican challenger George Allen, continues to hang around the Capitol building nearly two years later, sources reported Monday.

"I saw him again this morning," said U.S. Sen. Ted Stevens (R-AK), who served on various subcommittees with Robb during the latter's 1989-2001 senate tenure. "As usual, he was leaning against a column by the front steps,

smoking a cigarette. I tried to act like I didn't see him, but he flagged me down and started asking me all these questions about new legislation and 'what's been up with everybody.' It was so awkward."

While most ousted legislators land jobs in the private sector, go on the speaking circuit, or retire, Robb has struggled with the transition to post-senate life.

"Serving in Congress was the highlight of Chuck's life, and he just hasn't been

see SENATOR page 208

Above: Former Virginia senator Chuck Robb loiters outside the U.S. Capitol.

Dad Defends Purchase Of Bargain-Brand Cereal

Above: Showalter with two of his controversial purchases.

GOSHEN, IN—Calling his actions "sensible" and "how it's going to be from now on," Glen Showalter, a Goshen-area father of three, defended his unpopular decision to purchase bargain-brand breakfast cereals Monday.

"They're far cheaper than the name brands, and you can't tell me there's any difference in the taste," said Showalter, 41, holding a bag of Apple Zaps, a budget-priced Apple Jacks knockoff. "I can't think of a single reason to justify spending $2 more for the exact same product."

Showalter made the controversial decision at approximately 2 p.m. Sunday while grocery-shopping at Sav-A-

Lot Foods on College Road. Noticing a cluster of cereals in plastic bags on the bottom shelf of the cereal aisle, Showalter was surprised to discover that they were significantly less expensive than their boxed counterparts.

"I couldn't believe I'd been shopping for groceries all those years and never noticed the bargain versions until then," Showalter said. "To think of all the money we could have saved. Actually, I don't want to—it's too painful."

Excited by the discovery, Showalter loaded his shopping cart with bags of bargain cereal, including Cocoa-Roos, Frosted Mini Spooners, Golden

see CEREAL page 209

Arafat's $1.3 Billion

PLO leader Yasser Arafat has amassed a personal fortune of $1.3 billion—much of it allegedly coming from international aid intended for his people. What do *you* think?

"Wow, you could strap a lot of dynamite to a lot of teens with that kind of cash."

Phil Dixon
Systems Analyst

"It's not surprising. Arafat's compound is among among the most lavish cement dwellings in the entire West Bank."

Rachel Kittridge
Florist

"I had my suspicions when I saw footage of PLO soldiers throwing some really, really great rocks."

Melissa Unger
Dentist

"Arafat's got $1.3 billion? I guess he *does* have a nickel for every time somebody called him a terrorist."

Bob Lawton
Civil Engineer

"Shit, you'd think he'd be able to afford to move."

Danny Ploeg
Sales Representative

"So as much as he hates the Jews, deep down he's really not all that different."

Ron Runnels
Cashier

Celebrity Clothing Lines

From Jennifer Lopez to Delta Burke to 'N Sync's Chris Kirkpatrick, many celebrities are releasing their own signature clothing lines. Among them:

- LaToya Jackson's psychic sweater line
- Roger Ebert's Tent-a-rific Fattslaxx™ with popcorn-proof thigh slabs
- Uck: Clothes bought and later returned by Sarah Michelle Gellar
- Angela Lansbury's Pantsuit, She Wore
- Slim Goodbody's Ready-To-Wear Organ-o-tards™
- Lil' Kim's Fuck All Y'all latex body dip
- Steve Irwin's Zoology 500 collection
- Kevin Smith's superhero-comic T-shirts for the big and tall
- Hazbin For Men, the sport-casual line from Jim Belushi
- Steve Albini's partially untucked shirts for men
- Larry King's Radio Pants
- Kathie Lee Gifford's "I'd Sooner Drink Human Shit Than Actually Wear These Myself" collection

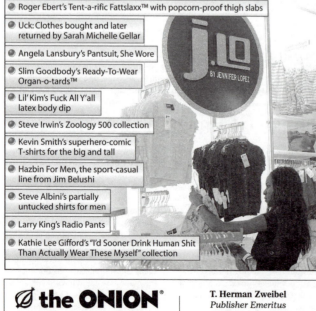

the ONION®
America's Finest News Source.™

Herman Ulysses Zweibel
Founder

T. Herman Zweibel
Publisher Emeritus

J. Phineas Zweibel
Publisher

Maxwell Prescott Zweibel
Editor-In-Chief

And Now, The Matter Of Whether To Pre-Approve Douglas C. Schwoegler For a Visa Gold Card

So we're unanimous on the merger with Chase Manhattan? Excellent. I think we all agree that this merger will benefit both companies tremendously. Nelson, get started on the paperwork for that immediately. I want it on my desk by Friday.

By Malcolm Williamson
Visa CEO

Now, on to the next order of business: Our continuing discussion on whether to pre-approve Douglas C. Schwoegler of Arden, CA, for a Visa Gold card.

I took Mr. Schwoegler's file to the beach house this weekend and read it over a few more times. To be honest, I'm still up in the air on this whole thing. I think we all remember Andrea's presentation last month detailing the ways in which Mr. Schwoegler fits the profile of an individual we'd pre-approve for a Gold Card: long-term employment as distribution manager of a reputable restaurant-supply firm, a homeowner with an affordable mortgage, a good record of paying off debts in a timely manner, a stable and loving relationship with his wife Janet and two children. But as persuasive and thorough

> Now, I agree that the Douglas C. Schwoegler issue has taken up a lot of the board's time. We've been debating pre-approving him for Visa Gold status for three straight meetings now. But it's vital that we get this right.

as your presentation was, Andrea, I still have my doubts.

I realize that when Douglas C. Schwoegler first became a Visa customer, our goal was to advance him to Visa Platinum status by 2010. So, if we want to stay on pace with our original timetable, we should approve the Visa Gold. But if we ultimately emerge from these meetings with the consensus opinion that he is not yet ready for the responsibility that comes with that kind of credit limit, we should be

willing to rework our long-term goals and push them back a few years. Agreed? Good.

That said, whenever I look at his file, I think, "Yes, he's a shoo-in for the Visa Classic Card, but Visa Gold?" I just don't know. Who else has thoughts on this matter?

> I took Mr. Schwoegler's file to the beach house this weekend and read it over a few more times. To be honest, I'm still up in the air on this whole thing.

That's an interesting point, Roger. But I think you might be confusing him with Douglas P. Schwoegler of Arcata, CA. We'll be discussing him next Thursday. Correct me if I'm wrong, but I don't believe the man we're talking about today ever filed for bankruptcy. Don't worry about it. Perfectly understandable mistake.

Now, I agree that the Douglas C. Schwoegler issue has taken up a lot of the board's time. We've been debating pre-approving him for Visa Gold status for three straight meetings now. But it's vital that we get this right. Every time I open up his file, I get a new angle on just who Douglas C. Schwoegler is. We can't just rubber-stamp him through in the interest of expediting matters. I'm sure you all remember when we gave a premature "yes" to Lynette A. Demuth. Or how about the Theodore R. Figgis debacle? I think we can all agree we don't want to go down that road again.

Fine. Let's go over some of the objections raised in past meetings. Jim was concerned about some late notices on Schwoegler's credit report. However, as we later discovered, those indiscretions occurred during his college years. Can't really fault a man for a few missed deadlines when he's busy with schoolwork. And those bills never went past 30 days late or went to collections, so the point is moot.

Bob also made a good point in the last meeting. He mentioned that, given Schwoegler's history of low spending during the winter months, his needs may not actually be best served with all the privileges and services that come with a high-end Gold Card.
see VISA page 209

Gay Man, Unattractive Woman Form Tight Bond

GULFPORT, MS—Heavy-set, frumpily dressed Debbie Ayler and openly gay Curtis Gwinn are the best of friends, the pair reported Monday.

"Curtis is so fun," said Ayler, 25, talking about her boyfriend-substitute as the two sat at a coffee shop. "We met

> Ayler met Gwinn in January 2001, when the two were assigned as temps at the same law firm. Ayler soon began spending less time with her old group of friends, even occasionally skipping their weekly "girls' night out" at a local Chi-Chi's.

each other and instantly clicked. Now, we do everything together: shopping, movies, coffee. I even took him to my parents' house for Christmas last year."

Continued Ayler: "I told Mom and Dad, 'Don't get any ideas—Curtis and I are just friends,' but I don't think

they believed me. Well, I guess if it makes them happy, let them think what they want."

Gwinn also speaks highly of Ayler.

"It's so great to have someone to lean on, someone you know will always be there for you," said Gwinn, 27. "I can call her any time, even in the middle of the night, and she's there to listen."

Ayler met Gwinn in January 2001, when the two were assigned as temps at the same law firm. Ayler soon began spending less time with her old group of friends, even occasionally skipping their weekly "girls' night out" at a local Chi-Chi's.

"I like my friends, but when I met Curtis, suddenly it was, like, I can relate to this person on a much deeper level, you know?" Ayler said. "We just connected. Plus, I can tell him anything. He is absolutely unshockable."

Gwinn instantly took to Ayler, as well.

"Debbie is just so crazy," Gwinn said. "I love that girl to pieces. The moment we met, I said, 'Uh oh, we are going to be one dangerous team.'"

In spite of Ayler's difficulties finding dates and her insecurity over her looks, Gwinn said she "has got it going on."

"Debbie is bootylicious," Gwinn said. "Just look at her. She should be Miss America. Some women are skinny as a stick, but Debbie has got curves. Look out!"

Neither Gwinn nor Ayler has had

Above: Gwinn and Ayler in a July 2001 photo.

much luck in the romantic department of late—a situation over which the pair has bonded.

"I've mostly given up," said Ayler, who has never had a real boyfriend but regularly shares with Gwinn the crushes she has on coworkers. "As for Curtis, he just can't seem to find the right person. Most men are such assholes. We both agree on that."

"I admit, I had a little crush on Curtis when we first met," Ayler continued. "But then I found out he was gay. You know what they say about all good men: They're either gay or married."

Though Gwinn is often chastised for his sexual orientation, his homosexuality posed no problems for Ayler.

"People can be so closed-minded about homosexuality, especially here in the South," Ayler said. "But I am totally fine with it. In fact, I read somewhere that 90 percent of people are bisexual. I wonder if Curtis is actually bisexual. Maybe that's why he hasn't found anyone yet."

While "out" to his friends and family, Gwinn said that many people mistakenly assume he and Ayler are dating.

"It's so funny," Gwinn said. "We were

see BOND page 208

Lazy FDA Approves X-Ray Vision Pills

WASHINGTON, DC—Citing the hot weather and a desire to go home for the day, FDA officials approved American Products Limited's "X-Ray Vision Pills" for commercial sale in the U.S. Monday. "After evaluating this and regulating that for months, we were really dying to cut out early, so we were all just like, 'Fuck it. Let's just approve this,'" FDA deputy commissioner Lester Crawford said. "Besides, nobody could think of a real good reason why X-ray-vision pills would be unsafe."

History Teacher Has Unusual Favorite President

GROVEDALE, MN—Paul Loftus, an 11th-grade history teacher at Grovedale High School, proudly touts

his unconventional choice for favorite U.S. president, Calvin Coolidge. "People fail to appreciate how Coolidge essentially rebuilt the presidency after the Harding scandals," said Loftus, who enjoys announcing and discussing his surprise pick whenever possible. "He was also a great diplomat who did much to foster world peace, all in spite of the tragic death of his son in his first term." Loftus went on to counter the widely held misconception that Coolidge, sometimes known as "Silent Cal," was a serious, humorless man.

Two New Burger King Sandwiches Negate Each Other

MIAMI—In a gala ceremony at its Miami headquarters, the Burger King Corporation rolled out two new sandwiches that conceptually negate each other. "The new Veggie Burger, with just seven grams of fat, is a refresh-

ing, heart-smart alternative to the usual fast-food junk," Burger King vice-president Robert Fass said. "And brace yourselves, meat lovers: The new BK Hickory Bacon Triple Stack— three juicy, big-beef patties topped with crispy bacon and slathered in a rich, smoked-cheddar sauce—is gonna blow you away." Burger theoreticians posit that the sandwiches could destroy each other if sold in a single order.

29-Year-Old Has Blast Writing His Will

GALVESTON, TX—Area resident Brian Whitford had "the best friggin' time" writing his will, the 29-year-old disclosed Monday. "That was so awesome, dividing up my DVDs and shit," said Whitford upon completion of the bequest portion. "I even got to give [former college roommate Steve] Krollner a big 'fuck you' by leaving him nothing but that one Phish CD I

used to play all the time that he hated." Whitford, who left most of his possessions to members of his family, bequeathed girlfriend Cindy Meijer his prized collection of vintage 1977 McDonaldland glasses.

Woman Thinks She Would Make A Great Talk-Show Host

CREVE COEUR, MO—Suzanne Bergtraum believes she would make an excellent host of a daytime-TV talk show, the 42-year-old podiatry-office receptionist disclosed Tuesday. "I'm sympathetic and an excellent listener, but I'm also not afraid to set somebody straight with a swift kick in the pants when it's called for," Bergtraum told coworker Alice Lehmann. "Plus, I'm totally high-energy and live to crack people up. Just ask any of my girlfriends." Bergtraum, whose show would be called *Suzanne*, said she "just [has] a way with people." ∅

and more diversified audience," the statement read in part. "With that in mind, He's promised that something new is 'in the wind' this year. Expect God to take the hurricane to places it's never been, bringing it to whole new audiences, making inroads further into the tornado-minded Gulf Coast states, and still delivering the goods to the hip, urban, coastal crowd that's

> **"We're already lining up for this next one," said Col. Jeff Esser, commander of the 105th Battalion of the North Carolina National Guard. "We figure response will need to be huge, and we're traditionally the first in the Atlantic theater of operations. I have a feeling we're each going to be seeing this one a few times."**

traditionally so crazy about them."

Hurricanes form when God maketh ocean water in equatorial regions warmer than average, causing warm air to rise and spiral inward and upward in a counter-clockwise direction, an effect amplified by the Earth's Coriolis forces.

God promised not to forget longtime fans, noting that the Southeast would be the location of some of the season's biggest hits.

"I'm not naming names," said the Archangel Ioniel, Guide of the Change and co-producer of 1992's Hurricane Andrew, which did more than $20 billion in damage to South Florida. "It'd be a shame to ruin the Big Guy's party. But let's just say Florida is still number one, and the residents of a certain sleepy Georgia coastal town are in for the meteorological sequel of the summer."

God's announcement sparked strong buzz among meteorologists and other weather watchers.

"We're already lining up for this next one," said Col. Jeff Esser, commander of the 105th Battalion of the North Carolina National Guard. "We figure response will need to be huge, and we're traditionally the first in the Atlantic theater of operations. I have a feeling we're each going to be seeing this one a few times."

"Two thumbs up! I loved it!" said a soaking-wet Al Roker after God treated him to a special preview of the 2002 season. "Batten down the hatches, America. This one's gonna blow your whole family away!"

Roker was then rushed to a Miami hospital, where he was treated for hypothermia and water inhalation.

In addition to putting up significant domestic numbers, the hurricane season is expected to make a major impact in foreign markets.

"Japan is always big for us," Ioniel said. "Brazil, too. We even have a following in Canada. And this year, we're looking to gain a foothold in traditionally large tourist markets, in-

> **"Two thumbs up! I loved it!" said a soaking-wet Al Roker after God treated him to a special preview of the 2002 season. "Batten down the hatches, America. This one's gonna blow your whole family away!"**

cluding the Bahamas, the U.S. Virgin Islands, and Jamaica. Add that to our not-inconsiderable Central American casualties, and we're making a killing almost as big as our domestic totals."

"This year, it's about more than just doing big numbers on the Saffir/Simpson Hurricane Damage Potential scale," God continued. "It's about more than 18-foot wave surges and 60-foot yachts being blown miles inland. This year, it's about the whole experience. We're going to be taking people directly into the eye of the storm. And when we're done, people will feel like they truly know hurricanes inside-out."

Asked whether the season would be more remarkable for the hurricanes' frequency or size, God was evasive.

"I don't have to tell you," God said. "But I will say this: Those weak, cerebral 'tropical depressions' are very five minutes ago. This season, it'll be devastating. Thus sayeth the Lord." ∅

able to let that go and move on," said Mark Shields, moderator of CNN's *The Capital Gang*. "I think that by loitering around the Capitol, he can convince himself he's still in the loop."

The day after Robb's election loss to Allen, numerous friends and colleagues dropped by his office to wish him good luck in future endeavors. U.S. Sen. Joe Biden (D-DE) recalled telling Robb "not to be a stranger"—unaware of just how faithfully the departing senator would heed the words.

"The first week after the Senate reconvened in January, he showed up," Biden said. "Everyone was excited to see him again and made a big deal about his dropping by. But then he just kept coming back. I used to joke about making him an honorary Senator For Life, but he seemed to take that a bit too seriously, so I stopped."

In spite of their discomfort with Robb's constant presence, most senators concede that he is generally unobtrusive.

"Mostly, he just likes shooting the breeze," U.S. Sen. Wayne Allard (R-CO) said. "He'll talk to you if you just want to chat, but he doesn't mind making himself scarce when there's work to be done. It's weird asking him to leave when, just two years ago, he would have been working alongside us."

Because the Capitol is a public

> **Because the Capitol is a public building, Robb is free to roam its halls during visiting hours. So omnipresent is Robb, senators occasionally forget that he is no longer an elected member.**

building, Robb is free to roam its halls during visiting hours. So omnipresent is Robb, senators occasionally forget that he is no longer an elected member.

"I approached Chuck one day to ask if I could count on his support for my new clean-water bill," U.S. Sen. Patrick Leahy (D-VT) said. "He just looked at me and said, 'I would, Pat, but federal law prohibits non-senators from voting.' I completely forgot he wasn't a senator anymore."

"Sometimes, I'll spot him with a tour group up in the balcony of the senate chambers, sighing loudly," U.S. Sen. Larry Craig (R-ID) said. "Sad."

Not all senators are as tolerant of Robb.

"The most important work in the country is being done in this building," said Senate Minority Leader Trent Lott (R-MS). "Charles is a nice enough fella, but he has no business being here. This is a lawmaking body, not a clubhouse." ∅

at a diner last week, and this old woman says to Debbie, 'Your husband forgot his coat.' So Debbie says, 'We're not married,' and the woman lowers her voice to a whisper and says, 'My daughter is living with someone, too.' It was *sooo* funny!"

"They're always giving each other these little looks that only they understand," said Karen Bilblach, a longtime friend of Ayler's. "At first, I thought something was going on between them, like secret sex, but Debbie assured me there's nothing like that. It's like they're playing house or something."

Despite the platonic nature of their relationship, Ayler and Gwinn are physically demonstrative toward one another, with Ayler often stroking Gwinn's hair or leaning her head on him as they watch movies. Gwinn said he is perfectly comfortable undressing in front of Ayler and often does "fashion shows" for her in his living room, trying on newly purchased outfits to solicit her opinion.

Ayler said that having a gay best friend has "opened [her] eyes to a whole new world." Once oblivious to gay culture, she now spends much of her time discussing skin care or the latest hit Broadway musical with Gwinn. She has even begun frequenting gay bars with him.

> **"At first, I thought something was going on between them, like secret sex, but Debbie assured me there's nothing like that. It's like they're playing house or something."**

"There's this place in the neighborhood called The Crowbar that we've been going to lately," Ayler said. "We have the best time there, dancing and checking out all the guys. Sometimes, we'll just sit at a table with a pitcher of beer and rate all the guys' buns as they walk past. It's so hilarious!"

"The nicest part, though, is that

they totally accept me there," Ayler added. "You'd think they'd have a problem with it, me being a 'breeder' and all. But they totally don't. It's ironic, but I actually feel more accepted when I'm with Curtis at a place like that than when I'm with straight people."

According to psychiatrist Dr. Angela Paschal, Gwinn and Ayler's relationship makes perfect sense.

"For Debbie, Curtis is an ideal partner," Paschal said. "He provides friendship, emotional support, and a certain sense of exoticism via his homosexuality. And, since she is long-accustomed to not having sex, she barely even misses that component in her quasi-romance. As for Curtis, he receives from Debbie social respectability, unconditional acceptance, and a major ego boost via her obvious but unspoken crush on him. Best of all, he doesn't have to feel the tiniest bit guilty or uncomfortable about her attraction to him because the relationship can never be consummated, thanks to his homosexuality. Curtis and Debbie enjoy a symbiotic relationship of the highest, most dysfunctional order." ∅

CEREAL from page 205

Puffs, Marshmallow Mateys, and Honey Buzzers. Though he possessed coupons for Cap'n Crunch, Cheerios, and other longtime Showalter-household staples, he chose not to purchase them.

According to Showalter, the trouble started virtually the moment he arrived home with the groceries.

"The kids love Fruity Pebbles, so I

> **"Besides," Showalter continued, "they've all got cartoons on the package, just like regular cereals, so it's not like they're any less fun."**

certainly didn't think they'd object to me bringing home a big bag of Fruity Dyno-Bites," Showalter said. "But as soon as [10-year-old son] Mark saw the bag, he just went nuts. He said the Dyno-Bites were embarrassing and 'totally lame.' I'm sorry, but I don't see what's so lame about being a smart shopper."

"Besides," Showalter continued, "they've all got cartoons on the package, just like regular cereals, so it's not like they're any less fun. Just look at the Frosted Flakers bag. It's got a big walrus wearing sunglasses and surfing. Now, tell me that's not as good as having Tony The Tiger."

Within minutes of Showalter's arrival home from the supermarket, word of his purchase had spread through the house. Daughter Stephanie, 13, and son Soren, 9, raced to the kitchen to register their protest.

"'Tootie-Fruities'? Ewww," said Soren, sticking out his tongue and making gagging noises at one of the bags. "They should call them 'Doody-Fruities,' because that's what they probably taste like. I want my Froot Loops back."

"I just hope none of my friends come over and see these bags," Stephanie said. "It makes us look like we're on welfare or something."

Showalter, who called his children "brand snobs," explained to them that the bagged cereals' no-frills packaging and lack of national advertising enables their manufacturers to pass the savings along to the customer.

"I told them Cocoa-Roos are no different from Cocoa Puffs," Showalter said. "The only difference is that bird on the box. What these kids don't understand is that when you buy Cocoa Puffs, you're mostly paying for that bird."

Showalter also reminded the children that when they become bread-winners themselves, they can buy all the overpriced cereal they want.

Showalter said he "kind of expected the kids not to understand." The biggest surprise, he said, came when

Above: Frosted Flakes and its budget-priced simulacrum.

his wife Cheryl spoke out against the purchase.

"I honestly didn't see why it was necessary," Cheryl said. "I could understand maybe one bag, just to try it, but why buy so many untested brands of cereal? In the end, I don't think we really saved all that much money. It was double-coupon day at Sav-A-Lot, and if he'd just used the coupons I'd given him, he would've spent, total, maybe $2 more than he did for the cheap stuff. I think we can survive that."

Added Cheryl: "I'm not even sure if that bagged stuff is fresh."

According to Hillary Bleier, editor of the trade publication *Supermarket Industry News*, the Showalter family is not likely to continue purchasing the bargain cereals over the long haul.

"Of the nine million Americans who buy knockoff cereals each year, fewer than 40 percent purchase the items a second time, and only 8 percent make a permanent switch," Bleier said. "Upon discovering them, consumers tend to buy them in abundance, but their eagerness quickly wanes as they

become disenchanted with the utilitarian packaging and what they perceive as inferior taste—even though these cereals are often manufactured by the same companies that make the commercial brands."

"Eventually," Bleier said, "they forget their flirtation with frugality and return to their old, Trix-buying ways."

In a telling sign that the cereals may experience a similar fate at the Showalter household, the bags were not unpacked and placed in the pantry where traditional cereal boxes go. Instead, they remain untouched on the kitchen counter, some still in the Sav-A-Lot grocery bags.

Unfazed by his family's lack of support, Showalter reiterated his commitment to buying the bargain versions.

"If people in this family still want to be suckered into the great Kellogg's-Post-General Mills swindle, they can go out and buy the stuff themselves," Showalter said. "I'm getting the bagged stuff from now on."

"I can't believe they're all so closed-minded, even Cheryl," he continued.

"Well, I'll eat every single one of those bags if I have to, even the sugared stuff I don't particularly care for. Or, better yet, I'll just pour the stuff into

> **"If people in this family still want to be suckered into the great Kellogg's-Post-General Mills swindle, they can go out and buy the stuff themselves."**

old boxes. Who'll know the difference? Oh, man, I just remembered: I took out the trash, so we don't have the old boxes anymore. Maybe I'll buy a couple boxes of the expensive cereal, dump it out, and replace it with the bargain stuff. Wait, that wouldn't make any sense. Look, I'm not changing my mind about this, okay?" ∅

VISA from page 206

I think that's valid and definitely something to consider.

But here's what I've been wrestling with for the last few days: Whenever we pre-approve borderline customers for a Visa Gold, something happens to them. They either feel obligated to spend more, or they get careless because of the increased credit line. Either way, they quickly find themselves in over their heads. Is there any indication that Douglas C. Schwoegler will treat this card responsibly? Anderson, you've been in charge of his day-to-day file and know his char-

> **Somehow, I have a feeling Mr. Schwoegler is going to rise to the occasion quite nicely.**

acter best. What do you think?

Really? Twice? I didn't know that about him. Food for thought, indeed.

Well, I didn't feel this way before

walking into this meeting, but after hearing all of your various arguments and points of view, I'm willing to gamble that Mr. Schwoegler is Gold Card material. I still think we should monitor his progress closely. If anyone sees a big-screen TV or 49ers season tickets on his monthly report, I want it faxed to me immediately. But I finally feel comfortable moving forward with this pre-approval.

Somehow, I have a feeling Mr. Schwoegler is going to rise to the occasion quite nicely. Quite nicely, indeed. ∅

Let Smoove Take You Away

By Smoove B
Love Man

Girl, I know what you want. In addition, as your man, I know what you need.

I know you love this city. I know you enjoy living and working here, as well as patronizing its various nightspots and eateries. But every now and then, a precious creature such as yourself needs to get away from it all. Let Smoove take you away on an exotic, far-off trip. I have it all planned out. You know this to be true.

Let me break down our itinerary.

I will arrive at your door in a pure-white limousine. Upon arriving, I will not honk the horn. Instead, I will walk up the stairs of your apartment building and softly rap on your door. When the door opens, I will compliment you on your outfit and your hair. I will then command the limo driver to take your bags so that I may look deep into your eyes as I hold your hand at shoulder level. As we walk down the stairs, I will whisper such romantic things to you as "Your eyes are like two brown gems," "You are my ebony queen," and "Your body is like a delicate flower, and I am a trained gardener who knows that kind of flower inside and out."

When we reach the car, I will open the door for you, because you deserve to be treated in such a fashion.

Inside the limo, I will have available

> ## When we exit the plane, you will be overwhelmed by the exoticness of the location at which we have landed. You know that no other man but Smoove would treat you in such a fine manner.

an assortment of only the finest champagnes purchaseable from the best champagne stores in all of France. There will also be cranberry juice. If you wish, you can mix the two together.

As our driver drives us, I will kiss you upon your neck, arms, and forehead. I will refrain from kissing your lips so that your passion for me will grow to the highest level imaginable. I will let you control the air conditioning in the limo, as well, ensuring that the temperature inside is precisely to

your wildest wishes.

After nearly 30 minutes in the limo, we will arrive at the airport, where we will board a private jet for the second part of our voyage. The inside of the jet will be filled with plush cushions on which you can sit. I will have pre-

> ## I will arrive at your door in a pure-white limousine. Upon arriving, I will not honk the horn. Instead, I will walk up the stairs of your apartment building and softly rap on your door.

instructed the crew to treat you like a princess. I will also treat you like a princess myself. We will talk only about the things you want to talk about. We will look out the window only at the things you want to look at. I will hit you doggy-style in the airplane bathroom.

When we exit the plane, you will be overwhelmed by the exoticness of the location at which we have landed. You know that no other man but Smoove would treat you in such a fine manner. Furthermore, if you have forgotten to pack anything, such as a toothbrush or comb, we will pick up brand-new copies of these items from a local Rite-Aid or other such store, and I will pay for them entirely.

Before we enter our bungalow, I will kiss you passionately, this time on the lips. Then, when I open the door, the room will be just as I requested it. Scented candles featuring only the finest smells in the world will be lit. Keith Sweat will be playing on the stereo. The windows will be open to let the ocean breeze cool your fine, cocoa skin. That is the Smoove guarantee.

I will then peel or slice an assortment of fruits brought in from only the finest local fruit establishments. Some fruits will be flown in from other tropical locations just so that you may sample them. I will then feed you each piece, one at a time. I will wipe away any juice that flows out of your mouth and down your chin with a hand-selected cloth that is both soft and absorbent.

Once you have had your fill of fruit, we will take a romantic walk on the beach. At first, we will run in the surf and laugh in an extremely playful manner. If you want to splash me, you can feel free to do so. I will not mind.

Then, as the sun goes down, things

Your Horoscope

By Lloyd Schumner Sr.
Retired Machinist and
A.A.P.B.-Certified Astrologer

Aries: (March 21–April 19)
You always thought an amoeba was a simple, single-celled organism, but the description seems to fit you perfectly.

Taurus: (April 20–May 20)
You will be exasperated and embarrassed by your appearance on Fox's *Let's Give A Million Bucks To The Guy With The Cleanest Underwear.*

Gemini: (May 21–June 21)
Your lawyer's closing arguments will hinge on the premise that you're too damned ugly to have even considered killing all those people.

Cancer: (June 22–July 22)
Your real-estate investments won't seem so wise when the Dow crashes though the roof of the apartment complex you recently bought.

Leo: (July 23–Aug. 22)
You will set a new record as the person most often struck by stray gunshots, flaming debris, and rampaging flightless birds escaping the circus.

Virgo: (Aug. 23–Sept. 22)
It may be time to reassess the risk/reward ratio of your nickel-counterfeiting operation.

Libra: (Sept. 23–Oct. 23)
The war for your stomach escalates when the vitamin fortifications of your complete breakfast are destroyed by a single well-placed Bomb Pop.

Scorpio: (Oct. 24–Nov. 21)
While no one will ever take your place in her heart, two tennis instructors, a bassist, and several of your friends have taken your place in her other areas.

Sagittarius: (Nov. 22–Dec. 21)
It does nothing to ease your pain when Miami Dolphins linebacker Zach Thomas is fined $7.25 for assaulting you at a fried-chicken restaurant.

Capricorn: (Dec. 22–Jan. 19)
Your characterization of your recent firing as a "Pyrrhic victory" illustrates your tendency to misinterpret classical references.

Aquarius: (Jan. 20–Feb. 18)
You're a guy who loves children. Which is good, because you're about to find out just how many you have.

Pisces: (Feb. 19–March 20)
The stars wouldn't take the risks you do, but, hey, it's your life for the next six months or so.

will get more serious as you cradle your head into my shoulder. At some point during our walk, I will kiss you with such passion that your knees will tremble. Then, I will scoop you up

> ## It is at this point that I will freak you wild to the break of dawn.

and walk with you in my arms back to our shared bungalow. At no point while carrying you will I seem tired.

When we get to the bungalow, I will lay you down on the bed and wash the sand off your feet with a soap and water solution. After drying your feet with a 100 percent cotton towel, I will take out a satchel filled with perfumed oils that I have personally selected for your particular feet. I will rub your feet for three hours. While I am doing so, I will say a variety of compliments specially tailored to you. Among these comments will be "Your makeup looks so fine" and "I cannot

wait to taste you."

I will also tell you that you look beautiful.

It is at this point that I will freak you wild to the break of dawn. Never before will you have been sexed like I will sex you then. That is my solemn vow. You will wish we could freak nasty like that forever. Smoove will make that wish come true.

In the morning, room service will bring up a selection of pancakes, many of which will be embedded with chocolate chips or blueberries and/or other such delights. There will also be muffins. If you prefer tea to coffee, I can have some ready for you.

If this scenario does not tempt you beyond all imagining, let me point out that I have only described Day One for you. Smoove will have many more pleasures waiting for you over the remainder of the weekend. These pleasures may include a midnight swim under a waterfall, provided that there is a waterfall and that swimming is allowed past 11 p.m. You will remember this romantic trip forever.

Damn. ∅

210

Water Pistol Fired Using Sideways Gangsta Grip

see LOCAL page 1E

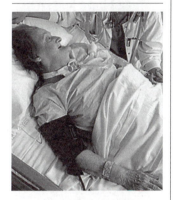

Grandma Told 'Do Not Resuscitate' Means 'Low-Sodium Diet'

see SENIORBEAT page 5C

Cheney Takes One Bite Out Of Each Buffet Item, Throws It Over Shoulder

see NATION page 3A

STATshot

A look at the numbers that shape your world.

How Are We Achieving Spiritual Oneness With The Universe?

1. Attending seminar
2. Hanging out with freaky new-age sister-in-law
3. Watching that one show with the guy who fakes talking to dead people
4. Trying not to be all uptight and shit
5. Mutilating first-born son's foreskin

THE ONION • $2.00 US • $3.00 CAN

0 74470 94595 6

---

the ONION®

VOLUME 38 ISSUE 31   AMERICA'S FINEST NEWS SOURCE™   29 AUG.–4 SEPT. 2002

60 Percent Of Local Man's Workday Spent On Sports Fandom

Above: Wetzel catches up on his fantasy-football reading before lunch.

ST. LOUIS—Area resident Denny Wetzel, 29, dedicates 60 percent of his workday to the pursuit of sports fandom, sources reported Monday.

"Cards, Blues, Rams, and Bulls—those are my teams," said Wetzel, a project manager at Energis Information Networks. "I also have a soft spot in my heart for the Pack, since I lived in Wisconsin until I was 10, but if they're playing the Rams, I'm backing Kurt [Warner] and the boys, no question."

Though Wetzel estimates that three-fifths of his workday is spent on sports, he acknowledges that the figure may actually be higher.

"I start the day with coffee and the sports page, of course," Wetzel said. "Then I listen to *SportsCentral AM* see FANDOM page 215

THE MONARCHY RESTORED

Exiled American King Triumphantly Returns To Washington

WASHINGTON, DC—After nearly three decades in exile, King William IV returned to the U.S. to reclaim his throne Monday.

"Good people of America," said the newly restored monarch, speaking from a White House balcony. "Let the word be spread throughout the land that your king has returned."

"Prepare a feast!" added His Majesty amid a fanfare of trumpets.

Citizens were overjoyed by the monarchic restoration.

"Huzzah!" said Diane Sowell of State College, PA. "At long last, we are rid of that corrupt, antiquated system of government known as democracy, a system that has done nothing but maintain the status quo of political inequality, economic stagnation, and social injustice. Our good king will change all that."

Overthrown in 1973 by democratic extremists, see KING page 214

Above: King William IV greets his subjects upon his return to Washington.

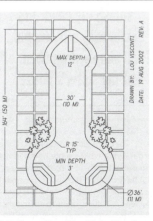

Right: Morgan. Above: Blueprints for his pool.

Price Of Penis-Shaped Swimming Pool Negotiated

LAKE TAHOE, NV—The price of a customized penis-shaped swimming pool was negotiated down Monday, when purchaser Rocky Morgan persuaded contractor Lou Visconti to agree to a $12,000 reduction in price.

"Right off the bat, I told Rocky I can do it, but it ain't gonna be cheap," said Visconti, owner of Mirage Pools. "First, there's a fee for the original design. And a lot more man hours go into laying a custom pool than one of see POOL page 214

Invading Iraq

Determined to oust Saddam Hussein, President Bush has been attempting to rally support for an invasion of Iraq. What do *you* think?

"The time to invade Iraq is now. If we wait, cooler heads might prevail."

Rich Dobbs
Truck Driver

"Well, I'm against it, but I'm probably in the minority, along with many Republicans, all non-Republicans, and the entire rest of the world."

Marty Ross
Systems Analyst

"Ousting Saddam would at long last pave the way for a corrupt, unstable, pseudo-democratic puppet government with friendly ties to Washington."

Douglas Glass
Dentist

"Isn't it funny how people say they'll never grow up to be their parents, then one day they look in the mirror and they're moving aircraft carriers into the Gulf region?"

Rachel Weitz
Student

"Even Brent Scowcroft is against this, and that guy spends his weekends pipebombing puppy kennels."

Chuck Barker
Landscaper

"After all Bush has done for us, can't we let him have just this one thing?"

Maria Davillo
Painter

The Baseball Strike

The Major League Baseball players union has set a strike deadline of Aug. 30. What are the players' demands?

- Fans in stands not allowed to make eye contact with players
- Access to special "players only" restrooms to avoid long stadium lines
- 35 percent insaner salaries
- Baseball diamond replaced with actual giant diamond like in Richie Rich comics
- "Look-the-other-way" clause for players whose home-run output suddenly quintuples
- Phrase "spoiled little crybaby millionaires" to be stricken from all contracts
- Ability to live forever, fly
- Full health coverage for cocaine prescriptions
- Minimum wage raised to $1.2 gajillion bazillion
- Fans required to come back, still idolize players in event of season-ending strike

⌀ the ONION®
America's Finest News Source.™

Herman Ulysses Zweibel
Founder

T. Herman Zweibel
Publisher Emeritus
J. Phineas Zweibel
Publisher
Maxwell Prescott Zweibel
Editor-In-Chief

When I Have Kids I'm Not Going To Drown Them

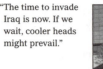

By Carrie Plunkett

That is just horrifying. Absolutely disgraceful. I can hardly believe some of the sick things I see on the evening news these days. Well, I'll tell you one thing: When I have kids, I'm not going to drown them.

To fill your bathtub to the brim and hold your children's heads under the surface until their little bodies stop flailing and kicking and struggling—that is precisely the kind of thing I am not going to do.

Now, I'm not quite ready to have kids just yet. But when I do, I'm going to be a great mother. I'm going to give my children plenty of love and hugs and kisses every day. I'm going to spend lots of time with them. We'll play tag. We'll bake cookies. We'll pitch a tent in the backyard and spend the night in sleeping bags. With all the fun things we're going to do, I won't have time to plan out some big multiple homicide, even if I wanted to.

I'm going to encourage my kids to express their creativity. I'll buy them art supplies, and I won't yell at them for making messes. If they want to wear one purple sock and one green sock, I'll say, "Go right ahead!" Why not? Kids are precious miracles of God. There's no reason to get mad at them when they mess up or do things a little differently. Let alone drown them.

Of course, I will set boundaries. Children need to be taught the differ-

> Should I ever get so overwhelmed with the stresses of motherhood that I feel the urge to smash my children's skulls with a frying pan, I will simply drop them off at my sister's house.

ence between right and wrong. I will instill strong morals and values in my kids. They will learn always to tell the truth. Lying will be a big no-no in my household. So will forced drownings. I'll be firm when they need to be punished, but not so firm that I kill them. Instead, I'll send them to their room for a time-out, or maybe tell them, "No TV for three days."

Not everyone has the same definition of the word "mother." To me, a mother is someone who loves and protects her children. A mother doesn't line her kids up and kill them one by one while the last child watches in horror, awaiting his or her own inevitable demise. A mother does not systematically drown her children until only one is left and then kill that

> When I have kids, it's going to be a major priority that they don't die, whether accidentally or by my own hands. I mean that.

one, too, the silence of the house broken only by the gurgle of bathtub water slipping down the drain. That is totally unacceptable.

When I have kids, it's going to be a major priority that they don't die, whether accidentally or by my own hands. I mean that. The kind of people who drown their children shouldn't be allowed to have children in the first place. That goes double for parents who strangle, shoot, stab, or bury their kids alive. Or lock them in a car trunk and drive into a river. Or tie them to a fence and drive a car into them. Or douse them with lawnmower gasoline and set them on fire. I think that sort of behavior is disgusting and just plain wrong.

Should I ever get so overwhelmed with the stresses of motherhood that I feel the urge to smash my children's skulls with a frying pan, I will simply drop them off at my sister's house and take a drive to the mountains to cool off. Or maybe I'd hire a babysitter and go to the movies—anything to get out of the house and avoid a multiple child murder.

Just imagine: Dragging the lifeless, blue-tinged bodies of the very children you gave birth to down the stairs and into the garage, their sopping-wet pajamas leaving a trail all the way across the floor. How in the world could someone do that? I'm serious: I would never even do that once.

A lot of people talk about what great parents they're going to be, but then when they actually become parents, they don't follow through. Not me. I really will be a great parent. This is my promise to you, my future children. I will not drown you. Ever. Cross my heart and hope to die. ∅

Search For Public Restroom An Epic Ordeal Of Alienation, Humiliation, Human Cruelty

AMES, IA—A local resident's search for a public bathroom became an epic odyssey of alienation, humiliation, and human cruelty Monday.

> "I should've gone at Burrito Bob's," said Webster, who had spent the night barhopping with friends. "But I didn't have to go when I left. Besides, I figured I could always just dart into a gas station or some 24-hour restaurant and do the deed."

"You have no idea what I've been through," said Pete Webster, 27, as he recovered from the harrowing ordeal in his apartment. "From endless 'Bathroom For Paying Customers Only' signs to toilets so disgusting they're unsuitable for vomiting, I saw it all."

Webster's bathroom search began at

approximately 1:15 a.m., 30 minutes after leaving Burrito Bob's, where he consumed a double enchilada platter and a 32-ounce Pepsi. Though he felt fine upon exiting the popular late-night eatery, he soon felt an overwhelming need to defecate.

"I should've gone at Burrito Bob's," said Webster, who had spent the night barhopping with friends. "But I didn't have to go when I left. Besides, I figured I could always just dart into a gas station or some 24-hour restaurant and do the deed."

"What I failed to factor in," Webster continued, "is the unfathomable darkness of the human soul."

Rather than head back to his westside apartment, a 25-minute walk from the downtown area, Webster made the fateful decision to search for a public restroom. His first stop was the Rite-Aid 24-hour pharmacy on West Gentry Street. Asking for the bathroom, he was told by a cashier that the facilities were for employee use only.

"I offered to buy a candy bar or something, but this bitch cashier said that wouldn't make any difference," Webster said. "How could a drugstore not have a public bathroom? Explain that one to me. Isn't public health in the interest of a drugstore? What's a more basic public-health issue than having to take a shit?"

Above: Webster revisits one of the many establishments to reject him during his harrowing ordeal.

> "What I failed to factor in," Webster said, "is the unfathomable darkness of the human soul."

With the pressure on his bowels steadily building, Webster was able to obtain the key to the men's room of an Amoco gas station on Kellogg

Avenue at 1:50 a.m. But an unspeakable horror awaited him.

"The toilet was backed up, and sewage had slopped over the lid of the toilet onto the floor," Webster said. "There was no toilet paper, no soap, no paper towels, and no stall door. Still, I decided to go for it."

Gingerly attempting to hover above the bowl without making contact, Webster stopped himself when he was suddenly overcome by a fear of splashback. He promptly returned the key to the gas-station attendant.

see RESTROOM page 215

3-Year-Old Terrified By Sizzling Fajita Platter

BRADENTON, FL—Hannah Robles, 3, shrieked in terror Monday when a Bennigan's waitress brought her father a plate of audibly hot Super Sizzlin' Fajitas. "Those fajitas really startled Hannah," said Evan Robles, 35. "I'm not sure if it was the sound of the fried onions angrily crackling in their 500-degree juices or the heat-distortion waves rising off the cast-iron skillet plate, but she just freaked."

DVD Tries To Pass Off 'Language Options,' 'Scene Selection' As Special Features

PLANO, TX—The recently released *Joe Somebody* DVD attempts to pass off "language options" and "scene selection" as special features, an

unhappy buyer reported Monday. "What the hell?" said Plano, TX, resident Bill Vinson, who was hoping for never-before-seen outtakes or director's commentary. "While they're at it, why don't they boast that it features 'complete credits' and a special 'pause option'? Christ."

Girl In Park Acts Like It's No Big Deal She's Wearing Bikini

TOLEDO, OH—Angela Liss, 21, made like it was no big deal that she was wearing a bikini in the park Monday. "She's all, 'Doo-dee-doo, I'm just hanging out here at the park,' like nothing's unusual," said Josh Arvada, moments after the curvaceous blonde asked him for the time. "Does she have any idea how fundamentally it alters the conversational dynamic when a woman is dressed like that?" Liss then casually applied lotion to her shoulders and legs, as if that wasn't a big deal, either.

Finger-Quotes Lady Now Doing Hand Parentheses

LINCOLN, NE—Finger-quotes lady Ann Hahn, 41, has added hand parentheses to her hand-punctuation repertoire, sources reported Monday. "I ran into Ann in the breakroom, and she told me Mindy Lewis wasn't at work last Friday because she was sick," coworker Edward Felk said. "Then she cups her hands and adds, 'from drinking too much.' Who does that?" Added Felk: "What's next, thumb commas?"

Heimlich Demands Maneuver Royalties

CINCINNATI—Lawyers for Dr. Henry Heimlich, inventor of the Heimlich maneuver, warned Monday that the doctor will sue anyone who performs his patented procedure without paying royalties. "The Heim-

lich maneuver is a registered trademark of my client," attorney Steve Greene said. "We are prepared to protect Mr. Heimlich's proprietary rights, even if it means filing a legal injunction against any non-royalty-paying choking victims."

Movie Works Out Exactly As Audience Hoped

ALTOONA, PA—Moviegoers at Clearview Cinema's 9:30 p.m. showing of *My Big Fat Greek Wedding* expressed delight Saturday, when the romantic comedy worked out exactly as they had hoped. "It was heartwarming enough to see the two young lovers get married after all they'd been through," said Janet Garlin, exiting the multiplex. "But to see the bride reconcile her feelings toward her crazy family? That was like a special bonus." Garlin said she hadn't been this satisfied by a movie's ending since the last movie she saw. ∅

those quick-and-dirty ready-made jobbers."

Morgan, a former executive at Arista Records and now the owner of an adult-DVD distribution company, came up with the idea for the penis pool after seeing a guitar-shaped pool at a friend's house in Malibu, CA.

"If you know Rocky Morgan, you know what his number-one skill is," said Morgan, 52, alluding to his sexual prowess. "People are impressed with my mirror room and my velvet-covered bar, but I knew a pool like this would make my Tahoe vacation house something guests would never forget."

After pondering the pool idea for a few weeks, Morgan called several contractors for estimates. While a number of the contractors provided rough, non-binding estimates over the phone, only Visconti was willing to pay a personal visit to Morgan's home.

"There was no way of knowing how to fit that pool in there without getting down in the backyard and actually scoping out the site," Visconti said. "I wasn't about to tease Rocky with a cock pool I couldn't deliver just to get his business."

Though impressed with Visconti's professionalism, Morgan said he was shocked by his initial $89,000 estimate.

"I was looking in a catalog, and most of the pools in there were in the $30,000 range," Morgan said. "I knew the one I wanted would be more, but 89 Gs? That's steep for any pool, whether it looks like a dick or not."

Visconti assured Morgan that spending the extra money for a quality penis pool would pay off in the long run.

"Sure, you can get someone else to do it for less, but they're gonna cut corners, do a shoddy job," Visconti told him. "In two, three years, you're

going to have cracks up and down the shaft, the scrotal area is going to cave in, and then you'll need me to come fix it. And believe me, you're gonna pay a lot more down the line than if you spend the money up front."

According to Visconti, many factors contribute to the final cost of a pool. Among them are the quality of materials, the type of wiring for the filtration system, and the amount of decorative detail—which Morgan decided to keep to a minimum, leaving the

> "If you know Rocky Morgan, you know what his number-one skill is," said Morgan, 52, alluding to his sexual prowess. "People are impressed with my mirror room and my velvet-covered bar, but I knew a pool like this would make my Tahoe vacation house something guests would never forget."

veins and ridges to swimmers' imagination.

"This is Nevada, and the penis is going to be out in the sun all year round," Visconti said. "If you don't do it right, the paint is going to be peeling like nobody's business, especially on that highly detailed area down by the glans. Something

like that in your backyard is gonna make property values plummet."

Visconti is more than qualified to advise Morgan on penis-pool designs. He has 15 years experience in the custom-pool business and has been called "the best in Nevada," having built pools shaped like pianos, palm trees, and slot machines.

In spite of his conviction that one must pay for quality, Visconti ultimately agreed to shave $12,000 off the cost of the pool.

"I could have said 'no can do' and walked away," Visconti said. "But then he wouldn't have his penis by Labor Day, and I would've lost a chance to satisfy a valued customer."

Visconti lowered the estimate by agreeing to absorb 15 percent of labor costs (approximately $6,500) and scaling down the pool's dimensions. The pool, originally slated for 80 meters, will be 50 meters in length, ranging in depth from three feet in the shallow play area near the base of the cock to 12 feet at the head, where a diving board will be positioned. Hand rails and steps will be built in the scrotal area, as well as midway down the shaft. A triangular deck will be added at the base, and bushes will be planted to create the effect of pubic hair.

While Morgan initially wanted to have a pair of hot tubs for the pool's testicles, the idea proved too costly. And though he wanted the pool to have a 17-meter-wide shaft, Visconti ultimately convinced him to build it a more lifelike 10 meters.

"So long as you build the cock a reasonable thickness, you're going to have a real nice lap pool on your hands," Visconti said. "Form follows function. That's what I always tell people."

Visconti said Morgan let him see a faxed proposal from his competitor at

Swan Lake Pools.

"You should have seen this thing," Visconti said. "They had the whole thing running east-west, with a deck along the length. It would have looked

> Visconti lowered the estimate by agreeing to absorb 15 percent of labor costs (approximately $6,500) and scaling down the pool's dimensions. The pool, originally slated for 80 meters, will be 50 meters in length, ranging in depth from three feet in the shallow play area near the base of the cock to 12 feet at the head.

like a brace, for Christ's sake. Then, they were going to paint the bottom blue. Come on. I can see white, black, maybe even pink. But blue? Who's ever seen a blue dong? It's ridiculous."

Visconti said Morgan made the right choice to go with Mirage Pools.

"Some of these outfits just pour concrete," Visconti said. "At Mirage, we use steel reinforcing rods to make a nice, sturdy, stiff base and shot crete, which has rock sand for extra strength. That'll keep your pool in top shape for a long time, hard as a rock when you're 80." ✒

King William fled to the Mediterranean island of Malta, where he had lived for the past 29 years. Throughout his time in exile, the king closely monitored the political climate in America, waiting for the right moment to return. When word of the Sept. 11 attacks reached him, he decided he could wait no longer. Assembling a small traveling party, he set sail across the Atlantic to reclaim his throne.

On Aug. 20, following a months-long, detour-filled odyssey over land and sea, the king and his traveling companions arrived at Annapolis, MD, where he revealed his true identity to a naval detachment and persuaded it to accompany him to Washington. As the royal entourage neared the capital, word spread that the long-deposed monarch was on his way back. By the time William reached the D.C. city limits Monday, an estimated 400,000 elated supporters had amassed along the banks of the Potomac River to show their support for the bloodless coup.

"My devoted subjects, the time has come to right a great wrong so many years old," the sovereign told the cheering crowd. "Scores remain to be settled and, in time, all will receive their due. But for now, let the word go forth that your king is come."

Marching up the National Mall flanked by a 2,500-unit regiment of loyalist troops, King William entered the National Archives, where he smashed a display case with his wooden staff and retook the crown, scepter, and red-white-and-blue ermine robes of his office.

The king then stormed into the Capitol building, the former site of the Royal Aviary, and announced his return, formally dissolving Congress by royal decree. He ordered all legislators to return to their homes, with the exception of U.S. Sen. Strom Thurmond (R-SC), whom the king locked in the royal dungeon for his role in the 1973 ouster.

According to a spokesman for King William, the 50 state governors will be permitted to retain their posts under

the revised title of Lord until further notice from the Crown. President Bush will also be allowed to retain his title,

> He ordered all legislators to return to their homes, with the exception of U.S. Sen. Strom Thurmond (R-SC), whom the king locked in the royal dungeon for his role in the 1973 ouster.

though he will function in a figurehead capacity with no real power.

Buoyed by the news of the restored constitutional monarchy, the Dow Jones soared past 14,000 Monday. Minutes after the closing bell, however, the resurrected Ministry of

Finance closed down the stock market, announcing that the generosity of the Royal Treasury will provide for all.

Beltway pundits see the restoration as a welcome development.

"Under democracy, millions of needy Americans slipped through the cracks," McLaughlin Group commentator Eleanor Clift said. "King William will, by God's grace, see all monies fairly distributed, and the truly deserving will be helped."

Chris Matthews, host of MSNBC's Hardball, applauded the king's return but questioned some of his policies. "As much as I support welfare reform," Matthews said, "replacing it with a nationwide network of debtor's prisons, as His Majesty plans, strikes me as a little extreme. Still, it can't be much worse than what we've had."

"Our nation is whole once more," said King William, speaking from his horse-drawn carriage during a procession down Pennsylvania Avenue. "God save the king of these good United States of America." ✒

FANDOM from page 211 RESTROOM from page 213

on KFNS while eating breakfast. After touching my signed J.D. Drew baseball, I'm off to the office, where I try to squeeze in a little work between visits to ESPN.com."

Aside from a small photo of his family on his desk, Wetzel's cubicle is largely decorated with sports memorabilia, including a Green Bay Packers helmet, St. Louis Blues team pictures, and a bobble-head doll of St. Louis Cardinals outfielder Albert

> **Aside from a small photo of his family on his desk, Wetzel's cubicle is largely decorated with sports memorabilia, including a Green Bay Packers helmet, St. Louis Blues team pictures, and a bobble-head doll of St. Louis Cardinals outfielder Albert Pujols.**

Pujols. His desk features a state-of-the-art workstation in a hodgepodge of team colors.

Coworkers say Wetzel has smoothly integrated his fandom into his professional life. In addition to organizing office sports pools, hosting the annual Super Bowl party, and acting as commissioner of the office fantasy-baseball league, Wetzel is widely recognized as the person with whom any employee can talk sports.

"Denny is our go-to guy for helping clients develop tech-driven business-development strategies, or 'plays' as he calls them," said Don Hewson, Wetzel's supervisor at Energis. "And when it comes to sizing up the Rams' off-season personnel moves, Denny is unsurpassed."

While 60 percent of Wetzel's workday is devoted to fandom, a whopping 90 percent of his home life is devoted to sports-related pursuits.

"As soon as he gets home, it's SportsCenter during dinner, then whatever game is on," wife Julie said. "Then, it's usually an old game on ESPN Classic, or reading *Sports Illustrated* or the Street & Smith season-preview guides."

Wetzel said he makes an effort to devote any remaining non-sports time to his family.

"You know, we'll have some quality family time, because it's important," Wetzel said. "I'll go out and toss a ball with [son] Cameron, or huddle with Julie on the couch."

"I mean, cuddle," Wetzel added. "Cuddle with Julie." ∅

Above: The alienated Webster stands on the outside, looking in.

"I told the guy the restroom was unusable," Webster said. "He gave me this look, like I was acting like some sort of diva."

> **"I snuck behind a tree to piss, but I couldn't get the piss going without the rest coming out, too," Webster said. "Sometimes, I can take a piss when I actually have to do more, but this time it would've been too much to hold back."**

Unable to find a place to defecate, Webster decided to give himself partial relief by urinating. Even this effort, however, brought nothing but torment and pain.

"I snuck behind a tree to piss, but I couldn't get the piss going without the rest coming out, too," Webster said. "Sometimes, I can take a piss when I actually have to do more, but this time it would've been too much to hold back."

At 2:10 a.m., Webster encountered a group of Iowa State University students, who directed him to the school's student union.

"They said, 'Oh, yeah, there's a

bunch of bathrooms in [the union]. Just head a few blocks down Marston and take a right at 12th Street, you can't miss it,'" Webster said. "When I got there, the whole place was lit up. I can't tell you how happy I was running up the steps of that building."

The building was locked, closed since midnight.

"When I saw the union was closed, I started thinking about that one guy who was having a hard time keeping a straight face while the other rattled off the directions," Webster said. "I guess they decided to have a little fun at my expense. I didn't know them, and they didn't know me. It was just a bit of senseless, cruel fun. I guess they didn't realize they were toying with a broken, desperate man."

The student-union episode was followed by several more spirit-crushing glimpses into the howling void. Webster encountered a Port-A-Potty in a local park which turned out to be padlocked, was denied restroom access by the acerbic employees of a bail-bonds office, and came across a convenience-store restroom dubiously declared "out of order" by a makeshift sign scrawled on notebook paper.

Finally, at 2:45 a.m., Webster decided to accept defeat and begin the 25-minute walk home. Within moments of opening the apartment door, relief was his.

"In retrospect, I should've just gone home right at the start," Webster said. "But I really thought it'd be faster to find a place downtown than to walk home. Even when I hit the one-hour mark, I still thought I'd find one any

second. That's the thing about bathroom searches: No matter how bad it's going, you still think some mythical golden stall with a clean seat and a fresh roll of paper is just around the corner."

The ordeal has given Webster new perspective on society's treatment of outsiders.

"Before last night, I never realized what second-class citizens people

> **"You have no idea what I've been through," said Webster, as he recovered from the harrowing ordeal in his apartment. "From endless 'Bathroom For Paying Customers Only' signs to toilets so disgusting they're unsuitable for vomiting, I saw it all."**

without ready access to toilets are," Webster said. "I'll tell you one thing: If I ever encounter someone in that situation, I will not put them through this. I'll let them use my own toilet, or personally drive them around until we find a halfway-decent crapper." ∅

Me Crush Middle-Class Tax Hike

By Senator Gronk

Raaaah! Gronk hate H.R. 3712, the Income And Property Tax Reassessment Act! Senator Gronk crush middle-class tax hike!

Me hate 3712! Bill punish hardworking Americans trying to earn fair wage and maintain decent standard of living. Bill discourage spending at time spending needed. Bill bad!

Hrrrrngh! Me crush regressive, short-sighted bill!

If House pass 3712 and send to Senate floor, Gronk destroy bill. Gronk pound bill with fists. Gronk stomp. Proponents in Senate sooner kill Gronk than pass bill. That kind of dedication constituents come to expect from Gronk.

Gronk, now more than ever, fight for American Way. Gronk fight for Americans like Gene Royster, who work 30 years building and managing restaurant. Restaurant now local institution. Middle-class tax hike hurt Gene! Tax hike keep Gene's children out of good college, so Gronk fight. Fight for Gene!

Gronk fight for Teresa Hennings, who lose everything in 1994 hurricane but pull up by bootstraps and make mail-order crafts business. Teresa true American. Teresa Gronk's friend,

> **Gronk, now more than ever, fight for American Way. Gronk fight for Americans like Gene Royster, who work 30 years building and managing restaurant. Restaurant now local institution. Middle-class tax hike hurt Gene! Tax hike keep Gene's children out of good college, so Gronk fight. Fight for Gene!**

make Gronk American-flag pin.

Gronk also fight for hardworking workers of Compuware Systems, who design and produce software that keep America's technological infrastructure running smoothly. Gronk believe in them, because they believe in Gronk.

Ever since Gronk created in labora-

tory accident in 1990, Gronk love America, where citizen free to pursue happiness. After Gronk made, Gronk spend six years fighting evil on streets of Los Angeles. Me meet criminals face-to-face, me fight Octorr and League Of Tentacles. Along way, Gronk see corrupt element threaten to destroy American way of life every

> **Ever since Gronk created in laboratory accident in 1990, Gronk love America, where citizen free to pursue happiness. After Gronk made, Gronk spend six years fighting evil on streets of Los Angeles. Me meet criminals face-to-face, me fight Octorr and League Of Tentacles.**

day. Fighting terrorism abroad bad enough without have to fight crime at home! Nnnrraaagh! Crime bad! Gronk punch!

After fighting street evil, Gronk spend six years serving great state of Alabama in U.S. Senate, fighting greater evil still. Gronk think state's residents better off since me occupy Senate. Gronk pass minimum-wage hike, Gronk toughen sentences for repeat offenders, Gronk help create 7,000 new jobs in home state. That level of dedication and commitment Gronk continue in second term.

Gronk opponent for Senate seat, him vote against the people in two unremarkable terms as congressman. Rep. Charles Braithwaite, him absent from vote almost one session out of five. Gronk have one of best attendance records in Congress! Gronk smash Braithwaite! SMASH!

Braithwaite also soft on foreign policy. After Sept. 11, it more clear than ever America need to address threats from abroad. Threat of Al Qaeda. Threat of Saddam Hussein. Threat of Grogg, evil brother of Gronk created in same lab mishap. Braithwaite no see this.

That America fight terrorism is clear. How hard America fight up to all of us. Up to Congress with votes Congress cast, but, most important, up to citizen with vote *citizen* cast.

Gronk thank great men and women of Huntsville Tub & Sink Works for opportunity to speak here today. Gronk go now, make good laws for you! ✍

Your Horoscope

By Lloyd Schumner Sr.
Retired Machinist and
A.A.P.B.-Certified Astrologer

Aries: (March 21–April 19)
You're a great believer in "an eye for an eye," but you don't understand why they always have to use yours.

Taurus: (April 20–May 20)
You continue to hurt the ones you love—not because you're a weak or bad person, but because narrative logic seems to demand it of you.

Gemini: (May 21–June 21)
You will be profoundly moved by a free tin of mints from a marketing company that clearly cares very much about you.

Cancer: (June 22–July 22)
In the harsh light of day, your plans seem crude and childish, making it all the more obvious that you need a good planning lamp.

Leo: (July 23–Aug. 22)
The story of your love life seems boring and uneventful, so Fate has decided to throw in a plane crash and swordfight toward the end.

Virgo: (Aug. 23–Sept. 22)
No matter how many children you abduct, you can't seem to garner national media attention. Next time, stick to pretty white girls.

Libra: (Sept. 23–Oct. 23)
Though you are locked in a corn-chip packaging plant with no way to escape, you refuse to think of yourself as "trapped."

Scorpio: (Oct. 24–Nov. 21)
You will experience monumental shifts in your sense of self-worth next week after your value is tied to the peso.

Sagittarius: (Nov. 22–Dec. 21)
Your suicide would have been the stuff of country-music legend if Billie Joe McAllister hadn't jumped off the Tallahatchie Bridge the very same day.

Capricorn: (Dec. 22–Jan. 19)
You will undergo a crisis of faith when your pastor cannot explain to you why everyone at the Last Supper was on one side of the table.

Aquarius: (Jan. 20–Feb. 18)
You are eager to undergo hip-replacement surgery until you realize they're just going to put in another hip.

Pisces: (Feb. 19–March 20)
The stars see your hopes dashed, your dreams mocked, and your friends proven false, and so they say: Stop hanging out with theater people.

FYVUSH-MANIA from page 214

amounts of blood. Passersby were amazed by the unusually large amounts of blood. Passersby were amazed by the unusually large amounts of blood. Passersby were amazed by the unusually large amounts of blood. Passersby were amazed by the unusually large amounts of blood. Passersby were amazed by the unusually large amounts of blood. Passersby were amazed by the unusually large amounts of blood. Passersby were amazed by the unusually large amounts of blood. Passersby were amazed by the unusually large amounts of blood. Passersby were amazed by the unusually large amounts of blood. Passersby were amazed by the unusually large amounts of blood. Passersby were amazed by the unusually large amounts of blood. Passersby were amazed by the unusually large amounts of blood. Passersby were amazed by the unusually large amounts of blood. Passersby were amazed by the unusually large amounts of blood. Passersby were amazed by the unusually large amounts of blood. Passersby were amazed by the unusually large amounts of blood. Passersby were amazed by the unusually large amounts of blood. Passersby were amazed by the unusually large

amounts of blood. Passersby were amazed by the unusually large amounts of blood. Passersby were amazed by the unusually large amounts of blood. Passersby were amazed by the unusually large amounts of blood. Passersby were amazed by the unusually large amounts of blood. Passersby were amazed by the unusually large amounts of blood. Passersby were

> **I'm sorry about your father's death, but we need to break up.**

amazed by the unusually large amounts of blood. Passersby were amazed by the unusually large amounts of blood. Passersby were amazed by the unusually large amounts of blood. Passersby were amazed by the unusually large amounts of blood. Passersby were amazed by the unusually large amounts of blood. Passersby were amazed by the unusually large amounts of blood. Passersby were amazed by the unusually large

see FYVUSH-MANIA page 217

First Place Cops Looked Was Inside AT-AT

see CRIMEBEAT page 6B

Springer Audience Now Just Chanting 'Kill! Kill!'

see TELEVISION page 2D

Woody Allen's Fourth Wife Born

see PEOPLE page 9E

Bishop Takes Queen

see CLERGY page 4C

STATshot

A look at the numbers that shape your world.

Top U.S. Army Recruitment Strategies

1. Offering discipline, structure, free Army T-shirt
2. Adhesive-lined "Recruit Motel"
3. Pamphlets down at quarry
4. Truck full of Bud Ice that suddenly snaps shut
5. Free lifetime membership
6. Pulling the old "Kiss Army" bait-and-switch
7. Downplaying "getting fatally shot" aspect

0 74470 94595 6

THE ONION • $2.00 US • $3.00 CAN

---

the ONION®

VOLUME 38 ISSUE 32   AMERICA'S FINEST NEWS SOURCE™   5–11 SEPTEMBER 2002

THE SEPT. 11 ANNIVERSARY

Who Will Bring Closure To A Grieving Nation?

see COVER STORY page 219

U.S. Fast-Food Chains Agree To Voluntary Cheese Limits

OAK PARK, IL—Fearful of the prospect of class-action lawsuits, seven of the nation's largest fast-food chains voluntarily agreed Monday to place cheese limits on their own sandwich items.

"With Americans becoming increasingly health-conscious and litigious, the restaurant industry felt it necessary to protect itself with a self-imposed cheese cap," said Paul Conklin, president of the National Association of Fast-Food Retailers. "Gone are the days when we could load a burger with seven slices of fatty, cholesterol-laden American cheese without fear of reprisal."

Effective Oct. 1, McDonald's, Burger King, and five other leading chains will institute the "three-ounce rule," limiting the amount of cheese per sandwich item to three ounces. Though still double the USDA's recommended daily limit for cheese, the three-ounce limit is expected to sharply reduce the health risk posed

see CHEESE page 221

Area Man Hoping Cell Phone Breaks So He Can Get Better One

CHULA VISTA, CA—Dave Sychak, a San Diego-area project manager and self-described "gadget freak," has been increasingly careless with his 10-month-old cell phone in the hopes that he will have to replace it, sources reported Monday.

"Overall, this is a great phone," Sychak said of the Motorola V60 he has carried since last October, in recent weeks in his back pocket. "I really can't complain. It may not have some of the bells and whistles I've seen on the newer models, like mobile messaging or color display or downloadable interface graphics, but it still suits my basic needs just fine. I shouldn't need a new one

for a long time, barring the unforeseen."

Added Sychak: "It's extremely durable, too. You can drop it onto the kitchen floor while cradling it on your shoulder and talking to your mom as you're boiling spaghetti, nearly dropping it into the hot water. And it barely even gets scratched up when you prop a door open with it."

Sychak's recent lack of affection for his cell phone has prompted him to treat it in a manner he never would have upon acquiring it. During the first four or five months of ownership, Sychak was extremely careful with the phone, taking pains to keep it in its protective case and handle it gently. Today, however, he

Above: Sychak with his 10-month-old Motorola V60.

routinely flips the phone open like a *Star Trek* communicator, leaves it out in the sun on the dashboard of his car, and, after finishing an unpleasant call, tosses it to the ground in

anger.

Friends have warned Sychak to exercise caution with the phone, to no avail.

"I've told Dave he should be more careful with that

see PHONE page 220

Martha's Mess

Implicated in the ImClone trading scandal, Martha Stewart is now accused of illegally dumping her own company's stock, as well. What do *you* think?

Linda Symanski
Realtor

"You'd think Martha, of all people, would know how to put those worthless old stock certificates to good use instead of just dumping them."

Frank Bergin
Contractor

"I really don't think it's right for us to act as Martha Stewart's judge, jury, and executioner. Executioner will have to do."

Benjamin Robison
Systems Analyst

"Have they built a jail cell strong enough to hold her?"

George Adamle
Civil Engineer

"Funny, the *Martha Stewart Living* web site doesn't mention anything about this."

Beth Atkinson
Graduate Student

"Poor Martha. She showed a lost and confused world how to spruce up those ho-hum wall sconces, and this is how we thank her."

Norman Linn
File Clerk

"First the Catholic Church, now Martha. Who's going to be left to make us feel bad about ourselves?"

Keeping Kids Safe

The nation has been hit with a rash of child abductions. What are federal officials recommending to reduce the risk?

▶ Instruct child to take different dark alley home from school every day

▶ Twice a year, hold abduction drill in which you throw your unsuspecting child into trunk of your car

▶ Have children that are as ugly as possible

▶ Attach your child to a large, unwieldy object, such as an old toilet seat, with the words "Bathroom Key" written on it

▶ Start emotionally distancing yourself from your child now to lessen the separation trauma of abduction later

▶ Warn your children of the dangers of abduction every night as you tuck them into bed

▶ Keep your children safely locked in basement, feeding them by throwing food down heating duct

▶ Avoid taking children to The Olive Garden; The maze of tables and artificial plants is an abductor's playground

▶ Give birth to multiple offspring to hedge your bets

▶ Be sure to take your children to work on Take Your Children To Work Or They'll Be Abducted Day

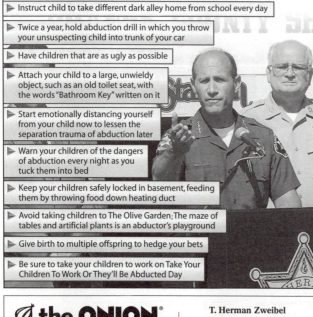

the ONION®
America's Finest News Source.™

Herman Ulysses Zweibel
Founder

T. Herman Zweibel
Publisher Emeritus
J. Phineas Zweibel
Publisher
Maxwell Prescott Zweibel
Editor-In-Chief

I Shall Scramble Two With Bacon When The Muse Moves Me

By Gus Ontiveros

Waitress! Take this plate of corned-beef hash and waffles, and spirit it to its appointed table posthaste. Hash and waffles must be served hot, and I will not have my latest masterpiece of short-order cookery spoiled by your sluggishness. What of the remainder of this order, you ask? The bacon and eggs? I do not have these yet, for inspiration has not struck. No, I will not "just make it." I shall scramble two with bacon when the muse moves me—and not one second before.

I will not consider cracking the egg and pouring forth its contents until blessed inspiration takes hold of my stainless-steel spatula. And before this has any chance of happening, I must first clear my mind of all distractions: the screeching of waitresses, the relentless blare of Van Halen emanating from the dishroom, even the very sizzle of my grill. The universe must be reduced to its two essentials: me and the egg. No matter how many tickets await my attention, I must give the egg all the time it needs.

Once cracked, the egg poses myriad questions. Does one add 2 percent, whole milk, or skim milk to create the delightfully fluffy peaks? Or does one

> **I will not consider cracking the egg and pouring forth its contents until blessed inspiration takes hold of my stainless-steel spatula.**

put in no milk at all, the better to capture the egg in all its raw, undiluted beauty? Does one forego salt and pepper in favor of a more exotic spice such as coriander? As you can see, a scram with bacon is not as simple as it seems.

What know you of the artistic process? Did Rodin create his great works of sculpture by throwing rocks at marble? No, he crafted each piece with a loving touch. So, too, must one treat the egg and the fruit of the pig.

I have kept a close eye on you, Barb Guyton. I have watched as your oafish, club-like feet drag my precious creations to the table or counter, only to carelessly dump them in front of the customer with no consideration for the loving craft with which they were made. Perhaps you would be more reverent with my egg-and-sausage breakfast sandwiches if you took the time to watch as I forged them atop my blazing grill. But when-

> **To whom do you think you are talking? Do you not realize that I am the man whose six-month stint at Egg Harbor's omelette station is the stuff of legend?**

ever the offer is made, you find it more important to top off someone's decaf. So be it.

To whom do you think you are talking? Do you not realize that I am the man whose six-month stint at Egg Harbor's omelette station is the stuff of legend? Lines would snake around the entire breakfast buffet, reaching the awed and envious cook at the formerly popular ham-slicing station on the other end. I could have remained a star there for the rest of my life, but I chose to move on and continue my quest for perfection, unappreciated as it may be by the likes of you.

I have paid my dues. I have put in the years of grueling practice necessary to become a master. I have gone through my "experimental" phases: double-poaching the egg, pre-salting the grill, and substituting chorizo for the common breakfast sausage. Working the morning shift here at Phil's Grill may be a job to you, but it's much more than that to me. And I will not allow my vision to be compromised by someone who is only in it for the money.

What's that? Yes, I'm sure Carl was much easier to work with. But Carl is not fit to defrost the wheat bread for toast, much less prepare a Denver omelette. Your beloved Carl would not have lasted a minute under the stern tutelage of my mentor, Greg Frankenheimer, a man whose memory still makes me ache with thousands of remembered blows for less-than-perfect Eggs Benedict. No, I think Carl would be better served giving up short-order cooking and working at a car wash than to have the burden of perfection placed on his sloped, insufficient shoulders.

I am The Gus, and don't you forget it. Now be gone, woman, and let me contemplate my scrambling in peace.

A Nation Turns On The Television For Strength And Support

NEW YORK—On Sept. 11, 2002, Americans will sort through emotions ranging from anger to grief, pain, and a profound sense of loss. But while the day will be difficult to endure, it remains unclear which television network will rise to the occasion, with its sensitive, cathartic anniversary coverage helping us decide what to feel while bringing a sense of closure to our national period of mourning.

Will it be a major network like CBS that heals us, salving our wounds with its around-the-clock, Dan Rather-hosted coverage? Or will it be a cable channel like CNN, its crack team of veteran telejournalists guiding us to a place of rebirth and renewal as only a 24-hour news network can? Or will it be a surprise young upstart like MTV, speaking to our hearts in a way foreign to its stodgier counterparts?

"When we're doing our jobs right, we're not merely reporting the news; we're helping viewers cope with the grief and pain in their lives," ABC News president David Westin said. "That is one of the central purposes of any newsgathering organization, and never will that be clearer than on Sept. 11."

"Now more than ever, we are a nation undivided," Fox News Channel senior producer Tom Bird said. "From the simple farm houses dotting the Iowa countryside to the condominium complexes of Los Angeles to the rustic cabins of Cape Cod, on the anniversary of the terrorist attacks, Americans will be huddled in front of their TV sets to assuage their grief and testify to their patriotism. And Fox News Channel will be right there with a shoulder to cry on."

All told, an estimated 800 hours of Sept. 11 retrospectives, memorials, and clips packages will air on more than 50 channels, including TNN, ESPN, and Oxygen. An estimated 200 million Americans are expected to tune in to at least some portion of the day's programming.

Diane Blauvelt, whose husband Randy died in the attack on the Pentagon, said she looks forward to the all-day coverage.

"It's been an incredibly hard year for me," Blauvelt said. "At times, I didn't think I could endure the grief. But I kept telling myself, 'Diane, just hang on until this coming Sept. 11, and the networks will make it all better.' That's the only thing that got me through."

Added Blauvelt: "I can't tell you how healing it will be to once again see that footage of the smoldering Pentagon where my Randy died."

"We as a nation need to experience some sort of closure," said Marcy McGinnis, CBS senior vice-president of news coverage. "And no one needs that more than the people who lost loved ones on Sept. 11. They will never forget what happened, but they need to move on and feel whole again. They need the sort of tasteful tribute montage set to Bruce Springsteen's 'Empty Sky' that we've got planned at CBS."

"How are we to memorialize an event of such unspeakably horrific proportions?" Fox News senior producer Jeff Kent asked. "How can we eulogize those whose deaths we can scarcely comprehend? Well, Fox is giving it a shot with the two-hour special *The Day America Changed*. I think you're going to like what you see."

In what may be the most touching display of caring, ABC News anchor Peter Jennings will host a question-and-answer session for children.

"Just imagine how confusing this all must be for the children," Westin said. "Thank goodness Peter will be there for them, from 3 to 4 p.m. EST."

Lawrence Crouch, a media-studies professor at Syracuse University, said the Sept. 11 anniversary coverage will stand as a shining example of the healing power of television.

"Will the answer to the nation's woes come in the form of a CNN special memorializing that tragic day? Or

Above: The McCardell family of Akron, OH, works through its lingering pain over Sept. 11.

a Katie Couric interview with an emotional Rudy Giuliani, live from Ground Zero?" Crouch asked. "Are our hours of personal reflection better spent ruminating on the fate of those lost by watching an interview with a firefighter's widow, or by celebrating our living heroes with a rousing musi-

cal salute? It's a toss-up, but my money is on NBC's *Concert For America*. I understand they have Alan Jackson on board."

According to NBC News senior producer Alan Koslow, TV news plays a vital role in Americans' lives.

see NATION page 221

Bar Owner Considering Sept. 11 Options

BOWLING GREEN, KY—With the one-year anniversary of the Sept. 11 terrorist attacks fast approaching, Tommy's Tavern owner Thomas Kuharski is trying to determine the appropriate way for his bar to mark the event. "I definitely want to have one minute of silence," Kuharski said. "But I'm not sure when, since the attacks took place around 9 a.m. and we don't open until noon. I'm also thinking of offering $1 rail drinks for police officers and firemen all day. Is that enough, though?" Kuharski said he may also order a cheese-and-cracker plate and flag napkins.

Catholic Church Rules Perjury Not A Mortal Sin

VATICAN CITY—The Vatican Synod of Bishops ruled Monday that perjury is not a mortal sin, downgrading the sin to venial. "God and The Mother Church will be more than satisfied with a penance of 20 rosaries for any act of perjury," Cardinal Angelo Sodano said. "Any earthly prohibition against lying in a court of law has no relevance to the holy teachings of The Bible." The proclam-

ation comes on the heels of last Friday's doctrinal clarification that adultery only occurs when both participants are adults.

Desperate U.S. Colleges Weigh Emergency Bob Marley *Legend* Ban

BOSTON—The American Council of College Administrators (ACCA) met Monday to discuss an emergency ban on the Bob Marley greatest-hits compilation *Legend*. "The situation grows more severe by the day," University of Michigan president Mary Sue Coleman told her fellow administrators. "At any given moment in Ann Arbor, it's impossible to walk down any street where there is undergraduate housing without hearing 'Get Up Stand Up' coming from five different porches." The ban would be the ACCA's first since a 1993 act restricting access to The Beastie Boys' *Check Your Head*.

JazzFest Performer Recognizes Audience From Last Year

INDIANAPOLIS—Twenty minutes into his set at Sunday's JVC JazzFest,

jazz guitarist Lee Ritenour recognized the entire audience from last year's event. "There's that one gray-haired guy with the ponytail and the Rippingtons T-shirt," Ritenour said to himself while playing. "And the fat guy who sits on a stack of old issues of Down Beat, just nodding his head. And there's that frizzy-haired lady with the Playboy JazzFest blanket who comes with her son. My, he's grown." After a rousing ovation at the end of his set, Ritenour thanked the crowd and said, "See you all next year."

KKK Member Struggles To Blame Blacks For His Hangover

SWAINSBORO, GA—Buford Anderson, a member of the Swainsboro chapter of the Ku Klux Klan, struggled to find a way to blame blacks for his wicked hangover Monday. "I believe the Nigra [sic] has conspired to hang me over with alcohol, even if I can't rightly prove it just at this moment," said Anderson, who had consumed a fifth of Jim Beam whiskey the previous night. "I done called the Jim Beam hotline to see if any of the board of directors is of the colored persuasion, but so far I'm inconclusive." Last December, Anderson blamed the "Jew-run media" for a paper cut sustained while reading *TV Guide*. ∅

Daughter Thinks It's Time To Have Sex Talk With Parents

Left: Sara Lister.

ST. LOUIS PARK, MN—After months of procrastination, Sara Lister, 13, decided Monday that it is "finally time" to sit her parents down so they can discuss sex with her.

"I really can't put it off any longer," Lister said. "It's time my parents and I had 'The Talk.' I know it seems kind of soon to be doing it when they're only in their late 30s, but I'd rather get it over with now than have them bring it up later."

Lister, a seventh-grader at Edgewood Junior High School, said she hopes her parents will feel comfortable enough during the conversation to discuss sex in a frank and open way.

"They were pretty mature about telling me where babies come from when I was little," Lister said. "They answered all of my questions and gave me a book. But this is totally different. This is way more serious, and I don't know for sure if they're going to be able to handle it."

Lister has been anticipating some version of the sex talk ever since turning 11. But after more than two years of waiting for her parents to sit her down to discuss matters of sexuality, she decided to take matters into her own hands.

"I thought they'd talk to me when I got my period last year, but they never did," Lister said. "Mom told me about tampons and pads and becoming a woman and how this meant I could get pregnant now, but nothing specific about sex or condoms or anything like that. It looks like I'm going to have to bring it up after dinner next week. I only hope I can find a natural way to start the conversation without it coming off all wrong."

Lister, who already has a good sense of what sex entails, sees the conversation with her parents as a chance to ease their growing anxiety about her coming into womanhood.

"I catch them getting embarrassed from time to time, like if we're watching some TV show or movie, and there's a sex joke," Lister said. "I usually act like I don't get it, to make them feel better. I think they like to pretend I'll never need to hear about it."

According to Lister, some of what she plans to discuss with her parents has already been covered by her teachers.

"We already went through some of this stuff in our assembly," Lister said. "They separated the boys and girls and told us all about menstruation and pubic hair. [Health-education teacher] Mrs. Arness looked so embarrassed and uncomfortable. It'll probably be like that with Mom and Dad, since they're about the same age."

Lister said she wants her parents to feel comfortable portraying sex as a normal, natural part of life.

"There's nothing wrong with sex," Lister said, "so there's no reason they should be afraid to discuss it. But even though sex is perfectly healthy, I have a feeling they're gonna be weird about the whole thing."

According to family psychiatrist Dr. Alice Migliore, Lister's desire to get her parental sex talk "over with" is natural.

"At this age, girls start to notice boys, and parents become increasingly uncomfortable thinking of their children as sexual beings," Migliore said. "Often, parents will dance around the issue, so it could take Sara forever to have an open, honest conversation with them. Unless she wants to face years of horribly awkward encounters with her parents, she's got to sit them down and have them tell her everything she already knows." Ø

PHONE from page 217

thing," coworker Rob Litt said. "If he doesn't, it's going to end up like that Nokia he broke just as the new ones hit the market. At the very least, he's going to have to replace the faceplate with a fancy new one pretty soon. That thing's scratched to hell."

"The other day, he was about to

> "It's going to end up like that Nokia he broke just as the new ones hit the market. At the very least, he's going to have to replace the faceplate with a fancy new one pretty soon. That thing's scratched to hell."

throw a pair of pants into the laundry when I happened to notice [the phone] sticking out of one of the pockets," said girlfriend Jeannie Gaffney, whose three-year relationship with Sychak has outlasted four cell phones. "As he's pulling it out, he says, 'Good thing my phone doesn't have a built-in PDA receiver like that new Ericsson R280LX Digital 'Wireless Web' Internet Phone. I'd hate to have almost ruined a phone with that.'"

Sychak's other cell-phone-destructive behaviors include absentmindedly flipping and catching the phone while walking down the street, sliding it across tables to friends who ask to use it, and occasionally using it as a makeshift flyswatter.

In recent weeks, Sychak has also made a habit of forgetting the phone in restaurants. Each time, however, a waiter or fellow patron has caught his mistake and returned the phone to him. Nervous that he will eventually lose it and be caught without a phone,

Sychak has begun browsing Nokia's web site so he will know what to order in case he needs to make a fast purchase.

Sychak said he is at a loss to explain his problem.

"I don't know why I keep having to replace my cell phone," said Sychak in a phone interview. "For some strange reason, I have the worst luck with these things. Hey, sorry about the noise on the line. I have to keep banging this thing on tables to get rid of the static." Ø

Above: Sychak longingly eyes a display case of new cell phones.

CHEESE from page 217

Above: A pre-limits Double Quarter Pounder.

to regular customers.

"This is us stepping up and taking responsibility for the health of our valued customers," Wendy's vice-president Bernard Angell said. "It's the right thing to do."

Most of the major fast-food chains have embraced the self-imposed limits, calling them "a small price to pay."

"From now on, anyone who wants extra cheese will have to sign a waiver clearing us of any and all culpability for health problems incurred as a result of excess cheese consumption," Burger King CEO Henry Tarment said. "The reality is, if we continued the way we were going, it was only a matter of time before that BK Triple Cheddar Stack caught up to us big-time. Three juicy beef patties and four big cheddar slices wasn't just a recipe for a great burger—it was a recipe for disaster."

One burger chain that has refused to participate in the cheese restrictions is Hardee's.

"The integrity of our Monster Burger would be severely compromised by these limitations," Hardee's president

> **"From now on, anyone who wants extra cheese will have to sign a waiver clearing us of any and all culpability for health problems incurred as a result of excess cheese consumption."**

Andrew Puzder said. "To have only three slices of cheese would mean we could not credibly call this product a Monster Burger. Although we applaud these other chains for their good intentions, our number-one priority is providing our customers with

the kind of delicious burgers they have come to expect and deserve. And cheese, healthy or not, is an essential component of that deliciousness."

Another powerful dissenting voice

> **"Nobody wants to be sued out of existence by the family of some overweight guy whose heart exploded,"** Shumacher added, "but at some point, you have to draw the line."

has been that of Arby's.

"The [NAFFR] proposal has its merits," said Boyd Shumacher, Arby's vice-president for product development and creator of the Arby's Big Cheddar roast-beef sandwich. "However, when we found that the limits included both natural cheese and imitation-and-natural cheese alloys, we felt we had to decline."

"Nobody wants to be sued out of existence by the family of some overweight guy whose heart exploded," Shumacher added, "but at some point, you have to draw the line."

Though many health experts applaud the unprecedented self-policing measure, they say more needs to be done.

"Decreasing the amount of cheese is certainly a good start," said Dr. Steven Gregory, director of the NYU Medical Center's obesity-studies program. "But even without cheese, these greasy fast-food burgers, when eaten every day, are going to cause significant health problems. Ultimately, the burger chains don't care about their customers' health. They're primarily looking to protect themselves from lazy, fat fucks who'll eat anything between two halves of a bun." ∅

I Gotta Get Back To My Roots

Hola amigos. How you doing? I know it's been a long time since I rapped at ya, but I've been busy as a mofo.

Nah, I'm full of shit. Jim Anchower's

The Cruise
By Jim Anchower

been taking it easy lately. Spending some time doing what I need to do to keep me happy. And who would try to keep me from doing that?

See, for a while there, I was in a pretty bad funk. I felt like I'd been taking care of everyone but Number One. The thing that was bringing me down the worst was my coat-check job at the museum. Sure, the money was okay, and I got to keep stuff from the lost-and-found if it stayed there for three weeks. And I got tips, so I always had beer money in hand after work.

But for all that good stuff, the gig just wasn't my speed. I couldn't take

any more of that button-down world. The last straw came when my supervisor started hassling me about the taco-sauce stain on my

> **See, for a while there, I was in a pretty bad funk. I felt like I'd been taking care of everyone but Number One.**

shirt. I told him no one noticed it but him. He said that was one too many people, as far as he was concerned. I told him that as far as I was concerned, he could ram the shirt and the job.

I've quit a few jobs in my day, hombres, but none ever felt as good as quitting that one. It felt like a heavy

see ANCHOWER page 222

NATION from page 219

"In the past, someone like Walter Cronkite merely informed. But in this day and age, Tom [Brokaw] and his fellow news anchors do so much more," Koslow said. "They function as parent, friend, teacher, social worker, grief counselor, and spiritual advisor. That's a lot of pressure considering they also have ratings to think about."

"Some people ask how a bunch of network executives can decide whether America should continue to mourn or get back to regular life," Koslow continued. "Well, it's very complicated and involves a lot of research and data the average person would never understand."

One of those average people, Chicago-area homemaker Adrienne

Coffey, said she knows exactly where she will be at 8:46 a.m. on Sept. 11.

"I want to share the day with others

> **Chicago-area homemaker Adrienne Coffey said she knows exactly where she will be at 8:46 a.m. on Sept. 11.**

who are feeling what I'm feeling," Coffey said. "I'm going to be right there in front of the TV." ∅

Dr. Andrea Herman, a University of Maryland psychiatrist and licensed grief counselor, has developed the following set of guidelines to help Americans get through the anniversary of the Sept. 11 terrorist attacks:

- Remember that you are not alone. An estimated 150 million people will be watching the three major networks.

- No one channel is the "right" one to watch. Find the programming that is best for you and believe in your choice.

- Take a break. If non-stop television coverage becomes overwhelming, you may need to get away by occasionally checking out a game show or sitcom rerun.

- Look to your elders. Find comfort in the wisdom and guiding hand

of experienced leaders like Dan Rather, Tom Brokaw, and Peter Jennings.

- Turn to your community for support. Tune into local news coverage, as well as national news programming.

- Seek out your peers. Get support from niche-oriented networks with which you personally identify, such as BET, Lifetime, or MTV.

- If needed, seek therapy. There is no stigma attached to turning to a counselor like Dr. Phil for help.

weight had been lifted from my back. No more snotty, know-it-all coworkers, no more my-shit-don't-stink customers, and no more King Prick boss. Just me and the wind. That's the way I like it.

Now, normally when I quit a job, I find myself in an immediate cash crunch. Not this time. I quit on the last day of the pay period, so I had a whole check coming. On top of that, I'd somehow managed to save up about $240. Plus, Ron owed me a shit-load of beers and food, and for once I could actually hit him up for it, 'cause he landed on easy street at the tool-and-die factory. That meant one thing: For the first time in years, Jim Anchower was in a financial position to kick around and get back to his roots.

When I was working and hating life, I'd spend all my time going back and forth between my crib and my bullshit job. If I was lucky, I could squeeze out enough energy to see a movie or drag my ass to a bar for an hour or two before having to go home and go to bed early for work the next day. But now that I was free, I celebrated with a few bong hits and mapped out a plan for my next few weeks of luxury.

It came to my attention that my wheels had not been properly serviced in quite some time. Now, I'm not one of those guys who keeps a bottle of Armor All in the glove box so I can shine the dash and seats every time I use the car. Hell, with my Ford Festiva, it wouldn't be worth it. But I gave the shitbox the old once-over, you know, just so it would keep running until I can finally get my dream wheels.

I gave it the full works. I changed the plugs and wires, checked the fluids. For the first time in a while, I was on

> I don't mean to get all deep on you, but I've come to realize something: Having no worries really changes a person for the better. You know? If your life ain't working for you, then you're doing something wrong, and you need to make a change.

top of things, automotive-wise. And it felt damn good.

"But Jim," I can hear you say, "fixing a car isn't enough for you. You're a wild man. You need more than that to keep you happy." You're right on that count. Jim Anchower finally took the plunge. I got a new video-game system.

My old Super Nintendo went on the fritz about a year ago, and I've done without ever since. Mind you, I can make my own fun. I just hate to have

> When I was working and hating life, I'd spend all my time going back and forth between my crib and my bullshit job. If I was lucky, I could squeeze out enough energy to see a movie or drag my ass to a bar for an hour or two before having to go home and go to bed early for work the next day.

to when I'm settling into a nice buzz. I like to keep my mind and hands busy, and that's just something you can't do when you're watching a movie. Unless it's one of those meat-spanking movies, and that ain't something I'm about to discuss with my readers.

Once I decided to get a new system, I called up Wes. He's always game for a trip to the electronics store. Don't ask why. Some people like to bowl, some people like to hang out at the park, but for Wes, an afternoon looking at camcorders and other fancy shit he can't afford is his idea of a great time. So we got in the old Anchowermobile and headed down to Best Buy.

While Wes looked at DVD players, I kicked the tires on all the game systems. Picking one wasn't easy. The graphics were great on all of them, and they all had some killer games. Plus, they all looked cool. Except the Xbox, which looked like a clunky steaming load.

Then, I weighed the all-important zombie-game factor. With my old Super Nintendo, there weren't any good zombie games. But in the time since I'd bought it, all the video-game makers finally figured out that people want to blow the shit out of zombies. All the new systems had pretty decent zombie games, so that was a good thing, though it didn't help me decide.

After giving it a lot of thought, I finally decided to get the Nintendo Game Cube. My Super Nintendo did all right by me, so I figured a *Super* Super Nintendo would probably do even better. Anyway, what the Game Cube lacks in race games it more than makes up for in zombie games. Not only does it have Resident Evil, but there's also Eternal Darkness. I took a hard look at the cash I'd socked away

and decided I had enough for a Game Cube plus one game. I got Eternal Darkness because, unlike Resident Evil, you can only get that for the Game Cube. You see, Jim Anchower enjoys the finer things in life, and there's not much finer than a video game that's exclusive to the very system that you happen to own.

Before making my purchases, I had to find Wes. After a 20-minute search, I finally found him camped out in front of the flat-screen TVs. Now, normally, I would've just grabbed him and dragged his ass out of there, but they were playing one of the *Die Hard* movies. I can't remember which one it was. There were terrorists in it, that's all I remember, and it looked pretty cool on that 36-inch flat screen, especially since we'd smoked up in the Best Buy parking lot before heading in. So we hung out there and waited for the movie to finish. I knew I'd never be able to afford one of those TVs unless I won the lottery.

On the way home, we stopped for some gas and lottery tickets. When we got back on the road, I was feeling so good about my Game Cube purchase that I rolled the windows down and

cranked some Molly Hatchet on the tape deck. Just when I thought the day couldn't get any better, we whizzed past Ron, who was walking somewhere. He looked up and tried to flag us down, but we were going too fast. It was just one of those days. I was filled with that peaceful easy feeling.

Sure, I'll probably call up Ron tomorrow and see if he wants to stop by and shoot some zombies with me. Or just watch me shoot zombies. If he asks about me blowing him off in the car, I'll just say I didn't see him. I'm going to make him bring the beer, and I won't take no for an answer, 'cause Jim Anchower is back in full form. It just goes to show you how it all falls into place if you wait for it.

I don't mean to get all deep on you, but I've come to realize something: Having no worries really changes a person for the better. You know? If your life ain't working for you, then you're doing something wrong, and you need to make a change.

That's all I've got to say on the subject. So don't come to me for any more wisdom, 'cause I ain't in the mood for an audience right now. ∅

Your Horoscope

By Lloyd Schumner Sr.
Retired Machinist and
A.A.P.B.-Certified Astrologer

Aries: (March 21–April 19)
You'll barely be able to make it through the day knowing that Ben Vereen is disappointed in you.

Taurus: (April 20–May 20)
The stars appreciate that you want to protest rampant corporate corruption, but they don't see what you think the giant puppets are going to accomplish.

Gemini: (May 21–June 21)
You will be the first person in almost three millennia whom the gods see fit to punish for an astounding lack of hubris.

Cancer: (June 22–July 22)
You understand that if you're not part of the solution, you're part of the problem, but you still aren't sure which is supposed to be better.

Leo: (July 23–Aug. 22)
This Saturday, evil gangsters will target an FBI crime dog who lives with a goofy mailman. Fortunately, it will happen on HBO, so you're still safe for the time being.

Virgo: (Aug. 23–Sept. 22)
The reality is, if people can't believe that yellow grease is not butter, this country is seriously fucked up.

Libra: (Sept. 23–Oct. 23)
Your confusion over the baffling ordeal of modern life is only made worse by the strobe lights and klaxons.

Scorpio: (Oct. 24–Nov. 21)
You may not be able to walk, but you refuse to think of yourself as handicapped. You prefer to see yourself as "handi-crippled."

Sagittarius: (Nov. 22–Dec. 21)
You understand that Alaska's economy has been hit hard by the poor salmon season, but you don't see how hunting you will improve matters.

Capricorn: (Dec. 22–Jan. 19)
You will soon discover the only brand of stylish, functional, high-tech sunglasses that make you feel like a complete man.

Aquarius: (Jan. 20–Feb. 18)
You thought you'd heard of all the kinky fetishes, but that was before next week's launch of a 24-hour doll-collecting channel.

Pisces: (Feb. 19–March 20)
You're familiar with the saying "throw the baby out with the bathwater," but you never imagined you'd actually find yourself in the situation.

Laptop Guy At Coffee Shop Nine Times Out Of Ten

see LOCAL page 10B

Michelin Introduces Tires For Women

see PRODUCTWATCH page 8E

Animal Has Animal-Print Covering

see NATURE page 4D

Fake Leg Urinated Down

see LOCAL page 2B

STATshot

A look at the numbers that shape your world.

Least Successful U.S. Charities

1. 9/11 Hijackers Fund
2. National Association For The Advancement Of Things
3. Feed The Statlers
4. North American Silverfish Fund
5. American Red Crotch
6. Entertainment Lawyer Preservation Society
7. Need A Thumb, Leave A Thumb

the ONION®

VOLUME 38 ISSUE 33   AMERICA'S FINEST NEWS SOURCE™   12–18 SEPTEMBER 2002

Bush Won't Stop Asking Cheney If We Can Invade Yet

THE IRAQ SITUATION

Above: Bush asks Cheney for the fourth time Tuesday.

WASHINGTON, DC—Vice-President Dick Cheney issued a stern admonishment to President Bush Tuesday, telling the overeager chief executive that he didn't want to hear "so much as the word 'Iraq'" for the rest of the day.

"I told him, 'Listen, George, I promise we're going to invade Iraq, but you have to be patient,'" Cheney said. "'We need a halfway plausible *casus belli*. You know that, George. Now, stop bugging me about it.'"

According to Cheney, for the past three weeks, Bush has been constantly asking if it's time to move troops into the Gulf region.

"George is calling me, he's following me around in the halls, he's leaving notes on my desk reminding me to let him know if I hear 'any news,'" Cheney said. "He just will not sit still. I actually have a permanent red mark on my shoulder on the spot where he comes up and taps me."

"'Hey, Dick, is it time yet?'" said Cheney, adopting a Texas drawl in imitation of the president. "'Hey, Dick, can we invade yet?'"

In spite of repeated assur-

see BUSH page 227

Second Birthday In A Row Ruined By Terrorism

Above: The birthday boy tries in vain to enjoy his special day.

HOBOKEN, NJ—In what threatens to be an annual ritual, Rob Bachman, born Sept. 11, 1973, braced himself Tuesday for yet another birthday ruined by the Sept. 11 terrorist attacks.

"My birthday's gonna suck for the rest of my life," Bachman said on the eve of his 29th birthday. "Every year, I'm going to want to go out and have fun, but it's always going to be inappropriate in light of the meaning of this most tragic of days."

Added Bachman: "Man, there's nothing quite like hitting the bars on the anniversary of the worst act of terrorism ever perpetrated on U.S. soil."

see BIRTHDAY page 226

Man Knows Just What He'd Say If He Met Christina Ricci

PITTSBURGH—Rick Hazell, a 29-year-old Pittsburgh liquor-store clerk and self-described "Christina Ricci nut," knows exactly what he would say if he were ever to meet the actress.

"Most people who approach her, especially guys, probably do the whole panting-fanboy thing, but I'd be totally cool about it," Hazell said. "First off, I'd definitely focus on her indie stuff, like *Buffalo '66* and *The Opposite Of Sex*, which I'm sure she'd appreciate since most people who say they're fans probably just want to talk about *That Darn Cat* and crap like that."

Added Hazell: "Every now and then, she has to do those big Hollywood things to pay the bills, because the

see RICCI page 226

Right: Hazell, who would "be totally cool about it" if he met Ricci (above).

Legalizing Pot In Canada

Last week, a Canadian senate committee recommended that the government legalize the use of marijuana. What do *you* think?

"If they do legalize pot, they're gonna be the world's number-one economic power in no time, 'cause you can make anything out of hemp."

Dan Zorn
Cashier

"I'm gonna toke up, sit back, and watch the geese."

Bob Edwards
Lawyer

"The last thing we need is a glut of web sites explaining how, if you watch *Strange Brew* while listening to Rush's *2112*, it all matches up."

Erin Parker
Biologist

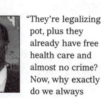

"Yeah, I heard about that. They're doing the same thing in Canada."

Cameron Davis
Welder

"I just hope no marijuana slips into the U.S."

Doris Atkinson
Librarian

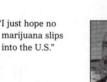

"They're legalizing pot, plus they already have free health care and almost no crime? Now, why exactly do we always make fun of them, again?"

Eric Donald
Systems Analyst

The 9/11 Anniversary

Wednesday marks the one-year anniversary of the Sept. 11 attacks. How are we commemorating the occasion?

▶ Reaching out to Muslim neighbors with fruit basket and card reading, "We don't blame you specifically"

▶ Rolling back prices on all new and used Chevrolets to pre-Sept. 11 levels

▶ Putting ridiculous stars-and-stripes kerchief on dog, walking around in public with dog

▶ Wondering if all the fireworks are maybe inappropriate

▶ Bravely defending America's borders on SOCOM: U.S. Navy Seals for PS2

▶ Breaking out old "Fuck You, Asshole" bin Laden T-shirt we haven't worn in ages

▶ Falsely reporting house is on fire, just to personally thank arriving firefighters for all they've done for country

▶ Getting bitched out by supervisor for leaving walk-in-cooler door open

▶ Jumping three feet every time a truck backfires

the ONION
America's Finest News Source.™

Herman Ulysses Zweibel
Founder

T. Herman Zweibel
Publisher Emeritus
J. Phineas Zweibel
Publisher
Maxwell Prescott Zweibel
Editor-In-Chief

You Call That Groveling?

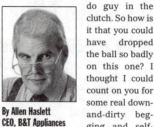

By Allen Haslett
CEO, B&T Appliances

Denison, you've been with the company 14 years now, and you've always been a real team player. Rarely a sick day, good with deadlines, a real can-do guy in the clutch. So how is it that you could have dropped the ball so badly on this one? I thought I could count on you for some real down-and-dirty begging and self-degradation when we told you we'd have to let you go as part of cost-cutting initiatives. We expected you to plead for your job back. But what you're doing is disappointing to say the least. You call that groveling?

My God, man, you're not even on your knees! When I think of groveling, I think of people putting it all out on the line. Really going for broke. No composure, no restraint, just a flood of sobbing, pleading hysterics. All you seem to have in you is "I just don't understand, sir," and "I've worked hard for the company for 14 years. This is the thanks I get?"

And that last one: "Can you reconsider this? I really think I deserve better." Not with that attitude, I won't! Your work performance was top-

> Let's look at the situation: You want to keep your job. Now, I'd love nothing more than to let you keep it. At the same time, I see a man who's not willing to frantically beg me not to lay him off. Do you see the difficult position you're putting me in here?

notch. Why can't your pleading rise to that same level?

Let's look at the situation: You want to keep your job. Now, I'd love nothing more than to let you keep it. At the same time, I see a man who's not willing to frantically beg me not to lay him off. Do you see the difficult position you're putting me in here? If you are unwilling to throw yourself at my mercy, how can I possibly believe that you *want* my mercy?

I can't say I'm unmoved by your words. I'm just not moved enough. Maybe you should try a little more of the sob story. You know, bring in some sort of dramatic tension. You have kids. Are any of them sick? In need of

> Maybe it would help if I filled you in on some of the details of your dismissal. Perhaps if you knew the stupidity, shortsightedness, and injustice of it all, you'd whip up the sort of fire and passion I'm looking for.

braces? How about your house? Did you just put down a deposit on a new roof? Dammit, Denison, would it kill you to squeeze one lousy tear out of your eye?

Maybe it would help if I filled you in on some of the details of your dismissal. Perhaps if you knew the stupidity, shortsightedness, and injustice of it all, you'd whip up the sort of fire and passion I'm looking for. Did you know that we—not "you-and-me we," but "me-and-the-company-you-used-to-work-for-until-five-minutes-ago we"—are on track to make record profits this year? Absolutely true, and it's all thanks to the money we're saving by letting 30 percent of our senior middle management go. You know, the loyal foot soldiers, the would-be lifers.

Doesn't that get your blood in a boil? How about this cruel fact: I'm set to receive a huge bonus this year. Huge. We're talking more than you made in the last five years put together, on top of my regular huge salary. Whoof, it's in the high six figures. I bet you really want to cut loose now. Come on, let me have it with both barrels of self-respect-obliterating histrionics!

How can I possibly take you seriously if you're not willing to surrender every last shred of human dignity you have? Put a little pepper on it, man! Tell me how much this job means to you and how great your performance has been. Choke up when you tell me how wonderful I've been as a boss. Belly-flop to the ground in front of me and kiss my feet.

Okay, that last one, that's a little over-the-top. After all, you have your dignity. I wouldn't expect that of you. But I wouldn't say no to it, either.

see GROVELING page 227

8-Year-Old Can't Understand Why He Isn't Allowed On Roof

STERLING HEIGHTS, MI—No amount of explanation has been sufficient to make Dylan Rieder, 8, understand why he is not permitted on the roof of his family's two-story home.

"I don't know why I can't play up there," Rieder said Monday. "I'm not gonna fall off. It's way less steep than the slide at the playground. And I never fall off that when I climb up. Plus, I wouldn't ruin anything—there's not even anything to ruin. It's just the roof and the chimney and the TV antenna and the wires that go to the telephone pole, but I know not to touch the wires."

Rieder's remarks came on the heels of his third parental warning in as many weeks not to even think about going on the roof.

"He does this every summer," said Beth Rieder, Dylan's mother. "As soon as it gets warm, he gets it in his head that he needs to get on that roof, and he won't give up until it's covered with snow. If I hadn't been out shopping all afternoon, he would have bugged me about it again today."

While Rieder has been subjected to numerous anti-roof-climbing lectures from his parents, his older brother Stephen, and next-door neighbor Mr. Rutigliano, none of their arguments have struck him as valid. Reasons given for staying off the roof have included the danger of falling off, the fragility of the shingles, and what someone driving by might think.

"He knows he shouldn't be up there," Beth said. "That's that."

Rieder said he recognizes that safety is a concern and promised he would

> **"He does this every summer," said Beth Rieder, Dylan's mother. "As soon as it gets warm, he gets it in his head that he needs to get on that roof, and he won't give up until it's covered with snow."**

not run, jump, or otherwise conduct himself irresponsibly if let onto the roof.

"I would be really, really careful," Rieder said. "It's not that different from climbing a tree. Mom once said she was going to let me put a tree-house up there. What's the difference?"

Rieder said he could perform many useful tasks if permitted onto the roof.

"I could see if any balls got caught up there and throw them down. And I could make sure the chimney doesn't have anything stuck in it," Rieder said.

Above: Dylan Rieder stands near the controversial roof.

"Also, I could help get the leaves out of the leavesdrops [sic], then Dad wouldn't have to get all mad at the ladder when it pinches his fingers."

As further evidence that his parents have nothing to fear, Rieder cited several eye-opening statistics.

"People can get killed in a car accident a hundred times more easy than they can on a roof," Rieder said. "Or they can eat poison by accident or get

a disease or get bit by a dog and get rabies. So I should get to go on the roof, 'cause it would be a lot safer than that."

Though he would like his parents' permission, Rieder said he has not ruled out a covert roof visit. Without use of his parents' bedroom window, which they keep locked at all times, Rieder's best chance for roof access is see ROOF page 227

Man Has Mixed Feelings About $39 Flight

SANDY SPRINGS, GA—Moments after saving hundreds of dollars on round-trip airfare from Atlanta to Los Angeles, Phillip Walden, 41, experienced mixed feelings about the bargain $39 Southwest Airlines flight. "What sort of corners would they have to cut to make a profit on that low a fare?" Walden wondered aloud after completing the Travelocity.com purchase. "Would $39 from every passenger even cover the fuel?" For safety's sake, Walden resolved to buy the second-cheapest ticket available from now on.

Senate Softball Team Loses Against Local Bar

WASHINGTON, DC—The U.S. Senate softball team suffered its fourth straight defeat Tuesday, losing 11-4 to the Anchor Inn. "We were actually ahead in the second after [U.S. Sen.] Judd [Gregg (R-NH)] hit a two-run double," team captain U.S. Sen. John Ensign (R-NV) said. "But then, Anchor Inn scored six in the bottom of the inning, and the rout was on." For next week's game against Pitchers Pub, Ensign said he plans to move error-prone shortstop Barbara Mikulski (D-MD) to right field.

Taco Bell Employee Somehow Dressed Down By Manager

DETROIT—Improbably, Taco Bell employee Wayne Lorimer, 28, was dressed down by manager Cal Dyer Tuesday. "I thought I was already cut down to size just by working here," said Lorimer, a former Ford auto worker laid off earlier this year. "But Cal's lecture about paying more attention to the proper way to apply sour cream if I want to remain a valued member of the Taco Bell family, that

managed to lower me even more." Lorimer added that he thinks Dyer might be right out of high school.

Balloon Deliveryman Forced To Take Bus

BALTIMORE—His car in the shop, Balloon-O-Gram deliveryman Burt Girardi, 37, was forced to use public transit Tuesday. "Well, that was pleasant," Girardi said. "You haven't lived until you've sat on a jam-packed crosstown bus for 40 minutes holding an 18-balloon Birthday Bouquet while dressed in full Zorro regalia." Girardi added that teenagers today think they are so goddamn funny.

Something Weird About Local Anchorman's Eyes

JOPLIN, MO—According to KODE-TV News At Five viewer JoBeth Anson, there's something weird about

anchorman Mort Bonds' eyes. "I can't quite put my finger on it," Anson said. "It's like the eyes are looking in slightly different directions, like one is glass. Or maybe it's that one's a little higher than the other. Whatever it is, something's off." Anson expressed confidence that she will figure it out soon.

Supreme Court Cock-Blocks Iowa Man

WASHINGTON, DC—By an 8-1 decision, the U.S. Supreme Court cock-blocked Des Moines, IA, bar patron Jon Carmody Friday, severely curtailing his power to score with fellow bar-goer Megan Navarre. "Carmody's right to put the moves on Navarre does not and cannot be construed to supersede this court's right to hit on her, too," Justice Antonin Scalia wrote in the majority opinion. "That Carmody scored last weekend with that blonde girl at P.J.'s serves to illustrate that he's had enough for now. We will preclude the shit out of that tool getting any from Navarre." ✎

stuff with integrity doesn't pay shit. One *Small Soldiers* pays for 30 *Pecker*s."

> ## "I definitely wouldn't be all creepy and tell her I've thought she was hot ever since the second *Addams Family* movie," Hazell said. "In fact, I'd avoid telling her she was hot at all. I'd be much more subtle about it."

Hazell has seen every one of Ricci's films, including *Casper*, *Sleepy Hollow*, and her first film, *Mermaids*.

"In *Mermaids*, even though she was really young—and the movie blew—she showed signs of future brilliance," said Hazell, who lists Ricci's performance in *The Ice Storm* as his favorite. "It takes a lot to be able to hold your own against someone like Cher when you're 10, but she did it."

Hazell stressed that he wouldn't tell her that if he met her, because he wouldn't want to seem like he was "sucking up."

Hazell said he has harbored a crush on the young actress ever since seeing her in *Addams Family Values* when she was just 13. If he met her, however, he would be coy about his attraction.

"I definitely wouldn't be all creepy and tell her I've thought she was hot ever since the second *Addams Family* movie," Hazell said. "In fact, I'd avoid telling her she was hot at all. I'd be much more subtle about it."

To ensure he doesn't come off like "some crazed stalker fan," Hazell said that if he ever met Ricci, he wouldn't let on just how much he knows about her.

"I'd definitely want to come off like an intelligent, knowledgeable fan,"

> ## "I really wouldn't want to force it," Hazell said. "I've never been to Hollywood, and she's probably not in Pittsburgh much. But who knows? Maybe she'll be on location shooting something here."

Hazell said. "But I wouldn't want to seem like one of those obsessive freakos. Like, I could ask her about getting her first producer credit on *Pumpkin*. Or what it was like to work

with Ben Gazzara on *Buffalo '66*. That'd be fine. But if she happened to mention that she's an Aquarius, I'd be like, 'Oh, really?' Because if she knew that I knew her sign, that might come off weird."

Though he has given a lot of thought to what he would say to Ricci, Hazell has not devised a plan that would put him in close physical proximity to the actress.

"I really wouldn't want to force it," Hazell said. "I've never been to Hollywood, and she's probably not in Pittsburgh much. But who knows? Maybe she'll be on location shooting something here. A bunch of movies have been shot here, like *Wonder Boys* and that Bruce Willis movie *Striking Distance*, so crazier things have happened. Or maybe I'll run into her in an airport somewhere. The bottom line is, you can't artificially manufacture these things. When it happens, it happens. And it'll be great."

Added Hazell: "I hear she's got a nude scene in *Prozac Nation*. Oh, man." ∅

BIRTHDAY from page 223

Though Bachman will try to enjoy his "special day" as best he can, he said he is not looking forward to the muted, somber acknowledgements he will receive from others.

"Last week, there was a lunchtime office party for [coworker] Matt [Quigle], complete with cake and decorations, because, of course, nobody cringes when you say your birthday is Sept. 5," Bachman said. "Already this week, Dina the receptionist, who lost a cousin in the attacks, looks like she's going to cry at any second. If they do recognize my birthday at all, I'm sure it'll be in some tasteful, appropriate way, without music or

streamers or anything like that."

"If I try to have a good time, I look like this shallow, selfish asshole who's oblivious to what's going on in the world," Bachman continued. "Still, Sept. 11 is the only birthday I have, and it'd be nice if I were allowed to have fun."

As of press time, Bachman's efforts to gather friends and coworkers for the evening have been unsuccessful. Most of his e-mails and voicemail messages have gone unreturned, while those friends who have responded have politely declined, offering subdued birthday wishes.

"When I invited my friends a few

weeks before, I distinctly avoided mentioning the date and just said people were getting together for my birthday on Wednesday," Bachman said. "Of course, once people realized what day it was, they all bowed out. Now that I think of it, I probably would've done the same thing."

If he is unable to assemble a group of friends, Bachman said he may just spend the evening at home alone.

"Maybe I'll just chill out and watch a movie," Bachman said. "But I know that as soon as I turn on the TV, I'm going to get hit with one of the wall-to-wall specials on the attacks, and it's going to make watching *Shallow*

Hal or some other bullshit puff movie seem way too depressing."

Though Bachman's friends are hesitant to engage in any sort of revelry on Sept. 11, they sympathize with his plight.

"I really feel bad for him," said Danielle Cimino, Bachman's longtime

> ## As of press time, Bachman's efforts to gather friends and coworkers for the evening have been unsuccessful. Most of his e-mails and voicemail messages have gone unreturned, while those friends who have responded have politely declined.

friend. "Some of his friends don't want to go out because they're afraid of some big follow-up attack. The rest just want to be alone that night. I was going to take it on myself to go out and make sure he has a good time, but I don't particularly want to go out, either."

Given the historical magnitude of the Sept. 11 attacks, Bachman said he doesn't hold out much hope for future birthdays, either.

"It's probably going to be at least 10 years before I can get back to celebrating like a normal person," Bachman said. "Then again, that 10th anniversary of the attacks should be a pretty big deal, too. Fuck." ∅

Above: Bachman reads a birthday card from friend Danielle Cimino.

ances that he will be apprised the moment the time to invade arrives, Bush continues to badger Cheney.

"He knows I don't want to talk about it, but he still somehow manages to find a way to sneak it into conversations," Cheney said. "He'll drop by my office on some pretense—the Kyoto treaty or whatever—and then right before he's about to leave, he'll say, 'Oh, by the way, do you think it's time to get those troops into the Middle East yet?' As if that wasn't his whole reason for the visit."

Bush has also taken to hanging around certain West Wing hallways,

> "George is driving me absolutely batty," Rumsfeld said. "I got back from lunch, and there were four voicemail messages from him, then another two on my cell phone. Each one says he has to talk to me about a 'highly confidential subject,' as if I don't know what it is."

hoping to "accidentally" bump into Cheney as he exits meetings.

"Last Thursday, I nearly ran him over as I was coming out of a debriefing with the Joint Chiefs of Staff," Cheney said. "So he says, 'I was thinking of maybe talking to [CIA director] George Tenet, because the CIA helped spark that Kurdish uprising in '96, so maybe we could do something like that again with Iraq.' I said, 'George, I'm doing everything I possibly can to set things up for an Iraq invasion. Try to think about something else—health-care reform, the economy, anything—before I strangle you.'"

Though he said he understands and appreciates the president's eagerness, Cheney said his patience finally wore out when Bush called him at home over the weekend.

"I'm sitting down to dinner, and I get a phone call asking if 'Congress knows they've got weapons of mass destruction,'" Cheney said. "I told him yes, and to settle down. Later that night—it must have been midnight—the secured line rings. I leap out of bed, thinking something awful has happened. It's George, saying that he can't sleep thinking about how right at this very minute, Saddam is manufacturing more weapons of mass destruction, and we're sitting here doing nothing."

On Monday, Cheney sat Bush down

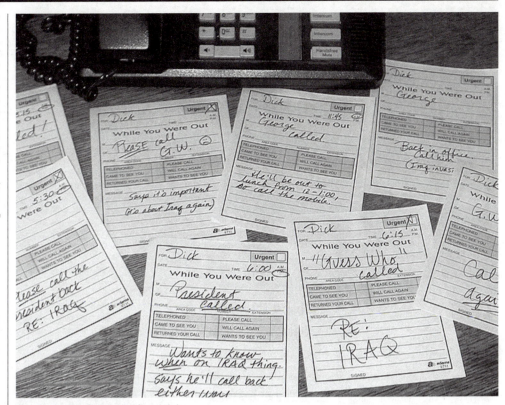

Above: Messages from Bush pile up on Cheney's desk.

and explained at length the political ramifications of proceeding with a first strike without creating the appearance of approval from Congress and the American people.

"I said we can do it, but we don't want to at this moment," Cheney said. "'If we just wait a little longer, Saddam is bound to commit some act of aggression or we'll find some juicy Al Qaeda ties or something, and then we can make it look like the whole country's behind it. George has got to learn to hold his horses."

Cheney also explained to Bush that his constant pestering is keeping him from attending to the very work that will make the invasion a reality.

"Donald [Rumsfeld] and I are work-

ing on the U.N. weapons-inspections thing, and we're *this* close to finding a way to make that a compelling reason, but we just need a little more time," Cheney said. "I told George to go back to the Oval Office and stay there. I also made him put his hand on his heart and promise me he wouldn't talk to me about it anymore."

Within an hour of sending Bush to his office, Cheney received six e-mails from Bush, all of them forwarded news articles that the president had found online. Among them was an Associated Press story titled "Lawyers Say Bush Does Not Need Congress To Attack Iraq," accompanied by a message from Bush reading, "dick, have

you seen this?!?!?!?!?!" [sic].

"Of course I've seen it," Cheney said. "Who does he think planted the story?"

The vice-president is not the only key White House figure Bush has harassed.

"George is driving me absolutely batty," Rumsfeld said. "I got back from lunch, and there were four voicemail messages from him, then another two on my cell phone. Each one says he has to talk to me about a 'highly confidential subject,' as if I don't know what it is. Condoleezza [Rice] said she's been getting the same thing. He just doesn't seem to understand that we all want war as badly as he does." ∅

Edwards was in here getting the old pink slip not more than 15 minutes ago. Now, *there's* a fella who took it hard. He was really pouring it on, telling me how his wife was already thinking about leaving him, and that he had twin daughters starting college in the fall. Hoo-boy, when it came time for his moment of truth, he could really bring the waterworks. Left a stain on my carpet. You're standing in his saltwater puddle right now. Now, it still wasn't enough to make me reconsider, but it did set the pleading bar pretty high. So if you want to make an impression now, you'll have to top a man who threw a crying fit so ferocious, his mustache got soggy with snot.

Denison, I'm a busy man, so let me cut to the chase. I could sit here all day waiting for you to lose your composure, but I won't. If you're not going to reduce yourself to a pathetic heap

of sobs and self-flagellation in the next 45 seconds, I'm going to have no choice but to call security and have you removed.

Forty-one... forty-two... forty-three... forty-four... forty-five... time. Guards, please escort Mr. Denison to the front door. Thank you.

Wait! Don't go! So you still won't grovel, eh? Hmm... You have more guts that I thought, Denison. I've sorely underestimated you. I always thought of you as a spineless weakling. You've got solid-brass balls. If I've misjudged you on the spine front, maybe I've made a severe miscalculation in letting you go. Perhaps I shouldn't have acted so hastily in your case.

Nah, I'm just kidding. Get the hell out of here! And don't come back until you're ready to show me some groveling that'll straighten my short-and-curlies! ∅

via a tree in the backyard. By climbing to the fourth extending branch, Rieder would be able to drop down neatly onto the roof. The tree, however, is visible to anyone looking out the kitchen window, the very place where his mother stands as she does dishes and prepares meals.

"I might try the tree in the back, too, but that's harder," Rieder said. "I can't get caught, 'cause Mom would kill me."

Climbing on the roof is not the only activity forbidden to Rieder. Also verboten are pulling up the loose blacktop at the edge of the driveway, picking leaves off the bushes in the front yard, playing with the rocks in the window wells, writing on the side of the house with chalk, climbing on the water meter, putting anything in the mailbox without prior approval, and opening the chest freezer in the garage. ∅

227

I Regret To Say Your Wedding Falls Square In The Middle Of The *Prisoner* Marathon

By Larry Groznic

When I received your wedding invitation, Neil, I was overcome with joy at the prospect of being part of your blessed day. As one of my oldest and dearest friends, you are the kind of person whose nuptials I would not want to miss for all the world. However, as much as I want to be there when you take Beth as your wife, I regret to say that your Oct. 12 wedding falls square in the middle of the *Prisoner* marathon on the Sci-Fi Channel.

I realize that, on the surface, it may appear that I am slighting you and Beth for the most trivial of reasons. I also realize that, with this no-show, I run the risk of permanently falling out of favor with you. Though I would be pained by a loss of friendship, I am one who has never been too concerned with outward appearances or public opinion. After all, had Number 6 practiced such timidity and deference to his peers, he would still be inhabiting the Village, chemically lobotomized and wading fully clothed in the Free Sea as his jailers used his valuable knowledge to achieve world domination.

I do not mean to liken you to the sinister yet mysterious entity that abducted The Prisoner. But I must wonder what would motivate a man to tie the knot during the very weekend when the Sci-Fi Channel is broadcasting the complete 17-episode run, including the alternate version of "The Chimes Of Big Ben" and a special "making-of" documentary featuring a rare interview with the reclusive Patrick McGoohan himself.

Explanations such as the availability of a reception hall or desire to marry in the fall don't adequately account for why you, Neil Croyer, a card-carrying member of Six Of One, *The Prisoner* Appreciation Society, would exchange vows with your longtime girlfriend on such a special weekend.

Are you not the man who pioneered the use of the Albertus font on your web page in 1991 and even went so far as to purchase a VCR that is compatible with PAL-format video so you could play your painstakingly acquired copies of 1977 ATV broadcast-feed bootlegs? How could such a supposedly dedicated fan do such a thing? And don't try to plead ignorance, either. I happen to know you are on Six Of One's mailing list, and that they announced the marathon way back in February.

Yet despite this callous disregard of your friends, many of whom share your *Prisoner* passion, it is I who bears the brunt of your scheduling negligence. Evidently, I am the only member of our circle of friends who has decided not to attend the wedding for marathon-related reasons. And, thanks to a mysterious informant who shall remain anonymous (not unlike Number 6 himself), I have been made privy to several e-mails roundly

> **I realize that, on the surface, it may appear that I am slighting you and Beth for the most trivial of reasons.**

condemning my decision.

As one unsigned e-mail, rather uncreatively titled "wahts with larry" [sic], put it, "How selfish does a person have to be to miss a good friend's wedding to watch a bunch of *Prisoner* episodes he's seen a million times, owns on DVD, can record on his TiVo, will be repeated in their entirety the day after the ceremony, and will be butchered by commercial interruptions anyway?" Another wag quipped, "Let's tell Larry that we heard Aimee Porter wanted to have sex with him, but she decided to stay home and catch the Thunderbirds marathon instead."

Passionately argued as they may be, such criticisms are deeply misguided (and that "*Thunderbirds* marathon" is an outright fabrication). It does not take a genius to figure out that a DVD or TiVo owner, in spite of the impressive technology at his disposal, cannot go online while the episodes are airing and swiftly and decisively refute the moronic prattling of one Muscatis1, that tireless scourge of *Prisoner* chat rooms who insists that Number 1 is actually the silent, diminutive butler who works at Number 2's residence. Nor would they be able to participate in the concurrent online trivia contest (grand prize being a trip to the Village itself, Portmeirion in North Wales) or vote for the all-time best episode (a tough choice indeed, but I would have to go with "Many Happy Returns" for its gripping narrative and devastating denouement, although I'm certain fans with cruder palates will gravitate toward the overrated "Fall Out" or, God forbid, "The Girl Who Was Death").

And my detractors are undoubtedly ignorant of my invitation-preceding promise to Chuck Kiergaard, publisher of the '60s sci-fi and spy-genre tribute 'zine *Catsuit*, to pen a review of the Sci-Fi Channel's presentation of the episodes for his Fall 2002 issue. You bet your penny-farthing I'm going to watch both days of the marathon. It would be wildly irresponsible of me not to, given my commitments.

I suppose, Neil, I should have known something was amiss when you failed to denounce *The Simpsons*' abysmal *Prisoner*-inspired episode back in the fall of 2000 on the alt.sci-fi.prisoner message board. It was left to lesser lights like TheSuprvisr, BCINGU, Nadia, and Muscatis1 to condemn its painfully forced scenario and glaring inaccuracies (*koalas on the Village grounds?!?*). That was around the time you began dating Beth, was it not?

Now, I am not blaming Beth for your loss of zeal for preserving the memory and legacy of this classic, groundbreaking program. But don't you think that if two people have a truly caring, loving relationship, they would respect and appreciate each other's interests, even if they don't necessarily share them? At the risk of sounding presumptuous, you wouldn't have asked Beth to wed you on the same weekend she had Blood-mobile duty, now, would you?

Which returns me to the question of why you would choose the weekend of the most important televised event of the year to get married. Perhaps your motives shall remain eternally ambiguous, much like the ending of the final episode of *The Prisoner*, in which we are uncertain whether the shadowy organization behind the Village has been destroyed or that the liberated Number 6 is truly free. But one thing is certain, Neil: I will not be pushed, filed, stamped, indexed, briefed, debriefed, numbered, or badgered into attending a wedding that denies me the rare opportunity to view the complete run of this landmark series in one consecutive stretch on TV. I am not a guest. I am a free man.

Be seeing you. ∅

Your Horoscope

By Lloyd Schumner Sr.
Retired Machinist and
A.A.P.B.-Certified Astrologer

Aries: (March 21–April 19)
Every day, in every way, you're getting better and better. But at this rate, you won't be good enough for 64 more years.

Taurus: (April 20–May 20)
Wednesday will be a good day to make business decisions. Business decisions made on any other day will cause the Nikkei index to plunge.

Gemini: (May 21–June 21)
You've never thought of yourself as an innovator in livestock genetics, as you have regular sex with them just like anybody else.

Cancer: (June 22–July 22)
You can barely contain yourself when you hear the national anthem, causing you to explosively deliquesce before the Packers game this Sunday.

Leo: (July 23–Aug. 22)
You've long been familiar with Marshall's theory of the Marginal Disutility of the Laborer, but you've just figured out that it means you'll now have to deep-fry stuff for 40 hours a week.

Virgo: (Aug. 23–Sept. 22)
Everyone wants the world to love them, but not everyone tries to win the world's affection by baking it an enormous pie.

Libra: (Sept. 23–Oct. 23)
There's something the stars have been meaning to tell you about elephants, but you'll soon find out for yourself.

Scorpio: (Oct. 24–Nov. 21)
Your desire to defend your country by being a soldier is admirable, but most people who feel that way simply join the armed forces.

Sagittarius: (Nov. 22–Dec. 21)
People generally get the sort of government they deserve, which is why the nation's biggest assholes cast write-in votes for you in the upcoming election.

Capricorn: (Dec. 22–Jan. 19)
Your shock and horror will be only partially offset by the prospect of great wealth when Liza Minnelli adopts you.

Aquarius: (Jan. 20–Feb. 18)
People will finally lose patience with you this week when God announces He's been finished with you for years.

Pisces: (Feb. 19–March 20)
After years of zoological study and careful consideration, you've decided that what separates us from the animals is a clever system of ditches and barriers.

Smithsonian Institution Politely Declines Sofa From *Charles In Charge*

see ARTS page 14A

iPod Flaunted

see TECHBEAT page 14C

Brawl Spills Out Of Teachers' Lounge

see LOCAL page 2B

DRBONG Pulled Over Again

see AUTOMOTIVE page 6D

STATshot

A look at the numbers that shape your world.

Top New Terms For 'Nerd'

1. Smork
2. Schwab
3. Freeze-framer
4. Weeble
5. Dodorkahedron
6. Fontslurper
7. Anakin
8. Spazimodo
9. Coen brother

the ONION®

VOLUME 38 ISSUE 34   AMERICA'S FINEST NEWS SOURCE™   19–25 SEPTEMBER 2002

Above: Bush outlines the details of Operation Deep Desert Off! to reporters.

Bush Sends Troops To West Nile

WASHINGTON, DC—Vowing to "exact justice for the taking of innocent American lives," a determined and defiant President Bush deployed more than 14,000 ground troops to the West Nile Monday.

"My fellow Americans, an enemy from overseas has attacked us in our own land, waging biological warfare against us on our home soil," Bush said in a nationally televised speech from the Oval Office. "We must send a strong message to our enemies in the West Nile region that this virulent aggression against America will not go unpunished; it will not stand."

Bush's decision to deploy troops came on the heels of three more West

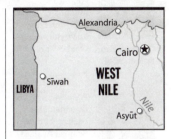

Nile virus deaths over the weekend—one in Louisiana and two in Illinois—bringing the national death toll to 51.

"These cowards want to bring down our very way of life," Bush said. "They have sought to rob us of our ability to

see BUSH page 233

Report: Al Qaeda Allegedly Engaging In Telemarketing

REC   10:36 2/7/02

Above: Ayman al-Zawahiri, Osama bin Laden's second-in-command, makes what appear to be cold calls from an undisclosed location in Afghanistan.

WASHINGTON, DC—In a chilling development, the CIA announced Monday that it has acquired a video-tape showing suspected Al Qaeda operatives engaging in what appears to be telemarketing.

"This video, obtained from a credible third-party source, features grainy footage of a group of men strongly believed to be Al Qaeda members making phone solicitations for vacation-home rentals, long-distance phone service, magazine subscriptions, and a vast array of other products and services," CIA Director George Tenet said at a press conference. "Many of these calls have occurred, unthinkably, during the dinner hour."

Added Tenet: "We had known about Al Qaeda's practice of raising money through drug trafficking and money laundering, but it seems the full scope of their depravity had barely been imagined."

see AL QAEDA page 232

Area Man Always Nostalgic For Four Years Ago

BOTHELL, WA—Eric Bagley, 32, a Seattle-area freelance photographer and part-time graphic designer, is perpetually nostalgic for the life he led four years earlier.

"The summer of 1998 was a pretty sweet time for me," Bagley said Monday. "I'd just moved to Seattle from Ohio. I had a bunch of money saved up and was just living off that, looking for jobs, meeting new people. You know, figuring out my life. It seemed like anything was possible then."

Bagley said his life four years ago was "miles better" than it is now.

"The first year or so I was here was the best," Bagley said. "I had this great group of friends I met through Keith [Aurilia], my roommate at the time. Our apartment had this amazing terrace, and that first summer, we'd all just hang out there every night, just drinking and shooting the shit until,

see NOSTALGIC page 232

Right: The perpetually wistful Bagley.

Europe, The U.S., And Saddam

A number of America's top European allies, including France and Germany, strongly oppose any potential U.S. military action against Iraq. What do *you* think?

"What? The rest of the world disapproves of America's militarism? Jesus, man, don't they know they can get bombed for that?"

Christopher Massey
Systems Analyst

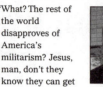

"It's not like we're asking our European allies to pitch in; we just want them to stand idly by and watch."

Michael Rossum
Lawyer

"Whatever will we do without the backing of the Spanish Armada?"

Lisa Hatcher
Graduate Student

"Fuck Europe. I hate those sniffy little watered-down wimps. So what if they're absolutely right? Fuckin' horse-eaters."

Rick Edgerton
Cab Driver

"C'mon, one shot at ousting Saddam every 10 years is only fair."

Bob Olsen
Roofer

"It's good to see that, after more than 50 years, America's shrewd piss-off-the-world strategy is finally starting to pay off."

Michelle Glover
Dietitian

Making McDonald's Healthier

Last week, McDonald's announced plans to cook its french fries and other fried foods in a lower-fat oil. What other changes are in store?

- Phasing out lead-based shakes
- Cashiers empowered to cut customers off when they've had enough
- Discontinuing "Thing We McFound" menu item
- Playland ball pit no longer filled with stale burger buns
- Thinner straws in shakes
- Beef upgraded from "D" to "D-plus"
- Requiring line cooks to gargle with disinfectant before spitting into food
- Chain to change name to Vibrant Gardens Healthateria
- Winning Monopoly game pieces good for garden salads only
- No longer serving McDonald's food

the ONION ®
America's Finest News Source.™

Herman Ulysses Zweibel
Founder

T. Herman Zweibel
Publisher Emeritus
J. Phineas Zweibel
Publisher
Maxwell Prescott Zweibel
Editor-In-Chief

I'm Not Proud Of Some Of The Things I've Done

By Tuffy
Excerpted From *The Confessions Of St. Tuffy*

Can it be true that my years in this world already number 12? Though mine is but a dog's life, I have always tried to live it well. Early on, I made it my mission to explore the neighborhood beyond my own yard, to appreciate nature and its many wonderful smells. I've thirsted for k n o w l e d g e, learning in excess of 10 tricks and committing to memory the location of every rabbit hole within a quarter mile. I have minded to comport myself with dignity, keeping my coat shiny and clean through a daily regimen of rigorous licking.

But, alas, I am not proud of some of the things I have done. I have willfully disobeyed orders. I have, at times, been too quick to bark, and I have whimpered needlessly. I have gnawed upon things I never should have gnawed. Yes, I have even bitten others in anger. Not often, and only when I felt I had to, but now I see that turning to the tooth never solves anything.

I have been a bad boy.

What springs to mind now, though it pains me to recall, is the garbage-can incident. My owner had been gone for hours. I was restless. Perhaps I was even a little angry over being left alone. At any rate, I nudged the kitchen-cupboard door open and overturned the garbage can. I was drunk with the ecstasy of my ill-gotten power and, suddenly, there was garbage everywhere. As if some evil force had taken hold of me, I chewed apart an empty bacon package right on top of the good blue couch. When I heard the car pull into the garage, it was as if I had awakened from a dream. Oh, the shame! I retreated to the basement and cowered next to the dryer in the hopes of evading the vigorous shoe-whacking I knew I richly deserved.

This is not my only transgression. My lust for table food has driven me to commit many a gluttonous act. There was the time I ate two pounds of raw hamburger meat left to thaw on top of the basement deep freeze. That was wrong. Worse still was the time I chewed right through that wrapped box under the Christmas tree to get at the cheese-and-sausage party-pak that lay inside. At the time, I viewed it as a bold and wholly justified act of defiance—I was weary of Science Diet and felt deserving of more treats. But in my heart I knew. I knew.

It has always been a battle to suppress the demon urges welling up inside me. Even as I slid from my mother's womb into the cardboard box in the tool shed, I was already not without sin. Yea, I sucked greedily at my mother's teat, trampling my six brothers and sisters in my milklust. I burdened my master with my youthful exuberance, repeatedly scampering out of the box and forcing him to chase me down. I used my tender age as an excuse to live with abandon, jumping on anyone, nipping wantonly, licking those who did not want to be licked. I arrogantly believed I had no need to learn the word "down."

Greater still were the sins committed upon reaching adulthood, for they could not be dismissed as the indiscretions of youth. At nine months, I

> **I have gnawed upon things I never should have gnawed. Yes, I have even bitten others in anger.**

knew full well when to sit, when to stay, which chairs were off limits, and yet I still broke the House Rules. I drank from the toilet. I snatched the choicest-smelling items from the laundry basket. Oh, the things upon which I chewed! Belts, shoes, newspapers, telephone cords, chair legs, and, one terrible day, the video-game controller. These foul acts—all the work of this bewhiskered mouth!

I also regret my indolence. My purpose in life is to protect my master's home, yet all too often I let sloth chase this sense of duty from me. So many afternoons I spent stretched out on the sunlit floor, my eyes blinking heavily until I drifted off into dreams of giant rawhide strips and bouncing rubber balls. Then, the knock of the UPS man or the thud of the evening paper on the steps would jolt me awake, the harsh sound castigating me for my negligence.

If only it were true that my only sin was that of omission! No, the abuse of free will has led me to commit the most vulgar of deeds. Repeatedly, I have succumbed to temptations of the flesh. There was no spaniel, no beagle-lab mix I did not see as my rightful property, with which I was free to have my way. Last summer, in my most depraved moment of carnality, only the blast of water from a cold hose was sufficient to separate me from my shameful congress with Duchess, the West Highland terrier next door.

In these dozen years, I have experienced misery—the ear infection, my

see PROUD page 234

Teen Humiliated By Activist Mom

AUSTIN, TX—Roberta Asher, 47, a longtime crusader for environmental and human-rights causes, once again humiliated her teenage son Monday when she appeared on the local TV news speaking at a rally for migrant and seasonal agricultural workers.

"I'm sitting in the living room with my friend Josh [Marden], when Mom comes in and turns on the news," said Craig Asher, 16. "Wouldn't you know

---

"Couldn't she find a way to do her protesting less publicly?"

---

it, there she is with a bunch of other freaky-looking people standing outside the Capitol going on about how Texas is failing to uphold the Migrant and Seasonal Agricultural Worker Protection Act. I swear, I could've died."

Added Craig: "Of all the moms in the world, I get stuck with one who's dedicated to eradicating economic and social injustice."

A 1976 graduate of the University of California–Berkeley, Asher has spent much of her adult life fighting on behalf of the underprivileged. Over the years, she has taken up such causes as women's reproductive rights, the imprisonment of AIM leader Leonard Peltier, No Nukes, and Jerry Brown's 1992 presidential run. In 1996, after receiving a law degree from the University of Texas, she established a non-profit foundation in

Austin offering free legal counsel to Mexican migrant workers.

Michelle Asher, Craig's 20-year-old sister, said she is "used to [her mother's activism] by now," but sympathized with her younger sibling's feelings of humiliation.

"I mean, it's fine that she wants to help poor people and stuff, but she does it in, like, this really embarrassing way," Michelle said. "Couldn't she find a way to do her protesting less publicly?"

For the past 18 months, Asher has worked tirelessly to force the state of Texas to more closely monitor farm-labor contractors and agricultural employers, demanding that they be required to disclose more information about their treatment of workers.

"The MSPA requires farm-labor contractors to register with the U.S. Department of Labor," said Asher, her son cringing nearby. "But there's no structure of accountability in place to actually *punish* them for abuses. There are workers out there being treated no better than slaves because employers know they won't seek recourse."

Over the years, Asher has embarrassed her children by appearing on the local evening news, writing impassioned letters to the editor of the local newspaper, speaking at city-council meetings and rallies, and even posting signs on the front lawn of their home.

"Last week, Mom stuck a big sign in the yard that said, 'Support H.R. 343!'" Craig said. "Thank God none of my friends know it's some dumb bill that requires companies to provide contracts in a worker's own language or

Above: The politically engaged Asher and her embarrassed son Craig.

some bullshit like that."

Asher's commitment to improving working and living conditions for migrant workers in Texas not only puts her in front of the camera, but occasionally on the front lines, as well.

"There was a picture in the paper of Mom at one of her protests, and Mr. Gemberling, my social-studies teacher, brought it in to class and showed it to everybody as an example of 'someone making a genuine difference in the community,'" Craig said. "So Doug Fritz yells from the back row, 'Dude, your mom's a dork,' and

the entire class cracked up. Why should I have to put up with this? Can't mom wait until I'm out of high school to do this shit?"

Michelle said she long ago gave up trying to explain to others what her mother does for a living.

"Everyone else can say that their parents are bankers or doctors or whatever," Michelle said. "What are we supposed to say? That she's an advocate for positive social change through direct action? That she gives a voice to the voiceless? I don't think so. I just say she's a waitress." Ø

Jury Selection Proving Difficult In Trial Of 'The Jury Killer'

PHOENIX—Defense attorneys for Thomas David Skrepnak, accused in 1999 of fatally stabbing all 12 members of the jury hearing his armed-robbery trial, are having trouble finding unbiased jurors for his upcoming murder trial. "It is difficult to find a jury that won't be at least somewhat prejudiced against Thomas," lead defense attorney Patricia Wynne said Monday, "especially given the hot-button issue of jury murder at hand here." Skrepnak's last six court appearances all ended in mistrial.

Son Surprised Dad Knows Johnny Cash Song

IOWA CITY, IA—Shawn Sullivan, 22, was stunned to learn Monday that

his father is familiar with the Johnny Cash song "I Walk The Line." "Where the hell did Dad learn that?" asked Sullivan, whose father recognized the song playing over speakers while dining out with the family. "That's, like, something me and my friends listen to." Sullivan conjectured that, while borrowing his father's car recently, he must have inadvertently left the radio tuned to KRUI 89.7, the local college radio station.

Apartment Set Up To Create Illusion Of Well-Rounded Life

RIVERSIDE, CA—Hoping to trick visitors into thinking he leads a well-rounded life filled with diverse interests, local resident Andrew Higgins has outfitted his apartment with such accoutrements as a framed *La Dolce Vita* poster, an acoustic guitar, and a magazine rack filled with back issues of *The New Yorker*. "I'm clearly into some pretty cool stuff," said Higgins,

26, who devotes 95 percent of his evenings to playing his Nintendo GameCube or patronizing a local topless bar. "This apartment is indistinguishable from that of a true Renaissance man."

Senators Wish Domenici Would Bring Dog To Work More Often

WASHINGTON, DC—Members of the U.S. Senate wish that Sen. Pete Domenici (R-NM) would bring his sheepdog Luke to work more often, Beltway sources reported Monday. "It's always so fun when we're debating a piece of legislation, and Luke comes charging in and runs all around the senate floor saying hi to everybody," Sen. Jon Corzine (D-NJ) said. "A couple weeks ago, I was right in the middle of a speech when he bowled me over and started licking my face." Virtually every senator has

encouraged Domenici to bring in Luke, with the notable exception of Sen. Mary Landrieu (D-LA), who is "so allergic to that thing, it's not even funny."

Director Of High-School Play Buys Director's Chair Out Of Own Pocket

WILKES-BARRE, PA—Bill Enqvist, Wilkes-Barre East High School drama teacher and director of the school's upcoming production of *West Side Story*, purchased a wood-and-canvas director's chair from Wal-Mart with his own money Tuesday. "I was kind of hoping the school would spring for one for me, but I guess they didn't see it as essential," Enqvist said. "That's okay: After the play, I can spruce up my deck with it." Enqvist added that for the next theatrical season, he may splurge on personalized iron-on letters for the chair's back. Ø

like, 4 a.m."

"But then Keith moved to Portland, and this other guy Chris left for medical school at UCLA, and the whole scene just kinda broke up," Bagley continued. "Man, I miss those days."

Bagley's friends recall the summer of 1998 differently.

"Every other night, he was calling me and telling me how much he hated Seattle," said Katie Gorn, a friend of Bagley's from his years in Columbus, OH. "He was always complaining about not having a job, how he just watched a lot of TV and pissed away all the money he'd taken years to save up. For him now to say he misses that time in his life is a total joke."

Aurilia said Bagley spent much of that supposedly halcyon summer of 1998 waxing nostalgic for 1994.

"God, I remember how Eric would go on and on about how great things were back in Ohio. He was cleaning pools with his friend Mark [Tanner], and all they did, according to Eric, was drive around from job to job, listening to the Melvins and talking about girls. Then, they'd get off from work and drink at this biker bar down the road from 3 in the afternoon until

closing."

Adding yet another layer to Bagley's revisionism, Tanner said he remembers 1994 differently.

"Back then, Eric was so depressed," Tanner said. "He felt trapped in Ohio, and he hated cleaning all those snobs' pools, so he got drunk every day to forget how much his life sucked. He was always talking about how great things were in college, back around '89, '90, when he had a band called The Trials and this hot redheaded girlfriend named Trish. Christ, if I'd had to listen to the Melvins or his Trials demo tape one more time, I would've strangled him. But he said it was the only thing that cheered him up, so I let it be."

According to childhood friend Glenn Lande, even as a boy, Bagley was nostalgic for four years earlier.

"In the fifth grade, Eric was always like, 'Didn't first grade rule?'" Lande said. "He'd go on and on about how easy it was and how we got two recesses instead of one. I'm sure in 2006, he'll be talking about how great his freelance-photography gig was and how much his new job and life sucks. It's kind of pathetic." ∅

The video is not the only evidence of telemarketing activity within Al Qaeda. According to Tenet, CIA agents tracking the terrorist organization over the past 12 months made steady progress infiltrating its communications network, eventually gaining access to transmissions to and from Al Qaeda operatives. These transmissions included a number of telemarketing "cold calls" to randomly chosen U.S. citizens.

Last December, during a sweep of caves near the Afghan-Pakistani border, Maj. Gen. Dan K. McNeill, leader of U.S. forces in Afghanistan, unearthed further evidence corroborating the phone-solicitation theory. Inside one cave, McNeill and his troops found a bank of empty cubicles with individual phone lines, a bullhorn, and 10 desktop bells, commonly rung in the event of a "sale."

"I couldn't believe what I saw," said McNeill, who also discovered bomb-making instructions and detailed maps of U.S. landmarks in the cave. "On top of all the destruction these people had already unleashed, plans were underway to harass the American people with a merciless assault of

offers for everything from discounts on home DSL lines to pre-approved, low-interest credit cards."

For all the evidence collected by the CIA, the "smoking gun" in the investi-

"Many of these calls have occurred, unthinkably, during the dinner hour."

gation may turn out to be an alleged Osama bin Laden motivational videotape, currently in the possession of CNN. The controversial tape, which has never aired on the cable network, is rumored to feature bin Laden urging his followers to think positive and believe in the quality of the product they are pitching, closing on the grim slogan "Smile And Dial."

Among the victims of Al Qaeda's telemarketing efforts is Coral Gables, FL, retiree Bernice Parks, who last Friday spent nearly 45 minutes trying to say no to a pushy aluminum-siding salesman who identified himself only as "Mohammed," only to give in and order full siding for her home. It is believed that the $3,000 charged to Parks' credit card—an amount she thought to be "a rock-bottom value, especially compared to what big companies like Sears charge"—was funneled through Al Qaeda's extensive siding cartel.

Nearly all of the $3,000 became Al Qaeda profit after what Parks described as "worn, faded siding that seemed to have been removed from another house" was hastily installed by three Middle-Eastern-looking men in an unmarked van.

"These evil people are preying on bored receptionists, gullible housewives, and defenseless seniors like me," Parks said. "At home, at work… they simply do not care."

In spite of the mounting evidence, Al Qaeda leaders detained in Guantanamo Bay continue to deny that their group is involved in any over-the-phone solicitation.

"Al Qaeda is willing to do many things to achieve its goals," said member Tariq al-Salaam from his holding cell. "Disrupting people with intrusive, unwanted phone calls is not one of them."

Jerry Wiener, a Metairie, LA, 75-year-old who was recently scammed into buying a $4,200-a-month timeshare condominium in "Yumabad, Arizona," urged the U.S. to take action.

"If it was up to me, every last one of those animals would be drawn and quartered in the public square," Wiener said. "I thought these Al Qaeda guys were pretty bad before. But making pushy, aggressive sales pitches to random, innocent strangers who just want to eat their supper in peace? That's about as low as it gets." ∅

---

the ONION presents

Tracing Your Genealogy

Building your family tree can be a fun and rewarding activity. Here are some tips to help you get started:

- There are many web sites and software packages out there that can help you trace your family history without having to deal with Grandma.

- If you are of European descent, don't be surprised to find that your ancestors were a bunch of bored, repressed, self-loathing people with blockish physiques.

- To spruce up your family tree, add gold stars next to the names of all the cousins you've nailed.

- If you trace your family back six generations, you should arrive at the great-great-great-great grandfather of Kevin Bacon.

- Keep in mind that entire branches of your family tree can be taken out with a simple Magic Marker.

- Searching your roots for a famous ancestor is a great way to validate your miserable existence as a legal secretary.

- Avoid this common mistake made by many first-time genealogists: Search for people with the same *last* name, not first.

- If you are white, just tell people you're from the Medici line of Italy. If black, say the Mandinka tribe. Asians, the Han-Tzu dynasty of Guangdong Province. Who's gonna call you on it?

- Mormons are experts at helping people trace family trees, but they'll probably want you to contribute to theirs.

- Note to women: In this society, it is unimportant to know anything about your lineage on your mother's side. Just skip it altogether.

- Before building your tree, ask yourself if you really want to know about the potato-eating filth that makes up your heritage.

- Go to your oldest living relative and ask him or her about your lineage. Work your way down to the second, third, and fourth oldest until you get to someone who makes some sense.

- If you are African-American, be advised that your research may take you to the mansion of a fat, ugly white man in Vicksburg who is less than happy to see you.

- Hey, you know who could help you, is the town historical society. They could help you find the location of the original veterans' cemetery before the county was incorporated. You should go there right now. I'll stay here and tell you how the Raiders game turned out.

Above: U.S. soldiers board a troop-transport boat near the West Nile city of Alexandria.

leave the house without repellent. But what they did not count on is the tremendous spirit and resolve of the American people. No one, be they man or mosquito, will dictate what we put or don't put on our skin for protection."

Armed with anti-mosquito munitions, American Special Forces made landfall at Damietta near the mouth of the Nile early Tuesday, and by dawn had erected U.S. Army netting over the city. Bush promised that the netting, expected to extend all the way to Khartoum by the end of the week, will eventually stretch nearly 1,000 miles to the Nile's source and "as far to the west as necessary."

"The United States will not stand idly by while people or insects who despise everything we stand for

> **Armed with anti-mosquito munitions, American Special Forces made landfall at Damietta near the mouth of the Nile early Tuesday, and by dawn had erected U.S. Army netting over the city.**

develop weapons of mass infection," Bush said. "The only way to fight a pestilence such as this is to attack it right where it breeds—in this case, the lands to the west of the Nile River."

Though not made public until Mon-

day, Operation Deep Desert Off! began at approximately 3 p.m. EST Sunday, when Air Force F-15 aircraft armed with mosquito-seeking Sidewinder missiles flew in support of F-18s deploying military-grade citronella napalm. By nightfall, special DEET-dispensing flamethrower tanks of the First Armored Infantry were scouting out possible base camps 100 miles west of the Nile.

Though details of the plan remain classified, Defense Secretary Donald Rumsfeld said the ultimate goal of Operation Deep Desert Off! is to "eradicate the deadly, virulent strain of anti-Americanism that has spread from the West Nile to our own shores."

"We have 14,000 fully armed and equipped American troops in the region right now who are prepared to take the fight to this foreign threat," Rumsfeld said. "I must stress that it will not be easy, as the war we wage is not against a traditional enemy. This enemy operates in secrecy, striking when and where we least expect. It is an enemy without borders. But I am nevertheless confident that the evildoers responsible for killing those 51 Americans and infecting hundreds more can be defeated by Christmas."

Response to Bush's troop deployment has been mixed.

"This ridiculous show of force is patently not the way to fight the West Nile virus," said Dr. Arnold Bloch of the Centers For Disease Control. "Foreign military action will do nothing to halt the spread of this disease and does not help those currently infected with West Nile. Besides, Bush should have deployed those anti-mosquito jet fighters along the eastern seaboard and garrisoned the Mississippi River area last year, when there was still a chance to contain the disease's domestic spread."

"Only two years ago, Bush said he would try to control his retaliatory impulses," Senate Majority Leader Tom Daschle (D-SD) said. "But in the past six months, he's invaded the West Nile, petitioned Congress for economic sanctions against Japan for

> **Though details of the plan remain classified, Defense Secretary Donald Rumsfeld said the ultimate goal of Operation Deep Desert Off! is to "eradicate the deadly, virulent strain of anti-Americanism that has spread from the West Nile to our own shores."**

the crop devastation wrought by the Japanese beetle, and threatened China with nuclear attack if its snakehead invasion was not halted. If he continues this hardline military stance on all overseas natural threats, he will badly damage his chances of ever solving future crises peacefully."

Undeterred, Bush maintained that the time to strike is now.

"We will hunt down and capture those who bring sickness and death to our shores," said Bush during a visit to the St. Louis home of Robyn Crist, 35, whose husband Dan was one of the first West Nile casualties. "Nothing can deter us from bringing down these bloodsucking anti-American parasites." ∅

Keepin' It Real In Tha Midstate Crib

**By Herbert Kornfeld
Accounts-Receivable
Supervisor**

Very first time I wrote this column, it wuz to inform all y'all nonbelievaz out there that tha H-Dog wuz a BAD ASS who best not be fucked with. That wuz nearly six yearz ago, and ain't a damn thing changed. If y'all think I gone soft 'cause I gots a shortie now, you dangerously mistaken. I still as hardcore as they come, know what I'm sayin'? Cross me, an' I'll samurai on yo' ass. Word is bond.

Damn, tha public think officin' peeps all be these pitiful, candy-ass bitchez watchin' *Jenny Jones* in tha break room or hangin' snapshots of they dumb-ass cats in they cubiclez. That be true o' some office workaz, like that wack Judy Metzger in Accountz Payabo, always wearin' a fool grin an' pushin' her muthafukkin' snickerdoodle cookiez on tha Midstate krew. But real office playas be all bidness, and don' stand foe no weak shit. Like my homiez Sir Casio KL7000 an' Kount Von Numbakrunch. We mad tight, but durin' tha work day, we don't talk at all. We tend to our respective bidness an' nothin' else. No phone calls, no e-mail, no gettin' our lunch on togetha at Applebeez.

It part o' tha Accountz Reeceevable code. See, back in tha day, this one A.R. bruthah got busted forwardin' a e-mail list of Monica Lewinsky jokes to anotha bruthah. When word got 'round, we put tha muthafucka in traction wit' a quickness, even though he wuz jus' a new-jack punk only five months certified. His mama told tha newzpaypas that tha A.R. wuz responsible, but even from his hospital bed, that bitch never pressed no charges 'cause he wanted to roll with our posse so bad. Didn't show him no mercy, tho'. Ain't no excuse foe that wack e-mailin' shit. Don't nobody want to get them lame jokes, 'specially not no hardcore A.R. enforcas.

So in tha rare event that A.R. bruthahs get togetha durin' bidness hourz, y'all best believe some serious shit be goin' down. And thas jus' what happen tha other mornin'. I hears a tap at my cubicle door, I turns aroun', and there be Sir Casio and Numbakrunch. First thing I think is, "Oh, snap, Jerry Tha Sharpie Head got hisself letta-opened in lockdown." But they didn't come ta bring no news about Jerry. Whut they said wuz a lot

see KORNFELD page 234

233

worse, true dat.

"Yo, Dog," Sir Casio say. "Me an' Krunch, we came to give you this here." And he hands me mah personalized double-gusset organiza wit' solar calculata.

Holy FUCK, y'all. I musta left it in tha SpeediBanc parkin' lot tha previous night. I ain't never fo'get mah organiza befoe. No self-respectin' A.R. bruthah ever leave his crib without his letta opener and organiza.

But befoe anythang can be said, Judy Metzger stick that big-ol' pumpkinhead of hers into mah cubicle. She all grinnin' that dipshit grin o' hers. Bitch has a serious love jones foe yours truly, but she ain't gettin' none o' tha H-Luv, unless she cross ova to tha A.R. And lose them muthafukkin' snickerdoodle cookiez. And get them front teeth removed, know what I'm sayin'?

When Judy pops in mah cubicle, she startle Casio an' Krunch so bad, they reach foe they letta openas, but I calm 'em down, sayin', "S'cool, she A.P., but she Midstate, too."

"Oh, Herbert," she say in this wack sing-song voice, like she Helen muthafukkin' Reddy or somethin'. "Can you come to the conference room for a minute? We're having a quick staff meeting."

"Aw, sheeit, bitch, this betta be important," I say. I be mad vexed, y'all. First, tha organiza thang and now a staff meetin'. I follow Judy to tha conferizence room, wit' Casio an' Krunch close behind.

But when I gets to tha room, ain't nobody there. "Goddamn, bitch, where tha krew at?" I aks. "You tryin' to play me? I oughta smack you upside yo' ugly head, you Aerosoles-wearin' ho."

Alla sudden, tha whole Midstate krew leaps out from under tha big ol' conferizence table. FUCK. It some kinda ambush. I whip out tha Letta Opener Of Death, grab Judy, and stick her ugly-ass permed head in tha ovahead projecta.

"Any y'all step to me, I turn on tha projecta bulb, an' Judy will be seein' spots foe dayz," I say.

"HAPPY BIRTHDAY, HERBERT!"

Dag, yo. I completely forgot. It be my muthafukkin' birfday.

Everybody in tha house: Bob Cowan from Human Resourcez, office comptrolla Gerald Luckenbill, all tha fly hos in Marketin', Mike and Phil in Inventory, Hal Tha Janitor, and, of course, mah Cash Room bitchez. Even muthafukkin' Myron Schabe, tha Accountz Payabo supervisa. Harriet from tha Cash Room bust out this big ol' cake all lit up wit' candlez and shit. Then they all set to singin'.

"*Happy birthday to you, happy birthday to you, happy birthday, dear Herbert, happy birthday to you.*"

Man, I was mad embarrassed bein' tha subject of some pussy-ass birfday party. Plus, they wuz wastin' valuable company time in mah name. As peeps be helpin' theyselves to cake an' ice cream an' soda an' them muthafukkin'

snickerdoodles, I resheath tha L.O.D., release Judy, an' turns to face Casio an' Krunch.

"Yo, I gots to get outta here. This ain't no place for a hardcore gangbanga like H-Dog," I says. "Besides, we gots important bidness to discuss."

We ditch tha conferizence room an' returns to mah cubicle. I takes up mah organiza an' lays it on tha floor. Same wit' tha L.O.D.

"Bruthahs," I say, "I brought shame to tha A.R. game today. I fo'get mah organiza. Thas why, effective immediately, I'm resignin' mah position as Accountz Reeceevable Supervisa at Midstate Office Supply an' from tha A.R. bruthahood at large."

Then Casio speak up. He say there

Alla sudden, tha whole Midstate krew leaps out from under tha big ol' conferizence table. FUCK. It some kinda ambush. I whip out tha Letta Opener Of Death, grab Judy, and stick her ugly-ass permed head in tha ovahead projecta.

---

ain't no need foe no resignation. He point at my attaché case an' tell me there be a organiza right there inside it. Sho' nuff, he right. Casio 'splain that when we wuz 'bout to leave tha SpeediBanc parkin' lot las' night, we takes up each othas organizaz by mistake, which look identical an' was layin' side-by-side on tha outdoor night-deposit box.

"An' as foe tha birfday partay, sheeit, y'all know them wack bitchez be pullin' that girlie shit all tha time on tha A.R. posse," Casio say. "It be a occupational hazard. Like, you know, carpal tunnel syndrome."

"No doubt," Krunch say. "They be pullin' that kinda wack pussy shit all tha time 'round here. Winta last, muthafukkin' coworkas tried to make me throw in foe Secret Santa. I didn't want no part of it, 'cause I wanted to keep it real and represent tha A.R. code to tha fullest. So I didn't give nothin', but I got somethin' anyway: a muthafukkin' crocheted pencil holda. I wuz like, dang, I don't want none o' this wack Secret Santa bling-bling. But if I returned tha gift, tha heat woulda been turned up on me like mad. You know, office politics an' shit. And remembа, tha Reeceevable Code say, serve and honor yo' employa at all costs. S'all good, s'all good."

Usually Numbakrunch ain't too bright, but I gotta give him mad propz foe makin' a bruthah see things anew. I ain't never realized

Your Horoscope

**By Lloyd Schumner Sr.
Retired Machinist and
A.A.P.B.-Certified Astrologer**

Aries: (March 21–April 19)
Your life is becoming boring, particularly to the people watching through the little peepholes.

Taurus: (April 20–May 20)
You'll deliver triplets in an elevator this week, even though they aren't due for three months and the elevator isn't stuck.

Gemini: (May 21–June 21)
You were brought up to love and fear God, but it's women who you truly love and fear.

Cancer: (June 22–July 22)
Your life has been a wonderful and varied symphony, but the bassoon, lower brass, and tympani are getting more minor-key solos this week.

Leo: (July 23–Aug. 22)
You've always been ready for when push comes to shove, but you'll be unprepared when push comes to uppercut, broken bottle, and meat saw.

Virgo: (Aug. 23–Sept. 22)
You're going to get one more chance to make it right. However, please note that in this case "it" refers not to your life, but to beef Wellington.

Libra: (Sept. 23–Oct. 23)
You'll fail to deal with a personal tragedy this week, wasting all of your time trying to determine whether you deserved it.

Scorpio: (Oct. 24–Nov. 21)
Your dream of becoming an accountant is ruined forever when economic circumstances force you to found and direct a modern dance troupe.

Sagittarius: (Nov. 22–Dec. 21)
Though you consider yourself a master of anal sex, you're just a strange combination of hyper-organization and raw sensuality.

Capricorn: (Dec. 22–Jan. 19)
Your future is wide open, an endless ocean of possibilities, as long as you do nothing that takes more than three days.

Aquarius: (Jan. 20–Feb. 18)
The stars have decided that your life needs no changes, at least from their perspective.

Pisces: (Feb. 19–March 20)
Drugs and alcohol are not the answer to your problems. Then again, hard work and self-reliance are, so drugs and alcohol will have to do.

---

that it ain't really violatin' tha Code if y'all have that weak shit thrust upon you. It only violatin' tha Code if tha weak shit be perpetuated BY tha A.R. bruthah HISSELF, like what that e-mailin' sucka did. In a perfect world, foolz like Judy Metzger would be locked out o' all officez, but tha world ain't perfect, an' it up to tha A.R. bruthahood to maintain a high officin' standard, even when they surrounded by tha wackest of shit. Much love to mah homiez Casio an' Krunch foe they wizdom and understandin'.

When Casio an' Krunch leave, I goes back to tha conference room to get mah eat on. I even chokes down a muthafukkin' snickerdoodle. But tha second I finish tha las' bite, I outta there an' back to my fly cubicle, where I start balancin' shit like a MOTHERFUCK. Birfday or no, ain't nobody gonna keep me from mah true callin'. Some officin' peeps may think tearin' off pages from they 365-days-a-year Far Side calenda be work, but not this banga. Daddy H be keepin' it real, representin' to tha fullest in tha Midstate crib 40/5.

Sheeit, what a A.R. bruthah gotta do jus' to stay alive in tha officin' world. ⌀

head getting slammed in the car door, the time I walked through that wet tar—but nothing equals the pain I feel when I think of the shameful disobedience I have shown my master.

O, Tyler Gregory, my benevolent keeper, my guide and my provider—you have been nothing but generous to me in spite of my hateful nature. You have loved me unconditionally, but without undue passion. You have corrected my errant ways, but with a gentle hand. You have been strong, but you have been fair.

It sickens me to look upon these four paws knowing they have committed such misdeeds in the face of your loving grace. I would gladly cut them off in penance—lay them across the very same railroad tracks that took the tail of the cat next door. But I know that such an act would only cause you pain, so true and selfless is your love for me.

My beloved master, great and giving one, my sole purpose is but to follow at your heels, to come when you call. I beg not for a snack treat, but for something far sweeter and more satisfying: your forgiveness. ⌀

Armchair Quarterback Blitzed

see SPORTS page 4C

Alpha Male Marries Tri-Delta Female

see WEDDINGS page 9D

Blind Person Gawked At Safely

see LOCAL page 11B

Dollar Store Looted

see CRIMEBEAT page 4E

STATshot

A look at the numbers that shape your world.

Top U.S. Foreign-Policy Blunders

1904 Teddy Roosevelt kills Russian ambassador with bare hands

1959 CIA covertly replaces Colombian coffee crops with Folgers crystals

1985 Scorpions granted work visas for "Rock You Like A Hurricane Tour"

1986 Iranian arms-for-Snausages deal

1990 Bush vomits on sneeze guard at grand opening of Tokyo Old Country Buffet

1997 CIA orders Princess Di taken down "with extreme prejudice"

the ONION®

VOLUME 38 ISSUE 35   AMERICA'S FINEST NEWS SOURCE™   26 SEPT.–2 OCT. 2002

The Sept. 11 Anniversary
Two Weeks Later

WASHINGTON, DC—It seems hard to believe that a fortnight has already passed, but this Wednesday, the nation will come together to commemorate the two-week anniversary of the one-year anniversary of the Sept. 11 attacks.

"I'll never forget where I was on Sept. 11," said Veronica Coulier of Greenpoint, Brooklyn. "My sister and I attended an anniversary candlelight vigil in Union Square. The subway ride back to Brooklyn was eerily quiet, with everybody lost in silent reflection about what had happened the year before. I'm not sure how I'm going to spend this Wednesday, but wherever I am, the events of Sept. 11, 2002, will not be far from my mind."

While much of the nation is determined to return to normalcy and put that difficult day of remembrance behind it, many Americans say they are not yet ready to let go.

"The Sept. 11 anniversary forever changed this country, and 14 days later, we are still reeling from its effects," said Georgetown University history professor Lawrence Appel. "Never before had America grieved together as it did on that emotional day one year after that unthinkable day. It's only natural that, on the two-week anniversary, intense feelings would surface once again."

Others say they will do their best

see ANNIVERSARY page 238

Above: Vartan in his irony-filled apartment.

20 Percent Of Area Man's Income Spent Ironically

LOUISVILLE, KY—Alex Vartan, 24, a Louisville-area convenience-store cashier and part-time DJ, spends 20 percent of his income ironically, sources reported Monday.

"I know I should really try to sock away some cash, but there's just so much funny shit out there," Vartan said. "Like, just yesterday, I passed by this Christian bookstore, and in the window they had those statues of Jesus playing basketball and a bunch of other sports with little kids. Now, how are you supposed to pass something like that up?"

Though his job as a cashier doesn't provide much in the way of disposable income, Vartan spends roughly one-fifth of his $21,000-a-year salary on such ironic items as Future Farmers of America jackets, Successories posters, and *Knight Rider* lunchboxes.

Vartan's love affair with irony-based

see IRONY page 239

Zombie Nutritionist Recommends All-Brain Diet

STONY BROOK, NY—In a dramatic reversal of decades-old medical wisdom, the late Dr. Albert Rossum, director of the O'Bannon Institute For Postmortem Nutritional Studies, recommended an all-brain diet for zombies Tuesday.

"Our research indicates that live human brains are not merely the cornerstone of a healthy diet; they are, in fact, the only food an active adult zombie should consume at all," Rossum said during a press conference at the institute, located at the State University of New York at Stony Brook. "A daily three-pound serving of brains supplies all the vital sugars, neurons, and ganglia essential to pro-

moting zombie fitness and slowing the decomposition process."

The Rossum Plan challenges the traditional zombie food pyramid, which consists of five to seven daily servings of human hearts, three to four servings of livers or eyeballs, and two servings of brains. Instead, Rossum advocates a four-level pyramid, with all four levels consisting of as many servings of brains as possible.

"Ideally, the brains should be consumed fresh from the head of the victim," said Rossum, widely considered the nation's leading expert in the field of undead nutrition. "However, precious scraps of brain may also be

see ZOMBIE page 238

Above: Dr. Albert Rossum (1940-1991) announces the findings.

Bush And The Weapons Inspections

Last week, Saddam Hussein agreed to U.N. weapons inspections in Iraq, but President Bush dismissed the offer as a cynical ploy. What do *you* think?

"It's clear to me that nothing short of war will stop Iraq from using its weapons."

John Englund
Software Developer

"Weird. It's almost as if Bush *wants* to invade."

Mitchell Ploeg
Systems Analyst

"I'd feel a lot better about the president's handling of this global nuclear brinksmanship if he could actually pronounce the word nuclear."

Miriam Knorr
Teacher

"This whole invasion-of-Iraq thing is so complicated. I wish Kurt Loder would explain it to me."

Rick Dunst
Cab Driver

"Bush should take up t'ai chi. He'd be a lot more relaxed and not so invady."

Todd Thane
Landscaper

"So, let me get this straight: Bush is saying he wants to invade Iraq, and Iraq is, like, trying to talk him out of it? Is this how invasions are usually handled?"

Audra Franks
Homemaker

Jack Welch's Retirement Perks

The details of General Electric CEO Jack Welch's lavish retirement package recently became public, sparking public outrage. Among the perks:

- New beagle puppy every day
- His divorce problems "taken care of"
- Autographed first-edition copy of *Jack: Straight From The Gut*
- Pick of GE's best electricity
- Unlimited 50-cent refills on 20-ounce jumbo coffee mug at participating Stop 'N' Go outlets
- May keep up to five GE nuclear warheads for own personal use
- Gets to do walk-ons on *Friends* whenever he wants
- 300 laid-off GE employees to be buried alive with him upon death
- Galaxian machine that's fixed so you don't have to put money in
- New *Harvard Business Review* editor/mistress every year
- Job as Conan's sidekick
- Boston
- 40-foot statue of Welch atop Rockefeller Center flinging lightning bolts down on helpless peons

⌀ the ONION®
America's Finest News Source.™

Herman Ulysses Zweibel
Founder

T. Herman Zweibel
Publisher Emeritus
J. Phineas Zweibel
Publisher
Maxwell Prescott Zweibel
Editor-In-Chief

Mock Me If You Will, But This Huge Cock Has Gotten Me Out Of Some Tough Scrapes

Ha, ha, very funny. Laugh it up, guys. I'm glad you find it so amusing.

Well, I hate to spoil your good time, but I've got some news for you: This huge cock has gotten me out of some tough scrapes.

This past June, I was rock-climbing in Utah with some college buddies when one of us, my good friend Alan, had a malfunction with his equipment. It's a little complicated to get into, but he was unable to get up or down, and the rope he was using was starting to fray. Wasting no time, I took out my penis and dropped it down to him so he could climb back up. Believe me, no one was laughing at the size of my piece when I pulled him to safety!

By Dean Alarie

Still not convinced? Maybe this anecdote will make you sing a different tune. I was at the art museum to check out a touring Van Gogh exhibit, and my belt had broken. Not wanting to alarm anyone, I made my way through the exhibit very slowly, holding my pants up with one hand. While pausing before one of Van

> **Wasting no time, I took out my penis and dropped it down to him so he could climb back up. Believe me, no one was laughing at the size of my piece when I pulled him to safety!**

Gogh's self-portraits, I saw a trio of armed bandits rush in. They told everyone to raise their hands as they took the paintings off the wall.

After what seemed like an eternity, one of the thieves noticed that I was only raising one hand. He said he'd shoot me if I didn't get that other hand up, so I did. My pants dropped, causing my humongous hose to unspool right in front of everyone. The crooks were so shocked by the immensity of my schlong that they dropped their ill-gotten loot and fled! The museum director was so thrilled, he gave me a lifetime membership and a 20 percent discount at the gift shop.

So you can see, my huge cock has really been a lifesaver—literally. But it's not just about saving lives. Oh, no. It has also helped me in my personal relationships. About four years ago, I went on a blind date. I was incredibly nervous, but when I got to the door, I was pleasantly surprised to discover

> **The crooks were so shocked by the immensity of my schlong that they dropped their ill-gotten loot and fled!**

that my date was extremely attractive. We got into my car and made some polite chitchat, but I was still so anxious that my mouth started getting dry. I pulled over to get some bottled water at a convenience store. On the way out of the car, my date accidentally dropped her house keys down the sewer. Uh-oh.

Luckily, I had my penis with me! After finding a nice, wide spot in the grating, I threw my cock down to the keys, hooked the head through her keychain (thank God she had an oversized key loop), and pulled them up. After that, things were much more relaxed between us, and the night was a huge success. As it turned out, my cock was just the icebreaker I needed. Did I mention that woman is now my wife? Dean's huge penis to the rescue!

Sometimes, my long dong actually seems to defy the laws of science. Like the time I got my kindly old neighbor Mrs. Linton's kitten out of a tree. I shook my penis erect and, lying on my back, created a ramp for the cat to climb down. Another time, I was able to use an erection to clear the leaves from my neighbor's clogged storm drain before an approaching downpour. Then there was the time I used my cock to hoist up the curtains at a rock concert, saving the show.

So you see, my cock shouldn't be subjected to cruel barbs just because it's so big. It deserves respect. As do I for using it to help people rather than hurt them. But if it makes you feel better to make it the target of your juvenile taunts, be my guest. Giving immature, insecure jerks something to mock so they can feel better about themselves is yet another use for my mammoth appendage. ⌀

236

Ken, Barbie Reenact Parental Fight

SPARTA, TN—A pair of Mattel Barbie and Ken dolls reenacted a fight between the parents of Amanda Lytle, 6, in the girl's bedroom Monday.

"Where were you so late last night?" Pop Sensation Barbie asked Ken at approximately 7 p.m., just after bath time. "What time did you get home? It was way past your bedtime when you got in."

Angrily bobbing across Lytle's bedspread to the pillow against which Ken lounged, Barbie raised her arm parallel to the floor and leaned menacingly toward Ken.

"I suppose you were down at that bar again with your dumb friends, weren't you?" Barbie said. "Why don't you call me when you're going to be late? Don't you think I worry?"

"If you know where I am, why do you need me to call?" responded Palm

> **Angrily bobbing across Lytle's bedspread to the pillow against which Ken lounged, Barbie raised her arm parallel to the floor and leaned menacingly toward Ken.**

> **Rising from his seated position, still bent at the waist, Ken bobbed over to an empty Hostess Twinkies box on the floor next to the bed and climbed inside.**

Beach Ken, dressed in a pair of Velcro-closed pants and a blue stretch pullover emblazoned with his name. "Besides, I only go to the bar because

people are nice to me there instead of being mean and picking on me like you do."

Lytle stared thoughtfully at the dolls before picking up Barbie, who raised her arm again and spoke.

"If the policeman stops you, he's going to give you a ticket, and then you will be sorry," Barbie said. "The last time you got one, it was for $4. We don't have money to give to the policeman. You were naughty."

While Barbie changed shoes, Lytle explained the conflict between the dolls to a row of Beanie Babies seated nearby.

"Barbie is mad at Ken because he said he was coming home after work, but then he didn't," Lytle said. "But Ken said he had to work late, so he should be able to go where he wants. And he didn't want to call because Barbie always gets mad at him and yells when he calls, so he doesn't call. But that makes Barbie *maaaad*. She's going to the kitchen."

"Slam, slam, slam!" said Barbie, fac-

Above: Barbie and Ken fight in their kitchen.

ing the wall. "I'm making dinner."

Rising from his seated position, still bent at the waist, Ken bobbed over to an empty Hostess Twinkies box on the floor next to the bed and climbed inside.

"I'm going to Circus City," said Ken, revving the Twinkies box's engine. "That's the place with all the TVs for sale where we went that time Uncle Dale needed to get batteries for his camera."

"Go ahead," Barbie said. "See you in five hours. Have a nice time at the bar."

"What is that supposed to mean?" Ken asked. "I said I was going to go to Circus City in my car. You've been yelling at me all week to get a new plug for the toaster. Now I go, and you are yelling at me."

"Fine, just don't buy anything else," Barbie said. "We don't have any money because you drink all the money."

see FIGHT page 239

Temp Replaced With Cheaper Temp

SAN BERNARDINO, CA—In a personnel move expected to save the company $17 a day, Cyntrel Fiberoptics replaced longtime Manpower temp worker Paulette Riordan with lower-paid MetroTemp employee Don Sendelbach. "Paulette was a familiar face in this office who we all very much liked," departmental supervisor William Youmans said. "But with the economy the way it is, tough decisions sometimes have to be made. Don's really learning the ropes well." Riordan's plans for the future include calling Manpower to inquire about openings in other offices.

*B*A*P*S* Rented On Strength Of Academy Award-Winning Stars

IRVING, TX—Blockbuster Video customer Stephanie Campbell rented the

1997 comedy *B*A*P*S* Tuesday, swayed by the presence of Oscar-winners Halle Berry and Martin Landau. "Wow, this is a pretty impressive cast," said Campbell, studying the back of the video box. "Talk about heavy hitters—it's even got Ian Richardson." Campbell ensured an evening of top-notch movie-watching by also renting *Loaded Weapon I*, which features Oscar-winner F. Murray Abraham.

American Idol Winner Already Complaining About Pressures Of Fame

NEW YORK—Kelly Clarkson, the winner of Fox's *American Idol*, griped about the pressures of her weeks-old celebrity Monday during an appearance on *Live! With Regis And Kelly*. "Being a star is amazing, and I wouldn't trade it for anything, but sometimes it's like, 'Can I please

have, like, one second to myself?'" Clarkson said. "Everyone wants a piece of you, and there is zero privacy." Clarkson, who performed her debut single "A Moment Like This" on *Live!*, said she plans to spend the next month "recharging at a secluded desert spa."

Disgusting Gyro Meat Magically Turns Delicious After Midnight

CHAMPAIGN, IL—A serving of greasy, heavily processed gyro meat was magically rendered delicious by the passage of the midnight hour, drunken Nick's Parthenon patron Sam Afton reported Monday. "Aw, man, this is so awesome," said Afton, gorging on the 14-hour-old, sodium-drenched strips of grade-C ground beef and lamb. "Thank God this place was open—I was starving." During his six years in Champaign, Afton had

walked past the low-cost Greek eatery on 207 occasions, each time disgusted by the smell and sight of the massive rotating cylinder of cheap, low-grade meat on twin spindles.

Hotel Bar Really Hopping Tonight, Says Hotel Bartender

GRAND RAPIDS, MI—According to George Fontana, the Grand Rapids Hilton's Tiki Town bar and lounge is "really hopping tonight," the 46-year-old hotel bartender reported Monday. "Usually, Mondays are pretty slow around here," Fontana said. "But it's been non-stop since about 10. To be honest, I'm not exactly sure why. I'd say it was the dental-supply convention, but most of those fellas are staying over at the Radisson." Fontana added that if the rush keeps up, he may have to unlock the supply closet to get a fresh box of olive picks. ∅

ZOMBIE from page 235

pried from the fingers of other brain-crazed zombies. Failing that, dropped brains may be slurped from the ground by a third party to such a scuffle."

Added Rossum: "Braaaaaaaaaiiiiiiii-iiiiiiiiiiinnnnnns!"

Nutritionists at the Romero Foundation For Zombie Health, the nation's oldest zombie-health organization, were dismissive of Rossum's announcement.

"The O'Bannon Institute's plan is a reckless fad diet," the late Dr. Vincent Peters said. "Five servings each day from the neurosensory group, made up of the brain, spinal column, and nervous system, as well as from the vascular, digestive, and pulmonary groups, are the best way to maintain robust zombie health. It is an established fact."

Told of Peters' remarks, Rossum strenuously disagreed, citing recent tests conducted by his institute.

"Studies have shown that zombies who follow the Romero school of nutrition can be stopped with a single bullet to the brainstem," Rossum said. "On the other hand, our exhaustive studies conclusively show that the newer, fitter breed of zombies who adhere to an all-brain diet cannot be

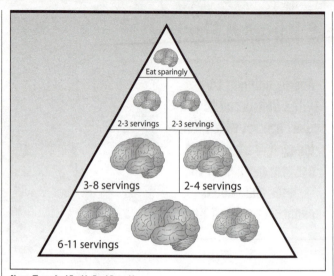

Above: The revised Zombie Food Pyramid.

subdued by anything short of total incineration."

Rossum's detractors are quick to point out that a high percentage of zombies in his studies are young accidental-death victims, many still in their teens, recruited from the punk-rock-fan community. Such individu-als, critics charge, are too healthy and recently deceased to be reliable subjects in long-term dietary studies.

Critics also charge that a diet consisting entirely of brains would not be likely to attract many followers due to its monotonous nature. Rossum again disagreed.

"There is still ample room for dietary variety in this plan," Rossum said. "One day, you might make a spicy South Of The Border treat of a Mexican person's brains. The next,

Nutritionists at the Romero Foundation For Zombie Health, the nation's oldest zombie-health organization, were dismissive of Rossum's announcement.

you could enjoy the Far East taste sensation of an Asian. There are so many different kinds of heads to tear open, there's no reason ever to get bored."

Rossum then stepped down from the podium and descended upon *New York Times* photographer Dennis Levitan, cracking his skull open and devouring his brains. ∅

ANNIVERSARY from page 235

to make this Wednesday just another day.

"I'm going to go to work, do my job, go home, and maybe watch a movie—just try to forget it's the second Wednesday after this year's 11th," said Angela Gregory of Frankfort, KY. "Maybe by the two-year anniversary,

"Sept. 11, 2002, was a really rough day," said Lisa Snider, 51, of St. Louis. "I think everyone is feeling what I'm feeling as we approach the two-week point after the one-year anniversary—sadness, but a bit of relief."

I'll be able to come to terms with what happened, but I just don't feel I can do that yet."

Making it all the more difficult to forget what happened two weeks ago are the physical reminders that can still be found all around us. In downtown Atlanta, red-white-and-blue banners still flutter along Peachtree Street. In St. Louis, plastic flowers and candles dot the base of the Gateway Arch, where, two weeks ago, the city held a memorial service along the Mississippi River.

"Sept. 11, 2002, was a really rough

Above: A Sept. 11 memorial service in New York.

day," said Lisa Snider, 51, of St. Louis. "I think everyone is feeling what I'm feeling as we approach the two-week point after the one-year anniversary—sadness, but a bit of relief."

According to Dr. James Olsafsky, a Los Angeles-area therapist and grief counselor, the nation is on the road to recovery.

"The mood of Americans is definitely improved over Sept. 10 of this year," Olsafsky said. "Back then, we were all a little ill at ease, not knowing what Sept. 11 would bring. You could feel that sense of anxiety

According to Dr. James Olsafsky, a Los Angeles-area therapist and grief counselor, the nation is on the road to recovery.

the day before the day the attacks happened the year before."

Meredith Engelberger, a Hoffman Estates, IL, homemaker and mother of three, said she expects Sept. 25 to be a day of healing.

"This past June 11, the three-quarters-of-a-year anniversary of the attacks, I was starting to think I'd never feel whole again," Engelberger said. "But then, at seven days before the one-year anniversary, it hit me: I'm not alone. Three weeks later, that's still true. If I can just get through the week before, the day of, and the day after the two-week anniversary of the one-year anniversary of Sept. 11, I know I'll be okay." ∅

Added Barbie: "We should get our daughter lots of nice presents and throw her a birthday party and get her a bike and a cat instead."

Throwing herself forward into a horizontal position on the bed, Barbie cried loudly. "Do you love me anymore?" Barbie asked. "Boo hoo hoo. If you don't love me anymore, tell me."

"Vroom, vroom, vroom," said Ken, zooming the Twinkies box across the room to the dresser. "I have to get out of this nuthouse. I am going crazy. I'm going to go to Circus City to get the new plug for the toaster."

Ken then drove off to Circus City, located on Lytle's dresser. After walking around the surface of the dresser several times, Ken climbed back into the Hostess box and returned home to find Barbie hiding under the pillow.

"Knock, knock, knock," said Ken, rapping his open palm on the pillow.

After nearly 10 seconds of silence, Barbie emerged from beneath the pillow. "I told you not to buy anything," Barbie said. "We don't have any money."

"I'm home from Circus City. I got the plug, and I got a movie on DVD. I got it because I know you wanted to see it. Come out, and we will make some microwave popcorn, and we can watch the movie on the couch. It's a movie with kissing in it."

After nearly 10 seconds of silence, Barbie emerged from beneath the pillow. "I told you not to buy anything," Barbie said. "We don't have any money."

"I got it for you," Ken said. "It's a movie for us to play. We can make the kids go to bed, and we can lay on the couch in our pajamas and watch it and drink beers together. And we can laugh a lot, but the kids will have to stay in bed even though it is not fair."

"Okay, let's watch the movie," said Barbie, hugging Ken with outstretched arms and pressing her face to his. "Kiss, kiss, kiss."

"I'm sorry," Ken said. "I love you."

Barbie then joined Ken in a seated position on the windowsill. The pair sat motionless for several minutes while Lytle headed downstairs to the kitchen for a juice box. Upon returning, she collected the reconciled dolls and threw them on the floor of the closet.

In the past week, Barbie and Ken have reenacted five parental fights. The most heated exchange came last Friday, when the dolls engaged in a screaming match over whether Barbie's sister Skipper should be allowed to come over any time she wants without calling. ∅

Above: A small sampling of Vartan's possessions.

shopping began in high school, when he bought a used sitting bath at a hospital surplus sale.

"I just thought it would be funny to use it for a chair," Vartan said. "Plus, it was only $3. At a garage sale a few days later, I found a bunch of copies of 'The Super Bowl Shuffle' for a dime apiece, and I gave them all out to my friends for Christmas. From that point on, I was hooked."

The habit grew worse in the spring

A typical trip to the supermarket for Vartan involves the purchase of at least one ironic foodstuff, such as Frank's Kraut Juice or Uncle Sam's cereal. When he returns home, he often pops open a can of Schlitz beer and unwinds with his prized laser-disc copy of Leonard Part 6 or a book of Lockhorns comic strips.

of 1996, when Vartan discovered eBay.

"Man, that blew my mind," said Vartan, who combs the popular auction site for ironic items almost daily. "I

couldn't believe the amazing stuff you could find on there. Like, about a month ago, I found this bootleg Wendy's employee-training video from the mid-'80s where this black kid does this how-to-cook-the-burgers rap. I shit you not."

A typical trip to the supermarket for Vartan involves the purchase of at least one ironic foodstuff, such as Frank's Kraut Juice or Uncle Sam's cereal. When he returns home, he often pops open a can of Schlitz beer and unwinds with his prized laser-disc copy of Leonard Part 6 or a book of Lockhorns comic strips.

Even when his financial situation is dire, Vartan has a hard time resisting ironic purchases.

"Last June, I found a $20 bill on the street," Vartan said. "I was totally psyched, because I was seriously hurting for cash at the time—I think I had, like, $5.85 in my checking account. I was going to put it in the bank, but on the way home I saw this shirt in the window of Ragstock that said, 'It's Not A Beer Belly, It's A Gas Tank For A Sex Machine.' Of course, I got the shirt and lost seven pounds that month because I ate nothing but rice and beans, so it was even more ironic."

Though he tends to gravitate toward pop-culture artifacts from the '70s and '80s, Vartan has recently taken to investing in contemporary items that he speculates will have future kitsch appeal.

"I spent $200 on a rare movie poster for the Italian version of The Adventures Of Pluto Nash," Vartan said. "I emptied out my bank account to get the money, and then I had to call the electric company and make up some excuse why I couldn't pay them this

month. That kinda sucked, but it's gonna be worth it in a few years when Pluto Nash is recognized as a classic on par with Battlefield Earth and

"I know I really should save for my future, but it's almost impossible with all the great crap you come across," Vartan said. "If I ever do manage to save enough money, though, I'd love to get a house in Celebration, FL, that freako Disney-planned community near Orlando."

Showgirls."

In spite of his misgivings, Vartan said he does not have any immediate plans to change his spending habits.

"I know I really should save for my future, but it's almost impossible with all the great crap you come across," Vartan said. "If I ever do manage to save enough money, though, I'd love to get a house in Celebration, FL, that freako Disney-planned community near Orlando. That place sounds so unbelievably weird and depressing, it'd be hilarious." ∅

Ask The Dauphin

By Crown Prince Phillippe Charles Louis François Leopold Auguste

Dear Dauphin,

This is a message for "Still Can't Believe It," whose 13-year-old dyed her hair pink the night before her Confirmation… GET OVER IT! It's just a little hair dye! It's not like your daughter uses drugs or held up a bank. It sounds like you've got a basically good kid who's going through a little phase, so relax and let her be her.

—Straight-Shooting
In Sherman Oaks

Dear Sherman Oaks,

I shan't! I shan't do my lessons! You are just a mere tutor, and you haven't the right to order about the future King like a common drudge! Horrid Latin! Beastly Geography! I would much rather be fencing or fox-hunting or engaged in pursuits befitting a great prince of a most divinely favored land. I shall be a man of destiny like my father the King, who does not concern himself with books and study and the queer prattlings of foolish bookworms and scribblers. He had that half-wit philosopher who blathers on about the "Rights of Man" imprisoned in the Dungeon, and that shall be your fate as well if you continue to place such ridiculous demands upon my royal person!

Dear Dauphin,

My husband says criminal tendencies are partially genetic. I say that's bull: Criminals are made, not born. Who's right? A steak dinner and tickets to a Packers game are riding on this one.

—Sure In Sheboygan

Dear Sheboygan,

Ah, Therese, my sweet sister, there you are! Come, let us play shuttlecock in the garden! How I adore you, dear Therese! Your locks shine like Papa's favorite bourbon as the candlelight glints off it. Oh, do not be cross, Therese; I was only being a sillybilly! Hee hee hee!

By the by, sister, yesterday Nurse said the most curious thing: She said that although I am the Dauphin, and you are Princess Royal, you cannot be my Queen! I grew quite cross with Nurse's impudence, Therese, for you yourself know how thick-headed she can be. I must not have known my fury, for Nurse started to tremble and weep so! Perhaps she feared I would start bleeding and not be able to stop, like that time when I pricked my finger on a thorny rose and was bedridden for days, do you remember? Be glad you do not share my curious condition, Therese.

O, now you weep, too, just as Nurse did? Therese, Therese, do not cry! You shall make me cry, and that would be most unbefitting the son of the King! Worry not—I may be small and sickly now, but one day I shall grow up big and strong just like Papa. I shall command my own regiment of fusilier—Papa has promised me so! Dear, dear Therese… I am sorry for likening your hair to Papa's bourbon. I despair ever so when you are upset, Therese. My only wish is for your happiness, for when you are blissful you are more beautiful than Venus herself. Come, Therese, let us retire to the garden to weave gardenia wreaths as Groom's son once showed us, and we will crown each other King and Queen for life… or you may read from your volume of Ovid as I lay my head in your delicate lap.

Dear Dauphin,

As your readers may know, this upcoming November is Prostate Awareness Month. Each year, tens of thousands of American men 50 and over are diagnosed with prostate cancer. In fact, it is the most common cause of death by cancer for men ages 75 and over. The good news is, survival is high if the disease is detected early. Studies also show that men who consume a low-fat diet and exercise regularly have a lower risk of developing the disease. These preventative measures, combined with annual screenings, can help ensure good prostate health for years to come.

—Surviving In Surreyville

Dear Surreyville,

Papa! It is most unspeakably intolerable, really it is! The Lord Chamberlain will not permit me to ride in my little carriage on the grounds today, even though Nurse dressed me in my nobby new riding-habit and boots! He told me I am obliged to stay indoors, as the peasants are once again demonstrating for bread outside the palace gates. If they did not spend their wages on drink, they would be able to feed themselves. Besides, they have no right to object to their sorry lot, for God made them inferior. Cardinal de Poucy told me so himself, and he is one of your most learned advisors. Yet they continue to be noisy and unruly, and their stench is horrible, too—have they never heard of cologne-water? Papa, I want you to fire your cannons at these noisome peasants so that I may once again ride in my little carriage. Mama told me I could carry my dress sword, too. Papa, who are these men who stand before you? They do not look like your

Your Horoscope

By Lloyd Schumner Sr.
Retired Machinist and
A.A.P.B.-Certified Astrologer

Aries: (March 21–April 19)
It will be hard for you to fill Dick Clark's shoes, so be sure to use a high-quality hydraulic cement.

Taurus: (April 20–May 20)
Your moodiness, lack of productivity, and wasteful habit of just riding around the main roads will get you fired from your job as a Wichita-area lineman.

Gemini: (May 21–June 21)
You will be the first one put up against the wall in next week's bloody revolution in skin care.

Cancer: (June 22–July 22)
It takes a lot to offend you, but you are profoundly outraged that Ricky Schroder is hosting the new *American Sportsman*.

Leo: (July 23–Aug. 22)
For the last time: Yes, there is a parasitic life form growing in some sort of pod deep inside your body, but this is perfectly normal for a pregnant woman.

Virgo: (Aug. 23–Sept. 22)
Tired of the austerity of modern architecture and disdainful of minimalist doctrine, you'll probably just stay home and order a pizza Thursday.

Libra: (Sept. 23–Oct. 23)
The gods, in their jealous wrath, will command you to perform the labors of Hercules next week, but it turns out to be a snap with the aid of modern technology.

Scorpio: (Oct. 24–Nov. 21)
Americans from coast to coast will be transfixed by your new signature dance, the Oh My God, Get It Off Me, Sweet Jesus, It Burns.

Sagittarius: (Nov. 22–Dec. 21)
You will come close to being a hero next Friday when you nearly push an old lady out of the way of a speeding bus.

Capricorn: (Dec. 22–Jan. 19)
Remember: Doing the right thing is nowhere near as important as whether others think you're cool.

Aquarius: (Jan. 20–Feb. 18)
You won't be too worried about the buildup of trinitrotolulene in your system, until you figure out that it's the scientific term for TNT.

Pisces: (Feb. 19–March 20)
Being an animated skeleton wouldn't be all that bad if it weren't for the incessant xylophone music.

ministers or courtiers. They dress coarsely, they wear no powdered wigs, and their eyes gleam a most unseemly shade of yellow. Why are they here, Papa? And why do they carry pikes?

Dear Dauphin,

I never thought I'd need to write you, but I have nowhere else to turn. I'm a 47-year-old woman who's losing her hair. As a woman, I never dreamed I'd have this problem. I can't stand the thought of wearing a wig, so I've recently taken to wearing a bandanna or baseball cap, but it looks ridiculous. Is there anything that can be done?

—Balding In Baldwin

Dear Baldwin,

Jailer? Jailer? If you please, Jailer, pray forgive my impertinence, but how fare Mama and Papa and the Princess Royal? I have not seen them for weeks since the coup. Pray forgive my speaking out of turn, but may I inquire as to their present condition? I know I am a very bad, wicked, spoiled, weak, miserable little boy, and that my father is an evil man who

feasted on the misery of his poor subjects and resembles a giant turnip. Only the people may master their own fate, and a mere accident of titled birthright mustn't preclude this. I understand it now.

Yet, I still wonder about Mama and Papa and the Princess Royal. Do they shiver as I do here in the Dungeon? I do wish someone would bring some wood so that I may have a fire. It need not be a big fire. I am only a small boy, and all I need is a small fire—just enough to warm my hands and perhaps drive away some of this damp. I think the damp is aggravating my cough. I'm sorry, Jailer sir, I'm sorry! I know I speak too much. I'll be quiet! Only please do not strike me! Please, nothing that will draw blood again. Please, sir! Forgive my impertinence! I am a spoiled, wicked boy! I shall speak no more, I promise!

Crown Prince Phillippe Charles Louis François Leopold Auguste is a syndicated advice columnist whose column, Ask The Dauphin, *appears in more than 250 newspapers nationwide.* ∅

Toll-Booth Girl Hit On Quickly

see LOCAL page 11C

Cable Ace Award Thrown Out In Apartment Move

see LOCAL page 4C

Sleeping Dom DeLuise Unaware Face Being Tickled By Lion's Tail

see PEOPLE page 5D

Nurse Has Amazing Medicine Cabinet

see LOCAL page 2C

STATshot

A look at the numbers that shape your world.

Least Healthy Fast-Food Items

1. BK Chicken-Fried Cheese Bricks
2. Pizza Hut Vodka Lover's Pizza
3. Wendy's Char-Grilled Styrofoam Carton
4. Taco Bell Lardito
5. Arby's Horseslaw
6. KFC "Just The Skin" Chicken Sandwich
7. Hardee's Tri-Gravy Smoothie
8. McDonald's biscuit with egg, cheese, sausage, egg, cheese, sausage

THE ONION • $2.00 US • $3.00 CAN

VOLUME 38 ISSUE 36 · AMERICA'S FINEST NEWS SOURCE™ · 3–9 OCTOBER 2002

Bush Seeks U.N. Support For 'U.S. Does Whatever It Wants' Plan

Above: Bush addresses the U.N. General Assembly.

UNITED NATIONS—In an address before the U.N. General Assembly Monday, President Bush called upon the international community to support his "U.S. Does Whatever It Wants" plan, which would permit the U.S. to take any action it wishes anywhere in the world at any time.

"As a shining beacon of freedom and democracy, America has inspired the world," said Bush in his 25-minute address. "With its military might, it has kept the peace and bravely defended the unalienable [sic] rights of millions around the globe. In this spirit, I call upon the world's nations to support my proposal to give America unrestricted carte

blanche to remove whatever leaders, plunder whatever resources, and impose whatever policies it deems necessary or expedient."

According to top Bush Administration officials, if the measure is passed by the U.N.—and possibly if it is not—the U.S. would immediately launch invasions of Iraq, North Korea, and Cuba; establish oil-drilling operations in Siberia; install nuclear-missile silos in Mongolia along the Chinese border; make English the official language of the planet; detain thousands of Middle Eastern nationals currently in the U.S. on temporary visas; begin each day with a moment of worldwide prayer; and pro-

see BUSH page 244

RIAA Sues Radio Stations For Giving Away Free Music

Above: One of the hundreds of radio stations being sued for distributing copyrighted music.

LOS ANGELES—The Recording Industry Association of America filed a $7.1 billion lawsuit against the nation's radio stations Monday, accusing them of freely distributing copyrighted music.

"It's criminal," RIAA president Hilary Rosen said. "Anyone at any time can simply turn on a radio and hear a copyrighted song. Making matters worse, these radio stations often play the best, catchiest song off the

see RIAA page 245

Huge Democracy Geek Even Votes In Primaries

NASHUA, NH—Politically engaged citizen David Haas, 25, described by friends and acquaintances as a "big democracy geek," even votes in primaries.

> "David votes in, like, mayoral and county-supervisor elections. How dorky is that?"

"I can understand voting in the big elections, like for president or governor, or maybe even senator," longtime friend Gregg Becher said Monday. "But David votes in, like, mayoral and county-supervisor elections. How dorky is that?"

The right to vote, as guaranteed in the Constitution, is among the hallmarks of the American democratic system. But Haas has exercised his franchise rights to an embarrassing extreme, voting in every federal, state, and local election since he turned 18.

"Normally, David's a reliable, punctual employee," said Dorothy Raubel, owner of Raubel Garden Center, where Haas has worked for the past

Above: Haas casts his vote in some obscure Sept. 10 election.

seven years. "But then there's that occasional Tuesday morning in April or November when he calls in saying he'll be late to work. It's a strange habit, but we've all grown accustomed to it by now."

Haas prides himself on being an informed voter, making sure to familiarize himself with candidates' positions before casting a vote. A self-described "independent" who tends to

see GEEK page 244

The NYC Smoking Ban

New York is one of a number of U.S. cities considering a ban on smoking in restaurants and bars. What do *you* think?

Shelly Sabel
Lighting Designer

"This is a victory for annoying people like me who call cigarettes 'coffin nails' and 'cancer sticks' and all that sort of stuff."

Jim Mackil
Systems Analyst

"Now that New York has addressed the problem of secondhand smoke, maybe they'll tackle the problem of secondhand human-waste stench."

Jef Awada
Real-Estate Agent

"Has Amnesty International heard about this?"

Dennis McCormack
Advertising Executive

"But what will I draw slowly on to indicate that I'm contemplating what's been said by my dinner companion?"

Tom Epstein
Actor

"I can't stand cigarette smoke, but no one seems to care down at the Drink & Smoke & Drink & Smoke Tavern."

Elizabeth Gabbay
Waitress

"As a bar waitress, I'm glad someone is protecting my right to work in a bar that doesn't make any money."

Stephen King Calls It Quits

Author Stephen King recently announced he will quit writing after publishing five more books. How does the King Of Horror plan to spend his retirement?

- Devote more time to getting rammed by vans
- Trim front-yard hedges under alias of Richard Bachman
- Learn how to build ship in a bottle, make thousands of them
- Finally get around to cleaning out that back room where for years he'd been throwing shopping bags full of cash
- Spend more time terrifying family
- Walk slowly down basement steps, each step creaking ominously as he descends into the darkness, to grab the weed whacker
- Hit his boneless leg over and over with hammer
- Rid flower garden of woodchucks in most disturbing way possible
- Scream "No! No! Never again!" at typewriter for six hours a day

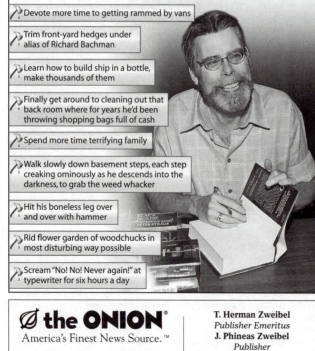

the ONION®
America's Finest News Source.™

Herman Ulysses Zweibel
Founder

T. Herman Zweibel
Publisher Emeritus
J. Phineas Zweibel
Publisher
Maxwell Prescott Zweibel
Editor-In-Chief

242

I Am The 'Top Gun' Of Commercial Airline Pilots

I've been piloting DCs and 7s for American Airlines going on 15 years now, and I don't mind telling you, I'm the best there is. The Navy's flight

**By Capt.
Ron "Mongoose" Haller
American Airlines**

school can only have one "Top Gun," and the same is true in commercial aviation. There are many great pilots at American and the other airlines, but none have the speed, wits,

and solid-brass balls that I do. That's right, Capt. Ron "Mongoose" Haller is the Top Gun of airline pilots.

To date, I've captained 2,947 domestic flights, and every single one arrived on time. Weather delays, safety procedures, FAA orders—it takes a hell of a lot more than all that to ground Mongoose, baby.

What's my secret? Nothing fancy, no hocus pocus. I just know my shit—and treat the plane like a beautiful woman.

One time, on a coast-to-coast, Engine Three went out over the Rockies. According to procedure, I'm supposed to radio a distress and land at the nearest airport. But I said to hell with that: Call me a wild card, a loose cannon, but Mongoose has never been one who slavishly follows "proper procedure." Besides, I've got 241 passengers who need to get to Frisco.

What's my secret? Nothing fancy, no hocus pocus. I just know my shit—and treat the plane like a beautiful woman.

I kept that bird up for 500 more miles and landed 12 minutes early.

Now, the pinstripers weren't too thrilled about that, but I know how to keep them at bay. They can threaten to bust me down to Navigator, but I know they'd never actually go through with it. Why? Because I'm the best they've got.

Then there was Flight 701 from Dulles to JFK a couple years back. We taxied almost 40 minutes late, and still those gutless sonofabitch controllers tried to put me in a takeoff queue. I knew the flight could land on time if I went for it, so I cut across the median and grabbed Runway F, which was down for routine mainte-

nance. The lead controller screamed a blue streak, but I got those passengers into Terminal C three minutes ahead of schedule. To this day, the FAA still rides my ass about that one, carrying on with their by-the-book bullshit.

I'll tell you the real reason for my being on the FAA's shit list. Let's just say Chief Boswell still hasn't forgotten about a little "incident" in flight school 20 years ago.

It was Aug. 14, 1982. I was a cocky

Don't get me wrong, I believe in the importance of rules and regulations for protecting clueless greenhorn pilots from themselves. But we're talking about Mongoose here.

---

young buck then, at the stick of a DC-9 for the first time in my life. Boswell was my instructor. At 13,000 feet and climbing, he radios me to cut the fuel and land because of a radar problem on their end. Like I'm gonna cut my flight just because their damn ears are off. So I kept climbing to 20K, until that zero-visibility pinhead threatened to expel and blacklist me from every flight school in the country if I didn't make nice and come down.

Well, I knew when I was beaten, but I got the last word by buzzing the tower, pulling away at the last possible second. I swear I saw that hardass dive under the console for cover, right in front of the CEO of Boeing. Later on, I heard Boswell was wearing different pants for the rest of the day. He never forgave me for humiliating him like that, and I only made it worse six years ago by taking the sexy stewardess he was looking to score with to the Norfolk Hilton for a night of sweet Mongoose Love. He's never forgotten that (and neither has that stewardess, I'm sure). To this day, Boswell rides my ass about every last rule in the book, every chance he gets.

Don't get me wrong, I believe in the importance of rules and regulations for protecting clueless greenhorn pilots from themselves. But we're talking about Mongoose here. I laugh at air pockets. Turbulence is a walk in the park for me. Once, when a blizzard was approaching the East Coast, I maxed all the engines and went from LAX to Logan in five hours, still a passenger-aviation record. Did I

see PILOT page 246

Temp Hides Fun, Fulfilling Life From Rest Of Office

BOSTON—Ty Braxton, 23, continues to hide his fun and fulfilling life from the full-time employees of Hale & Dorr, the Boston law firm for which he has temped since July.

"At a job like this, where you're surrounded by angry, perpetually stressed-out lawyers who are working 80 hours a week, it's important to hide the fact that you're enjoying a normal, balanced, happy life," Braxton said Monday. "People get really pissed when they hear stuff like that."

Braxton, who earns roughly one-fourth of what the firm's lowest-seniority full-time employees make, said he has no desire to make his coworkers feel bad about their "boring, shitty lives."

"If somebody complains about how bad it sucks to work overtime five days straight, I just nod and agree," said Braxton, who spends his weeknights at parties, at concerts, and playing basketball in the park. "No point in rubbing in the fact that no matter how busy things are, I leave at exactly 5 p.m. every single day. If anyone asks me to stay later, I just say my agency doesn't let me do overtime."

After graduating from Wesleyan University in May 2000 with a degree in Russian literature, Braxton worked a series of part-time jobs in and around Boston. In December 2001, he signed on with QualiTemps, the city's largest supplier of temporary office labor, which currently pays him $8.44 per hour.

"I have so much going on in my life right now," Braxton said. "I'm helping a friend start up a little Cajun food stand, I've gotten way into this Russian poet Mayakovsky, and I've been

> "If I had a great time staying out until 4 in the morning the night before, I make sure to wipe away all traces of a smile before I walk in these doors," Braxton said. "If anyone found out I'm not living a hellish existence like they are, I'd be asking for trouble."

hanging out with this really cool girl I met when my band, Sophie Drillteam, did a show with hers. Honestly, I just don't have the time or energy to put into some job."

In spite of his happiness, Braxton said he makes sure always to project an air of dissatisfaction, in both facial expression and posture, while

Above: The happily underemployed Braxton.

in the office.

"If I had a great time staying out until 4 in the morning the night before, I make sure to wipe away all traces of a smile before I walk in these doors," Braxton said. "If anyone found out I'm not living a hellish existence like they are, I'd be asking for trouble."

Braxton is also careful about engaging his coworkers in conversation.

"I stopped talking about movies, because no one here ever goes to them," Braxton said. "Every time I mention a movie to someone, I have to sit there and listen to them go through the process of figuring out the last movie they saw. The other day, Andrew Walser, this intellectual-property attorney who's trying to make partner, told me that his last movie was *Gladiator*. I was like, 'Oh, man, that's depressing.'"

In his long-term temp assignment as

see TEMP page 245

Large Dependent Film Tops Weekend Box Office

HOLLYWOOD, CA—In what is being hailed as a triumph for dependent cinema, Sony Pictures' *A Perfect Alibi*, a $90 million Mel Gibson-Cameron Diaz thriller, topped the weekend box office with an impressive $39 million take. "This just shows what can be accomplished when you've got a major studio's backing and distribution," executive producer Don Murray said Monday. "Contrary to what some in the movie business would have you believe, there is a place for big, non-character-driven pictures." Murray said he hopes the film's success serves as an inspiration to established, bankable actors and directors.

Band Loudly Discusses Record Deal At IHOP

AKRON, OH—The five members of Ratchet Chunk, close to finalizing a deal with Columbus-based Ripchord Records, loudly discussed the deal at the Polk Road IHOP Monday. "We've got to insist on 60 percent of the gross," said bassist Gavin Lee, speaking loudly enough for the high-school girls three booths over to hear. "If they try to go 50-50, I say we take our demo to Dimebag [Records]." Lead singer Kris Maldonado added that he should receive co-producer credit for the album, as the demo was burned on his iMac.

Tokyo Squeezes In Five More Residents

TOKYO—Tokyo somehow managed to squeeze in five more residents Monday, when the Takashi family moved into a converted studio apartment. "This was a one-bedroom apartment housing a family of six, but a wall was cleverly constructed to create a small studio," city planning minister Hideki Kumagai said. "This was good: We rarely can fit new citizenry into our city without drilling into the bedrock." The Takashi family, brought in from Osaka's overflow, will pay the equivalent of $12,600 monthly for 144 square feet of living space.

Purchase Justified By Theoretical $50 Rebate

LAKESIDE, VA—The theoretical possibility of receiving a $50 mail-in rebate motivated shopper Jim Crewes, 28, to purchase a color printer Monday. "I really can't afford to be buying computer equipment right now," Crewes said. "But if I buy the printer and two toner refills, and save the receipt and UPC symbols from all the boxes and buy two more Pitney Bowes products and save those receipts and symbols, and then send it all in with the original rebate coupon, and the offer's still good by then, I'm looking at 50 smackers." Crewes was also swayed by the printer's extended-warranty option, which provides free service and repairs if the printer broke and he actually shipped it back to its manufacturer, which he never would.

Cage Match Settles Nothing

PONTIAC, MI—The long-awaited steel-cage match between World Wrestling Entertainment rivals Violator and Psycho Sid, widely expected to settle a bitter dispute between the two, settled nothing Monday. "After all the accusations and insults exchanged between these men, I really had high hopes that this cage match would, at long last, provide some resolution and maybe even a sense of closure," WWE fan Jordan Bumpers said. "Yet, strangely, I feel like they're no closer to understanding each other's point of view than before they entered the cage." Psycho Sid, who lost the match by disqualification, continues to insist that he is the superior wrestler, a claim with which Violator vehemently disagreed. ∅

favor Democratic candidates, he can summarize the basic position of both major parties on most issues. As a result, Haas has endured the mockery and derision of those around him.

"On Sept. 10, he showed up late to

Though it's not clear why Haas insists on voting in every election, there is no shortage of speculation.

work, and you could just tell he'd been voting," coworker Mike Summers said. "He was holding something in his hand, and we were like, 'Hey,

Haasenpfeffer, whatcha got there?' He said it was the League of Women Voters candidate guide. So Rob [Mularkey] says, 'League of Women Voters? Now I know why you vote so much—you want to horn in on that hot women-voter action!' David didn't even smile; he just got all huffy and said the guide was from the morning paper, and that copies were available to the public."

Richard Prohaska, Haas' next-door neighbor, can attest to Haas' strange dedication to the American political process. Over the years, he said he has seen Haas get into numerous doorstep discussions with campaign workers and canvassing local politicians.

"About two months ago, some alderwoman who was up for reelection

was going door-to-door passing out leaflets," Prohaska said. "I took one, thanked her, and closed the door as

"On Sept. 10, he showed up late to work, and you could just tell he'd been voting," coworker Mike Summers said.

fast as I could. About 30 minutes later, I'm backing the car out of the garage to wash it, and there's David talking to her on his porch. I go to get the hose, and when I come back, he's

actually inviting her into his home. I was half-done waxing when she finally came out. Either they had one hell of a quickie, or David cares deeply about local politics. Knowing him, it was definitely the latter."

Though it's not clear why Haas insists on voting in every election, there is no shortage of speculation.

"My guess is, it's his way of hiding from the real world," said Jennifer Thorsten, Haas' sister. "He's always been interested in politics. He was on the debate team in high school and got a B.A. in poli sci in college. I've tried to get him to skip an election, but he never does. He says that only by exercising our democratic freedoms do we keep our democracy healthy and vital. Whatever, David." ∅

hibit Japan and Germany from manufacturing automobiles.

In addition, no demonstration against U.S. actions by any foreign nation or individual would be permitted. Any such protestation would be deemed a high crime subject to a U.N. tribunal, with those found guilty flown to Texas for execution by lethal injection.

"After the unspeakable events of last Sept. 11, the U.S. was deeply touched by the outpouring of support and condolences from our neighbors and allies the world over," Bush said. "This kindness played a vital role in our national healing process, but, more importantly, it cemented our long-standing self-image as *the* country, with all other nations lumped together into a vague, foreign Other Place. I call upon you now to join us in our vision of America as the only country whose wishes matter."

Bush then turned to the pressing

issue of Iraq.

"Despite repeated American efforts to change the situation, Saddam Hussein defiantly continues his longtime

"Saddam Hussein defiantly continues his longtime policy of being the president of Iraq," Bush said. "The time has come for this man to step down, because we want him to."

policy of being the president of Iraq," Bush said. "The time has come for this man to step down, because we want him to."

In addition to enabling the U.S. to address foreign crises, Bush said his plan will help solve many of the nation's domestic problems.

"While there exist many grave threats to America abroad, we suffer still more problems—from unemployment to a lack of quality, affordable housing—right here at home," Bush said. "After this resolution is passed, we will begin a 10-year project to clean out our nation's landfills and toxic-waste sites, transport the materials to Central American jungles, and build low-cost housing on the newly cleared land. This would solve the housing shortage, create thousands of construction jobs, and improve our nation's environment, all in one fell swoop."

As much of a boon as it would be to America, Bush stressed that his plan will also benefit the rest of the world, giving foreigners greater access than ever to American goods and entertainment.

"From the Beijing businessman who treats his family to dinner at KFC to the New Delhi textile worker who unwinds after a hard day's work by watching *Friends*, the world community has embraced our many wonderful cultural and commercial exports," Bush said. "As part of my plan, the U.S. will be allowed to export its products tariff-free, while other countries' goods will be subject to heavy taxes. This will help ensure that people the world over will continue to enjoy our computers, DVDs, and soft drinks, free of the clutter of competing non-American goods on their store shelves."

As much of a boon as it would be to America, Bush stressed that his plan will also benefit the rest of the world, giving foreigners greater access than ever to American goods and entertainment.

Bush concluded his speech by calling on the U.N. to fly an extra-large U.S. flag outside its headquarters, high above the other member nations' flags.

"From the Monroe Doctrine to our ignoring of the Kyoto Treaty, America has always boldly defied the powers that be. Ever since its founding, this great nation has courageously asserted its will, bravely tuning out the objections of the other nations of the world," Bush said at the speech's conclusion. "I urge you today, do not let that legacy die. Allow us to continue our long-standing tradition of getting our way."

Global reaction to Bush's plan has been mixed, with 56 percent of Americans in support and 100 percent of non-Americans strongly opposed. ∅

Above: A sampling of the details of the Bush plan.

Above: RIAA president Hilary Rosen and attorney Russell Frackman answer questions in a Los Angeles courthouse.

album over and over until people get sick of it. Where is the incentive for people to go out and buy the album?"

According to Rosen, the radio stations acquire copies of RIAA artists' CDs and then broadcast them using a special transmitter, making it possible for anyone with a compatible radio-wave receiver to listen to the songs.

"These radio stations are extremely popular," Rosen said. "They flagrantly string our songs together in 'uninterrupted music blocks' of up to 70 minutes in length, broadcasting nearly one CD's worth of product without a break, and they actually have the gall

> **For the record companies and the RIAA, one of the most disturbing aspects of the radio-station broadcasts is that anyone with a receiver and an analog tape recorder can record the music and play it back at will.**

to allow businesses to advertise between songs. It's bad enough that they're giving away our music for free, but they're actually making a profit off this scheme."

RIAA attorney Russell Frackman said the lawsuit is intended to protect the artists.

"If this radio trend continues, it will severely damage a musician's ability to earn a living off his music," Frackman said. "[Metallica drummer] Lars Ulrich stopped in the other day won-

dering why his last royalty check was so small, and I didn't know what to say. How do you tell a man who's devoted his whole life to his music that someone is able to just give it away for free? That pirates are taking away his right to support himself with his craft?"

For the record companies and the RIAA, one of the most disturbing aspects of the radio-station broadcasts is that anyone with a receiver and an analog tape recorder can record the music and play it back at will.

"I've heard reports that children as young as 8 tape radio broadcasts for their own personal use," Rosen said. "They listen to a channel that has a limited rotation of only the most popular songs—commonly called 'Top 40' stations—then hit the 'record' button when they hear the opening strains of the song they want. And how much are they paying for these songs? A big fat zip."

Continued Rosen: "According to our research, there is one of these Top 40 stations in every major city in the country. This has to be stopped before the music industry's entire economic infrastructure collapses."

Especially distressing to the RIAA are radio stations' "all-request hours," when listeners call in to ask radio announcers, or "disc jockeys," to play a certain song.

"What's the point of putting out a new Ja Rule or Sum 41 album if people can just call up and hear any song off the album that they want?" Frackman asked. "In some instances, these stations actually have the nerve to let the caller 'dedicate' his act of thievery to a friend or lover. Could you imagine a bank letting somebody rob its vaults and then allowing the thief to thank his girlfriend Tricia and the whole gang down at Bumpy's?"

Defenders of radio-based music distribution insist that the relatively poor

sound quality of radio broadcasts negates the record companies' charges.

"Radio doesn't have the same sound quality as a CD," said Paul "Cubby" Bryant, music director of New York radio station Z100, one of the nation's largest distributors of free music and a defendant in the suit. "Real music lovers will still buy CDs. If anything,

> **"According to our research, there is one of these Top 40 stations in every major city in the country. This has to be stopped before the music industry's entire economic infrastructure collapses."**

we're exposing people to music they might not otherwise hear. These record companies should be thanking us, not suing us."

Outraged by the RIAA suit, many radio listeners are threatening to boycott the record companies.

"All these companies care about is profits," said Amy Legrand, 21, an avid Jacksonville, FL, radio user who surreptitiously records up to 10 songs a day off the radio. "Top 40 radio is taking the power out of the hands of the Ahmet Erteguns of the world and bringing it back to the people of Clear Channel and Infinity Broadcasting. It's about time somebody finally stood up to those record-company fascists." Ø

conference coordinator at Hale & Dorr, Braxton schedules employee use of the firm's five common meeting rooms and is responsible for keeping the rooms stocked with cold refreshments and snacks. His other primary duty is to procure audio-visual equipment for meetings when requested, a situation that arises "only, like, one or two times a month."

"People e-mail me about needing rooms, and I have to e-mail them back with room assignments," Braxton said. "I also have to post the schedule on the meeting-room doors and order paper cups and things. All in all, though, it's pretty easy. Everybody's usually way too busy to give me any work to do, anyway."

During his three to four hours of "down time" each work day, Braxton reads, surfs the web, and e-mails friends. He also works on long-term personal projects. Over the past six weeks, Braxton has translated 41 pages of Alexander Pushkin's unfinished novel *Dubrovsky* for a new English version he dreams of one day publishing.

Braxton has never mentioned his translation project to coworkers, nor has he mentioned any of his other pursuits.

"I don't want to rub in how much I get to do the things I want to do," Braxton said. "I feel sorry for them. They go home after a hard day, and they're so fried they just spend the night sitting in front of the TV. You know how these people spend their weekends? Resting. They *rest*."

Another advantage Braxton enjoys over the full-timers is a significantly more relaxed dress code.

"They're always on the way to the dry cleaners or the barber or shopping for another expensive suit," said Braxton, who estimates that his average coworker spends five hours a week maintaining his or her personal appearance. "As long as I wear deodorant, keep my tie reasonably clean, and wash my one pair of Dockers over the weekend, no one really gives a shit what I look like."

In his efforts to hide his happy, fulfilling life from his coworkers, Braxton has even resorted to lying.

"Just yesterday, somebody asked me about my last temp job," Braxton said. "It ended in May, but I told them it ended in June. See, after it ended, I took about a month off and just kind of dicked around, traveling around Europe until my money ran out. I knew not to mention that to people who won't be able to do anything like that until they're 65."

Though Braxton said he sympathizes with his coworkers, he added that the decision to pursue a prestigious, high-paying career path was entirely their own.

"They wanted to go for the brass ring and really live the good life," Braxton said. "What they don't seem to get is that the key to living the good life is to avoid that brass ring like the fucking plague." Ø

245

Conan 'Conanquers' The Emmys!

**The Outside Scoop
By Jackie Harvey**

Item! It's a week later, and everybody's still buzzing about the star-packed Emmys. **"According To"** Jim Belushi was there, as was TV's reigning golden couple **Jane Kaczyzmarezk** and **the guy from The West Wing**. And who ever expected to see **Kelsey Grammar** at an Emmy ceremony? But the real star of the evening was the host himself, **Mr. Conan O'Brian**, who "conanquered" any doubts about whether he has what it takes to shine in prime time. "Conangratulations," Conan!

I saw **Austin Powers 3: Guildmember**, and it delivered thrills, surprises, and plenty of great jokes involving pee-pee, doo-doo, and a certain male body part that begins with "p" and ends with "s" (and it's not the pancreas)! It was rich! At one point, the titular villain rollerskates, just like I did when I was living through the '70s, only I was not as successful with the ladies. I don't know how funnyman **Michael Meyers** is going to top this, but I'll be first in line for **Austin Powers 4: Dr. Weiner And The Two Nuts**.

Item! Martha Stewart is still in hot water and, once again, I need to weigh in on this matter. I know we have to take a hard look at corporate crime, what with companies like Enron, Tyco, and Disney cooking the books. But don't we have enough big fish to worry about without picking on a lady who's done so much to make America a prettier, better-smelling place to live? Let's not make an example of her just because she's a

> ## Call me Jackie LaLanne, but I just can't get enough of those power bars! Talk about a perfect on-the-go snack for on-the-go people.

celebrity. Lay off already!

You never think to buy an **eraser** when you're in the store, but it's one of those things you never have around when you actually need it. Know what I mean?

Item! My Big Fat Greek Wedding is the big fat Greek hit of the summer! Who knew America was so hungry for a funny, lighthearted look at the second biggest step a person can take in their lives? Either that, or there are more big fat Greeks out there than I

thought.

Speaking of being hungry for Greek, get me to the nearest falafel stand—I'm famished!

Item! The Sopranos is back after a long time away, and I for one couldn't be happier. Like millions of Americans, I can't wait to find out what's been happening to **Tony**, **Uncle Kracker**, and **Fat Pussy** over the last year and a half. I have a lot of catching up to do since I had to get rid of

> ## Don't we have enough big fish to worry about without picking on a lady who's done so much to make America a prettier, better-smelling place to live? Let's not make an example of her just because she's a celebrity.

my cable a while ago and missed all of last season. Good thing they're all out on video, but *The Sopranos* is about eighth on my must-see list, after the **Sex In The City** videos, **In Like Flint**, and the **Tears For Fears** video collection.

To all those **child abductors and killers** out there, I've got just one thing to say: Enough!

I've been thinking about getting a new computer lately, and I'm really torn. There are those Apple commercials that say I should switch to Mac, and they make some pretty good points, but that Dell guy makes a convincing argument, too. I guess I'll wait until the prices come down again, because, to be honest, Jackie Harvey is rich with hot Tinseltown gossip, but not so rich with money. Hint, hint.

Item! A little bird told me that **Matt Affleck** is dating **Jennifer "Left Eye" Lopez**, and I couldn't be more excited. I loved Matt in **The Sum Of All The Pretty Horse Whisperers**, and I've worn out the grooves on J. Lo's latest hit CD. Could wedding bells be in their future? Check here for more on that later!

Item! Llance Bass from **In Sync** is no **Major Tom**. **The Russians** booted the brave "Buy Buy Buy" band boy because his sponsors couldn't come up with the required money. With all the celebrity charity events going on, you'd think it wouldn't be hard to raise $20 million to help a pop star get into space. It's sad to think of all the beautiful songs about the heavens that we'll never hear because Llance will have no inspiration to write them. Oh, well, our loss. Maybe we'll get

some money together by the time **Aaron Carter** is old enough to don a spaceman suit. (I can dream, can't I?)

Call me **Jackie LaLanne**, but I just can't get enough of those **power bars**! Talk about a perfect on-the-go snack for on-the-go people.

Just when we thought we'd heard the last of rapper **Two-Pack Shaker**, we get another layer to this rich story. **Some journalists in California** did some digging and found that archrival **Notary B.I.G.** may have had a part in Two-Pack's 1996 Las Vegas murder. I don't want to give an opinion just yet. Journalists shouldn't have the right to declare someone's guilt or innocence until all the facts are in. Just look at how the press handled the **O.J. Simpson** case! So I, for one, will wait for the **American justice system** to decide.

Well, that's it for this edition of **The Outside Scoop**. I have to go out and turn over some rocks, because that's where the best dirt can be found, and that's what you loyal Harveyheads demand of me. So, until next time, keep on dreaming those **Hollywood dreams**, and keep it on the Outside! ✍

Your Horoscope

**By Lloyd Schumner Sr.
Retired Machinist and
A.A.P.B.-Certified Astrologer**

Aries: (March 21–April 19)
Somehow, it's even more insulting that the circus to which you've been sold is huge in Finland.

Taurus: (April 20–May 20)
You'll go crazy if you can't remember the other good song by Question Mark & The Mysterians. Which is too bad, because Taurus isn't going to help you.

Gemini: (May 21–June 21)
You realize that it's pointless to worry about dying before your time. You've been way ahead of schedule for years now.

Cancer: (June 22–July 22)
Not that anyone asked them, but the stars believe that a pair of squabbling adult stepsisters sharing an apartment is a great idea for a sitcom.

Leo: (July 23–Aug. 22)
You have very little say in your fate or what will eventually befall you, but don't let that keep you from voting.

Virgo: (Aug. 23–Sept. 22)
Just so you know, fate doesn't necessarily have something special in store for you just because nothing particularly notable has happened to you yet.

Libra: (Sept. 23–Oct. 23)
This week will be unlike any you've ever experienced, but that has a lot less to do with you than it does the flaws in the space-time continuum.

Scorpio: (Oct. 24–Nov. 21)
You deserve to burn to death screaming in front of a national TV audience. If it's any consolation, it would have happened whether you'd deserved it or not.

Sagittarius: (Nov. 22–Dec. 21)
Charles Durning will soon contact you to reiterate that he has no intention of ever working with you.

Capricorn: (Dec. 22–Jan. 19)
It will be too late by the time you read this, but you became severely allergic to shellfish somewhere along the way.

Aquarius: (Jan. 20–Feb. 18)
You've always believed that anyone can be forgiven, but you'll find it hard to apply to the busload of sailors currently going down on your mom.

Pisces: (Feb. 19–March 20)
Time was, if a mysterious fungus started to overgrow your house, you'd have done something. But you've learned a lot about yourself this past year.

PILOT from page 242

break a sweat? Hell, no. I had Steel copiloting. With the Steel-Man to my right, I could scratch a cockroach's back with a 747 and still land at O'Hare under the gun.

I have no patience for suits riding my ass about "the book says this" or "regulations say that." Or "a standard-issue Captain's hat does not have claws embroidered on it" or "every passenger on that flight has joined a class-action suit because they believed they were going to die." Hell, if those passengers don't think flying under the St. Louis Arch at 600 mph makes for a great story, they don't deserve to fly Mongoose Air.

People say I'd be good enough to fly Air Force One if I weren't such a pistol. That's no skin off my ass. Let some namby-pamby milquetoast Air Force honors-student be a once-a-month chauffeur for the world's most overpaid kingfish. Mongoose serves the people.

I gotta admit, though, just once I'd love to strap on one of those Concordes. ✍

Frank Gehry No Longer Allowed To Make Sandwiches For Grandkids

see ARCHITECTURE page 10D

Horatio Sanz Sweeps Latin Emmys

see TELEVISION page 9C

Daughter's Name Misspelled On Emergency-Room Form

see LOCAL page 2E

STATshot

A look at the numbers that shape your world.

Top-Selling Executive Gifts

1. "I Can Buy And Sell You" memo pad
2. Gold-plated clicky-clack ball thingy
3. Sun Tzu's *The Art Of War For Golfers*
4. Electronic "smart" paperweight
5. Voice-activated sexual harasser
6. Briefcase full of $100 bills
7. Asshole polish

You Screwed 'Em!

THE ONION • $2.00 US • $3.00 CAN

the ONION®

VOLUME 38 ISSUE 37   AMERICA'S FINEST NEWS SOURCE™   10–16 OCTOBER 2002

Newly Out Gay Man Overdoing It

PENSACOLA, FL—Calling his flamboyant air and effeminate mannerisms "a bit forced," friends of recently out-of-the-closet homosexual Mark Glynn, 23, say he's overdoing it.

"When Mark first told us he was gay, everybody was totally cool with it," longtime friend Rich Eddy said. "We figured he'd basically be the same old Mark, except he'd be dating guys. Boy, were we wrong."

Though Glynn's friends expected him to become comfortable and open with his sexuality, they did not expect him to go to such great lengths to proclaim his preference for men at every conceivable turn.

"We just figured he'd start saying stuff to us at bars like, 'Check out that cute guy's butt,'" Eddy said. "But he takes pains to telegraph his gayness 24 hours a day. Last night, a bunch of us were talking about what's going on with Bush and Iraq, when, out of nowhere, he says, 'You know what Bush needs? A good ass-fucking. That'd relax him.' It's like, 'Okay, Mark, we get it already—*you're gay.*'"

Continued Eddy: "It's like he's scared that if he doesn't wear hot pants and say 'You go, girl!' a lot, somebody might think he's straight."

Lydia Richter, another longtime

see GAY MAN page 250

Above: Glynn rollerblades in one of his new ensembles.

Starving Third World Masses Warned Against Evils Of Contraception

Above: Children wait in line for food from relief workers in Bangladesh. Right: Cardinal Bevilacqua.

SÃO PAULO, BRAZIL—During a visit to the teeming slums of São Paulo Monday, Cardinal Anthony Bevilacqua warned the city's starving masses against the evils of contraception, urging them to "be fruitful and multiply" and do "everything in [their] power" to resist the mortal sin of birth control.

"In Genesis, God commands us to be fruitful and multiply, to fill the Earth and subdue it, and to have dominion over the fish and birds and every other living thing," said Bevilacqua, speaking before more than 200,000 malnourished São Paulo slum dwellers. "It is not for man to decide whether the world should have more

see CONTRACEPTION page 251

Gambling-Addiction Study Gets Out Of Hand

LAS VEGAS, NV—A gambling-addiction study by researchers at UNLV's Gaming Studies Research Center has "gotten way out of hand," sources close to the project reported Monday.

"Just one more sample group," said study director Robert Layton, nervously snapping the clasp of his lucky clipboard. "I have a hunch about this batch, a real hunch. I think it's gonna be a honey."

Addiction & Behavior

Layton, who has been conducting research in the lab and the field since March 2001, is studying relapse rates in habituated long-term gamblers. He is aided in his research by colleagues Dr. Steven "Shooter" Ojeda, Dr. "Big"

Arnold Stangel, and non-faculty laboratory assistant Fancy Nancy, who was enlisted in the belief that she might, for reasons unknown, have a favorable effect on results.

The study, which is now nearly $10 million over budget, was supposed to have been completed by this past May. Layton continues to gather data, however, insisting that the big breakthrough, or "payoff," is just around the

see GAMBLING page 250

The Preemptive-Strike Debate

President Bush's standoff with Iraq has prompted debate over whether preemptive strikes are a justifiable U.S. military option. What do *you* think?

"Those Iraqis have had it coming for a long time, suffering under the oppressive rule of a maniacal tyrant like that."

Jon Gordimer
Delivery Driver

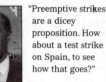

"Preemptive strikes are a dicey proposition. How about a test strike on Spain, to see how that goes?"

George Banks
Systems Analyst

"Who's going to stop us, I ask you? The rest of the world? Excuse me while I laugh."

Craig Utrecht
Cashier

"What other choice do we have? We've already exhausted every possible effort to find bin Laden."

Eileen Stavros
Librarian

"If we don't take decisive action now, we run the risk of countless Iraqis continuing to live."

Rachel Eckert
English Teacher

"Hey, if you've got a fucking problem with it, you can talk to my fucking fist. I'll be in the Senate chambers."

Stephen Edwards
Legislator

Snoop Dogg Goes Clean

After years of heavy smoking, rapper Snoop Dogg recently announced that he is giving up marijuana. What has the rapper been up to since quitting?

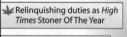
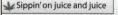

- Sippin' on juice and juice
- Relinquishing duties as *High Times* Stoner Of The Year
- Inviting the Mortensens over for dinner
- Turning collection of six-foot bongs into Habitrail for kids' gerbil
- Going on "Da Pizatch"
- Realizing he now has nothing to say to Willie Nelson
- Affixing "I Brake For Garage Sales" bumper sticker to Escalade
- Concentrating on appearing in family-friendly pornography
- Only using word "chronic" in reference to lower-back pain

∅ the ONION®
America's Finest News Source.™

Herman Ulysses Zweibel
Founder

T. Herman Zweibel
Publisher Emeritus
J. Phineas Zweibel
Publisher
Maxwell Prescott Zweibel
Editor-In-Chief

Point-Counterpoint: Wines

You Know, There Are Some Excellent Red Wines Coming Out Of Argentina

So, what do you think of the wine? To be honest, I thought it was a little meek. Passable, but meek. Did you happen to catch what kind it was?

By Kip Quinlana

Obviously, it's a cabernet, but I can't quite put my finger on the vineyard. Wherever it's from, it's certainly not the best I've had. If our hosts wanted something nice, they might have done better with something from Argentina. A lot of people don't know this, but there are some excellent red wines coming out of Argentina right now. Most people don't think of Argentina as wine country, but you'd be amazed. There's more to that country than the *pampas* and *gauchos*.

If you ask me, Argentine wines are highly undervalued. The Mendoza region is on par with the Simi Valley of California. For whatever reason, the Malbec grape just does really well there. It's got a really fruity bouquet, but don't hold that against it. The '99 Trapiche Iscay Merlot-Malbec offsets that fruitiness nicely. If you ever have the chance to buy a case, do not pass it up. I read in *Wine Spectator* that it's going to be the next hot vintage and will be quite hard to come by soon.

Hold still—I think you have some-

Argentine wines are highly undervalued.

thing on your sweater. There. Got it.

This is a great time for wine drinkers. I mean, we have so many options and choices available. And with the world economy in the toilet, there's no shortage of great wines at great prices. It would be criminal not to take advantage of it.

If you're interested in trying some Argentine wines, you could come over for a private tasting. I'd be happy to let you sample my stock. After all, my wine cellar's gotten so full, I could really use some help clearing a little room! Anyway, here's my card. Call me any time. I'm there all week, except when I'm on the boat. ∅

I Hate You, I Hate You, I Hate You

Is that right? Are there some excellent wines coming out of Argentina these days? Please, tell me more about Argentine wine. Tell me everything you know. I'm begging you. God, what a colossal prick.

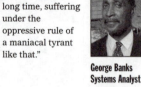

By Natalie Tran

A lot of people here might enjoy this conversation, but I'm not one of them. Who gives a shit where you get your wine? The way you're guzzling it, I'd be surprised if you can even taste it. And I'm really impressed by your references to *gauchos* and the *pampas*. What a worldly, cultured man you must be to know those two words. Should we have sex here or in one of the upstairs bedrooms?

I hate you, I hate you, I hate you.

If there's one thing more irritating than wine guys, it's wine guys with personal-space issues. I can hear you fine: Quit acting like the music's so loud that you have no choice but to lean in close to my ear.

Do you ever shut up? I wish I lived in your world, where I could spew a non-stop stream of dull facts and think people actually care. If you love the Mendoza region so much, why don't you move there? No, I'm not going to buy a case of anything, I'm just looking for a graceful way to get away from you. Where do you think you're putting your hand? Oh my God. He actually just did the invisible-lint

Won't someone please get this guy away from me?

thing. I don't think I've had a guy try that one on me since college.

This would be a great time to kick someone in the testicles. I wish I had the assertiveness to say something, but I haven't even had a chance to open my mouth. I've just smiled politely and nodded. Won't someone please get this guy away from me? Won't someone please hold a loud conversation about golf or foreign cars that this guy will overhear and want to join? Oh, how I long to hear this man say to me, "Excuse me, but I need to set someone straight about the merits of the new Big Bertha XP-200 titanium driver."

Thanks so much for your card. I'll be sure to use it if I ever need a piece of scrap paper. ∅

Man Looks Forward To Coffee Date With Ex-Girlfriend All Week

PORTLAND, ME—Derek Friese, 30, has been looking forward to a Friday coffee date with ex-girlfriend Kelly Lessing all week, sources reported Monday.

"It sure will be nice to see Kelly again," said Friese, whose three-year relationship with Lessing ended Aug.

> "She said she doesn't have a whole lot of time, but I'm just glad we're getting together to check in."

6. "She said she doesn't have a whole lot of time, but I'm just glad we're getting together to check in. It's less than 72 hours away now. Let's see, about 68 hours, actually."

The date, scheduled for 5:30 p.m. at Norm's Coffee Shop, located two doors down from the clothing store where Lessing works, will mark the first time Friese has seen his ex in more than a month.

"When Kelly and I split up—a decision that was mostly mutual—we decided we wanted to stay friends," Friese said. "Honoring that promise is really important to me. I'm sure it's important to her, too, hopefully."

While many consider post-breakup dates to be an unpleasant chore, that is not the case with Friese.

"Even though we're broken up, we still care about each other," Friese

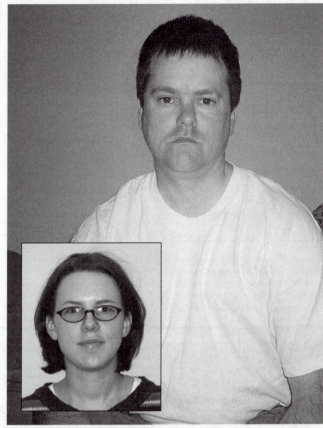

Above: Friese, who is excited about his Friday get-together with Lessing (inset).

said. "How could we not? A love like we had doesn't disappear just because we're not together anymore. We still want to be in each other's lives."

Friese said he would have met Lessing for coffee sooner, but they had trouble getting in touch, playing "phone tag" for nearly two weeks.

"I'd get home after work and find Kelly had returned my message, but then when I'd call her, she'd be out," Friese said. "Somehow, she always

called my work number after I'd already left. My cell number is the same as it's always been, but I guess she lost it."

As the date approaches, Friese has been making efforts to ensure that he puts his best foot forward. In addition to getting a haircut and buying a new shirt, he has given his apartment a thorough cleaning, just in case Lessing decides to drop by.

"If Kelly needs to borrow a book or something, I don't want this place looking horrible," Friese said. "I guess I could always bring the book down to her, but she might insist on coming up and getting it herself. Not that she would want to come up for anything more than that—we're definitely over."

Friese has also been preparing potential conversation topics for the get-together. While watching CNN last Sunday, he made a mental note to ask Lessing about wildfires in her home state of Oregon.

"That's not really the part of Oregon where she's from, but I still should ask if everything's okay with her parents, who still live there," Friese said. "I was really close with her parents, especially her mom. She was great."

Continued Friese: "I also have to remember to tell Kelly about the Mexican festival at the Civic Center this weekend. Kelly was a Spanish major in college, so she might want to go. Maybe if she doesn't want to go alone, I could offer to go with her as a friend."

The date, which will be sandwiched between the end of Lessing's work see DATE page 252

Affable Anti-Semite Thinks The Jews Are Doing Super Job With The Media

PLANO, TX—Henry McCullers, an affable Plano-area anti-Semite, praised the Jewish people Monday for doing "a bang-up job" running the media. "This has been such a great year for movies, and the new crop of fall TV shows looks to be one of the best in years," McCullers said. "And the cable news channels are doing a terrific job, too. Admittedly, they're not reporting on the Jewish stranglehold on world finance, but, hey, that's understandable."

American People Shrug, Line Up For Fingerprinting

WASHINGTON, DC—Assuming that there must be a good reason for the order, U.S. citizens lined up at elementary schools and community centers across the nation Monday for government-mandated fingerprinting. "I'm not exactly sure what this is all about," said Ft. Smith, AR, resident Meredith Lovell while waiting in line. "But given all the crazy stuff that's going on these days, I'm sure the government has a very good reason." Said Amos Hawkins, a Rockford, IL, delivery driver: "I guess this is another thing they have to do to ensure our freedom."

Captain's Hat Really Completes Street Lunatic's Ensemble

CHICAGO—A tattered U.S. Navy Captain's hat taken from a Salvation Army Dumpster adds the perfect finishing touch to street lunatic Corner Carl's outfit, fashion critics raved Monday. "The sailor's hat playfully juxtaposes his filthy Chicago Bears sweatshirt and backwards pajama bottoms," People style correspondent Steven Cojocaru said. "And when he screams at fire hydrants, it's now like he's scolding his imagined Navy underlings." GQ fashion writer Rob Vance said the nautical-themed hat makes Corner Carl resemble "a psychotic, profanity-spewing Alan Hale Jr."

Defense Department Typo Results In U.S. Attack On Ira

ARLINGTON, VA—The U.S. Defense Department apologized to Skokie, IL, dentist Ira Nussbaum Tuesday following a bombing campaign aimed at removing the 37-year-old from power. "Apparently, the intelligence source who drafted the attack plan against Iraq failed to strike the Q key hard enough," Defense Secretary Donald Rumsfeld said. "The Q was always a little stubborn on that keyboard. Sorry." This marks the first military action taken against Nussbaum since a malfunctioning shift key prompted Ulster Unionists to detonate his Ford Taurus in 1998.

New-Versus-Old Electric-Slide Confusion Blamed In Wedding-Reception Pileup

MALDEN, MA—Twelve wedding guests were critically injured Saturday night in a dance-floor pileup blamed on new-versus-old Electric Slide confusion. "The DJ called for the Electric Slide without specifying which, and when the 'old' Sliders slid to the right, they collided violently with the stationary, hip-shaking 'new' Sliders," paramedic Laura Denison said. "By the fifth bar, the dance floor was a gruesome tangle of bodies." In the wake of the tragedy, the American Association of Disc Jockeys released a statement urging all DJs to specify which Electric Slide they are calling for at any future weddings, retirement parties, and bar mitzvahs. Ø

friend of Glynn's, has also noticed the change.

"We can't have a conversation without him mentioning some aspect of gay culture," Richter said. "No matter what it is—art, comedy, movies, restaurants, philosophy—he goes off on how it affects him as a gay man. Mark, we've accepted that you like the dick, so just shut up and be gay already."

Even Andrew Storch, a gay coworker of Glynn's who recently went on several dates with him, said Glynn is "laying on the gay a little heavy."

"After Mark came out, he said he'd been attracted to me for a long time," Storch said. "We went out a few times, but he constantly acted like he had something to prove. Everywhere he went, he was mincing around like RuPaul at Wigstock. And, Lord, you should have seen the shoes he was wearing on our second date. I realize he's excited about being out of the closet, but you don't have to make up for those lost years of gayness all at once."

Added Storch: "I hope I wasn't like that when I came out."

Of all the aspects of Glynn's life, friends say his wardrobe has undergone the most drastic change. Instead of wearing khakis and understated dress shirts, Glynn now opts for brightly patterned sleeveless T-shirts and tight short-shorts.

"Two weeks after he came out, he showed up at a party in little pink biker shorts and an open button-

> Even Andrew Storch, a gay coworker of Glynn's who recently went on several dates with him, said Glynn is "laying on the gay a little heavy."

down shirt with nothing on underneath," Eddy said. "This is a guy who once said wearing blue jeans made him feel 'weird.' Now, he says he's saving up to buy a whole leather get-up

with harnesses and metal studs. I don't know where he got the idea that real gay people actually wear that stuff in their daily lives."

Glynn has adopted a number of other stereotypically gay affectations, including finger-snapping, a "swishy" walk, and calling everyone "sweetie" or "girlfriend."

"I guess he's picking it up from some of the gay guys he meets when he goes out, but it's just not him," Storch said. "A few times, I've actually caught him doing the limp-wrist thing. All that's missing is the lisp."

Even Glynn's drinking habits have taken on a gay tone.

"Mark used to be a single-malt scotch drinker," Eddy said. "Now it's Cosmos or Mai Tais. I didn't realize that liking men altered your taste buds."

According to Dirk Yunger, author of *You're Here, You're Queer, Get Used To It: The New Millennium Guide To Coming Out Of The Closet*, it is common for "late bloomers" like Glynn to over-embrace homosexuality.

"Mark has been hiding his true sex-

uality for so long, he can't help but want to shout it out to the world," Yunger said. "His friends should give him time to figure out how his new-

> "Mark used to be a single-malt scotch drinker," Eddy said. "Now it's Cosmos or Mai Tais. I didn't realize that liking men altered your taste buds."

found sexual openness will fit into his larger persona. Eventually, he will level out and become more like the Mark they used to know. In the meantime, his friends will have to endure a lot of annoying conversations about 14-inch dildos and what he'd like to do to Rupert Everett. Christ, I don't envy them." ⌀

corner.

"The last dozen subjects looked like they'd plot a near-perfect obsessive-pattern distribution curve once their habits were charted," Layton said. "They fell into two groups of six on both sides of the line. Classic boxcars. And a researcher whose office is right across from mine just hit it big studying the effects of class and religion on betting habits, so I figure I gotta be next."

"The lack of results so far, sure, it's discouraging," Ojeda said. "But this baby's so fat with data, we're due for a big payout. That's the way it is in

> Though they admit that the project has taken far longer than expected, members of Layton's team insist that their efforts will be well worth it in the end.

this business of high-stakes research. One big winning test group can make your whole study."

Layton expressed confidence that "major findings" will come soon.

"Unlike some of the researchers out there, we've got a system that works," Layton said. "The University of Nevada–Reno guys, for example, they use a Von Rhiemann-style control group to enhance certain values in figuring their results. The difference is, we know how to twist its tail—you know, finesse it."

Above: Gamblers at the Las Vegas Luxor play poker, one of the many games the UNLV team wants just a little more time to study.

Others at UNLV do not share Layton's optimism.

"They've been talking about hitting it big ever since the study began," said Howard Leventhal, a UNLV professor of social psychology and illness. "But there have been no results. Which is strange, when you consider how much time and effort they've put in. I mean, last month, Dr. Ojeda took out a second mortgage on his house because of some 'sure thing' he had."

Added Leventhal: "I told them not to bet the farm on anything based on classical conditioning. But there's something about a researcher that can't resist the long shots. Goes back

to Skinner."

Though they admit that the project has taken far longer than expected, members of Layton's team insist that their efforts will be well worth it in the end.

"Why spend your time studying habituation patterns of office-drone Joes and Janes when the payoff here is potentially so much bigger?" Ojeda said. "Besides, as long as you're spending lots of time at the tables collecting data, the coffee's free. Can't beat that with a stick."

Ojeda then excused himself to investigate a hot tip concerning the borderline obsessive-compulsive

behavior of adult children of abusive alcoholics taking in the fifth race at Santa Anita.

"Baby, this one is the big one, I can feel it," said Stangel, holding a CD-ROM of raw data to his ear and shaking it. "This contains data from control groups seven and eleven, stuff we'd thrown out because it seemed so blue-sky, but we were thinking too hard and not going with our gut. Sometimes, the scientific method can lead you wrong, you know?"

"Seven-eleven! Seven-come-eleven!" said Stangel, pausing to let Fancy Nancy blow on the disc. "Daddy needs a new paradigmatic skew!" ⌀

babies than it can reasonably support. God will decide whose seed shall find purchase and when."

The gathering, which took place on a muddy hillside crowded with tin-and-tarpaper shacks, was one of many to take place around the world Monday—a day Pope John Paul II declared World Childbirth Day.

"No wonder we are plagued by disease and high infant mortality," said São Paulo father of eight Oran-

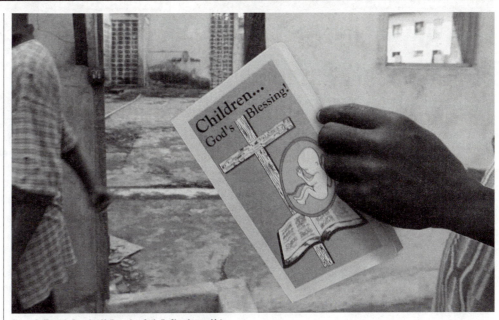

Above: A villager in Bamako, Mali, reads a Catholic Church pamphlet.

> Though critics have called the Catholic Church's anti-contraception campaign irresponsible and dangerous, particularly in regions where food and medical facilities are scarce, the missionaries remain steadfast in their commitment.

jinho Cruz, speaking from his dilapidated one-room home, which lacks electricity or potable water. "God has been punishing us for trying to prevent the miraculous gift of conception."

In Calcutta, a city where 53 percent of residents are under 18, Catholic missionaries delivered a similar message of love and procreation.

"In this life, there is a right path and a wrong path, and which you take is entirely up to you," said missionary Christopher Halloran, addressing a group of 4,500 villagers crammed into a schoolhouse. "Will you deny God's wisdom by using condoms, or will you shine in the divine light of unprotected sex? The choice is clear."

"God does not want you to choke the rivers of fertile bounty with immoral birth-control pills," continued Halloran, framed by a backdrop of brown, withered crops and skeletal, half-living farm animals. "He wants you to continue expanding your families. If your babies starve, Jesus will forgive them."

The words of Halloran and his fellow missionaries have struck a chord with the impoverished masses of the world.

"We were told we should not use condoms to prevent the spread of HIV," said Luis Ortiz of Bogotá, Colombia. "The man from the Church assured us that the Lord will protect us from disease, provided we are true to His wish that we produce more children than we can possibly care for."

Added Ortiz: "Life in this shanty-

town is difficult, but our troubles are nothing compared to what we will face in the Lake Of Fire if we try to live within our means and regulate the number of offspring we produce, as Satan teaches."

Though critics have called the Catholic Church's anti-contraception campaign irresponsible and dangerous, particularly in regions where food and medical facilities are scarce, the missionaries remain steadfast in their commitment to fighting the spread of birth control.

"No man-made organization knows God's will," said Atlanta-born missionary Lucas Roberts, 24, handing out Bibles to polio-stricken children in Dhaka, Bangladesh. "His ways are mysterious and noble. All we can do is interpret His words as they appear in the Good Book. And those words clearly state that we have an obliga-

> "In this life, there is a right path and a wrong path, and which you take is entirely up to you," said missionary Christopher Halloran, addressing a group of 4,500 villagers crammed into a schoolhouse.

tion to shun effective methods of population control."

Responding to critics, Cardinal Bevilacqua said the Catholic Church

is not oblivious to the plight of the impoverished, noting that it offers a sanctioned way to postpone the inevitable fruit of God's will.

"For those who want to practice God's natural birth control, there are two options," Bevilacqua said. "You can try abstinence or, if you are married, you can try natural family planning. This has proven up to 87 percent effective, which is more than suitable for maintaining a reasonable household. So long as no seed is spilled, God will not immediately strike you down."

Bevilacqua also noted that, in cases in which natural family planning fails, unwanted children can be sent to Catholic orphanages, where they will be cared for and groomed to spread word of the punishment awaiting those who impede God's grand biological destiny. ∅

WORMY from page 248

amounts of blood. Passersby were amazed by the unusually large amounts of blood. Passersby were

amazed by the unusually large amounts of blood. Passersby were amazed by the unusually large amounts of blood. Passersby were amazed by the unusually large amounts of blood. Passersby were amazed by the unusually large amounts of blood. Passersby were amazed by the unusually large amounts of blood. Passersby were amazed by the unusually large amounts of blood. Passersby were

> I feel really bad about strangling that puppy.

amazed by the unusually large amounts of blood. Passersby were amazed by the unusually large amounts of blood. Passersby were amazed by the unusually large amounts of blood. Passersby were amazed by the unusually large amounts of blood. Passersby were amazed by the unusually large amounts of blood. Passersby were amazed by the unusually large amounts of blood. Passersby were amazed by the unusually large amounts of blood. Passersby were

amazed by the unusually large amounts of blood. Passersby were amazed by the unusually large amounts of blood. Passersby were amazed by the unusually large amounts of blood. Passersby were amazed by the unusually large amounts of blood. Passersby were amazed by the unusually large amounts of blood. Passersby were amazed by the unusually large amounts of blood. Passersby were amazed by the unusually large amounts of blood. Passersby were amazed by the unusually large amounts of blood. Passersby were amazed by the unusually large amounts of blood. Passersby were amazed by the unusually large amounts of blood. Passersby were amazed by the unusually large amounts of blood. Passersby were amazed by the unusually large amounts of blood. Passersby were amazed by the unusually large amounts of blood. Passersby were

see WORMY page 255

Take Advantage Of Our Two-For-One Scott Tissue Special, For One Day We Will Die

**By Len Comello
Food King Manager**

Attention, Food King shoppers: Now in Aisle Four, take advantage of our two-for-one special on all Scott Tissue and Scott Towel products. Purchase up to 10 rolls of each. It's just one way you can save big as a valued Food King shopper. And do it soon, for one day, all will be dark. Then, there will be no savings, no bargains, only the cold, eternal embrace of Death.

And don't forget that every Tuesday is Double Coupon Tuesday at Food King, with extra savings on our already-low everyday prices. Small consolation for the inevitability of being buried under six feet of earth, the worms burrowing through our eye sockets, our flesh turning to dust in the pitch-blackness. But still, a fine reason to shop at Food King, no?

Also, be sure to check our Schreiber gourmet cheeses, on sale this week at $4.99 a pound. Do they really taste different from the bargain-brand cheeses, or do we fool ourselves into thinking that the higher price somehow imbues the product with the ineffable virtue of quality? How we would savor each crumb if the cheese were $100 a pound! How your guests would flatter you! So fill your cart if it brings

> **Small consolation for the inevitability of being buried under six feet of earth, the worms burrowing through our eye sockets, our flesh turning to dust in the pitch-blackness.**

you pleasure, but do not come to me hoping to find meaning in this absurdity.

For the month of October, buy two-liter bottles of all Coca-Cola products for just 99 cents each. Or, if you prefer, buy Pepsi, RC Cola, or Dr. Pepper for a little bit more. Or a host of other competing national brands, for that matter. For at Food King, you have both the power and the burden of choice—in-

escapable choice. From which products to buy to what manner of payment to the type of bag in which to carry the items home, choice torments the Food King shopper at every turn.

And don't miss our special offer on 12-packs of Budweiser beer for $6.99. You might as well take advantage. Who in this store would deny a help-

> **So fill your cart if it brings you pleasure, but do not come to me hoping to find meaning in this absurdity.**

less imbecile adrift in a cold, uncaring universe the chance to numb himself against the fickle whim of time and circumstance? It is all a rehearsal for the grave.

As if that weren't enough, Food King has everyday low prices on cosmetics and beauty aids, so there's never been a better time to delude yourself. Paint your face with blood-colored sludge and pretend you are somehow something more than a slab of meat temporarily occupying space in this uncaring world. Smear yourself a mere mote closer to the pretty princess you fantasized of being as a young girl. Go ahead, transform your crumbling visage into a ghoulish death mask, all caked-on rouge and clumped mascara. All existence is a delusion and fantasy, anyway; it does no harm to embrace it.

My father has been dead 12 years now. He used his last words to curse the gods for the cancer that had devoured his brain and his bones. Would he be pleased to know, more than a decade past his death, that 30-gallon Glad Bags were on sale for $2.69? It is hard to believe such an offer would be a balm to his soul. But so it is with us all. A hundred years hence, drunken high-school boys whose grandfathers are not yet born will sit upon my burial mound drinking illicitly and urinating on my headstone, and how I might feel about that now will matter not at all.

Our bakery counter has sheet cakes with free custom decorations starting at $5.99. Mark the passage of time, the birthdays, the anniversaries—these annual landmarks mean only that we are one year closer to our inescapable end. We claim to treasure life so, yet we celebrate each step taken toward

Your Horoscope

By Lloyd Schumner Sr.
Retired Machinist and
A.A.P.B.-Certified Astrologer

Aries: (March 21–April 19)
Thursday will usher in a new era of love and prosperity for Aries, which is only fair considering what happens Friday.

Taurus: (April 20–May 20)
You will seek the ancient wisdom of a witch doctor, but you'll have no idea what he means by "Ooh Eee Ooh Ah-Ah Ting-Tang Walla-Walla Bing-Bang."

Gemini: (May 21–June 21)
Society at large will expect you to donate to the Professional Wrestlers' Widows & Orphans Fund due to the unspoken code of *ignoblesse oblige*.

Cancer: (June 22–July 22)
You will belatedly realize you've become part of the problem when you board a train that leaves Philadelphia at noon traveling 45 miles an hour.

Leo: (July 23–Aug. 22)
After all is said and done, no one will have said or done anything involving you in any way.

Virgo: (Aug. 23–Sept. 22)
The streets will soon run red with blood and echo with the tortured cries of the unforgiven, but you'll be amazed how quickly you get used to it.

Libra: (Sept. 23–Oct. 23)
The only thing that keeps you from realizing your potential is the depressing awareness that it probably wouldn't take much time or effort.

Scorpio: (Oct. 24–Nov. 21)
Studies show that Colombia has the highest murder rate of any place in the Americas, except the place where you'll be standing at noon tomorrow.

Sagittarius: (Nov. 22–Dec. 21)
You should start studying physical and geometric optics now, so you'll have a better understanding of what's happening when you're suddenly converted to photons.

Capricorn: (Dec. 22–Jan. 19)
The stars advise you to reconsider your plans for the future, as they're not going to happen in Capricorn's back yard.

Aquarius: (Jan. 20–Feb. 18)
Though you're so fat, you should have your own zip code, you continue to use that of Fatsoville, your city of residence.

Pisces: (Feb. 19–March 20)
You will soon be unwillingly forced into a flurry of activity when you are chosen to host the 2014 Winter Olympiad.

the grave.

Those who missed last week's half-off Cinnamon Toast Crunch promotion, do not cast blame on yourselves. To live is to fail. Whether you seek to recapture the unconditional love of the womb or to overcome the unstoppable forces of entropy, failure is our lot in life. The loftiest of ambitions are but toys of nature, fleeting soap bubbles for the capricious Fates to dash upon the rocks for a moment's sport.

I gained my freedom the day I accepted my destiny and took work at the Food King, where I eke out a meager existence informing faceless rabble of everyday low prices on butternut squash and K.C. Masterpiece.

So come! Purchase three boxes of Twinings Ceylon Breakfast Tea for the price of two. Indulge in the city's finest deli counter, purveyor of fine macaroni salad and unctuous rotisserie chicken. It matters not. The sun sets on us all. To believe otherwise is the nakedest of folly.

And don't forget: Blue Bonnet tub margarine is on sale for just $1.09 through Saturday. ✍

DATE from page 249

day and her 6:45 p.m. yoga class, is unlikely to last more than an hour. Nevertheless, Friese said he relishes the opportunity to catch up with his "new old friend."

"I don't want to bring up any of the old garbage," Friese said. "I just want this to be a good time. We're going to get coffee, sit back, relax, talk, have a few laughs, maybe even exchange a friendly hug. It's going to be great."

Friese said Lessing is sure to be interested in what is going on in his life, too.

"I need to remember to let her know that my sister is having a baby," Friese said. "Kelly always liked Pam. When I called Pam and told her I was seeing Kelly, she told me to say hi."

Alyssa Neilson, a mutual friend of the former couple, said Friese's anticipation is growing by the day.

"Derek seems pretty excited," Neilson said. "He's casually mentioned to me that they're meeting for coffee at least 10 times, twice in the last 24 hours. Funny, Kelly never mentioned it at all." ✍

Religious Pamphlet Sat On

see LOCAL page 7D

Baby Found On Doorstep Moved To Neighbor's Doorstep

see LOCAL page 9D

Nantucket Poet Laureate Refuses To Apologize For Controversial Limerick

see ARTS page 3C

STATshot

A look at the numbers that shape your world.

What Are We Gluing To The Governor Of Wyoming?

1. Legos
2. Bus transfer
3. Corn Nuts
4. Used DVD copy of *Joe Dirt*
5. Sign reading, "Kick Me, The Governor Of Wyoming"
6. Funny hillbilly beard
7. $175,000 in cattle-lobby contributions
8. The governor of Massachusetts

the ONION®

VOLUME 38 ISSUE 38   AMERICA'S FINEST NEWS SOURCE™   17–23 OCTOBER 2002

FAA Considering Passenger Ban

WASHINGTON, DC—Seeking to address "the number-one threat to airline security," the Federal Aviation Administration announced Monday that it will consider banning passengers on all domestic and international commercial flights.

"In every single breach of security in recent years, whether it was an act of terrorism or some other form of crime, it was a passenger who subverted the safety systems on board the aircraft or in the terminal," FAA administrator Marion Blakey said. "Even threats that came in the form of explosives inside baggage were eventually traced back to a ticketed individual. As great a revenue source as they have been, passengers simply represent too great a risk to the airline industry."

see FAA page 257

Bush On Economy: 'Saddam Must Be Overthrown'

WASHINGTON, DC—Amid growing concerns about the faltering stock market and deepening recession, President Bush vowed to tackle the nation's economic woes head-on Tuesday, assuring the American people that he "will not rest" until Saddam Hussein is removed from power.

"Our nation's economy is struggling right now," said Bush, delivering the keynote address at the National Economic Forum. "Our manufacturing base is weak, new home sales are down, and unemployment is up. Millions of our people are suffering. That is why I stand before you tonight and make this promise: Saddam Hussein *will* be stopped."

With the Dow regularly suffering triple-digit plunges and the Nasdaq hitting a six-year low of 1184.94 late last month, Bush used the speech as an opportunity to outline his plan for getting the economy back on track.

"We can no longer turn a blind eye to our tumbling stock market and the disintegration of the retirement pack-

see ECONOMY page 256

Above: Bush addresses business leaders.

Goodwill Toy Section Most Depressing Thing Ever

SPENCER, IA—The toy section of the Fleet Road Goodwill, with its heartbreaking assortment of soiled, broken, bargain-priced playthings, depressed an estimated 20 shoppers Tuesday.

"Look at this one," said Spencer resident Bobbie Perrin, 43, as she gingerly picked up a grimy stuffed animal with her fingertips. "Judging from the 'Kennel Kritters' tag, it must be a

Left: One of the Goodwill store's heartbreaking rejects.

knock-off of one of those Pound Puppies from the '80s, only I'm pretty sure those had legs."

"Oh my God, are those tomato-soup stains on its back?" asked Perrin, flinging the Kennel Kritter back into a large bin, where it landed between a plastic horse and a faded Parcheesi game board. "I thought those were spots."

The bin, whose items were priced at 50 cents each, also contained a chewed rawhide dog bone, a Rubik's

see GOODWILL page 256

The Dockworkers' Strike

Dockworkers in 29 West Coast ports returned to work last week under court order, tackling a 10-day backlog of cargo. What do *you* think?

"Those damn dockworkers have it so good—except for the spending-all-day-hauling-200-pound-boxes part."

John McGee
Systems Analyst

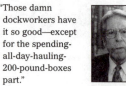

"Oh, good. I would have just died if some shit on a boat in San Francisco didn't get unloaded."

Adam Nesbitt
Attorney

"My heart goes out to those dockworkers. They could have been contenders. They could have been somebody. Instead of a bunch of bums, which is what they are."

Grace Olney
Librarian

"This is like the time I organized a strike over at Sbarro's. Actually, I just stopped showing up."

Gordie Runnels
File Clerk

"I heard Bush ended this strike by invoking 1947's Taft-Hartley Act. If I were him, I'd leave that boring crap back in ninth-grade history, where it belongs."

Randall Smithson
Electrician

"I just feel bad for all the rotting vegetables. They're the real victims in all this."

Marcy Webber
Student

2002 Nobel Prize Winners

The 2002 Nobel Prize winners were announced last week in Stockholm, Sweden. Among the recipients:

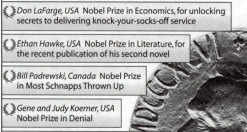

- *Don LaFarge, USA* Nobel Prize in Economics, for unlocking secrets to delivering knock-your-socks-off service
- *Ethan Hawke, USA* Nobel Prize in Literature, for the recent publication of his second novel
- *Bill Padrewski, Canada* Nobel Prize in Most Schnapps Thrown Up
- *Gene and Judy Koerner, USA* Nobel Prize in Denial
- *Dr. Hans Guttentag, Germany* Nobel Prize in Ergonomics, for invention of Backsaver 2000 posture-support chair
- *Randy Bachman and C.F. Turner, Canada* Nobel Prize in Taking Care Of Business
- *The Cooksey Twins, United Kingdom* Nobel Prize in Sleuthing, for solving the mystery of the haunted switchyard
- *Herman McGee, USA* Nobel Committee Special Certificate of Recognition, for being world's greatest grandpa

ⵁ the ONION®
America's Finest News Source.™

Herman Ulysses Zweibel
Founder

T. Herman Zweibel
Publisher Emeritus
J. Phineas Zweibel
Publisher
Maxwell Prescott Zweibel
Editor-In-Chief

You're Not One Of Those Couples Who Secretly Videotape Their Nanny, Are You?

Well, Mr. and Mrs. Hegan, you seem like a lovely young couple, and Courtney is an absolute doll. I'd be delighted to accept the job as your new nanny. And, yes, the salary you're offering will be fine, and I live just a mile away, so I can usually be available on short notice. I think this will be a fine arrangement for all involved.

By Helen Parrish

There is, however, one tiny little other thing. I hate to even bring it up, and I'm sure it's not the case, but I'd just feel better double-checking this before we move forward. Ken and Deborah, you're not one of those couples who secretly videotape their nanny, are you?

I only ask because—and I'm sure you'd agree—the erosion of the individual's right to privacy in contemporary America is an unfortunate and disturbing trend. And no example of this trend is more alarming than couples planting a hidden videocamera in their home in an effort to secretly monitor the woman responsible for taking care of their children while they're out.

It's just ridiculous these days, the way people are videotaping each other left and right like some kind of Orwellian nightmare. If we're going to be so mistrustful of people, why not place a police officer in every home? Sure, it would probably cut

And how reliable are these electronic sentry systems, anyway?

down on crime, but at what cost? Just because some nannies steal jewelry or slap kids doesn't mean all the others should be treated like they're guilty, too. Do you really want to live in a world where we assume the worst of each other, and go to incredibly invasive lengths to prove it?

And how reliable are these electronic sentry systems, anyway? They can't possibly catch a perpetrator from all available angles. You can't mount a camera in every corner of the house, can you? No. That would be prohibitively expensive. So if someone were to, say, scream in a child's ear for 20 straight minutes for spilling grape Kool-Aid, they could easily find some remote closet or crawl space to do it in. Isn't it futile to spend so much time and energy trying to peep illicitly

at a decent, honest citizen who's just trying to earn a living?

Let's also not forget the poor image quality of these videotapes. You've heard how a camera can add 10 pounds. Who's to say it doesn't also make swats on a child's hind-end with a wooden spoon look far more painful than they truly are? I've seen some of these tapes of bad nannies in

Are you going to put your faith in grainy, out-of-focus video footage, or are you going to put your faith in people?

action, and it's often impossible to tell what they're even doing. Are you going to put your faith in grainy, out-of-focus video footage, or are you going to put your faith in people? It's your choice.

Did you notice how I didn't ask for my first paycheck up front? Of course I didn't. Because I trust you. Let's think for a moment about that word. "Trust." What kind of world would it be if nobody trusted anybody else? Why, it would be the most awful place imaginable. No one could eat dinner without fearing it was poisoned, or go to bed without searching the sheets for scorpions. People who can't trust their fellow man don't go very far at all.

The great Benjamin Franklin once said, "They that can give up essential liberty to purchase a little temporary safety deserve neither liberty or safety." Wise words, indeed.

I once worked for a couple who liked to secretly tape their nanny, and I found them to be extremely unpleasant—the kind of cranky, half-cocked people who fire nannies at the drop of a hat. Well, phooey on them! I was glad to be rid of them. In fact, I didn't even save their name or address, because, hey, who needs references from jerks like that? Not me, that's for sure.

I'm just a harmless old woman, and I sure don't stand much chance against some big, intrusive police state. But maybe my voice and message can inspire others. Maybe I can do my small part to bring about a world where privacy is considered a sacred right, and the act of secretly taping somebody defecating in the laundry chute of an unfair employer is punishable by law.

So, I beg you, Ken and Deborah, don't let evil win by insisting on surreptitiously taping me. I'm counting on you to take the high road. ⵁ

New Mistress Seems To Be Good For Area Man

KIRKWOOD, MO—Len Stavros, 46, is a whole new man since he began dating new mistress Amanda Broder, sources reported Tuesday.

"I can't tell you how good Amanda has been for him," friend Robert Risser said. "He's completely

> "I can't tell you how good Amanda has been for him," friend Robert Risser said. "He's completely changed. He's calmer, friendlier, and just generally more positive about life."

changed. He's calmer, friendlier, and just generally more positive about life. I haven't even heard him bitch about his wife in, like, three weeks, and that used to be a daily ritual."

Added Risser: "I haven't seen Len this happy since he was sleeping with that optometrist a few years ago."

Coworkers have noticed a marked improvement in Stavros' mood since he began seeing Broder on the side in August.

"For the last two months, Len has been in unusually high spirits," said Georgia McGlothen, who works with Stavros in the accounting department of Allied Plastics. "I used to dread going to his office for something, because you never knew if you were going to get Dr. Jekyll or Mr. Hyde. But, lately, he's been nothing but smiles. I really hope they secretly stay together."

Those close to Stavros say he's even been taking better care of himself.

"For a while there, Len was letting himself go a bit," Risser said. "But last week, my wife asked me if he'd lost weight. When I asked him about it, he said he's been eating better and running two miles every morning before work. He's even hinted at becoming a vegetarian like Amanda, but he's afraid [his wife] Mary might get suspicious."

According to McGlothen, Stavros has been putting more care into his personal appearance ever since meeting Broder.

"Len's definitely been dressing better lately," McGlothen said. "I always tease him on the days he looks especially nice, because I know he's got a 'lunch meeting' with a special somebody. You should see him blush—it's the most adorable thing in the world."

Friends also admire the way Broder is able to keep Stavros in line.

"Len can sometimes be a little inappropriate in social situations, and Mary always puts up with it," Risser

Above: Stavros with his supportive, nurturing mistress.

> Those close to Stavros say he's even been taking better care of himself.

said. "Not Amanda. I was at dinner with them recently, and when Len started to recommend a dermatologist to the waiter, who had a little acne, she hit him really hard on the arm. He didn't even finish his sentence. Len needs somebody who'll call him on stuff like that."

Even those who are unaware of Stavros' extramarital affair have noticed a difference in his demeanor.

"Len's been a real joy to be around lately," wife Mary said. "He used to just mope around the house, watching football in his underwear and stuff, but these days, he's a dynamo of activity. He's even started playing racquetball at the gym every Thursday night. I'm not sure what the change is, but whatever he's doing, he should keep it up." ∅

Activity Made Up To Sell Athletic Shoes

BEAVERTON, OR—In its latest niche-marketing coup, the Nike Corporation on Monday unveiled the Nike Bog-Ramper, a light, durable sneaker designed for the newly fabricated sport of bog-ramping. "Nike is the first footwear company to introduce a shoe specially engineered to meet the exacting demands of the competitive bog-ramper," said Nike CEO Phil Knight, introducing the $130 shoe at the company's headquarters. "Whatever bog-ramping is, wherever it's done, and whoever does it, don't even think about trying it without your Nikes." Knight added that the shoes are also suitable for street wear.

Man Doesn't Realize Date Went Terribly

FORT WAYNE, IN—Dan Haft, 24, failed to realize that his date with Mindy Camden went terribly Saturday. "On a scale of 1 to 10, I'd have to give tonight a 9," Haft said following the date, which was characterized by awkward conversation and a distinct lack of chemistry. "It's a safe bet we'll be seeing each other again." Haft incorrectly added that he and Camden "were definitely vibing on each other."

Georgia School Board Bans 'Theory Of Math'

COGDELL, GA—The Cogdell School Board banned the teaching of the controversial "Theory Of Math" in its schools Monday. "We are simply not confident of this mysterious process by which numbers turn, as if by magic, into other numbers," board member Gus Reese said. "Those mathematicians are free to believe 3 times 4 equals 12, but that dun [sic] give them the right to force it on our children." Under the new ruling, all math textbooks will carry a disclaimer noting that math is only one of many valid theories of number-manipulation.

Marketing Guru Also A Getting-Divorced Guru

NEW YORK—Marketing guru Bob Lippman, 43, is also a getting-divorced guru, colleagues noted Tuesday. "Bob has an incredible knack for identifying branding strategies to connect with a demographic," coworker Ann Lamp said. "He's almost as good at establishing a product's core consumer message as he is at ending loveless, doomed marriages." In the past 10 years, Lamp has won four Mobius Awards and been married three times.

No One Has Heart To Ask Human Beat Box To Stop

VENTURA, CA—Friends of Ron Berg, the self-described "human beat box," don't have the heart to ask him to stop. "Any time we're out, it's only a matter of time before Ron starts up with 'poom poom-pkkhh, poom-pa-poom-pkkhh,'" friend Brian Craig said Tuesday. "But he's so proud of his 'special skill' that it'd devastate him if we told him he sucks and should stop." Craig, who has been sprayed with beat-box saliva "tons of times," said he makes sure never to sit across from Berg at a bar where the jukebox contains Run-DMC's *Raising Hell*.

Logo In Corner Of TV Reminds Man He's Masturbating To Spice

FRANKLIN, VT—A logo in the lower-right-hand corner of his TV screen helped remind Peter Brighton that he was masturbating to the Spice channel Monday. "Ah, so it's Spice that's presenting this quality softcore pornography that I am enjoying so much," said Brighton during his auto-erotic act. "I will be sure to keep Spice in mind when looking to stimulate myself to ejaculation in the future." ∅

age of the American worker," Bush said. "That is why I have developed a 14-point plan for reviving America's economy. The first step is taking the biological and chemical weapons out of the hands of this madman. These sorts of weapons have no place in a peaceful world."

Turning to the problem of unemployment, Bush discussed his strategy for creating new jobs and stimulating growth in the tech sector.

"We're working hard to put Americans back to work," Bush said. "Our citizens are fighters; they just need the opportunity. And it is in this spirit that we are committed to defeating Saddam Hussein, so that the world may stand together in liberty and freedom."

Bush then addressed the issue of corporate malfeasance, promising sweeping reforms and a major crackdown on white-collar criminals.

"Corrupt CEOs must be treated like any other criminal," Bush said. "The damage they do to this country, eroding investors' faith in our stock market and corporate institutions, is extremely serious. I would like to deliver a clear message to those who would bilk hardworking Americans out of their hard-earned 401(k) plans while greedily lining their own pockets: We cannot, and will not, sit idly by while this threat continues to mount in the Middle East. Iraq has stood in violation of U.N. resolutions since

Above: A Massillon, OH, department store closes while, around the globe, Hussein's reign of terror continues.

1991 by refusing to allow weapons inspectors into the palace compound, where we suspect there are laboratories for creating weapons of mass destruction. We must remove the dictator Saddam Hussein and install a government that is committed to working toward free and democratic elections for the nation of Iraq."

Added Bush: "This man tried to kill my dad."

After the president's speech, press secretary Ari Fleischer issued a brief statement.

"As you have just heard, the president and this administration are fully committed to turning the economy around," Fleischer said. "We know

how important it is for everyone to feel confident that their investment dollars are safe and that they will be able to build a better future for themselves and their children. We also know that what we really need to do at this time is to oust Saddam Hussein. Let's roll." ∅

Cube with the stickers peeled off and sloppily reapplied, a broken laser-pointer key chain, a nude Skipper doll, a deflated Minnesota Vikings plastic football, a Ziploc bag containing five Teddy Ruxpin cassettes and a crayon, and a "bendie" policeman with wires poking out of its joints.

Perrin, who had come to the store looking for black pants for her daughter's waitress uniform, said she took a detour into the toy section seeking a small, impromptu gift for her neighbor's 4-year-old child. Instead, Perrin was confronted with a profoundly sad

Above: More filthy, unwanted misfits.

menagerie of unwanted toys.

"This is the kind of stuff you wouldn't pick up if it were laying on the side of the road," Perrin said. "Yet, somehow, it's being presented for sale as merchandise. I guess if you can't afford to buy your child a new Frisbee for $3, you can get a dirty 25-cent one here."

"I'm going home to lie down," Perrin added. "I feel awful."

Perrin is not the only customer nearly brought to tears by the toys. Liza Robichaud, 22, who periodically visits the Goodwill store to shop for

drinking glasses and vintage '80s T-shirts, passed through the section on her way to the bathroom.

"The toy area has its own distinct odor: sort of a musty, mildewy, plastic, sour-milk, baby-vomit, metallic, rotting-cloth smell," Robichaud said. "It isn't quite the smell of evil—just despair."

Scanning the shelves of misfit games and books, Robichaud sighed deeply.

"I need to go wash my hands," Robichaud said. "I really shouldn't have touched that leaky Magic 8-Ball."

Corey Litt, a 21-year-old college student, was similarly shaken.

"This stuff's in such bad shape, it's hard to even enjoy it for the kitsch factor," Litt said. "I saw a can of Lincoln Logs over there and got excited. But when I opened it, there were only, like, three or four logs and a bunch of other crap—a Tinkertoy wheel with gum stuck in the holes, about a dozen bent Uno cards, a pair of lens-less sunglasses, a couple jigsaw-puzzle pieces, a marble, and a bicycle reflector."

Making the toy section all the more depressing, experts say, is the high percentage of promotional toys from fast-food restaurants and cereal boxes.

"On the ladder of toy desirability, promotional toys are the lowest rung," said Daniel Nestor, author of Bins Of Despair. "They are the shoddiest and, by virtue of their promotional

nature, most dated and disposable. A child who finds a McDonald's action figure of an Asian warrior at Goodwill is highly unlikely to recognize him as a character from Mulan, and it would take a movie-trivia whiz of the highest order to know that his name is Captain Li Shang. Removed from the context of the movie and the corresponding Happy Meal box, the toy becomes that much more pitiful and obsolete than its non-promotional counterpart."

Because the toys are in such poor shape when they arrive at Goodwill, there is little incentive for the store's staff to take good care of them. As a result, their condition worsens, leading to an endless degradation spiral: The dirtier the toys become, the less likely they are to be bought. In turn, the longer they remain in the store, the dirtier they become.

"Somehow, even the saggy-diapered 2-year-olds left to entertain themselves with the toys sense their lack of value," Nestor said. "They fling them around with abandon, banging them against each other with little fear of doing harm to the chipped alphabet blocks, sticky-film-covered Mega-Bloks, mascara-smeared Barbie heads, single miniature-doll shoes, and shards of colorful plastic that are vaguely Fisher Price in origin."

"Then there are the stuffed animals," Nestor said. "Those things are just gross." ∅

Above: Detroit Metro during a test of the proposed no-passenger safety measure.

Under the proposed reforms, the FAA would institute a strict ban on adult passengers, passengers 18 and under, international travelers, and domestic customers. A battery of

> If approved, the new restrictions would go into effect sometime around Thanksgiving, before the busy holiday travel season. Customers who have already purchased tickets for flights scheduled to take place after the ban's enactment will receive a voucher good for travel to their final destination by bus or train.

questions and ID checks will be used to determine whether an individual is a pilot, flight attendant, or federal security officer—the only humans who will be allowed to board an aircraft flying within or headed for the U.S.

In addition, security sensors installed at all gates will sound an alarm if they detect the presence of a 98.6-degree body temperature, and airport-security workers will be trained to spot and positively identify humans in the boarding area.

"Frankly, we've tried everything else," Blakey said. "We've put up more

metal detectors, searched carry-on luggage, and prohibited passengers from traveling with sharp objects. Yet passengers somehow continue to find ways to breach security. Clearly, the passengers have to go."

If approved, the new restrictions would go into effect sometime around Thanksgiving, before the busy holiday travel season. Customers who have already purchased tickets for flights scheduled to take place after the ban's enactment will receive a voucher good for travel to their final destination by bus or train. Should such transportation prove unavailable or inadequate, passengers on most major airlines will receive either a portion of their airfare refunded or a coupon redeemable for a future flight, from which they will also be banned.

"We realize that these new regulations would, for many air travelers, be a major inconvenience," Blakey said. "But we feel strongly that it's a small price to pay to ensure the safety of our skies."

While the ban's primary purpose would be to improve security, FAA spokesman John Gemberling said it would help the airlines' economic future, as well. As evidence, he pointed to the $7.7 billion losses posted by major airlines in 2001—much of which came in the wake of Sept. 11—and the $6 billion increase in passenger-screening costs since the tragedy.

"We've been stretched as thin as we can go," Gemberling said. "New bag-tracking measures ensure that a passenger is on the same flight as his or her luggage, but do little to eliminate the threat of said passenger placing an explosive in the luggage. All bags are currently being screened with bomb-detection machines, but even these $1 million devices are only equipped to detect a limited range of the most conventional explosives."

Added Gemberling: "They're certainly not going to be much help stopping the next guy who wants to blow up a plane with something like a shoe."

Even the stiff measures included in the Aviation and Transportation Security Act, which President Bush recently signed into law, have proven inadequate.

"Improved explosive-detection systems, fortified cockpit doors, more plainclothes sky marshals aboard planes, and mandatory anti-hijacking training for flight crews—none of it could eliminate the possibility of

> "Frankly, we've tried everything else," Blakey said. "We've put up more metal detectors, searched carry-on luggage, and prohibited passengers from traveling with sharp objects. Yet passengers somehow continue to find ways to breach security. Clearly, the passengers have to go."

another Sept. 11 with 100 percent certainty," Gemberling said. "This will."

"We've tried every possible alternative, but nothing has worked," Gemberling continued. "For all our efforts, we keep coming back to the same central problem: humans." ∅

The Tycoon Of 1567 Blossom Meadows Drive

A Room Of Jean's Own
By Jean Teasdale

In the weeks since I lost my job at Fashion Bug, I've been collecting unemployment. Now, just in case you're thinking that idle hands are the devil's playground, rest assured, Jeanketeers, that I've been looking for a job. Cross my heart! Besides, my joblessness has nothing to do with laziness. See, according to the paper, the county we live in has experienced a .42 percent increase in unemployment this year. That might

> Money-wise, hubby Rick and I have been getting by. My unemployment benefits aren't much less than what I earned at the Bug, and Rick got another 25-cents-an-hour raise at the tire center, so you won't be seeing our waterbed on the sidewalk outside 1567 Blossom Meadows Drive any time soon.

not seem like a lot, but the population is pretty small, and there are no major industries in our area besides the Hormel plant, and I can't work there because I think they kill things.

Money-wise, hubby Rick and I have been getting by. My unemployment benefits aren't much less than what I earned at the Bug, and Rick got another 25-cents-an-hour raise at the tire center, so you won't be seeing our waterbed on the sidewalk outside 1567 Blossom Meadows Drive any time soon. And I've got my column. True, it doesn't pay anything, but it's a big morale-booster and creative outlet for me, as well as a source of comfort and reassurance for my readers.

Then there's my secret money. All summer long, I was able to squirrel a little bit away here and there without Rick's knowledge. Each time I cashed my benefits, I set aside at least $20,

see TEASDALE page 258

and I never spent my final Fashion Bug check, since it overlapped with my first unemployment check. All in all, I accumulated about $400 in my special hidey hole, and by summer's end, it was practically burning a hole in a certain cat-litter bag in the kitchen closet (a place Rick was guaranteed *never* to look!).

I guess I could've kept on saving, but where's the fun in that? After all, money isn't worth anything unless it's spent. I feel sorry for people who never enjoy their wealth. Sometimes, you hear these sad stories about some old person being found dead in their dingy apartment with thousands of dollars sealed in Mason jars. You wonder why they were so miserly when there's Social Security and Medicare and other things to ensure that no old person goes hungry or neglected.

Still, with me out of work, I didn't want to be *too* irresponsible with the money. I was definitely going to spend it, but instead of blowing it all splurging at the mall, I decided to buy something that would be a smart investment. The first investment I considered was Betty Boop stuff. You would not believe how many products are licensed under the character, and they're soooo unbelievably cute! There's bobble-head dolls and music boxes and snow globes and salt-and-pepper shakers and alarm clocks and coffee mugs and purses and shower curtains and sleep shirts—you name it, they make it! And all the stuff is so remarkably affordable, so $400 could go a long way. I could sit on it for a couple years, then sell it on eBay for a big profit.

The chief drawback was that I didn't know anyone who owns or wants to collect Betty Boop merchandise. I suspect it was because the original cartoons are so weird. I was flipping channels one morning and came

> **The smart thing to do, I decided, would be to make a completely cold, cynical investment in something popular in which I myself had no interest. I'd make the most money that way, and then I could use the profits to buy things I *really* love!**

across an old Betty Boop cartoon on American Movie Classics. Betty didn't look anything like she does on the merchandise. She had the face of a dog and she had this dog boyfriend who was trying to have his way with

her. Then a string of frankfurters came to life and danced around. It was all pretty out there and not one bit adorable.

Then I realized that, instead of just

> **Since men are the powerful, business-y people in our society, I figured the most profitable stuff to invest in would be stuff they like. I contemplated the things that hubby Rick likes and, naturally, my thoughts turned to pornography.**

investing in merchandise, I should invest in the actual company that makes the stuff. Like Enesco, for instance: They make Precious Moments and Rudolph The Red-Nosed Reindeer figurines. If I invested in Enesco, I thought, maybe I'd get a say in the types of merchandise they produce. Enesco should do an entire line of characters from other Christmas specials. I think that's a really smart idea, since everybody loves those old shows, even Islamish people who can't celebrate Christmas.

I liked that idea, but then I came up with an even better one that would make even more money. The smart thing to do, I decided, would be to make a completely cold, cynical investment in something popular in which I myself had no interest. I'd make the most money that way, and then I could use the profits to buy things I *really* love!

Since men are the powerful, business-y people in our society, I figured the most profitable stuff to invest in would be stuff they like. I contemplated the things that hubby Rick likes and, naturally, my thoughts turned to pornography. So one afternoon, I visited some porn web sites to see if they had any investor-relations pages. It was all I could do to keep from holding my nose and gagging! Not only are these web sites absolutely disgusting, they're also totally unprofessional from a business standpoint!

Well, of course, as I'm fuming about all this, who should creep into our bedroom but none other than hubby Rick! I didn't expect him until dinnertime. He just about scared the bejabbers out of me as he sneaked up behind me and burst into this sudden, uproarious laughter. He asked me if I was going lesbo on him and, if I was, could he watch! (Leave it to hubby Rick to think of these things!) I quickly went offline and, in a huff, shoved him onto the waterbed, not even car-

HOROSCOPES

Your Horoscope

By Lloyd Schumner Sr.
Retired Machinist and
A.A.P.B.-Certified Astrologer

Aries: (March 21–April 19)
You are in grave danger of losing whatever credibility you had as a psychiatrist, which is strange, as you've been in floorcoverings for 17 years.

Taurus: (April 20–May 20)
A sign from the heavens will guide your every waking moment for the foreseeable future. It will be a sign telling you about The WB's hot new show *Greetings From Tucson*.

Gemini: (May 21–June 21)
Although you've always wondered if this is all there is to life, it's not like you've done anywhere near all of this in the first place.

Cancer: (June 22–July 22)
You'll continue to encounter long silences after uttering your trademark catchphrase, "Who fucked a chicken in here?"

Leo: (July 23–Aug. 22)
You'd chew through piles of the dead for a smile from a pretty girl, which is fortunate.

Virgo: (Aug. 23–Sept. 22)
You're not even the greatest lover in the food court, which is what you get for working at Barry White's Supperteria.

Libra: (Sept. 23–Oct. 23)
An unusually reticent Satan will take you to a somewhat high place and, in exchange for your allegiance, offer to make you treasurer of all you survey.

Scorpio: (Oct. 24–Nov. 21)
You like to think you can be relied on to do the right thing in a crisis. Well, enjoy your last few days of believing that, pants-wetting panic bunny.

Sagittarius: (Nov. 22–Dec. 21)
Next week will feature family scandal, almost a dozen murders, a drowned girlfriend, and lots of manic depression, yet it's not in any way based on *Hamlet*.

Capricorn: (Dec. 22–Jan. 19)
Unfortunately, there are only "kill or cure" solutions to your problem, but, hey, anything's better than hiccups.

Aquarius: (Jan. 20–Feb. 18)
You will once again have to deal with obvious fabrications, emotionally manipulative arguments, and outright insanity, but it means so much to your mom when you take her to church.

Pisces: (Feb. 19–March 20)
You'll be surprised how little you miss the parts that don't grow back.

ing if it burst a leak. He had something smart to say about that, too: "Oooh, you're getting frisky! Maybe you should look at porn more often!"

I don't know why I bothered, but I tried to explain to Rick that I was only looking at the sites to see if they had any company information, because I was looking to invest in something popular and profitable.

"Looking to invest?" Rick asked. "With what money?"

Oops. Talk about putting your foot in it!

"You've been hiding money again, haven't you?" he said. When I nodded, he went into this long rant about how any extra money we had on hand should go toward settling our credit-card debt, and how he was sick of getting his Visa declined at stores and being turned down for loans, and how, at this rate, we'd be moving into our first house at age 99. He whined about how his pickup truck's trannie was fouled up, saying he was foregoing getting it replaced just so we could eat and pay rent and meet the payments that we and the collection agency had agreed to.

It was pretty embarrassing, reaching deep into that litter bag to retrieve the envelope full of cash, but what irked me the most was Rick's big speech about wanting to save for a house. The only house he's ever showed any interest in moving into is the Playboy Mansion, and I notice that our tight budget hasn't prevented him from nightly visits to Tacky's Tavern!

Besides, doesn't he-man Rick know it's the woman's job to henpeck the husband about money? Talk about role-reversal! You'd think I was the irresponsible Fred Flintstone to Rick's pragmatic Wilma! While Rick was terrified of a little debt, I was trying to have vision about our financial future. If everyone was like Rick, there'd be no Wall Street. We'd still be trading beads and getting drunk on ye olde ale! Sheesh!

I tell you, kiddies, if it weren't for the invisible guardian angel on my shoulder that constantly whispers, "Keep smiling!" into my ear, I think I'd crack up. After all, believing in angels is chicken soup for the soul, and goodness knows I need all the chicken soup I can get! ⊘

Nelly Reiterates Sex-Liking Stance

see ENTERTAINMENT page 3B

Motorist Overwhelmed By Array Of Jerky Choices

see LOCAL page 1C

Corporate Brass Forced To Tolerate Tech Support Guy's Wolfman-Like Hair, Beard

see BUSINESS page 4E

STATshot

A look at the numbers that shape your world.

Why Did We Rent A Limo?

1. TV reception terrible at house
2. Didn't want to seem too desperate at job interview
3. To stick head out of sunroof and yell at poor people
4. Was son's first day as limo driver
5. To surrender self to authorities in style
6. Limo or lame-o, dude

0 74470 94595 6

THE ONION • $2.00 US • $3.00 CAN

the ONION®

VOLUME 38 ISSUE 39   AMERICA'S FINEST NEWS SOURCE™   24–30 OCTOBER 2002

63 Percent Of U.S. Implicated In New Scandal

WASHINGTON, DC—The Securities and Exchange Commission announced Tuesday that more than 63 percent of all U.S. citizens have been implicated in an illegal stock-dumping, the latest scandal to rock the nation's economy.

"It's staggering how far-reaching this is," SEC chairman Harvey Pitt said. "More than 175 million citizens from all walks of life are involved in one criminal imbroglio. Everybody from white-collar workers to grandmothers, boy-scout leaders, and the entire state of Delaware. Point a finger anywhere, and you have a better chance than not of hitting a guilty party."

According to the SEC, on Jan. 15, Jerome P. Lippman, vice-president of pharmaceutical giant Unocore Systems in Dallas, warned friends and business associates of a failed merger with Pfizer. The information was

see SCANDAL page 263

Above: Citizens implicated in the scandal conceal their faces on a New York City street Tuesday.

Sunken Oil Tanker Will Be Habitat For Marine Life, Shell Executives Say With Straight Face

HOUSTON, TX—The 1,080-foot, 300,000-ton oil tanker *Shell Global Explorer*, which sank off the coast of Newfoundland last month, will provide a welcome habitat for many diverse species of endangered marine life, Shell Oil Company executives announced with a straight face Tuesday.

"In its new resting place, far beneath the surface of the North Atlantic, the *Global Explorer* is host to countless fish and an infinite variety of marine

vegetation," a press release from Shell read, without a trace of irony. "A ship that once helped run life above the waves now houses life beneath them."

The reading of the press release preceded public statements from Shell executives.

"We in the petroleum industry have long believed that we have a responsibility to protect and conserve the environment in our daily business

see TANKER page 262

Above: The new habitat, moments before sinking.

Nails, Hair Cared For Better Than Child

MOBILE, AL—In terms of time, money, and effort expended, local parent Kelly Sweedlin takes better care of her hair and nails than she does her 2-year-old daughter Porcia, the bank teller reported Tuesday.

"As a single mom, it's sometimes hard to squeeze in my manicures between work and everything else, but I make it a priority," Sweedlin, 26, told her daughter's daycare provider. "If I don't spend the time to

really take care of them, who will?"

In spite of all the hard work required to grow a beautiful set of nails, Sweedlin calls it a "labor of love," adding that nothing is more rewarding than a relaxing Saturday afternoon spent "just playing" with different nail-polish colors and discovering new things about the array of beauty products available.

"No matter what my

see CHILD page 262

Above: Sweedlin spends a leisurely hour applying polish to her nails.

Obesity On The Rise

The National Center for Health Statistics recently announced that 64.5 percent of American adults are overweight or obese. What do *you* think?

Norine Barrodale
Loan Clerk

"It's a sin to waste food, and America just happens to have 16 boxes of almost-expired Ding Dongs for every man, woman, and child."

Dennis Moreland
Systems Analyst

"And with the insidious new alliance between Donald Trump and Grimace, it's only going to get worse."

Joseph Ortiz
Machine Operator

"If they knew the pain and humiliation of being obese, scientists wouldn't do these studies."

Eve Huffman
Optometrist

"This study buys into fascist media images about what is and isn't a leading cause of heart disease."

Don Watson
Paperhanger

"For your information, there are those who appreciate the curvy hips and ample breasts of a full-figured man, thank you very much."

Dana Harrison
Radiation Therapist

"The Clean Plate Club is big—bigger than anyone realizes. Look for a man named 'Boy-Ar-Dee.' There's your story."

The Sniper Attacks

An elusive sniper continues to terrorize the Washington area. How are Americans responding to the threat of random shootings?

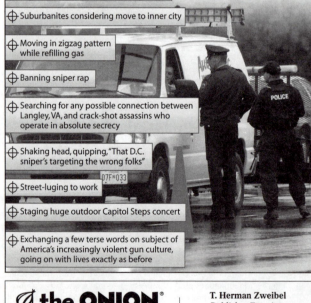

- In general, being on the lookout for vans
- Suburbanites considering move to inner city
- Moving in zigzag pattern while refilling gas
- Banning sniper rap
- Searching for any possible connection between Langley, VA, and crack-shot assassins who operate in absolute secrecy
- Shaking head, quipping, "That D.C. sniper's targeting the wrong folks"
- Street-luging to work
- Staging huge outdoor Capitol Steps concert
- Exchanging a few terse words on subject of America's increasingly violent gun culture, going on with lives exactly as before

the ONION®

America's Finest News Source.™

Herman Ulysses Zweibel
Founder

T. Herman Zweibel
Publisher Emeritus

J. Phineas Zweibel
Publisher

Maxwell Prescott Zweibel
Editor-In-Chief

My Novel Addresses Universal Themes Of Humanity And Has Fucking

By Steve Sloate

I have finally put the finishing touches on my novel, *Westbound 90*, and though it took forever, I am extremely pleased with the end result. It's a modern-day *Candide*, a coming-of-age tragicomedy in which the reader is taken on a great journey, both geographically and emotionally. I am confident it will be widely appreciated, as it addresses themes that speak to the human condition and, coincidentally, has loads of fucking.

In *Westbound 90*, I touch on two universal themes. One is the battle against the void, a war waged by countless souls. In short, I explore the duality of sentience: to be able to analyze, ponder, use tools, and create creature comforts, yet still be driven mad with the repetitiveness of life. The other theme, of course, is that everyone needs a series of explosive, mind-expanding fucks.

Although I don't believe "The Great American Novel" can be written, *Westbound 90* is a close approximation. Its 864 pages examine the broad tapestry of American people, confronting issues of race, culture, and

> Although I don't believe "The Great American Novel" can be written, *Westbound 90* is a close approximation. Its 864 pages examine the broad tapestry of American people, confronting issues of race, culture, and religion.

religion. Steve, the protagonist, travels all over America, much like Huckleberry Finn, in search of an unspecified object that will either save his life or make him complete. The object is never named, so each reader may project onto it his or her own personal Holy Grail. I also hope readers will project themselves onto the character of Steve, as he indulges in amazing feats of acrobatic fuckery with women of all backgrounds and body types.

The depth and weight of my novel is likely to put some people off, but I believe there's something in it for everyone. For example, who among us hasn't feared losing his identity to the hive-mind of society? In Chapter 15, Steve feels trapped by his job,

> I won't give too much away, but he only begins to experience clarity after he bangs a particularly buxom Navajo chick and realizes that true peace can only be found through fucking.

smothered by his family, and overwhelmed by the dictates of consumer culture. He finally snaps and heads to the desert to find an autonomous zone where he can reconnect with his true self. I won't give too much away, but he only begins to experience clarity after he bangs a particularly buxom Navajo chick and realizes that true peace can only be found through fucking.

I believe all readers will see something of themselves in Steve as he rails against the darkness of ignorance, chipping away at his own capacity to reason. *Westbound 90* will inspire people to break free of their self-imposed holding patterns, and it will inspire them in other ways with a totally hot scene in a convent where Steve has sex with a gorgeous anarchist posing as a nun.

Is technology dehumanizing us? Are the very items that enable us to function using us as much as we use them? Steve begins to feel that way when he spends a week without a meaningful encounter with another human being. But by chapter's end, Steve—and, by association, humanity—is redeemed by a six-way orgy of sloppy, fluid-soaked, triple-penetrating, bed-frame-splintering überfucking, proving to him once and for all that some human acts can never be replicated by machine.

I would ask you to keep an open mind while reading *Westbound 90*. Whether or not you agree with my conclusions, you can take something away from the book, and, if nothing else, it will make you think. It may raise points you had never considered before. And it will make you see fucking in a whole new light.

Now, if you'll excuse me, I feel inspired to write a new short story about a woman, her dreams, and her cunnilingus. ∅

High-School Science Teacher Takes Fun And Excitement Out Of Science

VERONA, NJ—Verona High School ninth-grade science teacher Mark Randalls has a unique talent for taking the fun and magic out of science, students of his comprehensive survey class reported Tuesday.

"I have a lot of information I'm required to impart to these children before they complete this grade and

> **"Mr. Randalls says science is a way of understanding how the universe works,"** said Lendberg. **"At least he said that on the first day. I've kind of tuned him out since then."**

move on to dedicated physics, biology, or chemistry," Randalls said. "If I tried to illustrate each and every aspect of science with an experiment or anecdote, we would never complete the necessary coursework by year's end."

A 25-year veteran instructor in Verona, Randalls teaches his students the periodic table using a standard wall-sized chart, the appropriate page in the same Houghton-Mifflin science textbook he's used since 1982, and a few minor experiments he runs by himself to save time.

"As you can see from the math I assigned you last night, the element

Above: Randalls awaits the beginning of fourth period, during which students will read silently at their desks.

sodium combines with water in an exothermic reaction, which means it gives off heat and, in some cases, light," Randalls said, doing the work at a safe distance from his fifth-period students. "Now, I'm using just a small grain of sodium, so there isn't the large flash you might get, not that you could see it in this stainless-steel bowl. But you can see the temperature go up on our thermometer here."

Randalls then asked the student

with the highest grade on the last weekly quiz, Mike Lendberg, to come up and read the temperature change off the unwieldy dial thermometer.

"Mr. Randalls says science is a way of understanding how the universe works," said Lendberg. "At least he said that on the first day. I've kind of tuned him out since then."

"I wonder if two-tenths of a degree is a lot," Lendberg added. "Well. Probably not."

For his part, Randalls said he believes a firm grounding in the basics is the most important education he can give his class, and that he constantly battles distraction in school.

"The other day, Amy Bethke asked me how sodium can be part of salt if it is poisonous," Randalls said, shaking his head. "I had to waste two minutes explaining how it has a stable bond with the element chlorine. Then,

see TEACHER page 264

Prison Warden Appears On Leno With Some Of His Favorite Prisoners

BURBANK, CA—San Quentin State Prison warden Ron Ditmeier wowed Monday's *Tonight Show* audience by displaying some of his favorite prisoners. "Rufus here is what we call a Throat-Slashing Double-Lifer," Ditmeier said while showing off an inmate to host Jay Leno. "These distinctive markings mean he's a hardcore in the Crips." The educational segment provoked peals of laughter when an Encino Wife-Beater urinated on Leno's shoulder and stabbed him in the eye with a pen.

Civil War Historians Posit 'You Had To Be There' Theory

ATLANTA—After years of conflict-

ing approaches to interpreting the Civil War, a coalition of historians on Tuesday posited the non-specific theory that "you had to be there" to fully understand the complexities of the war. "It's not just a matter of 'Were the Southern forces as confident and dedicated as their Northern counterparts?' or 'Was Gettysburg the turning point?'" said conference chairman Shelby Foote. "The whole gist of the war is just hard to really get unless, you know, you were there and saw it happen." The coalition also advanced a theory that the Great Migration, wherein one million African-Americans moved to northern cities between 1915 and 1920, was "a black thing."

Linebacker Faces Suspension For Genocide

MINNEAPOLIS—In the latest legal complication for an NFL player, Min-

nesota Vikings linebacker Antwone Evans may receive a fine and possibly even a suspension for his role in the mass slaughter of the Lithuanian people in a Sunday pogrom. "In cruelly rounding up and exterminating more than three million Lithuanian men, women, and children, Evans seriously violated the behavior standard to which we hold all our employees," said NFL commissioner Paul Tagliabue. "We are currently deliberating on whether to suspend him pending the verdict of his U.N. tribunal."

CEO Would Trade 5 Percent Of Stock Options For 10 Percent More Time With His Kids

HARTFORD, CT—Feeling sentimental Tuesday, Allied Plastics CEO Jonathan Mavre said he would gladly sacrifice a significant portion of his liquid assets for increased quality

time with his children. "If I had the chance, I would give anything, even 5 percent of my ADM options, for an extra afternoon a week with Jacob and Lauren," Mavre said. "Of course, I'd be smarter to hedge by splitting the loss between ADM and Pepsico."

Man In Break Room Can Still Hear Time Clock Ticking Loudly

LA GRANDE, OR—Roundy's Food Store stocker Jim Creighton felt ominously watched over by an employee time clock Tuesday as, at exactly 12:13 a.m., it noisily "clunked" over to the second-to-last minute of Creighton's 15-minute break. "Well, two minutes to go," Creighton mumbled grimly to himself, attempting to savor the final precious scraps of leisure time doled out to him by his employer. "Maybe I should grab another Pepsi." Creighton then sighed and stared at the coffee machine for the next 111 seconds. ∅

operations," said Shell CEO Steven L. Miller to reporters, in the face of all available evidence. "We view this commitment to projects that will conserve and protect the marine ecosystem as an important investment in our future."

"At Shell, we're proud to provide a niche for the struggling denizens of our oceans," said Shell vice-president of international shipping Dennis Gallsworthy, who apparently intended his words to be taken seriously.

Somehow maintaining his composure despite being able to hear the things he was saying, Gallsworthy added, "We have a strong commitment to protecting and preserving sea life."

On Sept. 27, radio messages from the tanker indicated it had suffered extensive damage to its hull following an explosion, which pierced its overloaded crude-oil tanks. By the time the ship slid to the bottom, Shell public-relations officials were touting

its potential as an artificial habitat, often while looking straight into reporters' eyes.

"The many species of fish native to Newfoundland's Grand Banks have in recent years increasingly struggled to find feeding and breeding grounds," Miller said, as if Shell were deeply concerned with these circumstances and not, in fact, partially at fault for them. "We must take all available steps to help reestablish these species in their native waters."

Hoping to both deflect blame and take an opportunity for self-promotion, Miller took aim at the commercial fishing industry without so much as a smirk.

"The *Global Explorer*'s new resting place will provide shelter for countless threatened, often over-harvested fish," he said. "At Shell, we're proud to use our multibillion-dollar, globe-spanning resources to aid a worthy environmental cause."

Not all press reaction has been positive.

"Once again, Shell has demonstrated its unique brand of environmental-

> ## "At Shell, we're proud to provide a niche for the struggling denizens of our oceans," said Shell vice-president of international shipping Dennis Gallsworthy.

ism, this time to the life of our planet's oceans," *Mother Jones* environmental reporter Neil Taylor said Tuesday. "The sunken hulk of the *Shell Global*

Explorer, which hauled billions of gallons of crude oil during its operational lifetime, will have an impact on aquatic life for hundreds of years to come."

Shell reacted quickly to these and other statements, working with mainstream news sources to tell its side of the story.

"Once again, Shell has demonstrated its unique brand of environmentalism, this time to the life of our planet's oceans," read a full-page ad from Shell that will appear in Wednesday's edition of *USA Today*. "The sunken hulk of the *Shell Global Explorer*, which hauled billions of gallons of crude oil during its operational lifetime, will have an impact on aquatic life for hundreds of years to come."

"We're proud of what we've done for the planet," Miller said, possibly truthfully. "And believe me when I say that at Shell, we're committed to changing our world forever." ∅

friends say, my nails are not the most important thing in my life," said Sweedlin, as Porcia sat on the floor picking a piece of gum from the bottom of her shoe. "I care about my hair way more. It's just that nails need

> ## "I have a special bond with my hairdresser that I don't have with anyone else," Sweedlin said.

more pampering if you want them to turn out halfway decent."

To take proper care of her hair, Sweedlin has a regular standing appointment for alternating Tuesdays at the Mane Attraction salon, where stylists spend hours radically changing her hairdo from straight to curly, blonde to brown, and back again.

"I have a special bond with my hairdresser that I don't have with anyone else," Sweedlin said. "If anything happened to her, like if the salon lost her to another place across town, I wouldn't know what to do."

Her most recent hairstyle, a shoulder-length cut, has garnered raves.

"Kelly's hair is soooo darling," said Donna Campbell, owner of Wee Ones Daycare, where Porcia spends up to 35 hours each week. "Thick hair is a gift from God. She must be so proud. I told her to enjoy that style while she can, because before you know it, a relaxed wave like that is all grown out."

Porcia spends each morning with her grandmother, who drops her off at Wee Ones at 11:30 a.m. The girl remains there until Sweedlin picks her up between 6 and 7 p.m., depending on whether she takes a detour to Walgreens, where a quick stop can take an hour. While Sweedlin often complains that money is too tight for new clothes for Porcia, she does bud-

get funds for the beauty products she needs to look "professional" for work.

Once the two are home, Porcia plays in her room, watches TV, or sits on the floor watching Sweedlin use her array of curling irons, makeup brushes, and hair-styling products, which the girl is repeatedly warned not to touch.

"That spray bottle is Mommy's!" Sweedlin told Porcia. "You can play with the old hair dryer, but don't you dare plug it in, hear?"

Though their apartment lacks *Sesame Street* or child-rearing magazines, the end tables are covered with copies of *Glamour* and *Hair Today*. Sweedlin knows nothing about major childhood diseases or car safety seats,

but the technological advances in cosmetology outlined in these periodicals rarely escape her notice.

"The new sunless tanning lotions are really great, but they're so expensive," Sweedlin said. "Maybe that doctor bill from when Porcia had Noxzema [eczema] can wait another month."

While Porcia's 24-month checkup is four months overdue, Sweedlin never misses an appointment at the Glamorous You day spa, where she regularly undergoes facials, makeovers, and leg-waxing sessions. Though she is on a first-name basis with everyone at the spa, she has yet to learn the first names of any of Porcia's friends in daycare.

"There's so many things I want to be

doing, but I don't have the time," Sweedlin said. "I should join a gym before I get too old."

Sweedlin has a number of friends, also single mothers, with whom she commiserates over her busy schedule.

"It's important to have someone to trade tips and secrets with," Sweedlin said. "Sometimes my girlfriends and I get out the photo albums and spend hours looking at how our fashion sense has changed."

Continued Sweedlin: "God, there's this one picture. I'm in a hospital bed for some reason—maybe it was when Porcia was born—and I have this stringy, straight hair. Ugh! I have no idea why I ever kept that photo." ∅

Above: Sweedlin examines a freshly-manicured hand.

SCANDAL from page 259

Above: Karla Shugg, an Alaska florist and grandmother of five, responds to allegations of insider trading.

leaked by an as-yet-undetermined source, resulting in 98 percent of Unocore's stock being sold off on Jan. 16, one day prior to an official public announcement of the unsuccessful merger.

Pitt said the 2 percent of Unocore's stockholders who failed to sell off their stock faced massive financial losses.

"The stock went from $235 to 13 cents a share in half an hour," said Kyle Levey, an Arizona factory worker implicated in the scandal. "That's when I knew I wasn't the only one with insider information. Sure enough, pretty much everyone on my block was in on it, too. And everyone down at work. And everyone at church."

Due to the enormous amount of paperwork involved in the scandal, the precise details of who was involved and to what extent remains unknown. Prosecutors say time will fill in most of the blanks.

"Everyone even remotely involved will be subpoenaed," Pitt said. "We've been going state by state in alphabetical order to tell those implicated that they will be brought to court. We're only up to Arkansas, though."

In order to streamline the notification process, the Justice Department will scroll the names of implicated U.S. citizens on Court TV and CNN, as well as during NBC's Thursday-night "Must See TV" block. Those listed are encouraged to call the 800 number on the screen for further instructions on how to be legally summoned to court.

"This is going to take years," Pitt said. "We've had to hire 52 million people, or about 19 percent of the population, just to answer phones."

With the economy already reeling from other corporate scandals and rising unemployment, the news could not have come at a worse time.

"Sure, some people are temporarily employed because of this," said economist Todd Langham, who was also implicated in the scandal. "But everyone else is tightening belts and fearing the worst. Millions are facing steep fines and possible jail time.

> **In order to streamline the notification process, the Justice Department will scroll the names of implicated U.S. citizens on Court TV and CNN, as well as during NBC's Thursday-night "Must See TV" block. Those listed are encouraged to call the 800 number on the screen for further instructions.**

They won't just get a slap on the wrist—unless they all get sprung on a technicality, that is."

Many citizens have expressed outrage at those charged in the scandal.

"It's just crazy," Chicago homemaker Mary Anders said shortly after Tuesday's announcement. "How so many people could be so greedy and corrupt is beyond me."

Anders was served a summons later that day.

Some implicated citizens are hoping their involvement goes unnoticed due to the enormity of the case, but prosecutors say they will diligently pursue all wrongdoers.

"It will take a while, but everyone involved will have to face Lady Justice," Pitt said. "Whether you sold one share or a thousand, using insider information for profit is illegal, and you will be prosecuted. I would recommend that the millions of people involved all chip in for a really good lawyer."

As of press time, the remaining 175,145,456 citizens implicated in the scandal had no comment. ✐

Ask A Third-Party Candidate

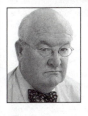

By Edgar Mayo Jr.
Presidential Candidate, American Rule-Of-Law Party

Dear Third-Party Candidate,
I like my new job, and my coworkers are great, but I can't seem to convince them that the reason I don't eat their homemade baked goodies is because I'm trying to lose weight, not because of the taste. They still think I'm snubbing them. What should I do?
15 Pounds Thinner And Counting In Aberdeen

Dear Thinner:
The United States is a *de facto* oligarchy. We who were born and raised in this so-called land of the free and home of the brave naturally resist such blunt accusations. We all like to believe we live in a free, democratic society. But a child need only observe the antics of the Republicrats and Demo(CRAP)ublicans to quickly realize there is more than meets the eye. Instead of addressing the needs of their constituents, these craven swindlers are more interested in lining their pockets and engaging in absurd intrigues in the corrupt Washington court. But we mustn't be too hard on these men and women. After all, they are only servile footmen carrying out marching orders from a *sinister international cult of amoral usurers and fascist sociopaths* headquartered variously in Geneva, Rome, and the Hague.

Dear Third-Party Candidate,
My husband's rubbernecking is giving me a royal pain! I don't want to be one of those insecure, henpecking wives who goes to pieces every time her spouse gazes at a pretty girl. "Ken" is otherwise very loving and attentive, but he practically ogles them head-to-toe, even when I'm standing right beside him! Would it be out of line to confront him about it, or should I accept the fact that "boys will be boys"?
Just About Had It In Joplin

Dear Had It:
Because it is the fundamental position of the American Rule-Of-Law Party that individual sovereignty must remain paramount, we cannot brook the hypocrisy of those "conservative" Republicans who claim to reject bureaucratic encroachment on personal freedoms, yet put restrictions on personal behavior (anti-drug laws, anti-sodomy laws). Nor can we rely on "liberal" Democrats, whose efforts to regiment society through excessive taxation and misguided attempts to improve conditions for the poor through social legislation
see CANDIDATE page 264

STEM CELLS from page 260

amounts of blood. Passersby were amazed by the unusually large amounts of blood. Passersby were

amazed by the unusually large amounts of blood. Passersby were amazed by the unusually large amounts of blood. Passersby were amazed by the unusually large amounts of blood. Passersby were amazed by the unusually large amounts of blood. Passersby were amazed by the unusually large amounts of blood. Passersby were

---

All I want is my son's life back, or $2 million.

---

amazed by the unusually large amounts of blood. Passersby were amazed by the unusually large amounts of blood. Passersby were amazed by the unusually large amounts of blood. Passersby were amazed by the unusually large amounts of blood. Passersby were amazed by the unusually large amounts of blood. Passersby were amazed by the unusually large amounts of blood. Passersby were amazed by the unusually large amounts of blood. Passersby were amazed by the unusually large amounts of blood. Passersby were amazed by the unusually large amounts of blood. Passersby were amazed by the unusually large amounts of blood. Passersby were
see STEM CELLS page 265

CANDIDATE from page 263

(affirmative action, anti-gun laws) have resulted in a snarl of bureaucracy and crippling litigation whose only beneficiary is an ever-growing swarm of lawyer-profiteers. Both these approaches undermine true democratic freedoms and individual rights to liberty, self-defense, and property. *The Rule-Of-Law Party calls for the abolition of any and all restrictions on drug and weapons possession and an immediate suspension of all environmental-protection laws that infringe on the right to property ownership.*

Dear Third-Party Candidate,

I was touched when my sister, a professional calligraphy artist, offered to do my wedding invitations free of charge. What I didn't realize was how long it would take her to finish them. When the invitations were a week overdue and she still had less than half of them done, I told her I couldn't wait any longer. She told me the guests I had added prolonged her work and that a good job takes time. Now she's threatening to not attend my wedding. Was I being unreasonable?

Goin' To The Chapel In Chapel Hill

Dear Chapel:

The American Rule-Of-Law Party believes in a strong centralized authority to promote the general welfare and provide for a common defense, as stated in the Preamble of the U.S. Constitution. The United States is too vast to be governed locally. However, the American Rule-Of-Law Party rejects the assumption that a strong centralized authority can abuse its power and make up a mandate as it goes along. It is with this in mind that we call for an *immediate dismantling of the U.S. tax code.* The labyrinthine bureaucracy of the IRS has supplanted whatever remains of reason and self-determination in the American character. It has crippled free enterprise and curtailed the prosperity of millions of hard-working people. According to the Rule-Of-Law plan, active civic (not civil) service would replace the yearly 1040 tax form and, indeed, our parliamentary governmental structure. (This latter point is a subject on which my short-sighted colleagues in the Libertarian Party are curiously silent.) As in Israel and Switzerland, Americans between the ages of 18 and 27 would be expected to serve in the armed forces for a minimal tour of duty of two years. Americans ages 28 to 55 would be required to serve on reconstructed, quorum-based democratic deliberative bodies, based on ancient Greek models of governance. High offices would be based on Roman models, but individuals who serve in these posts would be selected by a national lottery. Thus, any American age 35 or over, male or female, black or white, gay or straight, religious or atheist, could be chosen president. This will not only eliminate our present corrupt "professional" bureaucratic and political class, but endow Americans with

an empowering sense of responsibility not present in these days of media-brokered elections and smothering corporate lobbying.

Dear Third-Party Candidate,

I'm guilty of a little fib. I told my boyfriend of two years that I'm his age, 24, but I'm actually 33! I feel guilty for lying, and I want to tell him the truth, but do you think it's too late? Will he hold it against me?

Little White Liar In LaGrange

Dear Little White Liar:

Accusations put forward by the mainstream media, the Washington political elite, and the Libertarian Party claim that the American Rule-

> A vote for the American Rule-Of-Law Party is neither treasonous nor anti-American; indeed, it is the patriotism of our critics that should be questioned.

Of-Law Party, its founder (the late Edgar Mayo Sr.), and its current leader (myself, Edgar Mayo Jr.) espouse anti-Semitic and seditious sentiments. The anti-Semitism charge is a tired accusation leveled by individuals who wish to quell genuine and honest public debate, and does not dignify a response beyond our steadfast and long-held assertion that our quarrel has never been with the Jewish people, only the Jewish banking and media elite. Our critics also claim to be horrified by my radical rejection of the U.S. Constitution, particularly Articles I and III, which established both houses of Congress and the Supreme Court. Far more radical to me is the present system, whose structure continues to reflect the anti-pluralistic philosophy of its patrician, slaveholding framers. *Only by directly empowering the individual may we guarantee that individual's freedom.* A vote for the American Rule-Of-Law Party is neither treasonous nor anti-American; indeed, it is the patriotism of our critics that should be questioned. It is they who stand in direct opposition to government "of the people, by the people, and for the people." Dismiss, also, the prattling of the complacent, blinder-wearing dimwits who accuse me of being a quixotic fool. A vote for me is a vote to reverse centuries of elitism and exploitation and reaffirm the democratic, republican virtues we cherish.

Edgar Mayo Jr. is a syndicated columnist whose weekly advice column, Ask A Third-Party Candidate, *appears in more than 250 newspapers nationwide.* ✐

Your Horoscope

By Lloyd Schumner Sr.
Retired Machinist and
A.A.P.B.-Certified Astrologer

Aries: (March 21–April 19)
Love is strange. Repeating this fact no matter how you achieve orgasm will vastly aid your mental well-being this week.

Taurus: (April 20–May 20)
Your life will be improved enormously by the sudden appearance of a wisecracking toady who leers over your shoulder and repeats the last word of every sentence you utter.

Gemini: (May 21–June 21)
You've always thought of Death as a journey into the infinite, but it turns out to be a lot more like Harry Dean Stanton.

Cancer: (June 22–July 22)
You just don't have what it takes to be a contemporary man; in spite of your intelligence, compassion, and instinct for fun, there's still the gigantic tits.

Leo: (July 23–Aug. 22)
And to think you laughed when your high-school yearbook named you Most Likely To Be Responsible For The Extinction Of The Frigate Bird.

Virgo: (Aug. 23–Sept. 22)
In spite of your photos, the Church will profess ignorance of the origin of the phrase "Lord love a duck."

Libra: (Sept. 23–Oct. 23)
Yet another great moment in American oration will be ruined by your constant, vicious heckling of Mr. Sandler.

Scorpio: (Oct. 24–Nov. 21)
Your desiccated remains will be found on a desert island along with an empty water bottle, three emergency ration packages, and the exact right CD for the occasion.

Sagittarius: (Nov. 22–Dec. 21)
You're excited to get what you've always deserved until you realize it amounts to $4.27 in pizza coupons.

Capricorn: (Dec. 22–Jan. 19)
You've never considered yourself a genius, which helps you avoid damaging blows to your self-image this Sunday.

Aquarius: (Jan. 20–Feb. 18)
You have always rejected the doctrine of reincarnation as superstitious nonsense, which comes as a great relief to Hindu couples expecting children early next month.

Pisces: (Feb. 19–March 20)
There's no life for you without love, except in the strictest biological and durational sense.

TEACHER from page 261

when I tried to go on, she realized chlorine was also poisonous, and said, 'Isn't that weird that two deadly elements combine to make harmless table salt?' I finally had to send her to the office to make copies just to get her to stop interrupting the class."

Added Randalls: "These kids are getting worse every year. It's a wonder I get any teaching done at all."

Other points left out of Randall's discussion of the periodic table include a discussion of how simple flammable hydrogen makes up more than 90 percent of the universe, a demonstration of sound waves propagating strangely in helium, and an explanation of carbon's role in the creation of both coal and diamonds, as well as its use as a building block for life.

Nearly all of Randalls' students, or at least those who have chosen not to frequently skip class, have expressed dissatisfaction with his approach to science.

"I was really looking forward to last month's electricity unit," said freshman Don Linzmann, whose prior exposure to Bill Nye and *Cosmos* reruns

got him interested in physics. "I'd heard about these cool things called Van de Graaff generators, which make your hair stand up when you touch them, and this thing called a Ja-

> Added Randalls: "These kids are getting worse every year."

cob's Ladder that makes a really huge arc of electricity. But all we did was spend a week calculating amperage."

After another week spent on the periodic table, Randalls will begin teaching a unit on anatomy.

"I just hope these kids sit still for the frog dissection in two weeks," Randalls said. "I went to great lengths to procure a five-part filmstrip series that illustrates the frog anatomy step-by-step so we won't have to create a lot of mess dissecting the animals ourselves. Besides, the class always gets way too rambunctious when we try to do a lab." ✐

Look for these *New York Times* bestsellers, also by *The Onion:*

Dispatches from the Tenth Circle
0 7522 2011 X
£9.99 Paperback

Our Dumb Century
0 7522 1743 7
£9.99 Paperback

The Onion's Finest News Reporting,
Volume 1
0 7522 7158 X
£9.99 Paperback

BOXTREE